新东方 NEW ORIENTAL

NEW PERSPECTIVE GRAMMAR

英语语法新思维

中级教程——通悟语法

张满胜 著

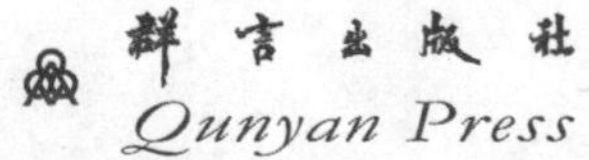
群言出版社
Qunyan Press

图书在版编目(CIP)数据

英语语法新思维中级教程——通悟语法 / 张满胜著.
北京：群言出版社，2008（2008.9 重印）
ISBN 978-7-80080-836-4

Ⅰ. 英…　Ⅱ. 张…　Ⅲ. 英语—语法—教材　Ⅳ. H314

中国版本图书馆 CIP 数据核字(2008)第 042800 号

英语语法新思维中级教程——通悟语法

出 版 人　范　芳
责任编辑　赵洪波
出版发行　群言出版社(Qunyan Press)
地　　址　北京东城区东厂胡同北巷 1 号
邮政编码　100006
网　　站　www.qypublish.com
电子信箱　qunyancbs@126.com
总 编 办　010－65265404　65138815
编 辑 部　010－65276609　65262436
发 行 部　010－65263345　65220236

经　　销　新华书店
读者服务　010－65220236　65265404　65263345
法律顾问　中济律师事务所
印　　刷　北京鑫丰华彩印有限公司

版　　次　2008 年 7 月第 1 版　2008 年 9 月第 2 次印刷
开　　本　787×1092　1/16
印　　张　23.75
字　　数　340 千字
书　　号　ISBN 978-7-80080-836-4
定　　价　48.00 元

写在前面

读者朋友，当你看到这套书——《英语语法新思维》，然后有勇气翻开这个“大部头”时，你真的应该为自己鼓掌、喝彩——为你的这份勇气，也为你自己对英语学习的这份热情和坚持！

我要高兴地告诉你：

你对英语的这份热情和坚持，会因为这套书而得到回报！

你对英语语法的学习，也会因为这套书而从此改变！

因为这套语法书“真的与众不同”，同时也是“与众不同的真”。它的“不同”与“真”体现在下列六方面：

- 不同于传统语法书只是机械地罗列教条式的“死规则”，《英语语法新思维》真的要告诉你规则背后的“活思维”。
- 不同于传统语法书追求“大而全”的规则排列，《英语语法新思维》真的要让你快速掌握“少而精”的思维规律。
- 不同于传统语法书那样本末倒置地给出较多生僻的“例外”，《英语语法新思维》真的让你高效掌握英语思维的本质。
- 不同于传统语法书采用枯燥的例句来讲解规则，读起来味同嚼蜡，《英语语法新思维》真的要让你在欣赏有趣例句、幽默故事以及精美短文的同时，领悟英语思维。
- 不同于传统语法书只给你孤立的、脱离语境的单一句子，《英语语法新思维》真的要让你知道例句背后的使用语境。脱离语境的句子，如同鸟的标本，失去了鲜活的生命力；融入语境的句子，才是自由飞翔的小鸟。
- 不同于传统语法书只教你语法知识，《英语语法新思维》真的要教你如何运用语法知识，从而把语法知识转化为你的语言技能，真正培养你创造性使用英语的能力。

以上这些“不同”与“真”正是本书的创作初衷和特色。如果想进一步深入了解，请读者继续翻开下一页，阅读“序言”的内容。

序 言

语法——新思维！
——学习语法是掌握英语思维的一条捷径！

一 一封读者来信——

在众多读者来信中，下面这封给我印象特别深刻：

“张老师，我学了许多年英语，还是不会写、不会说、听不懂。这些年学英文基本上是靠背单词应付考试过日子……我该怎样才能学好英语？”

这位读者的困惑我想是具有一定代表性的。长期以来，国人学英语都是重复着“背单词——应付考试——再背单词——再应付考试”这样一个循环。考四级背四级词汇，考六级背六级词汇，以及考研词汇、TOEFL词汇、GRE词汇、GMAT词汇——等等。这样一来，我们学英语的过程几乎就等同于一个背单词的过程，于是英语水平就简单的等同于词汇量的多少。这样造成的最终结果是，试考完了，单词也就忘记了，英语水平自然就直线下降。

单词学习固然重要。但是，学习一门语言，绝不能简单地等同于背单词。因为语言是人类思维的载体，语言表达本质上是一种思维的表达，即所谓“言传心声”。对于学习英语，如果只是死记单词，而没有训练出良好的英语思维，那么我们学到的充其量不过是英文这种文字(word)或文本(text)，而不是作为思想表达工具的英语这门语言(language)。书面上的英语文字，如果我们不能掌握其背后的思维规律，那终究不是活生生的交际语言，这就犹如一个“植物人”，虽然有人的生命，但不能成为有着思维表达的正常人。所以，训练和培养自己的英语思维才是学好英语的根本出路。

那么何谓英语思维？人人都知道用英文思维的重要性，但却没有人告诉我们到底如何用英文思维？其实，从语言本身去分析，这个问题就变得非常简单了。语言无非就是人们交流思想的工具。因此，首先要能发出声音，即语音；其次，还需要有记录声音的符号，即词汇。一门语言光有这两样还不行，如果真是这样，英语岂不就成了汉语的方言了？所以，语言还得有把词组成句子的造句规则即语法。因此，真正意义上的语言都离不开这三要素：语音、词汇、语法。语言作为思维的载体，而语法作为一种语言表达规律的归纳和总结，必然集中体现了该种语言的思维模式！因此毫无疑问，英语思维的训练必然落到了语法的身上！从这个意义上讲，语法即是思维，用英语思维，即是用英语语法思维！

二 《英语语法新思维》的特色

1. 死规则与活思维

说到“语法”，最容易让人联想到的恐怕要属“规则”了，于是我们很容易在二者之间划上等号：

语法＝规则

既然是规则，进而就会想到要严格遵守。这就容易让人产生如下误解：

第一，误认为语法先于语言。认为语法是由语法专家事先确定并要求人们去遵循的。这就相当于把“语法”当成“法律”，认为专门制定出来语法规则是为了规范人们的言语行为的。传统语法书也加强了人们这种错误印象。因为它们往往是先列出一些规则，然后再针对这些规则给出相应的例句，告诉读者，按照规则这么造句才是对的。久而久之，让人产生错觉：以为是先有一套语法规则、教条，然后必须按照这些规则才能制造出具体句子。《英语语法新思维》要告诉读者：事实恰恰相反，语法是源自语言，是先有语言，然后再从大量的语言实践中总结出人们在使用这种语言时所遵循的一般思维规律或表达倾向，即所谓的规则。套用鲁迅先生的一句话就是：世上本没有语法规则，说的人多了便成了规则。所以，语法规则不是什么不可逾越的清规戒律或天规，而是对人们的思维规律或语言表达习惯的归纳和总结。

第二，把语法规则当作一成不变的公式。把语法当作规则来遵守，这就容易让人们把语法规则当作一成不变的公式，学习语法就如同学习数学公式一样，死记一些“公式”般的规则，因而把英语学得非常死板。我们知道，数学公式往往都是来自于某些“公理”、“定理”，是比较确定的、不变的。但是，语言是灵活多变的，同时又具有规律性。语法规则就是对这些规律性的语言现象进行归纳和总结，但并不能涵盖所有的语言现象。从这个意义上讲，所谓的“语法规则”只不过是一种“权宜之计”的规则，是为了方便语言初学者的学习。因此，语法并不是一成不变的“公式”，也不是非此即彼、黑白分明的，而是存在很多“模糊区域”或“灰色地带”，因而总有“例外”存在。所以，语法规则不是绝对的，不是“死”规则。

第三，把语法规则当成随意的公式。语法规则常常似乎表现为随意的公式。比如，对于冠词的用法，一般语法书上会有这样一条规则：“第一次提到的单数可数名词前面用不定冠词 a 或 an，这一名词再次出现则要用定冠词 the”。传统语法书上往往只是给出这样的规则，但不解释为什么会这样选择冠词（详见本套书“初级”2.5.2 小节所给出的解释）。这样一来，英语学习者很容易误认为语法规则是随意的、专断的，没有什么道理可言的，因而容易死记规则，而忽略了规则背后的合乎情理的思维规律。《英语语法新思维》要告诉读者：很多看似随意的规则，其背后都有共同的思维规律。因此，学语法重在理解规则背后的合乎情理的思维，而不能“死记”规则。

由于以上种种误解，导致国人和老外（native speakers of English）在使用英语方面的最大的区别就是：我们记住了英语语法规则却没有英语思维，而老外是在用英语思维，尽管他们不懂语法规则。我们学的语法规则都用来对付英语考试的选择题了，而没有真正懂得规则背后的英语思维。我们往往只是僵化地牢记一些规则，然后简单地用这些规则来辨别一个句子“符合”与“不符合”自己牢记的规则，而不去关注句子所使用的语境。这样一来我们学到的只是一个“虚构”的英文句子，而不能把所学到的句子活用到真实的英语交际中。这就造成学英语与现实生活中的语言交际脱节。在说英语时，我们往往扮演的是“第三者”的角色，说出一些无关自己痛痒的句子，并没有融入英语思维去说英语。只有掌握了灵活的英语思维，我们才能如身临其境般地“言传心声”，否则只能是有口无心式地“鹦鹉学舌”或“言不由衷”。

《英语语法新思维》要告诉读者：语法是对语言表达习惯的归纳，总结出来的规律是为了对语言学习者正确引导，而不是严格限定；语法规则不是一成不变的“死”规则；学习语法不能“死记”规则，而要理解规则背后的思维。不能把“语法规则”看成是捆住自己英语手脚的“死规则”，而应该把它们当作是引导和帮助我们正确使用英语的“活思维”。简言之，语法不是“死规则”，而是“活思维”。

2. 结构形式与意义用法

笔者在上文中强调，应该把语法当作思维规律来理解，而不应该当作规则来死记。那么，如何才能把“死规则”转化为“活思维”呢？这就需要搞清楚学习语法规则应该包括哪些方面内容。

我们知道，词汇除了有发音外，还包括形式（即单词的拼写形式）、意义（即单词的含义）和用法（即单词的用法）。语法也有形式（form）、意义（meaning）和用法（usage）这三方面：

形式：某个语法结构是怎样构成的。比如“现在完成进行时”的构成形式是 have been doing。这是使用语法规则的起点，即首先要做到能够准确地构造某个语法结构，这是语法结构的准确性问题。

意义：某个语法结构表达什么意义。比如“现在完成进行时”可以表示“一个活动从过去一直延续到现在说话时刻”这样的含义，这就是现在完成时态这一结构所具备的语法意义。由此我们看到，特定意义一般是对应于特定结构形式的，或者说，特定的结构形式能够表达特定的意义（Particular forms will express their particular meanings）。这是关于语法结构的表意性问题。对于一个句子，它的含义不仅仅是来自于句中所使用的词汇的含义，而是还有来自于其中特定语法结构所含有的语法意义。

用法：关于何时 / 为什么使用某一语法结构的问题。这与在实际交流中的语境有关系，即在什么样的语境中，采用何种语法结构来表达特定的意义才合适，这是有关语法结构的合适性问题。意义和用法是密切相关的，有时难以严格界定。

某一特定的语法结构的形式、意义和用法这三者之间是相互联系的，图示如下：

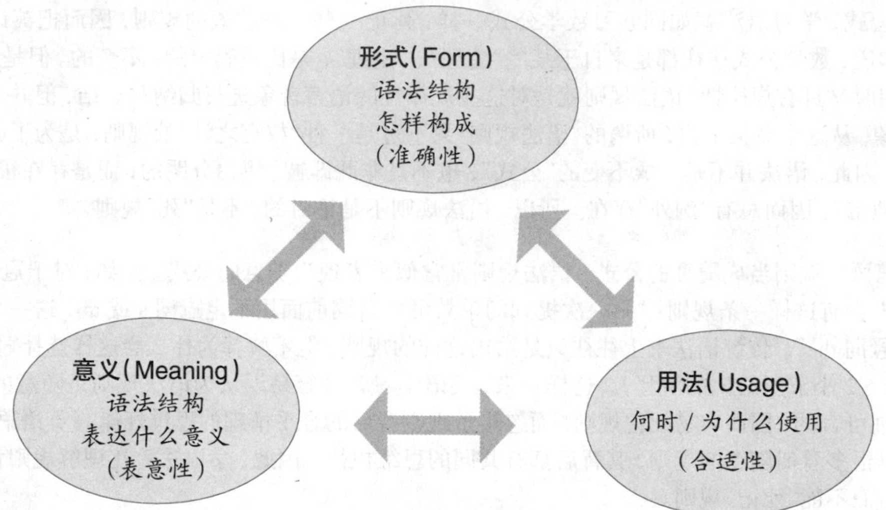

用一句话来概括三者间的关系就是：**英语学习者要能够准确地、有意义地、恰当地去运用英语语言结构**。做到这一点，才能够真正灵活使用语法规则，并进而在思维高度上来使用英语。

现在我首先来举例说明形式与意义的关系。比如下面这句话：

1 I ***have been coming*** to Beijing for fourteen years.

该如何理解其含义呢？看完这句话，对于它的意思，相信有读者第一反应是：

2 我来北京有 14 年了。

这样理解其实是错误的。还有人竟然这样曲解：“我到北京一路上走了 14 年”。相信本书读者都应该认识上句中的每一个单词，并且对其中的语法结构 have been coming 都知道是“现在完成进行时态”，尽管如此，但依然不知道这句话真正所要表达的意义是：

3 在过去这 14 年当中，我常常来北京。

这就是说，在 14 年期间，我多次“重复”来北京，而不是一直在北京住了 14 年（详见本套书“中级”6.5.1 小节所给出的解释）。由此可见，知道语法结构的形式并不一定就懂得语法结构的意义。

其实，这里的 have been coming 在英文里表示的是一个重复的活动，具体来说：用短暂动词（如 **come**）的完成进行时（如 **have been coming**）来表示到目前为止的一段时间内重复发生的动作。

下面我把这个句子稍加改动，说成：

4 I ***have been coming*** to Beijing ***fourteen times***.*

---

* 本书中所有标记“*”号的句子皆为错误范例。

显然这里说话人是想表达"我来北京有十四次了"这样的意思。这样对吗？这也不对。为什么？因为现在完成进行时态在表示重复活动时，不能说明具体的次数，比如这里的"十四次"（详见本套书"中级"6.6.1小节所给出的解释）。这就属于知道 have been coming 形式（现在完成进行时态）和意义（表示重复活动），但并没有真正掌握其用法，即不知道如何恰当地使用完成进行时态来表达重复意义。由此可见，知道语法结构的正确构造形式以及所能表达的意义，也并不一定就保证能够正确使用。

传统语法书和语法教学往往只强调结构形式，告诉学生如何构造出形式正确的英语句子；老师上课列举的例句，目的主要是为了让学生重点掌握句子构造的形式，很少把例句的真正意义及其所使用的语境交待给学生，因而学生对这些句子不知道该如何恰当地使用。这样就致使学生学到的只是一些句子"标本"，是毫无生命的死句子，而不是鲜活的交际语言。

《英语语法新思维》与一些传统语法书的一个主要不同点，就是始终坚持从交际的角度去看待语法，认识到语法不单是一个形式（句法学）问题，还包括在合适的语言环境（语用学）来表达某种意义（语义学）。因而在举例讲解某个语法结构时，笔者不仅要告诉读者如何在形式上达到准确性，同时也要帮助读者做到恰当地运用该语法结构，把握其意义。

3. 句子与语境

笔者在上文谈到了语法结构的形式、意义和用法的问题。其中用法问题往往与语言环境密切相关。我们知道，在真实的语言交际过程中，任何一个句子都不是孤立存在的，都有一个赖以生存的语境。甚至有时候，语境决定了一个句子真正要表达的意思（这是语用学研究的范畴）。比如下面这个电影对白发生在一位父亲与自己女儿的男朋友之间：

5 Father: Do you drink?

Young Man: No, thanks, I'm cool.

Father: I'm not offering; I'm asking IF you drink. Do you think I'd offer alcohol to teenage drivers taking my daughter out?

这位父亲问他女儿的男朋友（其正准备开车带他女儿出门）：Do you drink？他真正的意思是问这个年轻男子是否有饮酒的习惯，即是在询问情况，而不是问他现在想不想喝酒，即不是在提议。这就是语境对于句子意思的重要影响。

再比如对于 That was fun 这个句子，我们知道它的语法结构形式——一般过去时态（was），以及它的意思——"这很好玩"或"这很有趣"，但不一定知道该句在什么样的场合使用才正确、恰当。我们来看下面这个对话——一对男女在公园里学习滚轴溜冰：

6 Ted: Where did you learn to Rollerblade?

Anna: Here in the park. This is only my second time.

Ted: Well, it's my first time. Can you give me some lessons?

Anna: Sure. Just follow me.

（After a while）

Ted: Hey, that was fun. Thanks for the lesson!

这里我们看到，that was fun 被用在了溜冰活动结束之后，而不是在活动进行过程中（此时要说成 that is fun，详见本套书"初级"7.4.8 小节所给出的解释）。我估计，在上面这个对话语境中，大多数国人可能会说 that is fun。由此我们看到，如果不是提供这样完整的对话语境，读者就很难真正会恰当使用 that was fun。从更一般意义上来说，当一个句子脱离了它赖以生存的语境背景，这个句子就像一个句子"标本"，失去了鲜活的生命。打个形象的比喻来说，脱离语境的句子，如同鸟的标本，没有了生命；融入语境的句子，才是自由飞翔的小鸟。

所以，在学习语法规则时，我们不仅要能够构造出结构形式正确、能够表达意义的句子，更要关注这个句子所能使用的语境。传统的语法书和语法教学在这方面做得相当不够，他们提供例句主要是为解释某条语法规则服务的，而句子背后的使用语境没有展现给学生。规则下面罗列的例句都是僵化的、脱离了语境的死文字，像一具“木乃伊”一样没了生命。致使学生学到的只是一些句子“标本”，而不是鲜活的交际语言。另一方面，学生在学或老师在教语法规则时，往往都是一些死板教条的规则，而不探讨规则背后的思维规律。这就造成为什么中国学生学习语法但在交际中却不会运用。

《英语语法新思维》始终坚持从交际的角度去看待语法，在具体的语境中考查语法规则的使用，通过语篇、语境驾驭语法来达到十分具体的交际目的。基于这个认识，在本套书中，我们不是在设定英语“应该”怎样说(what learners ***should say***)，我们更感兴趣的是去分析、解释为什么英语本族语者要“这样”说(what native speakers of English ***actually do say*** and why)。在讲解某个语法规则时，我们不仅要告诉读者这个语法规则是什么，还要告诉读者这个规则背后的为什么以及如何使用这个规则；在举例时，不仅把句子的含义通过中文译文来告诉读者，还通过“妙语点睛”来向读者展现这个句子所使用的语境，或者是通过给出对话或短文来为例句提供一个完整的语境，这样就使得读者能够充分理解所学到的每个例句在具体交际中的使用。

4. 英语思维与汉语思维

从上面 That was fun 这个例句，我们看到，读懂句子意思，并不代表我们就真正会在口语或写作中使用这个句子进行交际，也就是说“读懂≠会用”。这背后的原因有很多，比如不知道这个句子的使用语境。这背后还有一个英语与汉语思维差异的问题。比如下面这个中文句子：

7 我已经结婚了，去年结婚的，到现在结婚有一年多了。

这几个看似简单的汉语句子该如何用英语地道表达呢？就拿“我已经结婚了”这句话来说，在一次课堂上，有许多学生为笔者提供了下列这些不同版本的译文：I ***have married***；I ***have been married***；I ***got married***；I ***married***；I ***had married***，等等。其实，这些译文都没能表达“我已经结婚了”这句话的含义。这三句话地道英文是这么说的：

8 I ***am married***. I ***got married*** last year. I***'ve been married*** for over a year.

简单比较一下，读者看到，汉语中的“结婚”一词，用英文表达却有 am married、got married 以及 have been married 这样的区分。而这样形式上的区分背后反映了英汉语言的一个重大思维差异：英文中有“动作(action)”与“状态(state)”的区分，以及时态方面的问题(详见本套书“中级”5.7.4 小节所给出的解释)，而这些话语特点在汉语思维中都是“盲点”，是天然缺失的。这就造成这样的窘境：我们可以轻而易举地把“I ***am married***. I ***got married*** last year. I***'ve been married*** for over a year.” 译成地道的中文，但反过来由中文却无法译成地道的英文，即能读懂英语句子，但在真正交际中不一定能准确地说出这样的句子，这就说明“读懂≠会用”。更严重的是，因为不懂英文思维特点，有时甚至都读不懂句子，而造成误解句义。比如下面这句：

9 He is interesting to listen to.

是要表达什么意思呢？一定有读者这么理解：

他对听别人讲话很感兴趣。

这么理解就错了。其实这句话意思是：

听他讲话很有趣。

不能正确理解这个句子的一个根本原因是没有真正理解这个句子的如下“深层结构”：

10 It is interesting ***to listen to him***.

也就是说，在表层结构上，he 是作句子的主语(He is...)，但在深层结构上，he 是作 listen to 的逻辑宾语(...listen to him)。这里不定式 to listen to 的逻辑主语是泛指大众，在句中没有明确给出，而只是隐含其中的(详见本套书“高级”分册 4.6.1 小节所给出的解释)。

所以，如果读者只满足于看懂句子意思就行了，而不去真正理解英语的思维规律，那么英语水平是无法真正提高的。这就是为什么大量中国英语学习者的英语水平就停留在能看懂英文文章但是说不出、写不来的尴尬境地，究其原因，还是因为没有真正“懂英文”！

传统的语法书及语法教学很少从思维的高度来探讨英语和汉语在思维表达上的差异，只是单纯地向学生灌输语法规则。学生利用这些规则也只是勉强读懂一些文章或句子。但在口语或写作中，依然是借用背诵别人的“优美句子”，而不能自己创造出句子，不能在语言交际中真正发出自己的声音。

笔者在创作《英语语法新思维》这套丛书时，始终想到这是一套为我们中国读者(尤其是成年读者)而写的语法书，他们在学习英语时，往往深受汉语思维表达的影响，这样就有必要对中英文的思维差异作比较。在这方面，本套书有大量精彩的讨论。只要遇到与我们中文思维方式有差异的英文语法规则时，笔者都会作详尽比较、总结，以求帮助读者加强理解，并灵活运用。

5. 语法知识与语言技能

语法知识本身不应该是读者学习英语的目的，也不是笔者写《英语语法新思维》这套丛书的目的。我们的目的是要让读者学会使用语法知识，进行语言交际，即把本套书中所介绍的语法知识转化为听、说、读、写这样的语言技能。如何转化呢？笔者认为要做到下列“两多”：

首先，要“多思考”(think much)，要认真领悟书中所讲到的语法规则。我这里之所以用“领悟”一词，就是希望读者要认真思考语法规则背后的合乎情理的思维规律，要把“课本上的语法”(a textbook grammar)变为“头脑中的语法”(a mental grammar)——即逐渐培养自己用英语思维的能力。不希望读者把书中的规则当成死规则来僵化地学习和背诵。我们不能再“背”语法规则了，而是要“理解”语法规则，让规则成为自己思维的一部分。否则花费了大量的时间学英语，学语法，记死规则，最后又很快遗忘，造成终难修成英语正果。

其次，要“多练习”(practice much)，这里的练习，不仅是指我们为了应付考试而做大量的阅读练习和单项选择题练习，而是包括听、说、读、写、译全方位的练习，尤其是口语和写作这种语言产出能力的练习。

所以，通过学习《英语语法新思维》这套丛书，读者是在掌握语法知识的同时也锻炼了语言技能。这样，读者既能够成为英语语法的专家，更是英语语言交流的高手。

三 《英语语法新思维》的逻辑体系

《英语语法新思维》不再像传统语法书那样，以词法和句法两条主线对英语语法进行大而全的、包罗万象的规则罗列。我们真正注重实用，循序渐进，科学地分为三个级别。给你设立明确的学习目标，增强你的学习信心，让你的英语学习不再半途而废。三级分工如下图所示：

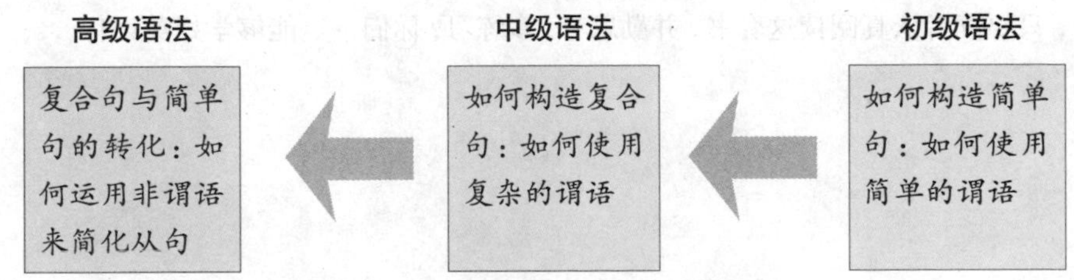

初级：以名词短语和动词作为两大主线。

在名词短语篇中，笔者首先帮助英语初学者建立起“名词短语”这个重要概念，以便于在“名词短语”这样的大背景下来学习接下来的各章内容，包括名词、限定词和形容词。有了“名词短语”这个概念，读者就能够很好地了解名词、限定词和形容词这三者之间的关系，从而可以慢慢地建立起科学的英语语法体系，以达到融会贯通、灵活运用的境界。通过本篇内容的学习，读者可以深刻认识到：语法的学习决不能是一堆凌乱不堪的散沙，而应该是一棵充满生机的“语法知识树”。

初级分册中的动词内容主要讨论了英语五种基本句型，让读者从一开始就树立正确的英语句型观念，这样为今后学习复杂从句奠定良好的基础。此外，详尽分析了一般时态和进行时态的思维用法，这些用法尤其适用于口语交际中。

中级：以从句和谓语动词作为两大主线。

中级分册中的从句内容主要是介绍如何将两个简单句合并成为三大从句，即名词从句、定语从句和状语从句。相当于英语从句的入门篇。

中级分册中的动词内容详尽分析了完成时态、完成进行时态、虚拟语气和情态动词等比较复杂的谓语形式，这些灵活多变的谓语形式尤其适用于口语交际中。并从思维的高度，比较了中英文的思维表达差异。

高级：以从句和非谓语动词作为两大主线。

高级分册中的从句内容主要是帮助读者分析和构造复杂的难句，以便于轻松应对各类国内外考试中的阅读理解及写作。相当于英语从句的提高篇。

高级分册中的动词内容详尽分析了英语中的三大非谓语：不定式、动名词和分词，并且在最后一章将三大从句与三大非谓语联系起来，考查二者之间的内在联系及相互转化的问题，使得读者不再是孤立地、僵化地看待各个部分的语法规则，而是在构造句子时能够对规则的使用应付自如。

四 《英语语法新思维》，让你一定能学好英语

这里笔者简单介绍一下读者该如何充分利用好这套书。

首先是关于学习顺序的问题。在对本套丛书的逻辑体系有一个大概了解的基础上，读者可以根据自己的个人英语水平，直接选择自己感兴趣的章节来进行有针对性的学习，也可以按照每本书的章节内容从前往后依次学习。

其次，关于每一章内容的结构安排。在各章当中，笔者都会把本章将要讨论的内容标题事先展现给读者，便于读者明确方向，理清思路。在各章内容中，很多小节后边都配有笔者精心设计的针对性练习，并且各章还配有综合练习。建议读者先认真阅读各章节的讲解内容，然后本着对自己负责的态度完成各章节后面的练习。通过这些练习，相信每个读者都会渐渐地掌握英语语法并建立起英语思维。此外，每一章都通过“写给读者的话”来进行总结，包括：本章学习思路、学习重点及难点、学习时间的安排，读者可以此作为参考，来指导自己的学习。

最后，我要强调的是，每学完一部分内容，读者应该停下来思考一下，看看自己是否真正理解我想说的意思了，可以通过每节后边的练习来检验。我不建议读者一气呵成地读完每章所有内容，而不做练习。所以，希望读者要踏踏实实地学，不要急于求成，囫囵吞枣。

我相信，只要读者认真阅读这套书，并勤思考，多练习，你们一定能够学好英语！

张满胜

目　录

第一章　简单句与复合句

第二章　名词从句

第三章　定语从句

第四章　状语从句

第六章　完成进行时态

第七章 虚拟语气

第八章 情态动词

Chapter 1

第一章　简单句与复合句

◇•

英语句子有长有短，结构有简有繁。从表面上看，英语句子似乎千变万化，难以捉摸；但从本质上来说，英语句子有其内在的结构规律，这个基本的结构规律就是简单句的五种基本句型。在《英语语法新思维初级教程——走近语法》里已经对这五种基本句型作过介绍，在此基础上，本章将更加深入而全面地介绍这五种重要句型。并且，本章将把简单句与复合句联系起来，以便让读者看到英语的复杂难句是如何由简单句叠加而成的。本章内容安排如下：

1.1 引　言

请读者先来看下面这个笑话：

A man was standing at a bus stop eating fish and chips（炸薯条）. An old lady and her little white dog stood next to him. The dog, excited by the smell of the fish and chips, started to bark and jump up on the man's leg.

"Do you mind if I throw him a bit?" the man said to the old lady.

"Not at all," she said. "Go ahead."

So the man picked up the little dog and threw it over a wall.

妙语点睛 也许有读者看完这个笑话心里还在纳闷：这笑话是什么意思呢？老太太为什么同意那个男的把她的狗扔出去呢？

看懂这个笑话的关键在于理解 Do you mind if I throw him a bit?这句话。在这里，男子和老太太对 a bit 的理解是不同的。具体来说，老太太是把 a bit 当作动词 throw 的直接宾语来翻译的，因此她把这句话理解成"我给你的狗扔点吃的你介意吗？"所以老太太说："不介意，你扔吧。"但是，这名男子是把 a bit 当作修饰谓语 throw 的状语来理解的，因而他的本意是"我把你这（讨厌的）狗扔远一点你介意吗？"听了老太太说"不介意，你扔吧"，于是他就真的把狗扔出去了。

精品译文 一名男子正站在一个公共汽车站吃着鱼和炸薯条。一个老太太带着她的小白狗站在他身旁。小狗由于闻到了鱼和炸薯条的香味，所以开始叫唤，还不住地往这男子的腿上跳。

"我给你的狗扔点吃的你介意吗（把 a bit 作直接宾语）？/我把你这（讨厌的）狗扔远一点你介意吗（把 a bit 作状语）？"该男子对老太太说道。

她说："不介意，你扔吧。"

于是，男子抓起小狗就把它扔到了墙那边。

由此可见，正确分析句子的成分是很重要的。老太太由于错误地判断了 a bit 所充当的成分，从而错误地理解了该男子的意思，导致自己的宠物狗被扔了出去。

当然这只是一个笑话而已。不过，对于中国的英语学习者来说，不能正确地分析句子的结构和成分，导致的后果就是不能正确地理解句子的意思，或者不知道正确地构造英语句子，这就直接影响到大家使用英语的水平。所以，正确地判断句子的结构和分析句子的成分，对于正确地理解和运用英语是至关重要的。

众所周知，英语的句子结构是非常有规律的，一个完整的句子都是由两部分组成：**"陈述对象＋陈述内容"**。这里的陈述对象一般是由名词或相当于名词的成分来充当，用语法术语来说叫主语。而陈述内容则是说明主语怎么样了，都是用动词来表达，我们称之为谓语。因此，一个完整的英文句子就是：**"主语＋谓语"**。

有了主语和谓语动词之后，一个句子的基本骨架结构就成形了，但意思往往还不完整，还需要在动词后面接其他成分。具体接什么成分，这是由**谓语动词**决定的，动词决定了一个句子是否有宾语，或者有几个宾语，或者是否需要补足语以及状语。因此，**谓语动词决定了一个句子的骨架结构**。这就给了读者两点启示：第一，在分析复杂的难句结构时，首先要找到句子的谓语，包括主句的谓语以及各个从句的谓语；第二，写句子时，一定要知道谓语动词的用法特点，比如该动词后面是否能接宾语，接什么形式的宾语，接不定式作宾语还是动名词作宾语等等，这些问题无不由谓语动词决定。所以，在下列的句型分析中，读者要特别注意每一种句型的谓语动词的特点。

根据动词的后面是否有**宾语**和**补语**，可以把句子分为五种，即构成英语简单句的五种基本句型。下面将详细论述。

思维训练

Exercise 1.1（Key: P325）

下面两个笑话故事都涉及到对句子成分的理解，请给出解释。

1. A: Father can lift a pig with one hand. Can your dad do that?

   B: I'm not sure. Where do you get a pig with one hand?

2. Hairdresser: I've had a lot of strange customers in my time.
Customer: Have you ever shaved a man with a wooden leg?
Hairdresser: No. I always use a razor.

1.2 句型一：主语 + 系动词 + 表语

我们先来分析该句型谓语动词的特点，然后举例说明这种结构的句子如何演变为复杂的难句。因此，本节内容安排如下：

1. 2. 1 谓语动词的特点
1. 2. 2 简单句叠加成复杂难句

1. 2. 1 谓语动词的特点

该句型的谓语动词是**系动词**(linking verb)(如 be 或其他系动词)。系动词，又叫连系动词，顾名思义，这种动词并没有具体的动作，而只是起连接主语和后面成分的作用。这种动词后面所接的成分是用来说明主语的特点，表明主语的性质特征的，因此被称之为主语补足语或表语(能表示主语特征的成分)，这就是读者熟悉的"主系表"句型。

在展开具体讨论之前，请读者先来看下面这个小故事，这个故事也许对各位读者学习英语会有所启示：

1 Losers look for quick fixes.

There are two ways of getting rid of weeds in your yard: the easy way and the not-so-easy way. The easy way may be to run a lawnmower and the yard looks fine for a while, but that is a temporary answer. Soon the weeds are back. But the not-so-easy way may mean getting down on your hands and knees and pulling out the weeds by the roots. It is time-consuming and painful, but the weeds will stay away for a longer time. The first solution appeared easy, but the problem remained. The second solution was not so easy, but took care of the problem from the roots. The key is to get to the root of the problem.

The same thing is true of our attitude in life. The problem with people today is that they want instant answer. They are looking for one-minute solutions to everything. Just like instant coffee, they want instant happiness. There are no quick fixes. This attitude leads to disappointment or even failure.

妙语点睛 在这篇短文中，"主系表"结构的句子有很多。比如：

1) The easy way ***may be*** to run a lawnmower.
2) The yard ***looks*** fine for a while.
3) But that ***is*** a temporary answer.
4) Soon the weeds ***are*** back.
5) It ***is*** time-consuming and painful.
6) The first solution ***appeared*** easy.
7) The second solution ***was*** not so easy.
8) The key ***is*** to get to the root of the problem.

这些句子谓语动词前面的名词短语都是主语，后面的则是表语。用作表语的形式有很多，可以是不定式(比如 to run a lawnmower 和 to get to the root of the problem)、形容词(比如 fine, time-consuming and painful, easy)、名词短语(比如 a temporary answer)、副词(比如 back)等。另外，这里的系动词主要是 be 的各种形式，如 may be, is, are 和 was 等，但除了 be 以外，还有其他系动词，如 looks 和 appeared。

精品译文 失败者寻找捷径

除掉院子里的杂草可以有两种方法：简便方法和不简便方法。简便方法可以是开动锄草机，然后院子里的草就没了。这可以管一阵子的事，但只是权宜之计，不久后杂草又长出来了。不简便的方法就意味着你自己得双膝跪地，然后用双手把杂草连根拔除。这既费时间又费力气，比较痛苦，但是杂草能够在很长一段时间内不会再长出来。第一个除草方案似乎简单易行，但只能治标不能治本，问题并没有真正解决。第二个方案比较费力，但是能根除问题。关键是要解决根本问题。

我们面对人生的态度也是如此。现代人的问题在于，他们想投机取巧，对一切事情都想快速解决。这就像速溶咖啡一样，他们想要的只是"幸福快餐"，而这样的幸福只是暂时的。生活中没有捷径，想找捷径最终会导致失望。

相信读者看完这个短文之后，应该有所启示，那就是学习英语的道理完全一样，要想真正学好它，是没有捷径可走的。学习英语可以有方法，但没有捷径，更不能投机取巧。英语学习是一个漫长的、需要点滴积累的"痛并快乐着"的过程。

接下来，我们来分析英语中的系动词的不同分类。主要有下面四大类：

一、单纯表示主语的特征、状态的

这样的系动词有 feel, look, sound, taste, smell, seem 和 appear 等。请看例句：

2 The iron ***feels*** hot. 这块铁摸起来很热。

3 The rose doesn't ***smell*** much. 这玫瑰花不是很香。

二、表示主语由一种状态转变为另一种状态的

这样的系动词有 become, grow, get, turn, fall, go 和 come 等。例如：

4 The leaf will ***turn yellow*** in autumn. 叶子秋天就会变黄。

5 The teacher ***became angry***. 老师生气了。

对于 fall, go 和 come 等词作为系动词时，这些系动词与形容词连用一般具有固定的搭配关系。请先看下面含有 fall 的例子：

6 Our supplies of sugar and rice ***fell short***. 我们的糖、米供应不足。

7 The jokes ***fell flat***. 玩笑毫无效果。

8 I've got to return the book this afternoon; it ***falls overdue*** a week. 我今天下午得还书，已经过期一周了。

9 fall due 到期

10 fall asleep 睡着

因为这里的 fall 都是作为系动词，所以其后面不能接副词，比如不能说 fall shortly* 或 fall flatly* 等。

请看 go 作为系动词的例子：

11 go hungry 饿了，挨饿

12 go mad 变疯了

13 go bad 坏掉了

14 go crazy 变得疯狂

15 go sour 变酸

16 go wrong 出错了

从上面的例子可以发现，go 作为系动词时，一般用于贬义，即表示主语是朝着坏的或消极的一面改变。相反，come 作为系动词，则是表示褒义的，即表示主语是朝着好的或积极的一面改变。请看例句：

17 Hope your dreams will ***come true.*** 祝你好梦成真。

18 The dream has ***come true.*** 梦想已经实现。

19 come right 纠正了，正确了

三、表示主语保持某种状态的

这样的系动词有 continue, remain, stay, keep, hold, rest 和 prove 等。请看例句：

20 He has fallen into the habit of doing morning exercises to ***stay healthy.***

妙语点睛 不要说 stay healthily，因为副词不能作表语。

精品译文 为了保持健康，他已经养成了晨练的习惯。

21 If you don't ***stay busy***, you die. I don't want to die right now.

妙语点睛 不要说 stay busily，因为副词不能作表语。

精品译文 如果你不辛勤忙碌，就等于死亡。我可不想现在就死去。

22 You may ***rest assured*** that he will come to the party.

妙语点睛 rest assured 是一个固定搭配。

精品译文 尽管放心，他会来参加聚会的。

23 The weather ***continued fine*** for several days. 天气连续几天都很晴朗。

24 He ***held silent*** for the whole day. 他一整天都沉默不语。

四、近似于不及物动词的系动词

近似于不及物动词的系动词有 sit, act, arrive, blush, marry, die 和 be born 等。有人将其称为"半系动词"，因为它们介于不及物动词和系动词之间。读者对这些系动词只需了解，并且在遇到相关句子时能够正确理解即可。

我们先来看下面这篇介绍阿诺德·施瓦辛格的短文：

25 Arnold Schwarzenegger grew up in Australia. His father was a policeman and his mother a housewife. Home didn't have a flush toilet or refrigerator until Arnie was 14. He ***arrived in the U. S. a penniless 21-year-old.*** His wife, Maria Shiver, is an anchor woman on U. S. TV news and niece of assassinated President John F. Kennedy. Andy Warhol and Grace Jones were among the 500 guests at their wedding. Others invited who were unable to attend included the Pope and the Reagans. His hobbies include reading, collecting art and attending classical music festivals.

我们来分析其中的一句话：He ***arrived*** in the U. S. ***a penniless 21-year-old***.

妙语点睛 首先，介词短语 in the U. S. 显然是表示地点的，修饰谓语 arrived，即是一个地点状语，表示"他到达了美国"。其次，名词短语 a penniless 21-year-old 起什么作用呢？作 arrived 的宾语吗？显然不行，因为 arrive 是不及物动词，不可能接宾语。从语义上来看，a penniless 21-year-old 显然是补充说明主语 he 的，表示"他到达美国的时候是一个身无分文的 21 岁的穷小子"，即 a penniless 21-year-old 是一个主语补足语，也就是相当于表语。可以把这个句子改写成：He was ***a penniless 21-year-old*** when he arrived in the U. S.

从而证明这里的谓语 arrived 相当于一个系动词的作用，连接主语 he 和表语 a penniless 21-year-old。

精品译文 阿诺德·施瓦辛格在澳大利亚长大。他父亲是一名警察，母亲是家庭主妇。直到小阿诺德 14 岁时家里才有了抽水马桶和电冰箱。21 岁的时候，他身无分文地来到美国。他的妻子玛丽亚·希弗是美国电视新闻的主持人，也是美国前总统约翰·F·肯尼迪的侄女。安迪·沃尔和格蕾斯·琼斯是参加他们婚礼的 55 名嘉宾之一，其他受到邀请却没能参加的客人包括教皇和里根家族的成员。他的爱好包括读书、收集艺术品和听古典音乐会。

请读者再来看下面这个小故事：

26 An eagle's egg was placed in the nest of a prairie（大草原）chicken. The egg hatched and the little eagle grew up, thinking it was a prairie chicken. The eagle did what the prairie chickens did. It scratched in the dirt for seeds. It clucked and cackled. It never flew more than a few feet because that was what the prairie chickens did. One day he saw an eagle flying gracefully and majestically in the open sky. He asked the prairie chickens, "What is that beautiful bird?" The chickens replied, "That is an eagle. He is an outstanding bird, but you cannot fly like him because you are just a prairie chicken." So the eagle never gave it a second thought, believing that to be the truth. He ***lived the life of and died a prairie chicken***, depriving himself of his heritage because of his lack of vision. What a waste! He was born to win, but was conditioned to lose.

我们来分析其中的这句话：He lived the life of and ***died a prairie chicken.***

妙语点睛 笔者认为，这是该故事中最难的一个句子了。这个句子原本地结构是 He lived the life of ***a prairie chicken*** and died a prairie chicken。也就是说名词短语 a prairie chicken 同时充当两个谓语部分 lived the life of 和 died 的成分。那在这里到底是什么成分呢？作宾语吗？可以肯定的是，a prairie chicken 是作介词 of 的宾语。但是 died 的宾语吗？我们知道，die 是不及物动词，不能接宾语。从语义的角度来看，即使把 a prairie chicken 看作是 died 的宾语，也是讲不通的，因为这样一来句子的意思就成了"它把一只草原鸡弄死了"，这显然不对，因为这里 he 就是 a prairie chicken，而不是两种不同的动物。其实，这里的 die 相当于一个系动词，其后面的名词短语 a prairie chicken 是用来补充说明主语的，也就是说是主语补足语，可以将其改写成：He was ***a prairie chicken*** when he died.（死的时候它也就是一只普通的草原鸡。）

精品译文 一只苍鹰的蛋被放置在一只草原土鸡的窝里。后来这枚蛋孵化成了一只小鹰。小鹰慢慢长大了，不过它就认为自己是一只草原鸡。它的生活习惯与草原鸡别无二致：也是在土里找种子吃；也是发出咯咯的叫声；也从不高飞，飞行距离不过几英尺，因为草原鸡就是这样飞的。有一天，它看见一只苍鹰在开阔的高空中优美地翱翔着，就问那些草原鸡："那是什么鸟？那么漂亮？"草原鸡回答道："那是一只苍鹰，是一只优秀的飞鸟。你不可能像它那样飞翔的，因为你只不过是一只草原鸡。"听了这番话，这只鹰信以为真，再也没有怀疑过。它就如同一只普通的草原鸡那样度过了一生然后死去。因为缺乏眼光而丧失了自己与生俱来的飞翔本领。这是多么浪费！他虽然生来就能取胜，但却注定要失败。

在我们的生活中，也不乏像这只鹰的人，因为缺乏远见或其他原因，最终只是碌碌无为地终了一生。

为了让读者更好地理解 die 作为系动词这一特殊的用法，请看例句：

27 1) Jane Austin ***died a spinster.***

2) He ***died a hero's death.***

妙语点睛 这两句话在表面上看都一样，就是在 died 后面接名词短语，分别是 a spinster 和 a hero's death。但实际上二者内在的深层结构是不同的。

在例句 1)中，a spinster 作表语或者说是主语补足语，即补充说明主语 Jane Austin 的性质特征，所以可以将原句改写成 Jane Austin was ***a spinster*** when she died. 但在例句 2）中，a hero's death 则不具有 a spinster 这样的特点，即并不是充当表语来修饰主语 he，因为 He was ***a hero's death*** when he died. * 是讲不通的。事实上，a hero's death 是一类较为特殊的宾语，英语里称为"**同源宾语**"。因为这里的 death 和 die 是同词源的，所以这里的 a hero's death 是同源宾语。除了同源宾语外，die 不能接其他正常的宾语。比如翻译这个句子"他把这个姑娘弄死了"，不能说 He ***died the girl.*** * 而要说 He ***killed the girl.*** 其他可以带同源宾语的不及物动词有 live（如 He lived a dog's life.），dream（如 He dreamt a beautiful dream.）等等。

精品译文 1)简·奥斯汀去世时，依然未嫁。

2)他英勇牺牲了。

下面将表语和状语进行比较。请看例句：

28 1) Lei Feng ***died young.***

2) Lei Feng ***worked hard.***

妙语点睛 在例句 1)中，young 是形容词，作表语（或者说是主语补足语），说明主语 Lei Feng 的性质特征，所以可将原句改写成 Lei Feng was young when he died。从这个句子里也可看出 young 不是用来修饰谓语动词 die 的。而在例句 2)中，hard 是副词，作状语，用来修饰 work，说明 work 的动作行为特征，而不是说明主语 Lei Feng 的性质特征的。所以，不能将这句话改写成：Lei Feng is hard when he works. *

精品译文 1)雷锋英年早逝。

2)雷锋工作很勤奋。

其他关于系动词 die 的句子还有：

29 He used to be very rich, but he ***died poor.***

妙语点睛 这句话相当于说 He was poor at the time of his death. 或者 He was poor when he died.

精品译文 他曾经非常有钱，但死的时候很穷。

30 He ***died a local company manager.***

妙语点睛 这句话相当于说 He was a local company manager when he died.

精品译文 他死的时候是一家公司的经理。

请看含有其他类似动词的例句。请比较：

31 1) Don't ***act stupid.***

2) Don't ***act stupidly.***

妙语点睛 这两句话里仅是一个形容词 stupid 和副词 stupidly 之别，则两句话的意思不同。在例句 1)中，act 是作为系动词，表示 to appear or seem to be，所以这个 act 不是讲行为动作，而只是讲故意装出某种样子。而在例句 2)中，由于是用副词 stupidly 作状语来修饰谓语动词 act 来说明行为动作的特点，所以这里的 act 是讲具体的行为动作。

精品译文 1)别装傻。

2)别笨手笨脚的。

再来比较一下 act 作行为动词和系动词时的词义区别。请比较：

32 1) I ***acted foolish.***

2) I'm ashamed I ***acted foolishly.***

妙语点睛 在例句 1)中，act 是系动词，后接形容词 foolish 作表语。在例句 2)中，act 是行为动词，后接副词 foolishly 作状语。

精品译文 1)我当时只是故意装傻。

2)我为自己的愚蠢行为感到羞耻。

讲到这里，笔者突然想起了我们常说的一句话：你到底是真傻还是装傻啊？如果是"真傻"，则说成 act foolishly；如果是"装傻"，则说成 act foolish，即此时 act 的内涵不同，作用也不同。

读者小时候有没有故意装病逃学的经历呢？这里的"装病"就应该说成 act sick，而不能说 act sickly。请看下面的对话：

33 (Lily is sick in bed.)

Mom: Lily! Why aren't you up and ready for school?

Lily: I don't feel so good, Mom.

Mom: Lily, if you're ***acting sick*** just because you want to play hooky...

Lily: (Coughing) No, Mom. I'm really sick.

Mom: Oh, that's a nasty cough. Let me feel your head (feels her forehead). You're on fire!

妙语点睛 这里的 act 是系动词，后接形容词 sick 作表语。

精品译文 (莉莉生病躺在床上。)

妈妈：莉莉！怎么还不起床准备上学？

莉莉：妈妈，我不舒服。

妈妈：莉莉，如果你是为了想逃学而装病……

莉莉：(咳嗽)不是，妈妈。我真的病了。

妈妈：喔，咳得蛮严重的。我摸摸你的头(摸她的额头)。你好烫！

请读者再看其他有关 act 的例句：

34 He ***acted quickly*** and seized the thief.

妙语点睛 这里的 act 是行为动词，后接副词 quickly 作状语。

精品译文 他动作很快，一下子就抓住了窃贼。

35 The crew, the passengers, and everybody else ***acted heroically***. Flying is all about teamwork and that's what we displayed.

妙语点睛　这里的 act 是行为动词，后接副词 heroically 作状语。

精品译文　机组成员、旅客以及其他所有人的表现都像英雄一样。飞行需要的是团队协作，我们恰恰体现了这一点。

这是英国航空公司 BA038 航班飞行员之一约翰·科沃德说的。这架从北京飞往伦敦的客机 2008 年 1 月 17 日在伦敦希思罗机场降落前，因突发故障导致动力全无，面临坠毁的危险。多亏飞行员的出色操作，飞机才成功地实现了紧急迫降，所有乘客和机组人员都安然无恙，只有十几人受了轻伤。

36 All men are created ***equal***.

妙语点睛　这句话可谓是美国的立国信条(creed)之一，写进了美国的宪法和《独立宣言》中。读者有没有这样的疑问：为什么这里使用了形容词 equal 而不是副词 equally 来修饰谓语 are created，并为这个疑问停下来认真思考过？

其实，这里的 equal 并不是修饰谓语 are created，而是补充说明主语 all men 的，因而可以很自然地改写成下面这样：***All men are equal*** when they are created (by God).

从这个改写后的句子，可以更清晰地看到其中的逻辑修饰关系。具体来说，这里的 equal(平等)的语义重点不在 created(创造)上，不是说"平等地被创造出来"(否则就要说成 are ***created equally***)，而在于说明主语 men 上，表示"人是平等的(all men are ***equal***)"。这就真正地理解了为什么要说 equal 而不是 equally。

精品译文　人人生而平等。

再看其他更多的例句：

37 All the audience ***sat silent.***

妙语点睛　这里的 silent 是说明主语 audience 的特征，而不是修饰 sat，故不用 silently。

精品译文　全场观众鸦雀无声。

38 He was ***born poor.***

妙语点睛　这里的 poor 是说明主语 he 的特征，而不是修饰 born，故不用 poorly。

精品译文　他出生贫穷。

39 People ***aren't born great***. They become great.

妙语点睛　这里的 great 是说明主语 people 的特征，而不是修饰 born，故不用 greatly。

精品译文　人不是生来就伟大，而是变得伟大。

40 I ***was born a leader.***

妙语点睛　这里的 a leader 是说明主语 I 的特征。

精品译文　我生来就是作领导的。

41 The boy ***blushed scarlet.***

妙语点睛　这里的 scarlet 是说明主语 the boy 的特征，而不是修饰 blushed。

精品译文　这孩子羞红了脸。

42 I ***married young.***

妙语点睛　这里的 young 是说明主语 I 的特征，而不是修饰 married，所以这句话可以改写成 I was young when I married。

精品译文　我早婚。

43 The caterpillars kept going in a circle in the pot. Eventually, after a week of circling around, they ***dropped dead*** of exhaustion and starvation with food only inches away from them.

妙语点睛　这里的形容词 dead 是说明主语 they 的特征，而不是修饰谓语 dropped。

精品译文　这些毛毛虫不停地在盆里绕圈。最终，这样过了一周之后，它们都因为疲劳和饥饿而死去，可是食物离它们只有几英寸远。

1.2.2 简单句叠加成复杂难句

了解“主系表”句型结构之后，下面将举例说明该句型如何演变为一个结构较为复杂的难句，以使读者了解简单句与复杂句之间的联系。请看例句：

1 Vitamins are organic compounds.

妙语点睛 这个句子的主语是 vitamins，谓语是系动词 are，名词短语 organic compounds 是表语。

精品译文 维生素是一种有机化合物。

这个句子很简单，但现在要逐步将其复杂化。比如在名词 compounds 后面添加一个后置定语，如下句：

2 Vitamins are organic compounds ***necessary for the normal growth of life.***

妙语点睛 这里我们添加了一个形容词短语 necessary for the normal growth of life，来后置修饰名词 compounds。

精品译文 维生素是一种有机化合物，是生命正常生长所必不可少的。

我们进一步把后置定语复杂化，比如下句：

3 Vitamins are organic compounds ***necessary for the normal growth and maintenance of life of animals, including man.***

妙语点睛 这里的形容词短语是 necessary for the normal growth and maintenance of life of animals, including man，依然后置修饰名词 compounds。

精品译文 维生素是一种有机化合物，是所有动物(包括人类)的正常生长和生命延续所必不可少的。

我们还可以把上句进一步复杂化，比如下句：

4 Vitamins are organic compounds ***necessary in small amounts in the diet for the normal growth and maintenance of life of animals, including man.***

妙语点睛 本句子是 1996 年考研完形填空真题的第一句话。这里是在 necessary 和 for 之间添加了介词短语 in small amounts in the diet，整个形容词短语是 necessary in small amounts in the diet for the normal growth and maintenance of life of animals, including man，依然后置修饰名词 compounds。

精品译文 维生素是一种有机化合物，尽管在饮食中的含量很少，但却是所有动物(包括人类)正常生长和生命延续所必不可少的。

比较上面各句可以发现，最后一句话显然要比第一句复杂得多，但是基本句型并没有改变，其核心结构依然是 vitamins are organic compounds 这一主系表句型。所以读者应该看到，对于难句的分析和解读，关键在于对句型结构的分析。

思维总结

本节重点讨论了四类不同的系动词，我们读者应该对其有所了解，尤其是对于近似于不及物动词的半系动词，遇到时要能够正确理解句子的意思。

思维训练

Exercise 1.2（Key: P325）

请翻译下列句子。

1. She lived the life of and died a spinster.
2. He arrived in Beijing a penniless 18-year-old and now is the CEO of a multinational company.
3. This book falls overdue a week; I must be fined.
4. Mr. Smith died a university president.

请比较下面两个句子的含义区别。

5. He acted stupid.
6. He acted stupidly.

请选择最佳答案填空。

7. I'm ashamed I acted ______.
   A. fool　　B. foolish　　C. foolishly
8. Lily acted ______ just to play hooky.
   A. sick　　B. sickly　　C. sickness
9. A: How about the ship then?
   B: It sailed back ______.
   A. safe　　B. safely　　C. safety
10. He has been working out in the gym to stay ______.
   A. healthily　　B. healthy　　C. health

1.3 句型二：主语 + 谓语

我们先来分析该句型谓语动词的特点，然后举例说明这种结构的句子如何演变为复杂的难句。因此，本节内容安排如下：

1.3.1 谓语动词的特点

1.3.2 简单句叠加成复杂难句

1.3.1 谓语动词的特点

该句型的谓语动词是**不及物动词**(intransitive verb)，所表示的动作没有作用对象，其本身意思完整，其后不需带宾语。比如 1.2.1 小节中关于苍鹰的那个故事，只含有"主谓"结构的句子包括：

1 The egg ***hatched.***

2 The little eagle ***grew up.***

3 It ***clucked*** and ***cackled.***

妙语点睛 这三个句子的主语分别是 the egg, the little eagle 和 it，而谓语动词分别是 hatched, grew up 和 clucked and cackled，其中，最后一句话的谓语是并列谓语，即有两个动词 clucked 和 cackled 充当谓语。这些动词都是不及物动词，所以没有接宾语。

精品译文 1. 这枚蛋孵化成了一只小鹰。

2. 小鹰慢慢长大了。

3. 它发出咯咯的叫声。

尽管这个句型里没有宾语，但是在谓语动词后面往往会接状语，用来修饰谓语动词，比如表示动作发生的地点等。请看例句：

4 An eagle's egg ***was placed*** in the nest of a prairie chicken.

妙语点睛 该句的结构分析图如下：

An eagle's egg (主语) was placed (谓语) in the nest of a prairie chicken (地点状语).

精品译文 一只苍鹰的蛋被放置在一只草原土鸡的窝里。

5 ***It scratched*** in the dirt for seeds.

妙语点睛 该句的结构分析图如下：

It (主语) scratched (谓语) in the dirt (地点状语) for seeds (目的状语).

精品译文 它在土里找种子吃。

我们看到，这句话里虽然没有宾语，但动词后面接了各种状语。

1.3.2 简单句叠加成复杂难句

下面举例说明该句型如何演变为一个结构较为复杂的难句，以使读者了解简单句与复杂句之间的联系。请看例句：

1 This trend began during the Second World War.

妙语点睛 该句的主语是 this trend，谓语 began 是一个不及物动词，后边没有带宾语。介词短语 during the Second World War 作时间状语。

精品译文 这种趋势始于第二次世界大战期间。

下面开始一步步把这个句子复杂化。比如：

2 This trend began during the Second World War, ***when several governments came to this conclusion.***

妙语点睛 这里加了一个定语从句 when several governments came to the conclusion，来修饰时间 Second World War。这个定语从句是一个“主语 + 谓语 + 宾语”的句型，主语是 several governments，谓语是短语动词 came to，宾语是 the conclusion。

精品译文 这种趋势始于第二次世界大战期间，当时一些国家的政府得出这样的结论。

我们再进一步把这个句子复杂化，比如：

3 This trend began during the Second World War, ***when several governments came to the conclusion that the specific demands cannot generally be foreseen in detail.***

妙语点睛 这里添加了一个同位语从句 that the specific demands cannot generally be foreseen in detail，补充说明 conclusion。这个同位语从句也是一个“主语 + 谓语”的句型，这里的主语是 the specific demands，谓语是一个被动结构 cannot generally be foreseen，介词短语 in detail 作状语。

精品译文 这种趋势始于第二次世界大战期间，当时一些国家的政府得出结论：具体要求通常是无法详尽预见的。

我们再进一步把这个句子复杂化，比如：

4 This trend began during the Second World War, when several governments came to the conclusion that the specific demands ***that a government wants to make of its scientific establishment*** cannot generally be foreseen in detail.

妙语点睛 这就是 1996 年的考研翻译真题，这里添加了一个定语从句 that a government wants to make of its scientific establishment，来修饰 demands。这个定语从句是一个“主语 + 谓语 + 宾语”的句型，主语是 a government，谓语是 wants，宾语是 to make of its scientific establishment。很多读者也许看不出这里 that 作定语从句的何种成分。其实，这里的 that 指代先行词 demands，在定语从句中作谓语 make 的宾语，从而构成一个 make demands of 的搭配，表示“对……提出要求”。很多读者由于不熟悉这个搭配而不理解定语从句的结构，结果造成不理解句子的意思。由此可见，掌握一定的短语搭配对于理解句子的结构是非常重要的。

精品译文 这种趋势始于第二次世界大战期间，当时一些国家的政府得出结论：政府想向科研机构提出的具体要求通常是无法详尽预见的。

综上所述，上面这个复杂的句子其实是由四个简单句复合而成的，即有两个“主语 + 谓语”结构的句子：this trend began during the Second World War 和 the specific demands cannot generally be foreseen in detail，还有两个“主语 + 谓语 + 宾语”结构的句子：several governments came to the conclusion 和 a government wants to make of its scientific establishment。

关于“主语 + 谓语 + 宾语”的句型结构，将在下一节中详细讨论。

1.4 句型三：主语 + 谓语 + 宾语

本节首先分析该句型谓语动词的特点，然后举例说明这种结构的句子如何演变为复杂的难句。因此，本节内容安排如下：

1.4.1 谓语动词的特点

1.4.2 简单句叠加成复杂难句

1.4.1 谓语动词的特点

该句型的谓语动词是**及物动词**(transitive verb)，这种动词告诉我们由主语发出的动作所作用的对象是什么，这个“所作用的对象”就是通常所说的**宾语**，即宾语是主语动作的承受对象。因此，这类动词是带有宾语的。英文中绝大多数动词都是及物动词。

比如 1.2.1 小节中的 Losers look for quick fixes 故事中，“主谓宾”结构的句子有：

1 But the not-so-easy way may ***mean*** getting down on your hands and knees and pulling out the weeds by the roots. 但是不简便的方法就意味着你自己得双膝跪地，然后用双手把杂草连根拔除。

2 They are ***looking for*** one-minute solutions to everything. 他们想投机取巧，对一切事情都想快速解决。

3 Just like instant coffee, they ***want*** instant happiness. 这就像速溶咖啡一样，他们想要的只是“幸福快餐”。

4 There are no quick fixes. This attitude ***leads to*** disappointment. 生活中没有捷径，想找捷径最终会导致失望。

在以上例句中，谓语动词 mean 和 want 都是及物动词。若是不及物动词，则可以加适当的介词，然后再接宾语，比如 looking for 和 leads to。

有人做过统计，英语中大约 80%的句子是“主谓宾”结构，由此可见这种句型的使用频率之高。

1.4.2 简单句叠加成复杂难句

讨论完“主谓宾”句型结构之后，下面将举例说明该句型如何演变为一个结构较为复杂的难句，使读者了解简单句与复杂句之间的联系。请看例句：

1 The emphasis helped to obscure the great importance.

妙语点睛 该句的主语是 the emphasis，谓语是 helped，宾语是 to obscure the great importance 不定式短语。

精品译文 这种强调模糊了这一重要性。

下面开始一步步把这个句子复杂化，比如：

2 The emphasis ***given by both scholars and statesmen*** helped to obscure the great importance.

妙语点睛 这里是在主语 emphasis 后面添加了一个分词短语 given by both scholars and statesmen，作后置定语，表明是谁在强调。

精品译文 学者和政治家们的这种强调模糊了这一重要性。

再进一步把这个句子复杂化，比如：

3 The emphasis given by both scholars and statesmen (***to the presumed disappearance of the American frontier***) helped to obscure the great importance.

妙语点睛 这里添加了一个介词短语 to the presumed disappearance of the American frontier。这个介词短语修饰哪个部分？其实这个介词短语是补充说明主语 emphasis 的，表明强调的内容是什么。

精品译文 学者和政治家们强调美国边疆消失的假设，这种强调模糊了这一重要性。

再进一步把这个句子复杂化，比如：

4 The emphasis given by both scholars and statesmen to the presumed disappearance of the American frontier helped to obscure the great importance ***of changes in the conditions and consequences of international trade.***

妙语点睛 这里在 importance 后面添加了介词短语 of changes in the conditions and consequences of international trade，作后置定语。这里还要搞清楚并列关系，不是 changes in the conditions 和 consequences of international trade 并列，而是 conditions 和 consequences 并列，然后介词短语 of international trade 修饰 conditions and consequences，表示"国际贸易的条件和后果"。最后整个介词短语 in the conditions and consequences of international trade 修饰 changes，表示在哪方面发生的变化，即"在国际贸易的条件和后果两方面发生的变化"。

精品译文 学者和政治家们强调美国边疆消失的假设，这种强调模糊了国际贸易的条件和后果方面发生变化的巨大作用。

再进一步把这个句子复杂化，比如：

5 The emphasis given by both scholars and statesmen to the presumed disappearance of the American frontier helped to obscure the great importance of changes in the conditions and consequences of international trade ***that occurred during the second half of the nineteenth century.***

妙语点睛 这里在 international trade 后面添加了定语从句 that occurred during the second half of the nineteenth century，作后置定语。这个定语从句则是一个"主语＋谓语"的句型，其主语是关系词 that，谓语是 occurred。

精品译文 学者和政治家们强调美国边疆消失的假设，这种强调模糊了在19世纪后半期发生在国际贸易的条件和后果两方面的变化的巨大作用。

综上所述，这个复杂的句子其实就是一个"主语＋谓语＋宾语"的句型，即 the emphasis…helped to obscure the great importance...。其内部又带有一个"主语＋谓语"的句型，即 that occurred...。

1.5 句型四：主语＋谓语＋间接宾语＋直接宾语

本节首先分析该句型谓语动词的特点，然后将举例说明这种结构的句子如何演变为复杂的难句。因此，本节内容安排如下：

1.5.1 谓语动词的特点

1.5.2 简单句叠加成复杂难句

1.5.1 谓语动词的特点

该句型的谓语动词是**双宾动词**(dative verb)，这种动词后面所接的成分有人又有物。一般来讲，这里的"人"表示动作的接受者，称作间接宾语(indirect object)；"物"表示动作作用的对象，是动作的承受者，称作直接宾语(direct object)。**间接宾语和直接宾语合起来称为双宾语。**请看例句：

1 He showed the guard his passport.

(the guard：间接宾语；his passport：直接宾语)

妙语点睛 对于这个句型，一般可以进行这样的改写，即把直接宾语提前置谓语后面，然后添加介词 to 或 for，再把间接宾语放在介词后面。比如上面这个句子可以改写成：

He showed ***his passport*** to ***the guard.***

精品译文 他把护照给门卫看了。

下面再来看一个带 for 的例句：

2 I am going to buy her a gift. =I am going to buy ***a gift*** for ***her.***

妙语点睛 这里的 her 是间接宾语，a gift 是直接宾语。改写后的句子用了介词 for。

精品译文 我打算给她买个礼物。

选择介词 for 还是 to，取决于谓语动词。具体详述如下：

1. 同 show 一样，当间接宾语后移时，间接宾语前需带介词 to，表示间接宾语是动作的接受者。这样的动词有：assign, award, bring, deliver, deny, feed, give, grant, hand, lend, offer, owe, pass, pay, promise, post, read, recommend, sell, send, show, take 和 write 等等。
2. 同 buy 一样，当间接宾语后移时，间接宾语前需带介词 for。这样的动词有：book（预订）, buy, build, change, choose, cook, fetch, find, get, keep, make, order, prepare 和 sing 等等。
3. 有个别动词只用于"主语 + 动词 + 间接宾语(+ 直接宾语)"的结构，而不用介词来替换。这样的动词有：charge, cost 和 bet 等等。比如：

1 I'll bet you ten dollars. 我跟你赌 10 块钱。

2 The repairman charged me ten dollars. 修理工收了我 10 块钱。

上面这些句子都是无法用 for 或 to 来改写的。比如不能说：I'll bet ten dollars of you/for you*.

此外，还有更特殊的动词（如 ask）当间接宾语后移时，间接宾语前需带介词 of。比如：

3 Can I ask you a question? = Can I ask a question ***of you***? 我能问你一个问题吗？

因此，类似的句子有：

4 I have a question to ***ask of*** you.

再比如，表示需要某人帮助，可以说：

5 I have a big favor to ***ask of*** you. 我想请你帮个忙。

对于这些特殊的动词用法，读者只需要了解即可，不要求掌握。

1.5.2 简单句叠加成复杂难句

讨论完"主谓双宾"的句型结构之后，下面将举例说明，该句型如何演变为一个结构较为复杂的难句，使读者了解简单句与复杂句之间的联系。请看例句：

1 Her work won her the Nobel Prize in 1983.

妙语点睛 该句的动词 won 是一个双宾动词，其后要接双宾语，即 win sb. sth.，表示"为某人赢得某物"。这里的 her 是间接宾语，the Nobel Prize 是直接宾语。

精品译文 她的工作使她赢得了 1983 年的诺贝尔奖。

可以把这句话稍微变得复杂一点，如下句所示：

2 Her work ***in genetics*** won ***United States scientist*** Barbara McClintock the Nobel Prize in 1983.

图解难句

her work in genetics	主语
won	谓语
United States scientist Barbara McClintock	间接宾语
the Nobel Prize	直接宾语
in 1983	时间状语，修饰 won

妙语点睛 这句话的间接宾语较长，即 United States scientist Barbara McClintock，直接宾语是 the Nobel Prize，原句型仍为 win sb. sth.，即表示"为某人赢得某物"。

精品译文 芭芭拉·麦克克林托克在遗传学领域的研究成果，使她赢得了 1983 年的诺贝尔奖。

上面两句虽然复杂程度不同，但句型结构完全一样，都是动词 win 后面带有一个双宾语的结构。

思维总结

掌握带有双宾语的句型，关键是在于谓语动词。所以，对于一些通常需要接双宾语的谓语动词，读者应该熟练掌握。此外，读者应该掌握介词 for 或 to 与谓语动词的搭配关系，以便对双宾语句型进行改写。

思维训练（Key: P325）

Exercise 1. 5

请分析下列句子中的双宾语，并试着用适当的介词改写句子。

1. Give a thief enough rope and he'll hang himself.
2. Can you recommend me a good novel?
3. He built them a hut.
4. He ordered himself a bottle of champagne.
5. Will you choose me an interesting novel?
6. Can you spare me a few minutes of your valuable time?
7. Jack doesn't owe me anything.
8. May I ask you a favor?
9. That will save you a lot of time.
10. The novel won the author a Nobel Prize.
11. It cost me three dollars.

1.6 句型五：主语 + 谓语 + 宾语 + 宾语补足语

本节首先分析该句型谓语动词的特点，然后将把这个句型与 1. 5 节的句型结构进行比较，最后举例说明这种结构的句子如何演变为复杂的难句。因此，本节内容安排如下：

1. 6. 1 谓语动词的特点
1. 6. 2 区分双宾语和复合宾语
1. 6. 3 简单句叠加成复杂难句

1. 6. 1 谓语动词的特点

该句型的谓语动词是**宾补动词**（factitive verb），这种动词后面接宾语，而此宾语后又接补充说明宾语的补足语（object complement）。**宾语和宾语补足语合起来称为复合宾语。**

△ 常见的带复合宾语的动词有：appoint, believe, call, choose, consider, declare, elect, feel, find, keep, leave, let, make, name, nominate, prove, see, suppose 和 vote 等等。请读者看下面的例句。

1 I very much hope that this new medium will ***make*** my Christmas message more personal and direct.

妙语点睛 该句的宾语是 my Christmas message，宾语补足语是 more personal and direct。这里是形容词作宾语补足语。

精品译文 我衷心希望，这种新媒体能让我的圣诞致辞更有人情味、更加直接。

我们再来看一个英语谚语，其意思类似于汉语中的“君子之交淡如水”：

2 A hedge（树篱）between ***keeps*** friendship green.

妙语点睛 该句的宾语是 friendship，宾语补足语是 green。这里是形容词作宾语补足语。

精品译文 保持距离，友谊常青（这句话可引申为“君子之交淡如水”）。

请再看其他例句：

3 They ***appointed*** John chairman.

妙语点睛 该句的宾语是 John，宾语补足语是 chairman。这里是名词作宾语补足语。

精品译文 他们任命约翰为主席。

4 I *believe* him to be true.

妙语点睛　该句的宾语是 him，宾语补足语是 to be true。这里是不定式作宾语补足语。

精品译文　我相信他是真诚的。

5 The chairman *declared* the meeting over.

妙语点睛　该句的宾语是 the meeting，宾语补足语是 over。这里是副词作宾语补足语。

精品译文　主席宣布会议结束。

6 You can *leave* the door open.

妙语点睛　该句的宾语是 the door，宾语补足语是 open。这里是形容词作宾语补足语。

精品译文　你就把门开着。

1.6.2 区分双宾语和复合宾语

有些读者不能区分双宾语和复合宾语，尤其是当两者都是“动词＋人＋物”这样的结构时。其实，区分这两种宾语的方法很简单，就是**在宾语后面加上 be 动词，若能构成一个语义通顺的句子，即是补足语**。因为宾语与宾语补足语的语义关系就相当于主语与主语补足语的关系，即类似一个主系表结构，所以，在宾语后面添上一个系动词 be，自然应该是能构成一个逻辑语义通顺的句子。而间接宾语与直接宾语二者之间就没有这样的语义关系，所以，添上 be 之后，自然是不能构成一个语义通顺的句子。请比较：

1 1) I made John our chairman.

2) I made John a cake.

妙语点睛　在例句 1)中，在宾语 John 后面添上一个 is，即 John is our chairman. 这说得通，所以例句 1)中的 our chairman 是宾语补足语。然而在例句 2)中，在宾语 John 后面添上一个 is，即 John is a cake*.(约翰是一块蛋糕。)这显然讲不通，所以例句 2)是一个双宾语结构，a cake 是直接宾语。

精品译文　1)我选了约翰当我们的主席。

2)我给约翰做了一块蛋糕。

再来看下面较难的句子：

2 1) She will make him a good husband.

2) She will make him a good wife.

妙语点睛　乍看起来，这两个句子仅 husband 和 wife 一词之差，但两者在句型结构上不同，意思的差别自然也很大。在例句 1)中，在宾语 him 后面添上一个 is，即 He is a good husband. 这说得通，所以例句 1)是一个复合宾语结构，句中的 a good husband 是宾语补足语。然而在例句 2)中，在宾语 him 后面添上一个 is，即 He is a good wife*.(他是一个好妻子。)这显然有悖常理，所以例句 2)是一个双宾语结构，a good wife 是直接宾语。另外，例句 2)可以改写为 She will make a good wife for him. 即表示“她可以成为他的一个好妻子”。

实际上，这里的 make 在两个例句中的意思是不一样的，在例句 1)中，make 是大家熟悉的使役动词，英文解释是 to cause to be or become，表示“使……成为”；而在例句 2)中，make 并非使役动词，英文解释是 to develop into，表示“变成为”。

精品译文　1)她会把他变成一个好丈夫的。

2)她会成为他的好妻子的。

从这对特殊的例句可以看出，利用上面介绍的方法来区分这两类宾语，对于正确理解句子是非常重要的。对于 make 作为“变成为”的意思，请读者再看下面这个例句：

3 I said to him, “Monsieur le President, I have no reason to refuse.” Carla is living an authentic love story. I think that they ***make a good couple.***

妙语点睛　这是意大利名模卡拉·布鲁尼的母亲玛丽萨·布鲁尼说的一句话。法国总统尼古拉·萨科齐于 2008 年 2 月与其女友卡拉·布鲁尼结婚，这是他的第三次婚姻，婚期距他与第二任妻子塞西莉亚离婚还不到四个月。

该句中的 make 就是表示“成为”的意思，相当于上一个例句中的 make (a good wife)。

精品译文　我对他说:“总统先生,我没有理由拒绝你。”卡拉正在经历一个真实的爱情故事。我想他们是很般配的一对。

请再看下面这个例句:

4 Recent technology gives computers both audio and video capability, making them multimedia machines with interactive potential.

妙语点睛　这里的 computers 与 both audio and video capability 的关系,不同于 them 与 multimedia machines with interactive potential 的关系,因为 Computers are both audio and video capability. *(计算机是视听功能。)讲不通,而 They (computers) are multimedia machines with interactive potential.(计算机是一个能与人类进行互动的多媒体机器。)讲得通。所以,这里的 computers 应是间接宾语,both audio and video capability 是直接宾语,而 multimedia machines with interactive potential 应是宾语 them 的补足语。

精品译文　近几年的技术发展,计算机具备了视听功能,这就使得它成为能与我们人类进行互动的一个多媒体机器。

1.6.3 简单句叠加成复杂难句

讨论完“主谓+复合宾语”的句型结构之后,下面举例说明该句型如何演变为一个结构较为复杂的难句,使读者了解简单句与复杂句之间的联系。请看例句:

1 Willa Cather considered ***this novel*** her best work.

妙语点睛　该句的动词 considered 是一个宾补动词,其后不但要带宾语 this novel,还要接宾语补足语 her best work,补充说明前面的宾语。若只说 Willa Cather considered this novel,这句话的意思显然不完整,于是要对 this novel 补充一下,加上补足语 her best work,说成 Willa Cather considered this novel her best work. 这样句子的意思才完整。

精品译文　维拉·凯瑟认为这部小说是她最好的一部作品。

现在可以把这句话稍微变得复杂一点,比如把宾语复杂化,如下句所示:

2 Willa Cather considered ***her novel of life in nineteenth-century Nebraska,*** **My Antonia** her best work.

妙语点睛　这句话的宾语较长,是 her novel of life in nineteenth-century Nebraska, My Antonia,其中 My Antonia 是小说的名字,与名词短语 her novel of life in nineteenth-century Nebraska 构成同位语。宾语补足语是 her best work。

精品译文　维拉·凯瑟认为她的那部描写19世纪内布拉斯加州生活的小说《我的安东尼奥》是她最好的一部作品。

上面两句话的复杂程度不同,但句型结构完全一样,都是动词 consider 后面带有一个复合宾语的结构。

思维总结

掌握带有复合宾语的句型,关键是在于谓语动词。所以,对于一些通常需要接复合宾语的谓语动词,读者应该熟练掌握。此外,读者应该学会判断双宾语和复合宾语。

思维训练

Exercise 1.6 (Key: P326)

请分析下列句子结构,找到宾语补足语,并将句子翻译成中文。

1. Absence makes the heart grow fonder.
2. The telescopes of the 1600's magnified objects thirty-three times their original size.
3. The boy's sharp remark left the teacher speechless.
4. The chairman has declared the meeting over.

5. I prefer my steak medium.
6. Dick set the caged animals free.
7. The pot calls the kettle black

1.7 从简单句到复合句

以上简单地介绍了英语的五种句型结构，它们是构成英语复杂难句的基础。换句话说，英文中各种复杂的难句都是由这五种基本句型通过扩展、组合、省略、倒装等各种形式的变化得来的，这一点已经通过以上各节中的例句不同程度的复杂变化有了初步的了解。下面再来简单考察一下从简单句如何过渡到复合句。

一般来讲，一个句子除了有主语和谓语之外，其他可能包含的成分还有宾语、表语、定语、状语、补语和同位语等。在这些成分中，谓语较为特殊，只能由动词来充当，而其他成分则可以由词、短语或者句子来充当。如果用一个完整的句子来充当另一个句子的某个成分时，即构成相应的从句。请看如下图表：

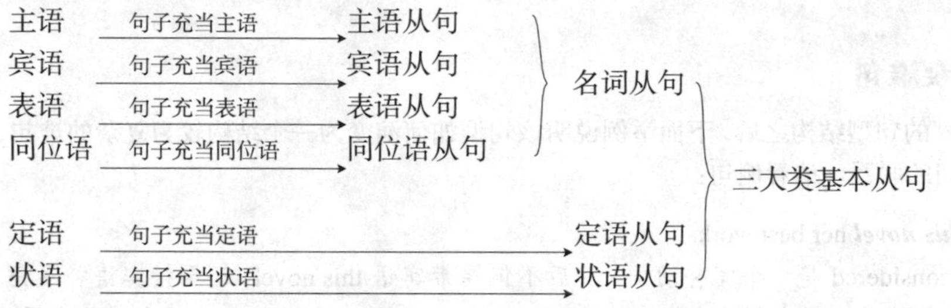

谓语：各种谓语动词的变化形式

从以上的图表看出，谓语是不能用句子来充当的，否则就会有“谓语从句”了。而其他成分可以用句子来充当，于是便有了各类从句。具体分类如下：

三大从句

1. 名词从句：包括主语从句、宾语从句、表语从句和同位语从句。我们知道，名词在英语中可作主语、宾语、表语和同位语这四种成分，因而这四种从句在句子中的作用相当于名词，故将此四类从句又统称为名词从句。

2. 形容词从句：或叫关系从句（relative clause）或定语从句。因为形容词最大的特点就是在句中起限定或修饰作用，用作定语，故常称为定语从句。

3. 副词从句：副词在英语中常用来修饰动词、形容词和副词，用作状语，故又称为状语从句。

在后面各章的讨论中都会涉及这些从句，在此就不再举例赘述。

其实，以上图表列出了英语中的重要语法项目，包括两大类：从句和谓语，这也正是本书的核心内容。本书将讨论三大从句以及英语中各种谓语动词形式，包括完成时、完成进行时、情态动词和虚拟语气等内容。

写给读者的话

一、本章学习思路

本章讨论的内容主要有三个方面：

第一，分析了英语中的五种基本句型，这是解读和构造英语句子的基础。

第二，通过举例，展示了简单句与复杂难句之间的联系。

第三，介绍了由简单句到复合句的演变关系，从而便于读者对整个英语语法体系的把握。

二、本章重点及难点

本章重点讨论了英语中简单句的五种基本句型。掌握英语句型的关键在于掌握谓语动词的用法，这些动词包括：系动词、不及物动词、单宾语动词、双宾语动词和复合宾语动词。真正能够灵活判断句子的骨干结构，是学习本章内容的重点和目的。

本章的难点内容包括：真正理解系动词的作用和掌握系动词的分类，对双宾语和复合宾语的辨别与判断。

三、本章学习时间安排

读者可以用三天左右的时间将本章内容读完一遍。本章主要是介绍性和基础性的内容，因此，想要真正灵活掌握本章所讲述的内容，关键还是在于平时的应用。比如对于特殊系动词用法的理解，关系到对句子意思的正确理解，这都体现在英语实践中。

综合练习（Key: P326）

请选择最佳答案填空。

1. Willa Cather considered her novel of life in nineteenth-century Nebraska, *My Antonia* ______.
   A. was her best work　　B. her best work
   C. her best work it was　　D. being her best work
2. The photographs of Carrie Mae Weems, in which she often makes her family members ______, are an affectionate and incisive representation of the African American experience.
   A. are her subjects　　B. her subjects
   C. are subjects　　D. which her subjects
3. One of Ulysses S. Grant's first acts as President of the United States was to name the Seneca chief Donehogawa ______ of Indian Affairs.
   A. as was Commissioner　　B. Commissioner
   C. was Commissioner　　D. him Commissioner
4. The novelist Edith Wharton considered the writer Henry James ______.
   A. that a strong influence on her work　　B. as strong influence on her work
   C. a strong influence on her work　　D. was a strong influence on her work
5. The sapphire's transparency to ultraviolet and infrared radiation makes ______ in optical instruments.
   A. it is of use　　B. it is useful　　C. it useful　　D. it uses
6. In 1993 the Library of Congress appointed author Rita Dove ______ of the United States.
   A. as was poet laureate　　B. was poet laureate
   C. poet laureate　　D. and poet laureate
7. In 1952 Ernest Hemingway published *The Old Man and the Sea*, ______.
   A. won him the Nobel Prize for Literature in 1954
   B. and the Nobel Prize for Literature won in 1954
   C. in 1954 won the Nobel Prize for Literature for this work
   D. a work that won him the Nobel Prize for Literature in 1954
8. Her work in genetics won United States scientist Barbara McClintock ______ in 1983.
   A. was the Nobel Prize　　B. the Nobel Prize was
   C. the Nobel Prize　　D. for the Nobel Prize

Chapter 2

第二章　名词从句

在第一章的 1.7 节，简单地介绍了简单句如何按照一定的造句规则构成复合句。本章将讨论简单句如何通过相应的英语操作规则而变成名词从句。本章内容安排如下：

2.1 简单句与名词从句

2.2 简单句与主语从句

2.3 简单句与宾语从句

2.4 简单句与表语从句

2.5 简单句与同位语从句

2.1 简单句与名词从句

在讨论简单句与名词从句之间的关系之前，首先要搞清楚什么是名词从句，然后再讨论不同种类的简单句如何转化为一个名词从句。因此，本节内容安排如下：

2.1.1 何谓名词从句？
2.1.2 陈述句作句子成分
2.1.3 一般疑问句作句子成分
2.1.4 特殊疑问句作句子成分
2.1.5 引导名词从句的连接词

2.1.1 何谓名词从句？

在英文中，**名词**或**名词短语**主要充当四种句子成分：主语、宾语、表语和同位语(见下表中的各例句 1)。如果把**句子**当作名词来用，分别充当另一句话的主语、宾语、表语或同位语（见下表中的各例句 2)，于是便构成了四种从句：主语从句、宾语从句、表语从句和同位语从句。因为这四种从句在本质上相当于名词的作用，所以将其统称为**名词从句**。请看下表：

四种成分	例句	解释	简单句还是复合句
主语	1. ***The book*** is interesting. 这本书很有趣。	在例句 1 中，名词短语 the book 作主语	简单句
	2. ***What I am reading*** is interesting. 我在看的这本书很有趣。	在例句 2 中，完整的句子 what I am reading 作主语，因此称为主语从句。该从句有自己的主语(I)和谓语(am reading)，what 在主语从句中作 am reading 的宾语	主语从句
宾语	1. No one knows exactly ***the life on other planets***. 没有人能够确切地知道外星人。	在例句 1 中，名词短语 the life on other planets 作宾语	简单句
	2. No one knows exactly ***whether there is life on other planets***. 没有人能够确切地知道是否有外星人存在。	在例句 2 中，完整的句子 whether there is life on other planets 作宾语，因此被称为宾语从句。该从句是 there be 句型，是一个完整的句子	宾语从句
表语	1. English is ***a useful tool***. 英语是一门有用的工具。	在例句 1 中，名词短语 a useful tool 作表语	简单句
	2. English is ***what I like most among all subjects***. 英语是所有科目中我最喜欢的。	在例句 2 中，完整的句子 what I like most among all subjects 作表语，因此被称为表语从句。该从句有自己的主语(I)和谓语(like)，what 在表语从句中作 like 的宾语	表语从句
同位语	1. I love the novel, ***The Old Man and the Sea***. 我喜欢《老人与海》这部小说。	在例句 1 中，名词短语 *The Old Man and the Sea* 作 novel 的同位语，用来补充说明 novel	简单句
	2. I love the saying ***that love, not time heals all wounds***. 我喜欢这句话：是爱而不是时间能够治愈一切创伤。	在例句 2 中，完整的句子 that love, not time heals all wounds 作 saying 的同位语，因此被称为同位语从句。该从句有自己的主语(love, not time)和谓语(heals)，that 在同位语从句中不充当成分	同位语从句

从上面的表格清楚地看到，一个完整的句子可以充当另外一个句子的某种成分，比如主语、宾语、表语或同位语，于是便构成相应的从句。看到这里，也许有读者会问：可以把哪种句子当作名词来用呢？经研究发现，相当于名词作用的句子有三类：陈述句、一般疑问句以及特殊疑问句。

因此，名词从句可简单概括为这样一句话：**名词从句就是用三种句子来分别充当另外一个句子的四种句子成分**，这构成了名词从句的本质特征。

但是，值得注意的是，这三种句子不是直接放在另一个句子中作成分，而是要作各种变化调整。接下来将对此问题进行讨论。

2.1.2 陈述句作句子成分

一、要在陈述句句首加上 that

当把一个完整的陈述句(见下表中的各例句 1)当作名词来使用时，需要在陈述句首加 that，然后可使"that+陈述句"这一结构分别充当另一个句子的主语、宾语、表语或同位语等四种成分(见下表中的各例句 2)，即构成主语从句、宾语从句、表语从句或同位语从句。请看下表：

陈述句	名词从句	解释
1. English is important.	2. That ***English is important*** is an undoubted fact. 英语很重要，这是毋庸置疑的事实。	陈述句作主语，构成**主语从句**
1. Love, not time heals all wounds.	2. I've learned that ***love, not time heals all wounds***. 我明白了，是爱而不是时间能够治愈一切创伤。	陈述句作宾语，构成**宾语从句**
1. The child should be sent to school.	2. My idea is that ***the child should be sent to school***. 我认为这孩子应该送去上学。	陈述句作表语，构成**表语从句**
1. He succeeded in the experiment.	2. The fact that ***he succeeded in the experiment*** pleased everybody. 他试验取得了成功，这让大家很高兴。	陈述句用作同位语，补充说明名词 the fact，构成**同位语从句**

二、为什么要加 that?

一般的语法书都是只讲"死"的规则，而不去追究规则背后合乎逻辑的语法思维，致使很多学生花费了大量的时间学英语、学语法，记死规则，最后又很快遗忘，造成最终难以修成英语正果。在此笔者要强调，对于英语的学习，一定要多去追问规则背后的"为什么"，一定要 think much(多思考)！

对于陈述句，为什么要在其句首加 that 后才能用它作成分呢？为什么在宾语从句中 that 又可以省去呢？请先来看这个例句：

1 ***That English is important*** is an undoubted fact.

主语从句　　　　谓语部分

妙语点睛 假如把 that 去掉，上句就变成：English ***is important is an undoubted fact***.

这句话就有两个中心谓语部分，即 is important 和 is an undoubted fact。但是，**在英文中，句子的核心意思主要是靠谓语部分来表达的，一个句子只表达一个核心意思**(因为我们说话要一句一句地说)，**也就只能有一个谓语部分**。现在这个句子有两个谓语部分，势必会造成 native speakers 混淆不清，因为他会先读出 English is important，这表示"英文很重要"，可是当他继续往下读时，又出现了 is an undoubted fact 这个谓语部分。于是整个句子 English is important is an undoubted fact. 就会让人感到"丈二和尚摸不着头脑(A Buddha, who is twelve feet, can't touch his own forehead.)"。native speakers 就会纳闷：你要表达的意思到底是"某个东西重要(something is important)"，还是要说"某个东西是事实(something is an undoubted fact)"？

为了避免混淆，在句首加上一个标志 that，这里的 that 就相当于一个指路牌，它的出现就等于是在告诉读者：that 后面紧接着的句子是要作为另一个句子的某一个成分来使用的，不是要表达的核心意思。因此，当读者读到 ***That*** English is important... 他也知道这个句子的核心意思并没有讲出来，他一定会期待着句子接下来的中心意思。当他读到 ...is an undoubted fact 时，他知道了，句子要表达的意思是"英语很重要，这是一个毋庸置疑的事实"，而不是要说"英语很重要"。

精品译文 英语很重要，这是一个毋庸置疑的事实。

关于 that 这种"指路牌"的作用，读者不妨利用下列例句自我测试一下。看下面这对句子，哪个更让你快速而准确地理解。

2 1) The criminal confessed his sins harmed many people.

2) The criminal confessed that his sins harmed many people.

妙语点睛 做这个测试的一个前提是，句中的单词读者都要认识。在单词都认识的情况下，相信一般读者对于例句 1)的解读时间肯定要比对例句 2)长。为什么？因为对于例句 1)，我们的大脑很容易这样断句：the criminal confessed his sins，即认为 his sins 作动词 confessed 的宾语，于是把例句 1)的前半部分 the criminal confessed his sins 理解成"这名罪犯坦白了自己的罪行"。但是，继续往下读，当看到了动词 harmed 时，我们的大脑这才"突然醒悟"，发现刚才的断句不对。这里的 his sins 不是 confessed 的宾语，而应该是 harmed 的主语，于是例句 1) 应该理解成是在 confessed 的后面接了一个宾语从句 his sins harmed many people。这样一来，我们的大脑必然要多花费时间来解读例句 1)，因为要推翻原来的错误判断 the criminal confessed his sins，转而要理解成 the criminal confessed 和 his sins harmed many people。

对于例句 2)，因为有了 that 的存在，我们大脑能轻而易举地判断出 the criminal confessed 是主句，而 his sins harmed many people 是宾语从句，所以我们的大脑就不会做出像例句 1) 那样的错误断句，因而缩短了理解的时间。

精品译文 这名罪犯承认，他的罪行伤害了很多人。

由此可见，一个小小的 that 的威力如此之大！我们再来看下面这个句子：

3 He said no word at the meeting was strange.

对于这个句子，很多读者自然会作宾语从句理解：He said ***that*** no word at the meeting was strange.

此时句子的意思是：他说，会上人们的发言都很正常，并没有什么奇怪的。

但是，如果在句首添加一个 that 而将其改写为：***That*** he said no word at the meeting was strange.

此时则要理解成：他在会上一言不发，这真让人觉得有些蹊跷。

再比如下面这两个句子：

4 ***That the seas are being overfished*** has been known for years.

妙语点睛 这里 that 引导的从句 that the seas are being overfished 即是一个主语从句。

精品译文 海洋正在被人们过度捕捞，许多年以来这已是尽人皆知的。

如果没有 that 而说成 The seas are being overfished has been known for years. * 就会出现 are being overfished 和 has been known 两个谓语部分连在一起，该句就无法理解了。再来看下面这个句子：

5 ***That the plates are moving*** is not beyond dispute.

妙语点睛 这里 that 引导的从句 that the plates are moving 即是一个主语从句。

精品译文 地球板块是在漂移的，这一点并非毫无争议。

同样，如果没有 that 而说成 The plates are moving is not beyond dispute. * 就会出现 are moving 和 is not beyond dispute 两个谓语部分连在一起，该句就无法理解了。

对于同位语从句和表语从句，若没有 that 作标志，同样会存在这种意思混淆不清的问题。例如：

6 My concern is ***that*** the child should be sent to school.

妙语点睛 这句话自然要理解成"我所关心的是，这孩子应该去上学"。若没有 that，句子写成 My concern is the child should be sent to school. 读者先读到 my concern is the child，他还以为是在说"我的担心是这个孩子"，而后面又接了 should be sent to school，这就让人觉得奇怪了。

那么为什么宾语从句中的 that 可以省去呢？这是因为对于宾语从句，主句的谓语已经出现，谓语后面所接的成分自然是宾语，所以在不会影响句子意思的情况下，可以把 that 省去。比如 I think you are right. 或 I think that you are right. 都可以。但是，如果遇到像上面的例句 2 那样，即使是宾语从句，that 也不宜省去。

综上所述，在陈述句作名词从句时，需要添加 that，**这个 that 相当于一个“指路牌”，能够帮助我们指明断句的方向，不造成对句子的误解。**

2. 1. 3 一般疑问句作句子成分

一、用 **whether** 或 **if** 引导

当把一个一般疑问句(见下表中的各例句 1)当作名词来使用时，需要先将疑问句的倒装语序变成陈述句语序，并在句首加上 whether 或 if(if 只用在宾语从句中)来引导，以保留原句的疑问意义。然后，把“whether+ 陈述句”这一结构分别充当另一个句子的主语、宾语、表语或同位语等四种成分(见下表中的各例句 2)，即构成主语从句、宾语从句、表语从句或同位语从句等四种名词从句。请看下表：

一般疑问句	名词从句	解释
1. Will he come to my party?	2. Whether ***he will come to my party*** makes no difference to me. 他来不来参加我的聚会对我来说无所谓。	一般疑问句作主语，构成主语从句
1. Does he need my help?	2. I don't know if/whether ***he needs my help***. 我不知道他是否需要我的帮助。	一般疑问句作宾语，构成宾语从句
1. Will people live on the moon someday?	2. My question is whether ***people will live on the moon someday***. 我的问题是，人类在未来的某一天是否真的能生活在月球上。	一般疑问句作表语，构成表语从句
1. Is there life on other planets?	2. Scientists have argued over the question whether ***there is life on other planets***. 科学家们一直就是否有外星人这个问题争论不休。	一般疑问句作同位语，补充说明 question，构成同位语从句

二、**if** 还是 **whether**?

对于 if 和 whether 这两个连词，其用法有以下区别：

1. if 一般只用于引导宾语从句，而 whether 可引导包括宾语从句在内的其他名词从句。

1 ***If*** he comes or not makes no difference. *

妙语点睛 这个句子不妥，应改为 ***Whether*** he comes or not makes no difference. 这里是主语从句，应由 whether 引导。

精品译文 他来不来无关紧要。

2 The question is ***if*** he will come. *

妙语点睛 这个句子不妥，应改为 The question is ***whether*** he will come. 这里是表语从句，应由 whether 引导。

精品译文 问题是他是否会来。

2. if 不和 or not 直接连用，即一般不说 if or not，但可以说 if...or not。而 whether 没有此限制。

3 1) I don't know ***if or*** not he comes. *

2) I don't know ***whether or not*** he comes.

妙语点睛 例句 1 错误，因为 if 和 or not 不能连用，即不能说成 if or not。例句 2)正确。

精品译文 我不知道他是否会来。

2. 1. 4 特殊疑问句作句子成分

一、变倒装语序为陈述语序

当把一个特殊疑问句(见下表中的各例句 1)当作名词来使用时，需要先将疑问句的倒装语序变成陈述句语序，然后分别充当另一个句子的主语、宾语、表语或同位语等四种成分(见下表中的各例句 2)，即构成主语从句、宾语从句、表语从句或同位语从句等四种名词从句。请看下表：

特殊疑问句	名词从句	解释
1. Why did dinosaurs become extinct?	2. ***Why dinosaurs became extinct*** is still a mystery. 恐龙为什么会灭绝目前还是个未解之谜。	一般疑问句作主语，构成主语从句
1. How many letters are there in the English alphabet?	2. I don't know ***how many letters there are in the English alphabet***. 我不知道英文字母表中有多少个字母。	特殊疑问句作宾语，构成宾语从句
1. What are we badly in need of?	2. Money is ***what we are badly in need of***. 我们急需的就是钱。	特殊疑问句作表语，构成表语从句
1. Where could we get the loan?	2. There arose the question ***where we could get the loan***. 现在的问题是我们去哪里弄到这笔贷款。	特殊疑问句作同位语，补充说明 question，构成同位语从句

从上面的表格看到，用特殊疑问句来充当句子成分时，一定要将特殊问句的倒装语序变成陈述句语序，而不用倒装语序。比如下面的例句都是错误的：

1 Why ***did dinosaurs become*** extinct is still a mystery. *

2 I don't know how many letters ***are there*** in the English alphabet. *

3 Money is what ***are we*** badly in need of. *

4 There arose the question where ***could we*** get the loan. *

二、特殊疑问词作主语，无需调整句子语序

需要注意的是，如果特殊疑问词在句中作主语，则特殊疑问句无需调整语序而直接作成分，因为此时的问句即是一个陈述句语序。请看例句：

5 1) Who will chair the meeting?

2) Who ***will chair the meeting*** has not yet been decided.

妙语点睛 在例句 1)中，特殊疑问词 who 作主语，此时整个问句 Who will chair the meeting?是一个"主语+谓语"结构的陈述句语序，因此用该问句作成分时，无需调整语序，而直接在例句 2)中充当主语，构成一个主语从句。

精品译文 1)谁将会主持这个会议？

2)谁将会主持这个会议，目前还没有决定。

2.1.5 引导名词从句的连接词

从以上各小节讨论的内容中，可以看出简单句与名词从句的对应关系，以及名词从句的连接词与简单句的疑问词的关系。现列表如下：

名词从句的引导词	对应的简单句类型	引导词是否作成分	引导词是否可以省略
连词 that	对应于陈述句	that 在从句中既不作成分，也没有实义	在不影响句子意思的情况下，宾语从句中的 that 可以省去
连词 whether 和 if	对应于一般疑问句	whether 和 if 在从句中不作成分，但具有"是否"的含义	不能省去，因为有"是否"的含义
连接副词 when, where, why 和 how；连接代词 who, whom, what, which 和 whose	对应于特殊疑问句	when, where, why 和 how 在从句中作状语；who, whom 和 what 作主语、宾语或表语；which 和 whose 作定语，后面接名词连用	不能省去，因为既作成分，又有意义

从上表我们看到：

第一，对于陈述句，连接词 that 是后来添加上去的，此时的 that 自然不充当从句里的任何成分，而且也没有任何意义，只起连接主句和从句的作用。

第二，对于一般疑问句，连接词 whether 也是后来添加上去的，目的是为了保留疑问的意义，表示"是否"，即 whether 是有意义的，这不同于 that。而与 that 相同的是，whether 也不充当任何句子成分。

第三，对于特殊疑问句，不需要添加任何连接词，因为特殊疑问词就充当了连词的作用，从而变成了相应的连接词，只需要把倒装语序还原成陈述语序就可以了。这些特殊疑问词都是在句中充当各种成分的，比如连接代词可以充当主语、宾语或表语，而连接副词则充当状语。

需要提醒大家注意的是，要特别关注这些连词是否在句子中充当成分。比如，that 不能作任何成分，只起连接作用，后面要接陈述句；what 一定是充当从句的主语或宾语等成分；which 和 whose 后面都要接名词等等。

思维总结

本节是整个"名词从句"一章的重点内容。读者需要掌握以下要点：

一、理解名词从句的本质，即三种句子（陈述句、一般疑问句和特殊疑问句）充当四种句子成分（主语、宾语、表语和同位语）。

二、理解为什么陈述句需要添加连词 that 之后才能变成名词从句。

三、掌握一般疑问句如何转化为名词从句，即要引入连词 whether 或 if。

四、掌握特殊疑问句如何转化为名词从句，即要变倒装语序为陈述语序。

思维训练

Exercise 2. 1（Key: P327）

请将括号里的疑问句变成名词从句。

1. ______ is unimportant to me.（Does she come?）
2. ______ remains uncertain.（Shall we have the match?）
3. I wonder ______.（Should we wait for him?）
4. No onc knows exactly ______.（Is there life on other planets?）
5. I am interested in the question ______.（Will people live on the moon someday?）
6. My question is ______.（Do we have enough time to go to the movie?）
7. Do you know ______ ?（Does sound travel faster than light?）
8. I don't know ______.（How old is he?）
9. ______ was interesting.（What was he talking about?）
10. Do you know ______ ?（What's on TV tonight?）
11. Please tell me ______.（Where do you live?）
12. I wonder ______.（Why did dinosaurs become extinct?）
13. ______ wasn't true.（What did she say?）
14. ______ is true.（What did he tell you?）
15. ______ is still a mystery.（Why did they refuse to cooperate with us?）
16. Do you know ______ ?（When are they coming?）
17. I can't remember ______.（How much does it cost?）
18. Let's ask him ______.（Which book does he want?）
19. I don't know ______.（Who is coming to the party?）
20. I don't know ______.（Who are those people?）
21. Do you know ______ ?（Whose pen is this?）
22. ______ is a secret.（Why did they leave the country?）
23. ______ is none of your business.（Where did she go?）
24. ______ will be forever etched in our memories.（What happened on the morning of September 11?）

25. I don't remember ______. (How many letters are there in the English alphabet?)
26. I need to find out ______. (How old does a person have to be to get a driver's license?)
27. The little boy wants to know ______. (Do animals have the same emotions as human beings?)
28. The little boy wants to know ______. (Why is the water of the sea salty?)

2.2 简单句与主语从句

从上一节的讨论中，已经把握了名词从句的本质，就是用三种句子(陈述句、一般疑问句和特殊疑问句)充当四种句子成分(主语、宾语、表语和同位语)。所以，当用这三种句子充当另外一个句子的主语时，就构成了主语从句。因此，本节内容安排如下：

2. 2. 1 陈述句作主语

2. 2. 2 一般疑问句作主语

2. 2. 3 特殊疑问句作主语

2. 2. 1 陈述句作主语

把"that+ 陈述句"这一结构放在主语的位置即构成主语从句。请看例句：

1 ***That the seas are being overfished*** has been known for years.

妙语点睛 这里 that 引导的从句 that the seas are being overfished 即是一个主语从句，直接置于主语的位置。

精品译文 海洋正在被人们过度捕捞，许多年以来这已是尽人皆知的。

2 ***That the plates are moving*** is not beyond dispute.

妙语点睛 这里 that 引导的从句 that the plates are moving 即是一个主语从句，直接置于主语的位置。

精品译文 地球板块是在漂移的，这一点并非毫无争议。

3 ***That English is important*** is an undoubted fact. 语很重要，这是毋庸置疑的事实。

4 ***That he doesn't understand English*** is obvious. 很显然，他不懂英语。

5 ***That the world is round*** is a fact. 地球是圆的，这是一个事实。

6 ***That the moon itself does not give off light*** is common knowledge. 月球本身不发光是一个基本常识。

对于陈述句作主语，更常见的是用 it 作形式主语置于句首，而将主语从句放在句末。因此上面各句可分别改为：

7 It has been known for years ***that the seas are being overfished.***

8 It is not beyond dispute ***that the plates are moving.***

9 It is an undoubted fact ***that English is important.***

10 It is obvious ***that he doesn't understand English.***

11 It is a fact ***that the world is round.***

12 It is common knowledge ***that the moon itself does not give off light.***

下列都是常见的主语从句句型(重点内容)：

一、It is +过去分词+that 从句

It's reported that...(据报道……) It's believed that...(人们相信……)

It is generally thought that...(人们普遍认为……) It should be noted that...(应当注意……)

It has been found that...(现已发现……) It must be pointed out that...(必须指出……)

类似动词还有 say, expect, know, estimate 和 forecast 等。请看例句：

13 As a child and as an adult as well, Bill Gates was untidy. ***It has been said that*** in order to counteract this, Mary drew up weekly clothing plans for him. 不论是在小时候还是长大成人以后，比尔·盖茨都是不修边幅的。据说为了让他改掉这个习惯，玛丽专门为他制定了一周的着装计划。

二、It is +形容词+that 从句

It is clear that...（显然……）	It is possible that...（很可能……）
It is likely that...（很可能……）	It is natural that...（很自然……）
It is certain that...（可以相信……）	It is strange that...（奇怪的是……）
It is fortunate that...（幸运的是……）	It is necessary that...（有必要……）

14 ***It is true that*** English is becoming an international language. 的确，英语正日益成为一门国际通用语言。

三、It is +名词短语+that 从句

常用的名词有：a pity, a shame, an honor, a good idea 和 no wonder 等等。

It is a pity that...（可惜的是……）	It is a fact that...（事实是……）
It is good news that...（……真是太好了……）	It is a good thing that...（……真是件好事……）
It is no wonder that...（难怪……）	It is a shame that...（遗憾的是……；……真是太不像话了）
It is an honor that...（真荣幸……）	It is common knowledge that...（……是常识）
It is my belief that...（我相信……）	It is a miracle that...（……真是奇迹）

15 ***It is common knowledge that*** the whale is not a fish. 鲸鱼不是鱼类，这是一个常识。

16 ***It is common knowledge that*** a flash of lightning is seen before a clap of thunder is heard. 人们先看到闪电，后听见雷声，这是一个常识。

17 ***It is a shame that*** you did not pass the test. 你没通过这次考试真遗憾。

2.2.2 一般疑问句作主语

一般疑问句作主语时，要把一般疑问句变成陈述句，并且用 whether 来引导，然后充当句子的主语，即构成主语从句。请看例句：

Whether he comes or not makes no difference to me. 他来不来对我来说无所谓。

2.2.3 特殊疑问句作主语

1 ***What we need*** is wholly new kind of police force.

妙语点睛 这里的特殊疑问词 what 是作 need 的宾语，所以需将原来的倒装句 what do we need 调整为陈述句语序 what we need，然后作主句的主语，即构成主语从句。

精品译文 我们需要的是一个全新的警察机构。

2 ***What he told*** you is true.

妙语点睛 这里的特殊疑问词 what 是作 told 的直接宾语，所以需将原来的倒装句 what did he tell you 调整为陈述句语序 what he told you，然后作主句的主语，即构成主语从句。

精品译文 他和你讲的都是实话。

3 ***When the meeting is to be held*** has not yet been decided.

妙语点睛 这里的特殊疑问词 when 是作从句的时间状语，所以需将原来的倒装句 when is the meeting to be held 调整为陈述句语序 when the meeting is to be held，然后作主句的主语，即构成主语从句。

精品译文 会议何时举行还没决定。

4 ***Why he refused to cooperate with us*** is still a mystery.

妙语点睛 这里的特殊疑问词 why 是作从句的原因状语，所以需将原来的倒装句 why did he refuse to cooperate with us 调整为陈述句语序 why he refused to cooperate with us，然后作主句的主语，即构成主语从句。

精品译文 他为什么会拒绝与我们合作，目前还不清楚。

5 ***How a person masters his fate*** is more important than what his fate is.

妙语点睛 这里的特殊疑问词 how 是作从句的方式状语，所以需将原来的倒装句 how does a person master his fate 调整为陈述句语序 how a person masters his fate，然后作主句的主语，即构成主语从句。

精品译文 对于一个人来说，重要的是如何掌握自己的命运，而不是被动地接受命运的安排。

6 September 11, 2001 started out as an ordinary day, but ***what happened that morning*** will be forever etched(铭刻) in our memories.

妙语点睛 这里的特殊疑问词 what 是作从句的主语，所以无需调整语序，而直接将疑问句 what happened that morning 作主句的主语，即构成主语从句。

精品译文 2001 年 9 月 11 号那天和平日一样到来，但是那天早晨发生的事情将永远铭刻在人们的记忆里。

思维总结

本节重点是掌握 that 引导的主语从句的句型。

思维训练

Exercise 2. 2 (Key: P327)

请把下列句子改写成 it 作主语的句子。

1. That the word is round is a fact.
2. That smoking can cause cancer is true.
3. That English is becoming an international language is true.
4. That Clint failed his English exam was strange.
5. That they are still alive is a consolation.
6. That he has been late for work over and over again is a serious matter.

2.3 简单句与宾语从句

名词从句的本质是用三种句子(陈述句、一般问句和特殊问句)充当四种句子成分(主语、宾语、表语和同位语)。所以，当用三种句子充当另外一个句子的宾语时，就构成了宾语从句。因此，本节内容安排如下：

2. 3. 1 陈述句作宾语

2. 3. 2 一般疑问句作宾语

2. 3. 3 特殊疑问句作宾语

2. 3. 1 陈述句作宾语

把“that+ 陈述句”这一结构放在宾语的位置即构成宾语从句。请看例句：

1 We know (*that*) ***the world is round.*** 我们知道，地球是圆的。

2 I think (*that*) ***a sound knowledge of grammar is indispensable to good writing.*** 我认为扎实的语法功底对良好的写作极为重要。

需要提醒读者注意的是，只有宾语从句中的 that 才可以省去（在不影响对句意的理解的情况下），而主语从句、表语从句和同位语从句中的 that 一般不能省去。

2.3.2 一般疑问句作宾语

把"whether / if + 陈述句"这一结构放在宾语的位置即构成宾语从句。请看例句：

1 I don't know ***if / whether he needs my help.*** 我不知道他是否需要我的帮助。

2 No one knew ***whether or not interest rates would rise.***

妙语点睛 这里原来的一般问句是 would interest rates rise，变成陈述句语序后成为 interest rates would rise，然后为了保留疑问的意义又添加了 whether or not，于是便有了 whether or not interest rates would rise，在主句的谓语 knew 后面作宾语，即构成宾语从句。需要提醒读者注意的是，因为一般不说 if or not，所以这里的连词不宜用 if，而要用 whether。

精品译文 没有人知道利率是否会提高。

注意：只有宾语从句才可以用 if 引导，主语从句、表语从句和同位语从句一般都要用 whether 引导。

2.3.3 特殊疑问句作宾语

把特殊疑问句变成陈述句语序后放在宾语的位置即构成宾语从句。请看例句：

1 I have not decided ***whom I should vote for.***

妙语点睛 这里的特殊疑问词 whom 是作 vote for 的宾语，所以需将原来的倒装句 whom should I vote for 调整为陈述句语序 whom I should vote for，然后作主句谓语 decided 的宾语，即构成宾语从句。

精品译文 我还没有决定该投谁的票。

2 No one knows exactly ***how speech began.***

妙语点睛 这里的特殊疑问词 how 是作 began 的方式状语，所以需将原来的倒装句 how did speech begin 调整为陈述句语序 how speech began，然后作主句谓语 knows 的宾语，即构成宾语从句。

精品译文 没有人确切地知道语言是如何产生的。

3 Could you tell me ***where the post office is?***

妙语点睛 这里的特殊疑问词 where 是作 is 的表语，所以需将原来地倒装句 where is the post office 调整为陈述句语序 where the post office is，然后作主句谓语 tell 的直接宾语，即构成宾语从句。

精品译文 你能告诉我邮局在哪里吗？

4 We don't know ***why he did not come yesterday.***

妙语点睛 这里的特殊疑问词 why 是作 come 的原因状语，所以需将原来的倒装句 why did he not come yesterday 调整为陈述句语序 why he did not come yesterday，然后作主句谓语 know 的宾语，即构成宾语从句。

精品译文 我们不知道他昨天为什么没来。

5 They gave ***who came to the meeting*** a pamphlet.

妙语点睛 这里的特殊疑问词 who 是作 came 的主语，所以无需调整语序，而直接将疑问句 who came to the meeting 作主句谓语 gave 的间接宾语，即构成宾语从句。另外，gave 的直接宾语是 a pamphlet。

精品译文 他们给所有到会的人员发了一本小册子。

6 You should vote for ***which candidate you assume best.***

妙语点睛 这里的特殊疑问词 which 是作定语，修饰名词 candidate，所以需将原来的倒装句 which candidate do you assume best 调整为陈述句语序 which candidate you assume best，然后作主句谓语 vote for 的宾语，即构成宾语从句。

精品译文 你应该投票给那些你认为最优秀的候选人。

7 The mother will buy ***whichever books her son wants.***

妙语点睛 这里的特殊疑问词 whichever 相当于 which，是 which 的强调形式，作定语，修饰名词 books，所以需将原来的倒装句 whichever books does her son want 调整为陈述句语序 whichever books her son wants，然后作主句谓语 buy 的宾语，即构成宾语从句。

精品译文 她儿子要什么书，这位妈妈就给他买什么书。

从以上例句看到，宾语从句可以是直接放在动词后面作宾语(如例句 1 和例句 2)，也可以是作双宾语动词的直接宾语(如例句 3)或间接宾语(如例句 5)，也可以放在介词后面作宾语(如例句 6)。也就是说，宾语从句的位置可以有很多种。关于宾语从句不同位置的详细讨论，请参见《英语语法新思维高级教程——驾驭语法》第一章第 1.3 节。

2.4 简单句与表语从句

从 2.1 节的讨论中，已经知道名词从句的本质，就是用三种句子(陈述句、一般疑问句和特殊疑问句)充当四种句子成分(主语、宾语、表语和同位语)。所以，当把三种句子充当另外一个句子的表语时，就构成了表语从句。因此，本节内容安排如下：

2.4.1 陈述句作表语

2.4.2 一般疑问句作表语

2.4.3 特殊疑问句作表语

需要注意的是，表语从句通常是置于系动词，尤其是 be 动词的后面。

2.4.1 陈述句作表语

把"that + 陈述句"这一结构放在表语的位置即构成表语从句。请看例句：

My idea is ***that the child should be sent to school.*** 我的看法是，应该把这个孩子送去上学。

2.4.2 一般疑问句作表语

把"whether + 陈述句"这一结构放在表语的位置即构成表语从句。请看例句：

My concern is ***whether he comes or not.*** 我关心的是他到底来不来。

2.4.3 特殊疑问句作表语

把特殊问句变成陈述句语序后放在表语的位置即构成表语从句。请看例句：

1 Change is ***what keeps us fresh and innovative.*** Change is ***what keeps us from getting stale.*** Change is ***what keeps us young.*** 唯有变革才能使我们保持思维敏锐，富有创造性。唯有变革才能防止我们思想僵化。唯有变革才能使我们永葆青春。

2 Money is ***what we are badly in need of.*** 我们急需的是钱。

3 Yesterday is history. Tomorrow is a mystery. Today is a gift. That's ***why it's called the present!*** 昨天是历史。明天是一个谜。今天是一个礼物。因此它才被称为 present!

4 The point is ***when you will become rich.*** 问题的关键是你何时才能有钱。

5 This is ***where our basic interest lies.*** 这是我们的根本利益所在。

2.5 简单句与同位语从句

所谓同位语，就是用来补充说明名词的成分。被补充说明的名词，叫作先行词。当用一个完整的句子来补充说明名词时，即构成同位语从句。所以，同位语从句都位于一个名词的后面，便构成了“名词 + 连词 + 同位语从句”这样的结构。本节内容安排如下：

2.5.1 陈述句作同位语

2.5.2 一般疑问句作同位语

2.5.3 特殊疑问句作同位语

2.5.1 陈述句作同位语

把“that + 陈述句”这一结构放在同位语的位置即构成同位语从句。请看例句：

1 He was prepared to prove **his theory** ***that two different weights would fall to the ground at the same time.***

妙语点睛 这里的先行词是 his theory，同位语从句是 that two different weights would fall to the ground at the same time。

精品译文 他准备证明他的这一理论：两个重量不同的物体将同时落地。

2 **The fact** ***that he succeeded in the experiment*** pleased everybody.

妙语点睛 这里的先行词是 the fact，同位语从句是 that he succeeded in the experiment。

精品译文 他试验取得了成功，这让大家很高兴。

3 **The rumor** ***that Tom was a thief*** turned out to be untrue.

妙语点睛 这里的先行词是 the rumor，同位语从句是 that Tom was a thief。

精品译文 有人曾谣传汤姆是小偷，结果证明是不对的。

注意：同位语从句可能与其修饰的名词被其他成分隔开。请看例句：

4 They spread **the lie** everywhere ***that Tom was guilty of theft.***

妙语点睛 这里的先行词 the lie 与同位语从句 that Tom was guilty of theft 被 everywhere 隔开。

精品译文 他们到处散布谣言说汤姆犯有盗窃罪。

5 **A saying** goes ***that practice makes perfect.***

妙语点睛 这里的先行词 a saying 与同位语从句 that practice makes perfect 被谓语 goes 隔开。

精品译文 俗话说，熟能生巧。

6 Dreary months dragged by before **the tragic news** reached her ***that her beloved brother had been killed for anti-Nazi activities.***

妙语点睛 这里的先行词 the tragic news 与同位语从句 that her beloved brother had been killed for anti-Nazi activities 被谓语 reached her 隔开。

精品译文 在狱中度过数月梦魇般的日子后，突然有一天传来噩耗：她亲爱的哥哥在反法西斯活动中被杀害了。

这种被分隔开来的情形在阅读文章中是比较常见的，遇到时一定要认真分析，才能正确地理解句子的意思。

2.5.2 一般疑问句作同位语

把“whether + 陈述句”这一结构放在同位语地位置即构成同位语从句。请看例句：

They are faced with the **problem** ***whether they should continue to work.*** 他们面临这样一个问题：他们是否应该继续工作。

2.5.3 特殊疑问句作同位语

把特殊疑问句变成陈述句语序后放在同位语的位置即构成同位语从句。请看例句：

1 There arose the **question** ***where we could get the loan.*** 现在的问题是我们去哪里弄到这笔贷款。

2 The **question** ***who should go abroad on this business tour*** requires consideration.
谁应该出差去国外，这个问题需要仔细考虑。

3 I have no **idea** ***when he will return.*** 我不知道他什么时候回来。

最后需要说明的是，**同位语从句主要是由that引导**，而很少用 whether 以及连接代词或连接副词引导，这是因为我们多是用陈述句来补充说明名词的内容，而很少用**一般疑问句**或**特殊疑问句**来补充说明名词的内容。

写给读者的话

一、本章学习思路

本章对名词从句的讲解完全是一种全新的思维，即名词从句可简单地概括为这样一句话：**名词从句就是用三种句子来分别充当另外一个句子的四种句子成分**。这里的三种句子是：陈述句、一般疑问句以及特殊疑问句；四种成分是：主语、宾语、表语和同位语。抓住了这一本质，名词从句的其他所有问题便能迎刃而解。

二、本章重点及难点

重点是掌握三种句子如何进行结构变化之后来作成分。具体如下：

1. 用陈述句作成分时，需要在句首加 that；
2. 用一般疑问句作成分时，需要先将疑问句转换成正常语序，然后在句首加上 whether 或 if（只用在宾语从句中），以保留原句的疑问意义；
3. 用特殊疑问句作成分时，只需要将疑问句转换成正常语序。

三、本章学习时间安排

名词从句是三大从句中难度最小的，读者可以用三天时间来学习本章讲解的内容，并做完所有的练习。

综合练习（Key: P328）

请选择最佳答案填空。

1. No one knows exactly __A__.
   A. how did speech begin　　B. how speech began
   C. how the beginning of speech　　D. of how beginning speech
2. It is obvious __D__ on more important things.
   A. which the money should we spend　　B. what the money should we spend
   C. that the money should we spend　　D. that we should spend the money
3. __C__ hard water does not mix well with soap.
   A. That is a well-known fact　　B. That is a well-known fact in which
   C. It is a well-known fact that　　D. It is a well-known that
4. __A__ every magnet is surrounded by a magnetic field.
   A. It believes that　　B. It believed that　　C. It is believed that　　D. It's believing that
5. __B__ was to return to school.
   A. That really interested him　　B. What really interested him
   C. Which really interested him　　D. That interested him really
6. Stopping pouring polluted water into the river is __A__ the factory has to solve at present.
   A. what　　B. that　　C. which　　D. why

7. ______ the mass of the nucleus is slightly less than the total mass of the protons and neutrons which made up the nucleus.

A. It found that　B. It was found that　C. It was found for　D. It finds that

8. He wondered ______.

A. what will be his wife's reaction　B. what would his wife's reaction be

C. how would be his wife's reaction　D. what his wife's reaction would be

9. He asked me ______ I intended to do after my graduation.

A. that what　B. what　C. that　D. which

10. Listening carefully to ______ in class means less work later.

A. what does the teacher say　B. what the teacher says

C. that the teacher says　D. which the teacher says

11. After the accident, I opened my eyes slowly and realized ______ I was still alive.

A. that　B. whether　C. what　D. which

12. John didn't say ______ he would return, but I presume he'll be back for dinner.

A. that when　B. when　C. if or not　D. where

13. He works too hard. That is ______ is wrong with him.

A. that which　B. that what　C. what　D. the thing what

14. ______ to space travelers is high acceleration or deceleration forces.

A. Danger can be　B. What can be dangerous　C. They can be dangerous　D. While danger

15. According to some educators, the goal of teaching is to help students learn what ______ to know to live a well-adjusted and successful life.

A. do they need　B. they need　C. they are needed　D. as they may need

16. ______ the trainer wanted to tell is ______ Asian elephants are easier to tame than African ones.

A. That, those　B. What, that　C. What, the　D. That, the

17. ______ the London Zoo will adopt as a measurement at the critical moment is to try all ways preserving the animals in the zoo.

A. That　B. What　C. It's　D. Whether

18. The problem now is ______ we can adopt to overcome the difficulties in shortage of funds.

A. what measure　B. that measure　C. measure that　D. measure which

19. The mountain was ______ many animals, such as wolves, badges and rabbits once haunted but now it is so silent.

A. that place　B. where　C. what　D. then

20. The reason we're so late is ______.

A. because of the car breaking down　B. due the care broke down

C. that the car broke down　D. because the car broke down

21. The question is ______ can be put into practice.

A. how you have learned　B. how that you have learned

C. that why you have learned　D. how what you have learned

22. There are signs ______ restaurants are becoming more popular with families.

A. that　B. which　C. in which　D. whose

23. ______ that the first cheese was probably made more than 4, 000 years ago by nomadic tribes in Asia.

A. The belief　B. Although they believe　C. It is believed　D. Believing

24. In the fourteenth century, ______ that glass coated with silver nitrate would turn yellow when fired in an oven.

A. the discovery　B. it was discovered　C. with the discovery　D. if it was discovered

25. We were all overjoyed at the news ______ the experiment turned out a success.

A. which　B. that　C. when　D. what

请选择括号中的连词填空。

26. A hinge joint is ______ (what/that/which) permits the forward and backward movement of a door.
27. It's doubtful ______ (whether/that/how/what) the government of that country can accept them as permanent residents.
28. It has always puzzled me ______ (that/why/where/what) the old man tied a red silk ribbon on the young tree in his courtyard.
29. The reason for my return is ______ (because/it/that/why) I left my keys behind.
30. Scientists have reached the conclusion ______ (what/that/which/when) the temperature on Earth is getting higher and higher.
31. I have no idea ______ (what/that/which/why) has happened to him.
32. An idea came to her ______ (that/what/when/which) she might do the experiment in another way.
33. One of the qualities ______ (that/what/who/why) separate us two-legged animals from the four-legged ones is compassion. It is ______ (which/that/what) makes us stand up tall instead of crawling about on all fours. And standing up tall is ______ (which/that/what) frees our arms to reach out to a fellow being and say, "Let me help you."
34. Change is ______ (which/that/what) keeps us fresh and innovative. Change is ______ (which/that/what) keeps us from getting stale. Change is ______ (which/that/what) keeps us young.

辨别改错。

35. Is there any proof which the food of the plant differs from that of animals?
    A: any proof　B: which　C: differs from　D: that of
36. A man cannot be really happy if that he enjoys doing is ignored by society as of no value or importance.
    A: that　B: is ignored　C: as of　D: importance
37. More and more people have realized such a fact of heart diseases are related to the way people live.
    A: have realized　B: such　C: of　D: are related to

Chapter 3

第三章　定语从句

定语从句是非常重要的一个语法项目。它有两个重要概念：先行词和关系词。定语从句的核心内容就是围绕先行词和关系词展开的。另外，定语从句有限制性和非限制性之分。最后，本章还将讨论定语从句与同位语从句的区别。因此，本章内容安排如下：

3.1 定语从句概述

3.1.1 形容词作定语与从句作定语比较

定语从句是英语里最为重要的语法项目之一，因为当要表达复杂的意思时，往往都要借助于定语从句来完成，即要用定语从句来修饰某个名词或名词短语。比如当我们说“我不喜欢懒人”，这时只需要用一个形容词 lazy 来作定语就可以。这句话可以这样说：

1 I don't like *lazy* people.

但是，如果要表达稍微复杂一点的意思，比如说“我不喜欢不守信用的人”，这时，简单地用形容词作定语就无能为力了，就要借助于**一个句子来修饰名词**，用作名词的定语，对名词进行限制。这句话可以这样说：

2 I don't like people ***who never keep their word.***

对于这两个例句，我们比较分析如下：

妙语点睛

两种定语	例句	比较
形容词作定语	I don't like ***lazy*** people.	形容词作定语要置于被修饰名词的前面
完整的句子作定语	I don't like people ***who never keep their word.***	从句修饰名词要置于被修饰名词的后面

这里，lazy 是作定语修饰 people，而 who never keep their word 也是作定语修饰 people，前者只是单个的形容词，而后者是一个有着完整主谓结构的句子，故称后者为定语从句，即用作定语功能的从句。说它是“从句”，因为这句话有主句，I don't like people 这是这句话的核心意思。

通过比较这两个例句，读者应该知道定语从句的作用了。下面将讨论定语从句的两个重要概念：**先行词**和**关系词**。

3.1.2 定语从句的两个重要概念：先行词和关系词

对于定语从句，一定要掌握先行词和关系词这两个重要概念，因为定语从句的核心内容就是围绕着先行词和关系词展开的。

一、先行词

被定语从句所修饰的对象称为先行词。上一节例句中的 people 即为先行词。

二、关系词

重复指代先行词、起连接主句和从句的作用，并且在定语从句中充当一定成分的连接词称为关系词。上一节例句 2 中的 who 即为关系词。关系词有两个作用：

1. 代词的作用：重复指代先行词并且在定语从句中充当一定成分，如上一节例句 2 中的 who 指代 people 并且作从句的主语；

2. 连接作用：即连接主句和从句，如上一节例句 2 中的 who 起着连接主句 I don't like people 和从句 who never keep their word 的作用。

接下来的各节内容都是围绕先行词和关系词展开的。因此，首先必须能够熟练判断先行词和关系词。请做下面的练习。

思维训练

Exercise 3. 1（Key: P329）

请找出下列短文中的定语从句，并指明先行词和关系词。

Passage 1:

Chris: Do you have a date for the party yet?

Kim: Actually, I don't. Do you think you could help me find one?

Chris: Hmm. What kind of guys do you like?

Kim: Oh, I like guys who aren't too serious and who have a good sense of humor. You know,...like you.

Chris: OK. What else?

Kim: Well, I'd prefer someone who I have something in common with—who I can talk to easily.

Chris: I think I know just the guy for you. Bob Branson. Do you know him?

Kim: No, I don't think so.

Chris: Let me arrange for you to meet him, and you can tell me what you think.

Passage 2:

Friendship is a very difficult thing. It is hard to handle. It creates many different problems. In fact I would say that friendship is as hard to handle as love is, or even marriage. Of course I am not talking about easy-come-easy-go friendship. I'm talking about friends who care deeply about each other, who support each other, who make life worth living. I'm talking about friends who you can share almost everything with.

Passage 3:

Beauty means this to one and that to the other. And yet when anyone of us has seen that which to him is beautiful he has known an emotion which is in every case the same in kind.

A ship in sail, a blooming flower, a town at night, a lovely poem, leaf shadows, a child's grace, the starry skies, apple trees in spring—thc thought of beauty—these are the drops of rain that keep the human spirit from death by draught. They are a stealing and silent refreshment that we perhaps do not think about but which goes on all the time. Beauty is the smile on the earth's face, open to all, and needs but the eyes to see, mood to understand.

3.2 关系词在定语从句充当的成分

在上一节中，在谈到关系词的“代词作用”时，提到它“重复指代先行词并且在定语从句中充当一定的成分”。因此接下来的分析思路是，以关系词为出发点，从两个角度来谈定语从句：一是关系词在从句中所能充当的各种不同成分（见本节）；二是关系词与先行词的对应关系，即不同的先行词要由不同的关系词来指代（见 3. 3 节）。

关系词必须在定语从句中充当某种成分，比如主语、宾语或表语等等。下面将进行详细讨论。本节内容安排如下：

3. 2. 1 关系词用作从句的主语（relative pronoun as subject）

3. 2. 2 关系词用作从句中动词的宾语（relative pronoun as object of verb）

3. 2. 3 关系词用作从句中介词的宾语（relative pronoun as object of preposition）

3. 2. 4 作宾语的关系词可以省去

3. 2. 1 关系词用作从句的主语（relative pronoun as subject）

我们先来比较简单句和定语从句，看看一个简单句如何变成定语从句。请读者先看两个简单句：

1 <u>The woman</u> is a famous dancer and <u>she</u> lives next door.

妙语点睛 上述两个简单句中有一个“重复元素”，这里的 she 就指代 the woman，即两句之间有一个交叉点，而通过这个交叉点建立起两句之间的联系。现在要用 she lives next door 来作定语修饰 the woman，以告诉对方哪个 woman 是舞蹈演员。而在定语从句中，指代"人"的关系词要用 who。前面说过，关系词既具有代词的作用又起着连词的作用，因此，上句可改写成：

The woman is a famous dancer ***who*** (=and she) lives next door.

由此看到，这里的关系词 who 既取代了代词 she 也取代了连词 and，也即 who 既具有代词的作用也起着连接的作用。另外，定语从句一般要紧跟在它所修饰的名词后面。因此，上句又可进一步改写成：

The woman ***who lives next door*** is a famous dancer.

到此，一个标准的定语从句"制造"完毕。整个转换过程如下：

The woman is a famous dancer ***and she lives next door***.

The woman ***who lives next door*** is a famous dancer.

由此看到，关系词 who 既指代 the woman，同时又在从句中作成分——从句的主语，而且还替换了 and，起着连词的作用。

精品译文 这位女士是一名著名的舞蹈演员，她就住在我家隔壁。

请再来看一下两个简单句如何合并为一个含有定语从句的句子：

2 1) I like guys ***and they have a good sense of humor***.

2) I like guys ***who have a good sense of humor***.

妙语点睛 这里的关系词 who 取代 and they，来引导定语从句 who have a good sense of humor，修饰名词 guys。这个 guys 就是先行词。

精品译文 我喜欢有幽默感的男士。

通过以上的变换操作过程，总结出以下三点，要提请读者注意：

一、用关系词 who 代替人称代词(如 she 或 they)后，定语从句里就不能再保留这些代词了。比如不能说：

3 The woman ***who she*** lives next door is a famous dancer. *

4 I like guys ***who they*** have a good sense of humor. *

因为这里已经有了 who 在从句中作主语，不必重复代词(如 she 或 they)了。

二、细心的读者也许已经注意到了，上述两个定语从句 who lives next door 和 who have a good sense of humor 分别修饰的名词 woman 和 guys，它们在各自的主句中充当的成分不同：woman 作主语（the woman is a famous dancer)，而 guys 是作宾语(I like guys)。事实上，定语从句可以修饰一个主句当中的任何一个名词。但是，我们关注的往往是**关系词在定语从句中所充当的成分**，不关心定语从句是修饰主句的哪个名词。

三、关于定语从句的主谓一致的问题。我们看到，同样是 who 作主语，但是 who lives next door 这个定语从句的谓语动词 lives 是单数第三人称的形式，即词尾加了-s；而 who have a good sense of humor 这个定语从句的谓语动词 have 却不是单数第三人称形式。这里读者或许就有一个疑问：为什么同样的主语 who 竟然会接两种不同形式的谓语呢？这里其实涉及关系词 who 的指代问题，也就是说，**定语从句的谓语动词形式是由关系词所指代的先行词来决定的**，而不是取决于关系词本身。定语从句 who lives next door 中的 who 指代的 woman 是单数名词，故谓语用单数的 lives；而定语从句 who have a good sense of humor 中的 who 指代的 guys 是复数名词，故谓语用复数的 have。这也进一步验证了，关系词是有指代作用的(同时具有连词作用)。

我们再来看更多的例句：

5 Anger is a thief ***who steals away the nice moments.*** 愤怒就如同一个窃贼，盗取了我们的幸福时光。

6 He ***who is not handsome at twenty, nor strong at thirty, nor rich at forty, nor wise at fifty***, will never be handsome, strong, rich, or wise. 一个人若在 20 岁时不俊美、30 岁时不健康、40 岁时不富有、50 岁时不明智，那么他将永远不会拥有这些。

7 There is this difference between happiness and wisdom: the person ***who thinks himself the happiest man*** really is so; but the person ***who thinks himself the wisest*** is generally the greatest fool. 幸福与智慧区别于此：认为自己

是最幸福的，他真的就最幸福；而认为自己是最有智慧的，他却往往是最大的傻瓜。

8 The world is a book, and those ***who do not travel*** read only one page. 世界犹如一本书，而那些从不出门旅行的人仅仅读了这本书的一页。

9 A rich person is not one ***who has the most***, but is one ***who needs the least.*** 一个富有的人，不是因为他拥有的最多，而是因为他需要的最少。

10 I like guys ***who aren't too serious*** and ***who have a good sense of humor.*** 我喜欢不过于严肃，并且具有幽默感的男士。

11 Of course I am not talking about easy-come-easy-go friendship. I'm talking about friends ***who care deeply about each other, who support each other, who make life worth living.*** 当然了，我这里所说的友谊不是那种"来得快去得也快"的泛泛之交，而是那种彼此之间能真正互相关心的朋友，能够互相支持的朋友，能够让你的人生更有意义的朋友。

在上面这些定语从句中，关系词 who 都是作从句的主语。

3.2.2 关系词用作从句中动词的宾语(relative pronoun as object of verb)

关系词除了像上面讨论的在定语从句中作主语外，还可以在从句中作宾语。而且，还可进一步区分为从句动词的宾语和从句介词的宾语。本节将讨论关系词作从句动词的宾语。同样，请读者先来看两个简单句如何合并为一个含有定语从句的句子。

1 1) I'd really like to find ***a friend*** and I can trust ***him*** completely.

2) I'd really like to find ***a friend***... I can trust ***who*** completely.

妙语点睛 在例句 1) 中，这里的 him 指代名词 a friend，可以用关系词 who 来替换 him，来充当动词 trust 的宾语。又因为 who 有连词的作用，所以此时 and 就要去掉了，如例句 2)所示。另一方面，关系词 who 要置于从句的开头，所以要把 who 移到 I 的前面，原句从而变成了下面的例句 3)：

3) I'd really like to find a friend ***who*** I can trust...completely.

这里的 who 虽然发生了移位，但依然是充当从句动词 trust 的宾语。这里用"..."表示 trust 的宾语是存在的，只不过发生了移位，移到了从句的开头，由 who 来充当。因此，这里的关系词 who 是充当从句的宾语。既然从句的谓语 trust 有宾语了，原来的 him 就要去掉，所以不能这样说：

4) I'd really like to find a friend ***who*** I can trust ***him*** completely. *

综上所述，最后带有定语从句的完整句子就是：

5) I'd really like to find a friend ***who I can trust completely***. 我想找一个我完全能够信任的人作朋友。

我们再来看更多的例句：

2 He is the best grammar teacher ***who*** I have ever ***seen.*** 他是我见过的最好的语法老师。

3 It's hard to have a friend ***who*** you can ***trust*** completely. 很难有一个你能完全信任的朋友。

4 He is the student ***who*** the teacher likes to ***praise*** for his hard work. 他就是那位因为学习用功而老师喜欢表扬的学生。

3.2.3 关系词用作从句中介词的宾语(relative pronoun as object of preposition)

关系词除了 3.2.2 小节中讨论的那样可以作从句动词的宾语外，还可以充当从句介词的宾语。例如：

1 1) I'm talking about friends and you can share almost everything with them.

2) I'm talking about friends ***who*** you can share almost everything ***with***.

妙语点睛 这里的 who 即是充当介词 with 的宾语。

精品译文 我这里说的朋友，是指那些你几乎可以把一切与之分享的人。

我们再来看更多的例句：

2 I hope I never have a boss ***who*** I can't talk ***to*** about my problems.

妙语点睛 这里的 who 即是充当介词 to 的宾语。

精品译文 我不希望有一个我无法与之沟通的老板。

3 I like the people ***who*** I work ***with.***

妙语点睛 这里的 who 即是充当介词 with 的宾语。

精品译文 我喜欢那些和我一同工作的同事。

4 I'd prefer someone ***who*** I have something in common ***with*** — ***who*** I can talk ***to*** easily.

妙语点睛 这里的关系词 who 分别充当介词 with 和 to 的宾语。

精品译文 我喜欢那些与我有共同点的人，这样易交流。

3.2.4 作宾语的关系词可以省去

综合 3.2.1、3.2.2 和 3.2.3 小节讨论的内容，我们看到，关系词在定语从句中主要可以充当两种成分：主语或宾语(动词的宾语或介词的宾语)。至此，将讨论关系词的省略问题。英语里有这样的习惯：**作宾语的关系词可以省去**，不论关系词是作动词的宾语还是作介词的宾语都可以省去。比如以上各节中讨论过的相关例句，可以分别改写成：

1 I'd really like to find a friend ( ) I can trust completely.

2 I'm talking about friends ( ) you can share almost everything with.

3 I hope I never have a boss ( ) I can't talk to about my problems.

顺便提一句，在从句中作主语的关系词无法省去。比如不能说：

4 I like guys ( ) have a good sense of humor. *

思维总结

本节主要讨论了两个问题：一是关系词在从句中充当两种成分，即主语和宾语；二是作宾语的关系词可以被省去。因此，判断关系词能否被省略，关键是看它充当何种成分，对此读者应该掌握。

思维训练

Exercise 3.2 (Key: P330)

请将左边的主句与右边的定语从句配对，答案可能不是唯一的。

1. It would be fun to go out with a person ______. a. who doesn't mind doing housework.
2. For me, the ideal spouse is someone ______. b. I have nothing in common with.
3. I'd really like to find a friend ______. c. that I can trust completely.
4. I hope I never have a boss ______. d. that doesn't criticize me all the time.
5. I don't want to be friends with anyone ______. e. I can't talk to about my problems.
6. The perfect English teacher is someone ______. f. who is a really good conversationalist.

请判断下列句子是否正确，错误的请改正。

7. He is the man who he is teaching us English.
8. I'd really like to find a friend that I can trust him completely.
9. I'd really like to find a friend I can share almost everything with him.

请给下列各主句配上定语从句。为每个主句分别写出三个定语从句，一个是关系词作从句的主语，一个是关系词作从句的动词宾语，一个是关系词作从句的介词宾语。

Example:

I don't like people ____.

I don't like people ***who say one thing but do something else.***（who 作主语）

I don't like people ***who I can't trust.***（who 作动词 trust 的宾语）

I don't like people ***who I have nothing in common with.***（who 作介词 with 的宾语）

10. I like people ______________________.
11. I don't like teachers ______________________.
12. A good friend is a person ______________________.
13. I have a good friend ______________________.

3.3 关系代词与先行词的搭配关系

在 3.2 节中，我们详细讨论了关系词在定语从句中所充当的成分，研究重心是放在定语从句本身。现在，我们把研究目光转向关系词与主句中的先行词之间的关系。细心的读者也许注意到了，在 3.2 节中所讨论的定语从句的关系词都是 who。但是在英语里，还有其他的关系词，比如 whom, which, that, whose, when, where 和 why 等等。这些关系词可以分为两大类：**关系代词和关系副词**。关系代词主要包括 who, whom, which, that 和 whose，这些词主要起着代词的作用，在定语从句里充当主语或宾语(但 whose 作定语)。关于它们的具体用法将在本节中详细讨论。关系副词则包括 when, where 和 why，这些词主要起着副词的作用，在定语从句里充当状语(不作主语或宾语)。关于它们的用法将在 3. 4 节中讨论。因此，本节内容安排如下：

3. 3. 1 先行词指"人"，用关系代词 who 或 whom

3. 3. 2 表示人或物的所有关系，用 whose

3. 3. 3 先行词指"物"，用关系代词 which

3. 3. 4 that 可以指代人，也可以指代物

提到的这些关系代词，他们与先行词有着严格的对应关系，据此可以分为三类。见下表：

who, whom	先行词只能是指"人"
which	先行词只能是指"物"
that, whose	先行词可以指"人"或"物"

3. 3. 1 先行词指"人"，用关系代词 who 或 whom

一、先行词指"人"才能用 **who** 或 **whom**

比如在 3. 1 和 3. 2 节中讨论的各个例句。再比如 3. 1 节的练习中出现的这段话：

1 Friendship is a very difficult thing. It is hard to handle. It creates many different problems. In fact I would say that friendship is as hard to handle as love is, or even marriage. Of course I am not talking about easy-come-easy-go friendship. I'm talking about ***friends who*** care deeply about each other, ***who*** support each other, ***who*** make life worth living. I'm talking about ***friends who*** you can share almost everything with.

妙语点睛 这里有两组定语从句。第一组 I'm talking about ***friends who*** care deeply about each other, ***who*** support each other, ***who*** make life worth living. 其中的先行词 friends 表示"人"，所以用了 who 来引导定语从句，这里有三个定语从句并列使用。第二组 I'm talking about ***friends who*** you can share almost everything with. 同样因为先行词是表示"人"，所以用 who 来引导定语从句。

精品译文 友谊是很难处理的，有时还会带来许多各种各样的麻烦。事实上，我想说的是，友谊与爱情甚至婚姻一样难以应付。当然了，我这里所说的友谊不是那种"来得快去得也快"的泛泛之交，而是那种彼此之间能真正互相关心的朋友，能够互相支持的朋友，能够让你的人生更有意义的朋友，是那种你和他们几乎可以分享一切的朋友。

那么，可以指"人"的关系代词 who 和 whom 有何不同呢？我们下面来讨论。

二、who 和 whom 的区别

1. who 的前面不能与介词搭配使用

因为 who 是主格形式，所以在介词的后面不能用 who，比如不说 with who*，而说 with whom。请看例句：

2 I'm talking about friends ***who*** you can share almost everything with.

不能说：I'm talking about friends ***with who*** you can share almost everything. *

而应该说：I'm talking about friends ***with whom*** you can share almost everything.

主格形式的 who 除了作定语从句的主语外，还可以充当定语从句的宾语或表语。

2. whom 在定语从句中不能作主语，但可作宾语或表语

3 A rich person is not ***one who*** has the most, but is ***one who*** needs the least.

妙语点睛 这里的 who 作从句的主语，所以不能用 whom，不说 whom has...

精品译文 一个富有的人，不是因为他拥有的最多，而是因为他需要的最少。

4 Only the people ***who*** have the patience to do simple things perfectly will acquire the skill to do difficult things easily.

妙语点睛 这里的 who 作从句的主语，所以不能用 whom，不说 whom have...

精品译文 只有有耐心圆满完成简单工作的人，才能够轻而易举地完成困难的事。

总之，who 可以作主语，也可以代替 whom 作宾语或表语，但不能用在介词后面。而因为 whom 是宾格形式，所以不能作主语。

3.3.2 表示人或物的所有关系，用 whose

whose 表示所有关系，其作用就如同物主代词 my, your, her, his, their 和 our 一样，whose 的后面要接名词。whose 可指人也可指物。"whose + 名词"在从句中可作主语、动词的宾语或介词的宾语。请看例句：

1 1) I know a friend. ***His*** brother is a pop singer.

2) I know a friend ***whose*** brother is a pop singer.

妙语点睛 例句 2)里的 whose 代替了例句 1)里的 his，指 friend，即表示人。

精品译文 我认识一个朋友，他哥哥是一名流行歌手。

2 1) These children sit in a schoolroom. ***Its*** windows are all broken.

2) These children sit in a schoolroom ***whose*** windows are all broken.

妙语点睛 例句 2)里 whose 代替了例句 1)里的 its，指 schoolroom，即表示物。

精品译文 这些孩子就坐在窗玻璃都打破了的教室里上课。

请再看其他例句：

3 When I looked through the window, I saw a girl ***whose beauty*** took my breath away.

妙语点睛 这里的 whose beauty 作从句的主语，whose 指人即 a girl。

精品译文 当我朝窗外看去，猛然看见一个美女，其美貌让我惊讶不已。

4 It was a meeting ***whose importance*** I did not realize at the time.

妙语点睛 这里的 whose importance 作从句动词 realize 的宾语，whose 指事物 a meeting。

精品译文 这个会议的重要性当时我并没有意识到。

5 Atlas (in Greek mythology) was a kneeling man ***on whose shoulder*** the world rested.

妙语点睛 这里的 whose shoulder 作从句中的动词短语 rested on 的宾语，这里 on 被提前。whose 指人即 man。

精品译文 阿特拉斯是(希腊神话中的)一个大力神，他跪在地上，肩上背负着地球。

3.3.3 先行词指“物”，用关系代词which

关系词 which 的造句结构完全类似于前面讨论过的 who，比如 which 可以作从句的主语或宾语，只不过 which 的先行词是“物”。请看下面的例句：

1 1）We are studying sentences. ***They*** contain adjective clauses.

2）We are studying sentences ***which*** contain adjective clauses.

妙语点睛 这里的先行词是 sentences，表示“物”，因此不能用 who。这里要用 which 代替 they，来指代 sentences，告诉对方“我们正在学习什么类型的句子”。

精品译文 我们正在学习带有定语从句的句子。

值得注意的是，关系词 which 所指代的先行词比较复杂，它除了可以指单个的名词外，还可以指代短语甚至是从句。下面将一一举例说明。

一、先行词是单个的名词

2 Anger is a wind ***which*** blows out the lamp of the mind.

妙语点睛 先行词是 wind，即 which 指单个的名词。

精品译文 愤怒是吹灭心灵之灯的风。

3 Perhaps it is human to appreciate little that ***which*** we have and to long for that which we have not.

妙语点睛 先行词是 that，即 which 指单个的名词。

精品译文 或许，“不惜已获，贪求不得”是人类共同的弱点吧。

二、先行词是一个短语

which 可以指代一个短语。请看例句：

4 He likes climbing mountains, ***which*** is a good exercise.

妙语点睛 先行词是主句中的一个动名词短语 climbing mountains。

精品译文 他很喜欢爬山，这可是一项好的运动。

三、先行词是一个句子

which 可以指代前面的整个句子。请看例句：

5 1）Tom was late. ***That*** surprised me.

2）Tom was late, ***which*** surprised me.

妙语点睛 例句 2）中的 which 替换了例句 1）中的 that，显然是指前面的整个句子 Tom was late。

精品译文 汤姆迟到了，这让我很吃惊。

6 He tore up my photo, ***which*** upset me.

妙语点睛 全句 he tore up my photo 作 which 的先行词。

精品译文 他把我的照片给撕毁了，这让我很生气。

再比如，一位单亲妈妈这样调侃道：

7 I became a single mother overnight, ***which*** is nothing like becoming famous overnight.

妙语点睛 全句 I became a single mother overnight 作 which 的先行词。

精品译文 我在一夜之间成了单亲妈妈，这跟一夜成名可完全不同。

3.3.4 that 可以指代“人”，也可以指代“物”

关系代词 that 的意义和用法主要有以下三点：一是 that 既可指“人”也可指“物”，即它指“物”时可以替换 which，指“人”时可以替换 who 来使用；二是 that 不用在非限制性定语从句中（关于限制性和非限制性定语从句，详见 3.5 节）；三是 that 不能用于介词的后面（同 who 一样）。

一、that 既可指"人"也可指"物"

因为 that 的先行词既可以是表示"人"也可以是表示"物"，所以 that 可以用来替换 which 或 who。比如下面这个句子：

1 Too many people spend money ***which*** they haven't earned, to buy things ***which*** they don't want, to impress people ***who*** they don't like.

妙语点睛 可以用 that 替换其中的 which 和 who 而将这句话改写成：Too many people spend money ***that*** they haven't earned, to buy things ***that*** they don't want, to impress people ***that*** they don't like.

这是影星威尔·史密斯(Will Smith)批评时下一些年轻人的生活方式时说的话。这里 that 的先行词有"物(money 和 things)"，也有"人(people)"。

顺便提一句，在前面 3.2.4 小节讨论过，作宾语的关系词可以省去，因此这句话也可说成：Too many people spend money (　　) they haven't earned, to buy things (　　) they don't want, to impress people (　　) they don't like.

精品译文 许多人花没挣到的钱，买自己不想要的东西，向自己不喜欢的人炫耀。

既然 that 可以指"物"也可以指"人"，那么就会涉及与 which 和 who 在用法上的区别的问题。为了便于记忆和使用，现列举出下面这些最好用 that 的情况，供参考：

1. 当先行词中同时出现"人"和"物"时，用 that

2 ***The writer and his novels that*** the article deals with are quite familiar to us.

妙语点睛 这里的先行词是 the writer and his novels，即同时有"人(writer)"和"物(his novels)"，所以要选用 that 引导定语从句。

精品译文 这篇文章里所说的这个作家以及他的小说，我们都比较熟悉。

2. 先行词为指"物"的 all, little, few, much, none 和 the first 时，用 that

3 ***All that*** glitters is not gold.

妙语点睛 这里的先行词是 all，所以用 that 来引导定语从句。另外要注意的是，这里有一个半否定的问题：all...not 要译成"并非都是"，不能译成全否定的"所有都不"。

精品译文 闪光的并非都是金子。

这句话是莎士比亚(Shakespeare)的剧作《威尼斯商人》(The Merchant of Venice)中的名句，它的意思是说凡事不能只看外表，外表显得贵重华丽的东西不一定真正有价值（Something which seems valuable at first may turn out to be worthless. Just because something appears valuable does not mean that it really is valuable.）。

请再看下面的例句：

4 This book contains ***little that*** is useful.

妙语点睛 这里的先行词是表示否定意义的代词 little(几乎没有什么)，所以用 that 来引导定语从句。

精品译文 这本书里有用的东西几乎没有。

5 There is not ***much that*** can be done.

妙语点睛 这里的先行词是代词 much，所以用 that 来引导定语从句。

精品译文 这没有什么办法了。

6 As long as you stand up to the difficulties, there are ***none that*** cannot be overcome.

妙语点睛 这里的先行词是代词 none，所以用 that 来引导定语从句。

精品译文 只要你勇敢地去面对困难，就没有什么克服不了的。

3. 先行词是不定代词 something, anything, nothing 和 everything 时，一般用 that

7 Greater expense does not always equal better gift. I would much rather receive a gift that was unique or that I knew my friend had put some thought into than ***something*** that cost a lot of money but that I didn't need or want. I would much rather receive ***something that*** made me laugh, made me reminisce, or fit my personality than ***something that*** cost a lot but ***that*** I will just throw in my closet and forget about.

妙语点睛 首先，对于这段话里先行词是 something 的定语从句，作者都是采用了 that 来引导。其次，这里还有其他先行词不是 something 的定语从句，比如 a gift that was unique or that I knew my friend had put some thought into。第三，从结构上来看，这段话里的句子稍微有些复杂，因为里面含有多个并列的定语从句，比如由 or 连接的 that was unique 和 that I knew my friend had put thought into 并列（注意这里的 I knew 是插入语，从句的主谓结构是 my friend had put...）；由 but 连接的 that cost a lot of money 和 that I didn't need or want 并列；由 but 连接的 that cost a lot 和 that I will just throw in my closet and forget about 并列，最后还有定语从句（something）that made me laugh, made me reminisce, or fit my personality。所以这篇短文里定语从句较多。最后，这里有一个重要句型：I would rather...than，表示"我宁愿……而不愿"。

精品译文 价格昂贵的礼物并不意味着贵重，我倒希望收到的礼物是很别致的，或是我知道是朋友精心为我准备的，而不是花了很多钱却不是我所想要或需要的。我希望收到的是能够让我开心，让我回味过去的时光，或是适合我口味的礼物，而不是价格不菲，但看完之后随手就扔进储藏室，抛在脑后的礼物。

4. 先行词被 any, only, all, every, no, some, much, few, little，序数词，形容词的最高级，the only, the one, the very, the right 和 the last 等成分修饰时，用 that

8 Tell us ***all*** things ***that*** you know. 把你知道的都告诉我们。

9 There is ***no*** difficulty ***that*** they can't overcome. 没有什么困难是他们不能战胜的。

10 ***The only*** thing ***that*** we should do is find our way home. 我们应该做的只有找到回家的路。

11 ***The very*** problem ***that*** I want to solve is like this. 我想解决的问题就像这个一样。

12 He is ***the only*** man ***that*** can speak four foreign languages in our company. 他是我们公司中唯一一个会说四种外语的人。

5. that 不用在非限制性定语从句中

不用 that 引导非限制性定语从句。比如要说：

13 I became a single mother overnight, ***which*** is nothing like becoming famous overnight.

而不能说：I became a single mother overnight, ***that*** is nothing like becoming famous overnight. *

精品译文 我在一夜之间成了单亲妈妈，这跟一夜成名可完全不同。

6. that 不能用于介词后面

不能在 that 前面使用介词。比如要说：

14 The world ***in which*** we live is made up of matter.

或：The world ***which*** we live ***in*** is made up of matter.

或：The world ***that*** we live ***in*** is made up of matter.

但不能说：The world ***in that*** we live is made up of matter. *

精品译文 我们所生活的世界由物质组成。

思维总结

本节是定语从句的重点内容，主要讨论了不同关系代词的用法特点，这与先行词有关。所以，换个角度来看，就是关系词与先行词之间的对应关系的问题。

思维训练

Exercise 3. 3（Key: P330）

请将下列每一组中的两个简单句合并为一个定语从句，用第二个句子作定语。

1. The girl is happy. She won the race.
2. The student is from America. He sits next to me.

3. The boy was not badly hurt. The boy fell from a tree.
4. The taxi driver was friendly. He took me to the airport.
5. I can't remember the name of the person. I gave the money to him.
6. The employees had to retire. They had reached the age of sixty-five.
7. The teacher spoke to the boys. Their work was below standard.
8. The people were friendly. I rented their houses.
9. He is the professor. I am taking his grammar course.
10. That is the man. His son died in that air crash.
11. The man called the police. His car was stolen.
12. The man is famous. His picture is in the newspaper.
13. I have a neighbor. His dog barks all day long.
14. The girl is a good friend of mine. I borrowed her camera.
15. The church was built in 1400. We were married in the church.
16. She told me her address. I wrote it down on a piece of paper.
17. We are studying sentences. They contain adjective clauses.
18. The exhibition was not very interesting. My friend took me to see it.
19. John isn't home yet. That worried me.
20. Jack was fired from his job. That surprised all of his co-workers.
21. My roommate always plays music at the dorm. That really gets on my nerves.

请判断下列句子是否正确，错误的请改正。

22. I enjoy the music that we are listening to it.
23. The people which live next to me are friendly.
24. He is the man who he taught me English.
25. I gave the book to him that he needed it.
26. The airline has a booklet who will tell you most of the important things about a trip to Europe.
27. The man which told me the news refused to give me his name.
28. The book which I bought it at the bookstore was very useful.
29. The woman was nice that I met yesterday.
30. I met a woman who her husband is a famous lawyer.
31. Let ABC be a triangle which sides are of unequal length.
32. Do you know the people who lives in that house?
33. The people who I met them at the party last night were interesting.
34. He dropped in on an old friend that day where he visited his club.
35. The day, when began brightly, ended with a violent storm.

请将下列定语从句中的 that 改为 who 或 which，并判断哪些关系词可以省去。

36. The girl that answered the phone was polite.
37. I didn't know any of the people that Bill invited to his party.
38. The woman that I saw in the park was feeding the pigeons.
39. I like the barber that usually cuts my hair.
40. The person that I admire most is my father.
41. The people that I met at the party last night were very nice.
42. The people that live next to me have three cars.
43. The soup that I had for lunch was too salty.
44. The pill that I took made me sleepy.
45. My daughter asked me a question that I couldn't answer.
46. The man that my sister goes out with is tall, dark and handsome.
47. I couldn't understand the woman that I talked to on the phone.

3.4 关系副词的用法

讨论完关系代词，我们现在来分析一下关系副词的用法。在英语中，引导定语从句的关系副词主要有when, where 和 why，它们在从句中分别作时间状语、地点状语和原因状语。本节内容安排如下：

3.4.1 when 的用法

3.4.2 where 的用法

3.4.3 why 的用法

3.4.1 when 的用法

一、先行词指时间

when 可以引导限制性和非限制性定语从句（关于这两类定语从句的区分，详见3.5节），其先行词须是表示时间的名词，如 day, year 或 time 等。

1 I'll never forget ***the day when I met you.***

妙语点睛 这里的先行词是表示时间的名词 day，所以要用 when 引导定语从句。这里 when 作从句的时间状语，修饰谓语动词 met。

精品译文 我永远不会忘记我们见面的那一天。

2 Most education experts today stress the importance of "life-long learning". They point out that education never ends. It is a continuous process. ***The day when we stop learning is the day when we die.***

妙语点睛 表示时间的名词 day 用作先行词，所以用了 when 来引导定语从句。这里 when 作从句的时间状语，修饰谓语动词 stop 和 die。这个句子让我们知道，我们现在身处一个"终生学习(life-long learning)"的时代。

精品译文 大多数的教育专家现如今都强调"终生学习"的重要性。他们指出，教育是一个连续的过程，永远不应该停止，除非是我们离开了这个世界。

3 April Fool's Day is ***that special day*** of the year ***when you should play a joke on someone***! Children's favorites are to put salt in the sugar bowl for Dad's morning coffee or put chalk on a desk chair at school so the teacher gets a white backside! But remember, if you play a joke after 12 noon, YOU are the April Fool!

妙语点睛 表示时间的名词 day 用作先行词，所以用了 when 来引导定语从句。这里 when 作从句的时间状语，修饰谓语动词 play。这句话向读者介绍了有关愚人节的一个小常识，不妨记住。

精品译文 愚人节就是一年一度的一个特殊的日子，在这一天人们可以捉弄别人。比如，孩子们最喜欢的把戏就是在老爸的早餐咖啡的糖罐里放入盐，或是在学校的桌椅上撒上粉笔灰，以弄脏老师的后背。不过千万要记住哟，若你在中午12点之后再捉弄人，那你就是"愚人"了！

我们再来看 when 引导的非限制性定语从句：

4 My favorite season is ***spring, when the earth seems born again.***

妙语点睛 这里是 when 引导的非限制性定语从句，先行词是表示时间的名词 spring。

精品译文 到了春天，万物复苏，所以春天是我最喜欢的季节。

5 We will put off the outing until ***next week, when we won't be so busy.***

妙语点睛 这里是 when 引导的非限制性定语从句，先行词是表示时间的短语 next week。

精品译文 我们要把出游推迟到下周，到时我们就不会这么忙了。

请再看其他例句：

6 March 10, 1876 was the ***day when the first complete sentence was sent over a telephone.***

在1876年3月10日，人类首次通过电话传出了第一个完整的句子。

7 The ***day*** may soon come ***when we don't bother to go to office but just work at home.***
也许在不久的将来，我们就不必去办公室上班了，而就在家里工作。

二、关系副词 when 在从句中作时间状语

在上面的例句中，我们反复强调 when 是在定语从句中作时间状语。换句话说，若定语从句不是缺少状语，**而是缺少主语或宾语，那么即使先行词是表示时间的名词，也不能用** when **而要用** which **或** that **来引导定语从句**。因为用 when 来引导定语从句的前提条件是：when 必须在其引导的定语从句中作**时间状语**。请比较：

8 1）I'll never forget the ***time which*** I ***spent*** on campus.
2）I'll never forget the ***day when*** we first met in the park.

妙语点睛 在这两句话里，尽管先行词分别是表示时间的名词 time 和 day，但用的关系词不同。在例句 1）里，由于定语从句中的谓语 spent 缺宾语，因此关系词要充当这一宾语，故要用 which。在例句 2）中，定语从句不缺主语或宾语，而是缺少时间状语，故关系词用 when，这里 when 作时间状语，修饰 met。

精品译文 1）我永远不会忘记在大学校园里度过的时光。
2）我永远不会忘记我们第一次在公园里见面时的情景。

9 The day, ***which*** began brightly, ended with a violent storm.

妙语点睛 这里的先行词是 day，表示时间。但由于定语从句缺少主语，所以用关系代词 which 来引导定语从句，作从句的主语，而不用关系副词 when，因为关系副词无法作主语，只能作状语。

精品译文 那天，开始的时候还是阳光明媚，后来就下起了暴风雨。

3. 4. 2 where 的用法

一、where 的先行词指地点

where 引导定语从句，其先行词一般是表示地点的名词，如 place 和 house 等。请看例句：

1 A: Since you work in the theater, can't you get me a free ticket now and then?
B: Certainly if you bring me a few notes now and then from the ***bank where*** you work!

妙语点睛 这里的先行词 bank 表示地点，而且 where 在从句中充当地点状语（定语从句中不缺主语或宾语），修饰 work。

精品译文 A：既然你在剧院工作，那你就不能时常给我弄些免费的票吗？
B：当然可以，只要你能够从你工作的那家银行里时常给我弄些票子出来。

请再看其他例句：

2 Do you know any ***place where*** I can buy Mr. Zhang's grammar book?
你知道我在什么地方可以买到张老师的语法书吗？

3 This is the ***town where*** I spent my childhood. 我的童年就是在这座小城里度过的。

二、关系副词 where 在从句中作地点状语

与 when 类似，并非凡是先行词表示地点的名词，都得由 where 来引导定语从句，这得看关系词在从句中充当的成分。若定语从句缺主语或宾语，则要用 which 或 that 引导定语从句。请比较：

4 1）This is the ***town where*** I spent my childhood.
2）This is the ***town which*** I told you about before.

妙语点睛 在这两句话里，尽管先行词都是表示地点的名词 town，但用的关系词不同。在例句 1）中，定语从句不缺少主语或宾语，而是缺少地点状语，故关系词用 where。这里 where 作地点状语，修饰 spent。在例句 2）里，由于定语从句中的谓语部分 told you about 缺少宾语，因此关系词要充当这一宾语，故要用 which。

精品译文 1）这就是我度过童年的小城。
2）这就是我以前告诉过你的小城。

5 1）The ***library where*** students often study was on fire last night.

2）The ***library, which*** was built in the 1930's, needs to be renovated.

妙语点睛 在这两句话里，尽管先行词都是表示地点的名词 library，但用的关系词不同。在例句 1）中，定语从句不缺少主语或宾语，而是缺少地点状语，故关系词用 where。这里 where 作地点状语，修饰 study。在例句 2）中，由于定语从句缺少主语，因此填入的关系词要充当这一宾语，故要用 which。

精品译文 1）学生们常常上自习的那个图书馆昨晚着火了。

2）这个图书馆建于 20 世纪 30 年代，现在需要翻修了。

6 I've never been to Beijing, but it's the place ______.

A. where I'd like to visit　　B. in which I'd like to visit

C. I most want to visit　　D. that I want to visit it most

正确答案 C。

妙语点睛 这是 1999 年的六级考试真题。本题考查定语从句关系词的选择。这句话中尽管先行词是表示地点的名词 place，但由于从句中的谓语 visit 缺少宾语，所以不能选 A，而 C 才是正确答案。这里相当于省去了关系词 that 或 which，因此原句应该是 that / which I most want to visit。

精品译文 我从未到过北京，但北京却是我最想去的地方。

3. 4. 3 why 的用法

why 用来表示原因，**只引导限制性定语从句**，先行词是 reason 等表示原因的名词。

This is the reason why I didn't come here.

妙语点睛 此处的 why=for which

精品译文 这就是我没来的原因。

思维总结

本节讨论了三大关系副词的用法，其中最常用的是 when 和 where。需要特别注意的是，它们只能充当状语，不能作其他成分。

思维训练

Exercise 3. 4（Key: P331）

请将下列每一组中的两个简单句合并为一个定语从句，用第二个句子作定语。

1. Monday is the day. We will come on that day.
2. He arrived in Shanghai that day. On the same day I left.
3. July is the month. The weather is usually the hottest in that month.
4. April Fool's Day is that special day of the year. On the day you should play a joke on someone!
5. March 10, 1876 was the day. On the day the first complete sentence was sent over a telephone.
6. The city was beautiful. We spent our vacation there.
7. That is the restaurant. I will meet you there.
8. The town is small. I grew up there.
9. This is the house. They put their tools in it.

请选择 where，when 和 which 填空。

10. I'll never forget the day ______ I met you for the first time.
11. I'll never forget the days ______ I spent with you.
12. The day, ______ began brightly, ended with a violent storm.
13. The day ______ we don't bother to go to office but just work at home may soon come.
14. I arrived in Beijing on the day ______ it was snowing heavily.

15. This is the town ______ I was born.
16. This is the town ______ I want to visit most someday.
17. The ripe fruit should be stored in a place ______ contains much carbon dioxide so that it can't decay rapidly.
18. The ripe fruit should be stored in a place ______ there is much carbon dioxide so that it can't decay rapidly.
19. The library, ______ was built in the 1930's, needs to be renovated.
20. I guess you can find him in the library ______ he works.
21. One of the places ______ I want to visit someday is Tibet.

3.5 限制性与非限制性定语从句

在前面各节讨论的定语从句中，细心的读者也许发现了，有的先行词与关系词之间有逗号分隔，有的没有逗号分隔，这其实涉及定语从句的限制性(defining relative clause)和非限制性(non-defining relative clause)之分。二者在形式上的区别是：在限制性定语从句中，先行词和关系词之间不用逗号隔开，而非限制性定语从句则有逗号隔开。这种在形式上的有逗号或没有逗号并不是随意的，换句话说，二者更重要的是在意义上有区别。根据意义上的差别，可以把定语从句分三种情况。最后，本节还将讨论非限制性定语从句的翻译特点。因此，本节内容安排如下：

3.5.1 限制性定语从句——不用逗号隔开
3.5.2 非限制性定语从句——用逗号隔开
3.5.3 用或不用逗号，句义有差别
3.5.4 非限制性定语从句的翻译

3.5.1 限制性定语从句——不用逗号隔开

限制性定语从句是用来对一个名词提供必要的信息(a defining relative clause defines or gives essential information about a noun)，以说明定语从句所修饰的先行词的身份或性质，或用来限制先行词所指的范围。若去掉限制性定语从句，则主句部分的含义不明确，或意义不完整，所以不能用逗号来分隔先行词和定语从句。

比如 I don't like people. 这句话的意思不明确，句义不完整，因此其后面必须加一个限制性定语从句，才能使句义完整。比如加上限制性定语从句后这么说：

1 I don't like people ***who are never on time.*** 我不喜欢不守时的人。

2 I don't like people ***who never keep their words.*** 我不喜欢不守信用的人。

以上句子黑体部分的定语从句都是用来说明 people 的性质的，是必不可少的信息，因此不能加逗号将其变为非限制性定语从句。再来分析下列例句：

3 There are two factors ***which determine an individual's intelligence.***

妙语点睛 这里若只是说 There are two factors. 则句义不够完整，现在有了限制性定语从句 which determine an individual's intelligence 来限制修饰名词 factors，就使得句义更明确。

精品译文 决定人的智力的因素有两个。

4 He is a man ***who is of value to the people.***

妙语点睛 这里若只是说 He is a man. 则句义不完整，现在有了限制性定语从句 who is of value to the people 来限制修饰名词 man，就使得句义完整而明确。

精品译文 他是一个有利于人民的人。

3.5.2 非限制性定语从句——用逗号隔开

非限制性定语从句用来提供附加的而非必要的信息，只是对先行词作进一步的解释、补充或说明(a non-defining relative clause gives optional information about a noun)。若去掉此定语从句，整个主句的意义一样很明确，不会引起误解和歧义。一般来讲，下面这两种先行词，其后都宜用非限制性定语从句。

一、专有名词

如果定语从句修饰一个专有名词，一般要用逗号分隔先行词与定语从句，也就是说要使用非限制性定语从句。这是因为专有名词本身的意思已经很完整，不需要限制，用定语从句只是对它进行补充说明。请看例句：

1 My mother, ***who is 50 this year***, lives with me now.

妙语点睛 这里的先行词 my mother 就是一个专有名词，其后的定语从句 who is 50 this year 只能是作为非限制性的定语从句来提供附加信息，不能使用限制性定语从句。若说 My mother ***who is 50 this year*** lives with me now. 则言外之意为“我有好几个母亲，目前和我住在一起的是今年 50 岁的那位母亲”。然而实际上，我们只可能有一位母亲。

精品译文 我母亲今年 50 岁了，现在和我生活在一起。

伊拉克首都巴格达的民众 2008 年 1 月 11 日早上醒来时惊见降雪。当地气象部门证实，这场雪是这座城市约 100 年来下的第一场雪。下面的例句就是 40 岁的巴格达居民法齐·卡里姆接受记者采访时说的：

2 I asked my mother, ***who is 80***, whether she'd ever seen snow in Iraq before, and her answer was no.

精品译文 我问我已经 80 岁的妈妈，她以前在伊拉克是否见过雪，她回答说没见过。

下面这个例句谈到美国现在(2008 年)的民主党总统侯选人奥巴马(Obama)的竞选策略：

3 Obama is trying to broaden our collective notion of the mainstream. On the one hand, his campaign is running television commercials in Iowa featuring his late mother, ***who was white.*** On the other, he touts his biracial, multicultural background as an advantage when it comes to representing the U. S. abroad.

精品译文 奥巴马也设法扩大我们对主流的集体概念。一方面，他的竞选包括在艾奥瓦州播放以他过世的母亲为主角的电视广告——他母亲是白人。另一方面，他使劲兜售自己的黑白混血多元文化背景，就代表美国来说，他的这种混血以及多元文化背景倒是一种优势。

在以上例句中，先行词都是 mother 这样的专有名词，都采用了非限制性定语从句。

请再看下面的例句：

4 Beijing, ***which is the capital of China***, has developed into an international city. 北京，中国的首都，已经成为了一个国际化都市。

5 Einstein, ***who was a great Jewish scientist***, created the theory of relativity. 爱因斯坦这位伟大的犹太科学家发明了相对论。

6 Hawaii, ***which consists of eight principal islands***, is a favorite vacation spot. 夏威夷包含八个主要岛屿，是一个度假胜地。

以上例句中的先行词 Beijing, Einstein 和 Hawaii 都是专有名词，因此，其后的定语从句都只能是非限制性的，以对其前面的先行名词进行补充说明，向读者提供附加的信息，故均不能变为限制性定语从句。

二、类指名词

上面谈到，专有名词作为先行词，其后接的定语从句一般都是非限制性的。现在来讨论普通名词作为先行词的情况。普通名词若是用来表示类指，即表示的是一类事物，而非具体的某一个事物，此时，其后也宜用非限制性定语从句。请比较下列例句：

7 1) An elephant, ***which is the earth's largest land mammal***, has few natural enemies other than human beings.

2) One of the elephants ***which we saw at the zoo*** had only one tusk.

妙语点睛 这两句的先行词都是普通名词 elephant，但例句 1) 用了非限制性定语从句 which is the earth's largest land mammal，而例句 2) 却用了限制性定语从句 which we saw at the zoo，原因就是因为两句中的 elephant 的意义是不一样的。例句 1)中的 an elephant 是类指或泛指，即表示“大象”这类动物，而不是指称具体的某一头大象。例句 2)中的 elephants 则不是类指概念，而是具体指代某一头大象，即“我们在动物园看到的那头大象”。

精品译文 1)大象作为陆地上体型最大的哺乳类动物，很少有天敌，除了人类之外。

2)我们在动物园看到一头大象只有一颗象牙。

3.5.3 用或不用逗号，句义有差别

在英文中，还有一类句子，用限制性或非限制性定语从句都可以，但强调的意义不一样，即句义不同。请比较：

1 1) He has a daughter ***who works in a hospital.***

2) He has a daughter, ***who works in a hospital.***

妙语点睛 例句 1) 表示他有多个女儿，其中有一个在医院工作。例句 2) 强调他有一个女儿，不是儿子，"在医院工作"纯粹是补充信息。

精品译文 1)他有一个在医院工作的女儿。

2)他有个女儿，是在医院工作的。

2 1) The food ***which wasn't in the fridge*** all went off.

2) The food, ***which wasn't in the fridge***, all went off.

妙语点睛 例句 1)表示部分食物坏了，即没有放在冰箱里的那部分食物坏了。例句 2)表示食物都坏了，因为没有放在冰箱里。此时定语从句补充说明了食物变质的原因，是因为没有放在冰箱里。

精品译文 1)没有放在冰箱里的那些食物坏了。

2)食物都坏了，因为没有放在冰箱里。

3 1) The cab drivers ***who knew about the traffic jam*** took another road.

2) The cab drivers, ***who knew about the traffic jam***, took another road.

妙语点睛 例句 1)的言外之意是"不知道的司机则没有换路线，只有部分司机换行驶路线了"。例句 2)的言外之意是"全部司机都知道，都换了行驶路线"。

精品译文 1)知道那里堵车的出租车司机换了另一条道。

2)出租车司机因为知道那里塞车了，他们都换了另一条道。

从以上非限制性定语从句的译文看出，非限制性定语从句的翻译非常灵活，不一定都译成定语"……的"结构。下面举例具体说明。

3.5.4 非限制性定语从句的翻译

最后，我们讨论一下上述两种定语从句在翻译上的差别。限制性定语从句一般翻译成定语的形式"……的"，而非限制性定语从句往往会译成各种状语形式。例如：

1 The food, ***which wasn't in the fridge***, all went off.

精品译文 食物都坏了，因为没有放在冰箱里(译成原因状语从句)。

2 The Ambassador gave a dinner to the scientists, ***with whom he especially wished to talk.***

精品译文 大使宴请了那些科学家，因为他特别想与他们交谈一下(译成原因状语从句)。

3 The people were desperate for work, any work, ***which could support their family.***

精品译文 人们急于找到工作，什么工作都行，只要能养家糊口(译成条件状语从句)。

4 The millionaire had another house built, ***which he didn't need at all.***

精品译文 那位百万富翁又建了一幢房子，尽管他并不需要(译成让步状语从句)。

5 They tried to stamp out the revolt, ***which spread all the more furiously throughout the country.***

精品译文 起义依然声势浩大地遍布全国，尽管他们试图镇压(译成让步状语从句)。

6 Both players, ***neither of whom reached the final***, played well.

精品译文 尽管两名选手都未进入决赛，但都表现得很好(让步状语从句)。

7 We know that a cat, ***whose eyes can take in many more rays of light than our eyes***, can see clearly in the night.

精品译文 我们知道，因为猫的眼睛能够比人的眼睛吸收更多的光线，所以猫在黑夜里也能够看得很清楚(原因状语从句)。

思维总结

本节重点讨论了限制性和非限制性定语从句在结构上、意义上和翻译上的差异。读者需重点掌握二者在意义上的差异，灵活掌握非限制性定语从句的两类名词。

思维训练

Exercise 3. 5（Key: P332）

请判断下列各个句子是否该加逗号而变成非限制性定语从句。

1. Seoul which hosted the 1988 Summer Olympics is well known for its shopping.
2. Seoul is the city that hosted the summer Olympics in 1988.
3. There are many temples and shrines in Kyoto which used to be the capital of Japan.
4. Kyoto which was the country's capital from 794 until 1868 has around 2, 000 temples and shrines.
5. Brasilia which is the capital of Brazil is less than 50 years old.
6. Montreal is a city where both French and English are spoken.
7. Bangkok which is the capital of Thailand has many beautiful temples.
8. Mexico City which has a population of around 20, 000, 000 is the largest urban area in the Americas.
9. Salvador which lies in the northeast was the country's busiest port from 1500 to 1815.

请分析下面句中所含定语从句分别属于前文所述 3 种情形中的哪一种，必要时请添加逗号。

10. I don't like stories that have unhappy endings.
11. A dictionary is a book that gives you the meaning of words.
12. It seems that the earth is the only planet that can support life.
13. The teacher who comes from Canada teaches us English.
14. We are studying sentences which contain adjective clauses.
15. I saw him stand under the apple tree which was behind the house.
16. The teacher thanked the students who had given her some flowers.
17. He has a daughter who works in a hospital.
18. An elephant which is the earth's largest land mammal has few natural enemies other than human beings.
19. One of the elephants which we saw at the zoo had only one tusk.
20. The rice which we had for dinner last night was very good.
21. Rice which is grown in many countries is a staple food throughout much of the world.
22. Jane was delighted when she opened the present which was from her ex-boyfriend.
23. A child whose parents are dead is called orphan.
24. Linda Watson who earned a cumulative grade point average of 3. 7 was graduated with highest honors.
25. Students who earn a cumulative grade point average of 3. 7 or more will be graduated with highest honors.

3.6 定语从句与同位语从句的区分

本节主要讨论由 that 引导的定语从句和同位语从句的区别。二者在结构上有相似性，都是“名词 +that 从句”，这里的名词都称作先行词。下面将从结构上和意义上来区分定语从句和同位语从句。因此，本节内容安排如下：

3. 6. 1 从结构上区分：that 是否作成分

3. 6. 2 从意义上区分：that 引导的从句的意义不同

3. 6. 1 从结构上区分：that 是否作成分

that 在定语从句中要充当成分，比如作从句的主语或宾语；而 that 在同位语从句中不作任何成分，仅起连词的作用。换句话说，定语从句的结构是“名词 + that + 不完整的句子”，而同位语从句的结构是“名词 + that + 完整的陈述句”。

1 1) ***The rumor that*** he spread everywhere turned out to be untrue.

2) ***The rumor that*** Tom was a thief turned out to be untrue.

妙语点睛 以上两句的先行词都是 the rumor，连词都是 that。但例句 1）中的 that 在从句中作成分，充当 spread 的宾语，故例句 1)为定语从句。例句 2)中的 that 在从句中不作任何成分，因为从句 Tom was a thief 是一个完整的句子，不缺少任何成分。故其为同位语从句，作 the rumor 的同位语，补充说明 the rumor 的具体内容。

精品译文 1)他到处散布的那个谣言，结果证明是假的。

2)有人谣传说 Tom 是窃贼，结果证明是假的。

2 1) ***The fact that*** we talked about is very important.

2) ***The fact that*** he succeeded in the experiment pleased everybody.

妙语点睛 例句 1)中的 that 作 talked about 的宾语，故例句 1)为定语从句。例句 2)中的 that 不充当成分，因为 he succeeded in the experiment 是一个完整的陈述句，故其为同位语从句。

精品译文 1)我们讨论的这些情况很重要。

2)他的实验成功了，这让大家都很高兴。

3.6.2 从意义上区分：that 引导的从句的意义不同

两类从句在意义上也不同：定语从句相当于形容词，对先行词起修饰、描述和限制的作用；同位语从句相当于一个名词，对其前面名词内容的具体表述，二者是同位关系。

1 1) ***The news that*** you heard is not true.

2) ***The news that*** Lincoln was murdered at a theater is true.

妙语点睛 例句 1)中的定语从句 that you heard 并不是表示 news 的内容，只是在限制 news 所指的范围，即“你听到的那个消息”。例句 2)中的同位语从句 that Lincoln was murdered at a theater 是表示 news 的具体内容，在意义上与 news 构成同位关系。

精品译文 1)你听到的那个消息并不是真实的。

2)有消息说林肯是在一个剧院被刺杀的，这是真的。

2 1) ***The fact that*** you pointed out made me interested.

2) ***The fact that*** there are no lives on the moon is known to us all.

妙语点睛 例句 1)中的定语从句 that you pointed out 并不是表示 fact 的内容，只是在限制 fact 的所指范围，即“你指出的这个事实”。例句 2)中的同位语从句 that there are no lives on the moon 是表示 fact 的具体内容，在意义上与 fact 构成同位关系。

精品译文 1)你指出的这一点，我很感兴趣。

2)众所周知，月球上并没有生命存在。

思维总结

本节主要讨论了由 that 引导的定语从句和同位语从句的区别。读者重点需要掌握二者在结构上的区分，即 that 引导的定语从句在结构上是不完整的，而 that 引导的同位语从句在结构上是完整的陈述句。

思维训练

Exercise 3.6（Key: P333）

请判断下列句子是定语从句还是同位语从句。

1. He turned down the proposal that she offered at the meeting.
2. He turned down the proposal that she should be sent abroad to study.

请分析下列 **that** 引导的是定语从句还是名词从句，并翻译成中文。

3. Studies show ***that*** the things ***that*** contribute most to a sense of happiness cannot be bought, such as a good family life, friendship and work satisfaction.

4. The mere fact ***that*** most people believe nuclear war would be madness does not mean that it will not occur.
5. An evidence ***that*** life may have existed on earth 3. 8 billions years ago has been discovered in these ancient rocks.
6. When reports came into London Zoo ***that*** a wild puma had been spotted forty-five miles south of London, they were not taken seriously.
7. The idea ***that*** some groups of people may be more intelligent than others is one of those hypotheses that dare not speak its name.
8. The ruler of an ancient kingdom wanted to disprove the rumor ***that*** their wives ruled the men of his domain. He had all the males in his kingdom brought before him and warned ***that*** any man ***that*** did not tell the truth would be punished severely. Then he asked all the men ***that*** obeyed their wives' directions and advice to step to the left side of the hall. All the men did so but one little man ***that*** moved to the right. "It's good to see," said the king, "***that*** we have one real man in the kingdom. Tell these chicken-hearted dunces（傻瓜）why you alone among them stand on the right side of the hall." "Your Majesty," came the reply in a squealing(长而尖锐的声音)voice, "it is because before I left home my wife told me to keep out of crowds."

写给读者的话

一、本章学习思路

定语从句是英文造句规则中的一个难点，也是重点。它有两个重要概念：先行词和关系词，定语从句的核心内容都是围绕着这两者之间的关系展开的。本章重点讨论了先行词和关系词之间的搭配关系，比如若先行词指"人"，关系词就要用 who 或 that；若先行词指"物"，关系词就要用 which 或 that；指时间一般用关系词 when(只作状语)等等。读者只需要抓住关系词与先行词的各个用法特点，就可以把握定语从句的核心内容。

二、本章重点及难点

1. 关系代词的用法；
2. 关系副词的用法，特别需要提醒读者注意的是关系副词只能作状语；
3. 灵活运用限制性和非限制性定语从句。比如在写文章时，一定要真正会判断何时该用限制性定语从句，何时该用非限制性定语从句。这两种形式上不同的定语从句其实是它们在思维上的差异的反映。
4. 区分 that 引导的定语从句和同位语从句。

对于某些读者来说，灵活判断和使用限制性和非限制性定语从句或许比较难，其次是熟练判断 that 引导的定语从句和同位语从句，这两点既是重点也是难点。

三、本章学习时间安排

对于从来没有接触过定语从句的读者，学习完本章内容至少需要用一周的时间，包括阅读讲解的内容和做完所有的练习。

综合练习（Key: P333）

请将下列中文翻译成英文。

1. 我昨天买了一本书，该书的作者是一位盲人。
2. 我的办公室在这栋大楼的二层，它很小。
3. 你昨天借给我的那本书很有趣。
4. 那位老师教我英文，他是加拿大的。
5. 和我一起工作的那个女孩已经有男朋友了。
6. 告诉我今天早晨你迟到的原因。
7. 他们到的时候天正在下雨。
8. 他是一个值得信赖的人。
9. 你住的那家酒店叫什么名字？
10. 接电话的那个男的告诉我你不在。

请选择最适当的词填空。

11. The professor and her achievement ______ you told me about are admired by us all.
A. who　B. which　C. that　D. whom

12. I don't suppose anything happens ______ he doesn't foresee.
A. that　B. which　C. what　D. as

13. They shouted with the loudest voice ______ they could.
A. when　B. that　C. which　D. what

14. This is the best book ______ on the subject.
A. which there is　B. that there is　C. which is　D. what is

15. He's written a book ______ name I've completely forgotten.
A. whose　B. which　C. of which　D. that

16. The meeting was postponed, ______ was exactly what I wanted.
A. that　B. which it　C. and that　D. this

17. Mr. Jones, ______ John was working, was very generous about overtime payment.
A. for whom　B. for who　C. whom　D. for that

18. There is not much ______ can be done now.
A. that　B. which　C. who　D. what

19. He showed me a book, ______ I could tell that it was pretty old.
A. which cover　B. of which cover　C. the cover which　D. from the cover of which

20. This kind of solar cooker can be used only in the daytime ______ the sun is shining.
A. when　B. as　C. while　D. since

21. Solomon was diligent, responsible and hardworking, ______ he was promoted from a clerk to a manager.
A. for which　B. which　C. for　D. that

22. What is ______ ordered the English book?
A. the lady's address in Beijing who　B. the lady's address in Beijing which
C. the address of the lady in Beijing who　D. the address of the lady in Beijing which

23. There comes a time in every man's life ______.
A. then he has to think　B. which he needs
C. when he has to think　D. therefore he has to work hard

24. No sample ______ we have received is satisfactory.
A. which　B. what　C. that　D. who

25. Obviously there was little certainty ______ the chairman would agree to this proposal.
A. which　B. why　C. what　D. that

26. There can't be any life on Venus, ______ the temperature is as high as 900F.
A. which　B. when　C. where　D. there

27. The reason ______ he died was lack of medical care.
A. which　B. for that　C. as　D. why

28. This is the shop ______ I often buy foodstuff.
A. where　B. which　C. of which　D. to which

29. The reason ______ he gave for his being late was unacceptable.
A. why　B. that　C. who　D. for which

30. The shop ______ I told you about before has closed down.
A. where　B. in which　C. at which　D. which

31. Those guilty of a serious crime ______ refuse to reform must be severely punished.
A. which　B. whom　C. when　D. who

32. Yet no firm evidence had come to light ______ the men arrested were actually responsible.
A. which　B. as　C. what　D. that

33. Another food crop raised by Indians ______ strange to the European was called Indian corn.
A. who were　B. that were　C. that was　D. who was

34. They helped us time and again, ______ very kind of them.
A. who were　B. which was　C. that was　D. which were

35. "Do you like the book your father gave you?"
"Very much. It's exactly ______ I wanted."
A. one which　B. that　C. one what　D. the one

36. When reports came into London Zoo ______ a wild puma had been spotted forty-five miles south of London, they were not taken seriously.
A. what　B. as　C. which　D. that

37. Many birds have feathers ______ with their surroundings.
A. colors blend　B. that colors blend
C. whose colors blend　D. of which the colors that blend

38. Civil rights are the freedoms and rights ______ as a member of a community, state, or nation.
A. may have a person　B. a person who may have
C. a person may have　D. and a person may have

39. In the early twentieth century, the "Model T" automobile was mass-produced and sold at a price ______ could afford.
A. the average person who　B. that the average person who
C. and the average person　D. the average person

请阅读下面的短文故事，并在空格中填入适当的关系词。

A story tells of two friends __40__ were walking through the desert. At a specific point of the journey, they had an argument, and one friend slapped the other one in the face. The one __41__ got slapped was hurt, but without saying anything, he wrote in the sand, "Today my best friend slapped me in the face."

They kept on walking until they found an oasis, __42__ they decided to take a bath. The one __43__ got slapped and hurt started drowning, and the other friend saved him. When he recovered from the fright, he wrote on a stone, "Today my best friend saved my life."

The friend __44__ had saved and slapped his best friend asked him, "Why, after I hurt you, you wrote in the sand and now your write on a stone?"

The other friend, smiling, replied, "When a friend hurts us, we should write it down in the sand, __45__ the winds of forgiveness can erase it away, and when someone does something good for us, we should engrave it in the stone of the memory of the heart, __46__ no wind can ever erase it."

Let's learn to write your hurts in the sand and to carve your blessings in stones.

请用适当的连词填空(名词从句与定语从句辨析)。

***Chicken Soup for the Soul* 心灵鸡汤**

Rose

****

Real love lies not in __47__ (what/which/that) is done and known, but in __48__ (what/which/that) is done but not known.

****

Red roses were her favorites; her name was also Rose. And every year her husband sent them, tied with pretty bows. The year he died, the roses were delivered to her door. The card said, "Be my Valentine," like all the years before. Each year he sent her roses, and the note would always say, "I love you even more this year than last year on this day." "My love for you will always grow with every passing year." She knew __49__ (what/which/that) this was the last time that the roses would appear.

She thought __50__ (what/which/*) he ordered roses in advance before this day. Her loving husband did not know __51__ (what/which/that) he would pass away. He always liked to do things early before the time. Then, if he got too busy, everything would work out fine.

She trimmed the stems and placed them in a very special vase and then put the vase beside the portrait of his smiling face. She would sit for hours in her husband's favorite chair, while staring at his picture, and the roses sitting there.

A year went by, and it was hard to live without her mate. With loneliness and solitude ___52___ (what/which/that) had become her fate. Then the very hour as on Valentines before, the doorbell rang, and there were roses, sitting by her door.

She brought the roses in, and then just looked at them in shock. Then went to get the telephone to call the florist shop. The owner answered and she asked him if he would explain ___53___ (what/which/that/why) someone would do this to her, causing her such pain.

"I know ___54___ (what/which/*) your husband passed away more than a year ago," The owner said, "I knew you'd call, and you would want to know." "The flowers ___55___ (what/which/that) you received today were paid for in advance." "Your husband always planned ahead, he left nothing to chance."

"There is a standing order ___56___ (what/which/that) I have on file down here. And he has paid well in advance, you'll get them every year. There also is another thing ___57___ (what/which/that) I think you should know, he wrote a special little card...he did this years ago."

"Then should ever I find out ___58___ (what/which/that) he's no longer here, it's the card ___59___ (what/which/that) should be sent to you the following year." She thanked him and hung up the phone, her tears now flowing hard. Her fingers were shaking, as she slowly reached to get the card.

Inside the card, she saw ___60___ (what/which/that) he had written her a note. Then as she stared in total silence, this is ___61___ (what/which/that) he wrote...

"Hello my love, I know it's been a year since I've been gone,
I hope it hasn't been too hard for you to overcome."

"I know it must be lonely, and the pain is very real.
For if it was the other way, I know ___62___ (what/which/that/how) I would feel.
The love ___63___ (what/which/that) we shared made everything so beautiful in life.
I loved you more than words can say, you were the perfect wife."

"You were my friend and lover, you fulfilled my every need.
I know it's only been a year, but please try not to grieve.
I want you to be happy, even when you shed your tears.
That is ___64___ (what/which/how/why) the roses will be sent to you for years."

"When you get these roses, think of all the happiness,
___65___ (what/which/that) we had together, and how both of us were blessed.
I have always loved you and I know I always will.
But, my love, you must go on, you have some living still."

"Please...try to find happiness, while living out your days.
I know it is not easy, but I hope ___66___ (what/which/that) you find some ways.
The roses will come every year, and they will only stop,
When your door's not answered, when the florist stops knocking."

"He will come five times that day, in case you have gone out.
But after his last visit, he will know without a doubt,
To take the roses to the place where I've instructed him,
And place the roses where we are together once again."

Chapter 4

第四章　状语从句

一般来讲，英语中的状语从句有九大类，分别可表示时间、地点、原因、目的、结果、条件、让步、比较和方式。因此，本章的主要内容安排如下：

本章主要是介绍引导这些状语从句常见的连词的用法。要想全面而深入地掌握状语从句，读者可以参阅《英语语法新思维高级教程——驾驭语法》第三章的内容。

4.1 时间状语从句

引导时间状语从句的连词较多，主从句时态搭配以及谓语动词的动作时间长短性等用法特点也各异。但本节只是简单地介绍一下 when, while 和 until 的用法特点，以及英语中表示“一……就”的结构。因此，本节内容安排如下：

4. 1. 1 时间连词 when 的用法特点

4. 1. 2 时间连词 while 的用法特点

4. 1. 3 时间连词 until 的用法特点

4. 1. 4 表示“一……就”的结构

需要提醒读者注意的是，更深入而全面的内容，读者可以继续研读《英语语法新思维高级教程——驾驭语法》第三章 3. 1 节的内容。

4. 1. 1 时间连词 when 的用法特点

一般来讲，when 的意思相当于 at that time(在……时刻)，因此从句的谓语动词通常是**短暂动词**，表示某一时刻的动作。不过，when 引导的从句也可接**延续动词**(continuous verb)，这时从句往往用过去进行时态，表示某一时间段内发生的动作。有关连词 when 常见的主从句时态搭配举例说明如下。

时间从句所表达的时间通常是过去和将来。首先，请读者来看 when 引导从句表示过去动作的四组时态搭配。

一、主句一般过去时+从句一般过去时

1 I ***started*** my dinner when he left. 他走了之后，我才开始吃晚饭。

2 He ***left*** when I ***got*** there. 我到了以后，他才离开。

从以上例句可以看出，若主从句都用一般过去时，则表示从句动作先发生。所以，从句还可以用过去完成时。于是，就有了下面的第二种时态搭配关系。

二、主句一般过去时+从句过去完成时

3 I ***started*** my dinner when he ***had left.***

4 He ***left*** when I ***had got*** there.

这两句的从句用了过去完成时，更强调了从句动作先发生，意思与上面两句区别不大。

在表示过去的动作中，when 引导的从句还有一个重要的时态搭配，即一般过去时(simple past)与过去进行时(past continuous)搭配。关于这一点，在《英语语法新思维初级教程——走近语法》中已详细讨论过。注意，**此时的时态搭配与主句、从句没有关系，而只与动作的长短有关系。短暂动作用一般过去时，延续动作用过去进行时**。这一时态配套使用所表示的意义是：在一个延续背景动作的过程中突然发生了一个短暂动作。既然此时的时态搭配与主从句没有关系，因此可以组合成下面两种时态搭配，即“主句过去进行时 + 从句一般过去时”，或“主句一般过去时 + 从句过去进行时”，即：

1. 主句一般过去时+从句过去进行时

5 The doorbell ***rang*** when I ***was telephoning.***

妙语点睛 这里的短暂动作 rang 用一般过去时，延续动作 telephone 用过去进行时。

精品译文 门铃响的时候，我正在打电话。

如上所述，这个句子也可以换成“主句过去进行时 + 从句一般过去时”这样的时态搭配，即：

2. 主句过去进行时+从句一般过去时

6 I *was telephoning* when the doorbell *rang*. 我当时正在打电话，突然门铃响了。

注意：由"主句一般过去时 + when + 从句过去进行时"变成"主句过去进行时 + when + 从句一般过去时"，此时 when 的意思发生了改变，即由 during the time（当……时候）变成了 at the time（正在那时）。这时 when 强调某个短暂动作突然发生，所以可以在 when 引导的从句中添加 suddenly 一词。请比较：

7 1）The doorbell *rang* when suddenly I *was telephoning*. *
2）I *was telephoning* when suddenly the doorbell *rang*.

妙语点睛 在例句 1)中，由于 when 的意思是 during the time，强调的是一个动作持续的过程，所以不能添加 suddenly 这样的词。在例句 2)中，由于 when 的意思是 at the time，强调的是一个短暂动作的发生，所以可以添加 suddenly 一词。

请比较：

8 1）I *was telephoning* Harry when she *arrived*.
2）I *telephoned* Harry when she *arrived*.

妙语点睛 我们看到，这两个句子仅主句的态不同。例句 1)用了过去进行时态的 was telephoning，例句 2)用了一般过去时态的 telephoned。不同时态表达的意思不同，并且说明主从句的动作发生先后也不同。在例句 1)中，telephoning（打电话）先发生，arrived（到达）后发生。在例句 2)中，则反过来了，telephoned（打电话）后发生，arrived（到达）先发生。另外，在例句 1)中，telephoning（打电话）是一个延续动作，arrived（到达）是短暂动作。但在例句 2)中，telephoned（打电话）变成了短暂动作，这里只强调动作的开始，而没有强调动作的持续性。

精品译文 1)她到的时候，我正在给哈里打电话。
2)她到了以后，我给哈里打了一个电话。

请再来看下面这两个句子：

9 I *was walking* along the road *when suddenly* someone *patted* me on the shoulder from behind.

妙语点睛 这是"主句过去进行时 + 从句一般过去时"的时态搭配，此时 when 强调短暂动作，所以可以添加 suddenly，表示"突然有人拍我"。

精品译文 当时我正在路上走着，突然有人从背后拍我的肩膀。

10 On a rainy day I *was driving* north through Vermont *when suddenly* I *noticed* a young man holding up a sign reading "Boston".

妙语点睛 这是"主句过去进行时 + 从句一般过去时"的时态搭配，此时 when 强调短暂动作，所以可以添加 suddenly，表示"我突然注意到"。

精品译文 在一个雨天，我正驾着车往北穿越佛蒙特州，这时我突然看见一个年轻男子，手里举着个牌子，上面写着"波士顿"。

我们下面来看 when 引导从句表示将来动作的一组时态搭配。

3. 主句一般将来时+从句一般现在时

在表示将来的动作时，主句显然要用一般将来时（simple future），而时间从句要用一般现在时（simple present）表示将来，不能使用将来时态。请看例句：

11 ***I'll speak*** to him when he ***arrives***. 等他到了我要和他说话。

12 ***I'll tell*** him about it when he ***comes*** back. 等他回来我要告诉他这件事。

4.1.2 时间连词 while 的用法特点

当 while 用作时间连词时，意思相当于 during that time（在……期间），表示某一时间段内发生的动作。因此，从句的谓语动词通常接延续动词。请看例句：

1 The phone rang ***while*** I was ***taking*** my bath.

妙语点睛 此句中 while 后面的谓语部分 taking my bath 是一个持续的动作。

精品译文 电话铃响的时候我正在洗澡。

2 The doorbell rang ***while*** we were ***watching*** TV.

妙语点睛 此句中 while 后面的谓语部分 watching TV 是一个持续的动作。

精品译文 当时我正在看电视，突然门铃响了。

时间连词 while 和 when 的含义有差别：while 的意思相当于 during that time(在……期间)，表示某一时间段内发生的动作，因此，从句的谓语动词通常接**延续动词**。when 的意思相当于 at that time(在……时刻)，从句的谓语动词通常是**短暂动词**，表示某一时刻的动作(从句也可接延续动词，这时从句往往用过去进行时态)。请比较：

3 A detective（侦探）arrested a criminal and was about to handcuff（给……戴手拷）him ***when*** a huge gust（一阵狂风）of wind ***blew*** the detective's hat ***off.***

"Shall I go and fetch it?" the criminal asked. "Do you take me for a fool?" asked the detective. "You wait here ***while*** I ***go*** and ***get*** it!"

妙语点睛 此句中的 go 和 get 尽管是短暂动词，但两动词连用表示的是在一段期间内的活动，所以用连词 while。而 when 的从句的谓语是 blew off，表示"吹落"，显然是一个短暂动作，所以不能用 while 引导。

精品译文 一个侦探逮着了一名罪犯。他正准备给罪犯戴上手铐，这时刮起了一阵狂风，把侦探的帽子吹落了。罪犯立即说："需要我去帮你把帽子捡起来吗？"侦探答道："你把我当傻瓜啊？你在这里等着，我自己去捡！"

我们再来看下面这道考题：

4 I was walking along the road ______ suddenly someone patted me on the shoulder from behind.

A. immediately B. when C. the moment D. while

正确答案 B。

妙语点睛 这是一道四级考题。这里从句的动词 patted 是一个短暂动作，所以不能选 D 即 while。

精品译文 当时我正在路上走着，突然有人从背后拍我的肩膀。

5 The phenomenon provides a way for companies to remain globally competitive ______ avoiding market cycles and the growing burdens imposed by employment rules, healthcare costs and pension plans.

A. but B. while C. and D. whereas

正确答案 B。

妙语点睛 这是 1997 年的考研完形填空第 48 题。这里的动词 avoid 表示的相当于一个状态，是延续动词，所以用 while。

精品译文 这种现象为公司开辟了一条道路，使它们既保持了自身的国际竞争力，同时也避免了市场周期的冲击和就业法规的限制，以及医疗费用和养老金带来的日益繁重的负担。

4.1.3 时间连词 until 的用法特点

在英语中，until 的用法有以下三个要点：

第一、until 既可以用作**介词**也可以作为**连词**，所以 until 的后面可以接名词短语也可以接时间从句。

第二、until 的本质思维是表示"一个(主句)动作一直持续到某一个时间点"。具体来说就是：**until 前面的主句或句子的谓语必须是延续性的，而 until 后面接的从句的谓语须是短暂性动词或接时间点。**

第三、由上面第二点，可以推导出 until 的句型结构有：

1. 作为连词引导从句时的句型：主句的**延续动词** + until + 从句的**短暂动词**；
2. 作为介词接名词短语的句型：**延续动词** + until + **时间点**(不是时间段)。

下面将从三个方面来详细讨论 until 的上述用法特点。

一、延续动词+until +短暂动词或时间点

当主句或句子的谓语动词是**延续动词**时，通常用**肯定**形式。until 的后面若接从句，则从句的谓语必定是短暂动词，或者接表示时间点(point of time)的名词短语。请看例句：

1 ***Wait*** until he ***comes*** back.

妙语点睛 这里主句的谓语 wait 是延续动词，从句的谓语 comes 是短暂动词。表示 wait 的动作一直持续到“他来了”这个时间点为止。

精品译文 等他回来吧。

2 Until I ***came*** back, he ***was waiting*** for me at my home.

妙语点睛 这里主句的谓语 waiting 是延续动词，从句的谓语 came 是短暂动词。表示 wait 的动作一直持续到“我回来了”这个时间点为止。

精品译文 在我回来之前，他一直在我家里等我。

3 We'll ***stay*** here until it ***stops*** raining.

妙语点睛 这里主句的谓语 stay 是延续动词，从句的谓语 stops 是短暂动词。表示 stay 的动作一直持续到“雨停了”这个时间点为止。

精品译文 我们将一直呆到雨停了再走。

4 When I showed my dad my report card, I said,“Remember, Dad, Thomas Edison got bad grades in school, too.” He said, “Fine, ***stay*** in your room until you ***invent*** the light bulb (灯泡).”

妙语点睛 这里主句的谓语 stay 是延续动词，从句的谓语 invent 是短暂动词。表示 stay 的动作一直持续到“发明出来”这个时间点为止。

精品译文 那天我把成绩单给我老爸看的时候，我对他说：“别忘了，老爸，爱迪生在上学期间学习成绩也是很差的。”他说：“那好啊，你就呆在房间里，等你发明了灯泡再出来吧。”

在以上例句中，until 都是用作连词，引导时间状语从句。前文说过，until 还可以作介词，后面接时间点。比如这个例句：

5 I ***will be away*** from my office until ***next Tuesday***.

妙语点睛 这里的名词短语 next Tuesday 表示一个时间点，until 是一个介词。

精品译文 我将要离开办公室，要到下周二才能回来。

二、短暂动词+until+短暂动词或时间点

值得注意的是，若主句或句子的谓语动词是**短暂动词**，则要用**否定**形式。因为否定之后表示的是一个状态，而状态则是延续的，这就是我们常说的 not...until(直到……才)的结构。请看例句：

6 He ***didn't leave*** the office until his boss ***came*** back.

妙语点睛 这里主句的谓语 leave 是短暂动词，不能与表示持续时间的 until 连用，所以必须否定成 didn't leave 表示一个持续的状态，才能与 until 连用。这里表示“没有离开”这个状态一直持续到“老板回来”这个时间点为止。从句的谓语 came 是短暂动词。

精品译文 直到老板回来后，他才离开办公室。

7 I ***did not realize*** how special my mother was until I ***became*** an adult.

妙语点睛 这里主句的谓语 realize 是短暂动词，不能与表示持续时间的 until 连用，所以必须否定成 didn't realize 表示一个持续的状态，才能与 until 连用。这里表示“没有意识到”这个状态一直持续到“我长大成人”这个时间点为止。从句的谓语 became 是短暂动词。

精品译文 直到我长大成人以后，我才真正懂得母亲是多么的不平凡。

8 One will ***never realize*** how much and how little he knows until he ***starts*** talking.

妙语点睛 这里主句的谓语 realize 是短暂动词，不能与表示持续时间的 until 连用，所以必须否定成 never realize 表示一个持续的状态，才能与 until 连用。这里表示“没有意识到”这个状态一直持续到“开始”这个时间点为止。从句的谓语 starts 是短暂动词。

精品译文 人们只有在与人进行交谈时才知道自己到底懂得多少。

在以上例句中，until 都是用作连词，引导时间状语从句。前文说过，until 还可以作介词，后面接时间点。请看例句：

9 Ice cream ***did not reach*** America until ***about the middle of the eighteenth century.***

妙语点睛 这里的名词短语 about the middle of the eighteenth century 表示一个时间点，until 是一个介词。主句的谓语 reach 是短暂动词，不能与表示持续时间的 until 连用，所以必须否定成 did not reach 表示一个持续的状态，才能与 until 连用。这里表示"没有到"这个状态一直持续到"18 世纪中叶"这个时间点为止。

精品译文 直到 18 世纪中叶，冰淇淋才传到美洲。

10 I ***didn't go*** to bed until ***12 o'clock last night.***

妙语点睛 这里的名词短语 12 o'clock last night 表示一个时间点，until 是一个介词。主句谓语 go 是短暂动词，不能与表示持续时间的 until 连用，所以必须否定成 didn't go 表示一个持续的状态，才能与 until 连用。这里表示"没有上床睡觉"这个状态一直持续到"昨晚 12 点钟"这个时间点为止。

精品译文 我昨晚 12 点才上床睡觉。

4.1.4 表示"一……就"的结构

在英文中，还有一些时间连词用来表达主句的动作和从句的动作相继发生，两者之间的时间间隔不长，相当于汉语里"一……就"的意思。此时，主句和从句的谓语都是短暂动词。

一、从句动作先于主句动作

确切地说，就是在从句动作发生之后，紧接着主句动作就发生了。表示这一时间关系的连词有：as soon as, once, the minute, the moment, the instant, immediately, directly 和 instantly 等等。这些连词的用法和句式结构是一样的，主从句时态一般一致。比如若表示将来的动作，则主句用一般将来时(simple future)，从句用一般现在时(simple present)表示将来。请看例句：

1 We will leave ***as soon as*** it stops raining.

妙语点睛 首先，这里主句的谓语动词 leave 和从句的谓语动词 stops 都是短暂动词。其次，这里主句谓语的时态是一般将来时 will leave，从句谓语的时态是一般现在时 stops，但表示将来的动作。再次，这里从句的动作 stops 先发生，紧接着主句动作 leave 发生，即"先雨停，再离开"。

精品译文 雨一停，我们就动身。

若表示过去的动作，则主句和从句都用一般过去时。请看例句：

2 It began to rain ***as soon as*** I arrived home.

妙语点睛 首先，这里主句的谓语动词 began 和从句的谓语动词 arrived 都是短暂动词。其次，这里主句谓语的时态是一般过去时 began，从句谓语的时态也是一般过去时 arrived。再次，这里从句的动作 arrived 先发生，紧接着主句的动作 began 发生，即"先到家，再开始下雨"。

精品译文 我刚到家，天就开始下起雨来。

再比如：

3 The doorbell rang ***as soon as*** we began having dinner.

精品译文 我们刚开始吃晚饭，这时候门铃就响了。

可以把上面例句中的连词 as soon as 换成其他连词，比如 immediately, instantly 或 directly。请看例句：

4 It began to rain ***immediately*** I arrived home.

5 The doorbell rang ***immediately*** we began having dinner.

或者换成带有定冠词 the 的连词，比如 the moment, the minute 或 the instant。比如下面两个谈论朋友的句子：

6 A fair-weather friend is like a banker who lends you his umbrella when the sun is shining and takes it back ***the minute*** it rains. 酒肉朋友就像一个银行家，正值阳光灿烂时他会把伞借给你，而一旦天下雨他就立即将伞收回。

7 Don't trust those who leave their friends ***the moment*** they get into difficulty! 一旦朋友陷入困境就会转身脱逃的人，我们不能信任！

请看下面这道四级考题：

8 You see the lightning ______ it happens, but you hear the thunder later.

A. the instant　　B. for an instant　　C. on the instant　　D. in an instant

正确答案 A。

妙语点睛 这是 1997 年 1 月份的四级考试题。本题考查考生对时间从句连词的掌握。首先，这里主句的谓语动词 see 和从句的谓语动词 happens 都是短暂动词，即表示"一……就"。只有选项 A 即 the instant 才能表示此意。其次，这里从句的动作 happens 先发生，然后紧接着主句动作 see 发生，即"先闪电，后看见"。

精品译文 闪电一发生你就能看见，但你要过一会才能听见雷声。

二、主句动作先于从句动作

确切地说，就是在主句动作发生之后，紧接着从句动作就发生了。表示这一时间关系的连词有：hardly...when, scarcely...when 和 no sooner...than。需要提醒读者注意的是，这些连词的用法和句式结构是不一样的，主从句时态一般也不一致。他们一般多用来表示过去的动作，此时，主句多用**过去完成时**，且常倒装，从句用**一般过去时**。可与 as soon as 等从句、主句互换。请比较：

9 1) No sooner ***had I arrived*** home than it ***began*** to rain.

2) It ***began*** to rain as soon as I ***arrived*** home.

妙语点睛 首先，在例句 1)中，连词 than 后面的 it began to rain 是从句，但在例句 2)中，it began to rain 是主句；在例句 1)中，had I arrived home 是主句，但在例句 2)中，I arrived home 是从句。其次，在例句 1)中，主句 had I arrived home 用了过去完成时且是倒装结构，从句 it began to rain 用一般过去时；在例句 2)中，主句 it began to rain 和从句I arrived home 都用一般过去时。

再来看更多例句：

10 A: The floor is awfully wet. What happened? 这地面太湿了，怎么回事啊？

B: No sooner ***had I got*** into the shower than the phone ***rang.*** 刚才我刚要进去洗澡，突然电话铃就响了。

11 No sooner ***had the storm started*** than all the lights ***went*** out. 刚一下起暴风雨，所有的灯马上就灭了。

12 No sooner ***had I started*** to type my paper than the telephone ***rang.*** 我刚准备开始打我的论文，这时电话铃响了。

还可以用 hardly / scarcely...when 这一结构来表达同样的意思。比如：

13 ***Hardly*** had I arrived home ***when*** it began to rain.

14 ***Hardly*** had I got into the shower ***when*** the phone rang.

15 ***Hardly*** had the storm started ***when*** all the lights went out

16 ***Scarcely*** had I started to type my paper ***when*** the telephone rang.

思维训练

Exercise 4. 1（Key: P335）

请选择最佳答案填空。

1. ______ she realized it was too late to go home.

A. No sooner it grew dark than　　B. Scarcely had it grown dark when

C. Hardly did it grow dark that　　D. No sooner had it grown dark when

2. The policemen went into action ______ they heard the alarm.
   A. promptly B. presently C. quickly D. directly
3. We held a meeting to sum up our experience ______ we finished the work.
   A. incidentally B. while C. immediately D. before
4. I was on the point of going out ______ it began to rain heavily.
   A. when B. while C. as D. before
5. ______ to speak when the audience interrupted him.
   A. Hardly had he begun B. No sooner had he begun
   C. Not until he began D. Scarcely did he begin
6. Doing your homework is a sure way to improve your test scores, and this is especially true ______ it comes to classroom tests.
   A. before B. as C. since D. when
7. On a rainy day I was driving north through Vermont ______ I noticed a young man holding up a sign reading "Boston".
   A. which B. where C. when D. that
8. I was walking along the road ______ suddenly someone patted me on the shoulder from behind.
   A. immediately B. when C. the moment D. while
9. We shall call on her as soon ______.
   A. as she will come B. as she came C. as she comes D. she comes
10. You see the lightening ______ it happens, but you hear the thunder later.
    A. the moment B. for a moment C. at the moment D. in a moment
11. The phenomenon provides a way for companies to remain globally competitive ______ avoiding market cycles and the growing burdens imposed by employment rules, healthcare costs and pension plans.
    A. but B. while C. and D. whereas

4.2 地点状语从句

地点状语从句通常是由 where 引导，用来表达主句的动作发生的场所。其结构通常就是“where+ 陈述句”，从句可以放在句首或句末。请看例句：

1. Stay ***where*** you are. 呆在原处别动。
2. Generally, air will be heavily polluted ***where there are factories.*** 一般在有工厂的地方，空气污染都会很严重。
3. A driver should slow down ***where*** there are schools. 在有学校的地方，司机应缓行。

地点状语从句若放在句首，在翻译时往往失去地点的含义，要灵活处理。请看例句：

4. ***Where there is a will,*** there is a way. 有志者，事竟成。
5. ***Where there is Love***, there is also Wealth and Success! 只要有爱，就会有成功和财富！

思维训练

Exercise 4. 2（Key: P335）

请选择最佳答案填空。

1. The picture is not hanging ______ it should on the wall.
   A. until B. wherever C. where D. when
2. ______, work songs often exhibit the song culture of a people in a fundamental form
   A. They occur where they are B. Occurring where
   C. Where they occur D. Where do they occur

3. I have kept that portrait ______ I can see it every day, as it always reminds me of my university days in London.
A. which B. where C. whether D. when

4.3 原因状语从句

本节主要讨论引导原因从句常见的连词的用法，此外还会涉及表示原因的介词或介词短语。因此，本节内容安排如下：

4.3.1 常见连词的用法
4.3.2 用介词表示因果关系

4.3.1 常见连词的用法

常用 because, for, as 和 since 这四个连词来引导原因状语从句。他们的意义和用法不完全相同。

在这四个连词中，because 的语气最强，只有它才能用来回答 why 的问句，所引出的原因往往是听话人所不知道的或最感兴趣的；也只有 because 才能被强调词如 only, just 和 perhaps 等来修饰。请看例句：

1 My friends dislike me ***because*** I'm handsome and successful.
妙语点睛 一般来说，"我"不被朋友喜欢的原因是听者感兴趣的，所以用 because 引出这个原因。
精品译文 我的哥们都不喜欢我，是因为我长相英俊又事业有成。

2 ***Perhaps because*** most of today's cross-cultural marriages occur because of "true love", these couples work hard to overcome their differences.
妙语点睛 一般就不会说 perhaps for*, perhaps as* 或 perhaps since*。
精品译文 可能因为现在的大多数跨国婚姻都是基于真爱，所以夫妇俩都很努力地克服双方的差异。

连词 since 表示人们已知的事实，是不需强调的原因，所以常译成"既然"，通常放在句首。请看例句：

3 ***Since*** we don't have class tomorrow, why not go out for a picnic?
既然我们明天没有课，那么为什么不出去野餐呢？

4 ***Since*** you are an English major, I guess you can help me with this sentence.
既然你是学英语专业的，我猜想你能帮我解决这个句子。

连词 as 与 since 的用法差不多，所引出的理由在说话人看来已经很明显，或已为听话人所熟悉而不需用 because 加以强调。请看例句：

5 ***As*** Monday is a national holiday, all government offices will be closed.
由于周一是法定假日，所有的政府机关都将休息。

连词 for 表示推断的理由，是对前面分句的内容加以解释或说明。请看例句：

6 It rained last night, ***for*** the ground is wet this morning. 昨晚下雨了，因为今天早上地都湿了。
试比较：***Because*** it rained last night, the ground is wet this morning.

相比较而言：
as 和 for 引导的主、从句，二者处于平等位置；
because 引导的从句显得比主句重要，强调原因；
since 引导的从句显得次要，而主句重要，以说明将要做什么事。

4.3.2 用介词表示因果关系

常用的介词有：because of, due to和 owing to。因为是介词，所以其后面不能接从句。请比较：

1. We had an accident ***because he was careless.***
2. We had an accident ***due to his carelessness.***
3. ***Owing to his carelessness*** we had an accident

妙语点睛 在例句1中，因为是从句，所以用连词如because引导。在例句2中，因为是名词短语his carelessness，所以用介词连接。此处不能说due to he was careless*。在例句3中，同样是名词短语his carelessness，所以要用介词。一般来说，owing to常置于句首，而due to通常不这么用。

精品译文 由于他的粗心大意，我们出了车祸。

思维训练

Exercise 4.3（Key: P335）
请选择最佳答案填空。

1. ______ you are leaving tomorrow, we can eat dinner together tonight.
   A. For　B. Since　C. Before　D. While
2. ______ the cold weather, we decided not to go out.
   A. Because　B. Due that　C. Owing to　D. Since
3. Neon is said to be inert ______ does not react with other substances.
   A. Because of it　B. it is because　C. because it　D. is because it
4. They looked so happy today, ______ they had a good bargain.
   A. for　B. in order that　C. when　D. except
5. ______ he has had a reputation for being a careful driver, his accident came as quite a surprise.
   A. Since　B. Since that　C. Because　D. For
6. It was ______ he was so young that he couldn't do it.
   A. as　B. since　C. for　D. because

4.4 目的状语从句

在英语中，常用的引导目的状语从句的连词有：so that, in order that 和 that。另外，在目的状语从句中常含有情态动词，比如may/might或can/could等。请看例句：

1. I turned off the TV ***in order that*** my roommate could study in peace and quiet.

妙语点睛 这里的从句由in order that引导，表示目的，意为"以便"。从句含有情态动词could。

精品译文 我关掉了电视，好让我的室友安静地学习。

2. When I was a child, I would take a flashlight to bed with me so ***that*** I could read comic books without my parents' knowing about it.

妙语点睛 这里的从句由so that引导，表示目的，意为"以便"。从句含有情态动词could。

精品译文 小的时候，我常常睡觉时带着手电筒上床，这样我就可以偷看连环画册而不被父母发觉。

3. Former Colorado governor Richard Lamm has been quoted as saying that the old and infirm "have a duty to die and get out of the way" ***so that*** younger, healthier people can realize their potential.

妙语点睛 这里的从句由so that引导，表示目的，意为"以便"。从句含有情态动词can。

精品译文 人们常引用科罗拉多州前州长理查德·兰姆的话说，老年多病者"有义务死去和让位"，以便让更年轻、更健康的人们发挥他们的潜能。

请再看其他更多例句：

4 I spoke slowly and clearly ***so that/in order that*** the audience could understand me. 我讲得既慢又清晰，以便观众能听懂我的话。

5 They carved the words on the stone ***so that/in order that*** the future generation should remember what they had done. 他们在石头上刻字，以便后人记住他们做过的事情。

6 We climbed high (***so***) ***that*** we might get a better view. 我们爬到高处，以便能看得更清楚。

7 The teacher raised his voice ***in order that*** the students in the back could hear more clearly. 老师提高了声音，以便坐在后排的学生能听得更清楚。

从以上例句我们看到，目的状语从句一般位于主句之后。但若要强调目的状语从句，可将 so that 或 in order that 引导的从句置于句首。请看例句：

8 ***In order that*** my roommate could study in peace and quiet, I turned off the TV.

思维训练

Exercise 4. 4（Key: P336）

请将下列简单句合并成目的状语从句，注意使用情态动词。

1. I am going to leave the party early. I want to be able to get a good night's sleep.
2. Harry brought his umbrella. He wanted to be sure he didn't get wet.
3. I turned on the TV. I wanted to listen to the news.
4. The little boy pretended to be sick. He wanted to stay home from school.
5. Clint took some change from his pocket. He wanted to buy a newspaper.
6. I put the milk in the refrigerator. I wanted to make sure it didn't spoil.
7. I unplugged the phone. I didn't want to be interrupted while I was sleeping.

4.5 结果状语从句

4. 5. 1 常见连词的用法

常用的引导结果状语从句的连词有：so...that 和 such...that。下面将详细讨论他们的用法。注意，结果状语从句都要放在主句之后，而不能提到句首。

一、连词 **so...that** 的用法

多数结果状语从句是由 so...that 引导的，这里 so 的后面接形容词或副词。请看例句：

1. 接形容词

1 Sensible Sam: I saw you pushing your bicycle to work this afternoon.

Foolish Fred: Yes, I was ***so late that*** I didn't have time to get on it.

妙语点睛 这里是 so...that 引导结果状语从句，so 的后面接了形容词(late)。

精品译文 聪明的萨姆：我今天下午看到你推着自行车去上班。

愚笨的弗雷德：是的，因为当时太晚了，所以我来不及骑上车子。

2 A geography teacher once told her class, "The moon is ***so large that*** several million people could live there." One boy started laughing, "It sure must get crowded when it's a crescent moon."

妙语点睛 这里是 so...that 引导结果状语从句，so 的后面接了形容词(large)。

精品译文 在地理课上，老师告诉全班学生说："月球的大小足以容纳几百万人口。"这时一个男生笑道："那么在新月时，月球上岂不是就会变得很拥挤。"

请再看下面这句话：

3 The food in our school canteen is ***so bad that*** flies go there to lose weight.

精品译文 我们学校食堂的饭菜质量真差，连苍蝇都飞到那里去减肥。

2. 接副词

4 He has put forward unquestioned claims ***so consistently that*** he not only believes them himself, but has convinced industrial and business management that they are true.

妙语点睛 这里是 so...that 引导结果状语从句，so 的后面接了副词(consistently)。

精品译文 他一直不断地提出确定不疑的主张，以至于不仅他自己对他们深信不疑，而且还使得工商管理界相信他们都是真的。

5 The newly described languages were often so ***strikingly*** different from the well studied languages of Europe and Southeast Asia ***that*** some scholars even accused Boas and Sapir of fabricating their data.

妙语点睛 这是 2004 年的考研翻译真题。这里是 so...that 引导结果状语从句，so 的后面接了副词(strikingly)。

精品译文 这些新近被描述的语言与已经得到充分研究的欧洲和东南亚地区的语言往往差别显著，以至于有些学者甚至指责博阿斯和萨皮尔编造了材料。

二、连词 such...that 的用法

可以用 such...that 来引导结果状语从句，此时 such 的后面要接名词。请看例句：

6 Diplomats and crabs are creatures who move in ***such*** a way ***that*** it is impossible to tell whether they are coming or going.

妙语点睛 这里是 such...that 引导结果状语从句，such 的后面接了名词(a way)。

精品译文 外交官和螃蟹是行为方式相同的动物，因为我们无法判断他们是要向前走还是想往后退。

请比较：

7 1) He is ***such a good teacher*** that everyone likes him.

2) He is ***so good a teacher*** that everyone likes him.

妙语点睛 注意这里的冠词 a 的位置关系：a 要紧跟在 such 的后面。

精品译文 他是一个好老师，所有人都喜欢他 。

4. 5. 2 结果状语从句的倒装

在英文中，such / so...that 引导结果状语从句，为了强调，还可以将主句中的 so 或 such 引导的部分置于句首从而构成倒装结构。请看例句：

1 ***So fast does*** light travel that it is difficult for us to imagine its speed.

妙语点睛 这句话的正常语序为：Light travels ***so fast that*** it is difficult for us to imagine its speed.

精品译文 光的传播速度是如此之快，以至于我们无法想象它的速度。

2 ***So terrible was*** the storm that the roofs were all ripped off.

妙语点睛 这句话的正常语序为：The storm ***was so terrible*** that the roofs were all ripped off.

精品译文 暴风雨是如此猛烈，把整个屋顶都掀翻了。

3 ______ that the pilot couldn't fly through it.

A. So the storm was severe　　B. So severe was the storm

C. The storm so severe was　　D. Such was the storm severe

正确答案 B。

妙语点睛 这是一道四级考题。正确的倒装结构应该是 B，这句话的正常语序为：The storm ***was so severe*** that the pilot couldn't fly through it.

精品译文 暴风雨是如此猛烈，飞行员无法驾驶飞机穿越。

我们下面来看一个 such...that 引导的结果从句变为倒装结构的例句：

4 ***Such a fool was*** he that he believed her.

妙语点睛 这句话的正常语序为：He ***was such a fool*** that he believed her.

精品译文 他真是愚蠢，连她都相信。

思维训练

Exercise 4. 5（Key: P336）

请用 so...that 和/或 such...that 合并句子。

1. This tea is good. I think I'll have another cup.
2. The car was expensive. We couldn't afford to buy it.
3. I had to wear my coat. It was a cold day.
4. I don't feel like going to class. We're having beautiful weather.
5. She talked too fast. I couldn't understand her.
6. The black leopard is very dark. Its spots are difficult to see.
7. I've met too many people in the last few days. I can't remember all of their names.
8. It took us only ten minutes to get there. There was little traffic.
9. There were few people at the meeting. It was cancelled.
10. I have too much trouble. I need your help.
11. The classroom has comfortable chairs. The students find it easy to fall asleep.

请选择最佳答案填空。

12. So involved with their computers ______ that leaders at summer computer camps often have to force them to break for sports and games.

 A. became the children　　B. become the children
 C. had the children become　　D. do the children become

13. It is ______ weather that I would like to go to the beach.

 A. so nice　　B. such nice　　C. such a nice　　D. so nice a

14. She told us ______ stories that we all laughed.

 A. so funny　　B. such funny　　C. funny such　　D. so fun

15. The music at the party was ______ that the neighbors complained.

 A. so loud　　B. such loudness　　C. so loudly　　D. such a loud

16. He's ______ man that everyone loves him.

 A. so kind　　B. such a kind　　C. such kindness　　D. so kindly

4.6 条件状语从句

本节主要分析真实条件句，而非真实条件句将在第七章"虚拟语气"中讨论。本节内容安排如下：

4. 6. 1 常见连词的用法

4. 6. 2 其他条件状语从句的连词

4. 6. 1 常见连词的用法

最常见的条件状语从句的引导词是 if 和 unless。连词 if 表示"如果"，unless 表示"如果不"或"除非"。请看例句：

下面这句话读者一定不会陌生：

1 ***If*** winter comes, can spring be far behind? 冬天来了，春天还会远吗？

有人说爱一个人完全是自己的事情，与对方无关。但不求回报地去爱，又有几人能做到？下面这个例句讲的就是这个道理：

2 Giving someone all your love is never an assurance that they'll love you back. Don't expect love in return, just wait for it to grow in their heart, but ***if*** it doesn't be glad it grew in yours. 为某人付出自己全部的爱，并不一定能够保证对方会同样爱你。不要期望爱的回报，就让爱在对方心中慢慢地成长。即使没有，也不要失望，而要为自己心中曾经爱过而感到高兴。

如果有一天你不经意间微笑起来，连你自己都无法解释为什么自己会笑，那原因就是：

3 Today ***if*** a happy smile comes to you, a happy smile that perhaps you can't explain...it is because at that moment, I am thinking of you, and smiling, too. 假如今天你不经意间开心地微笑起来，连你都无法解释自己为什么会笑……这是因为此时此刻我正在想着你，我也在微笑。

下面这句话是英国前首相撒切尔夫人(Margaret Thatcher)对男人和女人 woman 的评价：

4 In politics, ***if*** you want someone to make a speech, ask a man; ***if*** you want something done, ask a woman. 在政治领域，如果你想要有人发表演说，那就找男士去；而如果你想真正把事情解决，那就找女士。

我们再来看有关 unless 的例句。比如下面这则雅虎发表的免责申明：

5 The opinions expressed here are not necessarily the opinions of Yahoo! and we assume no responsibility for such content....Please do not post any private information ***unless*** you want it to be available publicly and never assume that you are completely anonymous and cannot be identified by your comments. 网友在本网站发表的任何评论并不代表雅虎的观点，因而我们对这些内容不承担任何责任。……请不要发布任何个人信息，除非你希望把个人信息公布于众；也不要认为在网络上你是完全匿名隐身的，别人不会因为你的评论而发现你。

一位美国老师指出，中国学生因为“面子”问题而不愿在口语课上开口说英语，下面是他建议其他外教该如何处理中国学生“面子”问题的作法：

6 Discussions about “face” can be difficult if one is not familiar with the significance and importance attached to it by many Asian people. It does have different meanings to different people and, ***unless*** a teacher is “comfortable” with broaching the subject, it is best left alone. 亚洲人非常看重“面子”问题，如果你对此不熟悉的话，讨论“面子”问题就会很困难。对于不同的人，“面子”问题的意味是不同的，除非作为老师你很善于把握这个话题，否则还是不要涉及为好。

下面两个例句都是关于英语学习方面的问题：

7 Read silently. Do not make a sound, move your tongue or lips. Reading aloud slows you down and will not help pronunciation ***unless*** you have a mentor who will correct your pronunciation. 默读。读英语的时候，不要出声、动舌头或者动嘴唇。大声朗读会降低你的阅读速度，而且并不有助于你正确地发音，除非你身边有老师能随时帮助你纠正发音。

8 Inside this book you will find a series of successful skills, strategies and suggestions for improving your English, but these will be useless ***unless*** you carry them out. 在本书里，你会看到一系列关于如何提高英语水平的成功技巧、方法和建议，不过你要真正运用和实践这些方法，否则它们对你依然毫无用处。

4.6.2 其他条件状语从句的连词

其他引导条件状语从句的连词有：suppose (that), supposing (that), providing/provided (that), so long as, as long as 和 on condition that 等。

下面这句中文谚语读者应该很熟悉：

1 ***So long as*** you work hard enough, an iron rod can be ground into a needle. 只要功夫深，铁杵磨成针。

关于年龄与心态的问题，下面这句话值得读者诵记：

2 A man is not old ***as long as*** he is seeking something. A man is not old until regrets take the place of dreams.

妙语点睛 这里是 as long as 表示条件，引导从句。

精品译文 一个人只要还有追求，他就不算老。只有当心中不再有梦想，而只是满怀遗憾，这时他才真正老了。

有人把人生比作自助餐厅，在这里，只要你愿意付出代价和努力，就什么都能得到，但关键是你必须主动、积极，为自己创造一切，你要为自己服务，而不是等着别人来为你服务：

3 Life's a cafeteria here. You can get anything you want ***as long as*** you are willing to pay the price. You can even get success, but you'll never get it ***if*** you wait for someone to bring it to you. You have to get up and get it yourself. 人生就是一个自助餐厅，只要愿意付出代价，你就什么都能得到。在这里，你甚至可以获得成功，但如果你只是等待别人来为你服务，你就什么也得不到。你必须行动起来，自己赢得成功。

下面这个例句是谈论人生目标方向的重要性：

4 Knowledge helps you to reach the destination ***provided*** you know what the destination is. 如果你知道自己的目标是什么，知识就能帮助你达到这个目标。

思维训练

Exercise 4.6（Key: P336）

请选择最佳答案填空。

1. You can arrive in Beijing earlier for the meeting ______ you don't mind taking the night train.
   A. provided　B. unless　C. though　D. until
2. He will surely finish the job on time ______ he's left to do it in his own way.
   A. in that　B. in case　C. as far as　D. so long as
3. ______ you fell in love with your boss, what would you do?
   A. Provide　B. Supposing　C. Unless　D. Except
4. Government cannot operate effectively ______ it is free from such interference.
   A. so long as　B. if only　C. unless　D. lest

4.7 让步状语从句

本节内容安排如下：

4.7.1 常见连词的用法

4.7.2 表示让步转折关系的介词

4.7.3 置于句首的 while 一般表示“尽管”

4.7.4 as 的倒装句表示让步

4.7.1 常见连词的用法

常见的引导让步状语从句的词有 though, although, even though 和 even if，此时，主句前不可用 but，但可用 yet 或 still。

1 ***Although*** he tried hard, (yet /still) he failed. 尽管他努力了，但他还是失败了。

2 ***Although*** I didn't know anybody at the party, I had a very good time. 尽管聚会上的人我一个都不认识，但我仍然玩得很愉快。

3 The family is the essential presence — the thing that never leaves you, ***even if*** you find you have to leave it. 对于每个人来说，家是不可或缺的，它永远为你守候，即使有一天你发现你要离开它。

再比如下面这道考研题：

4 Although Professor Green's lectures usually ran over (A) the fifty-minute period, but (B) none (C) of his students even objected (D) as they found his lectures both informative and interesting.

正确答案 B，应把 but 去掉。

妙语点睛 这是 1997 年的考研真题。本题考查的就是 although 和 but 不能连用这一知识点。

精品译文 尽管格林教授上课时间常超过 50 分钟，但是他的学生中没有一个人反对，因为他们觉得他的课既有趣又有收获。

4.7.2 表示让步转折关系的介词

上面讨论了常见的让步状语从句的连词，与此相关的是，在英文中，还可以用介词来表示让步转折关系。这些介词主要有 despite, in spite of 和 for all。需要提醒读者注意的是，although 和 though 是连词，因此后面只接从句（有时是省略形式的从句），而这里的介词只接名词（短语），不能接从句。请比较：

1 1）***Though he was inexperienced***, he did a very good job.

2）***In spite of his inexperience***, he did a very good job.

3）***In spite of his being inexperienced***, he did a very good job.

妙语点睛 在例句 1）中，连词 though 后面接的是从句 he was inexperienced。在例句 2）中，his inexperience 是一个名词短语，所以要用介词，比如这里用了 in spite of。在例句 3）中，his being inexperienced 是一个动名词短语的形式，也属于名词短语，所以这里也需要用介词，如 in spite of。

精品译文 尽管他没有经验，但是他表现得很不错。

其他类似的例子还有：

2 1）Although it was dangerous,...

2）Despite the danger,...

3 1）Though the weather was bad,...

2）In spite of the bad weather,...

需要提醒读者注意的是，介词后面除了接名词短语外，还可以接 what 引导的名词从句。请看例句：

4 ______ what he achieved in medicine, he remained modest.

A. Despite B. Although C. If D. Whereas

正确答案 A。

妙语点睛 本题考查的是状语从句连词的用法。因为这里 what=things that，引导的是一个名词性从句，其本质上相当于一个名词短语，故此处仍需用介词。若用连词 though，则只能说成：Though he achieved a lot in medicine, he remained modest.

精品译文 尽管他在医学领域取得了很多成就，但是他依然很谦虚。

5 ______ tired, he wouldn't stop working.

A. Despite B. For all C. Though D. Whereas

正确答案 C。

妙语点睛 本题考查的是状语从句连词的用法。因为这是一个省略的状语从句，原句相当于 Though he was tired, he wouldn't stop working. 所以要用连词，而不是介词，故 C 正确。

精品译文 尽管很累，但他依然坚持工作。

综上所述，我们可以总结出这样的规律：**介词后面可以接名词、名词短语、动名词或 what 引导的从句；连词后面可以接完整的陈述句、形容词（相当于省略句）、分词（相当于省略句）等。**

4.7.3 置于句首的 while 一般表示“尽管”

while 位于句首，一般意为“尽管”，引导让步状语从句。在很多阅读文章中常见到 while 的这一用法。请看例句：

1 ***While*** many countries of the world celebrate their own Mother's Day at different times throughout the year, there are some countries such as Denmark, Finland, Italy, Turkey, Australia, and Belgium which also celebrate Mother's Day on the second Sunday of May.

妙语点睛 while 出现在句首，表示让步转折。

精品译文 尽管世界上很多国家是在不同的日期庆祝母亲节的，但是仍然有些国家，比如丹麦、芬兰、意大利、土耳其、澳大利亚和比利时也是在五月的第二个周日庆祝母亲节。

2 ***While*** the government pushed for a total breakup of the software maker, Microsoft fought fiercely against any positions that would affect its ability to compete in the marketplace.

妙语点睛 while 出现在句首，表示让步转折。

精品译文 尽管美国政府积极要求彻底拆分微软这个软件巨人，但是微软公司极力反对任何影响其市场竞争力的动议。

3 ***While*** even the modestly educated sought an elevated tone when they put pen to paper before the 1960s, even the most well regarded writing since then has sought to capture spoken English on the page.

妙语点睛 while 出现在句首，表示让步转折。

精品译文 在 20 世纪 60 年代之前，当人们伏案写作时，即使受教育不多的人也追求一种高雅的风格，而从那以后，即使是令人景仰的文章作品也在追求一种口语风格。

4 ***While*** often praised by foreigners for its emphasis on the basics, Japanese education tends to stress test taking and mechanical learning over creativity and self-expression.

妙语点睛 这里 while 作为连词表示“尽管”。注意这里的从句是一个省略形式的状语从句，相当于说 while it is often praised by..., it 指代 Japanese education。

精品译文 虽然日本的教育常常因为重视基础知识而受到外国人士的赞扬，但是其教育往往强调应试和机械性的学习，而不是强调创造性及自我表现。

5 ***While*** history once revered its affinity to literature and philosophy, the emerging social sciences seemed to afford greater opportunities for asking new questions and providing rewarding approaches to an understanding of the past.

妙语点睛 while 出现在句首，表示让步转折。

精品译文 尽管历史学曾经崇尚它与文学和哲学的相似性，但新兴的社会科学似乎为人们开辟了更为广阔的天地，来提出新问题和提供了解过去的有效途径。

4.7.4 as 引导的倒装句表示让步

as 引导的倒装句可表示让步，这一结构有：

adj. / adv. / 分词 / 名词(无冠词) / 短语 } +as+ 主语 + 谓语动词

一、形容词提置句首

1 ***Young as*** he is, he is knowledgeable. 他虽然年轻，但知识渊博。

2 There are also desert insects which survive as inactive larvae. In addition, ***difficult as*** it is to believe, there are desert fish which can survive through years of drought in the form of inactive eggs.

妙语点睛 这句话是“形容词 +as+ 主谓”的结构，表示让步。

精品译文 还有一些沙漠昆虫，其幼虫靠着不活动来存活。此外，尽管很难以置信，但确有一种沙漠鱼，能够以不活动的卵的形式来抵御干旱，可以存活好几年。

3 ***Oldest in our workshop as*** he is, he works hardest.

妙语点睛 请注意在这结构中最高级前不加 the。

精品译文 尽管他是我们车间最年长的一位，他工作起来最努力。

二、副词提置句首

4 ***Much as*** I respect him, I can not agree with him. 虽然我非常尊重他，但是我仍旧不同意他的意见。

5 ***Again as*** he failed in doing this experiment, he didn't lose his heart.
尽管他的试验再次失败了，但是他并不灰心。

三、分词提置句首

6 ***Praised as*** he was, he remained modest. 尽管他受到了表扬，却仍旧很谦虚。

四、名词提置句首

7 ***Child*** as he is, he is knowledgeable.

妙语点睛 请注意这句话的名词前不带冠词。

精品译文 他虽然还是个孩子，却知识渊博。

8 ***Lazy a boy as*** he is, he is kind to help others.

妙语点睛 请注意这里名词短语的语序：lazy a boy。

精品译文 他虽然很懒惰，却乐于助人。

最后需要提醒读者注意的是，这里的 as 可以替换为 that 或 though，尽管较少这样使用。不可以用 although。

9 ***Odd though it sounds***, cosmic inflation is a scientifically plausible consequence of some respected ideas in elementary particle physics, and many astrophysicists have been convinced for the better part of a decade that it is true.

图解难句

odd though it sounds		让步状语从句
cosmic inflation is a scientifically plausible consequence of some respected ideas in elementary particle physics		并列主句 1
and many astrophysicists have been convinced	主句的主谓结构	并列主句 2
for the better part of a decade	时间状语，分隔了 convinced 与宾语从句	
that it is true	宾语从句，作 convinced 的宾语	

妙语点睛 这是 1998 年的考研翻译真题。这里作者用了 though 代替 as，来表示让步。

精品译文 宇宙膨胀理论虽然听似奇特，但它是基本粒子物理学中一些公认的理论在科学上看来可信的推论。许多天体物理学家十几年来一直确信这一论说是正确的。

请看下面的考题：

10 <u>Much although</u> I have traveled, I have never seen anyone <u>to equal</u> her in thoroughness, <u>whatever</u> <u>the job</u>.
A B C D

正确答案 A，应改为：Much as。

妙语点睛 这是 1998 年的考研真题。本题考查的就是 as 引导的让步从句。我们看到，这里用 although 代替as 是错误的。

精品译文 尽管我游历甚广，但我还从没有见过一个像她这样不论对什么工作都如此细致认真的人。

思维总结

让步状语从句的内容比较多，读者要掌握引导让步从句的各种连词以及各类句型结构。比如 as 的倒装句表示让步；while 放在句首，表示让步等等。同时，遇到时要能够正确翻译。

思维训练

Exercise 4.7（Key: P337）

请选择最佳答案填空。

1. ______, he does get annoyed with her sometimes.
   A. Although much he likes her　　B. Much although he likes her
   C. As he likes her much　　D. Much as he likes her
2. ______ lay eggs, but some give birth to live young.
   A. Although most insects　　B. Most insects　　C. Despite most insects　　D. Most insects that
3. Airsickness is produced by a disturbance of the inner car, ______ psychogenic factors, such as fear, also play a part.
   A. in spite of　　B. neither　　C. nor　　D. although
4. ______ his physical handicap, he ______ a successful businessman.
   A. Despite/has become　　B. Although/has become　　C. In spite/became　　D. Despite of/becomes
5. ______ all our kindness to help her, Sarah refused to listen to us.
   A. At　　B. For　　C. In　　D. On
6. ______, the policeman still has good command.
   A. Sophisticated as search techniques were　　B. Sophisticated were search techniques
   C. Search techniques were sophisticated　　D. Sophisticated as search techniques they were
7. ______, I still enjoy driving even after my accident.
   A. It may seem strange though　　B. Strange though it may seem
   C. Though strange it may seem　　D. Strange it may seem though
8. ______ I admire him as a poet, I do not like him as a man.
   A. Much so　　B. So much　　C. Much as　　D. As much
9. The engineers are going through with their project, ______ the expenses have risen.
   A. even though　　B. just because　　C. now that　　D. as though
10. ______ what she achieved in literature, she remained modest.
   A. Despite　　B. Although　　C. If　　D. Whereas
11. ______ annoyed by her words, he tried not to lose his temper.
   A. Despite　　B. For all　　C. Though　　D. Whereas

辨别改错：

12. Although Mr. Smith studied <u>art</u>(A) in Paris, <u>but his</u>(B) writings attracted <u>much</u>(C) more interest <u>than</u>(D) his paintings.
13. <u>Despite</u>(A) fats and oils are <u>nutritionally</u>(B) important <u>as</u>(C) energy sources, medical research <u>indicates</u>(D) that saturated fats may contribute to hardening of the arteries.

4.8 比较状语从句

比较状语从句的结构或句型较多，下面一一详细讲解。本节内容安排如下：

4. 8. 1 连词 as 的基本用法
4. 8. 2 连词 than 的基本用法
4. 8. 3 表示倍数比较的三种句型
4. 8. 4 the more..., the more 句型

4.8.1 连词 as 的基本用法

as 引导比较状语从句，其基本结构是 as...as，这里前一个 as 是副词，而后一个 as 才是比较状语从句的连词。具体用法如下：

一、结构 1：as+形容词或副词+as

1 The work is not ***as difficult as*** you think. 这项工作不像你想象的那么难。

2 Eyes are ***as eloquent as*** lips (are). 眼睛像嘴唇一样富于表现力。

3 An adult human must take eight steps to go ***as far as*** a giraffe does in one stride. 长颈鹿跨一步的距离相当于一个成年人走八步。

二、结构 2：as+形容词+a(n)+可数名词单数+as

这里前一个 as 作为副词来修饰一个形容词，而这个形容词同时又修饰一个名词。使用时要特别注意这里形容词置于不定冠词之前这一特点。请看例句：

4 Rarely has a technological development had ***as great an impact*** on so many aspects of social, economic, and cultural development as the growth of electronics.

妙语点睛 若没有 as 修饰 great，这句话原本的结构是 ***a great impact***，但现在将其放置在 as...as 结构中，则冠词和形容词的语序要互换，因此成了 as ***great an impact*** as。另外要注意的是，整个句子是一个倒装句，正常语序为：A technological development ***has rarely had as*** great an impact on...***as*** the growth of electronics.

精品译文 很少有哪项科技的发展能像电子技术的发展这样，对我们的社会、经济以及文化等诸多方面产生如此重要的影响。

5 Americans tend to think from small to large. Let us take ***as simple an example as*** the addressing of envelopes.

妙语点睛 若没有 as 修饰 simple，这句话原本的结构是 ***a simple example***，但现在将其放置在 as...as 结构中，则冠词和形容词的语序要互换，因此成了 as ***simple an example as***，译成“像这样的一个简单例子”另注：虽然这里 as...as 结构并不是引导一个比较状语从句，举这个例子主要是为了说明“as＋形容词＋a(n)＋可数名词单数＋as”这一结构。

精品译文 美国人的思维喜欢由小到大。我们举一个写信封地址的简单例子吧。

三、在否定句中第一个 as 可用 so 代替

6 This room is ***not so*** large as the one we saw yesterday. 这间房子没有我们昨天看到的那间大。

7 No other modern nation devotes so ***small a portion*** of its wealth to public health as the United States does.

妙语点睛 注意否定词(no)在句首，故此句为否定句

精品译文 没有一个现代国家像美国这样，只把自己的财富很少一部分投入到公共卫生事业中去。

四、为了保持句子平衡，从句还可以用倒装结构

此时的结构是“as...as＋助动词＋主语”，请看例句：

8 Small as it is, the ant is as much a creature ***as are*** all other animals on the earth.

妙语点睛 这里的 as are all other animals on the earth 是一个倒装结构，主语是 all other animals on the earth。另外，这里的 as much...as 表示的是“在同等程度上”，翻译时可以处理成“和……一样”。

精品译文 尽管蚂蚁很小，但是它同地球上的任何其他动物一样，也是一种动物。

9 The computer revolution may well change society as fundamentally ***as did*** the Industrial Revolution.

妙语点睛 这里的 as did the Industrial Revolution 是一个倒装结构。

精品译文 计算机革命对于我们人类社会的改变之深刻，就如同当年的工业革命。

4. 8. 2 连词 than 的基本用法

一、可比性问题

可比性问题，即指应是两个**同类事物**才能比较，如 he 和 I。不是两个同类事物是无法比较的。

1 He is taller than I (am). 他比我高。

2 The weather of the South is wetter than the North. *

妙语点睛 这是典型的句子错误，因为 the weather of the South 和 the North 是两个截然不同的事物，无法进行比较，只能是"南方的天气"和"北方的天气"这两个同类事物才能比较。故原句应改为：The weather of the South is wetter than **that of** the North.（为避免重复，用 that 代替 the weather。）

3 Young readers, more often than not, find the novels of Dickens far more exciting than Thackeray.
(A: not; B: of; C: far more; D: Thackeray)

正确答案 D，应改为：Thackeray's。

妙语点睛 这是 1992 年的考研真题。这里比较的对象是两个作家的小说，所以要用 Thackeray's，相当于说 Thackeray's novels。

精品译文 年轻的读者多半觉得狄更斯的小说要比萨克雷的小说有趣得多。

二、比较形式问题

即指在有 than 的比较句子里，主句中必须有**比较级形式**出现。

4 There are few electronic applications ______ to raise fears regarding future employment opportunities than robots.

A. likely B. more likely C. most likely D. much likely

正确答案 B。

妙语点睛 这是 1998 年的四级考试题。本题考查的是比较级的形式。这里只有 more 与后面的 than 构成结构上的搭配，故 B 正确。

精品译文 很少有任何一项电子技术的应用能够像机器人这样，引起了人们对未来就业机会的恐慌。

5 On the whole, ambitious students are much likely to succeed in their studies than are those with little ambition.
(A: On the whole; B: much likely; C: are those; D: little)

正确答案 B，应改为：more likely。

妙语点睛 这是 1996 年的考研真题。这个句子里有 than，那么其前面就应该有比较级形式与其构成结构上的呼应，所以把 much likely 改为 more likely。

精品译文 总的来说，一个有远大抱负的学生比起那些胸无大志的学生，更可能取得学业上的成功。

三、为了保持句子平衡，从句还可以用全部或部分倒装

此时的结构是：than + 助动词 + 主语。请看例句：

6 On the whole, ambitious students are more likely to succeed in their studies ***than are*** those with little ambition.

妙语点睛 这是上面讨论过的考研改错句子。我们看到这里 than are those with little ambition 即是一个倒装结构，这里的主语是 those with little ambition。

请再看更多的例句：

7 Foreign-born Asians and Hispanics "have higher rates of intermarriage ***than do*** U. S. -born whites and blacks". 在海外出生的亚洲人和西班牙人的通婚率"比出生在美国的白人和黑人的通婚率要高"。

8 In addition, far more Japanese workers expressed dissatisfaction with their jobs ***than did*** their counterparts in the 10 other countries surveyed. 另外，据调查，不满意自己工作的日本员工比另外 10 个国家的员工人数要多得多。

9 The surface conditions on the planet Mars are more like the Earth's ***than are*** those of any other planet in the solar system. 与太阳系中的其他行星相比，火星表面的情况同地球表面的情况最为相似。

10 Ichthyosaurs had a higher chance of being preserved ***than did*** terrestrial creatures because, as marine animals, they tended to live in environments less subject to erosion. 与其他陆生生物相比，鱼龙的遗体更易保存，因为它是水生生物，其生活环境使它不易腐烂。

4.8.3 表示倍数比较的三种句型结构

在英文中，除了用 than 和 as 来对两个事物进行比较外，还可以用 times 和 twice 等词来说明两事物之间的倍数关系。在英文中，表示两事物倍数关系的比较，可用以下三种句型（以三倍即 three times 为例）：

1. “倍数 + 比较级”结构：A is three times bigger（或其他形容词的比较级）than B
2. “倍数 + as...as”结构：A is three times as big（或其他形容词的原级）as B
3. “倍数 + 名词”结构：A is three times the size（或其他形容词对应的名词形式）of B

请看下列各例句：

1 When the United States entered just such a glowing period after the end of the Second World War, it had a market ***eight times larger than*** any competitor, giving its industries unparalleled economies of scale.

妙语点睛　这里是“倍数 + 比较级”结构。

精品译文　美国在二战后进入辉煌的历史时期时，它拥有比任何竞争对手大八倍的市场，这使其工业经济规模无可匹敌。

2 There are about 105 males born for every 100 females, but this ratio drops to near balance at the age of maturity, and among 70-year-olds there are ***twice as many*** women as men.

妙语点睛　这里是“倍数 + as...as”结构。

精品译文　每出生 100 名女婴，就会有 105 名男婴出生，但这个比例在他们成年时下降为基本平衡，在 70 岁的老人中女性是男性的两倍。

3 There are only ***half as many*** fisheries ***as*** there were 15 years ago.

妙语点睛　这里是“倍数 + as...as”结构。

精品译文　现如今的渔场数量仅是 15 年前的一半。

4 According to the Canadian Institute for Health Information, prescription drug costs have risen since 1997 ***at twice the rate*** of overall health-care spending.

妙语点睛　这里是“倍数 + 名词”结构。

精品译文　加拿大医疗信息协会的资料表明，自 1997 年以来，处方药的费用的增长速度是整个医疗费用增长速度的两倍。

5 Smoking is so harmful to personal health that it kills ______ people each year than automobile accidents.

A. seven more times　　B. seven times more

C. over seven times　　D. seven times

正确答案　B。

妙语点睛　这是 1999 年的考研真题。此题考查的就是倍数比较关系的表达。根据上面说到的“倍数 + 比较级”结构，这里的倍数 seven times 应该放在比较级的前面，故 seven times more 正确。其他的表达，如 seven more times, over seven times 均不符合上面的句型。

精品译文　吸烟对个人健康是如此有危害，以至于每年造成的死亡人数是交通事故导致的死亡人数的七倍多。

6 Americans eat ______ as they actually need every day.

A. twice as much protein　　B. twice protein as much twice

C. twice protein as much　　D. protein as twice much

正确答案　A。

妙语点睛　这是 1998 年的四级考题。此题考查的是倍数比较关系的表达。根据上面说到的“倍数 + as...as”结构，这里的倍数 twice 应该放在 as...as 前面，故 twice as much protein 正确，其他的表达均不符合上面说的这个句型。

精品译文　美国人每天摄入的蛋白质的量是他们实际所需要的两倍。

4. 8. 4 the more..., the more 句型结构

“the more..., the more”结构的基本意思是“越……，越……”。但很多英语初学者在使用这个句型时常常会犯错，究其原因，就是没有把握该句型的核心要点。正确使用这个句型的关键在于，要知道**这里的比较级部分都须在各自的分句中充当一定的成分**，换句话说，相当于是**将分句中的某个成分变为比较级之后提到了句首**。请读者先来翻译这样一个中文句子：

1 你用词越准确，人们就能越容易理解你的意思。

这里的“准确”可以用 exact 来表达。那么这句话该如何翻译呢？请读者不妨提笔练习一下。下面笔者来提供几个版本的译文，看看与大家刚才翻译的是否相同。

1）***The more exact*** you use your words, ***the easier*** people will understand you.

2）***The more exactly*** you use your words, ***the more easily*** people will understand you.

3）***The more exact*** your words are, ***the easier it is for*** people to understand you.

4）***The more exact words*** you use, ***the more easily*** people will understand you.

妙语点睛 上面的译文并不全对。要分析上面句子的对错，要牢牢抓住该句型的核心要点——**比较级部分都须在各自的分句中充当一定的成分。**

在句 1）中，两个分句的比较级部分分别是 the more exact 和 the easier，再往后看各自引导的分句 you use your words 和 people will understand you 就会发现，这里使用的形容词比较级 the more exact 和 the easier 是不能修饰句子的谓语 use 或 understand 的（因为形容词不能修饰动词），即比较级部分无法充当后面分句的任何成分，因此句 1）的译文不对。

在句 2）中，鉴于句 1）的错误原因，把比较级部分都改为副词的比较级 the more exactly 和 the more easily，此时就能修饰句子的谓语 use 或 understand(因为副词修饰动词)，即比较级部分充当了后面分句的某一成分，这里是作方式状语，因此句 2）的译文非常正确。

在句 3）中，鉴于句 1）的错误原因，只要使形容词的比较级 the more exact 和 the easier 能够在后面的分句中充当成分就对了，所以把后面的分句进行了改写，分别为 your words are 和 it is for people to understand you。这样一来，形容词的比较级 the more exact 就在其后的分句 your words are 中作表语，相当于说 your words ***are more exact***；形容词的比较级 the easier 就在分句 it is for people to understand you 中作表语，相当于说 it is ***easier*** for people to understand you，即比较级部分充当了后面分句的某一成分，这里是作表语，因此句 3）的译文非常正确。

在句 4）中，比较级部分 the more exact words 作后面分句的谓语 use 的宾语，相当于说 you ***use more exact words***；比较级部分 the more easily 作后面分句的谓语 understand 的方式状语，相当于说 people will ***more easily understand*** you，即比较级部分充当了后面分句的某一成分，因此句 4）的译文非常正确。

综上所述，我们总结出这个句型的三个用法要点：

1. 正确使用该句型的核心：**比较级部分都须在各自引导的分句中充当一定的成分。**
2. 从结构上来看，这个句型的前半部分是从句，后半部分是主句，即“the+ 比较级（**从句**），the+ 比较级（**主句**）”，这就是为什么前半句常用一般现在时态，而后半句常用一般将来时态，类似于其他状语从句的“主句用将来时，从句用一般现在时”的规则一样。
3. 翻译成汉语时，一般是按前后正常的语序，先译从句，后译主句。

我们再来看其他更多的例句。下面这个例句告诉我们，为什么说考古学家能够成为一个女人的最好丈夫：

2 An archaeologist is the best husband a woman can have: ***the older*** she is, ***the more interested*** he is in her.

妙语点睛 我们看到，这里的比较级 the older 在分句 she is 中作表语，the more interested 在分句 he is in her 中作表语。

精品译文 考古学家可谓是一个女人最好的丈夫人选：因为她越老，他对她就会越感兴趣。

在下面这个例句中，一位美国老年朋友把人类的衰老过程比作像在爬山，说得很有道理，他告诉我们，要以一种平和而积极的心态来面对自己已逝去的青春：

3 Aging is a part of life, and it can be an exciting and rewarding part. It has been said that aging is like climbing a mountain: ***the higher*** you get, ***the more tired and breathless*** you become, but the view becomes much more extensive.

妙语点睛 我们看到，这里的比较级 the higher 在分句 you get 中作表语，the more tired and breathless 在分句 you become 中作表语。

精品译文 衰老是生命的一个组成部分，而且可以说，它是生命中最激动人心和有意义的一部分。人们常说衰老就如同爬山，爬得越高，就会觉得越累和气喘吁吁，但是你看到的人生景致会更为丰富。

下面这个例句说明了“帮助别人就是在帮助自己”这样的道理：

4 ***The more*** we help others, ***the more*** we receive in return. We advance ourselves as we help others. 帮助别人越多，我们获得的回报也越多。帮助了别人，提升了自己。

朋友是什么？下面这个例句作出了回答：

5 Friends are lights in winter: ***the older*** the friend, ***the brighter*** the light.

妙语点睛 这个句子的比较部分是省略结构，完整的表达应该是 the older the friend is, the brighter the light is，即这里省去了系动词 is。所以，比较级都是在各自引导的分句中作表语。注意，在这个句型中，系动词常常会被省去。

精品译文 朋友犹如冬日里的暖阳，越是老朋友，就越让你感觉温暖。

下面这个例句讲了该如何学习英语，说的就是要多花时间和老外“泡”在一起，和他们“泡”的时间越多，你的英文就会越地道，有条件的读者不妨效仿：

6 For a Chinese person to write in English, he or she must first be able to think in English. This can only be done after a long time of reading foreign books and magazines and interacting with other foreigners. ***The more time*** you spend with native speakers, ***the more*** you will understand how they think and ***the better*** you will be able to write in a way that is similar to theirs.

妙语点睛 我们看到，这里的比较级 the more time 在分句 you spend with native speakers 中作 spend 的宾语，the more 在分句 you will understand how they think 中作状语，修饰 understand，the better 在分句 you will be able to write in a way that is similar to theirs 中作状语，修饰 able，因为我们要说 you will be ***better able*** to...。由此可见，所有的比较级都充当了各自分句的某一成分。

精品译文 中国人要想具有良好的英语写作能力，他们首先必须能够用英语进行思考。而要想达到这个目的，就必须长期进行大量的阅读，比如阅读原版的书刊杂志，还要多和老外交流。你越是多花时间和老外“泡”在一起，你就越能够理解他们的思维方式，因而也就越能够以类似于他们的思维方式来进行英文写作。

上面讲到了学习的例子，下面这个例子讲了学习有什么用。为什么这么说呢？我们来看它的“魔鬼逻辑”：

7 Why study?
The more we study, ***the more*** we know.
The more we know, ***the more*** we forget.
The more we forget, ***the less*** we know.
So, why study?

精品译文 为什么要学习呢？
学的越多，知道的就越多。
知道的越多，忘记的就越多。
忘记的越多，知道的就越少。
那么，为什么要学习呢？

面对2007年火爆的股票市场，很多人摩拳擦掌，按捺不住想进入：

8 John: The stock market is really hot now. I'm thinking of getting into it.
Casey: Well, I suggest you be careful. It's easy to get your fingers burnt.
John: My uncle works for a securities company. He will help me to make an investment portfolio.
Casey: But I think ***the hotter*** the market is, ***the more risk*** there is.
John: Yes, you are right. But ***the more risk*** there is, ***the more profit*** there might be.

精品译文 约翰：现在股市可真火啊！我也想投身其中。
凯西：我建议你小心。如果判断失误，那你会损失惨重的。
约翰：我叔叔在一家证券公司工作，他会帮我掌握好投资组合的。
凯西：但我觉得市场越火，风险就越大。
约翰：是，你说得没错。但风险越大，收益也会越大。

思维总结

比较状语从句应该是九大状语从句中内容最多的，涉及各类句型结构。读者应该重点掌握有关 as 和 than 的用法。此外，要熟练掌握表示倍数比较的三种句型。

思维训练

Exercise 4. 8（Key: P337）
请选择最佳答案填空。

1. An adult human must take eight steps to go ______ as a giraffe does in one stride.
   A. as far B. the farther C. how far D. farther
2. The harder you work, ______ you have of passing your exam.
   A. more chance B. more chances C. the more chance D. the chances
3. The knee is ______ most other joints in the body because it cannot twist without injury.
   A. more likely to be damaged than B. much likely to be damaged than
   C. likely to be more damaged than D. more than likely to be damaged
4. I would have paid ______ — for my car if the salesman had insisted, because I really wanted it.
   A. as much twice B. much twice C. twice as much D. two times
5. Any preexisting illness, even ______ the common cold, increases the chances of contracting another disease.
   A. as mild one as B. as one mild as C. as a mild one as D. as mild a one as
6. After retirement my father earns only ______ as he used to. However, he lives happily enjoying his leisure time.
   A. a half as much B. a half as many C. half as many D. half as much
7. In China the South generally receives much less snow than ______ the North.
   A. does B. it does C. does in D. it does in
8. The number of registered participants in this year's marathon was half ______.
   A. of last year's B. those of last year's C. of those of last year D. that of last year's
9. The air inside a house or office building often has higher concentrations of contaminants ______ heavily polluted outside air.
   A. than does B. more C. as some that are D. like of
10. The atmosphere is as much a part of the earth as ______ its soils and the water of its lakes, rivers and oceans.
    A. are B. do C. is D. has
11. Do you enjoy listening to records? I find records are often ______, if not better than, an actual performance.
    A. as good as B. as good C. good D. good as

辨别改错：

12. In the long run, however, this hurry to shed full-time staff may be more harmful to industry as it is to the workforce.
    A: In the long run B: hurry C: may be D: as

4.9 方式状语从句

方式状语从句表示动作的方式，引导词有：as, like, as if, as though 和 the way 等。请看例句：

1 When in Rome, do as the Romans do.

妙语点睛 这是一个英语谚语，意思是说 When traveling, follow the customs of the local people. 相当于汉语中的"入乡随俗"。

精品译文 入乡随俗。

我们来看上面这个例句在口语中的应用：

2 Hazel: Yak burgers? What's a yak?

Nina: It's a kind of long haired ox. Tibetans put yak butter in their tea as well as eating yak.

Hazel: Yak! Yuk! I wouldn't touch it with a barge-pole!

Nina: Come on! Be adventurous! ***When in Rome do as the Romans do***!

Hazel: I'm not in Rome. I'm in Beijing. And when we get to Lhasa you can try it first!

精品译文 黑兹尔：牦牛汉堡？牦牛是什么？

尼娜：是一种长毛的牛。藏民在茶里添加牦牛油，也吃牦牛肉。

黑兹尔：牦牛！哈哈！我才不碰那东西呢！

尼娜：别啊！有点冒险精神好不好？入乡随俗嘛！

黑兹尔：我没在"乡下"，我是在北京，所以不用随俗。咱们到了拉萨你可以先试试！

请再看其他例句：

3 Do it ***the way*** you were taught. 按照教给你的那样做。

4 He looks ***as though/as if*** he is an actor. 他看上去像个演员。

我们来看一个 like 作连词引导方式状语从句的例句。笔者很喜欢这段话，它表达了一种人生态度：

5 Work ***like*** you don't need the money.

Love ***like*** you've never been hurt.

Dance ***like*** nobody's watching.

Sing ***like*** nobody's listening.

Live ***like*** it's heaven on earth.

精品译文 去工作吧，犹如你不需要金钱。

去爱吧，犹如你从未曾被伤害过。

去舞蹈吧，犹如无人在一旁观看。

去歌唱吧，犹如无人在一边谛听。

热爱生活吧，犹如这里是人间乐土。

写给读者的话

一、三大从句的比较

到本章为止，我们已详细讨论了英语中的三大从句：名词从句、定语从句和状语从句。因此，有必要对它们进行一个比较，以便于读者更好地认识这三大从句的特点。具体如下：

最简单的是名词从句。这一点毫无疑问。

最难的是定语从句，但相比较而言也是最重要的。真正要全面掌握并运用好定语从句，着实有点不容易。

最繁杂的是状语从句。九大类就够我们费费脑筋的了，何况还有各个不同的连词的用法以及句型结构，所以的确是够多、够杂的。不过，状语从句在结构上理解起来并没有定语从句那么难，正如笔者一再强调的，读者只要掌握连接词即可翻译句子。

二、本章学习思路

从本质上来讲，状语从句就是用不同的连词将几个分句连接起来，以表达分句之间特定的逻辑语义关系。因此，掌握引导九类状语从句的有关连接词的用法特点和意义是学习状语从句的关键。只要记住连接词就能够识别是何种状语从句，从而正确分析句子的结构并理解句子的意思。在具体的学习过程中，要掌握不同状语从句的各个常用的连词和句型结构，一方面便于自己在阅读中遇到时能够正确地理解和翻译，另一方面便于自己在写作等英语应用过程中使用。

三、本章重点及难点

本章重点内容包括：

1. when 的用法特点，以及其各种时态搭配关系，比如其中的"过去进行时＋一般过去时"这样的时态搭配用法；
2. until 的用法特点；
3. 常见的表示原因的连词和介词，注意连词后面不能用名词短语，而介词后面不能接从句；
4. 结果状语从句 so...that 与 such...that 在用法上的区别；
5. 结果状语从句的倒装结构；
6. 常见的表示让步的连词和介词，注意连词后面不能用名词短语，而介词后面不能接从句；
7. 引导比较从句的 as 和 than 的用法特点，包括他们的倒装结构，以及表示倍数比较的三种句型。

本章内容理解起来并不难，但由于内容多而杂，所以建议读者在学习这一章时要有耐心和细心，不要混淆了各个状语从句连词的含义。

四、本章学习时间安排

读者可以花七天左右的时间认真研读本章所讲解的内容。在学完第一遍之后，建议读者再反复研读几次，这样在自己造句写作时，方能做到信手拈来、运用自如。

综合练习（Key: P338）

请选择最佳答案填空。

1. Poor ______ he is, he is honest and kind.
   A. that　　B. however　　C. because　　D. although
2. ______ apparently rigid, bones exhibit a degree of elasticity that enables the skeleton to withstand considerable impact.
   A. In spite of　　B. As　　C. Although　　D. Despite
3. ______ native to Europe, the daisy（雏菊）has now spread throughout most of North America.
   A. Although　　B. In spite of　　C. If it were　　D. That it is
4. Not until I shouted at the top of my voice ______ his head.
   A. that he turned　　B. did he turn　　C. he didn't turn　　D. he had turned
5. Dew is formed ______ the grass is thick.
   A. while　　B. where　　C. when　　D. until
6. You can find him ______ he works.
   A. when　　B. where　　C. which　　D. as
7. ______ some flowers contain more nectar than others, how does a honeybee worker, faced with a patch of flowers containing variable amounts of nectar, decide when to stop collecting.
   A. Given that　　B. Giving that　　C. To give　　D. Being given
8. He wrote down the address ______ he should forget it.
   A. in case not　　B. lest　　C. in order that　　D. of fear that
9. Let's take the front seats ______ we may have a better view.
   A. so as to　　B. in order to　　C. in order　　D. that

10. ______ many children have bought balloons ______ the store is now out of stock.
A. So—that　B. Such—that　C. Such a—that　D. So—as to
11. Let's finish our work ______ we can be free this evening.
A. now that　B. than　C. because　D. so that
12. Batteries must be kept in dry places ______ electricity should leak away.
A. where　B. lest　C. that　D. unless
13. The motorist looked over the engine carefully ______ on the way.
A. so that it should go wrong　B. lest it should go wrong
C. in order that should not go wrong　D. for fear that it should not go wrong
14. This approach is superior to that one ______ it provides explicit accounts.
A. in which　B. in this way　C. in that　D. in order that
15. ______, he remains stupid.
A. Though his learning　B. Through all his learning
C. For all his learning　D. However his learning
16. ______, electrons are still smaller.
A. As small atoms are　B. Small as atoms are
C. As atoms are small　D. Are small atoms
17. It was not until the eleventh century that ______
A. the detective found out the truth　B. did the detective find out the truth
C. had the detective find out the truth　D. had the detective found out the truth
18. ______, he failed to pass the test.
A. Hard although he tried　B. He tried hard, though
C. Hard as he tried　D. Though hard as he tried
19. ______, the fire men were unable to quench the fire.
A. Try they would　B. As they tried　C. What they tried　D. Try as they would
20. Angiosperms inhabit relatively diverse environments and may be found ______ higher plants can survive.
A. there　B. where　C. somewhere　D. then
21. ______, he still retained the use of all his faculties.
A. Because he was old and weak　B. As he was old and weak
C. Unless he was old and weak　D. Old and weak as he was
22. The agency agreed to do the job ______ that the fee was high enough.
A. so long　B. only　C. such　D. provided
23. No sooner had we started the experiment ______ we stopped it because of the cut-off of water.
A. than　B. when　C. then　D. as
24. It was not until she had arrived home ______ remembered her appointment with the doctor.
A. when she　B. that she　C. and she　D. she
25. The lower ______ in a room, the more slowly our eyes focus.
A. the level of lighting　B. light level　C. leveling of light　D. lighting is level
26. ______ no conclusive evidence exists, many experts believe that the wheel was invented only once and then diffused to the rest of the world.
A. Even　B. But　C. Although　D. So
27. Gorillas are quiet animals, ______ they are capable of making about 20 different sounds.
A. whether　B. which　C. even though　D. as well as

辨别改错：

28. Since rats are destructive and may carry disease, therefore many cities try to exterminate them.
A (destructive)　B (may carry)　C (therefore many)　D (exterminate)

29. The southwestern portion of the United States is a land of little rain, and parts of it are too dry that they are called
A B C D
deserts.

30. The black leopard is very dark that its spots are difficult to see.
A B C D

31. The speaker claimed that no other modern nation devotes so small a portion of its wealth to public assistance
A B
and health than the United States does.
C D

32. Saturn is the second largest planet after Jupiter, with a diameter nearly ten times those of Earth.
A B C D

Chapter 5

第五章　完成时态

本章首先介绍完成时态的基本构成，然后总体介绍完成时态的基本意义，即表示"回顾"性思维。在此基础上，将以现在完成时态为例，深入分析完成时态的三种用法，即表示"延续事件"、"重复事件"和"单一事件"，并对这三种用法进行详细的比较。接着，介绍用于完成时态的最高级句型，以及时间连词since的用法特点。最后，介绍过去完成时和将来完成时的用法。因此，本章内容安排如下：

5.1 完成时态的构成

完成时态(perfect tense)的构成分为两部分：一是助动词 have，二是实义动词的过去分词-ed。具体来说，用助动词 have 表示"时(tense)"，以表明动作发生的时间是在过去、现在还是将来；用过去分词来表示动作的"体态(aspect)"，以表明该动作已经完成。用-ed 来代替过去分词，于是完成时态的构成是"have+-ed"。以动词 work 为例，三种完成时态的构成形式如下：

现在完成时：have worked

过去完成时：had worked

将来完成时：will have worked

在《英语语法新思维初级教程——走近语法》中给出过进行时态谓语的如下公式：

Tense	(Modal)	Continuous	Verb
PAST or PRESENT	(WILL)	BE + -ING	VERB

同理，现在可以给出完成时态谓语的公式，如下：

Tense	(Modal)	Perfect	Verb
PAST or PRESENT	(WILL)	HAVE + -ED	VERB

现在用这个公式分别表示现在完成时、过去完成时和将来完成时的谓语构成形式，仍以 work 为例。

现在完成时(have worked)可以具体表示为：

Tense	Perfect	Verb
PRESENT	HAVE+ED	work

或简化为：have worked=present+perfect+work

过去完成时态(had worked)可以具体表示为：

Tense	Perfect	Verb
PAST	HAVE+ED	work

或简化为：had worked=past+perfect+work

将来完成时态(will have worked)可以具体表示为：

Tense	Modal	Perfect	Verb
PRESENT	WILL	HAVE+-ED	work

或简化为：will have worked=present+modal+perfect+work

从以上公式看到，现在完成时态、过去完成时态和将来完成时态具有共同的"态(aspect)"，即"完成(perfect)"态。在意义上是表示动作完成了(complete)，在结构上用动词的过去分词-ed 来表示。所以三种完成时态的本质意义是相同的，区别只是动作发生的时间不同而已。关于这一点，读者在 5. 2 节里会有更深入的理解。

5.2 完成时态的意义

完成时态的本质思维或者说其核心意义就是用来表示"回顾(retrospect)"(详见 5.3 节)。既然是"回顾",就必然要涉及两个时间点,即从一个时间点回顾到另外一个时间点,因此完成时态必定涉及前后两个时间。

比如,现在完成时(present perfect tense)就是站在"现在(present)"的时间角度回顾一个"过去"的事件,是把"过去"和"现在"这两个时间点联系在一起,来表达一个事件。如图所示:

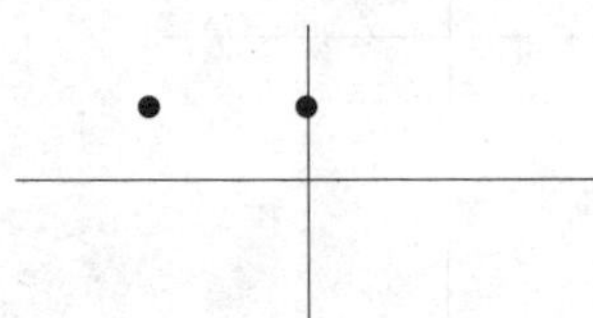

过去完成时(past perfect tense)就是站在"过去(past)"的时间角度回顾"更远的过去"的事件,是把"更远的过去"和"过去"联系在一起来表达一个事件。如图所示:

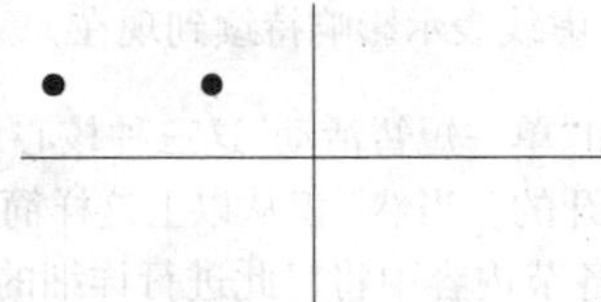

将来完成时(future perfect tense)则是以回顾的角度去看待将来的某个事件,或者说是站在未来的时间角度回顾在此之前发生的事件。如图所示:

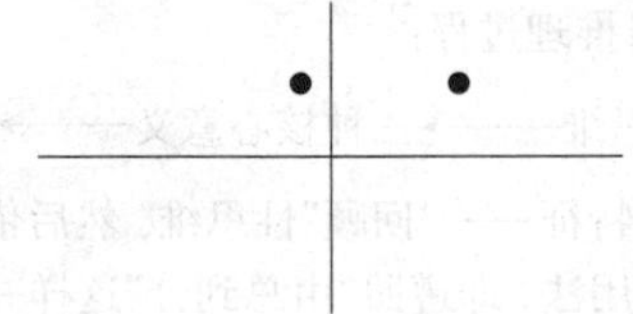

简言之:

现在完成时态就是站在"现在"回顾"过去";

过去完成时态就是站在"过去"回顾"更远的过去";

将来完成时就是站在未来的时间角度回顾在此之前发生的事件。

所以,完成时态表示的就是一个横跨前后两个时间点的事件。那么这个事件是如何把两个时间点联系起来的呢?主要通过下列三种方式:

1. 一个事件从一个时间点"延续(continue)"到另外一个时间点;
2. 一个事件从一个时间点"重复(repeat)"到另外一个时间点;
3. 一个事件在前一个时间点已经结束,但它的影响"延续"到另外一个时间点。

以现在完成时为例,一个过去的事件是如何与现在发生联系的呢?其实,一个过去的事件与现在发生联系的方式有上述三种,对应于三种事件:

1. 延续事件(continuous event):一个过去发生的事件"延续"到现在;
2. 重复事件(repeated event):一个过去发生的事件"重复"到现在;
3. 单一事件(single event):一个过去发生的短暂事件没有"延续"或"重复"到现在,但它的影响"延续"到了现在,或者说一个过去发生并结束了的事件对现在仍然有影响。

这三种联系的方式图示如下：

1. 一个事件从过去“延续”到现在：

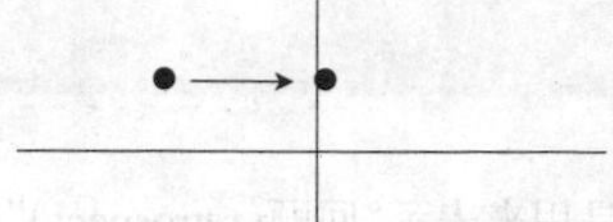

2. 一个事件从过去“重复”到现在：

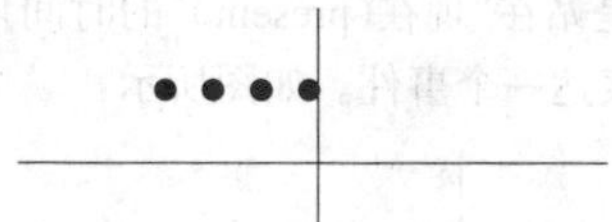

3. 过去某一短暂动作对现在的影响：

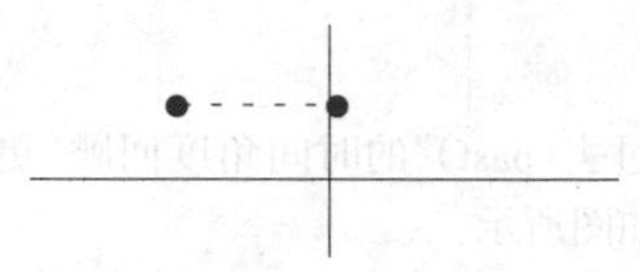

（虚线表示影响持续到现在）

所以，完成时态具有“延续”、“重复”和“单一短暂活动”这三种核心意义和用法。在整个“完成时态”一章所讨论的内容都是围绕这三种用法来具体展开的。当然，仅从以上这样简单的表述，读者朋友一定无法真正领悟完成时态的这三种思维特征，在接下来的各节内容中将对此进行详细的讲解。本章**将以“现在完成时”**（详见5.3-5.9节）**为例，深入细致地分析完成时态的思维特征**。这么做主要有两个原因：一是现在完成时远比过去完成时（见5.10节）和将来完成时（见5.11节）更为常用；二是掌握了现在完成时态的三种思维特征（延续、重复以及单一短暂活动），其他两种完成时态的意义完全可以同理类推。

本章的内容的阐述遵照这样一个逻辑推理过程：

回顾性思维——→三种核心意义——→具体用法

首先，我们将讨论完成时态总的思维特征——“回顾”性思维，然后依次详细讨论其三个核心意义。在讨论的同时，详细分析这三种核心意义的具体用法，即遵照“由总到分”这样一个思维逻辑来展开。核心内容包括下面五节：

5.3 “回顾”思维

5.4 延续事件

5.5 重复事件

5.6 单一事件

5.7 “延续事件”、“重复事件”与“单一事件”之间的相互关系

掌握了上述五节的内容，即可真正领会完成时态的精髓。在接下来的一节中，笔者开始讲解完成时表示“回顾”性这一本质思维。

说句心里话

老实说，5.2节的内容是非常笼统和抽象的，因为这节的内容是总结性的和概括性的，它一方面总结了完成时态的核心思维，另一方面表明了本章的讨论思路。所以，这一节内容非常重要，贯穿了完成时态的整个内容。如果读者不能理解或深刻理解这些抽象的说明，这是非常正常的，请读者不要着急和沮丧。在接下来的各节内容中，都会有对此极为详尽的描述和讲解。

现在完成时态有着极为广泛的语义功能（a wide range of functions），从以上简单的、定义式的描述中，读者朋友是无法真正理解现在完成时态极为丰富的内涵的。在英文所有的时态当中，现在完成时态是被最为广泛研究和探讨的，这主要是集中在上个世纪70至80年代，大量的欧美语言学专家从各个不同的角度（如语用学、语义学、语法化等角度）对现在完成时态进行了深入的研究。为了真正深谙这些

"烦人的"完成时态的意义和用法，笔者在剑桥大学(Cambridge University)读书时曾经阅读过一百多万字的英语时态文献资料，其中讨论现在完成时态的就占到了一半。不同的研究角度，对现在完成时态的用法分类是不一样的。笔者上面所述的三种分类是充分考虑到汉语的思维习惯以及英汉时态的差异而作出的。

读者朋友在学习本章内容时，需要有耐心、恒心和信心。要有耐心和恒心，是因为本章内容多、理解难，读者可能难以抓住；有信心，是要相信通过笔者详细而全面的举例分析，你们一定能够真正掌握完成时态的思维和用法。

请读者现在就真正开始完成时态之旅吧！

5.3 "回顾"思维

在前面提到过，**完成时态的本质思维就是用来"回顾(retrospect)"**。这一本质思维应用到现在完成时中，就是表示站在"现在时间"的角度回顾"过去"。既然是回顾自己从过去到现在的经历，因此现在完成时态的这种思维用法在个人自传中应该是少不了的。下面这篇短文是选自英国著名的哲学家、数学家和散文家伯特兰·罗素(Bertrand Russell, 1872-1970)的自传(The Autobiography of Bertrand Russell)的前言部分，请读者注意里面现在完成时的表达。

1 What I ***Have Lived*** for

Three passions, simple but overwhelmingly strong, ***have governed*** my life: the longing for love, the search for knowledge, and unbearable pity for the suffering of mankind. These passions, like great winds, ***have blown*** me hither and thither, in a wayward course, over a deep ocean of anguish, reaching to the very verge of despair.

I ***have sought*** love, first, because it brings ecstasy — ecstasy so great that I would often have sacrificed all the rest of life for a few hours of this joy. I ***have sought*** it, next, because it relieves loneliness — that terrible loneliness in which one shivering consciousness looks over the rim of the world into the cold unfathomable lifeless abyss. I ***have sought*** it, finally, because in the union of love I ***have seen***, in a mystic miniature, the prefiguring vision of the heaven that saints and poets ***have imagined***. This is what I ***have sought***, and though it might seem too good for human life, this is what — at last — I ***have found***.

With equal passion I ***have sought*** knowledge. I ***have wished*** to understand the hearts of men. I ***have wished*** to know why the stars shine. And I ***have tried*** to apprehend the Pythagorean power by which number holds sway above the flux. A little of this, but now much, I ***have achieved***.

Love and knowledge, so far as they were possible, led upward toward the heavens. But always pity brought me back to earth. Echoes of cries of pain reverberate in my heart. Children in famine, victims tortured by oppressors, helpless old people a hated burden to their sons, and the whole world of loneliness, poverty, and pain make a mockery of what human life should be. I long to alleviate the evil, but I can't, and I too suffer.

This ***has been*** my life. I ***have found*** it worth living, and would gladly live it again if the chance were offered me.

妙语点睛 读者朋友看到了，罗素在其自传中回顾自己一生的时候，频繁地使用了现在完成时态，如标题中的have lived，以及从开篇的have governed直到最后的结语has been和have found。作者通过使用这些完成时态，来表明自己"从过去一直到现在"这段有生之年一直被三种激情所控制(have governed my life)：对爱的渴望、对知识的探索和对人类所遭受的苦难的同情。随后，作者用了大量的现在完成时来说明自己为什么一生在追求这三种激情，因为"爱和知识能够把人类引向天堂，而同情却把人类带回尘世"。他渴望减少人间的痛苦与邪恶，但却无能为力，所以他也心受折磨。在最后，罗素用现在完成时总结说：This ***has been*** my life. 因为他是在回顾自己的一生经历，所以必然要用"现在完成时"这样一个横贯过去与现在的时态来作出"这就是我的一生"这样的结语。若单纯地用一般现在时说成 This is my life. 那只表明他目前的生活状态——

"这就是我现在的生活"，而失去了"回顾过去、纵观一生"的思想内涵。由此可见，两句话的含义完全不同，而这种差别就是通过句子谓语动词的时态变化(由 has been 到 is)表达出来的。由此也足以证明，完成时态具有"回顾"性这一本质的思维特征。只要抓住这一本质思维，完成时态的各种用法便迎刃而解了。

精品译文　我生之所求

我的一生被三种简单却又无比强烈的激情所控制：对爱的渴望，对知识的探索和对人类苦难难以忍受的同情。这些激情像狂风，把我恣情吹向四方，掠过苦痛的大海，乃至使我濒临绝望的边缘。

我寻求爱，首先因为它使我心为之着迷，这种难以名状的美妙迷醉之感，使我愿意用所有的余生去换取哪怕几个小时这样的幸福。我寻求爱，还因为它能缓解我心里的孤独，在这种可怕的孤独中，我感觉心灵的战栗，仿如站在世界的边缘而面前是冰冷、无底的死亡深渊。我寻求爱，还因为在我所目睹的爱的结合中，我仿佛看到了圣贤和诗人们所设想的天堂之景。这就是我所寻找的，虽然对人的一生而言似乎有些遥不可及，但至少是我用尽一生所领悟到的。

我用同样的激情去寻求知识。我希望能够理解人类的心灵，希望能够知道群星闪烁的原因。我试图领悟毕达哥拉斯所景仰的"数即万物"的思想。我已经悟出了其中的一点点道理，尽管并不是很多。

爱和知识，用它们的力量把我引向天堂，但是同情却总把我又拽回到尘世中来。痛苦的呼喊声回荡在我的内心。饥饿中的孩子，压迫下的难民，被儿女们当作负担的无助的老人，还有这整个充满了孤独、贫穷和痛苦的世界，都是对人类所憧憬的美好生活无情的嘲弄。我渴望能够减少邪恶，但是我无能为力，甚至连我自己也难免于备受其折磨。

这就是我的一生。我已经找到了它的价值，而且如果有机会，我很愿意能再活它一次。

我们下面再看看美国前总统克林顿在 2001 年 1 月 18 日作卸任演说时，是怎样通过现在完成时态来"回顾"和吹嘘自己的政绩的：

2　In all the work I ***have done*** as president, every decision I ***have made***, every executive action I ***have taken***, every bill I ***have proposed*** and ***signed, I've tried*** to give all Americans the tools and conditions to build the future of our dreams, in a good society, with a strong economy, a cleaner environment, and a freer, safer, more prosperous world. (Selection of President Bill Clinton's farewell address to the nation on Jan. 18, 2001.)

妙语点睛　克林顿用了现在完成时表明他从 1993 年 1 月 20 日上台当总统以来到目前为止（即 2001 年 1 月 18 日，他演说的当天），是如何尽心尽力地"为美国人民提供途径和创造条件，来实现美国未来的梦想"的。克林顿在演讲时，显然还是美国总统，所以这种"回顾"性的演说，他当然要用"现在完成时态"来向世人宣称自己在过去八年里的"丰功伟绩"。

精品译文　(在过去的八年里)作为总统，我所做的每一项工作，作出的每一个决策，采取的每一个行政措施，以及提议并签署的每一个法案，都是在尽力为全体美国人民提供途径和创造条件，来实现美国未来的梦想——社会稳定、经济繁荣、环境美好，进而使得全世界更自由、更安全、更繁荣。

同时值得注意的是，如果克林顿现在(比如 2008 年)再说这番话，那他就该用"一般过去时态"了，因为他现在已不是总统。比如他要这么说：

In all the work I ***did*** as president, every decision I ***made***, every executive action I ***took***, every bill I ***proposed*** and ***signed***, I ***tried*** to give all Americans the tools and conditions to build the future of our dreams, in a good society, with a strong economy, a cleaner environment, and a freer, safer, more prosperous world.

由此可见，**英语时态是与说话的时间点和语境密切相关的活生生的思维表达，而不是僵化的死规则**。

2002 年 2 月 22 日是美国前总统尼克松秘密访华 30 周年的纪念日，在这一天，美国总统小布什应邀访华，并在清华大学发表了演说。我们来看看小布什是如何使用"现在完成时态"来"回顾"中美外交这 30 年的风雨历程的：

3 During the 30 years since, America and China ***have exchanged*** many handshakes of friendship and commerce. And as we ***have had*** more contact with each other, the citizens of both countries have gradually learned more about each other. And that's important.

精品译文 自从那时以来的30年当中(作者注：指1972尼克松首次访华到2002年这30年)，美国和中国已经握过多次的友谊之手和商业之手。随着我们两国间接触的日益频繁，我们两国的国民也逐渐地加深了对彼此的了解，这是非常重要的。

(作者注：尼克松总统于1972年2月22日秘密访华，从而打破了中美两国外交的坚冰；1978年1月1日中美两国正式建立外交关系；同年3月1日，两国互派大使，在对方首都建立大使馆。)

小布什作完演讲后(注：本节后面附有小布什这次演讲的节选，供读者欣赏)，接受了清华大学学生的提问。当有位学生问到有关台湾问题时，小布什作了如下表态：

4 We***'ve had*** many discussions with your leaders, and I***'ve reiterated*** support for the "One China" policy. It***'s been*** my government's policy for a long period of time, and I ***haven't changed it.***

妙语点睛 我们看到，这里短短的几句话，小布什全部用了现在完成时态，强调自从尼克松总统首次访华及后来的中美建交以来，中美两国之间在不断地交流、交往、增加接触、加强了解，以及美国政府对"一个中国"政策的一贯支持。

精品译文 我同你们的领导人有过很多的沟通和交流，我本人也一再重申支持"一个中国"的政策，而且这也是我们政府的一贯政策，我不会改变。

我们可以想象，如果小布什用了一般过去时态，说成：

The "One China" policy was my government's policy for a long period of time. (我们美国政府曾经在很长一段时间内坚持了"一个中国"的政策。)

这句话地言外之意是，现在美国政府不再坚持这个重要政策了，那么接下来的一句话他就不会说：I haven't changed it.

而是要说：I have changed it. (但我现在已经改变了这个政策。)

果真如此，那真是中美两国人民的灾难，但愿也相信这样的事情不会发生！

思维总结

本节通过三段经典短文，想让读者真正理解完成时态的核心思维意义是"回顾"。另外，需要提醒读者注意的是，虽然这里列举了现在完成时态的例子，但这种"回顾"性的思维特征对于过去完成时态和将来完成时态同样适用。

思维训练

Exercise 5. 3 (Key: P339)

请分析和体会第一句话中的完成时态 has been 所反映出来的"回顾"性思维，并把该对话翻译成中文。

1. A: So here we are at the end of the 20th century, and what a century it ***has been***!

   B: Yes. When the century began, who would have ever imagined that cars, planes, movies, radios, televisions, telephones, videos and Internet would be taken for granted.

   A: I wonder what it will be like in the 21st century?

   B: From the great advances in these past years I assume that we will be entering a new golden age of miracles and wonders.

   A: Yes, life will be fantastic in the next century.

请判断下列语境中该用何种时态。

在每周的周末回顾这一周的忙碌经历时，你可以说：

2. This ______ (be) a hectic week.

   在年末总结时，你可以说：

3. This ______ (be) a difficult year.

如果你是在年初时预测，你可以说成：

4. This ______ (be) a difficult year.

附录：2002 年 2 月 22 日小布什清华大学演说节选：

My visit to China comes on an important anniversary, as the vice president mentioned. Thirty years ago this week an American president arrived in China on a trip designed to end decades of estrangement and confront centuries of suspicion. President Richard Nixon showed the world that two vastly different governments could meet on the grounds of common interest in the spirit of mutual respect.

As they left the airport that day, Premier Zhou Enlai said this to President Nixon: "Your handshake came over the vastest ocean in the world — 25 years of no communication."

During the 30 years since, America and China have exchanged many handshakes of friendship and commerce. And as we have had more contact with each other, the citizens of both countries have gradually learned more about each other. And that's important.

Once America knew China only by its history as a great and enduring civilization. Today we see a China that is still defined by noble traditions of family, scholarship and honor. And we see a China that is becoming one of the most dynamic and creative societies in the world, as demonstrated by the knowledge and potential right here in this room.

China is on a rising path, and America welcomes the emergence of a strong and peaceful and prosperous China.

5.4 延续事件

上一节讲到完成时态是用来表示“回顾”(比如站在“现在”回顾“过去”的现在完成时)的，这是完成时态一个总体的思维特征。“过去”和“现在”发生联系的方式有三种(见 5.2 节)，这一节我们将探讨“延续”事件。本节内容安排如下：

5. 4. 1 过去的事件“延续”到现在

5. 4. 2 “延续事件”与时间状语的关系

5. 4. 1 过去的事件“延续”到现在

所谓“延续事件”，是指**“一个开始于过去的动作或状态(action or state)一直延续到现在”，这是现在完成时态最基本、也是最容易理解的意义和用法。**请看下面这个笑话：

1 An old woman walked out into the middle of the street. The policeman yelled to her, "Don't you know what it means when I hold up my hand?"

The lady said, "Sure I do. I ***have been*** a school teacher for 28 years now."

妙语点睛 在这个笑话中，那位 old woman 对警察说的这句话：

I ***have been*** a school teacher for 28 years now.

表示她从事“老师”这个职业是从过去，即 28 年前开始并且一直延续到了现在，她现在仍然是老师，所以她说 28 years ***now***。这是现在完成时态最常见的一个用法，具体来说就是，如果要表示某一动作或状态(action or state)从过去开始，并且一直持续(continue)到说话时，而且还可能持续下去，就要采用完成时态形式。我们可以用下图说明：

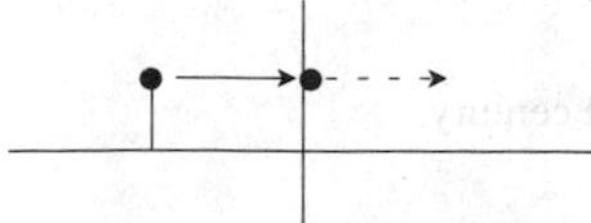

说明：两个黑点表示现在和过去两个时间；实箭头表示动作在延续；虚箭头表示动作可能持续到将来。

精品译文 一个老太太走到马路中央，这时一个警察朝她大声嚷道："我把手举起来，难道你不知道是什么意思吗？"

这位老太太答道："当然知道，我做了28年的老师了！"

比如，如果你现在有了男 / 女朋友，要告诉别人你们两人恋爱多长时间了，就可以这样说：

2 We ***have been*** in love for eight years and we are getting married next month. 我们恋爱有八年了，下个月就要结婚了。

如果已经结婚，在谈到自己的幸福婚姻时，可以这样说：

3 I ***have been*** married for over a year. I am happily married. 我结婚有一年多了，现在婚姻很幸福。

这两句话里的现在完成时态都表示"延续"思维，即从过去一直延续到现在的"恋爱"或"已婚"的状态。

再比如，谈到自己学英语的历史时，可以这样说：

4 I ***have learned*** English for over ten years now, but I still can't speak it well.

妙语点睛 在这句话里，"我"是在10年前开始学习英语的，但这个过去的动作一直延续到了现在，所以用了现在完成时态 have learned。

精品译文 我学英语都超过10年了，但现在还是说不好。

在电影《特洛伊》中，特洛伊的大王子郝克托尔（Hector）面对希腊联军的强劲攻势，为了鼓舞士气而说道：

5 All of my life I ***have lived*** by a code and the code is simple: honor the gods, love your women and defend your country. Troy is mother to us all. Fight for her! 整个一生我都信奉一条简单的准则，这就是：敬重神灵，深爱妻子，保卫国家。特洛伊就是我们的母亲。为她而战吧！

这里郝克托尔用了完成时态，表示从过去到现在自己一直所坚持的人生价值理念。

5.4.2 "延续事件"与时间状语的关系

从上一小节的讨论中可以看出，现在完成时表示"延续"性的意义时是很好理解和掌握的。但要想更深刻和全面地理解这一用法，还要注意以下三点：

一、谓语要表示"延续"

显然，既然是表示延续思维，句子的谓语动词就要给予配合，即要能够表示延续。具体来说，谓语必须是延续动词，如前面例句中的 learn/live，或者是能够表示延续状态的词，如 be 动词。如果是短暂动词，则不能表示这种延续思维，比如上一节中的例句 2 和例句 3，就不能说：

1 I ***have fallen*** in love for eight years. *

2 I ***have married*** for over a year. *

因为这里的 fall 和 marry 都是短暂动词，无法与延续性的时间状语（如 for eight years）连用。所以，上一节中的例句都用了表达状态的词，如 be in love 和 be married。注意，这里的 married 是形容词，所以 be married 并不是一个被动语态。

另外，大家需要注意的是，之所以说 I have fallen in love for eight years. * 这样的句子是错误的，是因为这里的 fall in love 是一个短暂动作，而短暂动词不能与延续性的时间状语（如 for eight years）连用。但这并不是说像 fall in love 这样的短暂动词不能用于现在完成时态。换句话说，句子错误的原因是**fall in love 这样的短暂动作与 for eight years 这样的延续性时间状语有语义上的冲突，而不是 fall in love 这样的短暂动作与现在完成时态有冲突**。笔者发现很多中国学生误解了这一点，他们干脆认为"短暂动词不能用于现在完成时态"，因此，像 I have fallen in love. 这样的句子是错误的。其实，像 I have fallen in love. 这样的句子是完全正确的。短暂动词用于完成时态时的含义和用法，我们将在 5.6 节详细讨论。所以，这里要再次强调的是，**短暂动词完全可以用于现在完成时态，此时不能和延续性的时间状语连用，而不是说短暂动词不能用于现在完成时态。**

二、要与“延续性时间状语”连用

表示延续思维的完成时态除了要有延续性的谓语之外，还必须有延续性的时间状语（durational adverbials）。具体来说，这种表示延续性动作或状态的完成时态一般必须接一个表示“一段时间”的延续性时间状语，以说明某个动作或状态持续到现在有多久了。下列例句均是“从过去开始并一直延续到现在”的时间表达方式，所以通常会和现在完成时态搭配。

1. since+时间点或从句

3 ***Since time began***, man ***has lived*** in fear of fire. 自古以来，人们就害怕发生火灾。

since 作时间引导词的用法将在 5. 9 节详细讨论。

2. for+时间段

4 Great changes ***have taken place*** in Beijing ***for the past few years.*** 近几年来，北京发生了巨大的变化。

3. “到目前为止”，“迄今为止”

这样的时间短语有：until now, up until now, up to now, up till now 和 so far 等。请看例句：

5 We ***have up until now failed*** to take any action to decide on a common language that would further communication between nations.

迄今为止，我们尚未采取任何措施来一种国际通用语言，以促进各国之间的交流。

4. “在最近几个/年/月以来”

这样的时间短语有：in the past few years, over the past few years, during the last three months, for the last few centuries, through centuries 和 throughout history 等。请看例句：

6 ***Throughout history*** man ***has had*** to accept the fact that all living things must die, for the very nature of life includes death. 自古以来，人类就不得不接受这样的事实：一切生物最终都会死亡，因为生命的本身包含了死亡。

最后需要提醒大家的是，除了与现在完成时态连用外，“for + 一段时间”还可以与一般过去时连用（详见《英语语法新思维初级教程——走近语法》中“一般过去时”的相关用法）。比如：

7 1) I ***have lived*** in China for 3 years.

2) I ***lived*** in China for 3 years.

妙语点睛 例句 1)表示现在“我”还在中国居住。既然到目前为止已经生活三年了，因此我们可以明确计算出“我”是三年前开始居住在中国的。例句 2)则只是说明“我”曾经在中国生活过三年，而且现在已经不住在中国了。这里三年的起止时间，即何时开始在中国居住，何时离开中国，我们都无从知晓。

精品译文 1)到目前为止，我已在中国住了三年了。

2)我曾经在中国生活过三年。

三、没有延续性的时间状语，则表示一个“完成了（complete）”的动作

以上其实已经给出了完成时态要表示延续思维所必须具有的两个条件：

一，谓语要表示延续；

二，要有延续性的时间状语。

具体来说，延续性思维的完成时态必须和延续性的时间状语连用才能表示一个延续到现在的动作或状态。

但是如果没有这个延续性的时间状语，句子用完成时态还正确吗？若正确，那又是什么意思呢？回答是：若没有延续性的时间状语，可以用完成时态，但表示的是一个**在过去已经完成的动作，而没有延续到现在**。

先看下面的例句：

8 John has lived in Paris ***for ten years.***

精品译文 约翰在巴黎生活 10 年了。

妙语点睛 这句话用了现在完成时态，表示 John 现在还在巴黎生活（John is still living in Paris now.）。但是如果没有延续性的时间状语而说成：John has lived in Paris.

则要理解成“约翰在巴黎生活过”，但现在他已不住在巴黎了。这句话可以接着往下说：

9 John has lived in Paris. That was ten years ago. He is now living in Beijing.
约翰在巴黎生活过，不过那是10年前的事了，他现在住在北京。

请注意，只有在特殊的上下文语境中，John has lived in Paris. 这句话才有可能当"延续"讲。比如：

10 A: Where has John lived since he left Beijing?

B: He ***has lived*** in Paris.

妙语点睛 这里，B的回答相当于说：He has lived in Paris ever since he left Beijing.

精品译文 A：约翰离开北京后一直在哪里生活？

B：他一直生活在巴黎。

再看下面这个笑话：

11 Dr. Findlay was passing one of his patients in the street. "Hello, Mrs. Merton. You haven't visited me for ages." "I know, doctor. I***'ve been*** ill."

妙语点睛 在这个语境中，虽然没有延续性的时间状语，但这里的完成时 have been ill 表示"一直在生病"，即表示延续事件。

精品译文 芬德雷医生在街上遇到他以前的一个病人，他问候道："你好，莫顿太太，你好久没有来我这里了。""我知道，医生。我最近一直在生病。"

请比较下列例句：

12 1）I ***have been*** a school teacher ***for 28 years now.***

2）I ***have been*** a school teacher.

妙语点睛 例句1）表示从事老师这个职业延续到了现在，即现在还是老师。例句2）则表示自己当过老师，有过当老师的生活经历，但现在已经不是老师了。

精品译文 1)我当老师到现在有28年了。

2)我曾经当过老师。

请读者分析下列短文中现在完成时态的意义：

13 You***'ve been*** in love, of course. If not, you've got it to come. Love is like the measles; we all have to go through it. Also like the measles, we take it only once. One never need be afraid of catching it a second time. No, we never sicken with love twice. Cupid spends no second arrow on the same heart.

妙语点睛 这句话中的 have been in love 后面没有接延续性的时间状语，所以这句话的意思是"你曾经恋爱过吧"，而不是说"你一直恋爱到现在"。这就不同于上面分析过的例句 I have been in love for eight years. 表示"恋爱延续到了现在"。

精品译文 你曾经恋爱过吧？如果没有，那你得尝试一次。恋爱就如同患麻疹，我们都得经历一次，且仅有一次。你根本不必担心会得上两次。的确，我们是不会二度"为伊消得人憔悴"的。爱神丘比特不会往同一颗心上射上第二支箭。

讲完关于恋爱的句子，下面再回到这个大家都很熟悉的关于结婚的例句：

14 I ***have been married*** for a year.

这个英文句子的意思不难理解，相信所有的读者朋友都能正确翻译，它的意思是：我结婚已经有一年了。

但是，如果将这个句子稍作如下改变：I have been married.

即把句末的时间状语 for a year 去掉，又该如何理解呢？这时这个句子的意思不是"我已经结婚了"，而是"我曾经结过婚"。

这句话的言外之意是："我"现在要么离婚了，要么丧偶了，总之是单身(single)。所以可以说，没有延续性的状语，延续状态顿时变成一个在过去完成的事件，而没有持续到现在。比如这里的"已婚"状态在现在已经结束。接下去还可以这么说：

15 I have been married. It ***was*** a troubled marriage. I am afraid I will never get married again. 我结过婚，那是一次很不幸的婚姻，我想我再也不敢结婚了。

讲到这里，笔者想起中国学生常犯的一个错误。比如当你向外国朋友介绍自己时说“我已经结婚了”，很多人以为这里有“已经”，那当然得用完成时态，于是就把这句话说成 I have been married.（我结过婚，后来离婚了。）听完这句话，你的外国朋友很可能是对你报以同情地说 I'm sorry to hear it. 听他这么说，你可能会糊涂了，或者还以为他对你有什么企图呢！其实，要表达“我已经结婚了”，就是 I am married. 这一简单的句子。由此可见，在交流的过程中正确使用时态是很重要的。

思维总结

本节讨论了现在完成时态的一个最简单的思维规律，即表示一个延续事件。这种延续性思维必须有两个条件：一是谓语动词必须是表示延续的，如延续性动词或延续状态；二是必须接有延续性的时间状语，才能表示延续到现在的活动。没有这样的时间状语则表示一个完成了的活动，而没有延续到现在。

下一节我们将讨论现在完成时态的第二种思维——“重复”动作。

5.5 重复事件

本节内容安排如下：

5. 5. 1 过去的事件“重复”到现在

（一）

在展开具体的讨论之前，请读者先来欣赏下面这篇美文：

1 **Teachers of Love**

I ***have had*** so many teachers in my life. I ***have had*** teachers in school. I ***have had*** teachers at home. I ***have had*** teachers in stores, on streets, and at playgrounds. I ***have had*** teachers in books. I ***have had*** teachers in nature. I ***have had*** teachers everywhere I***'ve gone, stayed, and lived.***

The teachers that I ***have valued and enjoyed*** most of all, though, ***have been*** the teachers who taught me about love. Teachers of love are not as rare as you would think either. I ***have seen*** teachers of love everywhere. The person who smiles happily when they drop money in a charity box is a teacher of love. The handicapped child who offers smiles, laughter, and hugs more freely than we adults ever will is a teacher of love. The person who sets corn out for starving deer and seed out for hungry birds in the winter time is a teacher of love. The big dog who shares half his food and a place in his doghouse with a little neighborhood puppy on a cold winter's night is a teacher of love. Everyone who spends their lives sharing great love through countless little acts of kindness is a teacher of love.

妙语点睛 作者用众多的现在完成时态“回顾”自己曾经遇到过的很多可以作为自己老师的人，这是因为他们的善行和爱心，所以作者把他们称为“爱心老师”。因此，这里的完成时态是表示“回顾”性的意义。但如果再仔细分析一下，就会发现它和前面表示“延续”的完成时态的思维有所不同。比如第一句：I ***have had*** so many teachers in my life.

这里 have had 真正的含义是表示“多次遇到”，这从 so many 以及名词复数 teachers 可以看出来。也就是说，这里的现在完成时态表示一个“重复”的事件(repeated events)。作者接下来使用的众多完成时的句子，无一不是表示这种重复的意义：

I ***have had*** teachers in school.

I ***have had*** teachers at home.

I ***have had*** teachers in stores, on streets, and at playgrounds.

I ***have had*** teachers in books.

I ***have had*** teachers in nature.

上面这些句子中的现在完成时都表示一个从过去重复到现在的事件，这从复数 teachers 就可以看出，这里表示"多个老师"。随后作者用下面这句话对上面的陈述作了一个总结：

I ***have had*** teachers everywhere ***I've gone, stayed, and lived.***

即表示"在我所到过的、停留过的、生活过的地方，都曾遇到众多老师"。紧接着作者笔锋一转，说道：The teachers that I ***have valued and enjoyed*** most of all, though, ***have been*** the teachers who taught me about love. Teachers of love are not as rare as you would think either.

即表示"最让我珍视和欣赏的老师，一直是那些教我懂得爱的人"。然后作者以下面这句话：I ***have seen*** teachers of love everywhere.

作为一个主题句来总领下文。于是，作者接下来铺排了众多的"爱心之师"：

The person who smiles happily when they drop money in a charity box...

The handicapped child who offers smiles, laughter, and hugs more freely than we adults ever will...

The person who sets corn out for starving deer and seed out for hungry birds in the winter time...

The big dog who shares half his food and a place in his doghouse with a little neighborhood puppy on a cold winter's night...

显然这些"爱心之师"是作者"重复不断"地在生活中遇见的，所以，这里用的现在完成时态都表示一个重复的事件。

所谓"重复事件"，就是表示站在现在的角度回顾到目前为止的一个时间段内(a time period up to now)，某一活动或事件重复发生了多次。其实，我们可以把完成时态这一"重复性"思维用法看作是上述"延续性"思维的一个特例——动作不是毫不间断地在连续发生，即不是一个延续性的活动（continuous activity)，而是断断续续地在重复，是一个重复活动(repeated activity)。我们可以用下图来表示：

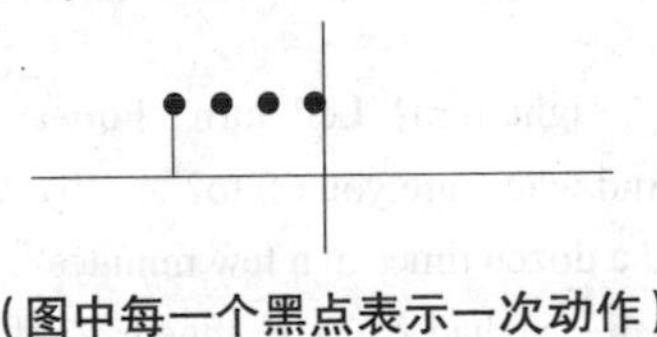

（图中每一个黑点表示一次动作）

精品译文 爱心老师

在我的人生中，我曾遇到过很多老师：在学校、在家里、在商店、在街上、在运动场、在书本中、在自然界。总之，在我所到过的、停留过的以及生活过的地方，都曾遇到过老师。

不过，最让我珍视和欣赏的老师，一直是那些教我懂得爱的人。这样的老师并不像你想象中那么少，我在各处都曾遇到过这样的"爱心老师"：把钱丢进募捐箱时，脸上洋溢着快乐微笑的人；比我们成年人更乐于给予人们微笑、快乐和拥抱的残疾儿童；在严寒的冬日里，喂饥饿的小鹿和小鸟吃玉米和种子的人；在寒冷的冬夜里，能把自己的食物和狗舍与附近的幼狗分享的一只狗。所有这些人、这些动物，无论他们行的是多么微不足道的善行，只要是点点滴滴的付出和爱心，都可以成为我们的"爱心老师"。

（二）

下面来分析在 5. 3 节提到的克林顿在 2001 年 1 月 18 日所作的卸任演说：

2 In all the work I ***have done*** as president, every decision I ***have made***, every executive action I ***have taken***, every bill I ***have proposed*** and ***signed***, ***I've tried*** to give all Americans the tools and conditions to build the future of our dreams, in a good society, with a strong economy, a cleaner environment, and a freer, safer, more prosperous world. (Selection of President Bill Clinton's farewell address to the nation on Jan. 18, 2001.)

妙语点睛 在这里，克林顿不厌其烦地使用完成时态，正是表示在他的八年总统任职期间，他"重复不断"地在 have done, have made decisions, have taken action, have proposed and signed bills。比如说"签署法案"，克林顿不可能是一直毫不间断"持续"地(continuously)在签署，这一签就持续了八年，而是表示在八年的总统任职期间，他"多次重复"签署各种不同的法案。

精品译文 （在过去的八年里）作为总统，我所做的每一项工作，作出的每一个决策，采取的每一个行政措施，以及提议并签署的每一个法案，都是在尽力为全体美国人民提供途径和创造条件，来实现美国未来的梦想——社会稳定、经济繁荣、环境美好，进而使得全世界更自由、更安全、更繁荣。

再看下面美国影星汤姆·克鲁斯(Tom Cruise)的从影经历：

3 Tom Cruise ***has been*** Hollywood's leading man for the last over 20 years. But when he was young, he didn't want to be an actor. In fact when he was at school he wanted to be a priest and spent a year training in a monastery. When he realized that this wasn't the life for him he turned to acting. He moved to New York and appeared in a few teen movies before starring in his first big hit, Top Gun in 1986. Since then he ***has made*** hit after hit movies.

妙语点睛 这段话里有两个现在完成时态：has been 和 has made，但两者的意义显然是不一样的。has been 表示一个延续的状态，所以属于完成时态的"延续"性思维；has made 则说明阿汤哥一次又一次地好戏不断，所以属于完成时态的"重复"性思维。

精品译文 过去二十多年来，汤姆·克鲁斯一直是好莱坞的一线男演员。但他少年时的梦想并不是当一名演员。事实上，在上学的时候，他曾经渴望成为一名牧师，并在修道院进修了一年。当他发现这种生活并不适合他时，才转而投身演艺事业。他移居纽约，在一些青少年电影里亮相。直到1986年，他主演了《壮志凌云》一片，才一炮打响，此后他便好戏不断。

由此可见，完成时态的这两种思维表达经常同时出现。比如，当我们在一个新地方生活了一段时间之后，往往会回顾说：我来某地方多久了，认识了很多新朋友。此时我们会说：

4 I***'ve been*** in Canada for six months. I***'ve met*** many new friends.

妙语点睛 这里的 have been 是完成时的延续性思维；而我们"结识(met)"新朋友不可能在一天完成，也不是一刻不停地时刻在延续，而是不断重复的一个过程，即属于典型的重复性思维。

精品译文 我来加拿大已经六个月了，我认识了很多新朋友。

请看这样一个笑话：

5 The coach commands the players: "Right turn! Left turn! Forward march!..." One of the players leaves the line shrugging his shoulders. "And where are you off to?" "I***'ve had*** enough! You don't know yourself what you want! You***'ve changed*** your mind a dozen times in a few minutes!"

妙语点睛 这里有两个现在完成时态：'ve had 和 've changed，但两者的意义是不一样的。首先，我们来看 've changed，这显然是典型的完成时态重复性思维，因为这名队员是抱怨他的教练在短短的几分钟之内多次改变主意，以至于让他们一会向左转、一会向右转，结果该队员不耐烦了，离开了队伍。其次，这里的 I've had enough(我受够了)是一个很好的表示"愤怒"的用语。同时注意这里的完成时态，既不是"延续"思维，也不是"重复"思维，而是完成时态的第三种思维——"单一短暂事件"的意义。关于这一点，我们将在第 5.6 节详细讨论。

精品译文 一名教练正在训练队员："向右转！向左转！齐步走！……"这时，有个队员不屑一顾地走出了队伍。"你要去哪里？""我受够了！你自己都不知道到底要怎样！几分钟之内你改变了多次主意！"

从以上的例子可以看出，完成时态表示重复性思维时，句中往往都会有较明显的表示重复概念的词语或语言标示(如复数-s)。比如：

6 I have had ***so many*** teachers in my life.

7 I have had ***teachers*** in school.

8 ...***every*** decision I have made, ***every*** executive action I have taken, ***every*** bill I have proposed and signed,...

9 Since then he has made ***hit after hit*** movies.

10 I've met ***many*** new friends.

11 You've changed your mind ***a dozen times*** in a few minutes!

上面的黑体字部分(如 so many)、名词复数-s(如 teachers, movies, friends)、every、hit after hit、many 以及表示次数的 a dozen times 等"语言标示"都表示多次重复的事件或活动，表示完成时态的重复性思维。

(三)

但是有时候，句中并没有出现上述这样明确表示重复活动的"语言标示"，但重复性思维隐含在说话的语境中。这时就要细心体会其中的重复意味，从而正确理解句子的内涵。我们来分析下面这个例句：

12 "For us this ***has been*** the most perfect way to remember her, and this is how she would want to be remembered."

妙语点睛 首先，应了解一下这句话的语境背景。这句话是英国的威廉王子在纪念母亲戴安娜的音乐会上说的。1997年8月31日，戴安娜在巴黎出车祸，香消玉殒。2007年7月1日是戴安娜诞辰46周年纪念日，威廉王子与哈里王子希望用戴安娜喜爱的音乐来纪念她。于是，由两位王子发起，7月1日当天在英国伦敦温布利体育场(Wembley Stadium)举办"献给戴安娜的音乐会"，借音乐会的形式纪念戴安娜王妃去世10周年(They organized the event to mark the 10th anniversary of their mother's death.)。整场音乐现场有六万多英国观众，并同时向世界各地140个国家现场转播，约有五亿观众观看。音乐会结束时，威廉王子说了上面这番话。国内媒体在报道这则新闻时是这么翻译的：

对我们来说，这是纪念她的最佳方式，这也是她所希望的纪念方式。

虽然说这么翻译也未尝不可，但它并没有很好地传达英语原句的意思。这里关键是要理解威廉王子为什么要用完成时态 has been，而不是直接说 is。

其实，这里的完成时态 has been 就是我们本节讨论的重复性思维表达。我们知道，自从戴安娜王妃去世10年来，英国举办过各种活动来纪念她。也就是说，到目前为止，纪念戴安娜的活动已经多次举办过，可以说是从过去到目前为止的重复发生的活动。现在，威廉王子在音乐会现场，他显然是在"回顾"过去10年的各种活动，然后得出结论说，这次音乐会"是纪念她的最佳方式"，这正是完成时态"回顾"性思维的体现，并且是表示一个重复到现在的活动，因而他要用完成时态说 For us this ***has been***...他用完成时态的另外一个意义还在于，完成时态还表明活动依然可以重复到将来，换句话说，以后一定还会有其他纪念戴安娜王妃的活动，因而也就可能出现比这次音乐会更好的其他纪念方式。因此，确切地说，这次音乐会是"迄今为止(up until now)"纪念她的最佳方式，这正是威廉王子用 has been 所要传达的意义。如果威廉王子用一般现在时态说成 For us this ***is*** the most perfect way to remember her,... 根据一般现在时态的思维特征——表示从过去到现在直至将来的一个永恒的状态，则意味着这次音乐会作为纪念戴安娜的方式是"前无古人，后无来者"的，是永远无法被超越的了。相信这不是威廉王子所期望的，所以他要用 has been 来给这次音乐会精确定位——这是**迄今为止**纪念她的最佳方式。

由此可见英语语言的特点，借用时态(如 has been)可以潜含如此丰富的"言外之意"，这对于一个中国英语学习者来说是比较难以把握的。如果不是深谙英语的思维表达之道，我们很难理解 has been 与 is 在这句话中的细微差别。比如笔者曾经拿这个句子做过试验，先让对方看一遍这个英语句子，并且在确认他们理解这句话的中文意思之后，又立即让他们复述这个英文句子，他们毫无例外地都用一般现在时态说 For us this ***is*** the most... 显然，他们在读这个英语原句的时候，对其中的 has been 所要传达的"言外之意"并没有真正理解，而只是想着中文的"这是"就对应英文的 this is。对于这种在英语阅读过程中"丢失"英语原文所要传达的"言外之意"的现象，笔者称之为英语阅读过程中的"信息过滤"或"信息失真"。这主要是由中英文思维表达上的巨大差异造成的。比如笔者发现很多英语学习者在读英语时，注意力主要集中在实词上，如动词、名词和形容词，而很少关注**动词的时态变化、情态动词和介词的微妙含义以及连词的使用，殊不知，后者才是英文思维表达规律的附着载体**。国人英语学不好，不会说、不会写，主要原因就在于此。现在请读者测试一下自己，不看英语原文，将下面这句中译文还原成英文：这也是她所希望的纪念方式。

现在请努力回忆一下，上面的英语原文是怎么说的，然后写下你自己的译文……

写完后，将你的译文和下面的原文比较一下：

...and this is how she would want to be remembered.

现在你们自己已经有了比较结果。当然笔者不可能知道你们的译文，但有几点要注意：

首先，译文中的"也"对应着 and；

其次，"方式"对应着连词 how；

再次，"纪念"应该是被动语态，这在中文里是看不出来的，但在英文的逻辑表达中要说成 be remembered，因为主语 she 与 remember 是被动关系；

最后，"希望"要译成 ***would*** want，这里 would 是最难的。这个测试的主要目的是希望读者能够写出 would，所以，如果你的译文里有 would，应该为自己喝彩和鼓掌！

为什么非要加 would？这是英语虚拟语气的思维表达所要求的(我们将在第七章中讨论虚拟语气)。因为在音乐会现场，戴安娜已经不在人世，她无法"希望"了，所以要说"她所希望"只能有一个虚拟的条件——如果她现在还活着的话(if she ***were*** alive)，她则会希望(she ***would want***...)。也就是说，这是一个对现在情况的虚拟，表示与现在事实相反的情况，此时主句的谓语要用 would do(从句谓语用过去时，be 动词要用 were)，所以我们要表示 would want。

因此，对于上面这个英语句子，读者关键要用心体会两个动词形式：一个是 has been，这是动词时态的问题；一个是 would want，这是情态动词的问题。这就是我们在上面强调的——动词时态、情态动词的微妙含义等才是英文思维表达规律的附着载体！

分析至此，可以对上面的译文作一个修改，以使译文能够反映出 has been 和 would 的精确含义。比如我们可以这样翻译：

对我们来说，这是迄今为止纪念她的最佳方式。如果她在天有灵的话，我想这也是她所希望的纪念方式。

上面的 has been 表达的就是一个重复思维，但句中并没有名词复数、many 或 every 等表示重复活动的“语言标示”，但在上下文语境中已经潜含了重复意味(5. 8 节还会再次讨论这个句子，到时候读者就能更深刻地理解这里 has been 的重复意义)。

美国前总统吉米·卡特 (Jimmy Carter)2007 年 5 月 19 日在接受《阿肯色民主公报》(Arkansas Democrat-Gazette)的采访时，严厉批评了布什政府是有史以来在国际关系上表现最差的美国政府。他说：

13. I think as far as the adverse impact on the nation around the world, this administration ***has been*** the worst in history. The overt reversal of America's basic values as expressed by previous administrations, including those of George H. W. Bush and Ronald Reagan and Richard Nixon and others, ***has been*** the most disturbing to me.

妙语点睛 这里的 has been 也表示重复思维。卡特在说这番话时，是拿布什政府与美国历史上历届总统领导的政府作比较（这种比较可以从下文他提到的 previous administrations, including those of George H. W. Bush and Ronald Reagan and Richard Nixon and others 看出来)，然后得出结论说“本届政府是有史以来最糟糕的”，这即体现了重复思维，也体现出完成时态表示“回顾”性这一核心意义。他说这番话的时间是 2007 年 5 月，当时布什还是美国总统。如果在布什不是美国总统的时候再作这番评论，则要用一般过去时 was 了。

精品译文 我认为，就在全球范围内对美国造成的负面影响而言，本届政府是有史以来最糟糕的。现任政府公然违背了老布什、罗纳德·里根、理查德·尼克松等往届政府所展现的美国基本的价值观，这使我最感恼火。

卡特一向反对伊拉克战争，而且经常直言不讳地批评布什总统。卡特对布什政府的中东政策和“先发制人”打击伊拉克的做法提出强烈批评，认为现政权背离了美国历届政府阐述的基本价值观。民主党人卡特在 1977 年到 1981 年间任美国总统，2002 年，他获得了诺贝尔和平奖。

除了抨击布什政府的政策，卡特还对英国首相布莱尔及其与美国的关系进行了同样强烈的批评。在接受英国广播公司的采访时，卡特说，英国“盲目”地支持美国发动伊拉克战争，这对于世界来说是个“重大的悲剧”。在回答如何评价布莱尔对于布什的支持时，卡特对英国广播公司(BBC)形容说：“令人厌恶、忠诚、盲目、明显的奉承……我认为，英国几乎坚定不移地支持布什政府并不明智的伊拉克政策，已经成为这个世界的重大悲剧。”对此，卡特进一步解释说，因为有了英国对布什政府在伊拉克问题上的支持，使得各方反对伊拉克战争的努力变得更加困难。如果英国当时反对伊战的话，整个情况将会有所不同。我们来看卡特的原话是怎么说的：

14 Carter also lashed out at British prime minister Tony Blair. Asked how he would judge Blair's support of Bush, the former president said: “Abominable. Loyal. Blind. Apparently subservient. And I think the almost undeviating support by Great Britain for the ill-advised policies of President Bush in Iraq ***has been*** a major tragedy for the world,” Carter told British Broadcasting Corp. radio.

妙语点睛 这里的 has been 并不是表示“重复”意义，而是表示“延续”意义——因为布莱尔一直支持布什政府的伊拉克政策，所以他的存在一直是一个灾难。

2007 年 10 月，卡特在接受英国 BBC 采访时对现任(2007 年 10 月时)美国副总统切尼(Cheney)也提出了批评。他说切尼是一个好战分子，自己逃避兵役，在过去的 10 年中却一直强硬地通过军事手段在世界其他地方谋求美国霸权。他说切尼在很多问题上都是错误的，并说他对于美国来说是一场灾难：

15 You know he***'s been*** a disaster for our country. I think he***'s been*** overly persuasive on President George Bush and quite often he***'s prevailed.***

妙语点睛 这里的 has been 并不是表示"重复"意义，而是表示"延续"意义——从切尼担任美国副总统一直到目前说话时为止，所以，我们采用"一直"来对应翻译。同样道理，如果切尼不再担任美国副总统，那么要对他作出如此评论，则应该用一般过去时 was 了。

精品译文 你们知道，他一直是我们国家的灾难，我想他一直对总统布什过度诱导，并且经常取得成功。

对于卡特的这番批评，网上有读者这么回应：

16 Disaster? Please, he's more than just a disaster. He is a catastrophe, we may never recover from the harm he***'s done*** to our country. The best we can hope to do is heal and move on. This administration, particularly because of Cheney, ***has been*** a great embarrassment and shameful blemish on the United States.

精品译文 灾难？得了吧，他何止是灾难，简直就是一个巨大的祸根！我们国家或许再也无法从他造成的伤害中恢复了。我们能做的最好的事就是尽量治愈创伤，然后继续前行。布什这届政府已经给美国带来了巨大的尴尬，使美国蒙羞，这尤其是因为切尼的原因。

不过，他对美国国务卿赖斯却赞誉有加。在接受英国 BBC 的采访时，卡特表示："我对赖斯勇敢抵抗（切尼）充满惊叹，她甚至在担任安全顾问时就这样做了。现在作为国务卿，她的影响显然大于过去，我希望她能获胜。"

（四）

最后，需要说明的是，正如前文所说，"重复意义"的完成时态可以看作是"延续事件"完成时态的一个特例，所以，这两种完成时的思维方式是如此地密切相关，以至于有时我们很难对二者进行严格的界定区分。比如：

17 For more than eighty years, scientists ***have argued*** over whether life exists on the planet Mars.

妙语点睛 如果把 have argued 当作延续性思维来理解，则可译为"八十多年以来，科学家们一直在争论火星上是否有生命存在"。强调争论一直在持续，已经持续了八十多年。

如果把 have argued 当作重复性思维来理解，则可译为"八十多年以来，就火星上是否有生命存在这一问题，科学家们不断地挑起争论"。表示争论了一段时间告一段落，若干年后，争论又被再次挑起或被多次挑起。强调八十多年当中，"争论"多次被挑起，每一次争论只持续若干年。

精品译文 延续思维：八十多年以来，科学家们一直在争论火星上是否有生命存在。

重复思维：八十多年以来，就火星上是否有生命存在这一问题，科学家们不断地挑起争论。

比较模糊的翻译：八十多年以来，科学家们一直就火星上是否有生命存在这一问题不断地进行争论。

正如前文图示，对于完成时态的"延续"和"重复"两种思维表达，我们可以分别用"直线"和"重复的点"来表示，如图所示：

延续：▬▬▬▬▬▬▬▬▬▬▬▬

重复：● ●

其实，用"重复的点"来表示重复活动相当于一种比较极端的情况，我们完全可以用各种虚线来表示重复。比如：

▬ · ▬ · ▬ · ▬ · ▬ · ▬ · ▬

▬ ▬ ▬ ▬ ▬ ▬ ▬ ▬ ▬ ▬ ▬

▬ · ▬ · ▬ · ▬ · ▬ · ▬ · ▬

▬▬ ▬▬ ▬▬ ▬▬ ▬▬ ▬▬ ▬▬

可以看到，由上往下的虚线越来越接近一条不间断的直线，也就是说，正如从不连贯的"点"到连贯的"直线"中间存在一个过渡区域一样，在重复思维与延续思维中间也存在一个过渡区，而不是"一刀切"，非此即彼。这就解释了为什么重复活动与延续活动有时难以区分。比如说：

18 I ***have lived*** in Beijing for 10 years.

这句话可以表示"我"一直生活在北京，一刻也没有离开过北京；也可能是表示在北京前后断断续续地生活了10年，中间也离开过北京。此时相当于说：

I *have lived* in Beijing *on and off* for 10 years.

我们还可以说：

I *have lived* in Beijing *every winter* for 10 years.

表示"我"每年冬天都回到北京生活，前后已经持续了10年了。这同样是重复与延续兼而有之的活动，相当于这样一条虚线：

— — — — —

因此，在实际使用中，我们不必非得严格地界定一种活动是"重复发生"还是在"一直延续"，只要真正理解完成时有这两种思维方式即可。

5.5.2"重复事件"与时间状语的关系

正如上面指出的，重复与延续难以严格区分，因此5.4.2小节列举的时间状语也都可以用于重复思维表达的句子中，在此不再赘述。

本一小节要讨论重复活动与时间状语的关系，将涉及现在完成时态与一般过去时态的区别问题。先来比较下面这两个例句：

1 1) I *have called* him three times this morning.

2) I *called* him three times this morning.

妙语点睛 这两句话的区别仅一字(have)之差，但意思的差别很大。这两句接的时间状语都是this morning，那为什么可以同时采用两种不同的时态呢？

在例句1)中，既然采用了现在完成时态，而且是表示重复的活动(因为有three times这样的"重复标示")，所以该句强调的是到目前为止的一个时间段内重复的活动，或者说过去的动作called重复到了现在，这里的"现在"显然就是this morning。也就是说，例句1)的说话时间是"今天上午"。而例句1)要表达的意思其实相当于说：

I *have called* him three times *so far* this morning.

即表示"我今天上午到目前为止已经给他打过三次电话了"。言外之意是，随着现在的说话时间this morning往将来推移，"我"还可能继续给他打电话，可能打第四次、第五次……等等。由此可见，这里的"打电话(have called)"具有"将来可重复性(repeatable)"这个特点。

相比之下，例句2)与例句1)有很大的不同。既然采用了一般过去时态，则表明事情发生在过去，与现在没有什么联系，因此例句2)的说话时间可能是在"今天下午"或"今天晚上"。进而也就决定了"我""今天上午"给他打电话的次数仅为三次，没有继续重复的可能性("我"当然可以继续给他打电话，但已经不属于"今天上午"的活动次数了)。由此可见，这里的"打电话(called)"不具有"将来可重复性(repeatable)"这个特点。

简言之，例句1)和例句2)有下列两点区别：

一，说话的时间点不同：例句1)是在"今天上午"说的，例句2)则是在"今天下午"或"今天晚上"说的。而这一差别不是从句子的字面上能看出来的，而与具体的交际语境密切相关，这就是由语言之外的信息(即"超语言信息extra-linguistic information")决定的。这也证明了时态表达的灵活性，以及说话的语境对语言表达的重要性。

二，可重复性不同：例句1)中的have called具有"可重复性"，而例句2)中的called不具有"可重复性"。

精品译文 1)我今天上午到目前为止已经给他打过三次电话了。

2)我今天上午给他打了三次电话。

由这个例句所揭示的have called与called在"可重复性"方面的差别可以推而广之，**即现在完成时态具有"将来可重复性"，而一般过去时态不具有"将来可重复性"**。这是判断用现在完成时态还是用一般过去时态的重要原则，笔者称这个原则为**"可重复性"原则**(Principle of Repeatability)。下面举例详细说明。

一、可重复原则是现在完成时态的一条根本原则

我们先来看下面这个例句:

2 His father ***has been dead*** for three years.

这个英文句子的意思不难理解(相信所有的读者朋友都能正确翻译),意思是“他爸爸去世已经有三年了”。但是,对这个句子稍作如下改变:

His father has been dead. *

即把句末的时间状语 for three years 去掉,又该如何理解这句话呢?我相信,看到这个句子,一定有读者说,这有何难,不就是把时间状语去掉了嘛!部分读者会把这句话理解成:他爸爸已经死了。

其实,这样理解是不正确的,这句英文真正的意思是:他爸爸曾经死过。

不需笔者解释,大家都知道这就意味着人死了是可以复活的——他爸爸曾经死过,后来又复活了,现在还活得好好的。显然,除非你真的相信人都像耶稣一样,死后是能够复活的(unless you believe in resurrection),否则这个句子就有问题了。因而,在英文里,这个句子一般被认为是错误的,因为没有使用它的场合——人是不能死而复生的。

说到这里,也许有读者会追问一句——那么“他爸爸已经死了”用英文该怎么说?其实,这句话要看上下文的语境。比如,说到你某位朋友的爸爸,如果你只是要说明他爸爸已经过世了这一事实,只需说 His father ***is dead***. 但若是你这位朋友的爸爸刚刚去世,你的朋友当然很悲痛伤心、精神恍惚,当别人问你他怎么了,你就可以说是因为 His father ***has died.*** 这里的现在完成时态就是我们将在 5.6 节讨论的第三种用法——过去发生的事件(比如朋友的父亲去世)对现在有影响(比如你朋友现在悲痛的表现)。

所以,对于像“死亡”这样天然不具有重复性的事件,即不能表示来回往复的发生,就不能用现在完成时来表示“过去经历”。同样,人不能返老还童,所以我们不能说:

I have been old. *

这句话的意思是“我曾经老过”,言外之意是我现在又年轻了。显然,人是不能返老还童的。套用王朔在说到“80后”一代时的一句话:谁没年轻过呀,但你们老过吗?谁也不能说自己曾经老过(I have been old. *),只能说自己曾经年轻过(I have been young.)。

综上所述,我们看到,事件的可重复性对于现在完成时态具有重要意义。如果是一个天然不具有重复性的事件,就不能用现在完成时来表达。

二、可重复原则与将来的时间有关

这种可重复性往往与将来的时间有关。我们知道,现在完成时是一定要与现在发生联系的,而“现在”又处在过去与将来的临界位置,是一个随时会成为过去的动态时刻,所以要想保证与“现在”有联系,现在完成时态往往会把“现在”延伸至“将来”。也就是说,现在完成时态所表达的动作或状态往往都含有持续或重复到将来某一个时间点的意味,即现在完成时与将来的时间有关,也就是笔者这里说的“将来可重复性”原则。**现在完成时态可以说是以现在的时间为参照来谈一个可以持续或重复到将来的事件。**请读者认真体会下列例句:

3 1) How many people ***have entered*** for the race?

2) How many people ***entered*** for the race?

妙语点睛 虽然这两个句子都可以译成“有多少人报名参加这个比赛”,但在英文中,两个句子所使用的语境以及要表达的时间是不同的。

在例句 1)中,完成时态表达了一个重复活动,真正的含义是“到目前为止有多少人报名参加这个比赛”,相当于说 How many people ***have entered*** for the race ***so far***?其言外之意是,这个比赛还没有开始举行,是一个将来的活动。说话人关心的是到现在为止报名参加的人数。所以,这正是上面提到的“现在完成时是以现在的时间为参照来谈一个可以持续或重复到将来的事件”。这里是重复到将来的事件——不断有人报名参加,即具有“将来可重复性”。如果比赛已经结束了,成为了一个过去的事件,则“(报名 enter for)”就已没有“将来可重复性”了,此时我们就不能用现在完成时态,而只能用一般过去时态,这正是例句 2)要表达的意思。在例句 2)中,用一般过去时态表明这个比赛已经结束了,而不是一个将来事件。该句真正的意思是“有多少人报名参加了那次比赛”,显然,此时我们不能加 so far 说成 How many people ***entered*** for the race ***so far***?*

精品译文 1)到目前为止,有多少人报名参加这个比赛?

2)有多少人报名参加了那次比赛?

再比如下面这个例句：

4 Many athletes ***have entered*** for the Olympic Games this year.

妙语点睛 这里用了现在完成时态，表明奥运会还没有举行，这里的"报名"是一个可以重复到将来的活动。

精品译文 很多运动员报名参加了今年的奥运会。

以上谈到的是重复事件的现在完成时与将来的时间有密切联系。其实，即使是一个单一的事件而不是一个重复活动，如果使用了现在完成时态，同样与将来时间有关系。请看例句：

5 I ***have entered*** for the examination but I don't want to take it.

妙语点睛 这个句子用了现在完成时态，表明是将来的事件——考试是在将来举行。

精品译文 这次考试我已经报名了，但我不想考。

我们再来分析下面的对话：

6 A: ***Have*** you ***visited*** the new exhibit?

B: Not yet, but it will be at the student center until June.

妙语点睛 从B的回答中我们知道这个"展览会(exhibit)"还没有结束，是一个可以持续到将来的事件，因而具备了将来可持续性，所以用了现在完成时态。如果说话人问的是 Did you visit the new exhibit?则表明这个展览会已经撤展结束了，已是一个过去的事件。

精品译文 A：这次新的展览会你去参观了吗？

B：还没有去，不是一直在学生中心展览到6月份才结束嘛。

7 A: I***'ve been invited*** to a dinner party at Janet's. Do you think I should bring something?

B: You could pick up a cake. Chocolate is her favorite.

妙语点睛 从这个对话的语境中我们知道，这个 dinner party 还没有举行，是一个将来的事件。不过，"邀请(invite)"现在已经发生了，它的影响会一直持续到现在及未来直到 dinner party 结束，所以用了现在完成时态。如果用一般过去时说 I ***was invited*** to a dinner party at Janet's. 则只表示一个过去的事件，即 dinner party 已经结束了。

精品译文 A：我受到邀请去珍妮特家参加晚宴，你认为我该带点什么东西去吗？

B：你可以买一份蛋糕嘛，巧克力口味的她最喜欢。

三、可重复性原则与过去时间

大家知道，在英文中，确定的过去时间状语(如 yesterday 和 last night)不能用于现在完成时态，这可以用可重复原则来解释。因为过去时间状语表明事件在过去已经完成而无法延续或重复到现在及未来，这就违背了完成时态的将来可重复性原则，故现在完成时不能使用确定的过去时间状语。请比较：

8 1) I ***was*** absent four times ***last semester.***

2) I ***have been*** absent twice ***this semester.***

妙语点睛 在例句1)中，过去时间状语 last semester 表明"缺课(absent)"这个事件已经结束，即上学期只有确定的四次缺课。该事件不具有可重复性，所以不能用完成时态。在例句2)中，这学期还没有结束，随着时间的推移还可能有更多次数的"缺课(absent)"。该事件具有未来可重复性，所以要用现在完成时态。

精品译文 1)我上学期逃课四次。

2)这学期到目前为止我逃过两次课。

四、可重复性原则与现在时间

所谓现在时间，是指诸如 today, this week 和 this year 等这样的时间状语。这样的时间状语一般都会用于现在完成时态，如果有特殊的语境信息表明某个事件无法继续延续或重复到现在及将来，就用一般过去时。换句话说，现在时间可以用于现在完成时态或一般过去时态。请比较：

9　1) ***I haven't seen*** him ***this morning.***

2) I ***didn't see*** him ***this morning.***

妙语点睛　这个例句类似于本节开头的第一个例句，即“打电话”场景的那个例子。不同的时态，表明了说话的时间不同：

例句1）用了现在完成时，而完成时是要与“现在”发生联系的，故例句1）说话的时间是this morning。该事件具有可重复性，随着时间的推移，“我”有可能会见到他。例句2)用的是一般过去时，说明this morning已经成为过去的时间，故例句2)说话的时间是在“今天下午”或“今天晚上”。该事件不具有可重复性，“我今天上午没有见到他”已是确定无疑的事件，不可改变了。

精品译文　1)今天上午到现在我还一直没有见到他。

2)我今天上午没有见到他。

以上例句是通过“说话时间”的不同来确定句子的时态，而这里的“说话时间”不能从该句的字面上反映出来，属于“超语言信息(extra-linguistic information)”，这与说话的真实语境相关。所以，对于现在时间，若是用于一般过去时态，则往往是由这些“超语言信息”决定的，这在书面语上看不出来，只能通过解释来澄清。但若是在口语交际中，这些“超语言信息”是再明确不过的了，而无需过多地说明。所以说，时态的使用是灵活的，是与语境密切相关的。比如下面这个例句：

10　1) I ***have made*** five phone calls ***today.***

2) I ***made*** five phone calls ***today.***

妙语点睛　这里的例句1)用现在完成时态，则表明“打电话”这个活动还会重复到未来，今天很可能会继续打第六个、第七个电话。而例句2)用一般过去时态，则表明“打电话”这个活动在今天不会再重复了，今天总共就只打了五个电话。

我们可以随便想象一下这两个句子不同的使用语境：比如你在一家公司做电话销售员，你的工作就是每天不断地打电话联系你的客户，推销产品。在今天上午10点钟的时候，你和同事交流时说“我今天打了五个电话了”，此时显然你就得用现在完成时态说I have made five phone calls today. 而如果你在下午下班后和同事交流时说“我今天打了五个电话”，此时显然你不会再打电话了，所以要说I made five phone calls today.

精品译文　1)我今天打了五个电话了。

2)我今天打了五个电话。

五、可重复性原则与一般时间

上面我们讨论了过去时间和现在时间与时态表达的关系，现在我们来看一般时间与时态的关系。所谓一般时间，是指诸如in the morning这样不确定是现在还是过去的时间。

大家都知道，一个句子如果出现了具体的过去时间状语，那就不能使用现在完成时态。比如我们不能说：

11　I ***have gotten up*** at five o'clock ***this morning.*** *

但是很多人据此就误认为，只要出现了表示某一时刻的时间状语，句子就一定不能使用现在完成时态。其实不然，比如我们看下面这个例句：

12　I ***have gotten up*** at five o'clock ***in the morning.***

很多读者看了上面这个句子，也许很快就认为这是错误的句子，认为有具体时间状语at five o'clock in the morning就不能和现在完成时连用。其实这是误解。仔细比较11、12两句就会发现二者的不同：前一句用了this morning(今天早晨)，而在说话的时候，“今天早晨”一定已经成了过去，所以有了这样具体的过去时间状语，就不能用现在完成时态。但是后一句是用了in the morning(在早晨)，而“在早晨”并不是指“今天早晨”。因此，at five o'clock this morning是一个具体的过去时间，但at five o'clock in the morning并不是指一个具体的过去时间；前者只有一次，但后者可以无数次地重复。所以，具备了这样的“可重复性(repeatable)”，完全可以用现在完成时态来表达。后一句就是表示到目前为止的一个“重复活动”，是一个典型的现在完成时用法，翻译成“我曾经在早晨五点钟起过床”，说话人这样表达的言外之意是要强调“五点钟”是一个很早的时间，而自己曾经这么早就起床，即表明自己具有早起这样的“过去经历”。类似的我们还可以说：

13 I ***have gone swimming*** at 12 ***at midnight.***

这句话的意思就是"我曾经在夜里 12 点去游过泳"，同样表示自己的"重复经历"。当然，我们不能说：

14 I ***have gone swimming*** at 12 ***last night.*** *

六、可重复性原则与地点表达

有时，地点状语起着表明说话时间的作用，因为地点的转化总是伴随着时间的变化。请比较例句：

15 1) ***In my hometown***, I ***had*** five jobs.

2) ***In this city***, I ***have had*** two jobs.

妙语点睛 在例句 1)中，地点状语 in my hometown 表明"我"现在人不在老家，这个地点状语暗含了过去的时间，所以该句要用一般过去时态，该事件不具有可重复性。在例句 2) 中，地点状语 in this city 表明"我"现在人在这个城市，这个地点状语暗含了现在的时间，该句的意思是"到目前为止我做过两份工作"，该事件具有可重复性，所以用现在完成时态。

精品译文 1)我在老家的时候，做过五份不同的工作。

2)在这个城市，我到目前为止做过两份不同的工作。

七、可重复性原则与死人情况

一般来说，谈到有关死人的情况，往往都是无法持续和重复的，即不具有将来可重复性，所以，涉及死人的句子通常要用一般过去时态（If you refer to the experiences of a dead person, you must use the simple past tense because nothing more can be added to that person's experience.)而不能用现在完成时态。这里举一个关于电影明星的例句。我们知道，美国著名影星玛丽莲·梦露(Marilyn Monroe)已不在人世，所以谈到关于她的情况时，往往要用一般过去时态。而美国人称"大嘴美人"的茱莉亚·罗伯茨(Julia Roberts)现在(至少在笔者 2007 年 10 月写这本书的时候)还活着，所以谈到关于她的情况时，就会用到现在完成时态。请比较：

16 1) Marilyn Monroe ***starred*** in many movies. She died in 1962.

2) Julia Roberts ***has starred*** in many American movies.

精品译文 1)玛丽莲·梦露于 1962 年去世，她生前出演过多部电影。

2)茱莉亚·罗伯茨出演过很多美国电影。

如果将对茱莉亚·罗伯茨的介绍改为一般过去时态，说成：

17 Julia Roberts ***starred*** in many American movies.

则会有两种情况：一是等她去世之后这么说，二是她明确宣布退出影坛了。但这两个条件现在都不满足，所以上面这个句子在 native speaker 听来就显得有点奇怪(sounds odd)。而后一种情况适合日本影星山口百惠，虽然她还活着，但已息影多年，所以要用一般过去时来谈她的从影经历。

再比如上面讲阿汤哥的从影经历的这个例句：

18 Since then he ***has made*** hit after hit movies.

在上面讲解第四点"可重复性原则与现在时间"时我们提到了"超语言信息(extra-linguistic information)"，这与说话的真实语境相关，有时需要说话人具备一定的背景常识。其实，这里谈到的死人的情况也属于超语言信息的一种。如果一个说话者不知道玛丽莲·梦露为何许人，没有这个娱乐常识，那么他很可能会用现在完成时态来谈她的情况。

下面我们要谈到的也是一种"超语言信息"的情况。

八、可重复性原则与特定语境

有时，这种"超语言信息"的背景知识并不是一个众所周知的常识，而只是交际双方共有知识(shared knowledge)的一部分，此时到底用现在完成时态还是一般过去时态，则取决于具体语境。如果有语言外的信息决定了某一活动不再延续重复，就要用一般过去时态。请比较：

19 1) ***Have*** you ever ***fallen off*** a horse?

2) ***Did*** you ever ***fall off*** a horse?

妙语点睛 在例句 1)中，用了现在完成时态，意味着“骑马”这个活动没有结束，将来还要骑马，因此 fall off a horse 这个事件可能重复发生。在例句 2)中，用了一般过去时态，意味着“骑马”这项活动不再持续，说话人不再骑马了，因此，fall off a horse 这个事件不可能重复发生。

精品译文 1)到目前为止，你骑马从马背上摔下来过吗？

2)你以前骑马的时候，从马背上摔下来过吗？

我们来看下面这个完整的对话。如果现在还骑马，我们就说：

A: ***Have*** you ever ***fallen off*** a horse?

B: Yes, I***'ve fallen off*** quite often.

精品译文 A：到目前为止，你骑马从马背上摔下来过吗？

B：是的，我经常从马背上摔下来。

如果现在不骑马了，就要说：

A: ***Did*** you ever ***fall off*** a horse?

B: Yes, I ***did*** occasionally.

精品译文 A：你以前骑马的时候，从马背上摔下来过吗？

B：摔过，不过只是偶尔摔下来。

由此可见，“可重复性(repeatability)”是现在完成时态的一个重要的思维特征，但这一特征是很多英语学习者所忽略的甚至是根本不知道的，这必然会影响到他们正确理解和有效使用现在完成时这一重要时态。

在下一节，我们还会结合“单一事件”完成时态来讲解可重复性原则的应用。

思维总结

本节重点讨论了现在完成时态表示重复意义——到目前为止的一个时间段内重复发生的活动，并提醒读者，由于我们可以把“重复”活动看作是“延续”活动的特例，所以有时“延续”和“重复”难以区分，对此不必严格界定。5.5.2 小节着重讨论了完成时态的一个重要特征——将来可重复原则，通过这个原则，可以区分现在完成时态与一般过去时态。

思维训练

Exercise 5.5（Key: P339）

请用括号中动词的适当时态填空。

1. Tanya ______（be）very persistent about talking to me. She ______（call）six times!
2. I ______（tell）you five times how to use this computer program, but you keep making the same mistakes over and over.
3. A total of 36, 832 fires in China ______（kill）971 people during the first quarter of the year, injuring 1, 228 and causing 310 million yuan in direct economic losses, a source with the statistics said.
4. Give him another chance

   Husband: I've got to get rid of my chauffeur; he ______（nearly, kill）me four times.

   Wife: Oh, give him another chance.
5. 下面短文是关于美国著名黑人歌星 Quincy Jones 的：

   And now, in time for Valentine's Day, Jones ______（release）a new 25-song double-CD entitled “From Q, With Love”, a collection of his favorite love songs that he ______（produce）since 1966. Quincy Jones ______（nominate）for 77 Grammys, and he ______（win）26.
6. A: Did you see this article on the exhibit of eighteenth-century prints that opened today?

   B: Yes, and I ______（already, buy）a ticket to see it next month.
7. A: They've just announced the flight ______（delay）until four o'clock.

   B: Oh no! How are we going to kill two hours?

8. A: How many interviews ______ you ______ (have) this month?
   B: I ______ (have) two interviews so far this month.
9. A: How many interviews ______ you ______ (have) last month?
   B: I ______ (have) four interviews last month.
10. Audrey Hepburn ______ (star) in many movies. She died on January 20, 1993 in Tolochnaz, Switzerland, from colon cancer.

附录: Teachers of Love

I ***have had*** so many teachers in my life. I ***have had*** teachers in school. I ***have had*** teachers at home. I ***have had*** teachers in stores, on streets, and at playgrounds. I ***have had*** teachers in books. I ***have had*** teachers in nature. I ***have had*** teachers everywhere I***'ve gone***, ***stayed***, and ***lived***.

The teachers that I ***have valued*** and ***enjoyed*** most of all, though, ***have been*** the teachers who taught me about love. Teachers of love are not as rare as you would think either. I ***have seen*** teachers of love everywhere. The person who smiles happily when they drop money in a charity box is a teacher of love. The handicapped child who offers smiles, laughter, and hugs more freely than we adults ever will is a teacher of love. The person who sets corn out for starving deer and seed out for hungry birds in the winter time is a teacher of love. The big dog who shares half his food and a place in his doghouse with a little neighborhood puppy on a cold winter's night is a teacher of love.

Everyone who spends their lives sharing great love through countless little acts of kindness is a teacher of love. Do you want to know something wonderful? You can be a teacher of love, too. You can be a person who gives encouragement and joy to a soul in need. You can be a person who cares for a sick friend, who helps out a hurting heart, and who shares cheerfulness and kindness with everyone everywhere. You can be a person who picks up trash off the ground and plants flowers and trees in it. You can be a person who saves a dog or cat by adopting it and offering it your love. You can be a person who works hard everyday to make the world a better place by choosing and sharing all the love and joy you possibly can.

You can be what God wants each and every one of us to be: a teacher of beautiful, glorious, and unconditional love.

5.6 单一事件

笔者相信，凡是学过现在完成时态的读者，耳边都会经常回荡着这样一句话：

"过去的事件对现在有影响。"

本节将对这句话进行详细讨论，因为它是现在完成时态三大思维用法之一。简言之，现在完成时可以表示**影响现在的过去"单一事件"**。正是这一用法困扰着广大的英语学习者，它是完成时态最难理解和应用的一种用法，因为它与说话的语境密切相关，也即与上一节提到的"超语言信息"有关。笔者将把这句话拆分成两方面来解释：一，何谓"对现在有影响"？二，何谓"过去事件"？因此，本节内容安排如下：

5.6.1 何谓"对现在有影响"？
5.6.2 何谓"过去事件"？
5.6.3 新闻热点(hot news)——近的过去
5.6.4 过去的经历(past experience)——远的过去
5.6.5 "单一事件"与时间状语的关系

5.6.1 何谓"对现在有影响"？

有这样一个小笑话，说的是一个衣着前卫的摩登女郎，有一天她身穿吊带背心，脚蹬一双拖鞋就去了音乐厅。门口的检票员看她这身装束就很礼貌地拒绝让她进场：

"Miss, NO ADMISSION WITH SLIPPERS."(小姐，穿拖鞋是不准进剧场的。)

这位小姐听完之后立即脱掉拖鞋并提在手中，说道：

"Really? Then I will go in barefootedly."(哦，是吗？那我就光脚进去！)

这时，这位目瞪口呆的检票员惊叫道：

"Oh, my god! Fortunately, I ***have not told*** her NO ADMISSION WITH A VEST."(天啊！幸好我刚才没有对她说穿背心不准进！)

这个笑话的原文是：

A modern girl went to the theater with a vest and a pair of slippers. The ticket-examiner turned her away very politely: "Miss, NO ADMISSION WITH SLIPPERS." "Really?" the girl took off the slippers and carried them in her hands, "Then I will go in barefootedly." "Oh, my god!" the ticket-examiner cried out, "Fortunately, I ***have not told*** her NO ADMISSION WITH A VEST."

我们现在来分析其中用了现在完成时态的句子：

1 "Oh, my god! Fortunately, I ***have not told*** her NO ADMISSION WITH A VEST."(天啊！幸好我刚才没有对她说穿背心不准进！)

这里检票员说 have not told，而没有用 did not tell，这种时态差别的背后反映了重大的意义差别。如果用一般过去时态说成 did not tell，这只是在陈述过去的事实"没有告诉"，而与现在没有任何关系。但是用现在完成时态说成 have not told，则不仅是在陈述一个过去的行为事实，更重要的是强调这个"过去"的行为对"现在"造成的影响，是把"过去"和"现在"联系起来了。根据前几节说明的，这种横贯"过去"和"现在"的时态就是现在完成时。

但是，深入分析后，我们就会发现这句话中的现在完成时态与前面讨论的"延续"思维和"重复"思维的两种完成时态的用法显然又是不同的：首先，"告诉(told)"这一动作并没有延续到现在，因为它是短暂动作；其次，该动作也不是重复发生多次。所以这里的完成时态是这节要详细讨论的第三种完成时态用法：**表示过去发生的事件对现在有影响**。如下图所示：

图解：

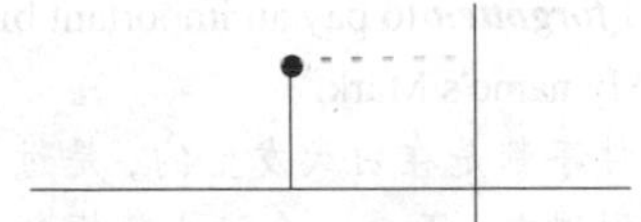

图中黑点表示过去某一时刻发生的动作；虚线表示过去发生的动作对现在有影响。

具体来说，就是某一个短暂事件是在过去发生并结束的，但是这一事件产生的影响是一直到现在都还存在的（We use the present perfect to refer to an activity that happened at an indefinite time in the past and that still has importance or relevance to the present situation.）。为了表述方便，我们姑且把它称为"单一事件"完成时，所以前面讨论的延续性思维和重复性思维的完成时也可分别称为"延续事件"完成时和"重复事件"完成时。

笔者知道，这种现在完成时的意义和用法对很多学生来说很难理解，而且很多读者从中学就学过或者是背过完成时的这一用法——表示过去发生的事件对现在有影响，但一直没有真正理解这句话，因此一直不会运用。

症结何在?

这个"对现在有影响"就是困扰我们的症结所在。前面讨论过的**"延续事件"及"重复事件"两种完成时，单从句子的字面即可理解其意。而"单一事件"完成时表示的"对现在有影响"，从句子的字面本身是反映不出来的，而是与真实的说话的语境密切相关，往往表现出一种"言外之意"。**

比如在上文中，那位 ticket-examiner 说："Fortunately, I ***have not told*** her NO ADMISSION WITH A VEST."

显然，"告知(told)"这一事件是发生在刚刚的过去，用了完成时态 have not told，说话人的"言外之意"是：假如我"刚才"告诉她穿背心不准进入——这是过去的行为，那么她"现在"一定会把背心脱掉，然后进去的——这就是"对现在的影响"。可见这种"对现在的影响"单从英语句子 I have not told her NO ADMISSION WITH A VEST. 是看不出来的，只有结合上下文的语境才能体会出这个完成时态句子的言外之意：她现在一定会把背心脱掉，然后进去。

由此可见，**"单一事件"完成时从句子的字面看不出"影响"，须结合上下文的语境方能理解"对现在的影响"，体会言外之意**。所以，在实际使用时，我们要真实再现句子背后的语境及言外之意，这就与"超语言信息"即语言之外的信息有关。

比如，我们说：

2 David ***has fallen*** in love.

精品译文　大卫恋爱了。

这句话中的 has fallen 是一个短暂动作，不表示延续或重复，所以是"单一事件"完成时。这一过去事件翻译成中文很简单——"大卫恋爱了"，但这简单译文的背后所反映的言外之意或说话的语境是很多读者不去关注的。显然，我们不可能平白无故地突然冒出这句话来，换句话说，这句话是出现在一定的语境背景下的，或者说这句话有一定的言外之意。那么这句话背后到底有何语境？这里只要再简单添上一个句子就能使该句的语境更完整，比如这样说：

David ***has fallen*** in love, and that's why he's becoming excited.

精品译文　大卫恋爱了，你看他那兴奋的样子。

这里的第二句说"他很兴奋"，就是 has fallen in love 这个过去的短暂动作对现在造成的影响，或者说就是"单一事件"完成时的言外之意。而这一言外之意无法从 David has fallen in love. 这句话的字面看出来。

下面我们再通过下列几个笑话来使读者加深理解"单一事件"完成时所表示的"对现在有影响"，即它所产生的"言外之意"：

3 **A Surprise**

Mr. Odds works in a bank and lives on his own. The only family he has is in the next town: his sister lives there with her husband, and her son, Mark. Last week Mr. Odds had a surprise. He drove home from the bank at the usual time, driving neither too slowly nor too fast; he parked his car where he always parked it, out of the way of other cars, and he went inside to make his evening meal. Straight away, there was a knock at the door. Mr. Odds opened the door, to find a policeman standing on the doorstep.

"What ***have*** I ***done*** wrong?" Mr. Odds asked himself. "***Have*** I ***driven*** on the wrong side of the road? ***Has*** there ***been*** some trouble at the bank? ***Have*** I ***forgotten*** to pay an important bill?"

"Hello, Uncle," said the policeman, "My name's Mark."

妙语点睛　欧兹先生怀疑自己做错的四件事都是在白天发生的，是过去的事件，而且它们既没有"延续"到现在，也没有"重复"发生到现在，而是一个过去的短暂事件。但强调对现在的影响是：警察为什么会来找他。而这一影响从上述四个完成时句子本身是看不出来的，只能反映在上下文语境中。

精品译文　**虚惊一场**

欧兹先生在一家银行工作，独自生活。他唯一的亲人——他的姐姐和她的丈夫及儿子麦克住在邻近的一个镇上。上周欧兹先生受了一次惊。那天，他照常从银行下班后开车回家，车速不快也不慢。他把车停在老地方，没有挡住其他车的路。然后进门就开始做晚饭。很快，就有人敲门。欧兹先生打开门，看见台阶上站着一位警察。

欧兹先生心想："我做错什么了吗？是开车逆行了？是银行工作中出了问题？还是某个重要的账单我忘了付钱？"

"你好，舅舅，"那位警察说道，"我是麦克。"

4 **He's Been Rude**

The exceedingly stout lady indignantly tackled a bus inspector at a busy stopping-place.

"I want to report the conductor of that bus that's just gone," she shrilled. "He***'s been*** rude!"

"How?" asked the bored official.

"Why?" went on the lady. "He was telling people the bus was full up, and when I got off he said: 'Room for three inside.'"

妙语点睛　在这个故事中，"他无礼(he's been rude)"这一事件发生在过去，对现在的影响是：胖女人很生气，要投诉他。所以，这一"对现在的影响"要通过上下文中另外的句子反映出来，而不是现在完成时的句子 he's been rude 本身所能反映出来的。

精品译文　**他刚才太粗鲁无礼了！**

在一个繁忙的公共汽车站，有位极其肥胖的妇女怒不可遏地去找公共汽车监察员交涉。

“我要投诉刚开走的那辆车的售票员，”她尖声叫道，“他刚才太粗鲁无礼了！”

“怎么了？”不耐烦的监察员问道。

“怎么了？”她接着道，“刚才他还说车上已满员，而当我一下车他就说：‘里面有三个人的位置。’”

5 He’s Just Been to the Zoo

When I was waiting in line at the bank, I noticed a woman holding a small child at one of the windows. The boy was eating a roll, which he thrust at the teller. The teller smiled and shook his head.

“No, no, dear,” said the boy’s mother, and then, turning to the teller, “I beg your pardon, young man. Please forgive my son. He***’s just been*** to the zoo.”

妙语点睛 “去动物园”这个事件是发生在过去的，对现在的影响是：小男孩拿自己吃的面包卷去“喂”银行柜员（The little boy thrust the roll at the teller.）他还以为自己在喂一只动物呢！这一“对现在的影响”从完成时的句子 He’s just been to the zoo. 本身是看不出来的。

精品译文 **他刚去了动物园**

那天我在银行排队办事时，看到一位妇女抱着一个小孩在站在一个窗口前。小男孩正在吃一个面包卷，并把它往一个柜员面前送。这位营业员微笑着摇了摇头。

“宝贝，别这样，”孩子的母亲说道，然后转过脸对柜员说：“对不起，先生，请原谅这孩子，他刚刚去了动物园。”

另一方面，He’s just been to the zoo. 这一过去的事件可能会对现在造成很多不同的影响。比如我们还可以这样说：

6 He now knows what the elephant is like. He ***has just been to*** the zoo.

妙语点睛 在这句话中，“刚去动物园”这一过去的事件对现在的影响就是：他知道了大象的模样。而这些影响都是只能在上下文中通过另外的句子反映出来，而不是完成时句子本身能告诉我们的。

精品译文 他现在知道大象长什么样了，因为他刚刚去了动物园。

可见，同样一个“过去的事件”，可能有多种“对现在的影响”。而这些诸多影响从完成时句子本身是反映不出来的，而是需要上下文更多的句子来解释，比如上面的 He now knows what the elephant is like. 或 The little boy thrust the roll at the teller. 小男孩的这一奇怪动作就是 He has just been to the zoo. 这句话的前提语境，也就是所谓的“对现在有影响”。

由此可见，“单一事件”的完成时态是与说话的语境密切相关的，若单独拿出完成时态的句子，我们很难理解其所要表达的真正含义，因为它所要表达的言外之意潜含在上下文的语境中，或通过上下文的其他句子反映出来。所以，在使用中绝不应死记规则，而要真正理解完成时态的这一用法特点，要融入自己的思维。因为语言表达本质上是一种思维表达，语言只是载体，它的背后是说话人的思维！

下面我们以一封读者来信以及笔者的回复来结束本小节的内容。读者看完之后，一定会更加深刻地理解何谓“对现在有影响”！

读者潘×× 的来信：

张老师：

您好，我是《新东方英语》的爱好者，您说的语法很详细易懂。非常谢谢您！在这，我有一个小问题，请您指导一下！我在向别人解释如何区别“现在完成时”和“一般过去时”，就说“凡是过去做的事情影响到现在就要用现在完成时，如不是就用一般过去时。”还提到“就是有具体过去时间就用一般过去时。”但我的朋友就反驳我说，如何得知是有影响的？我举了一个例子是“如果你昨天看了电影，今天你的朋友邀请你去看你就会不去了！因为昨天看了！影响到现在！”但她立即反驳，请问我再看一次不行吗？有何影响？现在我也是觉得一头雾水！麻烦您在百忙中抽空帮我解释一下“一般过去时和现在完成时”的区别好吗？谢谢！

学生：潘××

笔者的回复：

潘××，你好！

谢谢来信及所提出的问题。

你问到"一般过去时和现在完成时"的区别。从你的来信举例中可以看出，真正的问题是：一般过去时与"单一事件"现在完成时的区别。对于完成时的"延续"用法，一般都好理解。但"单一事件"用法一直困扰中国学生，原因很简单，因为现在完成时态的这种用法表示的是在过去开始并结束的动作，这与一般过去时一样，都是同样表示过去开始并结束的动作。尽管在时间上两者是一样的，但一般过去时和现在完成时看待这一过去事件的角度(perspective)是不同的。就举"看电影"这个例子来说明吧。

1. I ***saw*** a movie.

2. I ***have seen*** the movie.

我们可以假想这样一个场景：你和你的朋友在闲聊中，你们说到她和她男朋友上周末的约会，你就问她约会时都有什么"节目"，都干什么了。她回答说，就是和男朋友看了一场电影。在这种场景下她就会说 I saw a movie with my boyfriend. 我们看到，这个"看电影"的过去事件与现在没有任何联系，只是谈论过去事件本身。

再想象另一个场景：你的朋友们在谈论一部电影，然后你就插话进来，对这部电影大加评论或大发感慨，随后有人问你是怎么知道这部电影的，你可以说 I ***have seen*** the movie. 即你看过这部电影。这里"看电影"这一过去事件没有延续到现在，但是它的影响——你对这部电影内容的熟知，却一直延续到了现在，这就是我们常说的"对现在有影响(current influence)"。

你的朋友对你反驳得很好："如何得知是有影响的？"这里需要提醒的是，一个完成时的句子所产生的"对现在的影响"不是一成不变的，而是依据说话的语境而定的，换句话说，**同样一个完成时的句子，语境不同会导致我们从不同的角度来解释"对现在的影响"**。这一点，是我们的很多英语学习者所不知道的或忽略的。比如，同样一句 I have seen the movie. 用在下面这样的语境中就会产生不同的"对现在的影响"：你的朋友邀请你去看电影，而这部电影你已经看过了，于是当他问你是否愿意和他一起看电影时，你说 I have seen the movie. 在这样的语境中，"对现在的影响"就是你不想再去了，因为你已经看过这部电影了。所以，这里的"对现在的影响"不是说你知道该电影的内容，而是在拒绝他的邀请。由此可知，**所谓"对现在的影响"是与真实对话的语境密切相关的，单从完成时句子本身很难看出或者说根本看不出来，"对现在的影响"往往体现出一种言外之意**。这是造成我们对现在完成时难以把握的一个重要原因，因为我们讨论完成时态的时候，往往是脱离了语境的，只是看一个孤零零的英文句子本身，这样当然无法领略完成时态"对现在的影响"的实质内涵。这时候，就需要老师在讲解的时候要再造出一个，甚至是多个完成时句子背后的真实生活的语境。比如我说：

3. She ***has been*** to the bank.（她去过那家银行了。）

我为什么要说这句话？这句话背后的"言外之意"或者说"对现在的影响"是什么？我们只要发挥想象就可以很容易地造出很多不同版本的"对现在的影响"，比如比较直接的影响有：1)为什么她现在有钱花了(She has some money.)因为她去银行取过钱了；2)她已经把手里的支票存到银行了(The checks are deposited.)。比较间接的影响有：1)她为什么知道那家银行的地点位置，因为她以前去过(即 She has been to the bank.)；2)她为什么现在很高兴，因为她曾去这家银行应聘工作，她刚去过这家银行(即 She has been to the bank.)。现在知道自己被录用了，等等。

所以，我们看到，一个完成时地句子若是用在真实的语境中，可能产生多少种"对现在的影响"。另一方面，同样一个 She has been to the bank. 可以理解成较远的过去事件——"她以前去过这家银行"，也可以理解成较近的过去事件——"她刚去过这家银行"。关于"近的过去事件"和"远的过去事件"，请读者继续看 5. 6. 2、5. 6. 3 和 5. 6. 4 小节的解读。

事实上，一个句子背后往往有着各种复杂的语境前提，这其实就是"语用学(pragmatics)"研究的范畴。因此，这里要强调的是，**对于"对现在的影响"的解释，很多时候不是从句子意思本身可以得到的，而是在很大程度上依赖于语境或语用知识**（The interpretation of the current influence is thus not derivable directly from the meaning of the sentence itself but is heavily dependent on context or pragmatics.）

思维总结

本节详细讨论了完成时态的第三种用法——表示过去的事件对现在的影响。通过举例说明这一"影响"从句子本身是看不出来的，只能反映在上下文的语境中，由此看出"单一事件"的完成时态是与说话的语境密切相关的，往往体现出一种言外之意。这一节着重分析了何谓"对现在的影响"，在下一节中我们将讨论何谓"过去事件"，从而更全面地掌握"单一事件"完成时的复杂用法。

思维训练

Exercise 5. 6. 1（Key：P340）

下面短文是一篇关于美国前总统约翰·肯尼迪的一个笑话故事，请体会文中现在完成时的言外之意，想象出或解释出各自的"现在影响"：

1. Joke about Kennedy

After President Kennedy's assassination, his colleagues worried over whether he would be admitted to Heaven. They well knew of his insatiable appetites for women. His chief aides were so concerned that one made a telephone call to Heaven. The call was answered, "This is Virgin Mary. May I help you?" "Yes, ***has President Kennedy arrived yet?***" "No, he hasn't."

A little later the call was repeated and answered with "This is the Immaculate Mary, Mother of God. May I help you?" the aide asked the same question and was given the same answer. He waited a short time and anxiously called Heaven again. The call was answered, "This is Mary. May I help you?" The aide put down the phone, turned to his fellow mourners and said, "The President is in Heaven."

下面短文讲的是英国大侦探夏洛克·福尔摩斯和他的好友华生医生去外野营中被盗的故事。请想象出或解释出各自的"现在影响"：

2. Camping Trip

Sherlock Holmes and Dr. Watson go on a camping trip. After a good dinner and a bottle of wine, they retire for the night, and go to sleep. Some hours later, Holmes wakes up and nudges his faithful friend. "Watson, look up at the sky and tell me what you see."

"I see millions and millions of stars, Holmes." Replies Watson.

"And what do you deduce from that?"

Watson ponders for a minute . "Well, astronomically, it tells me that there are millions of galaxies and potentially billions of planets. Astrologically, I observe that Saturn is in Leo. Horologically, I deduce that the time is approximately a quarter past three. Meteorologically, I suspect that we will have a beautiful day tomorrow. Theologically, I can see that God is all powerful, and that we are a small and insignificant part of the universe. What does it tell you, Holmes?"

Holmes is silent for a moment. "Watson, you idiot!" he says, "Someone ***has stolen*** our tent!"

请分析下列句子的言外之意，想象出或解释出各自的"现在影响"：

3. He ***has brok***en his leg.
4. A: What ***has happened*** to Jane? She is crying.
   B: She broke the dining-room window. She has to face the music when her father gets home.
5. A: Frank is certainly in a good mood.
   B: The bargain he got on his new stereo ***has made*** him happy.

5. 6. 2 何谓"过去事件"？

在上一小节中，我们讨论了"单一事件"完成时，通过举例详细分析了何谓过去的事件"对现在有影响"。分析完"对现在的影响"之后，这一节将讨论"过去事件"。看到这里，一定有读者感到甚为奇怪——这"过去事件"有什么好讨论的？不就是过去发生的事件嘛？其实不然，这里的"过去"大有文章可做。比如下面这个对话：

1 A: Has the postman left any newspapers?

B: Yes, he did *six months ago.* *

精品译文 A：邮差把报纸送来了吗？

B：送了，他六个月前送的。

看了这个对话，各位读者是不是觉得有些怪怪的？问题就出在B的回答上，B的回答除非是在开玩笑，否则就会显得很荒唐，因为我们期待的答案应该是一个比较近的过去时间。比如他可以说：

B: Yes, he did this morning.（送了，他今天上午就送过来了。）

这里B的回答在上下文的语境中显然就比上面的回答真实、自然。由此可见，**"过去事件"中的这个"过去"应该有离现在较近和较远之分**。因为，从时间的角度来看，"过去事件"是表示**"到目前为止的过去任何某一时间点发生的事件"**，这个"过去任何某一时间点"当然是不确定的，因此可以指离现在很近的过去，也可以是离现在较远的过去。于是，**"单一事件"的完成时既可以表示发生在最近的动作，也可以表示发生在较远的过去的动作，具体情况要看上下文的语境**。比如上面这个例句就应该是"近的过去"事件。再比如，读者一定还记得下面这个例句：

2 David ***has fallen*** in love, and that's why he's becoming excited.

妙语点睛 这个例句就应该理解为恋爱这个事件是发生在"近的过去(quite recently)"，而且对现在的影响是 he's becoming excited（The action took place in the past, but it is implied that ***it took place quite recently.*** Furthermore, it is implied that is still relevant at the time of speaking — David has fallen in love, and that's why he's becoming excited or behaving strangely.）

精品译文 大卫恋爱了，所以他为什么那么兴奋。

上面这两个例句讲的是，根据上下文只能作为"近的过去"事件来理解。但是有时对于同一个句子，按照"近的过去"与"远的过去"两种意义都可以理解，但两者表达的意思不一样。再看看下面这个 TOEFL 听力考试中的句子：

3 ***Have*** you ***asked*** your little brother to do the dishes?

这句话到底该如何翻译呢？请读者现在不要继续往下读，给自己 30 秒的时间思考，然后给出你的答案。

……

OK, time is up!(时间到！)各位都有答案了吗？

首先，大家要知道，这里的短语 do the dishes 是 wash the dishes 的意思，也就是"刷碗"的意思。这个句子该如何翻译呢？首先，它不能译成延续状态，因为我们强调过，表示延续状态的完成时一般必须同时满足两个条件：句子的谓语是延续性动作或状态（continuous action or state）；句子带有延续性的时间状语（durational adverbials）。这里，ask 不是延续性动词且句中没有延续性的时间状语，因此这里的完成时态不是表示延续状态，所以不能把它翻译成"一直让你弟弟刷碗"。

其实，这个英语句子是有歧义(ambiguous)的。产生歧义的原因是我们既可以把 asked 作为"近的过去"来理解，也可以作为"远的过去"来理解。请看下面的译文：

1)你让你弟弟把碗刷了吗(近的过去)？

2)你有没有让你弟弟刷过碗(远的过去)？

妙语点睛 显然，这两句译文所使用的语境是不同的。

在句 1)中，问话的人一般应该是你的家人，比如说你妈妈。设想这样一个场景：因为正要开饭了，而她找不到干净的碗碟，所以她问你："你让你弟弟把碗刷了吗？"她现在关心的是有没有干净的餐具可以用——这就是用现在完成时所要表达的"对现在的影响(current influence)"。在句 2)中，问话的人一般不可能是你的家人，应该是你的朋友。设想这样一个场景：你和朋友们正在聊兄弟之间的关系，你告诉你朋友说，你喜欢让你弟弟做各种各样的事情，比如让他为你洗衣服、替你做功课、给你做饭等等，这时候你的一个朋友问你："那你有没有让你弟弟刷过碗呢？"

比如我们把上面两个译文分别放在下面两个不同的语境中：

3) A: Have you asked your little brother to do the dishes?(你让你弟弟把碗刷了吗？)

B: No. I did that myself this morning.（没有，今早我自己刷的。）

4) A: Have you asked your little brother to do the dishes?(你有没有让你弟弟刷过碗?)

B: Thousands of times.(无数次了。)

可以看到，同样一个句子 Have you asked your little brother to do the dishes? 可以用在两个截然不同的语境中，从而产生两种不同的中文解释——一个表示最近发生的"单一事件"，另一个表示比较远的过去事件。

由此可知，对于"单一事件"的完成时态，虽然该事件发生的过去时间是不确定的，但我们可以大概地区分为"近的过去(near past)"事件和"远的过去(distant past)"事件，因而所表达的意思也不一样。不过，这种时间上的远近是需要借助上下文的语境才能作出区分的，单从完成时态句子的本身是无法区分的。因此可以说，"单一事件"的完成时态，若是离开语境，几乎无法理解它所要表达的真正含义。再来看一个例子：

4 I *have cleaned* the car.

该如何理解这句话？是作为"近的过去"事件译成：

我已经把车洗干净了。

还是作为"远的过去"事件译成：

我曾经洗过汽车。

对此，需要更多的上下文才能确定其确切含义。我们可以为这个英文句子补充更完整的语境如下：

1) ***I have cleaned the car***. So it's ready for tomorrow.

精品译文 我已经把车洗干净了，明天可以用了。

2) A: You've never cleaned the car yourself. You've always paid someone to do it.

B: That's not true. ***I have cleaned the car***, you know. Several times.

精品译文 A：你从来都不自己洗车，总是花钱找别人替你洗。

B：这你可就错了，我自己洗过车，还洗过好几次。

当然，在实际的口语交际中，一般都会有比较完整的语境来帮助我们判断该如何理解"单一事件"完成时句子。比如下面这个句子来自笔者的一位美国朋友给笔者的邮件：

5 Sorry, but something ***has come up***. I won't be able to teach at this time. Maybe in a few months. I'll let you know.

妙语点睛 这里的 has come up 显然是表示"近的过去"事件。

精品译文 对不起，因为有其他事情要做，所以我现在不能教课了。也许再过几个月可以教，到时候我再告诉你。

对于上面讨论的有歧义的完成时态的句子，笔者做过测试，发现大多数中国学生一般只能理解一个意思，即作为"近的过去"事件来翻译，而很少有人作为"远的过去"事件来理解。对于这两类过去事件，接下来的两节中将有更详细的讨论，并将讨论在汉语译文中如何区分这两类事件。

思维总结

本节内容给读者两点启示：一，**完整的语境对于语言理解非常重要，尤其是"单一事件"的完成时态，若是离开语境，我们几乎无法理解它所要表达的真正含义；二，"单一事件"的完成时态有"近的过去"与"远的过去"这两种意义上的区分，因而所表达的意思也不一样。**

思维训练

Exercise 5.6.2 (Key: P340)

请分析下列句子可能有的含义。

Have you passed your driving test?

5.6.3 新闻热点(hot news)——近的过去

在上一小节中我们区分了"近的过去"和"远的过去"。这一小节将详细讨论"单一事件"的完成时态用于"近的过去"事件所表达的意义，下一小节将讨论"单一事件"的完成时态用于"远的过去"事件所表达的意义。

当"单一事件"的完成时态用于"较近的过去"时，往往会产生一些特殊的语义效果，包括：

1. 所造成的现在结果往往是直接具体或依然清晰可见的；
2. 具有最新热点新闻的效果；
3. 完成时提起话题，过去时继续详谈内容。

一、所造成的现在结果往往是直接具体或依然清晰可见的

这种表示“最近”动作的现在完成时态用在日常生活当中，表示**所造成的现在结果往往是直接具体或依然清晰可见的**。例如：

1 A: Look! Somebody ***has spilt*** milk on the carpet.
B: Well, it wasn't me. I didn't do it.
A: I wonder who it was then.

妙语点睛 这里对现在造成的“清晰后果”是：地毯被弄脏了，上面现在还有牛奶渍。

精品译文 A：瞧，谁把牛奶泼在地毯上了.
B：不是我，我没泼。
A：那会是谁呢？

再来看下面这个关于电脑报错的句子：

2 A problem ***has been detected*** and Windows ***has been shut down*** to prevent damage to your computer. If this is the first time you***'ve seen*** this stop error screen, restart your computer. If this screen appears again, follow these steps.

妙语点睛 操作电脑时，如果出现了病毒或其他原因导致电脑死机，有时会出现电脑报错信息，这时往往出现蓝屏，上面就出现这样的几行字，读者以后不妨注意一下。这里的完成时态表示的显然就是“刚刚”发生的错误，然后导致的直接后果就是出现了死机、无法操作等等。

精品译文 有故障被发现，Windows 操作系统已被关闭，以免损坏你的电脑。如果这是你第一次看到这个终止操作的屏幕错误信息，请重新启动电脑。若该错误屏幕再次出现，请按照下列步骤操作。

另外，关于该句中的...you***'ve seen***...这个现在完成时态，我们将在 5.8 节讨论。
其他例句如：

3 Who's ***taken*** my dictionary? It isn't on my desk. 谁拿走了我的词典？它不在桌上了。

4 Someone ***has broken*** the window. 有人把窗户打破了。

5 The car ***has arrived.*** 车子到了。

二、具有最新热点新闻的效果

因为是表示最近才发生的动作，因而具有“新闻”的性质，常常**用来提供最新热点新闻**(hot news)，所以往往用在新闻报道中。比如 2003 年 12 月 14 日萨达姆被抓时，各大媒体立即在新闻报道中说：

6 Saddam Hussein ***has been captured*** alive in his hometown of Tikrit, the U. S. military said Sunday Dec. 14, 2003.
美国军方 2003 年 12 月 14 日说，萨达姆·侯赛因在其家乡提克里特被抓获。

再比如，2004 年 10 月 11 日美国著名影星、“超人”的扮演者克里斯托弗·里夫(Christopher Reeve)去世时，路透社用现在完成时态这样报道：

7 "Superman" actor Christopher Reeve, paralyzed when he fell from a horse nine years ago, ***has died*** in a New York hospital of heart failure, his publicist said on October 11, 2004.
“超人”的扮演者克里斯托弗·里夫在纽约的一家医院死于心脏病，他的发言人 2004 年 10 月 11 日对外发布了这一消息。他在九年前由于从马背上摔下来而全身瘫痪。

在日常对话中，完成时态的这个用法常常用来提供最新消息。比如某个名人刚刚去世，这往往是个大新闻，这时就会用到现在完成时态。比如：

8 I hear that famous Chinese comedian ***has died.*** 我听说那位著名的中国喜剧明星死了。

9 The President ***has been assassinated.*** 总统被暗杀了。

但是，如果某个名人的“死亡”不是刚刚发生的，而是离现在的时间比较远了，就要改用一般过去时态了。比如肯尼迪总统是被刺杀的，但因为是很久远的事情了，所以要用一般过去时态来表达：

10 John F. Kennedy ***was assassinated.***

妙语点睛 如果用现在完成时态则听起来会比较奇怪：

John F. Kennedy ***has been assassinated.*** *

因为这个句子听起来给人的感觉是"肯尼迪刚刚被暗杀"，这显然不符合现实的语境了，所以这个句子被认为是错误的。

精品译文 约翰·F·肯尼迪被刺杀。

三、时态搭配：现在完成时+一般过去时

另外值得注意的是，口语对话中常出现"现在完成时＋一般过去时"的时态搭配使用。此时，我们用**"现在完成时"提起一个新闻话题，用"一般过去时"继续详谈内容(Topic: Present Perfect; Details: Past Simple)**。这是因为，现在完成时属于现在时态，所以我们并不关心动作发生的具体的过去时间是远还是近，而是关注这一过去事件对现在的结果或对现在造成的影响，即不关注事件的发生时间，而关注事件的内容。因而，在实际生活对话中，通常先用现在完成时开始提出一个谈论的话题，随着对话的继续，动作发生的过去时间在说话人的脑子里已经确定了。所以，如需进一步详细说明事件的内容，如 when, where, how 和 why 等，则通常用一般过去时(In hot news texts, present perfect regularly contrasts with past simple in the same text, where the topicalizing sentence uses present perfect, while the details of the narrative are in past simple.)(注意："现在完成时＋一般过去时"这一时态搭配同样适用于将于下一节讨论的"远的过去"完成时，但意义有所不同。)

比如，上文关于萨达姆被捕的新闻报道中，接下去详谈细节内容，就需要改为一般过去时态了。请看下面继续报道的内容：

11 Saddam Hussein ***has been captured*** alive in his hometown of Tikrit, the U. S. military ***said*** Sunday Dec. 14, 2003. A force of 600 American soldiers ***captured*** Saddam Hussein in a raid on Saturday night on an isolated farm near Tikrit, American military officials ***said.*** U. S. administrator L. Paul Bremer ***told*** a news conference that Saddam ***was captured*** Saturday at 8:30 p. m. in a cellar in the town of Adwar, 10 miles from Tikrit. The former Iraqi president ***was found***, haggard and grubby but alive, hiding at the bottom of an 8-foot-deep hole.

精品译文 美国军方 2003 年 12 月 14 日说，萨达姆·侯赛因在其家乡提克里特被抓获。美国军方官员说，一个由 600 名美国士兵组成的特遣部队于周六晚在对提克里特附近一个偏僻的农场的突袭中抓获萨达姆。伊拉克临时管理委员会美驻伊最高长官 L. 保罗·布莱默 14 日在新闻发布会上说，萨达姆是于周六晚 8:30 在距提克里特 10 英里的一个名叫阿德瓦的小镇的一个地窖里被抓获的。当时这位伊拉克前总统面色憔悴，蓬头垢面，但依然是活着的，正躲藏在一个约 8 英尺深的洞里。

所以，这种"现在完成时＋一般过去时"的时态搭配关系在新闻报道中常常出现，读者在阅读报纸时不妨多多关注。这一用法与上面第二点提到的用完成时来"提供最新热点新闻"有关。比如，若你要把萨达姆被捕这一新闻告诉你的朋友，你一开始应该用现在完成时，接下去的对话则应改为过去时：

12 A: The former Iraqi President Saddam ***has been captured.***

B: Really? When ***did*** that happen?

A: He ***was captured*** Saturday at 8:30 p. m. in a cellar on an isolated farm near Tikrit.

精品译文 A：伊拉克前总统萨达姆被抓了。

B：真的？什么时候？

A：他是周六晚 8:30 在提克里特附近一个偏僻的农场的地窖里被捕的。

比如，对于克里斯托弗·里夫病逝的消息，路透社用"现在完成时态＋一般过去时态"这样报道：

13 "Superman" actor Christopher Reeve, paralyzed when he fell from a horse nine years ago, ***has died*** in a New York hospital of heart failure, his publicist said on October 11, 2004. Reeve, 52, ***went*** into a coma on Saturday when he ***suffered*** a heart attack during treatment for an infected pressure wound and ***died*** on Sunday afternoon without regaining consciousness, publicist Wesley Combs told reporters. (Marion Curtis/Reuters)

精品译文 “超人”的扮演者克里斯托弗·里夫在纽约的一家医院死于心脏病，他的发言人2004年10月11日对外发布了这一消息。他在九年前由于从马背上摔下来而全身瘫痪。他的发言人威斯利·考姆斯告诉新闻记者说，里夫现年52岁，在他因为伤口感染接受治疗时突发心脏病，于周六进入昏迷状态，以后就再没有苏醒过来，于周日下午去世。

再比如，2007年12月27日，巴基斯坦前总理贝·布托（former Pakistani prime minister Benazir Bhutto）遇刺身亡。英国的《卫报》（The Guardian）在一篇“讣告（obituary）”中是这么说的：

14 The Pakistani opposition leader Benazir Bhutto, ***who has been killed***, aged 54, in a bomb attack at a political rally in Rawalpindi — the northern town where she had once gone to school — ***died*** as she ***had lived***, plunged deep in the chaotic political life of Pakistan, a victim, as well as in part a culprit, of its chronic instability. She was back in the country after spending more than eight years in exile to avoid corruption charges.

精品译文 巴基斯坦前反对党领导人贝·布托在拉瓦尔品第举行的一次政治集会上遭到炸弹袭击，她在这次袭击中遇害。贝·布托现年54岁。拉瓦尔品第是位于巴基斯坦北部的一座城镇，贝·布托曾在这里上学。贝·布托深深地卷入了巴基斯坦混乱的政治生活中，是巴基斯坦长期动荡的政治的受害者，同时从某种程度上来说亦是一名犯罪者。在为躲避对其腐败罪行的指控而流亡海外八年后，她回到了巴基斯坦。

当天该报有记者撰文猜测这是谁干的：

15 Benazir Bhutto ***has been assassinated.*** Who ***did*** it? The blunt answer is no one knows and no one is likely to know for the foreseeable future. The range of suspects is of course vast. 贝·布托被刺杀了。这是谁干的？直言不讳地讲，现在没人知道，在可预见的将来也不可能有人知道。当然，疑犯有很多。

读者可以看到，上面的英语新闻报道中的时态使用是**用“现在完成时”提起一个新闻话题**，如 who ***has been killed*** 和 Benazir Bhutto ***has been assassinated***；**用“一般过去时”继续详谈内容**，如 who ***did*** it。如果在多年以后再谈起这次刺杀事件时，就不会再用现在完成时态了，因为已不再是新闻。

再比如，上面提到的例句8和例句9，接下去继续对话可能会是这样的：

16 A: I hear that famous Chinese comedian ***has died.***
B: Really? When ***did*** she die?
A: She ***was dead*** late last night.

精品译文 A：我听说那位著名的中国喜剧明星死了。
B：真的吗？她什么时候死的？
A：她昨夜晚些时候死的。

17 A: The President ***has been assassinated.***
B: Really? When ***did*** that happen?
A: He ***was killed*** last night when he spoke in crowd.

精品译文 A：总统被暗杀了。
B：真的吗？什么时候啊？
A：他昨晚在公众面前讲话的时候被暗杀的。

思维总结

这里讨论的是“单一事件”的现在完成时态用于“近的过去”所表达的意义和用法，即用来表示较近的过去：谈论热点新闻，或某事件的直接后果。同时，要注意这样的时态搭配规律：现在完成时提起话题，过去时继续详谈内容，简言之就是“现在完成时＋一般过去时”。

至于“单一事件”的完成时用于“较远的过去”，我们将在下一节讨论。

思维训练

Exercise 5. 6. 3（Key: P340）

请用适当的时态填空。

1. A: Clint ______（break）his leg.（报告最新消息）
   B: Really? How ______ that ______（happen）?（询问具体经过）
   A: He ______（fall）off a ladder.（阐明过去原因）
2. A: Look! Somebody ______（spill）milk on the carpet.
   B: Well, it ______（be, not）me. I ______（do, not）it.
   A: I wonder who it ______（be）then.

5. 6. 4 过去经历（past experience）——远的过去

一、表示过去经历的现在完成时

5. 6. 2 小节讨论了"单一事件"可以区分为"近的过去"和"远的过去"。5. 6. 3 小节讨论了"近的过去"单一事件的意义和用法。现在要讨论的是"远的过去"单一事件的意义和用法。

当谈论一个发生在离现在时间较远的过去的某个事件时，常常含有回顾自己曾经的经历的意味。所以，如果**把现在完成时用于指较远的过去的事件，这时的完成时往往用来谈论人们过去的经历或经验**（past experience）。

先来看看下面这篇很有趣的文章，它是美国《读者文摘》（*Reader's Digest*）杂志做过的一项关于"你有多诚实（How honest are you?）"的调查。有近 3, 000 人参加了这次调查，结果，他们的回答让他们自己都大吃一惊。很多人在参加这个调查之前，都信誓旦旦地说自己很诚实，但在接受了这个调查之后，有些人便不再如此自信了。所以，在这里如果有读者自信自己够诚实，那么请先"诚实"地回答下列这些问题吧：

1 ***Have*** You Ever...?
（你是否曾经……？）
Called in sick at work when not ill?
（没病装病不去上班？）
Taken office supplies from your company?
（从公司拿办公用品？）
Taken anything valuable from your company for personal use?
（从公司拿东西留做己用？）
Misstated facts on a resume/job application?
（在简历 / 求职信上歪曲事实？）
Shifted blame to a co-worker for something you did?
（把自己的罪责转嫁到同事身上？）
Been undercharged/received too much change from a cashier and not told him?
（遇到收银员少收或多找钱的情况时不告知对方？）
Downloaded music from an Internet site without paying for it?
（从互联网上下载音乐但并不付费？）
"***Cheated***" on your tax return（not declared income or even-reported deduction）?
（在缴税上有欺诈行为〈不公开收入或夸大扣除的所得税额〉?）
Switched price tags to get a lower price for something you want to buy?
（把你想买物品的价签拿掉而换一个低价的标签？）
Lied to friends or family members about their appearance, to avoid hurting their feelings?
（为了避免朋友或亲人不高兴而在评价其外形时撒谎？）
Knowing you had little chance of getting caught, ***driven*** more than 20 m. p. h. over the speed limit or gone through a red light?
（在知道不大可能会被发现的情况下，在限速 20 英里 / 小时的区域超速驾驶或者闯红灯？）

Lied to your spouse or partner about the cost of a recent purchase?
（在新买物品的价格上欺骗你的伴侣？）

Lied to your spouse or partner about your relationship with another person?
（虽然有外遇，却对你的伴侣撒谎说没有？）

回答完上面的13个问题之后，是不是发现自己对很多问题的回答都是Yes呢？其实这也没什么，因为“人非圣贤，孰能无过”。《读者文摘》的调查结果显示，在被访问者中，几乎每个人都承认自己曾经有过不诚实的行为。只有39位“圣人”级人物（约占1.5%）声称他们没有做过上述13种不诚实行为中的任何一种——当然这前提还得是他们要完完全全说了实话。只有一个受访者良心发现承认做过所有的行为。平均而言，受访者对5个问题的回答是肯定的。下面是对每个问题回答“是”的百分比统计结果：

问题1：63%	问题2：63%	问题3：16%	问题4：18%
问题5：13%	问题6：50%	问题7：37%	问题8：17%
问题9：12%	问题10：71%	问题11：71%	问题12：32%
问题13：28%			

做完这个测试，读者应该是更加清楚地知道自己到底有多诚实了。现在我们从语言的角度分析一下这篇短文的造句规律。读者一定发现了，13个句子中的谓语都是用了过去分词，然后与标题中的Have you ever...一起构成了在完成时态，比如：

1）***Have*** you ever ***called*** in sick at work when not ill?

2）***Have*** you ever ***taken*** office supplies from your company?

3）***Have*** you ever ***taken*** anything valuable from your company for personal use? 等等。

这些问题涉及的时间跨度很长，其中伴有时间副词ever（曾经）来强调这个时间跨度。正如有受访者所言：“‘曾经’是一个很长的时间范畴（Ever is a long time.）”，它包括从出生以来到目前为止的任何一个过去的时间点，这正是现在完成时态的第三种思维——“单一事件”完成时。所以，上述句子都用了现在完成时态。另外，这里的完成时句子都是表示过去的经历，具有“远的过去”事件的意味。

在美国史诗巨片《特洛伊》里有这样一个场景：特洛伊王国的大王子海克特（Hector）发现弟弟帕里斯（Paris）将斯巴达王后海伦（Helen）偷偷带上船后，他敏感地预知一场战争将会不可避免地爆发。作为长兄，他严厉地批评了弟弟这种仅为自私的爱情而置国家命运于不顾的愚蠢做法，他质问弟弟帕里斯道：“你说你爱海伦，那你对父王的爱呢？你对整个特洛伊王国的爱呢？你知道父王为了特洛伊的和平，征战了多少年？现在你把这个女人带到船上，整个特洛伊都将会为之毁灭！”听了哥哥的这番训斥，帕里斯说道：“如果你想把海伦送回斯巴达，那就送回去好了，但我将和她一起回去！（If you want to take Helen back to Sparta, so be it! But I go with her!）”但是作为特洛伊的大王子，海克特肩负着父王普利安（Priam）的重托和保护弟弟帕里斯的责任，他不可能看着弟弟去送死，但同时他严肃地警告帕里斯战争和死亡的残酷性：

2 Hector: To Sparta, they'll kill you.

Paris: Then I'll die fighting.

Hector: Oh, and that sounds heroic to you, doesn't it? To die fighting. Tell me, little brother, ***have*** you ***ever killed*** a man?

Paris: No.

Hector: ***Ever seen*** a man die in combat?

Paris: No.

Hector: ***I've killed*** men and ***I've heard*** them dying and ***I've watched*** them dying and there's nothing glorious about it, nothing poetic. You say you're willing to die for love but you know nothing about dying and you know nothing about love!

Paris: All the same, I go with her. I won't ask you to fight my war.

Hector: You already have.

在这里，海克特质问他弟弟：“你说你要奋战到死，这听起来像个大英雄，是吧？那我来问你，你杀过人吗（have you ever killed a man）？你见过战争中死人吗（Ever seen a man die in combat）？我杀过人，我见过无数的人在战争中死亡（I've killed men and I've heard them dying and I've watched them dying），这些并不光荣和诗意。你说你愿意为爱而死，可你对死亡一无所知，对爱也一无所知！”我们看到，海克特在这里用了五个现在完成时态，一方面显示出弟弟帕里斯对于战争的残酷性的无知，另一方面表明了自己拥有丰富的作战经历。

我们现在来分析这里的五个现在完成时态：

1）...***have*** you ***ever killed*** a man?

2）(***Have***) ***Ever seen*** a man die in combat?

3）I'***ve killed*** men and I'***ve heard*** them dying and I'***ve watched*** them dying and there's nothing glorious about it, nothing poetic. You say you're willing to die for love but you know nothing about dying and you know nothing about love!

妙语点睛　这里的第一个完成时 have ever killed 是海克特问弟弟帕里斯：“……你杀过人吗？”这显然是表示曾经的经历，相当于一个“远的过去”事件，而不是表示“近的过去”事件，否则会译成“你刚刚杀了人了吗？”这里的 ever 排除了这个意思；第二个完成时 Ever seen a man die in combat? 同样是表示曾经的经历，是一个“远的过去”事件；最后三个现在完成时态 I've killed...I've heard... I've watched 则是相当于前面说的“重复”事件，这里的动作 killed, heard 和 watched 显然是多次重复发生的。

精品译文　海克特：　去斯巴达，他们会杀了你的。

帕里斯：　那么我会奋战到死。

海克特：　哦，你说你要奋战到死，这听起来像个大英雄，是吧？那我来问你，兄弟，你杀过人吗？

帕里斯：　没有。

海克特：　你见过战争中死人吗？

帕里斯：　没有。

海克特：　我杀过人，我听过无数的人在战争中呻吟，目睹他们死亡，这些并不光荣和诗意。你说你愿意为爱而死，可你对死亡一无所知，对爱也一无所知！

帕里斯：　无所谓，我跟她一起走。我不会请你来为我战斗。

海克特：　你已经这样了。

二、时态搭配一：现在完成时+一般过去时

5.6.3 小节中提到过，在“现在完成时＋一般过去时”这个时态搭配中，一般用完成时提起一个新闻话题，然后用一般过去时继续详谈这个新闻的内容。那里的现在完成时是表示“近的过去”事件。现在，这一时态搭配中的现在完成时也可以用来谈“远的过去”事件，此时用完成时询问对方过去的经历，然后用一般过去时继续详谈这个经历的具体情况（The present perfect often serves to introduce a topic, which in turn becomes a definite event and is talked about using the past tense.）比如：

3　A: ***Have*** you ***seen*** the film Forrest Gump?（询问对方过去的经历）

B: Yes, I ***have***.（现在知道电影的内容）

A: When ***did*** you see it?（关心看电影的过去的具体时间）

B: I ***saw*** it last spring.（给出具体时间）

A: ***Did*** you see it alone?（询问当时的情况）

B: No, I ***saw*** it with my boyfriend.（提供过去的事实）

精品译文　A：你看过电影《阿甘正传》吗？

B：是的。

A：你什么时候看的？

B：去年春天。

A：你自己去看的吗？

B：不是，我和男朋友一起去的。

4　A: Hey, this sounds good — snails with garlic! ***Have*** you ever ***eaten*** snails?

B: No, I ***haven't***.

A: Oh, they're delicious! I ***had*** them last time. Like to try some?

B: No, thanks. They sound strange.

精品译文 A：嘿，这道菜听起来不错——蒜蓉蜗牛！你吃过蜗牛吗？

B：没有。

A：哦，好吃极了！我上次吃过。你想尝尝吗？

B：不了，谢谢，这菜听起来怪怪的。

可见，在“现在完成时+一般过去时”这个时态搭配中，现在完成时可以表示“远的过去”事件，来询问某人过去的经历。另一方面，这种表示“远的过去”完成时还可以用于下列时态搭配，即“一般过去时+现在完成时”。

三、时态搭配二：一般过去时+现在完成时

我们刚才讨论的是“现在完成时+一般过去时”的搭配使用：用“现在完成时”提起新闻话题，用“一般过去时”继续详谈内容。有趣的是，也可以用相反的时态搭配，即“一般过去时+现在完成时”：用一般过去时讲述自己过去的经历，然后用现在完成时探询对方是否有相似的经历，以期望获得更多的理解或共鸣。请看下列口语对话中是如何使用这一时态搭配的：

5 John: We went down into Juarez and through El Paso, and oh, we had a ball.

Louise: Really?

John: Yeah. ***Have*** you ever ***been*** t- ***have*** you ever ***heard*** of Juarez?

Louise: I***'ve heard*** of both of them because my girlfriend's old boyfriend was stationed in El Paso.

John: Well, we went to Juarez...

妙语点睛 这里约翰在用一般过去时讲述自己在图阿雷兹的经历，但在继续讲故事之前，他从过去时态的叙述转到一个现在完成时态的询问(Have you ever been t- have you ever heard of Juarez?)以此来探询路易斯是否了解图阿雷兹这个地方。而路易斯在展示自己的有关知识时也使用了现在完成时(I've heard of both of them...)，表明自己对图阿雷兹有所了解。而这个“现在的了解”是因为过去听说过那个地方——即过去的事件对现在有影响。

精品译文 约翰：我们南下去了图阿雷兹，穿过了整个埃尔帕索市，哦，我们玩得开心极了！

路易斯：真的？

约翰：是的。对了，你曾经去过——你听说过图阿雷兹吗？

路易斯：这两个地方我都听说过，因为我的女朋友的前男友就是驻扎在埃尔帕索的。

约翰：噢，我们去了图阿雷兹……

请再看下面这段文字，这里作者在讲述自己一次去看摔跤比赛的经历：

6 We got to the Civic Center about an hour early, since I didn't have tickets yet, and I knew that it would be crowded. If you***'ve never been to*** a professional wrestling match, you really should go — not for the wrestling, but for the crowd — eight to ten thousand people, wearing their favorite wrestler's T-shirts and screaming their heads off. I***'ve been to*** rock concerts that weren't as loud.

妙语点睛 作者在if引导的条件状语从句中使用了现在完成时态If you've never been to...来探询读者是否有观看职业摔跤比赛的经历，并建议如果没有看过就应该去看一场。作者接下来用摇滚音乐会作比较时，也用了现在完成时I've been to...谈自己的经历，随后即转为一般过去时weren't来具体谈过去的情况。

精品译文 我们提前一个小时左右到达市府中心，因为我还没买票，而且我知道那里会非常拥挤。如果你从来没有看过职业摔跤比赛，那你真的要去看看了——不是为了看摔跤，而是去看人群——八千至一万名观众，穿着印有自己喜爱的摔跤手的T恤，疯狂地叫喊。我去过的摇滚音乐会也没这么吵。

同样的时态搭配用法也见于《老友记》(Friends)里的一个场景：菲布斯(Pheebs)有一个双胞胎妹妹叫乌尔苏拉(Ursula)，两人感情十分不和。据菲布斯说，原因是乌尔苏拉从小就爱抢菲布斯的东西，然后故意把它弄坏。这一恶习发展到她们长大以后，乌尔苏拉还爱抢菲布斯的男朋友。比如，菲布斯有个男友，同时也是她最好的朋友叫兰迪·布朗(Randy Brown)，后来乌尔苏拉生生地把他从菲布斯手中抢走了，然后又故意把兰迪甩掉，让他伤心。结果，弄得兰迪和菲布斯连朋友都做不了了，他怕见到菲布斯会想起乌尔苏拉，因为两人长得太像了。

从此，兰迪再也不和菲布斯说话了。这当然让菲布斯很郁闷，所以她向雷切尔（Rachel）和莫尼卡（Monica）诉苦，讲述自己这个痛苦的经历：

7 Monica: Are you alright?

Phoebe: Yeah. It's just, you know, it's this whole stupid Ursula thing, it's...

Rachel: Okay, Pheebs, can I ask? So, he's going out with her. I mean, is it really so terrible?

Phoebe: Um, yeah. Look, I mean, I'm not saying she's like evil or anything. She just, you know, she's always breaking my stuff. When I was eight, and I wouldn't let her have my Judy Jetson thermos, so she threw it under the bus. And then, oh, and then there was Randy Brown, who was like...***Have*** you ***ever had*** a boyfriend who was like your best friend?

Monica and Rachel: (Wistfully, shaking their heads) No.

Phoebe: Well, but that's what he was for me. And she, you know, kind of stole him away, and then...broke his heart...and then he wouldn't even talk to me any more. Because he said he didn't wanna be around... anything that looked like either one of us.

Rachel: Oh...Oh, Pheebs.

Phoebe: I mean, I know Joey is not my boyfriend, or my thermos, or anything, but...

妙语点睛 这里菲布斯先用一般过去时态讲述她和乌尔苏拉从小就不和（...she's always breaking my stuff. When I was eight, and I wouldn't let her have my Judy Jetson thermos, so she threw it under the bus. And then, oh, and then there was Randy Brown, who was like...）。然后，菲布斯从一般过去时态换为现在完成时态问道***Have*** you ***ever had*** a boyfriend who was like your best friend? 以此来探询莫尼卡和雷切尔是否有"男朋友同时也是最好朋友"的经历。这里菲布斯问的目的当然是希望博取两人更多的理解和同情了，但两人没有这样的经历（尽管很渴望有〈wistfully〉）。不过，菲布斯还是自顾自地把自己的遭遇讲出来了（Well, but that's what he was for me. And she you know, kind of stole him away, and then...broke his heart...and then he wouldn't even talk to me any more. Because he said he didn't wanna be around...anything that looked like either one of us.）

精品译文 莫尼卡： 你没事吧？

菲比： 没事。只是，你知道，都是愚蠢的乌尔苏拉干的，这……

雷切尔： 好吧，菲布斯，我能问个问题吗？那么，他与她约会了。我的意思是说，这有这么严重吗？

菲比： 嗯，是的。瞧，我的意思是，我不是说她有多么邪恶或者其他的什么，她只是，你知道，她总是弄坏我的东西。我八岁那年，我不想把我的茱迪·杰特森牌暖水瓶给她，于是她就把它扔到公共汽车底下去了。接下来，哦，接下来就是兰迪·布朗了，他就像个……你们有没有过男朋友同时又是你最好的朋友？

莫尼卡和雷切尔：（惆怅地摇了摇头）没有。

菲比： 嗯，但是他对于我来说就是这样的。而她，你知道，就好像是把他偷走了那样，然后……伤了他的心……然后他就再也不想和我说话了，因为他说他不想在……任何长得像我们俩的人身边了。

雷切尔： 哦……哦，菲布斯。

菲比： 我是说，我知道乔伊是不我的男朋友，也不是我的暖水瓶或者其他什么属于我的东西，但是……

四、时态搭配三：一般现在时+现在完成时

在上面讲的"一般过去时＋现在完成时"搭配中，说话者用一般过去时讲述自己过去的经历，然后用现在完成时探询对方是否有相似的经历，以期望获得更多的理解或共鸣。但是如果说话人谈到的是一般常见的经历，而不是指某一次具体的过去的经历，那么他会用一般现在时态，然后接一个现在完成时态，来探寻听话者／读者是否有过类似的经历。比如在下面这个例子中，作者谈论到中国餐馆服务质量差的现象：

8 **Give Me Some Service, Will Ya?**

All you want is a fresh pot of tea. First, you snap your fingers. Then you wave your hand. Finally, you yell for some service. *Fuwuyuan* (waiter)!

You've been there, right?

In my opinion, the threat of withholding a tip — or the reward of handing it out — is the only tool the customers have in the long struggle for decent service.

妙语点睛 这里作者一开始采用一般现在时态来描述一个常见的情景，然后用现在完成时态来探寻读者是否也有过类似的经历。作者最后认为，要想提高中国餐馆的服务质量，付小费是唯一的出路。

精品译文 **给我来点服务吧，好吗?**

(在一个餐馆里)你所要的就只是一壶茶而已。开始时，你打着响指想引起服务员的注意，这招不行，于是你挥舞着手想引起对方注意，这招还不管用，最后你只好大声叫道："服务员！"你有过类似的经历吧?

在我看来，顾客要想得到很好的服务，采用付小费制是唯一的出路，因为给或不给小费是一个很好的杀手锏。

注意，上面这段话里的 you have been there 的意思不是"你去过那个地方吧"，而是"你也有过类似的经历吧"。比如下面这个句子：

9 I'm going through this divorce. I know ***you've been there*** before, but mine is turning into a real legal battle.

精品译文 我正在办离婚。我知道你也经历过这个，但我的离婚手续完全是一场法律战。

思维总结

本小节讲的是"单一事件"的完成时用于"远的过去"，往往表示人们过去曾经的经历。在口语中，现在完成时态有时会和一般过去时搭配使用，说话者先用一般过去时讲述过去的经历，然后用现在完成时探询对方是否有相似的经历，即为"一般过去＋现在完成(远的过去意义)"。同时请注意，这不同于"现在完成(通常是近的过去意义)＋一般过去"。

思维训练

Exercise 5. 6. 4（Key: P340）

请根据不同的回答，使用正确时态填空。

1. A: Have you ever worked in a restaurant?
   B: Yes. I ______ (work) in many ones.
   B: Yes. I ______ (work) in a French one last year.
2. A: Have you ever been to the Great Wall?
   B: Yes. I ______ (be) there many times.
   B: Yes. I ______ (go) there last spring.
3. A: Have you read this book?
   B: Yes. It ______ (be) interesting.
4. A: Have you ever taken a French course?
   B: Yes. I ______ (take) a French course in high school.
5. A: Have you graduated from college?
   B: Yes, I ______ (study) French for two years.

请用完成时态询问你的朋友可否有下列经历。

6. Lend money to a friend
7. Be on television
8. Meet a famous person
9. Break an arm or leg
10. Go to court
11. Find money on the street
12. Be cheated

13. Tell a lie
14. Take a flight
15. Go to Disneyland
16. Study abroad
17. Order products over the Internet.

看看在下面工作面试场景中，native speaker 是怎样谈自己以往工作经历的。请在空格中填上适当的时态。

18. A: May I help you?

 B: Yes. I would like to apply for one of the security guard positions you advertised in the local paper.

 A: Good. May I ask you a few questions first?

 B: Certainly.

 A: ______ you ______ (ever, work) as a security guard before?

 B: Yes, at shopper's plaza San Francisco and at the Regency Hotel here in town.

 A: How many years of experience ______ you ______ (have) as a security guard?

 B: a little over four years.

 A: ______ you ______ (have) experience monitoring alarm systems?

 B: Yes. I ______ (monitor) several types of alarm systems in my previous job.

 A: Very good. You seem to meet our minimum qualifications. Complete this application form and bring it back to me. Then I'll schedule you for another interview.

 B: Thank you. I'll fill this out now.

请用正确的时态完成下面对话。

19. A: What jobs ______ (did you have/have you had)?

 B: Well, I once ______ (have had/had) a job on a cruise ship.

 A: What ______ (have you had/did you have) to do?

 B: I ______ (have organized/organized) activities for the passengers.

 A: What ______ (have you liked/did you like) about it?

 B: Well, working on a cruise ship ______ (has been/was) terrific. I really enjoyed...

 A: ______ (Were there/Have there been) any bad points?

 B: Oh, sure. Every job has its bad points. I didn't like...

20. Isabel: I went to Sunrise Beach last week. ______ (Did you ever go/Have you ever been) to Sunrise Beach, Andy?

 Andy: Yes, ______ (I did/I have). It's beautiful. ______ ______ (Did you go/Have you gone) there on the weekend?

 Isabel: Yeah, ______ (I did/I have). I ______ (went/have gone) on Sunday. ______ (I got up/I've gotten up) at 4:00 a. m.

 Andy: Wow! ______ (I never woke up/I've never woken up) that early!

 Isabel: Oh, it wasn't so bad. I ______ (got/have gotten) to the beach early to see the sun rise. ______ (Did you ever see/Have you ever seen) sunrise, Andy?

 Andy: No, ______ (I didn't/I haven't). I prefer sunsets to sunrises.

 Isabel: Really? Then I ______ (went/have gone) swimming around 6:00, but there were some strange dark shadows in the water. ______ (Did you ever hear/Have you ever heard) of sharks at Sunrise Beach?

 Andy: Yes, ______ (I did/I have). I ______ (heard/have heard) a news report about sharks last summer.

 Isabel: Gee! Maybe I ______ (had/have had) a lucky escape on Sunday morning! Why don't you come with me next time?

 Andy: Are you kidding?

5.6.5 "单一事件"与时间状语的关系

本小节将探讨"单一事件"的现在完成时态与时间状语的搭配关系。

一、"单一事件"完成时的肯定句不与持续的时间状语连用

这种完成时态的谓语动词通常是短暂动词，即指动作在短时间或瞬间内就已终止，而不再延续。常见的这类动词有：come, go, leave, kill, die, lose, buy, start, give, marry, join 和 bring 等。因为动作本身无法延续，因此与它连用的时间状语不能是指"一段时间"的，如 for a year 等。这正好与"延续事件"的完成时相反——"延续事件"的完成时必须加持续的时间状语，而"单一事件"完成时态不能加持续的时间状语，这在 5.2.3 节中曾提到。比如不能说：

1 I ***have bought*** this pair of shoes ***for a year.*** *

2 I ***have married for over a year.*** *

3 I ***have fallen*** in love ***for eight years.*** *

4 He ***has left*** his hometown ***for three years.*** *

再比如，汉语里完全可以说"这部电影我看了有两年了"，但在英语里却不能用现在完成时态这样表达：

5 I ***have seen*** the movie ***for two years.*** *

因为这里句子的谓语动词都是短暂性的，不能表示延续，因而不能与 since 或 for 等引导的持续性的时间状语连用。只要把"动作(action)"转化为"状态(state)"即可，因为状态是可以延续的。比如上面几个错误的句子可以改为相应的"状态"：

6 I ***have had*** this pair of shoes for a year. 这双鞋我买了有一年了。

7 I ***have been married*** for over a year. 我结婚有一年多了。

8 I ***have been*** in love for eight years. 我恋爱有八年了。

9 He ***has been away*** from his hometown for three years. 他离开家乡有三年了。

若句中的"动作"表达无法转化成"状态"表达，就不能用现在完成时态，而只好改为一般过去时态。比如 see 没有对应的状态表达，所以上面的例句 5 只好改成一般过去时：

10 I ***saw*** the movie ***two years ago.***

这完全能够表达汉语的"这部电影我看了有两年了"这句话的意思。其他句子也可以作同样的时态改变，比如说：

11 I ***bought*** this pair of shoes ***a year ago.***

12 I ***got married over a year ago.***

13 He ***left*** his hometown ***three years ago.***

二、"单一事件"完成时的否定句表示状态意义，可与持续的时间状语连用

不过，短暂性动词的完成时句子若用否定式，来表示尚未发生的事情，则可作为一种状态 (state)，从而可以表示延续。所以，这种否定句就相当于前面介绍过的"延续事件"完成时态。来看下面这个可怜的乞丐：

14 Beggar: Madam, I ***haven't seen*** a piece of meat ***for weeks.***
Lady: Mary, please show this poor man the ham we bought just now.

精品译文 乞丐：夫人，几个星期以来我都没见过一片肉了。
夫人：玛丽，把我们刚才买的那根火腿给他瞧瞧。

这位乞丐说 I haven't seen a piece of meat for weeks. 显然其言外之意是"给我一些肉吃吧"，但那位妇人故意从字面上理解他的意思，所以让玛丽只是给他"看肉"。这里短暂动词 see 的否定式与延续的时间状语 for weeks 连用了。

下面这个笑话与上面那个有异曲同工之妙：

15 **Beggar and Woman**

A beggar walked up to a well dressed woman and said, "I ***haven't eaten*** anything ***in four days.***"

She looked at him and said, "I wish I had your willpower (毅力)."

精品译文 乞丐与妇女

一个乞丐走到一位衣着华丽的夫人面前说道:"我四天来没吃一点东西了。"

她看看他然后说道:"我希望自己能有你这样的毅力。"

还有口语中，我们见面时常说的:

16 I ***haven't seen*** you ***for ages***! 我很久没见到你了!

再比如下列句子:

17 I ***haven't bought*** a pair of shoes ***for a year.*** 我有一年没买过鞋了。

18 I ***haven't seen*** a film ***for weeks.*** 我有好几个星期没看电影了。

19 I ***haven't heard*** from my girlfriend ***since I came to America.***

自从我来到美国以后就一直没收到过我女朋友的来信。

三、"单一事件"完成时常与不确定的时间状语连用

以上讨论的是"单一事件"的完成时与延续的时间状语的搭配关系，但是这种现在完成时更多的是与过去的不确定的时间搭配使用(the present perfect with indefinite past time)。如: already (已经), yet (只用在疑问句或否定句中), lately (最近), just (刚刚，方才), never (从不，从未发生过), ever (曾经)和 before (以前)等，而且还可以按照前面讨论的"远近过去"把它们划分为:

1. 较远的过去: ever(英文意思是 any time between the past and the present，表示"曾经"，一般指较远的过去时间); before;

2. 较近的过去: yet, already, lately 和 recently;

3. 更近的过去: just，表示"刚刚"，常与完成时态连用。

如上一小节的练习中的例句:

20 A: ***Have*** you ***ever worked*** in a restaurant?

B: Yes. I've worked in many ones.

B: Yes. I worked in a French one last year.

21 A: ***Have*** you ***ever been*** to the Great Wall?

B: Yes. I've been there many times.

B: Yes. I went there last spring.

看到朋友发怒，可以这样规劝:

22 Get a hold of yourself! ***I've never seen*** you so upset ***before***! 你要控制一下情绪。我以前从未见你这么生气!

注意 yet 要用在否定句或疑问句中:

23 A: Have you found a job ***yet***? 你找到工作了吗?

B: No, ***not yet.*** 还没有。

24 Has it ***stopped*** raining ***yet***? 雨停了吗?

25 He ***hasn't arrived yet.*** 他还没到。

在肯定句中，用 already 代替 yet 表示"已经":

26 A: Have you found a job ***yet***? 你找到工作了吗?

B: Yes. I've found a job ***already.*** 是的，我已经找到工作了。

27 He *has already arrived.* 他已经到了。

表示"刚刚的过去"，用 just：

28 A: Would you like something to eat? 你想吃点什么吗?

B: No, thanks. *I've just had* dinner. 不了，谢谢。我刚吃过饭(现在不饿)。

思维总结

本小节的重要内容包括：

1. "单一事件"完成时的肯定句不与持续的时间状语连用；
2. 否定句表示状态意义，可与持续的时间状语连用；
3. "单一事件"完成时常与不确定的时间状语连用。

思维训练

Exercise 5. 6. 5（Key: P342）

请用正确的时态填空。

1. Jenny's policy is to be friendly with everyone she meets. I ______ (never, see) her be rude to anyone.
2. You ______ (never, see) a baseball game before? We can fix that! I'll take you to one next week.
3. Perhaps the animal is ill; it ______ (not, eat) anything since Monday.
4. What kind of vessel is that? I ______ (never, see) that sort of boat before.
5. What a novel idea! I ______ (never, see) anything like this before.
6. I ______ (never, see) such a large concentration of horses. They're everywhere!
7. This room ______ (not, clean) for months.

5.7 "延续事件"、"重复事件"与"单一事件"之间的相互关系

到目前为止，我们终于把现在完成时态的三种思维用法讨论完毕。为了进一步巩固学习战果，在接下来的这一节将对三种思维用法作一个系统的比较，以便于大家对现在完成时态有更深入的理解和灵活运用。

我们将从两方面来讨论三者的关系：一是三者之间思维上的相关性，二是三者之间语义上的相关性，这时要注意区分谓语是"动作"还是"状态"，即与动词本身的体态(lexical aspect)有关。

先来简要回顾一下现在完成时态的三种思维用法。图示如下：

用法一：延续事件

(图 1：延续状态)

典型例句：

1 I have lived here since 1980. 从 1980 年以来，我一直住在这里。

用法二：重复事件

(图 2-1：重复活动 1)

典型例句：

2 I have lived here on and off since 1980. 从 1980 年以来，我断断续续在这里生活过。

(图 2-2：重复活动 2)

典型例句：

3 He has been fired four times so far. 到目前为止，他被开除过四次。

用法三：单一事件

（图 3：单一事件）

典型例句：

4 He has just died. 他刚去世。

从以上图示来看，不妨这样理解三者间的关系：重复事件可以看作是延续事件的一个特例，即表示延续事件的一条直线（如图 1 所示）变成了表示重复事件的一条虚线（如图 2-1 所示），进而变成了多个点（如图 2-2 所示）。比较图 1 和图 2-1，也可以看出，延续事件与重复事件两种用法之间具有相关性，有时甚至是难以明确区分的（这一点在 5.5.1 小节中讨论过）。比较图 2-2 和图 3，也很容易看出，单一事件可以看作是重复事件的特例——事件只发生了一次，而没有多次重复。

还可以换一个角度这样理解三者之间的关系：延续事件与单一事件这两种用法代表了两个极端，分别用一条直线（如图 1）和一个黑点（如图 3）来形象直观地表示。而联系这两个极端的就是重复事件，而且是各种各样不同特点的重复活动（这里仅列出两种，其实还可以有更多种）。下面来详细分述三者间的相互关系。内容安排如下：

5.7.1 延续事件与单一事件

5.7.2 延续事件与重复事件

5.7.3 重复事件与单一事件

此外，我们还要结合谓语动词的“体（lexical aspect）”的特点——动作（action）和状态（state）来讨论它们之间的相关用法特点，因此还会涉及下列内容：

5.7.4 “动作表达”的完成时态与“状态表达”的一般现在时态

5.7.5 “动作表达”的完成时态与“状态表达”的完成时态

5.7.1 延续事件与单一事件

这二者的区别和联系主要与是否带有持续的时间状语有关。这可以从两方面来阐述：带有持续的时间状语（with durational adverbials）和不带持续的时间状语（without durational adverbials）。

首先，由于单一事件的谓语动词往往是短暂动词，所以它不与持续的时间状语连用（详见 5.6.5 小节），而延续事件则必须带有一个持续的时间状语（详见 5.4.2 小节）。请比较：

1 1) He ***has been married*** for a year.

2) He ***has married*** for a year. *

3) He ***has gotten married*** for a year. *

妙语点睛 这里例句 1) 正确，而例句 2) 和 3) 错误，因为 marry 和 got married 都表示短暂动作，不能与持续的时间状语 for a year 连用。

精品译文 他结婚有一年了。

2 1) His father ***has been dead*** for three years.

2) His father ***has died*** for three years. *

妙语点睛 这里例句 1) 正确，而例句 2) 错误，因为 die 表示短暂动作，不能与持续的时间状语 for three years 连用。

精品译文 他父亲去世三年了。

但要注意的是，短暂动词可以用于现在完成时态。比如：

3 He ***has married.*** 他已经结婚了。

4 His father ***has died.*** 他父亲已经去世了。

此时，一般只能表示单一事件中的"近的过去"事件。

其次，5.4.2 小节讨论过，延续事件的完成时在没有持续时间状语时不能表示延续，只能表示过去曾经的经历，这正是单一事件中的"远的过去"事件。请比较：

5 1）I have been married for a year.

2）I have been married.

妙语点睛 例句 1)表示"我结婚已经有一年了"，现在还是已婚状态；例句 2)则表示"我结过婚"，而现在是单身。

综上所述，延续事件与单一事件的联系是：**没有持续的时间状语的延续事件立即变成了单一事件中的"远的过去"事件——表示过去的经历。**

5.7.2 延续事件与重复事件

前面多次提到过，延续事件与重复事件有着密切的联系，有时难以明确区分一个事件究竟是一直在延续还是在多次重复发生。比如下面这个典型的表示延续事件的例句：

1 I have lived here since 1980. 从 1980 年以来，我一直住在这里。

但将其稍作改变，即可变成重复事件。比如：

2 I have lived here on and off since 1980. 从 1980 年以来，我断断续续在这里生活过。

也可以变换一下时间状语，变延续事件为重复事件。比如：

3 1）He has lived here ***for ten years.***

2）He has lived here ***several times.***

妙语点睛 这里的例句 1)表示延续事件，而例句 2)表示重复事件。

精品译文 1）他住在这里已经有 10 年了。

2）他断断续续地在这里住过几次。

4 1）He has been married ***for a year.***

2）He has been married ***a couple of times***.

妙语点睛 这里的例句 1)表示延续事件，而例句 2)表示重复事件。

精品译文 1)他结婚有一年了。

2)到目前为止他结过两次婚。

5.7.3 重复事件与单一事件

前面谈到过，单一事件可以区分为"近的过去"单一事件和"远的过去"单一事件(参见5.6.2、5.6.3 和 5.6.4 小节)，所表达的意思是不一样的。下面将分别讨论重复事件与这两种单一事件的关系，并更精确地定义何谓"重复事件"和"单一事件"。

一、重复事件与"远的过去"单一事件

先来讨论重复事件的完成时与"远的过去"单一事件的关系。请看下面例句：

1 I have been married. 我结过婚。

这句话的意思是"我结过婚"，是表示"过去曾经的经历(a past experience)"，也即是一个"远的过去"单一事件。但它并没有告诉我们"结婚"经历了几次，只是我们知道"结婚"这一事件到目前为止至少发生过一次(at least one occurrence up to the present)。说"至少发生过一次"其实就潜含了重复的意味，也就是说"结婚"至少有一次，也可能是多次。因此，我们很容易就能把上面这句变成一个重复事件，即在句末加一个"重复标示"——频度状语(比如 three times)说成：

2 I have been married ***three times***. 到目前为止我结过三次婚。

这是一个典型的表示重复事件的完成时。所以，从表示过去经历的“单一事件”到“重复事件”，只需迈一小步，即加上一个表示具体次数的频度状语就可以了。可以把表示“过去经历”称为“隐性”的重复事件(implicitly repeatable events)，而把说出了具体次数的情形称为“显性”的重复事件(explicitly repeatable events)。I have been married. 这个句子也说明了单一事件与重复事件的“边界模糊性”(比如这里不知道“我”是结过一次婚还是结过多次婚)。

再比如下面这些例句：

3 ***Have*** you ***ever killed*** a man?

4 (***Have***) ***Ever seen*** a man die in combat?

5 I'***ve killed*** men and I'***ve heard*** them dying and I've watched them dying and there's nothing glorious about it, nothing poetic. You say you're willing to die for love but you know nothing about dying and you know nothing about love!

妙语点睛 例句3中的完成时 have ever killed 是海克特(Hector)问弟弟帕里斯(Paris)“你杀过人吗？”这显然是表示曾经的经历，相当于一个“远的过去”事件，而不是表示“近的过去”事件，否则会译成“你刚刚杀了人了吗？”这里的ever排除了这个意思。例句4中的完成时 ever seen a man die in combat 同样表示曾经的经历，是一个“远的过去”事件。例句5中的三个现在完成时态 I've killed...I've heard...I've watched 则是相当于前面说的“重复”事件，这里的动作 killed, heard 和 watched 显然是多次发生，但同样具有过去经历的意味。

精品译文 3. 你杀过人吗？

4. 你见过战争中死人吗？

5. 我杀过人，我听过无数的人在战争中呻吟，目睹他们死亡，这些并不光荣和诗意。你说你愿意为爱而死，可你对死亡一无所知，对爱也一无所知！

“远的过去”单一事件与重复事件的密切相关性从下列对话中也可以揭示出来：

6 A: ***Have*** you ever ***seen*** the movie ***Titanic***? (询问过去的经历——单一事件意味)

B: ***Over ten times***, I think. (该经历重复了多次——重复事件意味)

精品译文 A: 你看过电影《泰坦尼克》吗？

B: 我想我看过十多遍了。

7 A: ***Has*** Sandy ever ***missed*** coming to one of our parties? (询问过去的经历——单一事件意味)

B: Only once or twice at the most. (该经历重复了一两次——重复事件意味)

精品译文 A: 桑迪以前错过我们的聚会吗？

B: 最多一两次而已。

另一方面，用现在完成时来谈论过去的经历时，这个经历一定得是具有可重复性的。如果一个活动或状态天然不具有重复性，即不能表示来回往复的发生，就不能用现在完成时来表示“过去的经历”。比如说“死”，因为人死不能复生，所以不能说：

8 His father has been dead*.

同样，人不能返老还童，所以也不能说：

9 I have been old*.

综上所述，重复事件与“远的过去”单一事件的关系体现在两个方面：一是“远的过去”单一事件相当于一个“隐性”的重复事件，只需添加一个表示次数的重复标示就可以把它变成“显性”重复事件，即一个真正意义上的重复事件；另一方面，用现在完成时来谈论过去的经历时，这个经历一定得是具有可重复性的。因此，可以把单一事件完成时表示“过去经历”的用法包含在“重复事件”完成时的思维里。由此可以把“重复事件”定义为：**到目前为止的一个时间段内，某个事件至少发生过一次(at least one occurrence)。**

二、重复事件与“近的过去”单一事件

上面把“重复事件”定义为：到目前为止的一个时间段内，某个事件至少发生过一次。但真正意义上的重复事件应该是发生过多次的。在这多次重复的活动当中，如果要明确指出是“**离现在最近的一次活动 (the latest**

occurrence or the occurrence nearest to now)”，那么这就变成了“近的过去”单一事件了。于是，重复事件与“近的过去”单一事件产生了密切联系。下面用下列例句来说明二者的关系：

10 He has been fired.

这个句子该作何理解呢？其实，在没有上下文的情况下，上面这个句子是有歧义的（产生歧义的原因见5.7.5小节的详细解释）。它既可以解释成“远的过去”事件，即表示“过去的经历”：

他被开除过。

也可以理解成“近的过去”单一事件：他被开除了。

为了消除歧义和更明确地表达意思，我们可以添加相应的时间状语来加以区分。比如说：

He has been fired ***before***.（他以前曾被开除过。）

He has ***just*** been fired.（他刚被开除了。）

对于上述两句中文译文，相信读者都能理解它们的区别。说“他被开除过”，表明“被开除(being fired)”这一事件至少发生过一次，而且这样的事件是具有可重复性的(repeatable)，即他在将来有可能还会被开除，所以这里可以用现在完成时态(has been fired)来表示他“被开除的经历”。这相当于一个“隐性”的重复事件。还可以加上具体的次数(如 three times)从而把它变成一个“显性”的重复活动：

He has been fired three times so far.（到目前为止，他已被开除过三次。）

另外，“他被开除过”只是说明他过去的经历，并不涉及他现在的就业状况，或者说，这句话与他现在是否有工作没有必然的联系。比如不能说“他被开除过，所以他现在没有工作”，这是不符合思维逻辑的。不过，我们完全可以说“他曾被开除过，但现在他有工作”：

He has been fired before, but he is now at work.（他曾被开除过，但现在他有工作。）

另一方面，说“他被开除了”，此时的“被开除”事件一定是强调“最近的一次”，即表示“近的过去”单一事件。这一“最近被开除事件”导致对现在的直接影响就是“他失业了”。所以可以说“他被开除了，所以现在没有工作”：

He has just been fired, so he is now out of work.（他刚被开除了，所以现在失业了。）

综上所述，重复事件与“近的过去”单一事件的关系体现在：在这重复事件当中，**离现在最近的一次事件(the latest occurrence or the occurrence nearest to now)**就是“近的过去”单一事件。

事实上，He has been fired. 这个句子存在歧义，这本身就说明了重复事件、“远的过去”单一事件以及“近的过去”单一事件这三者之间是密切相关的。像上面论述的那样，这个句子稍作改变就可以更明确地传达出这三个不同事件的含义。比如通过添加不同的状语 three times, before 和 just 说成：

11 He has been fired ***three times***.（到目前为止，他已经被开除过三次了。——重复事件）

12 He has been fired ***before***.（他以前被开除过。——“远的过去”单一事件）

13 He has ***just*** been fired.（他刚刚被开除了。——近的过去单一事件）

最后，对于三者间的关系，不妨这样来看：“远的过去”事件因为潜含了重复的意味，所以相当于“隐性”重复事件；“近的过去”单一事件可以看作是重复事件的一个特例(这从“重复事件”和“单一事件”两种思维的图示可知)，即某一动作在从过去到目前的一个时间段内只发生了一次，而且是离现在最近的一次，而并没有多次重复。因此，具体到某一个句子，可能既有“单一事件”的含义，也有“重复事件”的意味。

5.7.4 “动作表达”的完成时态与“状态表达”的一般现在时态

以上讨论了延续事件、重复事件以及单一事件三者之间的语义关系。接下来我们结合谓语动词“体(lexical aspect)”的特点——动作(action)和状态(state)来讨论它们之间的相关性。

“动作表达”和“状态表达”的区别往往与现在完成时态有着密切的联系。比如上面关于“结婚”的例子，如果要表达“我结婚有一年了”这样的延续状态时，只能用“状态表达”即 be married，而不能用“动作表达”即 married 或 get married，所以这句中文用英文表达就是：

1 I've ***been married*** for a year.

而不能说：

2 I've *married* for a year. *

3 I've *got married* for a year. *

这些句子前面曾经介绍过，在此不再赘述。关于“动作表达”和“状态表达”与完成时态的关系，有两条思维规律值得掌握。

规律一：在英语中，“动作表达”的完成时态在意思上相当于“状态表达”的一般现在时态。这里的动作往往指的是短暂动作，即表示一个“近的过去”单一事件。

比如谈到“死亡”时，既可以用“动作表达”的 die，也可以用“状态表达”的 be dead。要表达“他爸爸已经去世了”，就可以用“动作表达”的完成时态这样说：

4 His father ***has died.***

也可以用“状态表达”的一般现在时态这样说：

5 His father ***is dead.***

不过要注意，这两句话的语境背景还是稍有不同的。比如，说到你某位朋友的爸爸，如果你只是要说明他爸爸已经过世了这一事实，只需说 His father is dead. 此时他爸爸去世的时间往往不是在最近；但是，如果你的一位朋友的爸爸刚刚去世，你的朋友因此很悲痛伤心、精神恍惚，当别人问起你他怎么了，你就可以说是因为“他爸爸刚刚过世(His father ***has died.***)”这句话表达了我们谈到现在完成时态的用法时常说的“对现在有影响”，这个“现在”的影响对应于一个一般现在时态(如 is dead)。

再以“结婚”为例。看到 I have been married. 要理解成“我结过婚”。但要表示“我已经结婚了”，英文里可以用“动作表达”的完成时态这样说：

6 I ***have married.***

也可以用“状态表达”的一般现在时态这样说：

7 I ***am married.***

同上面谈论“死亡”的例句一样，这两句话的语境背景还是稍有不同的：I am married. 只是很客观地、平静地说明“我已经结婚了”这个事实；而 I have married. 则带有感情色彩，只适用于新婚不久的情况，比如“我”表现出兴奋的样子，见到朋友，满脸幸福地向朋友们宣布“我已经结婚了(I have married.)”——这即是完成时所要表达的“对现在的影响”。这种新婚时的兴奋劲一过，以后再向别人作自我介绍时说“我已经结婚了”，就只能说成 I'm married. 由此看来，能说 I have married. 的语境是相当有限的，正因为如此，一般外国人可能会认为 I have married. 这个句子听起来有点奇怪，甚至认为不正确，这一点请读者注意。

再比如：

8 My boss ***has arrived.***（我的老板来了。）

这样的“动作表达”完成时在意思上相当于：

My boss ***is here*** or is in his office now.（他现在就在这里或在他的办公室里。）

这样的“状态表达”的一般现在时态。

再比如，在酒店场景的英语中，问客人是否有预定，既可以用“动作表达”的完成时态这样说：

9 ***Have*** you ***made*** a reservation?

也可以用“状态表达”的一般现在时态这样说：

10 ***Do*** you ***have*** a reservation?

再比如，你去某个公司找人，说“我来找某某”，这时既可以用“状态表达”的一般现在时态这样说：

11 I'***m here*** to see...

也可以用“动作表达”的完成时态这样说：

12 I'***ve come here*** to see...

下面这个句子中的 have come 就是这种用法。这句话讲的是一个人在找过夜的地方：

13 Good evening. I*'ve come* to see if you've a room for just one night. I came for a treatment this morning from the eastern shore, and there's no bus till morning. 晚上好。请问你们有没有房间可供我住一晚？今天一早我从东海岸赶到这里来接受治疗，我要等到明天早上才有公共汽车回去。

再来看 have come 在下面两个笑话中的使用：

14 A: Mummy, you know that old vase in the hall?

B: Yes.

A: The one that has been handed down from generation to generation?

B: Yes.

A: Well, this generation ***has come*** to apologize for dropping it!

精品译文 A：妈妈，你知道客厅里的那件古董花瓶吗？

B：知道。

A：就是代代传下来的那件古董？

B：知道。

A：噢，现在"我这一代"来向你道歉，因为刚刚我把它摔了！

15 A man walked into a police station and said, "I*'ve come* about the job that's advertised outside."

"What job?" asked the policeman.

"The one on the poster outside that says: MAN WANTED FOR BURGLARY."

精品译文 一名男子走进警察局说道："我来是应聘你们外面广告上的那份工作。"

"什么工作？"警察问道。

"外面海报上说的'MAN WANTED FOR BURGLARY'。"

（注：wanted 在英文中既可以是"招聘"的意思，也可以是"通缉"的意思。）

我们看到，上面这两个笑话中都用了 have come 表示"我来是为了……"，这里不能用一般时态说成 I come，不过可以用"状态表达"I'm here。这是英文里很常见的一个语言表达现象，**即用最近发生的动作的"现在完成时态"来表达现在的状态**。需要提醒大家注意的是，这里的动作应该是"最近发生"的，即是一个"近的过去"单一事件，动作发生的过去时间离现在不能太远。比如萨达姆刚刚被美军抓住时，新闻报道就可以用现在完成时态说：

16 Saddam ***has been captured.***

意思相当于：Saddam ***is captive.***

肯尼迪刚刚被暗杀后，就可以说：

17 Kennedy ***has been assassinated.***

意思相当于：Kennedy ***is dead.***

但是，随着时间的改变，语境也就变了，"萨达姆被抓"、"肯尼迪被杀"离现在都比较久远了，因此，现在就不便说：Saddam ***has been captured***. 和 Kennedy ***has been*** assassinated. 而只能用一般过去时并加上具体的过去时间状语说成：Saddam was captured on 14 Dec. 2003. 和 Kennedy was assassinated on 22 Nov. 1963.

5.7.5 "动作表达"的完成时态与"状态表达"的完成时态

我们在上面的讨论中分别涉及下面这些例句：

1 He has been fired.

2 1) I have been married.

2) I have married.

3 1) His father has been dead. *

2) His father has died.

4 1) I have been old. *

2) I have become old.

细心的读者也许会有下面这些疑问：

为什么 He has been fired. 会有“他被开除了”和“他被开除过”这样的歧义？

为什么 I have been married. 没有歧义，只能理解为“我结过婚”，而不能理解成“我已经结婚了”？

为什么 His father has been dead. 不可以理解成 His father has died.（他爸爸已经去世了）而转化为正确的句子？同样，为什么 I have been old. 不能理解成“我已经老了”？

对于上述这些问题，的确有细心的读者（笔者在《新东方英语》杂志上的读者）来信提出过：

张老师：

你好，一直很喜欢贵刊的《语法新思维》专栏，这种“新思维”让我原本混乱的语法概念变得清晰易解。在最近一期（第4、5期）的《语法新思维》中我有一些不理解的地方需要您的指点。

在这里您提到了这个句子 He has been fired. 可以理解成“被开除过”或“被开除了”，那么 I have been married. His father has been dead. 和 I have been old. 这三个句子是否也都有这两种理解呢？——“我结婚了”，“他的爸爸过世了”和“我老了”，要是像这样理解，那后两个句子就不会是错的了。还有一点就是文中提到 His father has died. 这句在具体的语境中可以理解成对现在的影响，而 His father has bean dead. 是错误的，同样的是现在完成时，这两句有什么本质上的区别呢？

期待着您的回复，谢谢！

这些问题就是第二条规律可以来解释的了。现在请看规律二：

规律二：在英语中，“动作表达”的完成时态强调最近发生的事件，而“状态表达”的完成时态强调“较远的过去”经历。

“规律一”和“规律二”是有联系的，“状态表达”的一般时态相当于“动作表达”的完成时态（如 is dead 相当于 has died）；而“状态表达”若用了完成时态，则与“动作表达”的完成时态在时间上离现在的远近是不同的，前者较远，强调过去的经历（past experience），后者很近，强调现在的影响或结果（current influence）。这就是为什么：

5 His father ***has died.***

表示“他爸爸已经死了”，因为 has died 是“动作表达”，此时通常要理解成最近的事件。而

6 His father ***has been dead.*** *

这是“状态表达”，强调过去的经历，所以表示“他爸爸曾经死过（但现在又活过来了）”，显然不通，因此被认为是错句。同样道理：

7 I ***have been*** old. *

表示“我曾经老过（现在又返老还童了）”，意思不通，所以是错句。把它改为“动作表达”就可以了，比如说：

8 I ***have become*** old.

表示“我已经变老了”。同理，be married 是“状态表达”，所以它的现在完成时态一般表示“曾经的经历”，因此：

9 I ***have been*** married.

表示“我曾经结过婚”。再比如：

10 He ***has come*** here.

这样的“动作表达”的完成时表示“他来了”，相当于说 He is here. 即“他人现在在这里”。若改为“状态表达”：

11 He ***has been*** here.

则表示“他来过这里”，但现在他人不在这里了，已经走了。

值得注意的是，像上面 has come here 与 has been here 这样明确地表示动作 / 状态的谓语，在翻译时是不会有歧义的，即前者译成刚刚发生的动作——“他来了”，而后者译成曾经的经历——“他来过这里”。但是，对于

不能明确区分是动作还是状态的谓语，则会产生歧义。比如下面这个句子：

12 He ***has been fired.***

因为 be fired 既可以是"动作表达"也可以作为"状态表达"（这与"动态被动"和"静态被动"有密切联系，在此不再赘述），所以这个句子自然就会有两个意思：既可以理解成最近一次动作——"他被开除了"，也可以理解成曾经的经历——"他曾经被开除过"。

同样道理，5.6.2 小节讨论过的下面这个句子：

13 Have you asked your little brother to do the dishes?

之所以有两个意思——"你让你弟弟把碗刷了吗？"或"你有没有让你弟弟刷过碗？"就是因为这里的谓语既可以看作是"动作表达"，也可以是"状态表达"。

如果混淆了"动作表达"和"状态表达"的完成时态的不同意思，显然就会出现上面那位读者那样的疑问。正如他问到的"His father has died. 这句在具体语境中可以理解成对现在的影响，而 His father has bean dead. 是错误的，同样的是现在完成时，这两句有什么本质上的区别呢？"可以说，这两句的时态是一样的，本质的区别就在于前者是死的"动作表达"（即 die），而后者是死的"状态表达"（即用 be dead），从而有不同的意思理解。如果不知道这一点，就可能把 He has been dead. 这样的句子错误地理解成"他已经死了"，从而误认为它是正确的。

进一步分析，还可以有下列发现：

第一，如果句子的谓语已经明确区分了动作和状态，此时英文里没有歧义。比如 He has been here. 是"状态表达"，那么就只能作为"远的经历"理解，即"他来过这里"；而 He has come here. 是"动作表达"，那么就只能作为"最近的事件"理解，即"他来了"。同理，I have been married. I have been old. * 和 His father has been dead. * 均是"状态表达"，所以都只能作为"远的经历"来理解。但又因为后两个句子不具有重复性，所以是错误的。相应地，I have married. I have become old. 和 His father has died. 均是"动作表达"，所以都只能作为"最近的事件"来理解，分别译成"我刚刚结婚了"、"我已经老了"和"他爸爸刚刚过世"，都讲得通，所以都是正确的。

第二，如果句子的谓语既可以作为动作，也可以作为状态，此时英文就有歧义，区分要靠语境。比如 He has been fired. 就属于这种情况。

第三，有意思的是，与英语相比，汉语能轻易区分"过去的经历"和"最近的事件"——汉语**用语助词"过"表示"过去的经历"，而用语助词"了"表示"最近的事件"**，从而不会产生歧义。这不论是上面第一种情况，还是第二种情况，汉语中都能很好地区分。

可见，在这点上英语显得很 stupid！正是英语的这种 stupidity 给我们造成了翻译或理解上的麻烦：因为一个英语句子若没有语境就会产生歧义（ambiguity），既可以把它当作"过去地经历"译成"过"，也可以把它当作"最近地事件"译成"了"。对此，请读者倍加小心！

通过上面的详细举例讲解，希望各位读者从今以后能真正开始区分英文里的"动作表达"和"状态表达"，以及它们与时态搭配时产生的不同意义。我们这里讲的"动作表达"和"状态表达"是英语里非常基本的一个思维规律，平时大家在学英语时一定都有过接触，只不过以前没有从思维这样的高度去领悟并运用它，所以未能领略其精髓。没有掌握英语的思维规律，我们就永远只能停留在"鹦鹉学舌"的阶段，机械地模仿老外讲英语，而不能创造性地运用英语这门语言工具来深入地交流思想，这就像笔者的一个英国朋友说的"Chinese students are just parrots（中国的学生都是在鹦鹉学舌）"。这句话，听了虽然让人很不舒服，但却是中国英语教育和英语学习的现状和事实。我们背了那么多的单词，只是为了应付考试，到头来，背了的单词也不会用，简单的话不会说，简单的文章不会写。这就是因为我们没有学到英语这门语言的基本思维特点和表达规律，于是等到了说话或写文章，只好把英语单词按照汉语思维的表达规律进行机械的堆砌，造出的英语句子"汉语腔"十足。大家知道，我们的语言表达是一种思维的表达，我们说出来的句子只是传达我们内在思维的一个表面形式，而它的背后是有思维表达规律的，这些英语思维规律就是英文表达的最核心的秘诀。如果我们不掌握这些英语最底层的秘密，我们就永远只能停留在机械的模仿阶段。我们的"语法新思维"就是通过向大家揭示这些秘诀，帮助大家掌握英语的思维规律，从而能真正地驾驭英语，让自己的语言表达成为鲜活灵动的思维表达，而不再是"鹦鹉学舌"！

思维训练

Exercise 5.7 (Key: P342)

请说明下列三句意思差别并译成中文。

1. He has come here.
2. He has been here.
3. He has been here for three hours.

请用括号动词的适当的时态填空。

4. ______ you ______ (make) any vacation plans?
5. ______ you ______ (have) any vacation plans?
6. ______ you ______ (make) a reservation?
7. ______ you ______ (have) a reservation?

请判断下面句子的正误，错误的请说明原因。

8. John Kennedy has been assassinated.
9. His father has been dead.
10. This woman has been old.

请试着用两种方式翻译下列句子，并解释产生歧义的原因。

11. I have been fired.
12. I have cleaned the car.

5.8 完成时态用于最高级的句型

（一）

先来看一则笑话：

有一次，在飞机上，一名男子身边坐着一位怀抱小孩的母亲。这位母亲很为她的孩子骄傲，于是她给这位男子看她的孩子。可这位男子却不顾情面地说出了他的真心话：

1 I don't mean to offend you, madam. But this is the ***ugliest*** baby ***I've ever seen*** in my life.

精品译文 我无意冒犯您，夫人，但这是我平生所见到过的最丑的婴儿。

听完这句话，这位母亲简直不敢相信自己的耳朵，她问："你说什么？"男人回答：

2 I mean ***I've seen*** ugly babies before, but this baby is the ugliest of all.

精品译文 我的意思是说，我以前也见过长得丑的小孩，但你这个孩子是最丑的一个。

这话真是伤了一位母亲的心。她生气地哭叫起来："你怎么敢侮辱我和我的孩子！我要去控告你！"

这时，空中小姐听到吵闹声后马上跑了过来，她也不知道发生了什么，但她想安慰这位母亲，于是很关心地说道："夫人，放松点。我去给您倒杯茶，顺便拿根香蕉给您的猴子，您看好吗？(Excuse me, madam, why don't you just relax while I get you a cup of tea and a banana for ***your monkey***?)"

我想，听了这位空姐的话，这位母亲肯定都要气得背过气去！

真实往往是很残酷的。

这个笑话的英语原文请看本节后面的附录。我们先来分析一下这里的现在完成时态。英文常常把现在完成时态用于这样的结构中：

"最高级 + 名词 +that 从句 + 现在完成时谓语"

也就是说，**在形容词最高级修饰的名词后面若接有一个 that 从句，此时从句的谓语要用现在完成时态。**

这一结构虽然不需要理解就能轻而易举地记住，从而能够知道何时该用现在完成时态。但是正如前面多次强调过的，如果光是死记结构，而不了解结构背后的思维规律，终究是不能真正学好英语的。其实这一结构中的现在完成时态符合 5.5 节讨论的完成时"重复事件"的思维规律，同时也是符合完成时表示"回顾"这一核心意义的。要比较说某事物“最怎么样”，显然是“回顾”了自己以前类似的经历，并把它们与现在相比较，然后得出结论，才说现在这事物“最怎么样”。比如上面这个笑话中，那位男子说“这孩子是我平生所见到的最丑的婴儿”时，他显然是在“回顾”自己曾经见过的所有孩子，所以他后来接着说 I mean I***'ve seen*** ugly babies before, but this baby is the ugliest of all. 然后作比较，最后得出结论说“这个孩子是最丑的”。这非常像汉语中说的，“我见过长得丑的孩子，但没见过长得这么丑的”。可以看出，这里的现在完成时 I***'ve seen*** ugly babies before 就是表示一个重复的事件。

由上面的理性分析能看出，最高级与现在完成时态有一种“天然”的内在联系（The superlative adjective and the present perfect tense are intrinsically related），原因在于二者都具有“重复”的意义——表示从过去到目前为止的一个时间段内的重复事件。

大家应该还记得 5. 5. 1 小节中讲过的这个句子：

3 For us this ***has been*** the ***most perfect way*** to remember her, and this is how she would want to be remembered.

这是威廉王子在纪念他的母亲戴安娜的音乐会上说的一番话。在这个句子里，完成时 has been 与最高级 the most perfect way 就很好地结合在一起了。

进一步分析后会发现，为了配合最高级所表达的“重复”意义，要采用现在完成时态来造句，即我们可以把最高级所在的句子的谓语直接用现在完成时态，比如说成 this ***has been*** the most perfect way；也可以像本节讨论的那样在最高级后面的从句中使用现在完成时谓语，比如 this is the ugliest baby I***'ve ever seen***。此时，最高级所在的主句的谓语就要用一般时态了，如这里的 this is the ugliest baby I've ever seen。这相当于是把现在完成时态“后移”了——由原来的主句谓语移至从句谓语。

说到这里，也许有读者就会问了：那么该如何把 For us this ***has been the most perfect way*** to remember her... 这个句子的现在完成时“后移”到从句谓语呢？请大家现在就动笔试试看如何改写这个句子。

下面给大家提供一个改写的版本：

This ***is the most perfect way*** that we ***have had*** to remember her...

这里的现在完成时态由原句 For us this ***has been*** the most perfect way to remember her 中的 has been 位置“后移”至 This is the most perfect way that we ***have had*** to remember her...这个句子的 that 从句的位置 have had，而原来的 has been 变为现在的 is。

因此，对于较难理解其中完成时态的句子 For us this ***has been*** the most perfect way to remember her... 可以将其改写成 This ***is the most perfect way*** that we ***have had*** to remember her... 还可以进一步解释这个句子为 That means, we ***have had*** lots of different ways to remember her, but this is the most perfect of them all.（到目前为止，我们有过很多纪念她的方式，但这次音乐会是最佳的纪念方式。）这里的“重复”意义就非常明显，从而易于理解为什么要用现在完成时态。5. 5 节分析这个句子时强调过，这里的 has been 隐含了“重复”的意义。到这里，相信读者应该更能理解 has been 所具有的“重复”意义，以及这个句子谓语为什么要用 has been 而不是简单的 is 了。

下面这个例句讲的是当时的英国球星贝克汉姆（David Beckham）也出席了纪念戴安娜的音乐会，请看他是如何评价戴安娜的：

4 When the footballer took to the stage to huge cheers, he said: “I am truly honoured to be here today to help celebrate the incredible life of ***the most amazing lady*** this country ***has seen*** for many, many years. She was the nation's lady, the nation's princess, always has been and always will be.”

妙语点睛 小贝在他的讲话中同样是在最高级 the most amazing lady 后面的从句中使用了现在完成时态 has seen。

精品译文 当这位足球明星在热烈的欢呼声中走上舞台后，他说道：“我非常荣幸地出席今天这个音乐会，以此来纪念这位英国多年来一直是最有魅力的女性。她作为英国的王妃，过去是，现在是，将来也永远是。”

下面再来看一位牙医是如何“残酷而真实”地对待病人的：

5 “Good grief, you've got the ***biggest*** cavity（牙洞）that I***'ve ever seen***!” the dentist exclaimed as he examined a new patient.

"***The biggest*** cavity I***'ve ever seen***!" The patient snapped（厉声说）, "You don't have to repeat it."

"I didn't," replied the dentist, "That was an echo."

妙语点睛 这里，这位牙医真实的回答同样招来病人的不快。所以，有时人们还是爱听"美丽的谎言(white lies)"的。这个句子因为有了最高级 biggest，而具备了"回顾"过去的意义以及"重复事件"的意义，所以，从句谓语用了现在完成时。

精品译文 "天啊，这是我见过的最大的一个牙洞！"牙医在给病人看牙时大声喊道。

"我所见过地最大的牙洞！你不必非得重复说两遍啊。"病人生气地说道。

"我没有说两遍啊，刚才那是回声。"牙医答道。

我们再来看下面这个句子：

6 He is ***the cockiest*** guy I ***have ever met*** in my life.

妙语点睛 墨西哥前总统比森特·福克斯如此描述美国总统布什。在其出版的回忆录中，福克斯还透露，尽管布什总是表现出美国西部牛仔的做派，但他实际上很害怕骑马，他的得州农场也没有马。该从句中的 that 被省略了，原句相当于 He is the cockiest guy that I have ever met in my life.

精品译文 他是我有生以来见过的最自负的人。

5.5 节中提到过，美国前总统吉米·卡特 2007 年 5 月 19 日对布什政府提出强烈批评，认为布什政府在处理国际关系方面堪称"史上最差"。有专家认为，这是卡特迄今针对一名美国总统提出过的最强烈的指责。美国图兰大学历史学家暨卡特传记作者道格拉斯·布林克利说，卡特这么强烈地批评一名现任总统是"史无前例"的(Douglas Brinkley, a Tulane University presidential historian and Carter biographer, described Carter's comments as unprecedented.)下面来看他的原句是怎么说的：

7 This is ***the most forceful*** denunciation President Carter ***has ever made*** about an American president. When you call somebody the worst president, that's volatile. Those are fighting words.

妙语点睛 这里最高级 the most forceful 后面的从句中使用了现在完成时态 has ever made。

精品译文 这是卡特总统对一名美国总统最猛烈的斥责，当你把一个人称为"最差劲总统"时，这过于咄咄逼人，这是斗争用语。

在日常口语中，要告诉别人这是自己的"最怎么样"的经历时，就要用现在完成时态。比如：

8 This is ***the most interesting*** novel that I***'ve ever read.*** 这是我看过的最有趣的小说。

9 This is ***the hardest*** job that I***'ve ever done.*** 这是我做过的最难的工作。

10 A: This is ***the longest*** assignment we***'ve had*** all semester

B: You're telling me. We'll be lucky if we can do half of it.

A：这是我们这学期做过的最长的作业。

B：没错。我们能做完一半就算走运了。

11 Living with a roommate in a dorm has to be ***the hardest*** thing I***'ve encountered.***

和一个室友同住一间宿舍是我遇到过的最难的事情。

对于这样的表达，请读者注意模仿，今后可以用在自己的口语中。

(二)

在这个句型结构中，除了用最高级外，还可以用序数词(如 second)来修饰名词。此时，从句的谓语同样要用现在完成时态。比如下面这位喝咖啡上瘾的人：

12 A: This is the ***tenth*** cup of coffee that I***'ve drunk*** this evening.

B: How are you going to be able to fall asleep later if you keep on like this?

妙语点睛 从这个对话中，同样可以看出完成时态的"重复"意义：说话人是在"回顾"自己今晚"重复"喝了 10 杯咖啡。

精品译文 A：这是我今晚喝的第 10 杯咖啡了。

B：如果你一直这样喝下去，一会儿怎么能睡着觉啊？

再来看下面这个笑话：

13 A: Doctor, I'm very nervous. This is ***the first time*** I'***ve ever needed*** an operation.

B: Don't worry, I feel the same. This is ***the first operation*** ***I've ever performed.***

精品译文 A：医生，我现在很紧张。这是我第一次需要做手术。

B：别担心，我也很紧张，因为这是我第一次给人做手术。

在口语中，如果要告诉别人自己是第几次来某地方，都要用现在完成时态。比如：

14 This is ***the first time*** that I'***ve come*** to Beijing. 这是我第一次来北京。

15 This is ***the third time*** that I'***ve come*** to Paris. 这是我第三次来巴黎。

再来看下面这个关于电脑报错的句子：

16 A problem has been detected and Windows has been shut down to prevent damage to your computer. If this is ***the first time*** you'***ve seen*** this stop error screen, restart your computer. If this screen appears again, follow these steps.

妙语点睛 这里的主句中有序数词 first，所以后面从句的谓语用完成时态 have seen。另外两个完成时 has been detected 和 has been shut down 在 5. 6. 3 小节介绍过。

精品译文 有故障被发现，Windows 操作系统已被关闭，以免损坏你的电脑。如果这是你第一次看到这个终止操作的屏幕错误信息，请重新启动电脑。若该错误屏幕再次出现，请按照下列步骤操作。

最后，需要顺便提及的是，在上述句型中，主句的谓语若是一般过去时，比如 was（如 It was the second/best...），that 后面的句子的谓语要用过去完成时态。例如：

17 That ***was*** the ***tenth*** cup of coffee that I ***had drunk*** that night. 那是我那天晚上喝的第 10 杯咖啡。

思维总结

本节的内容较为简单，大家只要记住下列结构须用现在完成时态即可：

(This/That/It is+)最高级或序数词修饰名词 + that 从句，从句谓语用现在完成时。

同时，要能真正理解这一结构背后所反映的"重复"意义的现在完成时。

思维训练

Exercise 5. 8 (Key: P342)

请用适当的时态填空。

1. It is the third time that I ______ (come) to Beijing.
2. It is the fifth time that someone ______ (knock) at my door.
3. A: This is the longest assignment we ______ (have) all semester

   B: You're telling me. We'll be lucky if we can do half of it.
4. A: This is the most fascinating article that I ______ (ever, read).

   B: Oh, really? I would have thought that anything about electronics would be tedious.
5. This is the most interesting movie that I ______ (ever, see).
6. This book is huge. It has the most extensive collection of World War II photos that I ______ (ever, see).

请翻译成英文。

7. 这是我喝过的最美的酒。
8. 这是我读过的最糟糕的一本书。
9. 这是所有我做过的工作当中最难的一份。

附录：开心一刻

On a plane, a man sits next to a mother holding her baby. The mother is very proud of her baby. She shows it off to the man.

"I don't mean to offend you, madam. But this is the ***ugliest*** baby I***'ve ever seen*** in my life," the man said.

The woman cannot believe her ears, she asks, "Excuse me?"

"I mean I***'ve seen*** ugly babies before, but this baby is the ugliest of all," answers the man.

The woman is very angry and sad, and she starts shouting and crying. "How dare you insult me and my baby! I'm going to sue you."

The air stewardess hears the shouting. She quickly goes over to the woman and tries to calm her down. "Excuse me, madam, why don't you just relax while I get you a cup of tea and a banana for your monkey."

5.9 时间连词 since 的特殊用法

最后，我们来讨论一下 since 作为时间连词的用法，因为这与现在完成时态密切相关。先来看一个例句：

1 I ***have worked*** in this company since I left school. 自从毕业离校以来，我就一直在这家公司工作。

这个例句中的 since 作为时间连词，意思是"自从……以来"。与它有关的主句和从句时态搭配关系是：since 后面所接从句的谓语要用一般过去时态，如上面例句中的 left；与其搭配的主句谓语则用现在完成时态，如上面例句中的 have worked。

相信很多读者对 since 的上述用法非常熟悉。上述 since 的这一用法固然不错，但是如果据此就认为 since 后面的从句只能用一般过去时态而不能用其他时态，那就是只知其一，不知其二了，有时甚至会造成对句子意思完全错误的理解。比如，下面这个英文句子该如何理解？

2 It ***has been*** three years since I ***worked*** in this company.

很多读者看完这句话，就会很自然地将其理解为：

我在这家公司工作已经有三年了。

也就是将这句话完全等同于：

I ***have worked*** in this company ***for three years now.***

看到这里也许有读者会纳闷了：不就是这个意思吗？难道还能有其他意思？

其实，这句英文真正要表达的意思是：

It has been three years since I ***last worked*** here in this company. I ***have NOT worked*** in this company during the past three years.

也就说，这句话是要强调"我最后一次在这家公司工作是在三年前，换句话说，我过去三年间都没有在这家公司工作，也即我离开这家公司已经有三年了"。

看到这里，一定有读者觉得难以理解，为什么这个句子真正的意思与我们对其字面的理解相差如此遥远，甚至正好相反？要想弄清个中缘由，还得从动词的特点来分析。

通过比较上述两个 since 引导的从句的谓语动词 left 和 worked，会发现，left 是典型的"短暂动词"，而 worked 则是"延续动词"。问题就出在这动词延续性的长短上，因为 since 后面接延续性或短暂性动词，用于不同时态，所表达的意义是有区别的。具体思维规律如下：

一、since + 短暂动词

时间连词 since 接短暂动词的用法是最常用的，也就是大家常记住的这种时态搭配：主句用现在完成时，since 后面的从句用一般过去时。比如上面的这个例句：

3 I ***have worked*** in this company since I ***left*** school. 自从毕业离校以来，我就一直在这家公司工作。

再比如：

4 It ***has been*** three years since I ***came*** to China. 我来中国已经有三年了。

以上这两个例句里的 since 引导的从句的谓语动词 left 和 came 都是典型的短暂动词，而且这些动作都是在过去发生的，所以自然要用一般过去时态。

实际上，这里的谓语动词也可以采用现在完成时态，句子的意思不变。比如上面这两个句子也可以这样说：

5 I ***have worked*** in this company since I ***have left*** school.

6 It ***has been*** three years since I ***have come*** to China.

综上所述，since 后面接短暂动词时，用一般过去时态或现在完成时态均可，而且意思一样，都表示从句动作“结束”以来，主句活动在持续。翻译成中文时，句子的意思就按英文字面去理解。比如 leave 是短暂动词，不论用于一般过去时态（left）还是用于现在完成时态（have left），都表示 leave 的动作结束后，主句活动 work 才开始并且一直在持续（即离开学校后就一直在这家公司工作）。

二、since + 延续动词

当 since 接延续动词时，用一般过去时态或现在完成时态均可，但意思不一样。若用一般过去时态，则表示从句动作“结束”以来，主句活动在持续；若用现在完成时态，则表示从句动作“开始”以来，主句活动在持续。请比较：

7 1）It's been three years since I ***worked*** in this company.

2）It's been three years since I ***have worked*** in this company.

妙语点睛 在例句 1）中，worked 是延续动词用于一般过去时态，主句时间则是从 work 这个活动已经“结束”后开始算起到现在有三年了，即例句 1）表示“我”不在这家公司工作已经有三年了。在例句 2）中，have worked 是延续动词用于现在完成时态，主句时间则是从 work 这个活动“开始”以来算起到现在有三年了，即例句 2）表示“我”开始在这公司动作已经有三年了。

精品译文 1）我不在这家公司工作有三年了。

2）我在这家公司工作有三年了。

所以，如果只是死记 since 引导的从句都一定要用一般过去时态，若是从句碰巧接短暂动作还不至于造成误解，因为此时按英文字面翻译即可；但若是 since 引导的从句接延续动词并且用了一般过去时态，则往往会造成误解，因为此时就不能按照英文字面去理解了。

来看下面这封私人信件，请读者注意其中现在完成时态的用法：

8 Hi Clint!

It ***has been*** a while since we ***talked***...wow. I'm doing well. In some ways it has been a very difficult semester for me. I have been very busy with work, much more so than at Cambridge. I feel drained a lot of the time. I think the main thing that has made it hard is that Jenny has had a harder semester. She is under a lot of stress all the time, but she does a good job being patient and working hard. She is really amazing. In any case, I feel like both of us have just not had much energy to do things.

精品译文 你好，克林特！

我们好久没有交流了……哇！我一切都挺好的，不过这学期对我来说过得一直很辛苦，因为我一直在忙于学习，甚至比我在剑桥大学时更忙。我感觉时间不够用。这么辛苦还有一个原因是珍妮这学期也很累，她的压力一直很大，不过因为她很用心和勤奋，所以她也还挺顺利。她真是了不起。总的来说，我感觉我们就是没有力气参加别的活动了，主要精力就是放在了学习上。

这是笔者的美国朋友给笔者的来信，他在“回顾”自己忙碌的一学期时用了很多的现在完成时态，比如：

In some ways it ***has been*** a very difficult semester for me. I ***have been*** very busy with work, much more so than at Cambridge.

这两个完成时态都是表示延续状态，是完成时“延续”性思维的体现。接下来他讲到这么辛苦的原因时也用了两个现在完成时态：

I think the main thing that ***has made*** it hard is that Jenny ***has had*** a harder semester.

这里的 has made 相当于完成时“单一事件”的用法，而 has had 又是一个表示延续状态的用法：因为忙于学习了，所以其他活动没法参加，此时他也用了一个现在完成时：

In any case, I feel like both of us ***have*** just ***not had*** much energy to do things.

这里 have just not had 同样是表示延续状态意义的现在完成时。

现在回到第一个完成时的句子：

It ***has been*** a while since we ***talked***...wow.

这句话是不是很像上面分析的这个句子：

It ***has been*** three years since I ***worked*** in this company.

这里的 talked 是一个延续动词，用了一般过去时态，表示"我们最后一次交流到现在有好长时间了"，换句话说就是"我们好久没有交流了"，用英文解释就是：

9 It has been a while since we ***talked last time*** when we were both at Cambridge. We have NOT talked ever since then. 从我们最后一次交流到现在有很久了，当时我们俩都还在剑桥大学。从此以后我们就一直没有联系了。

事实上，这封信是在我们离开剑桥大学很长一段时间之后他写给我的，也就是"我们很长时间没有交流了"——这正是英文 It has been a while since we talked...要表达的意思。所以，这句话不能理解成：

我们谈了很长时间了*。

这样理解既不符合英文的思维表达，也不符合事实。

请看下面这个例句：

10 Since China ***has been*** open she'***s traveled*** to Australia, where she always dreamed of going, many times.

妙语点睛 这里的 since 引导的从句提前了，但这对时态没有影响。这里的从句用了现在完成时态 has been，表明中国"一直"在开放。如果用一般过去时态说成 Since China was open...则是表示中国不再奉行改革开放政策了，这显然不符合现实。另外，主句的完成时 has traveled 显然是表示重复活动，与 many times 呼应。

精品译文 自从中国开放以来，她已经多次到澳大利亚旅游，澳洲一直是她梦想去的地方。

再比如：

11 It's two years since I ***was*** in this university.

这里表示延续状态的动词 be 用了过去式 was，应该是表示从 was in this university 的状态结束后开始计算时间，所以此句应翻译为：我大学毕业已经有两年了。

而不能按照字面理解为：我上大学已经有两年了*。

"我上大学已经有两年了"应该说成：It's two years since I ***have been*** in this university.

注意：since 引导的主句如果单纯表示时间，可以说：It ***is*** 或 ***has been*** + 时间段 + since... 所以这句话也可以说成 It***'s been*** two years since I have been in this university。

现在通过更多的场景对话来深入理解 since 引导的从句的动词与时态的复杂关系。

12 **场景一：谈转学**

约翰和珍妮正在谈论自己想转学到剑桥大学(Cambridge University)去，但又担心不能成功……

John: I am thinking about Cambridge University. It has an excellent reputation. But it's probably very selective.

Jenny: But you ***have gotten*** good grades in the three semesters since you ***have been*** in here at the college, haven't you?

John: Yeah, mostly As in my major and a few Bs in sciences.

Jenny: So what are you worried about? Just ask your professors to write letters of recommendation for you and give you portfolio together, and you'll be set.

妙语点睛 这里用表示延续状态的 be 动词的完成式 have been，表示约翰一直在目前这个学院上学已有三个学期了。若是用表示延续状态的 be 动词的过去式 was，则表示约翰已经离开他现在的学院有三个学期了，这显然不符合上下文的语境。

精品译文 约翰：我在考虑转到剑桥大学去，那可是名校啊，但她对学生一定是要精心筛选的。

珍妮：但你现在在这个学院三个学期下来的成绩不是一直很好吗？

约翰：是啊，专业课基本上是优秀，其他课程有几门是良好。

珍妮：那你还担心什么呢？先让你的教授给你写几封推荐信，再准备其他一些申请材料，不就搞定了嘛。

13 场景二：要与家里保持联系

A: Are you keeping current on the news from home since you***'ve been*** here?

B: I've been getting weekly updates.

妙语点睛 这句话同样用了表示延续状态的be动词的完成式have been，以说明"你"一直在这，而不是离开了这个地方。另外，我们还发现，这里的主句改用了现在进行时态are you keeping...，因为进行时也可以表示持续，这类似于完成时的延续。

精品译文 A：你来这之后一直和家里有联系吗？最近有什么消息？

B：有的，我每星期都收到家里的消息。

14 场景三：锻炼有效果

A: I must admit that since I ***started*** the exercises I've been feeling less tired.

B: What did I tell you?

妙语点睛 这里从句的谓语start是一个短暂动词，所以就用一般过去时态，这是since引导的从句的谓语最常见的时态用法。

精品译文 A：我得承认，自从开始锻炼以来，我就再也不像以前那么觉得累了。

B：你看，我说什么来着！有效果吧！

另外，since引导的从句除了用一般过去时态或完成时态外，也可以根据具体语境用完成进行时态。比如下面的场景：

15 场景四：锻炼有效果

A: You look great since you***'ve been taking*** those exercise classes.

B: Thanks. I've never felt better in my life.

妙语点睛 这里的从句用完成进行时态have been taking，表示的是一个"重复活动"，即说明从过去到目前为止的一段时间内"你"多次参加锻炼。

精品译文 A：自从你经常参加那些锻炼以来，你的气色看起来好极了。

B：谢谢。我比以前感觉好多了。

下面这段话选自英国著名作家毛姆(W. Somerset Maugham, 1874-1965)的《午餐》(The Luncheon)：

16 I caught sight of her at the play and in answer to her beckoning I went over during the interval and sat down beside her. It ***was*** long since I ***had last seen*** her and if someone had not mentioned her name I hardly think I would have recognized her. She addressed me brightly.

"Well, it's many years since we first met. How time does fly! Do you remember the first time I saw you? You asked me to luncheon."

妙语点睛 这里since引导的从句用了过去完成时态，以便与主句中的一般过去时态was呼应。

精品译文 我在看演出的时候瞥见了她，她也朝我示意了一下，于是幕间休息的时候，我走过去坐在她的身边。我上次见她已经是很久以前的事了，如果不是有人提起了她的名字，我想我很难认出她来。她愉快地同我打招呼。

"哎呀，我们第一次见面是在许多年以前了，时间过得可真快！你记不记得我第一次见你时的情景？你邀请我去吃午餐。"

思维总结

从以上的讨论可知，since引导的从句的谓语不仅可以使用一般过去时态，还可以用其他时态，比如完成时态或完成进行时态。Since引导的从句的动词与时态的关系如下：

1. 接短暂动词，常用一般过去时态，翻译时按英文字面的意思理解即可。这是since最常见的用法。

2. 接延续动词，此时分两种情况：一是用一般过去时态(did)表示从句动作已经结束，翻译时不能按照英文字面的意思理解，这是本节内容讨论的重点，也是容易混淆的用法；二是用现在完成时态(have done)表示从句动作开始延续，翻译时可按照英文字面的意思理解。

3. 从句动作也可用完成进行时态(have been doing)，此时动词的延续性或短暂性不限。

思维训练

Exercise 5.9（Key: P342）

请翻译下列句子。

1. a. How long is it since you were a teacher?
   b. How long is it since you have been a teacher?
2. a. He has written to me frequently since I was ill.
   b. He has written to me frequently since I have been ill.
3. It's been three years since I had a holiday.

5.10 过去完成时态

5.3节中讲过，完成时态的本质思维就是用来"回顾"。比如现在完成时就是站在"现在时间"的角度回顾过去，表示一个从过去持续到现在的事件。同理类推，过去完成时就是站在"过去时间"的角度回顾更远的另一个过去，表示一个事件从这个更远的过去持续到离现在较近的过去。所以，对于过去完成时态的用法，关键首先是要确定过去时间的坐标，这一点将在下一节中详细讨论。过去完成时同现在完成时一样，可以表示延续事件、重复事件和单一事件这三种意义。因此，本节内容安排如下：

5.10.1 在"过去"回顾"更远的过去"

5.10.2 延续事件、重复事件和单一事件的过去完成时

5.10.3 过去完成时的其他意义和用法

5.10.4 过去完成时与一般过去时的比较

5.10.1 在"过去"回顾"更远的过去"

完成时态本质的思维特征就是"回顾"。现在完成时态就是站在"现在"回顾"过去"，而过去完成时态就是站在"过去"回顾"更远的过去"。现在完成时态以"现在"作为时间参照物来谈论过去，过去完成时态则是以"过去"作为时间参照物来谈论更远的过去。因此，可以说现在完成时和过去完成时本质的思维是一样的，区别只是参照的时间不同——前者是"现在"，而后者是"过去"。

现在完成时态的参照时间"现在"往往潜含在语境中，并不需要明确地表达出来。比如我们说：

1 I have been a school teacher for 28 years.

妙语点睛　这里的 for 28 years 就是表现距离现在有"28年"了，相当于说：I have been a school teacher for 28 years ***now***.

精品译文　我当老师到现在有28年了。

再比如，其他用于现在完成时态的典型时间状语，如 since 1980 表示"自从1980年以来"，这里显然是指从1980年一直到"现在"。所以，**现在完成时态的参照时间"现在"可以隐含在语境中而不明确地说出来。**

但是，对于过去完成时态，其参照时间"过去"则一般是要明确地在上下文中给出来的。说得更具体点，就是必须先有一个过去时，然后以这个过去时作为参照的时间点，来谈论更远的过去，此时这个更远的过去才能用过去完成时态。因此，**过去完成时态可以说是一个不能独立使用的时态，它必须依附于一个在上下文中出现的一般过去时。**下面我们通过一个故事——《最珍贵的礼物》，来阐明过去完成时与一般过去时的这种依赖关系。

（一）

最珍贵的礼物

曾经读到过这样一个故事，说的是一个小男孩从一个老人那里听说，在这个世界上有一份最好的礼物，谁要是能得到它谁就会永远幸福（It is the best present a person can receive because anyone who receives such a gift is happy forever.）这个礼物叫做 The Precious Present。

小男孩心想："真希望有人能把它作为圣诞节礼物送给我。"进而又一想，他就十分纳闷了："什么样的礼物会如此神奇呢，竟然能让拥有它的人永远幸福？"他发现自己很难找到答案，于是，就去问那位老人。

“它是一个魔戒吗？带上它之后就能让我所有的愿望都实现？”老人说：“不是。The Precious Present 与你的愿望无关。”

“它是一块神奇的飞毯吗？坐上它就能带我去任何我想去的地方？”老人说：“不是。The Precious Present 能让你无论身在何处，都会感到无比幸福。”

岁月流逝，小男孩现在已经长大成人，但他心中对那份神秘的礼物依然念念不忘。于是他又去问那位老人。

“您说的 The Precious Present 难道是海底的珍宝吗？比如说，是很久以前被海盗埋在海底的金币？”老人说：“不是。或者说它的确是珍宝，但与金币无关。”

对于老人一再否定的回答，这位年轻人备受打击，他开始有些不耐烦了，甚至是生气。他对老人愤愤地说：“如果您想让我幸福，那您为什么不直接告诉我 The Precious Present 到底是什么呢？还有，为什么不告诉我在哪里才能找到它呢？”老人无奈地说：“我的孩子，我无法告诉你，也无法给你，因为这个礼物除了你自己，其他任何人都无法送给你(The Precious Present is not something that someone gives you. It is a gift that you give yourself.)”

听了老人这番话，年轻人更加糊涂了。但不管怎样，他已决定自己去寻找 The Precious Present。

于是，他背起背包，动身去寻找那梦想中最珍贵的礼物。

然而，他历经数年苦苦寻求，却终无所获，失望而归。他现在已渐渐对找寻礼物失去了信心，因为他已经翻阅无数典籍，走访众人，足迹踏遍险峻的山巅、阴冷的山洞、湿热的密林和浩淼的大海。他已历经千辛万苦，因为他曾经如此想得到这份珍贵的礼物。但他苦苦的寻求换来的却是身心疲惫，一无所获。

最后，他又重新回到老人的身边……

(He packed his bags. He left where he was and went elsewhere to look for The Precious Present.

After many frustrating years, the man ***grew*** tired of looking for The Precious Present. He ***had read*** all the latest books. He ***had looked*** in the mirror and into the faces of other people. He ***had looked*** for it at the tops of mountains and in cold dark caves. He ***had searched*** for it in dense, humid jungles and underneath the seas. He ***had gone*** to extraordinary lengths. He ***had wanted*** so much to find The Precious Present. But it was all to no avail. His stressful search ***had exhausted*** him.

The man returned wearily to the old man's side...)

故事讲到这里，聪明的读者朋友一定知道了，这份能让我们永远幸福的“最珍贵的礼物”是什么了吧？现在言归正传，来分析一下上文中的过去完成时态(had done)的思维和用法。

在上面的故事中，开头几句用的是一般过去时态(如 the man ***grew*** tired of looking for The Precious Present)，但其他黑体部分用的是过去完成时态：

2 He ***had read*** all the latest books.

3 He ***had looked*** in the mirror and into the faces of other people.

4 He ***had looked*** for it at the tops of mountains and in cold dark caves.

5 He ***had searched*** for it in dense, humid jungles and underneath the seas.

6 He ***had gone*** to extraordinary lengths.

7 He ***had wanted*** so much to find The Precious Present.

8 His stressful search ***had exhausted*** him.

这是因为在英语思维里，陈述一件过去的事件（如上文中的 the man ***grew*** tired of looking for The Precious Present）的时候，再回顾联想到在这个过去的事件之前所发生的另外一个事件（如 He ***had read*** all the latest books.)，对这个“过去之前的过去(the past before the past)”就须用“过去完成时态(had done)”的动词形式。换言之，过去完成时是站在“过去时间”的角度回顾更远的过去，即谈的是“过去的过去”的情况。从这个意义上讲，**过去完成时态是一个不能独立存在的时态，它必须依附于一个一般过去时态，也就是说，要先有一般过去时态，才可能有过去完成时态。**

比如在上文中，grew 表示过去，而接下来的一系列活动都是发生在 grew 之前的，所以都用了过去完成时态，说成 had read, had looked in, had looked for, had searched, had gone, had wanted 和 had exhausted 等。

现在我们再回到刚才讲的故事中。当历经数年苦寻而终无结果之后，这位 unhappy young man 决定放弃寻找。而此时奇迹出现了，他突然顿悟：原来自己苦苦寻找的、希望能带给自己永远幸福的“最珍贵的礼物”——不是过去，不是将来，而是现在，是最宝贵的当下的生活（The Precious Present is just ***The Present, not the past and not the future, but The Precious Present.***）！

最珍贵的礼物 The Precious Present 不就是最珍贵的现在时刻(The Precious Present)吗？而每一个现在时刻的幸福不就是永远的幸福吗？

其实，这个故事要告诉我们的道理很简单，就是要活在当下！因为：

My past was the Present; my future will be the Present. The Present moment is the only reality I ever experience. As long as I continue to stay in the Present, I am happy forever: because Forever is always the Present! ***The Precious Present*** is something precious that I can give to and receive from myself, for I am precious. I am ***The Precious Present***!

（二）

下面来看第二个故事。这是马克·吐温(Mark Twain)写的一篇关于自己母亲的文章，题目是 This Was My Mother：

9 This Was My Mother

She was 82 and living in Keoluk when, unaccountably, she insisted upon attending a convention of old settlers of the Mississippi Valley. All the way there, and it was some distance, she was young again with excitement and eagerness. At the hotel she asked immediately for Dr. Barrett, of St. Louis. He ***had left*** for home that morning and would not be back, she was told. She turned away, the fire all gone from her, and asked to go home. Once there she sat silent and thinking for many days, then told us that when she was 18 she ***had loved*** a young medical student with all her heart. There was a misunderstanding and he left the country; she ***had immediately married***, to show him that she did not care. She ***had never seen*** him since and then she had read in a newspaper that he was going to attend the old settlers' convention. "Only three hours before we reached that hotel he ***had been*** there," she mourned.

She ***had kept*** that pathetic burden in her heart 64 years without any of us suspecting it. Before the year was out, her memory began to fail. She would write letters to school-mates who ***had been dead*** 40 years and wonder why they never answered. Four years later she died.

妙语点睛 文章一开始，作者就说 This Was My Mother，过去时 was 表明“母亲”已经不在人世，那么后面的经历都是过去的，这个 was 就为下文的过去完成时态奠定了“过去”的时间视角。在翻译时，如果把 This ***Was*** My Mother 简单直白地译成“这是我的母亲”，那么显然没有译出 was 的含义。我们不妨把它译成“回忆母亲”，用“回忆”表明母亲已不在人世——与英语的 was 有异曲同工之妙。

文章最后说道，母亲的记忆力差了，但尽管如此，母亲依然记得自己的初恋。这一段感情母亲深藏了 64 年，而且至今依然爱着，这就是为什么母亲非得坚持去参加那个聚会。

精品译文 **回忆母亲**

那年母亲 82 岁高龄，生活在科鲁克小镇。有一天，她无缘无故地非得坚持要去参加密西西比河谷老居民聚会。尽管离聚会地点还有挺长的一段路程，但是在去那里的一路上，她青春焕发、神采奕奕的，心中满是兴奋与盼望。一到聚会的酒店，她就立即打听有没有来自圣路易斯市的巴雷特医生的消息。有人告诉她说，他那天一早就回家了，再也不回来了。母亲马上转过脸去，神色黯然，并要求回家。有一次，她静静地坐着，呆呆地想了好几天，然后告诉我们说，她在 18 岁的时候曾经全心地爱过一个医学院的年轻学生。后来两人之间产生了误会，他离开了那个乡村，而她很快就结了婚，以向他表示自己并不在意(两人间曾经的感情)。从那以后，母亲就再也没有见过他了。后来，她在一份报纸上读到一则消息说，他要来参加那个居民聚会。“就在我们到达那家酒店三个小时前他还在那里”，母亲哀伤地说道。

从那以后的 64 年间，母亲心里一直有这么一个感情的疙瘩，可是我们谁也不知道。随着岁月的流逝，母亲的记忆力开始衰退，所以，尽管她当时的那些校友去世了都有 40 年了，但母亲依然经常给他们写信，还纳闷他们为什么从不回信。四年后，母亲去世了。

现在来分析其中的过去完成时态：

1） At the hotel she ***asked*** immediately for Dr. Barrett, of St. Louis. He ***had left for*** home that morning and would not be back, she was told.

妙语点睛 这里的 had left 是发生在过去的动作 asked 之前的，所以用了过去完成时。

另外值得注意的是，这里还有一个具体的过去时间 that morning。对于这样一个具体的过去时间，句子若采用一般过去时态是没有问题的，而这里用了过去完成时态。由此可见，**过去完成时态可以与具体的过去时间状语连用**。这不同于现在完成时态，因为现在完成时态是绝对不可以与具体的过去时间连用的。具体的过去时间之所以可以与过去完成时连用，是因为只要这个具体的过去时间是表示"过去的过去"，就符合过去完成时态的根本使用原则——表示"过去的过去"之情况。比如这里的 that morning 是在 asked 这个过去的时间之前，所以出现 that morning 与过去完成时 had left 搭配使用的情形。

精品译文 一到酒店，她就立即打听从圣路易斯市来的巴雷特医生的消息。有人告诉她说，他在那天一早就回家了，再也不回来了。

2） Once there she sat silent and thinking for many days, then ***told*** us that when she was 18 she ***had loved*** a young medical student with all her heart.

妙语点睛 这里的 had love 发生在过去的动作 told 之前，所以用了过去完成时。

精品译文 有一次，她静静地坐着，呆呆地想了好几天，然后告诉我们说，她在 18 岁的时候曾经全心地爱过一个医学院的年轻学生。

3） ...she ***had immediately married***, to show him that she did not care.

妙语点睛 这里的 had married 是相对于 was 而言的，发生在过去的动作 was 之前，所以用了过去完成时。

精品译文 ……她很快就结了婚，以向他表示自己并不在意(两人间曾经的感情)。

4） She ***had never seen*** him since and then she ***had read*** in a newspaper that he was going to attend the old settlers' convention.

妙语点睛 含有 since 的主句中一般是用现在完成时态，但这里用了过去完成时 had never seen，这是因为这里的 since 所表示的时间段不是到目前说话时为止，而是到当时为止——即她去世时为止。所以，要用过去完成时。

精品译文 从那以后，母亲就再也没有见过他了。后来，她在一份报纸上读到一则消息说，他要来参加那个居民聚会。

5） "Only three hours before we ***reached*** that hotel he ***had been*** there," she mourned.

妙语点睛 这里的 had been 是发生在过去的动作 reached 之前的，所以用了过去完成时。

精品译文 "就在我们到达那家酒店三个小时前他还在那里"，母亲哀伤地说道。

6） She ***had kept*** that pathetic burden in her heart 64 years without any of us suspecting it.

妙语点睛 这里的 had kept 是相对于 was 而言的，是在 was 之前持续了 64 年，所以用了过去完成时。

精品译文 从那以后的 64 年里，母亲心里一直有这么一个感情的疙瘩，可是我们谁也不知道。

7） She would write letters to school-mates who ***had been dead*** 40 years and wonder why they never answered.

妙语点睛 这里的 had been dead 是相对于过去的动作 would write 而言的，所以用了过去完成时。

精品译文 尽管她当时的那些校友去世都有 40 年了，但母亲依然经常给他们写信，并纳闷他们为什么从不回信。

下面来比较一篇文章，这篇文章讲的不是 mother 而是 grandmother：

10 My Grandmother

My grandmother ***is*** a woman who used to crack Brazil nuts open with her teeth, a woman who once ***lifted*** a car off the ground, when there ***was*** an accident and it had to be moved. She ***has been*** representing her death as imminent ever since ***I've known*** her — twenty-five years — and ***has discussed***, at length, the distribution of her possessions and her lamb coat. Every time we said goodbye, after our annual visit to Winnipeg, she'd weep and say she'd never see us again. But in the meantime, while every relative of her generation, and a good many of the younger ones, ***has died*** (usually nursed by her), she ***has kept*** making knishes, shopping for bargains, tending the healthiest plants I***'ve ever seen.***

妙语点睛 作者在文章的一开头用了一般现在时的is，向读者表明，他的祖母还没有去世，所以，说话的时间视角是“现在”，那么下文中要“回顾”过去的经历时，就自然会用到现在完成时态（比如has been, have known, has discussed, has died, has kept和has ever seen），而不可能出现过去完成时态。

精品译文 **我的祖母**

我的祖母年轻时，可以用牙齿嗑开巴西坚果；她还曾经把一辆汽车抬离地面，因为当时发生了交通事故，汽车必须挪动开。不过，自从我认识她这25年来，她就一直常常把死挂在嘴边，认为自己将不久于人世，而且还煞有其事地、十分认真地和大家商讨，在她死后，她的财产要如何分配，她的那件羔羊皮大衣该给谁。每年我们去温尼伯看望她后向她告别时，她总是流着泪说她再也见不到我们了。可这么多年来，尽管她那一辈的亲戚们都相继去世，甚至有好些比她还年轻的、她曾经照看过的亲戚先她而去，她老人家的身子依旧硬朗，还可以做煎饼、上街买东西、侍弄花草植物，而且她的花草养得比谁家的都好，是我见过的最茁壮的。

（三）

下面我再给出几个场景，读者可以体会一下过去完成时对一般过去时的这种依附关系。

11 **场景一：当国会下院议员的感受**

A: You have been a member of Parliament for five or six weeks now. Is it as you expected it to be?

B: I ***had*** an idea of what being a member of Parliament was like. I ***had been*** on a local authority for four years, and as a journalist and as a political activist I ***had visited*** the House of Commons, so it's more or less what I expected.

妙语点睛 在这段对话中，B一开始回答就用了一般过去时态had an idea，表示他以前就对当议员的生活有所了解，而不是在当上议员之后才知道的。后面他紧接着就解释他为什么会对议员的生活有了解，因为他自己以前曾经在（had been）一个政府机关（a local authority）工作过四年，并且常常拜访（had visited）国会下院。这里的had been和had visited都是基于前面的一般过去时态的had an idea基础上的一个更远的过去事件，所以都用了过去完成时态。也就是说，因为前文先有了had an idea，所以后文再往过去回顾就得用过去完成时had been和had visited。

但如果B是在做了五六个星期的议员后到现在才了解议员工作的，那么他就会用一般现在时态这样说：Since I have been a Member of Parliament for five or six weeks now, I ***have*** an idea of what being a member of Parliament ***is*** like.

言外之意，他以前对议员工作是不了解的。没有了一般过去时态作为时间参照，那么后文再对过去的事件进行陈述就无法用过去完成时态了，而应该改用一般过去时态。比如他会说：...I ***was*** on a local authority for four years and...I ***visited*** the House of Commons,...

但是，从前后两部分的逻辑关系来看，后文的had been和had visited是对前文的had an idea...的解释，如果改成一般现在时态后说成have an idea，那么后文的was和visited就与前文的have an idea在逻辑语义上没有联系了，因此也就无法对have an idea进行解释说明了。由此可见，时态在上下文语境中的灵活与正确的使用对于句义及话语的逻辑关系的表达是多么重要。

精品译文 A：你担任下院议员到现在已有五六个星期了，当议员和你以前所想象的是一样的吗？

B：我以前就知道当议员会是什么样的，因为我在当地的政府部门工作过四年，而且曾经以记者和政治活动家的身份与国会下院打过交道。所以，议员的工作跟我以前想象的差不多。

作者注：英国的国会叫做Parliament，the House of Commons是英国国会下议院，the House of Lords指英国国会上议院。

12 **场景二：母羊如何辨认小羊羔**

I ***had*** always ***wondered*** how the ewes knew their own lambs; now I ***learned*** that it was partly by voice, but chiefly by smell, looks not entering into it.

妙语点睛 在这句话中，had wondered 同样是表示在 learned 之前的过去，即过去的过去，所以用了过去完成时态。如果后面说成 now I ***learn*** that...，那么前面就得改为一般过去时态说成 I always ***wondered***...，因此整个句子就需要这样说：I always ***wondered*** how the ewes knew their own lambs; now I ***learn*** that it ***is*** partly by voice, but chiefly by smell, looks not entering into it.

精品译文 过去我一直不明白母羊是怎样认出自己生的羊羔的，后来我才知道，它们一方面是靠听声音来辨认，但主要是靠闻气味，根本就不用看长相。

13 **场景三：大风吹毁花园**

Yesterday the wind blew very hard. It ***had never blown*** that hard before. I knew when it first began that it would be bad for my garden. The plants that grew out in the open were hurt badly. Only a few which ***had already grown*** strong survived the windstorm. If I had only known, I would have planted them closer to my house.

妙语点睛 这里的 yesterday 就为下文定下了时间基调，所以才会出现 has never blown 和 had already grown 这样的过去完成时。

精品译文 昨天风很大，这是以前从来没有过的。一开始起风的时候我就知道，这下子我的花园可要遭殃了。园子里露天生长的花花草草被大风吹得惨不忍睹，只有那早些时候栽种的花草因为已经长大了，才在这次风暴中幸免于难。如果我早知道要刮风，我就会把它们种在离屋子近点的地方了。

前面讲过，过去完成时可以和过去的具体时间连用，而现在完成时态是不可以的。请看下面的短文：

14 **The Call of the Wild**

Sheba the shark floated just centimeters away from me. I could have reached out and touched her. Could have, that is, if the thick Plexiglas wall ***hadn't been*** there. The wall curved above my head, forming a tunnel through the aquarium. The tunnel allowed me to visit the home of Sheba and 3, 000 other sea animals.

When my undersea tour ***had ended***, I rode the escalator back to the mall. I felt a little strange. Moments ago, ***I'd been*** in the dark, beautiful world of the ocean floor. Now crowds of people and brightly lit stores surrounded me.

Located in Minnesota's Mall of America, Underwater Adventures offers visitors a virtual tour of the ocean floor. It does so in the convenience of a shopping center. This park is just one of many in the rapidly expanding world of animal parks.

妙语点睛 这里有 moments ago 这样的过去的具体时间，但它与过去完成时的 ***I'd been*** in the dark, beautiful world of the ocean floor. 连用。

精品译文 **野性的呼唤**

鲨鱼示巴在离我就几厘米远的地方浮游。我本来伸手就能摸到她的。说"本来能够摸到"，那就是说如果没有一道厚厚的玻璃墙挡在我们中间的话。这层玻璃墙在我头顶上方是弯曲的，这样形成一个通道，直达水族馆。透过这个玻璃通道，我能看到示巴以及其他三千多种海洋动物生活的家园。

当我的海底之旅结束的时候，我乘坐电梯回到了购物中心。我感觉有点奇怪。就在刚才，我还在黑暗而美丽的海底世界中，而现在，我处在人群和灯火通明的商店的包围之中。

水下探险世界位于明尼苏达州的美国购物中心里，它让游客们享受到一次真正的海底之旅，而享受这样的旅行非常方便，因为水下探险世界就在购物中心里面。这个探险世界就是正在迅速增加的诸多动物园中的一个。

另外，by the time 常常可以与过去完成时搭配使用，具体结构是：过去完成时 + by the time + 一般过去时。请看下面这个笑话：

15 A: It was my grandmother's birthday yesterday.

B: Is she old?

A: Well, ***by the time*** we ***lit up*** the last candle on her birthday cake, the first one ***had gone out***!

妙语点睛 因为 by the time 本身的意思是"在……之前"，所以过去的动作 lit 之前发生了 had gone out 的动作，故用过去完成时态。

精品译文 A：昨天是我奶奶的生日。

B：她年纪很大吗？

A：哦，等我们点完她生日蛋糕上的最后一支蜡烛时，第一支蜡烛都已经烧完了！

最后，请读者做下面的这道 2001 年的考研题：

16 She felt suitably humble just as she ______ when he had first taken a good look at her, hair waved and golden, nails red and pointed.

A. had B. had had C. would have had D. has had

正确答案 A。

妙语点睛 这道题有一定的难度，它考查考生对时态的掌握。首先看到这里主句的谓语 felt 是表示过去的时间。其次，时间状语从句 when 的谓语 had taken 是过去完成时。综合这两点，现在需要判断 as 引导的方式状语从句的谓语需要用什么时态。显然，as 引导的从句的谓语动作发生在 felt 之前，故也需要用过去完成时态，因而可以排除 C 和 D 选项。而选项 B 即 had had 是一个完整的谓语，谓语动词是 had，但该句中没有"had(有)"的意思。于是只能填 A 即 had。

分析到这里，也许还是有读者不明白为什么要填 A。其实，这里的 A 是一个省略形式，完整的谓语应该是 had done，done 可以省去。这里的 done 代替了 felt。因此，真正的谓语是 had felt，相当于说 as she ***had felt humble***，即表示"就像他当初见到她时，她感到谦卑那样"。

精品译文 她举止谦逊、得体，就像他当初见到她时，她所表现的那样。她的头发依然是波浪形、金黄色的，指甲涂成了红色，尖尖的。

从以上的分析可以看出，这道题其实是测试考生对过去完成时态的灵活运用。如果没有深厚的时态功底，这道题很难理解和答对。

思维总结

本小节的内容是过去完成时态的核心。在这里，我们强调了过去完成时态是一个不能独立存在的时态，它必须依附于一个一般过去时态，也就是说，要先有一般过去时态，才可能有过去完成时态。对此，读者应该真正地理解并灵活运用。

思维训练

Exercise 5. 10. 1（Key: P342）

请用括号中动词的适当形式完成下面句子。

1. I ______（just, sit）down in the recliner to watch TV when I ______（hear）a knock on the door. When I ______（open）the front door I ______（see）a young man standing there staring at me.
2. I ______（just, pour）myself a cup of tea when the phone ______（ring）. When I ______（come）back from answering it, the cup ______（be）empty. Somebody ______（drink）the tea or ______（throw）it away.
3. A: It's already 10 o'clock. I guess Bob and Amy won't be coming to the party.
   B: They ______（call）at nine to say that they ______（hold up）.

用括号中动词的适当形式完成下面笑话故事：

4. Surgeon: How ______ the patient ______（be）since I ______（operate）on his heart?
   Nurse: He is fine except that he seems to have a double heartbeat.
   Surgeon: Ah, so that's where it's gone! I was wondering where I ______（lose）my watch!
5. When her daughter ______（arrive）home from a party, Mrs. Thompson asked her if she ______（thank）her hostess. "No," she said. "The girl in front of me thanked her and the lady said 'Don't mention it' so I didn't."
6. Kenneth is so stupid. He phoned his teacher at school yesterday to say he couldn't come to school because he ______（lose）his voice!
7. A: A beggar stopped me the other day and said he ______（not, have）a bite for days.
   B: What did you do?

A: I bit him!

8. A: Mum! Mum! Dad ______ (fall) over a cliff.

B: Is he okay?

A: I don't know. He ______ (not, stop) falling when I left.

5.10.2 延续事件、重复事件和单一事件的过去完成时

现在完成时是站在“现在时间”的角度回顾过去。同理类推，过去完成时是站在“过去时间”的角度回顾更远的过去(The Past Perfect indicates “the past before the past” — what film-makers call a “flashback” in time.)即谈的是“过去的过去”的情况。这里同样涉及两个时间点：一个事件从更远的过去开始发生，然后“延续”到另一个较近的过去，或者“重复”到另一个较近的过去，或者在过去的某一时刻已经结束，这就分别构成了延续事件、重复事件和单一事件，完全类似于现在完成时，区别只是“坐标时间”由“现在”移至“过去”。因此，过去完成时态同样具有三种含义——延续事件、重复事件和单一事件。具体来说，过去完成时是用来表示在过去的某一时刻之前(即过去的过去)就已开始的动作，这一动作：

1. 在该过去时刻仍然在继续，或在该过去时刻刚刚停止(延续性思维)；
2. 在该过去时刻之前的一段时间内重复的动作(重复性思维)；
3. 在该过去时刻之前的某一时刻停止的动作(单一事件)。

下面分别举例解释说明。

一、过去完成时表示“延续事件”

如同现在完成时，**过去完成时可以表示开始于过去之前(即过去的过去)的动作或状态在过去这一时刻仍在持续**。具体来说，就是表示一个动作或状态在过去的某一时间之前已经开始，这一动作或状态一直持续到这一过去时间，并且到这一过去时间还未结束并仍有可能继续持续下去。

图解：

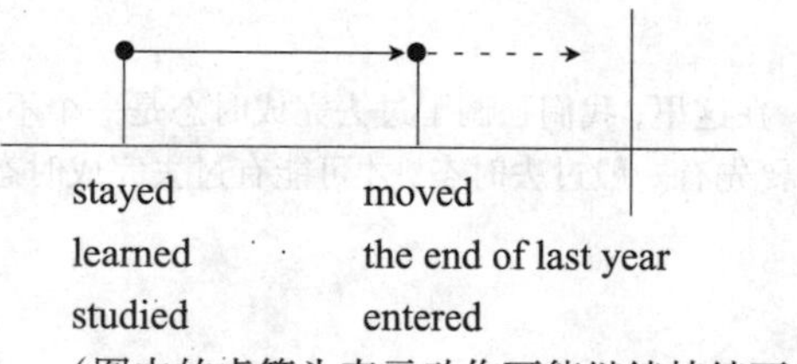

(图中的虚箭头表示动作可能继续持续下去)

请看例句：

1 I *had stayed* in America for two years when he moved here.

妙语点睛 moved 是过去的动作，stayed 发生在 moved 之前，即过去的过去，并且在 moved 之后还将会继续下去，因此用过去完成时 had stayed。

精品译文 他搬到美国时，我在这里已经生活了两年了。

2 I *had learned* 1, 000 words by the end of last year.

妙语点睛 learned 在过去的时间 the end of last year 之前已开始发生，到“去年年底”之后还将可能持续下去，因此用过去完成时 had learned。

精品译文 到去年末，我已经学会了 1, 000 个单词。

再比如，谈到学英语的时间，可以这么说：

3 We *had studied* English for six years when we entered college.

妙语点睛 studied 在过去的动作 entered 之前已开始发生，并且继续延续，因此用过去完成时 had studied。

精品译文 进入大学的时候，我们已经学了六年英语了。

当然，也可以谈一般的情况，此时 when 引导的从句的谓语可以用一般现在时态，那么主句就要改成现在完成时态了。比如说成：

4 We *have studied* English for six years when we *enter* college.

再来看其他例句：

5 A: It's already 10 o'clock. I guess Bob and Amy won't be coming to the party.

B: They ***called*** at nine to say that they***'d been held up.***

妙语点睛 现在的时间是 10 点，在 9 点钟这一过去的时间打电话时，Bob 和 Amy 已经"有事被耽误了"，所以"被耽误"应该用过去完成时 had been held up。

精品译文 A：现在已经 10 点了。我猜想鲍勃和艾米不会来参加聚会了。

B：他们 9 点钟来过电话说他们有事被耽误了，不来了。

6 **Why Did the Easter Islanders Disappear?**

Isolated in middle Pacific Ocean, Easter Island has attracted anthropologists ever since its discovery in 1772. This civilization ***had lived*** for 1, 200 years on this small island. Who were they, and why did they sculpt those big stone heads with staring eyes?

妙语点睛 这里的过去完成时 had lived 一直持续到另外一个过去的时间 its discovery in 1772。

精品译文 复活节岛上的居民为何消失了？

复活节岛位于太平洋中央，自从人们于 1772 年发现它以来，已经吸引了许多考古学家。该文明在这座小岛上延续了 1, 200 年。他们是谁？他们为什么要雕刻那些大头、瞪眼的雕像？

或由上下文明确告知动作或状态持续到过去这一时刻即停止。

图解：

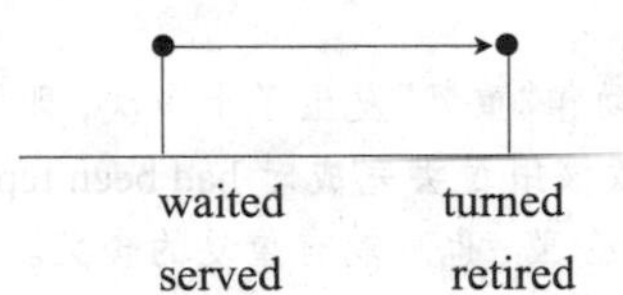

请看例句：

7 Former Japanese Prime Minister Keizo Obuchi, who ***had been*** in a coma（昏迷）for six weeks, ***died*** of a cerebral（大脑的）infarction（梗塞）at a Tokyo hospital.

日本前首相小渊惠三，在昏迷了长达六个星期后，因患脑梗塞死于东京的一家医院。

8 I ***had waited*** for her for two hours in such a severe winter when she eventually ***turned*** up, which of course drove me mad. 我在这样严寒的冬日里等了她两个小时，所以当她终于出现的时候，我当然气得要命。

9 He ***had served*** in the army for ten years; then he ***retired*** and ***married***. His children were now at school.

他当过 10 年兵，后来退伍并结了婚。他的孩子当时都在上学。

10 There ***had been*** fifty colleges in our city up till 1993. 到 1993 年时，我们的城市里已经有了 50 所大学。

二、过去完成时表示"重复事件"

如同现在完成时，过去完成时可以表示在过去之前开始的动作，**在过去之前的一段时间内重复发生。**

图解：

下面这篇短文谈到了著名影星奥黛丽·赫本(Audrey Hepburn)：

11 In 1988, Audrey became a special ambassador to the United Nations UNICEF fund helping children in Latin America and Africa, a position she retained until 1993. She was named to ***People'***s magazine as one of the 50 most beautiful people in the world. Her last film was Always in 1989. Audrey Hepburn died on January 20, 1993 in Tolochnaz, Switzerland, from colon cancer. She ***had made*** a total of 31 high quality movies. Her elegance and style will always be remembered in film history as evidenced by her being named to ***Empire*** magazine's "The Top 100 Movie Stars of All Time".

妙语点睛 这里的过去完成时 had made 显然是表示过去重复的动作，且该动作只重复到过去，没有一直持续到现在，所以用过去完成时。读者可以将该句与 5.5.1 小节的有关汤姆·克鲁斯(Tom Cruise)的这个例句进行比较：He moved to New York and appeared in a few teen movies before starring in his first big hit, Top Gun in 1986. Since then he ***has made*** hit after hit movies.

因为阿汤哥现在还在世，因此他拍电影这一活动就可能一直重复到现在直至将来，所以这里要用现在完成时 has made。

精品译文 1988 年，奥黛丽·赫本成为了联合国儿童基金会的一名特殊的大使，致力于帮助拉丁美洲和非洲的儿童，她在这个职位上一直干到了 1993 年。她被《人物》杂志评为世界上 50 个最美丽的女人之一。她平生的最后一部影片是拍摄于 1989 年的《永远》。奥黛丽·赫本因患结肠癌，于 1993 年 1 月 20 日在瑞士的托洛那茨去世。她一生中共拍摄了 31 部高水平的影片，她的优雅和风格将永载电影史册。为此，她被《帝国》杂志评为"历史上最耀眼的 100 名影星"。

再来看一个关于 2003 年爆发的 SARS 的新闻报道：

12 Students at Northern Jiaotong University are welcomed with flowers after being discharged from quarantine yesterday afternoon in Beijing. Nearly 400 students were in isolation in a dormitory compound for a fortnight. More than 10 severe acute respiratory syndrome (SARS) cases ***had been reported*** in the building before it ***was sealed off*** on April 24. No new cases were found during the isolation period. Quarantine measures were also lifted yesterday at a residential building of Beijing's Central University of Finance and Economics, where some 38 families ***had been isolated*** since April 24.

妙语点睛 在过去的动作 was sealed off 之前，reported 的动作"重复"发生了十多次，即文中说的 more than 10 severe acute respiratory syndrome (SARS)，故该用过去完成时 had been reported。另外，对于过去完成时 had been isolated，既可能有延续的含义，也可能有重复的含义。这里出现了 since，虽然与 since 搭配的主句一般是现在完成时态，但这里用了过去完成时态的 had been isolated，因为"被隔离"只持续到上文出现的 yesterday afternoon，而没有持续到现在。这里的 yesterday afternoon 就相当于一个过去的参照时间。

精品译文 昨天下午，北京的北方交通大学的学生们被解除了检疫隔离，受到了学校热烈的迎接。近 400 名学生在一座单独的宿舍楼中被隔离了两周。在该宿舍楼于 4 月 24 日被封锁之前，这里报告了十几个"非典"病例。在隔离期间，没有发现新的病例。北京的中央财经大学中的一座居民楼也于昨日解除了检疫隔离，自从 4 月 24 日起，这座楼里大约 38 户居民被隔离。

请看其他例句：

13 I ***had proposed*** to her five times, but she still refused to marry me. 我已经向她求婚五次了，但还是被拒绝。

14 I ***had written*** her 100 letters when she finally promised to marry me.
我给她写了 100 封信，她最后终于答应嫁给我了。

15 Clint ***had written*** three letters by the time she arrived. 她到达的时候，克林特写了三封信。

三、过去完成时表示"单一事件"

如同现在完成时，过去完成时可以表示**开始于过去之前的动作到过去这一时刻之前即已停止**。具体来说，就是表示一个动作或状态在过去的某一时间之前已经开始，并在这一过去的时间之前即告结束，而没有持续到这一过去的时刻。这时过去完成时的动作通常是短暂动作。

图解：

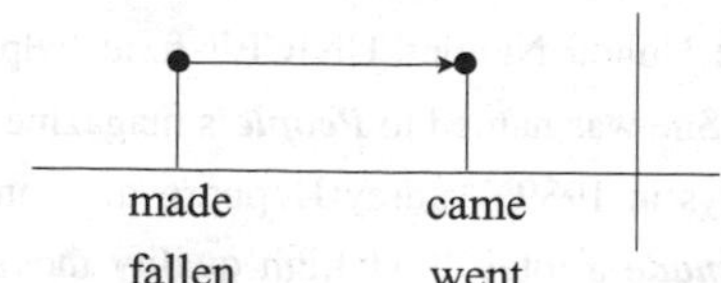

请看例句：

16 She ***had made*** everything ready before I ***came***.

妙语点睛 这里 made 的动作在 came 之前已经完成，故用过去完成时 had made。

精品译文 在我来之前，她已经把一切都准备好了。

17 Her baby ***had fallen*** asleep when she ***went*** into the room.

妙语点睛 这里 fall 的动作在 went 之前已经完成，故用过去完成时 had fallen。

精品译文 她进房间时，孩子已经睡着了。

18 I ***had just poured*** myself a cup of tea when the phone ***rang***. When I came back from answering it, the cup was empty. Somebody ***had drunk*** the tea or ***thrown*** it away.

妙语点睛 在过去的动作 rang 之前 pour 的动作已经完成，故用过去完成时 had poured。同理，在过去的状态 was empty 之前 drink 和 throw 的动作已经完成，故两者都用过去完成时 had drunk 和(had) thrown。

精品译文 我刚刚给自己倒了一杯茶，这时电话铃响了。于是我去接电话，接完电话回来的时候，发现杯子空了。有人已经把茶喝了或者是倒掉了。

19 I ***had just sat*** down in the recliner to watch TV when I ***heard*** a knock on the door. When I opened the front door I saw a young man standing there staring at me.

妙语点睛 在过去的动作 heard 之前 sat 的动作已经完成，故用过去完成时 had sat。

精品译文 我刚坐在躺椅上准备看电视的时候，听到有人敲门。打开前门，我看见一个年轻人站在门前凝视着我。

5.10.3 过去完成时的其他意义和用法

本节将来总结一下过去完成时的其他用法。

一、表示"非真实"的过去

主要是指 intend, mean, hope, want, plan, suppose, expect, think, propose 和 wish 等动词用于过去完成时，可表示过去未能实现的计划、设想、意图或希望等。请看例句：

1 I ***had intended*** to watch just one program, but somehow I couldn't make myself switch off the TV.
我本来打算只看一个电视节目，可不知怎的，电视打开之后我就关不了了。

2 I ***had intended*** to see you, but I was busy. 我本打算去看你，但是我太忙了。

3 I ***had planned*** to go shopping with you, but my mother came to see me just when I was about to go.
我本打算和你一起去逛街，但正当我要出门的时候，我妈妈过来看我了。

4 She ***had hoped*** that he would come to date her, but he didn't show up.
她本来希望他能来约会她，但是他没露面。

5 They ***had hoped*** to see you off at the airport, but they got there too late.
他们本来希望去机场给你送行，但是他们到得太晚了。

6 A: Peter ***had hoped*** to have his apartment painted by this time.
B: But he hasn't even started yet, has he?
A：彼得本来是希望到现在已经把他的公寓粉刷完了。
B：可他不是还没有开始刷吗？

7 A: Are you glad you came to China?
B: Yes. Indeed. I***'d considered*** going to Tokyo or Singapore, but I've never regretted my decision.
A：你来到中国之后感到高兴吗？
B：是的，非常开心。我本来是考虑去东京或新加坡的，但现在我从不后悔当初的决定。

二、用于最高级句型

这一点完全类似于我们在 5. 8 节中讨论过的现在完成时的用法，即用在 "It was the + 序数词（first, second...）或最高级…… that……"句型中。例如：

8 It ***was the third time*** that someone ***had interrupted*** me that night. 那是那天晚上我第三次被打断。

9 On his next trip he arrived a little after seven in the morning. As a gift, he ***brought*** a big fish and a quart of ***the largest oysters I had ever seen***. He said he ***had shucked*** them that morning before he left so that they'd be nice and fresh. I knew his bus left at 4:00 a. m. and I wondered what time he had to get up in order to do this for us.

妙语点睛 因为有过去时的 bought 表明是过去的时间，所以在最高级 the largest 的后面要用过去完成时态 had seen。

精品译文 他再次来的时候，早上七点刚过就到了。为了答谢我们，他给我们带来了一条很大的鱼，还有一夸脱重的牡蛎，那是我所见过的最大的牡蛎。他说，他那天早上出发之前才把牡蛎去壳，这样能保持肉质鲜美。我知道他乘坐的公共汽车是凌晨 4 点启程的，那他究竟要多早起床为我们做这些事啊！

5. 10. 4 过去完成时与一般过去时的比较

比较 1：两个或两个以上相继发生的动作，用and 或 but 按动作发生的先后顺序连接，此时要用一般过去时，而不用过去完成时。过去完成时则强调主语在过去的某一时刻"回顾"更早的动作。具体来说，如果在谈论过去某一事件时，又想到在这之前已发生的某事，就要用过去完成时态。例如：

1 He ***opened*** the door and ***entered***, but ***found*** nobody. 他打开门进去了，但一个人都没看见。

请读者比较：

2 1) He ***served*** in the army for ten years; then ***retired*** and ***married***. His children ***are*** now at school.

2) He ***had served*** in the army for ten years; then he ***retired*** and ***married***. His children ***were*** now at school.

妙语点睛 在例句 1)中，因为有了 are 表示现在的时间，作为现在的参照时间，所以在此之前的 serve 的动作，应该用一般过去时 served。在例句 2)中，因为有了 were 表示过去的时间，作为过去的参照时间，所以回顾在此之前的 serve 的动作，应该用过去完成时 had served。

精品译文 1)他当过 10 年兵，然后退伍并结了婚。他的孩子现在都在上学。

2)他当过 10 年兵，后来退伍并结了婚。他的孩子当时都在上学。

3 He ***had served*** in the airforce for ten years before he ***died*** in the jet-crash incident.

妙语点睛 因为有了 died 表示过去的时间，作为过去的参照时间，所以回顾在此之前的 serve 的动作应该用过去完成时 had served。

精品译文 在上次的坠机事故中他牺牲了，在那之前他在空军中服役了 10 年。

4 I heard voices and ***realized*** that there ***were*** several people in the next room.

我听见说话的声音，知道隔壁房间里有人。

5 I saw empty glasses and cigar butts on the table and ***realized*** that someone ***had been*** in the room.

我看见桌子上有空杯子和烟蒂，知道了屋子里有人来过。

6 I ***realized*** that we ***had met*** before.

我意识到我们以前见过面。

这里不说：I ***realized*** that we ***met*** before. *

比较 2：在表示两个相继发生的动作时，用过去完成时可以表示一个动作完成以后，另一个动作才开始发生，从而使得两个动作相互独立，彼此脱离开来。用一般过去时，则可能表示一个动作"导致"另一个动作的发生，或两动作之间有一种因果关系。例如：

7 When I ***had opened*** all the windows, I sat down and had a cup of tea.

不宜说：When I ***opened*** all the windows, I sat down and had a cup of tea. *

我把所有的窗子都打开后，就坐下来喝了杯茶。

8 When I ***opened*** the window the cat jumped in.（比说 When I ***had opened***...更自然。）

我刚把窗子一打开，就有只猫跳了进来。

9 When I ***had written*** my letters I did some gardening.

不宜说：When I ***wrote*** my letters I did some gardening. *

我把信写完后，就到花园里干了些活。

10 When I ***wrote*** him a letter, he came at once. 我给他去了封信后，他立即就来了。

11 When the singer ***had sung*** her song, she sat down. 这名歌手唱完歌以后，就坐下了。

上面这句话若说成：When the singer ***sang*** her song, she sat down.

则可能给人造成这种印象：这位歌手喜欢坐着唱歌。

思维训练

Exercise 5. 10（Key: P343）

请读者研读下面故事，并认真分析其中黑体部分的过去完成时态的含义。

Appointment with Love

Six minutes to six, said the clock over the information booth in New York's Grand Central Station. The tall, young Army lieutenant lifted his sunburned face and narrowed his eyes to note the exact time. His heart was pounding with a beat. In six minutes he would see the woman who ***had filled*** such a special place in his life for the past 13 months, the woman he ***had never seen***, yet whose written words ***had sustained*** him unfailingly.

Lieutenant Blandford remembered one day in particular, during the worst of the fighting, when his plane ***had been caught*** in the midst of a pack of enemy planes. In one of his letters he ***had confessed*** to her that he often felt fear, and only a few days before this battle he ***had received*** her answer, "Of course you fear...all brave men do. Next time you doubt yourself, I want you to hear my voice reciting to you: Yeah, though I walk through the Valley of the Shadow of Death, I will fear no evil, for thou are with me..." He ***had remembered***, and it ***had renewed*** his strength.

Now he was going to hear her real voice. Four minutes to six.

A girl passed close to him, and Lieutenant Blandford started. She was wearing a flower, but it was not the little red rose they ***had agreed upon***. Besides, this girl was only about 18, and Hopis Meynell ***had told*** him she was 30. "What of it?" he ***had answered***. "I'm 32." He was 29.

His mind went back to that book he ***had read*** in the training camp. Of Human Bondage it was, and throughout the book were notes in a woman's handwriting. He ***had never believed*** that a woman could see into a man's heart so tenderly, so understandingly. Her name was on the bookplate: Hopis Meynell. He ***had got*** hold of a New York City telephone book and found her address. He ***had written***, and she ***had answered***. Next day he ***had been shipped out***, but they ***had gone*** on writing.

For 13 months she ***had faithfully*** replied. When his letters did not arrive, she wrote anyway, and now he believed that he loved her and that she loved him.

But she ***had refused*** all his pleas to send him her photograph. She ***had explained***, "If your feeling for me has any reality, what I look like won't matter. Suppose I'm beautiful. I'd always be haunted by the feeling that you ***had been taking*** a chance on just that, and that kind of love would disgust me. Suppose I'm plain (and you must admit that this is more likely), then I'd always fear that you were only going on writing because you were lonely and had no one else. No, don't ask for my picture. When you come to New York, you shall see me and then you shall make your decision."

One minute to six...he pulled hard on a cigarette. Then Lieutenant Blandford's heart leaped.

A young woman was coming toward him. Her figure was long and slim, her blond hair lay back in curls over her delicate ears. Her eyes were as blue as flowers, her lips and chin had a gentle firmness. In her pale-green suit, she was like springtime come alive.

He started toward her, forgetting to notice whether she was wearing rose or not, and as he moved, a small, provocative smile curved her lips.

"Going my way, soldier?" she murmured. He made one step closer to her. Then he saw Hollis Meynell.

She was standing almost directly behind the girl, a woman well past 40, her graying hair tucked under a worn hat. She was more than plump, her thick ankle feet were thrust into low-heeled shoes.

But she wore a red rose on her rumpled coat. The girl in the green suit was walking quickly. Blandford felt as though he were being split into two, so keen was his desire to follow the girl, yet so deep was his longing for the woman whose spirit had truly companioned and upheld his own, and there she stood. He could see her pale, plump face was gentle and sensible and her gray eyes had a warm twinkle.

Lieutenant Blandford did not hesitate. His fingers gripped the worn copy of Human Bondage, which was to identify him to her. This would not be love, but it would be something precious, a friendship for which he had been and must ever be grateful...

He squared his shoulders, saluted, and held the book out toward the woman, although even while he spoke he felt the bitterness of his disappointment. "I'm John Blandford, and you...you are Miss Meynell. May...may I take you to dinner?"

The woman smiled. "I don't know what this is all about, son," she answered. "That young lady in the green suit, she begged me to wear this rose on my coat. And she said that if you asked me to go out with you, I should tell you she's waiting for you in that restaurant across the street. She said it was some kind of a test."

5.11 将来完成时

本节先来讨论将来完成动作的开始时间，然后简单介绍将来完成时的三种思维用法。因此，本节内容安排如下：

5.11.1 将来完成动作的开始时间
5.11.2 将来完成时的三种思维用法

5.11.1 将来完成动作的开始时间

现在完成时是以“现在”作为“坐标时间”，来描述开始于现在之前（即过去）的动作持续到现在。过去完成时是以“过去”作为“坐标时间”，来描述开始于过去之前（即过去的过去）的动作持续到过去。同理，将来完成时是以“将来”作为“坐标时间”，来表示开始于**将来之前**（可能是**过去**、**现在**或**将来**）的动作持续到将来。注意，这里说动作开始于“将来之前”，意味着动作开始的时间可能是过去的某一时刻、可能是现在的某一时刻，或者也可能是将来的某一时刻。但动作开始的时间并不重要，关键是说话人要站在**将来的某一时间**来谈某一动作的完成情况。例如：

We ***will have taken*** five exams ***by next Friday.***

妙语点睛 1）“我们”可能是昨天开始考试的，比如说成：

We started our exam yesterday and we ***will have taken*** five exams by next Friday.

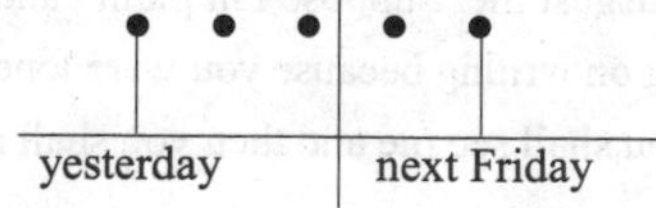

2）可能是今天开始考试的，比如说成：

We have started our exam today and we ***will have taken*** five exams by next Friday.

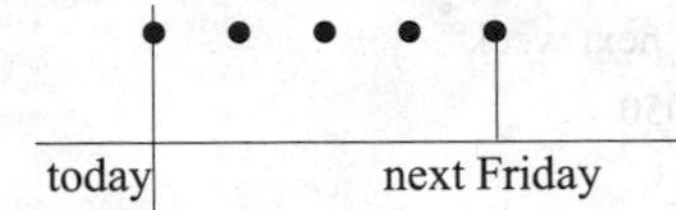

3）也可能是明天才开始考试，比如说成：

We will start our exam tomorrow and we ***will have taken*** five exams by next Friday.

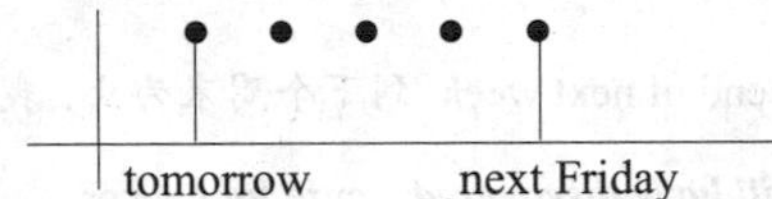

但具体是哪一天开始的并不重要，说话人强调的是他们一共有五门考试。

精品译文 到下个星期五之前，我们将完成五门考试。

5.11.2 将来完成时的三种思维用法

同前面其他的完成时态一样，将来完成时态有三种基本用法。

一、延续事件

表示在将来某一时刻之前开始的动作，一直延续到该时刻，并可能继续延续下去。

图解：

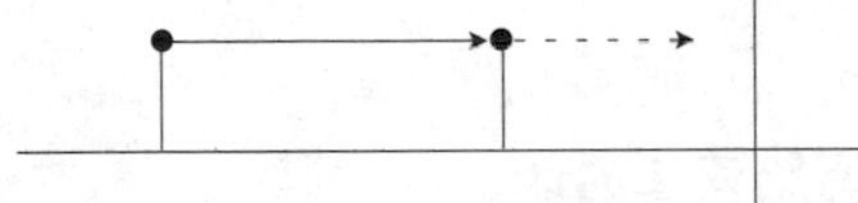

（虚线表示这一动作可能开始于现在或过去；虚箭头表示这一动作可能继续延续下去）

请看例句：

1 I ***will have taught*** English in New Oriental School for five years by the end of next month.
到下个月底之前，我在新东方学校教英语将满五年了。

2 I ***will have learned*** 8, 000 words by the end of next year. 到明年年底之前，我就将学过 8, 000 个单词了。

3 I ***will have waited*** for her for two hours when she arrives at 2 o'clock this afternoon.
她今天下午两点钟到达的时候，我就将已经等她两个小时了。

4 The old man ***will have worked*** in this factory for 50 years when he retires next month.
那个老人到下个月退休的时候，他在这家工厂工作就将满 50 年了。

二、重复事件

表示在将来的某一时刻之前开始的动作，并在该时刻之前的一段时间内重复发生。这如同现在完成时的第三种用法。

图解：

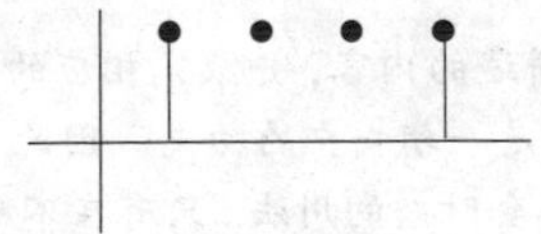

请看例句：

5 By five o'clock this afternoon the spaceship ***will have traveled*** eleven times round the world.
到今天下午五点钟之前，这艘宇宙飞船就将绕地球飞行 11 次了。

三、单一事件

表示在将来的某一时刻之前开始的动作，到该时刻之前已经完成。

图解：

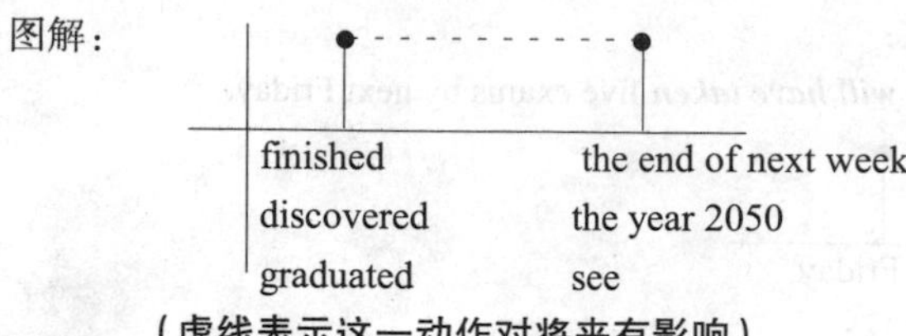

（虚线表示这一动作对将来有影响）

请看例句：

6 We ***will have finished*** our exam by the end of next week. 到下个周末为止，我们就将完成考试了。

7 By the year 2050, scientists probably ***will have discovered*** a cure for cancer.
到 2050 年时，科学家们可能就会找到治愈癌症的方法。

8 I will graduate in July. I will see you in September. By the time I see you, I ***will have graduated.***
我将于 7 月份毕业，于 9 月份与你见面，到我见到你的时候，我将已经毕业了。

9 I ***will have finished*** my homework by the time I go out on a date tonight.
到我今晚出去赴约的时候，我将已经做完作业了。

10 The construction company ***will have completed*** the stadium by the end of next July, when the Olympic Games is to be held here. 这家建筑公司将于明年 7 月底之前把体育场建成，奥运会将在那里举行。

写给读者的话

一、本章学习思路

在这一章里，我们重点阐述了现在完成时态的三种思维用法，即延续事件、重复事件和单一事件，并在 5.7 节中详细地比较了三种思维用法之间的内在相关性和统一性。这是完成时态的核心重点。笔者认为，学习完成时态的成败，关键就在于理解现在完成时态的这三种思维特征。掌握了这三种思维规律，那么过去完成时态及将来完成时态的用法就可以同理类推了。所以，我们在前面讨论现在完成时态的过程中费了不少笔墨。笔者之所以如此费尽心思，就是希望读者看完这些内容后，能比较清晰、全面而深刻地理解完成时态——这一英语中最难的时态。

二、本章重点及难点

本章重点是 5.3 节至 5.7 节的有关现在完成时态的内容，这包括了完成时态的三种思维用法及其相互之间的内在联系。读者在学习这些章节的内容时，一定要边阅读，边停下来思考，要能真正地理解和掌握其中所描述的内容。

本章的难点在于 5.6 节“单一事件”和 5.7 节有关三种用法的比较。但这些内容同样是本章的重点，需要读者掌握。

三、本章学习时间安排

读者可能需要用 10 至 15 天左右的时间来研读一遍本章所讲述的内容，并做完相应的练习。但是，要想真正地掌握英语时态的用法，并形成很好的英语思维，绝不是一朝一夕的功夫。因此，读者即使看完了本章所讲解的内容，也依然需要在平时的英语阅读中注意体会时态的用法。只有在不断的英语实践中，才能逐渐培养出良好的英语思维。

综合练习（Key: P343）

请用适当的时态填空。

1. I began to teach in New Oriental School in 1997. This year is 2001. So far I ______ （teach）here for 4 years. By 2000, I ______ （teach）for 3 years. By 2002, I ______ （teach）for 5 years.

2. Don't spend your money like water. If you keep on like this, you ______ (spend) all your money before the end of the trip.
3. A: Was Clint at the party when you arrived?
   B: No, he ______ (already, go) home.
4. A: Was Clint at the party when you arrived?
   B: Yes, but he ______ (go) home soon afterwards.
5. I felt very tired when I got home, so I ______ (go) straight to bed.
6. The house was very quiet when I got home. Everybody ______ (go) to bed.
7. Sorry I'm late. The car ______ (break) down on my way here.
8. We ______ (drive) along the road when we saw a car that ______ (break) down, so we stopped to see if we could help.
9. Yesterday I had a phone call from Clint. I was very surprised. I ______ (write) to him many times but he ______ (never, reply) to my letters.
10. I met Clint a few days ago. He ______ (just, come) back from holiday. He looked very well.
11. The man sitting next to me on the plane was very nervous. It was his first flight. He ______ (never, fly) before.
12. This traffic is terrible. We're going to be late. By the time we ______ (get) to the airport, Bob's plane ______ (arrive, already), and he'll be wondering where we are.
13. Last spring I went to France. It was the first time that I ______ (be) there.
14. This is the only novel that he ______ (write).
15. This is the first time that I ______ (take) the flight.
16. This is the most difficult job that I ______ (ever, do).
17. I hope you ______ (read) all the material before you make the final decision.
18. Clint is phoning his girlfriend again. This is the fourth time that he ______ (phone) her this evening.
19. I ______ (lose) my key. I can't get into my house.
20. I ______ (lose) my key, so I couldn't get into my house. But now I ______ (find) it.
21. A: I need to find a dermatologist. You're familiar with Dr. Smith. Do you recommend her?
    B: Well, I ______ (see) by her a few times. And the best I can say for her is she has interesting magazines in her waiting room.
22. It's reported that by the end of this month the output of cement in the factory ______ (rise) by about 10%.
23. A: May I speak to your manager Mr. Williams at eight tonight?
    B: I am sorry. Mr. Williams ______ (go) to a conference long before then.
24. A: I ______ (think) this shirt ______ (be) a great deal but I washed it once and it ______ (shrink) so much that I can't wear it.
    B: Some bargain. You should ask for a refund.
25. A: Look! It ______ (snow).
    B: It's wonderful! This is the first time I ______ (see) snow. It ______ (snow, not) in my hometown.
26. A: I hear you ______ (get) lost on your way to the hotel.
    B: I ______ (not, know) how I ______ (do) it. I ______ (be) there a million times.
27. A: ______ the parts we need for the copier ______ (arrive) yet?
    B: I ______ (order) them last week, but something's holding them up.
28. A: ______ you ______ (see) this postcard from Ron? He's in Florida.
    B: Oh, so he ______ (be) able to get time off.
29. A: I wish I hadn't hurt Mary's feelings like that. You know I never ______ (mean) to.
    B: The great thing about Mary is that she ______ (not, hold) the grudge. By tomorrow she ______ (forget) all about it.
30. A: Look at the time. I'm going to miss my bus.
    B: Don't worry. I ______ (drive) you to the stop. And if the bus ______ (already, leave), I can get you to your apartment.

31. Newcomers and Old-timers

There's a newcomer to the World Cup this year: China ______ (qualify) for the first time. The team's new Yugoslav manager ______ (help) four other national teams qualify in past competitions. And what about soccer powerhouse Brazil? Brazil ______ (compete) in every World Cup since its beginning in 1930. Surprisingly, though, Brazil ______ (almost, lose) hope of qualifying until they beat Chile in October. That victory ______ (assure) them of a place among the 32 finalists.

请判断下面各句的时态使用是否正确，错误的请改正。

32. I have entered the university for two years.
33. He has come here for three hours.
34. The old lady has died for ten years.
35. He has left his native place for three years.
36. I have married for one year.
37. He has joined in the army for five years.
38. I have come to Beijing for seven years.

根据场景提示，请用括号中的内容正确造句，在合适的地方填入 **just, already, yet, before** 等。

39. A man sitting next to you on a flight seems very nervous but feels very excited. You can ask: ______ ? (take a flight)
40. Jack is skiing from the top of the mountain. He doesn't look very confident. You can ask: ______ ? (ski from the top of the mountain.)
41. After lunch you go to see a friend at her house. She says "Would you like something to eat?" you say: No, thank you. ______. (have lunch)
42. You know that a friend of yours is looking for a job. Perhaps he has been successful. Ask him: ______ ?(find a job)
43. You are eating in a restaurant. The waiter thinks you have finished and starts to take your plate away. You say: Wait a minute! ______.(not/finish)
44. John goes out. Five minutes later, the phone rings and the caller says "Can I speak to John?" You say: I am afraid ______. (go out)

请阅读下面笑话，说出其中完成时态是什么思维和用法。

45. Mary: How long have you ***been married***?

    Lisa: This time—or altogether?

46. A Perfect Record

    Teacher: Young man, you ***haven't handed*** in one homework assignment since we started this class. Won't you please do tonight's assignment?

    George: What? And ruin a perfect record?

47. I Don't Know

    Lucy: Do you believe kissing is unhealthy?

    Lily: I couldn't say— I've never....

    Lucy: You ***have never been kissed***?

    Lily: ***I've never been sick.***

48. Will He Lose His Job?

    First Clerk: Poor old Watkins ***has completely lost*** his hearing. I'm afraid he'll lose his job.

    Second Clerk: Nonsense. He's to be transferred to the Complaint Department.

请把下列各句中的中文翻译成英文。

49. 我来美国到现在有三个月了，交到了很多好朋友。但是他们都是男生，我希望我能认识些女生。
50. 你是不是一直在减肥(on a diet)呀？看你现在皮包骨(skin and bones)的样子！
51. 中国历来就一直反对任何形式的恐怖主义(terrorism)。

52. 这几天晚上他一直睡在地板上。
53. A: 我想我以前没见你穿过那件羊毛衫。It's great!
    B: You think so? 这是我奶奶前几年为我做的。But this is the first time I dare to wear it in public.
54. A: 我还以为你打算读 this book by today.
    B: Oh, but 我已经读过了。
55. A: Are you glad you came to China?
    B: Yes. Indeed. 我本来是要考虑去 Tokyo or Singapore, but 我从不后悔我的决定。
56. A: 我们篮球队到目前为止赢得了每一场比赛。
    B: Isn't that because of the new coach?
57. 我不知道该如何解这道数学题，我试过的每一个方法 just leads to a dead end.
58. A: I'm really not interested in seeing that film
    B: 可是它赢得了那么多的奖项啊。
59. A: Denis told us he likes to play cards.
    B: 可是我们邀请过他三次，他一次也不来。
60. A: Did you tell Carl that the concert starts at eight?
    B: 我试过好几次，但电话一直占线。

Chapter 6

第六章　完成进行时态

本章先介绍完成进行时态的基本构成，然后总体介绍完成进行时态的基本意义。在此基础上，以现在完成进行时态为例，深入分析完成进行时态的两种用法，即表示“延续事件”和“重复事件”，并将它们与现在完成时态进行比较。最后，介绍过去完成进行时和将来完成进行时的用法。因此，本章内容安排如下：

6.1 完成进行时态的构成

在结构上，完成进行时态(perfect continuous tense)是由完成时态和进行时态复合而成。完成时态的构成是“have+ 过去分词”，若用-en 表示过去分词，则可表示为 have +-en；进行时态的构成是 “be+ 现在分词”，若用 doing 代替现在分词，则可表示为 be+doing。因此，完成进行时可以表示为 have -en+be doing=***have been doing***。由此可见，完成进行时态的构成分为三部分：一是助动词 have，二是助动词 be 的过去分词形式 been，三是实义动词的现在分词形式 doing。具体来说，用助动词 have 表示“时(tense)”，以表明动作发生的时间是在过去、现在还是将来；用 been doing 这一“过去分词 + 现在分词”的构成形式来表示动作的“体态(aspect)”，以表明该动作“完成 + 进行”。以动词 work 为例，三种完成进行时态的构成形式如下：

1. 现在完成进行时：have been working
2. 过去完成进行时：had been working
3. 将来完成进行时：will have been working

《英语语法新思维初级教程——走近语法》给出过进行时态的谓语公式，如下：

Tense	（Modal）	Continuous	Verb
PAST or PRESENT	（WILL）	BE+-ING	VERB

本书第五章给出过完成时态的谓语公式，如下：

Tense	（Modal）	Perfect	Verb
PAST or PRESENT	（WILL）	HAVE+-ED	VERB

现在，只要把上面两个公式复合在一起，即可以得到完成进行时的谓语公式，如下：

Tense	（Modal）	Perfect	Continuous	Verb
PAST or PRESENT	（WILL）	HAVE+-ED	BE+-ING	VERB

现在用这个公式分别表示出现在完成进行时、过去完成进行时和将来完成进行时的谓语构成形式，还是以 work 为例。

现在完成进行时态 have been working 可以具体表示为：

Tense	Perfect	Continuous	Verb
PRESENT	HAVE+-ED	BE+-ING	work

或简化为：have been working=present+perfect+continuous+work

过去完成进行时态 had been working 可以具体表示为：

Tense	Perfect	Continuous	Verb
PAST	HAVE+-ED	BE+-ING	work

或简化为：had been working=past+perfect+continuous+work

将来完成进行时态 will have been working 可以具体表示为：

Tense	（Modal）	Perfect	Continuous	Verb
PRESENT	WILL	HAVE+-ED	BE+-ING	work

或简化为：will have been working=present+modal+perfect+continuous+work

从以上公式可见，现在完成进行时态、过去完成进行时态和将来完成进行时态具有共同的“态(aspect)”，即“完成(perfect)+进行(continuous)”态。所以，三种完成进行时态的本质意义是相同的，区别只是“时(tense)”，即动作发生的时间不同而已。关于这一点，读者在接下来的“完成进行时态的意义”一节以及后面6.7节中会有更深入的理解。

6.2 完成进行时态的意义

从结构(structurally)的角度来看，完成进行时态是由完成时态与进行时态复合而成的，这种结构上的复合也必然会反映到意义上，因此完成进行时兼备“完成体”和“进行体”这两种时体的意义。

比如，对于现在完成进行时而言，一方面，完成体赋予了它“始于现在之前”的概念，即表示一个动作或状态是从过去持续或重复到现在；另一方面，进行体赋予它暂时的、不间断的延续性。所以，结合这两者的特点，现在完成进行时的核心意义是表示：**被描述的事件开始于现在之前，而且是有限地(不会无限期地)持续下去**。简言之，完成进行时的核心含义是表示“**有限的延续性**”。深刻地理解这一核心意义，有助于掌握完成进行时态的具体意义和用法。

6.7节(尤其是6.7.2小节)将更加具体而深入地分析完成进行时的意义，因为只有在掌握了完成进行时的基本用法之后，才能比较容易理解笔者的理性分析，否则就会显得抽象而笼统。因此，对于完成进行时的意义，在此不再赘述，留待以后详述。

在接下来的6.3到6.6节这四节内容中，我们将以现在完成进行时态为例，深入分析完成进行时态的两种用法，即表示“延续事件”和“重复事件”，并将它们与现在完成时态的“延续事件”和“重复事件”进行比较。

6.3 延续事件

6.3.1 延续事件概述

现在完成进行时强调动作的持续性，表示一个到目前为止尚未完成的活动(an incomplete activity)。具体来说，它表示开始于过去的活动持续到现在，并且活动往往还没有结束，将继续持续下去。此时的完成进行时常与for+时间段、since+时间点、all morning、all day、all week等这样的表示一段时间的时间状语连用，以强调在这一段期间内，某项活动正在持续。如下图所示：

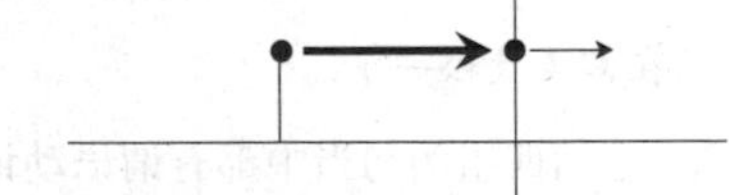

图中的黑点表示现在和过去两个时刻；粗箭头表示动作一直在持续；
细箭头表示该动作还将继续持续下去

先来看下面几个例子：

在谈到自己学英语的历史与英语水平的现状时，恐怕很多学生会很没底气地说：

1 ***I've been studying*** English for over ten years now, but I still can't speak it well.

妙语点睛　该句的谓语have been studying采用了现在完成进行时态，表示从10年前开始学习英语，一直持续到目前说话的时候，并且还将继续持续下去。

精品译文　我英语都学了有十多年了，但现在还是说不好。

如果是辛辛苦苦地学习了一个学期，那么到了假期就真该好好犒劳自己一下，出去度个假。比如下面的对话：

2 A: I ***have been studying*** too much and need a change. So I'm just making plans to go away during January break.

B: Really? Where are you going?

A: I'm planning to visit New Mexico.

B: My sister and I had the vacation there last year and we had a great time.

A: Did you get into Albuquerque?

B: Sure. Whenever we were skating.

妙语点睛 该句的谓语 have been studying 采用了现在完成进行时态，虽然这里没有像上句中的 for over ten years 那样的表示持续的时间状语，但从上下文的语境可以判断出“学习”这个活动是在持续。

精品译文 A：最近我一直学得很辛苦，需要换换脑子了，所以我正计划在1月份的假期里出去玩。

B：真的？你打算去哪玩？

A：我想去新墨西哥州。

B：我和我姐姐去年就去的那里，玩得非常开心。

A：那你们去阿尔伯克基了吗？

B：当然，只要是滑雪我们就去那。

比如，你正在专心看书，准备应考。这时你的朋友过来要你放松一下，一起去看电影：

3 A: You*'ve been studying* that one page for over an hour.

B: Well, I'm being tested on it tomorrow.

A: Come to the movies with us. Everybody needs to take a break every once in a while.

B: I guess I might as well. I*'ve been studying* so long I can hardly concentrate.

妙语点睛 该句的谓语 have been studying 采用了现在完成进行时态，虽然这里没有像例句1中的 for over ten years 那样很长的表示持续的时间状语，但这里持续较短的时间状语 for over an hour 并不妨碍我们把“学习”理解为一个持续的活动。

精品译文 A：光那一页内容你就看了有一个多钟头了。

B：噢，我明天要考这个啊。

A：和我们一起去看电影吧，谁都需要偶尔休息休息的。

B：我想也是啊，我一直这么学习有好长时间了，现在都无法集中精力了。

你妈妈看到你正在看电视，不高兴地说：

4 A: Hey, you're watching TV again.

B: I*'ve been studying* for the whole morning. I need to relax now.

妙语点睛 该句的谓语 have been studying 采用了现在完成进行时态，但“学习”这个活动在说话时并没有在持续，而是在说话之前的一段时间内持续进行。

精品译文 A：嘿，你又在看电视！

B：我刚刚学了一上午了，现在需要放松一下。

从对以上例句的分析中可以发现：首先，上面四组例句当中都有谓语动词 have been studying，而且都是表示延续事件。其次，从活动持续时间的长短来看，从第一句到第三句，study 的持续时间应该是越来越短的，比如从第一句的 over ten years 到第三句的 over an hour。再次，比较第三句和第四句，我们发现，第三句中的 study 持续到说话的时刻，而第四句中的 study 没有持续到说话的时刻，是在说话之前就结束了。

可见同样是延续事件，但仔细分析起来，还是有很大的不同的。为此，根据延续时间长短的不同，可以区分四种不同的延续事件：长期在延续的一个一般性活动；近期在延续的活动；在说话时刻仍在延续的活动；在说话时刻之前在延续的活动，或者说刚刚在延续但现在已结束的活动。接下来将对这些含义不同的延续活动进行详细讨论和比较。内容安排如下：

6.3.2 延续事件(一)：长期在延续的事件

6.3.3 延续事件(二)：近期在延续的事件

6.3.4 延续事件(三)：在说话时刻仍在延续的事件

6.3.5 延续事件(四)：在说话时刻之前在延续的事件(即刚刚在延续的事件)

在6.2节中就讲过，完成进行时是由完成时和进行时两种时态复合而成的，因此完成进行时兼备“完成体”和“进行体”两种时体所反映的意义。所以，在讨论上述这四类延续事件的特点时，还要考察它们是更接近**现在完成时**还是更接近**现在进行时**，这样有助于真正地理解完成进行时的内涵。

此外，完成进行时态对动词的延续性很敏感，所以在讨论这四种延续活动时，我们将重点比较动词延续性的不同特点。

6.3.2 延续事件(一)：长期在延续的事件

现在完成进行时可以表示从过去到现在的一个相当长的时期内在持续的一个一般性活动。请看例句：

1 ***I've been learning*** English ***for over ten years now.*** 不是我学英语到现在有十多年了。

2 I ***have been living*** here ***since 3 years ago.*** 我从三年前就一直住在这里。

3 I ***have been teaching*** in this school ***for 25 years.*** 我在这所学校教书有25年了。

4 He ***has been working*** in the same job ***for 30 years.*** 他干同样的工作一干就是30年。

5 A: Winter is over at last. Time to pack up my gloves and boots.

B: ***I've been waiting*** for this ***for months.***

A: 冬天终于过去了，现在该把手套和长靴收拾起来了。

B: 我等了好几个月了！

从以上例句可以看到，这些现在完成进行时表达的都是在相当长的一个时间段内(比如 for 30 years)持续的一般性活动。说它们是"一般性活动"，是因为这些活动并不具有很强的"正在进行"的动作的意味，或者说这些活动在说话的时刻一般并不正在持续。这些活动类似于一个持续的状态，**更具有状态的意义，而没有多少动作的意义**。所以，**现在完成进行时的这一用法与"现在进行时态"的关系较远，而与"现在完成时态"的关系更近**，完全类似于现在完成时所表达的"延续事件"的意义。比如，如果把上述句子的时态改成现在完成时态，也同样是正确的表达，而且意义上没有多大差别(详见6.4.2节)，所以可以这样说：

6 ***I've learned*** English for over ten years now.

7 I ***have lived*** here since 3 years ago.

8 I ***have taught*** in this school for 25 years.

9 He ***has worked*** in the same job for 30 years.

10 A: Winter is over at last. Time to pack up my gloves and boots.

B: ***I've waited*** for this for months.

关于现在完成进行时与现在完成时在表示"延续事件"方面的异同点，6.4.2节中将有详细讨论。

6.2节中讲过，现在完成进行时往往表示有限的延续性，这是进行体赋予它的这个特点。而这里提到现在完成进行时表示长期在延续的事件，二者就有了语义上的冲突，这也就解释了为什么现在完成进行时的这一用法与现在进行时关系较远的原因。这一语义上的冲突其实也是在告诉我们：能够表示长期延续事件的现在完成进行时对谓语动词有特殊要求。换句话说，并不是所有的动词用于现在完成进行时都能表示一个长期在持续的事件。来看下面这个句子：

11 He ***has been repairing*** his car ***since 6:00 this morning.***

妙语点睛 这里的现在完成进行时 has been repairing 也是表示延续事件，但不是长期在延续的事件，而是一个"从早上6点到现在"短短几个小时的延续活动。整个句子的意思是"从早上6点到现在，他一直在修理他的车"，这个句子的言外之意就是，他现在仍然在修车，也就是说，在说话的时刻，repair 的动作依然在进行。这完全不同于上述表达状态意义的 wait 等动词。

精品译文 从早上6点到现在，他一直在修理他的车。

下面来看看，如果这种动作意味很强的动词用于表达较长时间的状语，会产生何种语义效果。比如说：

12 He ***has been repairing*** cars ***for almost 20 years.***

妙语点睛 当我们说"他修理汽车有将近20年了"，显然不是表示 repair 这个动作一直不间断地持续了将近20年，也就是说，这里的 has been repairing 与表达较长时间的状语 for almost 20 years 连用时，就不能把它解释成一个长期延续的事件了，而只能把它解释成“重复事件”，即在将近20年当中，他不断“重复”地修理汽车，这就强烈地表明，他是专门从事汽车维修工作的，修车是他的职业。而如果说“从早上6点到现在，他一直在修理他的车”，则并不能说明修车是他的职业，只是表示他一直在做的一项活动而已。

精品译文 他修理汽车有将近20年了。

从对以上两个例句的比较可以看出，像repair这样的表示**单一具体动作的动词**用作谓语时，若句子接有一个表示较短时间的状语，则表示延续的活动；但若句子接一个表示较长时间的状语，则表示一个重复的活动。也就是说，像repair这样的动词虽然具有一定的延续性，但持续的时间不能太长，所以这类动词被称为**有限延续动词**。英文中的大多数动词都是有限延续动词。关于像repair这样的动词用于表示较短时间的状语和用于表示较长时间的状语时产生的不同语义，6.5.2节将有详细讨论。

由此可见，能够表示长期延续事件的谓语动词不能是那些动作意味很强的动词。在英文中，像study, live, work, learn, teach和wait这样的动词并不能表达出某一具体的动作，它们近乎于一种状态的延续，这样的动词被称为**无限延续动词**。这一部分动词在英文中比较少。因此，现在完成进行时在表示长期持续的事件时，其谓语动词必须是一些无限延续动词。再比如下列例句：

13 Yeah, I really need a change. I*'ve been working* in this company for over five years now, and I'm just not learning anything new. It's the same routine every day, and I am really sick of sitting in front of a computer. I think I need to try something totally different. I want to be in a profession that involves meeting people.

妙语点睛 这里的work不表现一个具体的动作，而是一个具有状态意义的动词。

精品译文 是的，我真的需要换个工作了。我在这个公司都干了五年多了，现在学不到什么新的东西，每天都是重复做同样的工作，我真的很厌烦坐在电脑前。我想我需要尝试一些完全不同的东西，我想找一个能与人打交道的工作。

14 “Someday, when I have some time, I'd like to...” Heard that one lately? I think I use that phrase at least 10 times a week. But “someday” never seems to arrive. Now is the time for those little activities you*'ve been saving* for the future.

妙语点睛 这里的save不表现一个具体的动作，而是一个具有状态意义的动词。

精品译文 “哪天等我有了时间，我一定就会去做……”经常听人这么说吧？我自己一星期至少要说10次这样的话。可是，“哪天”似乎从来就没有来过。对于那些你一直攒着想等将来做的事情，现在就应该去做。

当然，对于无限延续动词来说，其所接的时间状语不论长短，都表示延续事件的意义。例如work是无限延续动词，表示一种状态，所以下面两句不论是表达短时间的状语for two hours还是表达长时间的状语for 30 years，都是表示延续事件：

15 He *has been working* on the puzzles for two hours. 他玩这个拼图游戏有两个小时了。

16 He *has been working* in the same job for 30 years. 这个工作他做了有30年了。

对于wait是同样的道理，表达长时间与短时间的状语都表示延续事件：

17 I*'ve been waiting* for you for three hours! 我等你有三个小时了！

18 A: Winter is over at last. Time to pack up my gloves and boots.

B: I*'ve been waiting* for this for months.

A：冬天终于过去了，现在该把手套和长靴收拾起来了。

B：我等了好几个月了！

在英文中，像study, live, work和wait这种无限延续动词并不多，更多的是有限延续动词。因此，当这些有限延续动词用于完成进行时的时候，往往都是接表达较短时间的状语才能表示延续事件。这正体现了现在完成进行时所具有的“有限延续性”的特点。将在下面的6.3.3、6.3.4和6.3.5三节中讨论的延续事件，都是在较短时间内持续的活动。

6.3.3 延续事件(二):近期在延续的事件

先来看下面这段话:

1 Rose and John ***have been dating*** for a year. They really like each other. Recently, they ***have been considering*** getting married. They face a serious obstacle on the path to marriage, however. Rose's parents don't think John is the right guy for their daughter. They think Rose can do better. Although John is a decent and likeable man, he doesn't have a very large income. They advise Rose to break up with John and to find someone more suitable.

妙语点睛 这里有两个完成进行时:have been dating 和 have been considering,但二者在持续的时间上不完全一样,前者表示较长时间的持续活动,而后者表示近期在持续的活动(这句话中的 recently 一词也表明了这一点)。

精品译文 罗丝和约翰恋爱有一年了。他们彼此深爱着,最近他们一直在考虑要结婚。不过,他们的婚姻道路似乎并非坦途,而是遇到了一个严重的障碍。原因是罗丝的父母认为约翰和自己的女儿并不般配,他们认为罗丝能找到更好的。尽管约翰的素质修养都很好,但他收入不高。他们建议罗丝和约翰分手,去找一个更合适的。

从上面这个例句可以看到,现在完成进行时除了可以表示一个长期持续的活动(见 6.3.2 节)之外,还可用来表示**最近一段时期内正在持续**的一般性活动,比如上面这个例句中的 have been considering。再请看下面的例句:

2 A: ***Has*** Cynthia ***been working*** hard on her term paper?

B: Day in and day out.

妙语点睛 根据 B 的回答 Day in and day out.(天天如此忙着。)就可以知道,A 的意思并不是在问 Cynthia 在说话的时刻是否一直在忙着写论文,而是问她近期是否在忙着写论文。

精品译文 A:最近辛西娅是一直在忙着做学期论文吗?

B:是的,天天在忙着她的论文。

从上面这个例句也可以看到,现在完成进行时的这一用法的语义重点,不是关心某个活动在说话时是否正在进行,而是关心该活动在最近一段时期内是否在持续。比如可以设想这样一个对话语境:A 看到辛西娅非常疲倦的样子,于是就很关心地问 B:***Has*** Cynthia ***been working*** hard on her term paper? She looks so tired.(最近辛西娅是一直在忙着做学期论文吗?她看起来那么疲倦。)在说话的时刻,很可能辛西娅并没有在忙着写论文,而是在干别的事情,比如在睡觉,此时 A 的问句 Has Cynthia been working hard on her term paper? 依然成立,因为这句话的意思是强调"最近是否在忙着",而不是"现在是否在忙着"。说到这里,或许有读者联想到了现在进行时一样可以表示一个在近期持续的一般性活动(详见《英语语法新思维初级教程——走近语法》第八章 8.2.2 小节)。比如:

3 Cynthia ***is working*** hard on her term paper these days.

妙语点睛 这里有时间状语 these days 就表明,该句的语义重点不在于辛西娅在说话的时刻是否在写论文,而是表达她近期的一般性活动。

精品译文 辛西娅这几天一直在忙着做学期论文。

由此可见,**现在完成进行时表示"近期在延续的事件"这一用法与现在进行时的关系更密切。**

再来看下面更长的一个对话场景,体会其中现在完成进行时表示一般性活动的用法。请看对话:

4 Jo: You look tired. What ***have*** you ***been doing***?

Emily: ***I've been burning*** the midnight oil. ***Been writing*** my mid-term essay.

Jo: Oh no! I feel sorry for you. I thought you'd finished it already!

Emily: Yes, I did. But my teacher wasn't happy with it. She told me to do it all again!

Jo: No way! Your teacher is mean.

Emily: Well, I had to do it. Otherwise, she would have given me a low score.

Jo: I suppose if you look at it like that then your teacher is not mean at all. After all she gave you a second chance.

Emily: Yeah, and I have to admit that my essay is better now. I really need to do well so that I can get a scholarship.

Jo: Well, good luck then.

Emily: Thanks, and I'm going to sleep like a log tonight!

妙语点睛 这里的第一句 What have you been doing?中的现在完成进行时 have been doing 表示的是近期在持续的一般性活动，而不是表示刚刚在延续的活动(见 6.3.5 小节)，所以应理解成"你最近在忙什么"，而不是"你刚刚一直在忙什么"。第二句 I've been burning the midnight oil. 中的现在完成进行时 have been burning 同样也是表示在近期持续的一般性活动，应理解成"我最近一直在挑灯夜战"。如果理解成刚刚在延续的活动，就是另外的意思了，即"我昨晚刚刚一夜没睡都在挑灯夜战"。但这从上下文来看是不通的。注意这里的 burn the midnight oil 是英语的成语，是"挑灯夜战，开夜车"的意思。第三句 Been writing my mid-term essay. 是一个省略句，相当于说 I've been writing my mid-term essay. 其中的现在完成进行时同样是表示近期在持续的一般性活动。

精品译文 乔：你看上去很疲惫，最近都在忙什么？

艾米丽：我最近一直在开夜车，写我的期中论文。

乔：天啊！我还以为你早就弄完了呢！

艾米丽：我是弄完了。可我的老师不满意，让我全部重写一遍！

乔：不会吧！你们老师也真可恶！

艾米丽：没办法啊，我就得重写，不然她就会给我很低的分了。

乔：要是这么说的话，你的老师也还不错，毕竟她又给了你一次机会。

艾米丽：没错，而且我必须承认，这次我的论文的确有进步了。为了得到奖学金，我必须把它做得好一点。

乔：那么祝你好运！

艾米丽：谢谢！我今晚得好好睡一觉！

下面例句中的现在完成进行时均是表示近期在持续的一般性活动，请认真体会：

5 Nina: Do you have a sec?

Chandler: Ah, sure, Nina. What's up?

Nina: I don't know. For the past couple days, people ***have been avoiding*** me and ***giving*** me these really strange looks.

Chandler: Oh, well, ah...maybe that's because they're ah...jealous, of us.

妙语点睛 这里有表示持续的时间状语 for the past couple days，明确表示 have been avoiding...giving 是一个近期在持续的活动。

精品译文 尼娜：你现在有空吗？

钱德勒：啊，当然有空。尼娜，怎么了？

尼娜：我不知道这是为什么，最近几天人们总是故意逃避不理我，看到我时表情总是很奇怪。

钱德勒：噢……嗯……啊……可能是因为他们……呃……妒忌咱们。

6 A: Alice ***has been spending*** a lot of time at the library lately.

B: Well. She's got a paper due and two final exams next week.

妙语点睛 这里有时间状语 lately，明确表示 have been spending 是一个近期在持续的活动。

精品译文 A：爱丽丝最近花了很多时间在图书馆学习。

B：是啊，因为她下周要交一篇论文，还有两门期末考试。

7 All the students ***have been studying*** hard, for final exams start next week.

妙语点睛 后面的从句 for final exams start next week 可以表明，have been studying 表示一个近期在持续的活动。

精品译文 最近学生们都在用功学习，因为下星期就要期末考试了。

来看看下面的例句都是如何表达"我最近一直在考虑"的：

8 I *have been thinking* about changing my job. 我最近一直在考虑换个工作。

9 I'*ve been flirting* with the idea of changing my job, I probably won't.
我最近一直有换工作的念头，但我想我还是不会换的。

10 I *have been thinking* it over. 我最近一直在考虑这件事。

11 I *have been thinking* about what you said and I've decided to take your advice.
我最近一直在考虑你说过的话，我已决定听从你的建议。

向自己心仪的人表白时，可以这样说：

12 I'*ve been doing* a lot of thinking and the thing is I love you.

妙语点睛 这里用现在完成进行时说 have been doing a lot of thinking，表示“最近我一直想了很多”，这就表明你爱慕这个人已有许久，而且是经过慎重考虑后，才郑重地向对方大胆地说出“我爱你”的。

精品译文 最近我一直想了很多，我想对你说的是“我爱你”！

与自己仰慕已久的人见面时，可以这样说：

13 I *have been looking* forward to meeting you.

妙语点睛 这里用现在完成进行时 have been looking 显得相当正式，所以要注意使用的对象。如果对象不妥，这么说则显得有点虚伪和矫情。

精品译文 久仰大名！

在口语中，如果想要表达“我一直想干什么”或“我早就想干什么”，可以说 I *have been wanting* to do sth. 或 I *have been meaning* to do sth.；如果要表达“一直想要什么”，可以说 I have been wanting。请看下列例句：

14 Thank you so much for the binoculars. I'*ve been wanting* a pair for ages.
非常感谢你送我这副望远镜，我一直想要一副。

15 I *have been wanting* to meet you for long. 我早就想见你了。

16 A: Oh, Larry, I *have been meaning* to talk to you.
B: Hi, Denise. What's up?

妙语点睛 A 用了 have been meaning 的形式，表示想找 B 谈话的急切心情。

精品译文 A：嗨，拉里，我一直想找你聊聊。
B：嗨，丹尼斯，怎么啦？

17 A: Have you had a chance to wear your new shirt yet?
B: That reminds me. I'*ve been meaning* to exchange it for a larger size.
A：你有没有机会穿过那件新衬衫啊？
B：你这倒提醒我了，我一直想着要去换一件大号的。

对于上面的众多例句，完全可以套用到日常口语中，所以请读者注意模仿使用。

从上面这些例句可知，现在完成进行时的这一用法在大多数情况下是不带有持续时间状语的，不过也可以带有持续时间状语(如 for the past couple days)，都可以表示一个近期在持续的一般性活动。

另外要注意，这里的“近期”是一个相对概念，可能是近几天，也可能是近几个星期，甚至是近几个月。所以，这里所讨论的“近期”与上一小节讨论的“长期”并没有明确的界限，完全是根据实际生活经验来判断的。比如上面的例句：

Thank you so much for the binoculars. I'*ve been wanting* a pair for ages.

I *have been wanting* to meet you for long.

也可以看作是“长期在持续的事件”。

最后顺便要说的是，现在完成进行时表示“近期在延续的事件”的用法，与下面的 6.3.4 小节将要讨论的现在完成进行时表示“说话时刻仍在延续的事件”的用法不同，因为前者关心某个活动在“最近一段时期内”是否在持续，而后者的语义重点是关心某个活动在“说话时”是否正在进行。

6.3.4 延续事件(三):在说话时刻仍在延续的事件

现在完成进行时可以表示一个在说话时刻之前一段时间内延续的活动，并且这个活动在说话的时刻仍然在进行。比如：

1 A: You*'ve certainly been reading* that one page for a long time now.

B: Well, I'm being tested on it tomorrow.

妙语点睛 这里 read 的动作从过去开始并且持续到了现在说话的时刻，在说话的时刻 A 仍然在看书。

精品译文 A：那一页内容你显然已经看了很长时间了。

B：噢，我明天就要考这页内容啊。

再比如：

2 I'm staring at this computer. I*'ve been staring* at this computer screen for hours and my eyes hurt.

妙语点睛 stare 的动作从几小时之前开始并且一直持续到现在，现在仍然在盯着电脑看。

精品译文 我正在盯着电脑，我盯着电脑屏幕看了几个小时了，现在眼睛很痛。

现在把这个例句放在一个更大的语境中，就更能看出这里的现在完成进行时态所表示的"说话时刻仍在延续的事件"。请看下面的对话：

3 A: Hi, Tom. How is your chemistry paper going?

B: It's coming along. But I*'ve been staring* at this computer screen for hours and my eyes hurt.

A: Yeah. Doing that can make your eyes really dry and tired. You should take a break.

B: I can't. I have to get this paper written. It's due tomorrow.

A：嗨，汤姆，你的化学论文进展如何？

B：正在写，不过我盯着电脑屏幕看了几个小时了，现在眼睛很痛。

A：是啊，一直看电脑会让你的眼睛又干又累，你应该歇会。

B：可是不行啊，我得把这篇论文写完，明天就得交。

从上面这两个例句可以看到，**现在完成进行时表示"说话时刻仍在延续的事件"这一用法与现在进行时很接近**，比如上面这个例句中，可以同时使用现在进行时 am staring 和现在完成进行时 have been staring。只不过，现在进行时态不能接持续的时间状语(durational adverbials)，而现在完成进行时往往都会接一个这样的状语。请比较：

4 1) I*'m staring* at this computer.

2) I*'ve been staring* at this computer screen for hours and my eyes hurt.

一般不能说：I*'m staring* at this computer ***for hours.*** *

再来看一个例句：

5 I*'m trying* to study. I*'ve been trying* to study ***for the last hour***, but something always seems to interrupt me. I think I'd better go to the library.

妙语点睛 可见，这里的现在完成进行时 have been trying 与持续的时间状语 for the last hour 搭配了，而现在进行时 am trying 却没有。

精品译文 我正想学习，一直努力试图进入学习状态都有一个小时了，但老是有东西干扰我。我想我最好还是去图书馆算了。

现在完成进行时与现在进行时的这种相关性，以及现在完成进行时与持续的时间状语的搭配关系，从下面这些例句中都可以看得出来：

6 It began raining two hours ago and it's still raining. It ***has been raining*** for two hours.

两个小时前开始下雨，现在仍然在下雨，所以雨一直下了两个小时了。

7 It began raining at 8 o'clock. Now it's still raining. It ***has been raining*** since 8 o'clock. It ***has been raining*** all day.

8点钟开始下雨，现在仍然在下，所以说，从 8 点钟开始到现在一直在下雨，都下了一整天了。

8 It *has been snowing* all day. I wonder when it will stop. 雪一直下了一整天了，我不知道它何时会停。

9 Clint is surfing the Internet now. He *has been surfing the Internet* for five straight hours. He must be tired.

克林特现在正在上网，他连续上网五个小时了，他一定很累了。

以上例句都表示一个活动由过去开始并且持续到现在的说话时刻，而且还一直在持续。不过，可能由上下文告知，开始于过去的动作持续到现在为止不再继续。如图所示：

图解：

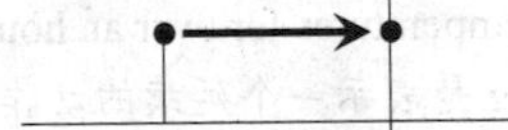

图中的黑点表示现在和过去两个时刻；黑箭头表示动作一直在持续，该动作到现在时刻即告终止

请看例句：

10 A: Come to the movies with us. Everybody needs to take a break every once in a while.

B: I guess I might as well. I'*ve been studying* so long I can hardly concentrate.

妙语点睛 由上文"不妨休息(I guess I might as well)"可以推断，study 的动作持续到说话时为止，不再延续。

精品译文 A：和我们一起去看电影吧，谁都需要偶尔休息休息的。

B：我想也是，我一直学习好长时间了，现在不能集中精力了。

下面的例句都表示开始于过去的活动持续到说话时刻为止不再继续下去了：

11 Where have you been? I'*ve been looking* for you for the last half hour. 刚才去哪里了？我一直等了你半个小时。

12 I'm so sorry I'm late. *Have* you *been waiting* long? 对不起我迟到了，你等了很久吗？

6.3.5 延续事件(四)：在说话时刻之前在延续的事件(即刚刚在延续的事件)

一个事件在说话时刻之前一直在延续，换句话说，就是刚刚在延续但到说话时刻已经结束了(a recently finished activity)。从下面这个例句可以明确看出事件"刚刚在延续"：

1 He returned home yesterday. He *has been traveling.*

妙语点睛 这里前一句话明确说"他昨天回家了"，这就表明他的旅行到现在说话时刻已经结束了，所以 has been traveling 就是表示一个"刚刚在延续的事件"——刚刚结束旅行。

精品译文 他昨天回到家里了，在这之前他一直在外旅行来着。

再比如：

2 What *have* you *been doing* while I have been away?

妙语点睛 这个句子表示"我刚才不在的时候，你们都一直在干什么了"，所以，这里的 have been doing 也由于从句 while I have been away 的存在而明确表明一个刚刚在延续的事件。

精品译文 我刚才不在的时候，你们一直在干什么？

但是，更多的时候，某个事件"刚刚在延续"并不会像上面这两个例句这样明确地表达出来，而是通过上下文来表明这个事件是"刚刚在延续"。先来看下面这个例句：

3 A: You look hot.

B: Yes, I'*ve been running.*

妙语点睛 此句中的 have been running 是表示一个延续的动作，但这个动作并没有延续到现在（说话人现在不在 running 了），而是一直延续到离现在不远的过去时间结束的，即表示刚才一直在延续，但现在已结束的活动(a recently finished activity)。"刚才在延续"的活动所导致的"现在"结果往往清晰可见。比如在这个对话当中，"跑步"的活动不久前刚刚结束，而并没有延续到说话时刻，但导致现在依然清晰可见的结果是 You look hot.

精品译文 A：看你很热的样子。

B：是的，我刚刚一直在跑步来着。

从上面这个例句可知，现在完成进行时的这一表示“刚刚在延续的事件”的用法往往是**强调一个持续活动所带来的、现在清晰可见的后果**。简言之，就是表示刚刚停止、现在能看到结果的一个事件。通过这个事件的清晰可见的后果可以表明该事件刚刚在延续。

比如看到一个朋友瑟瑟发抖的受冻的样子，你问道：“你看起来这么冷，怎么了？”他可能这样告诉你原因：“在这样冷的天气里，我刚才一直站在外面等车等了一个多小时。”请看下面的对话：

4 A: You do look cold. What happened?
B: I***'ve been standing*** outside in Arctic temperatures for over an hour waiting for a bus.

妙语点睛 此句中的 have been standing 是表示一个延续的动作，但这个动作并没有延续到现在（说话人现在不再 standing 了），而是一直延续到离现在不远的过去时间结束的，即表示刚才一直在延续，但现在已结束的活动（a recently finished activity）。“刚才在延续”的活动所导致的“现在”结果往往清晰可见。比如在这个对话中，“在寒冷的外面站着”的活动不久前刚刚在延续，导致现在依然清晰可见的结果是 You do look cold.

精品译文 A：你看起来这么冷，怎么了？
B：在这样冷的天气里，我刚才一直站在外面等车等了一个多小时。

看到你的朋友眼睛红红的样子，你可以这样问：

5 Your eyes are red. You***'ve been crying***? 看你眼睛红肿的，你刚刚哭过吧？

笔者有时一天要连续上课 10 个小时，从早晨 8:30 一直站着讲到晚上 9:10，这样一天下来腰酸腿疼不说，嗓子也成了“公鸭嗓”，于是一天的课程结束后，笔者可以这样说：

6 My throat is husky because I***'ve been talking*** too much.

精品译文 我现在嗓子沙哑的，因为一直说了太多的话了。

从以上这些例句可以看到，现在完成进行时的这一用法往往都伴随有刚刚在延续的事件所带来的后果。在日常口语中，如果看到某一个现状或后果，就可以用现在完成进行时来推导出刚刚在持续的、与这个后果有关的事件。比如下面这些场景中的句子：

看到你的朋友在喘气，你可以问：“刚刚是一直跑步了吧？”来看这句话用英语怎么说：

7 Your friend is out of breath. You ask, “***Have*** you ***been running***?”
你的朋友上气不接下气的，你问他：“你刚刚是一直在跑步吧？”

在街上碰到一个朋友，他的脸和手都很脏，你就可以问他“你刚才干什么了？”来看这句话用英语怎么说：

8 You meet a friend in the street, whose face and hands are very dirty. You ask, “What ***have*** you ***been doing***?”
你在街上碰到一个朋友，他的脸和手都很脏。你问他：“你刚才在干什么了？”

一个小男孩从头到脚都很脏，因为“他刚才一直在玩泥”：

9 The little boy is dirty from head to foot because he ***has been playing*** in the mud.
小男孩从头到脚都很脏，因为他刚刚一直在玩泥巴。

“衣服为什么会这么脏？刚刚一直在干什么了？”这句话用英文说就是：

10 Why are your clothes so dirty? What ***have*** you ***been doing***? 你的衣服怎么这么脏？你刚刚都在干什么？
再比如下面这个小笑话：

11 Mother: Paul, ***have*** you been ***fighting*** again? You've lost your two front teeth.
Son: No, I haven't, Mom. They're in my pocket.
母亲：保罗，你刚才又和人打架了吧？你两个门牙都没了。
儿子：妈妈，门牙没有丢，它们在我的口袋里。

偶尔，某个动作的明显后果并不是在句子的字面上能反映出来的，而是体现在语言之外的现实世界中。比如巴菲特（Warren Buffett）的这个名言：

12 It's only when the tide goes out that you learn who*'s been swimming* naked.
只有当潮水都已退去，你才能知道是谁刚刚在裸泳。

该句虽然没有从字面上反映出 has been swimming 之后的后果，但在真实场景中，看看就知道了。

在以上所讨论的众多例句中，细心的读者可能注意到了，现在完成进行时在表示"刚刚在延续的事件"时，一般不接持续的时间状语（除了 I*'ve been standing* outside in Arctic temperatures for over an hour waiting for a bus. 这个句子）。若接持续的时间状语时，则往往表示一个延续至今的事件。请比较：

13 1) Be careful! I*'ve been painting* the door!
2) I*'ve been painting* the door *for half an hour.*

妙语点睛　在例句 1)中，painting 的活动刚才在延续，或者说刚刚结束。在例句 2)中，一般表示 painting 的活动还没结束。

精品译文　1)小心，这门我刚刚刷完漆！
2)这门我刷了有半个小时了。

不过也不尽然。对于某个句子到底是"刚刚在延续"还是"一直在延续"，需要结合上下文的具体语境来看。如果没有上下文，那么就可能有歧义，也就是两种情况都可能存在。比如：

14 A: You do look cold. What happened?
B: I*'ve been standing* outside in Arctic temperatures for over an hour waiting for a bus.

这里既然 A 问 B"你怎么看起来这么冷"，就表明此时 B 没在等车，即等车的活动刚刚结束了。所以这里 B 的话里尽管带有一个持续的时间状语 for over an hour，但它表示的是一个刚刚在延续的事件。可以译成：

在这样冷的天气里，我刚才一直站在外面等车等了一个多小时。

如果 B 在说话的时刻依然在外面等车，他用这句话来抱怨他已经等得不耐烦了：

I*'ve been standing* outside in Arctic temperatures *for over an hour* waiting for a bus.

此时可以把它译成：

在这样一个大冷天，我站在外面等车到现在都等了一个多小时了(可是车还没来)。

由此可见，同样一个带有持续的时间状语的句子，在不同的语境中，既可以表示"刚刚在延续"(刚刚一直在外面等车，但现在没有等)也可以表示"一直在延续"(现在依然在等车)。再比如：

15 ***I've been running for half an hour.***

这句话既可以理解成"一直在延续"：

到现在为止我一直跑了有半小时了。

也可以理解成"刚刚在延续"：

刚才我跑步跑了半小时(所以为什么我现在满头大汗的)。

前者表明现在"我"还在跑步，这个活动并未结束；后者表明"我"现在没有在跑步，这个活动已经结束。

这种歧义在真实的口语交际中一般不会存在，因为具体的语境告诉听者该如何理解说话人的意思。比如你的朋友在正健身房的跑步机(treadmill)上跑步时对你说 I've been running for half an hour. 显然你就要理解成"跑步的活动一直在持续"；而如果他现在满头大汗地站在你面前说 I've been running for half an hour. 显然你就要理解成"跑步的活动刚刚在持续"。

不过，**在没有上下文语境帮助排除的情况下，对于带有持续的时间状语的完成进行时的句子，我们一般会解释成"一直在延续"的事件。**

对于不带有持续的时间状语的句子同样会存在歧义。比如：

16 It*'s been snowing.*

这句话可以有两种意思。如果在说这句话时外面还在下着雪，则表示"一直在延续"而并未结束的动作：

外面一直在下雪哩。

或者，如果说这句话时外面的雪已经停了，则表示"刚刚在延续"——延续至不久前刚刚结束的动作：

(瞧，地上是白的)刚刚下过雪。

由此可见，把这句话放在具体的语境中，结合说话时的语境来理解，就不会产生歧义了。

不过，**在没有上下文语境帮助排除的情况下，对于没有持续的时间状语的完成进行时的句子，我们一般会解释成“刚刚在延续”的事件。**

综上所述，能得出这样的结论：

在有持续的时间状语的情况下，现在完成进行时通常都表示一个延续至今的活动，除非有上下文明确表明这个活动刚刚结束。

在没有持续的时间状语的情况下，现在完成进行时通常都表示一个刚刚结束的活动，除非有上下文明确表明这个活动至今仍在延续。

思维总结

本节重点讨论了现在完成进行时所表示的四种不同的延续事件，它们与现在进行时或现在完成时都有某种联系，具体如下：

表示“长期在延续的事件”的现在完成进行时与现在进行时态的关系较远，而与现在完成时态的关系更近，完全类似于现在完成时所表达的“延续事件”的意义。

表示“近期在延续的事件”的现在完成进行时与现在进行时态的关系更密切，完全类似于现在进行时所表示的“一个在近期持续的一般性活动”的意义。

表示“在说话时刻仍在延续的事件”的现在完成进行时与现在进行时态的意义很接近，因为二者都表示这个活动在说话的时刻仍然在进行。

表示“刚刚在延续的事件”的现在完成进行时与现在完成时态的关系更接近，类似于完成时表示的“单一事件”。与现在进行时的关系较远，因为现在进行时没有表示事件在说话时刻已经结束的用法。

思维训练

Exercise 6. 3（Key: P345）

请用括号中动词的适当的形式填空。

1. Your friend is out of breath. You ask, “______ you ______ (run)?”
2. Why are your clothes so dirty? What ______ you ______ (do)?
3. The little boy is dirty from head to foot because he ______ (play) in the mud.
4. You meet a friend in the street, whose face and hands are very dirty. You ask, “What ______ you ______ (do)?”

6.4 延续事件比较：完成进行时与完成时

上一节详细讨论了现在完成进行时可能表示的四种“延续事件”，而第五章“完成时态”的 5. 4 节讨论了现在完成时态也可以表示“延续事件”。因此，读者现在自然要问：既然两种时态都可以表示“延续事件”，那么有何异同?这就是这一节要回答的问题。因为 6. 3. 5 小节刚刚讨论过“刚刚在延续的事件”，因此，接下来先比较它与完成时的区别，然后再比较两种时态的其他有关“延续事件”的区别。内容安排如下：

6. 4. 1 比较(一)：完成进行时“刚刚在延续的事件”与完成时“单一事件”

6. 4. 2 比较(二)：完成进行时的“延续”与完成时的“延续”

6. 4. 1 比较(一)：完成进行时“刚刚在延续的事件”与完成时“单一事件”

上一节讨论的现在完成进行时的这一用法涉及刚刚结束的事件所产生的后果，这就让我们联想到现在完成时态的“单一事件”的用法(详见 5. 6 节)，尤其是“近的过去单一事件”的用法(详见 5. 6. 3 节)。二者有三个共同点：

第一，二者都表示一个事件在说话的时刻已经结束；

第二，二者都伴随有现在清晰可见的后果；

第三，二者都不接持续性的时间状语。不过，需要注意的是，现在完成进行时可以接持续的时间状语，但意思往往会不同；而现在完成时"单一事件"的用法是不能接持续的时间状语的。

现在通过下面这个例句来讨论二者的区别。请看例句：

1 1) My hands are dirty. I***'ve been cleaning*** the car.

2) I***'ve just cleaned*** the car.

妙语点睛 在例句1)中，现在完成进行时强调活动本身的持续性(emphasis on duration)，然后推导出一个与这个持续的活动本身有关的结果——手很脏了。从动词的延续性角度来看，这里的clean是一个延续活动。在例句2)中，现在完成时强调活动的结果，或者说强调活动的成果(emphasis on achievement)——车子现在干净了。从动词的延续性角度来看，这里的clean是用作一个短暂动词，而不是表示延续活动。

精品译文 1)我的手很脏，我刚刚一直在洗车来着。

2)我刚把车洗干净了。

从这个例句可以得出二者的两点区别：

第一，现在完成进行时强调活动本身的持续性(emphasis on duration)；现在完成时强调活动的结果，或者说强调活动的成果(emphasis on achievement)。

第二，从谓语动词的延续性的角度来看，现在完成进行时的"刚刚在延续的事件"的用法所采用的动词一定都是**延续性动词**，以表示一个延续活动；现在完成时的"单一事件"的用法所采用的动词都是**短暂动词**，或者用作表达短暂性的动词，不表示一个延续活动。所以，现在完成进行时可以接持续的时间状语，但意思往往会不同；而现在完成时"单一事件"的用法是不能接持续的时间状语的。这就证明二者在谓语动词的延续性方面有差别。

再来看下面这组例句：

2 1) Be careful! I***'ve been painting*** the door!

2) I***'ve painted*** the door green.

妙语点睛 在例句1)中，现在完成进行时强调活动本身的持续性——"我"刚刚一直在给门刷漆，由此推导出一个与这个持续活动本身有关的结果——门上的油漆现在还没有干，所以"你"要be careful(小心)。从动词的延续性的角度来看，这里paint是一个延续活动。在例句2)中，现在完成时强调活动的结果，或者说强调活动的成果——门现在变成绿色了(比如说原来是白色的)。从动词的延续性的角度来看，这里的paint是用作一个短暂动词而不是表示延续活动。

精品译文 1)小心！这门我刚刚刷过油漆。

2)我把门漆成了绿色。

这里也可以看到，**现在完成进行时的这一用法与现在完成时态的关系更接近，而与现在进行时的关系较远**，因为现在进行时没有表示事件在说话时刻已经结束的用法。

6.4.2 比较(二)：完成进行时的"延续"与完成时的"延续"

大家知道，现在完成时和现在完成进行时都可以表示"延续事件"，现在就来比较二者此类用法的异同点。这里主要考察在带有持续的时间状语或没有持续的时间状语时，两种时态的异同。

一、与持续的时间状语连用

在带有持续的时间状语时，用两种时态几乎没有多大区别，都表示一个开始于过去的动作一直延续到现在。比如如果要表达：

1 我学习英文有10年了。

就可以用两种时态来表达如下：

1) I ***have been learning*** English for ten years.

2) I ***have learned*** English for ten years.

要表达：

2 自从三年前开始，我就一直住在这里。

可以用两种时态来表达如下：

1) I ***have been living*** here since 3 years ago.

2) I ***have lived*** here since 3 years ago.

要表达：

3 我教书有25年了。

可以用两种时态来表达如下：

1) I ***have been teaching*** for 25 years.

2) I ***have taught*** for 25 years.

不过也有这样一种观点，认为此时二者的细微区别在于：现在完成进行时会强烈暗示动作会继续持续下去；而现在完成时则往往表示动作有可能会持续下去。如上面的例句3，很可能分别有以下的言外之意：

1) I ***have been teaching*** for 25 years, and I can't imagine doing anything else.

我教书都教了25年了，我真想象不出还能干什么别的事情。

2) I ***have taught*** for 25 years, so now it's time to think about doing something else.

我教书都教了25年了，现在是该考虑改行做别的事情的时候了。

这种细微的区别在下面这个例子中也得到了印证：

4 It is amazing that the Leaning Tower of Pisa ________ for so long.

A. has stood　　B. has been standing　　C. stood

妙语点睛 来分析备选答案中的三种时态填进去之后分别会产生何种含义。首先，若是用一般过去时stood，则表示比萨斜塔现在已经倒掉，已成为历史，这显然不符合事实，所以可以排除C(这种情况倒是符合中国杭州的“雷峰塔”，若谈到“雷峰塔”，则应该用stood)。剩下的has stood和has been standing其实都是可以填入的。但笔者的美国朋友告诉笔者说，选has been standing表示比萨斜塔现在一定还是“巍然耸立”的，即到现在还依然standing；而若是选has stood则可能表示比萨斜塔刚刚倒掉，然后我们回顾它的历史时说了这么一句话。

精品译文 比萨斜塔至今依然屹立不倒，这真是了不起。

由此可以得出结论：**完成进行时比完成时更强调活动本身的持续性**，这是进行时态赋予它的特点。

二、不与持续的时间状语连用

接下来分析在没有持续的时间状语时，二者在时态上的区别（the present perfect vs. the present perfect continuous with no time mentioned）。第五章5.4.2节分析过，表示“延续事件”的现在完成时必须具备两个条件，其中之一就是必须与持续的时间状语连用，如果没有持续的时间状语，则不表示延续至今的事件，而表示一个在过去完成了的事件，即表示“单一事件”中的过去的经历。而现在完成进行时在没有持续的时间状语的情况下，依然可以表示延续至今的事件。请比较：

5 1) I ***have worked*** in this company.

2) I ***have been working*** in this company.

妙语点睛 在例句1)中，现在完成时have worked表示曾经的经历，即现在不在这家公司工作了。在例句2)中，现在完成进行时have been working表示一直在延续的事件，即现在还在这家公司工作。

精品译文 1)我在这家公司工作过。

2)我一直就在这家公司工作。

6 1) ***Have*** you ever ***worked*** in a foreign-funded company?

2) You look tired. ***Have*** you ***been working*** hard?

妙语点睛 在例句1)中，现在完成时have worked表示询问对方曾经的经历，动作已结束。在例句2)中，现在完成进行时have been working表示询问对方最近是否一直是这样辛苦，相当于现在完成进行时所能表示的“在近期持续的一般性活动”。

精品译文 1)你在外企工作过吗?

2)你看起来很累,最近工作一直很辛苦吧?

7 1) He ***has slept.***

2) He ***has been sleeping.***

妙语点睛 在例句1)中,现在完成时has slept表示他睡过了,所以现在不困了。我们可以接着往下说:He has slept well and is ready for his interview. 表示"他刚才好好地睡了一觉,所以现在准备好去面试了"。在例句2)中,现在完成进行时has been sleeping表示他一直在睡觉,现在还在睡。相当于说He has been sleeping and he is still asleep now.

精品译文 1)他睡过了。

2)他一直在睡觉。

从以上这些例子可以看到,在不带有时间状语时,现在完成时指的是在过去某一时间完成了的动作(refer to a singular occurrence at an indefinite time in the past),现在完成进行时则表示一个正在持续的活动(refer to an ongoing activity),活动还没有结束。下面的例句也可以证明这一区别。请比较:

8 1) ***I've been cleaning*** the house, but I still haven't finished.

2) ***I've cleaned*** the house, but I still haven't finished. *

妙语点睛 在例句1)中,因为现在完成进行时have been cleaning表示一个一直在持续的活动,活动并没有结束,相当于汉语中说的"我一直在打扫房间",所以接下去可以说but I still haven't finished,表示"但是还没有打扫完",这样来明确表示活动还没有结束。在例句2)中,因为现在完成时have cleaned表示一个过去完成了的活动,相当于汉语中说的"我把房间打扫完了",所以接下去无法说but I still haven't finished(但是还没有扫完),这样前后语义矛盾,故例句2)是错误的。

精品译文 1)我一直在打扫房间,但现在还没有打扫完。

9 1) ***I've been writing*** a novel, but I still haven't finished it.

2) ***I've written*** a novel, but I still haven't finished it. *

妙语点睛 在例句1)中,因为现在完成进行时have been writing表示一个一直在持续的活动,活动并没有结束,相当于汉语中说的"我一直在写一部小说",所以接下去我们可以说but I still haven't finished it,表示"但是还没有写完",这样来明确表示活动还没有结束。在例句2)中,因为现在完成时have written表示一个过去完成了的活动,相当于汉语中说的"我写完了一部小说",所以接下去我们无法说but I still haven't finished(但是还没有写完),这样前后语义矛盾,故例句2)是错误的。

精品译文 1)我一直在写一部小说,但现在还没有写完。

综上所述,现在完成进行时不论是带有还是没有持续时间状语,同样可表达"一直在持续的活动"。这进一步证明了上述结论:完成进行时比完成时有更强的持续性。

思维总结

完成进行时表示的"刚刚在延续的事件"与完成时的"单一事件"的用法类似,因为:二者都表示一个事件在说话的时刻已经结束;都伴随有现在清晰可见的后果;二者一般都不接持续性的时间状语。二者最大的区别在于谓语动词的延续性。现在完成进行时的"刚刚在延续的事件"的用法所采用的动词一定都是**延续性动词**,以表示一个延续活动;现在完成时的"单一事件"的用法所采用的动词都是**短暂动词**,不表示一个延续活动。

二者在表示"延续事件"方面最大的区别在于持续的时间状语。一方面,在带有持续的时间状语时,两种时态几乎没有多大区别,都表示一个开始于过去的动作一直延续到现在。另一方面,如果没有持续时间状语,完成时则不表示延续至今的事件,而表示一个在过去完成了的事件(即表示"单一事件")。但是,现在完成进行时在没有持续的时间状语的情况下,依然可以表示延续至今的事件。由此可见,完成进行时比完成时更强调活动本身的持续性。

思维训练

Exercise 6.4（Key: P345）

请用括号中动词的适当形式填空。

1. I ______（clean）the house, but I still haven't finished.
2. I ______（write）a novel, but I still haven't finished it.
3. Be careful! I ______（paint）the door!
4. I ______（paint）the door green.

6.5 重复事件

前面各节中主要讨论了现在完成进行时态表示"延续事件"的用法，以及这一用法与现在完成时的"延续事件"用法的区别。这一节开始讨论现在完成进行时的另一种用法——重复事件。

现在完成进行时可表示重复事件，具体来说，就是表示到目前为止的一段时间内重复发生的活动（a repeated activity, a habitual action in a period of time up to the present）。

现在完成进行时表示"重复事件"的用法主要分为两种情况：一种是"短暂动词"用于现在完成进行时可以表示一个重复事件，这是最典型的重复事件的用法；另一种是"有限延续动词"用于现在完成进行时可以表示一个重复事件。因此，本节内容安排如下：

6.5.1 重复事件(一)：短暂动词

6.5.2 重复事件(二)：有限延续动词

6.5.1 重复事件(一)：短暂动词

笔者曾经在和一位外国朋友聊天时，问他是否是第一次来北京，他是这么回答我的：

1 I *have been coming* to Beijing for 14 years.

看完这句话，对于它的意思，相信大多数读者的第一反应是：

我来北京有14年了。

也就是说14年来，他一直长期生活在北京。但实际上，笔者的这位朋友并不是生活在北京。

还有人这样曲解："我到北京一路上走了14年。"也就是说，他从某个地方来北京，由于路途遥远，这一长途跋涉竟花了他14年的时间——非也，若果真如此，那可不亚于"唐僧西天取经"啊！

相信只要学过英语的人都认识该句中的每一个单词，但对于这一看似简单的句子，要想真正理解它的意思却并不那么简单。

问题的关键在于该如何正确理解have been coming的意思。其实，这里的have been coming表示的是一个重复的活动，所以这句话正确的意思应该是：

在过去的14年中，我常常来北京。

这也就是说，在14年期间，他多次重复来北京，而不是一直在北京住了14年。

从这个例子，可以看到现在完成进行时的另一种思维表达——**用短暂动词(如come)的完成进行时(如have been coming)来表示到目前为止的一段时间内重复发生的动作。**

再来看一个短暂动词come用于现在完成进行时表示重复活动的例句：

2 *I've been coming* to see him for 10 years.

妙语点睛　这里的have been coming同样是表示一个在10年当中不断重复的活动。

精品译文　10年来，我常常过来看望他。

再来看下面这个句子：

3 They *have been going* there for 10 years.

虽然这句话译成汉语可以是：他们去那里已经有10年了。

但这并不是表示他们一直生活在那里，而是表示“10年期间，他们屡次去那里”，即表示一个重复活动。可以把这个句子放在一个更完整的语境中：

4 Every Sunday they meet in the bar. They ***have been going*** there for 10 years.

妙语点睛 这里的 have been going 表示一个在10年当中不断重复的活动，即在10年期间，每周日他们都去那家酒吧。所以，“他们去那里已经有10年了”并不是表示他们一直生活在那里。

精品译文 他们每周日都会在那家酒吧会面，他们去那里已经有10年了。

再比如下面的对话：

5 A: Guess what? Michael and Jane are getting married!
B: Really? I didn't even know they were going together.
A: They ***have been going*** together for over three years now.

妙语点睛 大家知道 go together 是一个短暂活动，这里要表示一个在三年当中不断重复的活动，所以用了现在完成进行时 have been going together。

精品译文 A：知道吗，迈克尔和简要结婚了！
B：真的？我连他们俩在谈恋爱都不知道。
A：他们恋爱都三年多了。

另外值得注意的是，这里的 go together 在口语中是表示“谈恋爱”的意思。所以中文的“恋爱三年多了”用英文就可以说成 have been going together for over three years now。如果不知道这个短语，有的读者也许会想到 fall in love 这个短语。但是如果说一个人 have been falling in love for three years，则往往表示在三年当中，他不断地恋上不同的人，恋事不断，但终无结果，因为 fall in love 也是一个短暂动词，它的完成进行时就表示一个不断重复的活动。

再来看一个关于“恋爱”的例子：

6 You***'ve been going*** with Nancy for over three years now. Why don't you pop her the question?

妙语点睛 大家知道，go 是一个短暂动词，这里要表示一个在三年当中不断重复的活动，所以用了现在完成进行时 have been going。另注：pop the question 是俚语，表示“求婚”的意思。

精品译文 你与南希交往已经有三年多了，怎么还不向她求婚呢？

谈完“恋爱”，现在说说“结婚”。“结婚”的英文是 marry，它是一个短暂动词，所以，如果要表示“我结婚有一年了”，要用“状态表达”说成 I***'ve been married*** for a year. 而不是 I***'ve married*** for a year. * 因此，如果把 marry 用于现在完成进行时，则是表示一个重复的活动。请看下面的例句：

7 Koreans ***have been marrying*** U. S. soldiers stationed here since the 1950s. The peak years were during the 1970s, when more than 4, 000 Koreans married U. S. soldiers each year.

妙语点睛 这里的 have been marrying 是表示一个不断重复发生的事件，即重复事件，所以翻译时要注意体会，比如译成“不断嫁给”。

精品译文 自20世纪50年代以来，就有韩国人不断嫁给在当地的美国驻军，70年代达到了高峰，每年有四千多人嫁给美国大兵。

再来看其他的例句：

8 Over the past few years, many towns in the United States ***have been joining*** with neighboring communities to share the costs of government.

妙语点睛 这里 join 的动作不是一次完成的，而是在近几年当中（over the past few years）不断重复发生的，所以要说 have been joining 来表示这一重复活动。

精品译文 在近几年中，美国的许多城镇不断合并，以降低政府的费用开支。

9 In recent years, railroads ***have been combining*** with each other and ***merging*** into supersystems, causing heightened concerns about monopoly.

妙语点睛 这里的 have been combining...merging 同样是表示重复发生的活动。

精品译文 近些年来，铁路公司相互合并，而成为超大型集团，这引起人们对垄断的日益关注。

10 I've ***been hearing*** from my girlfriend regularly since I came to America.
自从来到美国后，我就不断地收到女朋友的来信。

11 The price ***has been going*** up recently. I wonder whether it will remain so.
最近物价一直看涨，不知是否会一直这样。

12 I've ***been taking*** French lessons this year. 今年我一直在上法语课。

比如，在过去的几年里，笔者收到来自全国各地读者朋友的来信，从这些来信中，笔者更好地了解到他们在英语学习中的困惑，于是笔者可以用现在完成进行时来这样说：

13 From the letters I've ***been receiving*** from my readers for years, I understand where their difficulties lie in learning English.

妙语点睛 这里的 receive 是一个短暂动词，所以笔者就得用现在完成进行时 have been receiving 来表示重复事件，即这几年不断地收到读者的来信。

精品译文 从这几年的读者来信中，我能理解他们学习英语的难点在哪里。

最后需要提醒大家注意的是，短暂动词用于完成进行时态（如 have been coming）一般不宜接"短的时间状语"。比如：

14 Mike ***has been winning*** that race ***for two hours.*** *

这句话是没有太大的实际意义的，因为一个人不可能在两个小时内连续两次、甚至多次赢得某个比赛的胜利。所以，后面接的都应该是表达较长时间的状语，表示在一段相对较长的时间内重复的动作。比如这么说：

15 Mike ***has been winning*** that race ***for years.***

这就表示"麦克多年以来多次赢得那个比赛"。这里的 win 同样是一个短暂动词，它用于现在完成进行时，可以被解释成一个重复发生的事件。

6.5.2 重复事件（二）：有限延续动词

上一小节讨论了现在完成进行时态（have been doing）用于短暂动词（如 come）时表示"重复事件（repeated events）"时的意义和用法，这一节将讨论"有限延续动词"用于现在完成进行时是如何表示"重复事件"的。先来看看下列关于"网恋（Internet dating）"的一个例句：

1 I've ***been chatting*** online for a little over three years and have met hundreds of people. One common thing of those who have met others in real life is "Don't base the rest of your life on a week or two", meaning don't spend a week or two with your online lover, then move in with them and get married.

妙语点睛 这里的 chat 虽然是一个可以延续的动词，但它用在 I have been chatting online for a little over three years 这句话里面，显然就不能表示一个不间断的延续活动了，因为"聊天"不可能是一直不间断地"延续"了三年多。所以，根据日常的实际经验，只能把它解释为是在三年之中"重复"上网聊天，也即这里的 have been chatting 应该是表示一个重复事件（repeated events），而不是延续事件（continuous events）。

精品译文 我上网聊天已经有三年多了，也认识了很多人。那些已经和现实生活中的网友见过面的人总说："别因为一两个星期的感情就搭上你一辈子幸福"，这就是说，别仅仅因为和你的网上情人相恋一两个星期后就谈婚论嫁。

另一方面，也可以将上面这个例句中的"三年"的时间段缩短为"三小时"，而仍然保留完成进行时 have been chatting，于是可以换个语境这么说：

2 I began chatting online three hours ago and I am chatting online now. I ***have been chatting*** online for three hours now.

妙语点睛 在这一句里面，have been chatting 则显然表示的是一个延续活动而不是重复活动，即"聊天"这一活动是一直不间断地持续了三个小时。

精品译文 我是三个小时之前开始上网聊天的，现在还在聊，因此，我上网聊天到现在已有三个小时了。

尽管上述两个语境中用的都是完成进行时态 have been chatting，但它们所表达的意义是不同的，而这种差异是由于两个语境中所用的时间长短不一样造成的。对比上述两个不同的场景，会发现这样一个有趣的现象：have been chatting 如果接一个"较长的时间段"，则表示的是一个"重复活动"；如果接一个"较短的时间段"，则表示的是一个"延续活动"。

为了能从中找出一般规律，下面来进一步分析其他例句。请比较：

3 1）Frank likes to eavesdrop on his boss's phone conversations. His boss doesn't know Frank ***has been listening*** to him talk on the phone for the past three years.

2）Frank is eavesdropping on his boss's phone conversations. He ***has been listening*** to him talk on the phone ***for ten minutes now.***

妙语点睛 在例句 1）中，现在完成进行时 has been listening 与表达较长时间的持续时间状语 for the past three years 搭配使用，这就表示在近三年当中，他不断"重复"地偷听他老板的电话，所以，这里的 has been listening 表示重复活动。在例句 2）中，现在完成进行时 has been listening 与表达较短时间的持续时间状语 for ten minutes now 搭配使用，则表示他偷听老板的电话是一直在"延续"的，已经延续了 10 分钟了，所以，这里的 has been listening 表示延续活动。

精品译文 1）弗兰克喜欢偷听他老板的电话，他老板还不知道他偷听电话有三年了。

2）弗兰克现正在偷听他老板的电话，他老板还不知道他偷听电话有 10 分钟了。

4 1）Larry King ***has been interviewing*** important people ***for more than 40 years***. King ***has been asking*** famous people questions ***throughout his career***, having accumulated more than 40, 000 interviews. He has talked with every American president since Richard Nixon.

2）Larry King ***has been interviewing*** the President ***for over an hour.***

妙语点睛 在例句 1）中，完成进行时 has been interviewing 接了表达较长时间的时间状语 for more than 40 years，这就表示在过去的 40 多年中，拉里·金多次重复采访众多要人，所以，这里的 has been interviewing 表示重复活动。同样道理，has been asking 与表达较长时间的时间状语 throughout his career 搭配使用，所以，这里的 has been asking 也是表示一个重复活动。在例句 2）中，has been interviewing 则表示一个一直在延续的活动，且持续了一个多小时。（另注：拉里·金为美国 CNN（有线新闻网）最为著名的节目主持人，主持脱口秀节目 Larry King Live，被称为 the most remarkable talk-show host on TV ever）。

精品译文 1）拉里·金从业 40 多年来，采访过众多名人，向他们提出各种问题，累积采访达四万多人次。自从尼克松总统以来，历届美国总统都接受过他的采访。

2）拉里·金一直在采访总统，到现在有一个多小时了。

5 A: I'm going out to pick up a sandwich. Can I get you something?

B: Hmm. I'***ve been eating*** too much lately. I'll just have the yogurt I brought, but thanks for the offer.

妙语点睛 这句话中的 have been eating 显然也是表示最近（lately）在重复的活动。但如果你此时正在吃饭，有人问你吃了多长时间了，你说 We have been eating for two hours 就是表示一个延续的活动。

精品译文 A：我想出去买块三明治，要我替你捎点什么吗？

B：嗯，最近我吃的太多了，我还是就吃我带来的酸奶吧，多谢了。

从对以上众多例句的分析中可以发现，像动词 chat, listen, interview, ask 和 eat 等，都是表示可以延续的动作，所以这些动词用于完成进行时都可以表示延续的活动。这不同于 come 这样的瞬间即结束的动词，因为它不能延续，所以它的完成进行时 have been coming 用于较长的时间段时，只好把它解释为重复的动作（见 6. 5. 1 节）。但在另一方面，像动词 chat, listen, interview, ask 和 eat 等，虽然比瞬间动词 come 具有较强的延续性，但它们所表达的延续性也是有限的，因为它们都是表达某一个单一具体的动作，而对于一个能体现出具体动作的动词，一般不可能持续太长的时间。因此，当它们用于表达较长时间的时间状语时，就不能说某一活动在"延续"，而只能解释成"重复"了。比如前文中的一个"采访（interview）"不可能持续 40 多年的时间，实际情况是在 40 年期间，拉里·金在"重复"采访，即他从事新闻采访这个职业。

对于这样具有一定的延续性但又不能长时间延续的动词，我们称之为"有限延续动词"，所以可以得出这样的结论：

“有限延续动词”用于完成进行时态，若接表达较长时间的状语表示“重复活动”，若接表达较短时间的状语则表示“延续活动”。

此时的现在完成进行时态体现了“现在进行时态”的“有限持续性”的特点，因此，它的持续时间不宜太长，这是进行体赋予它的特点。再比如：

6 1) He ***has been repairing*** cars ***for almost 20 years.***

2) He ***has been repairing*** his car ***since 6:00 this morning.***

妙语点睛 在例句1）中，有限延续动词 repair 的完成进行时 has been repairing 与表达较长时间的状语 for almost 20 years 连用，所以这里的 repair 可以解释成重复事件，表示“他修理汽车有将近 20 年了”，这强烈表明他是专门从事汽车维修工作的，修车是他的职业。在例句 2)中，有限延续动词 repair 的完成进行时 has been repairing 与表达较短时间的状语 since 6:00 this morning 连用，所以这里的 repair 可以解释成延续事件，表示“从早上 6 点到现在，他一直在修理他的车”。这并不能说明修车是他的职业，只是表示他一直在做的一项活动而已。

精品译文 1)他修理汽车有将近 20 多年了。

2)从早上 6 点到现在，他一直在修理他的车。

7 1) We***'ve been writing*** to each other ***for years.***

2) ***I've been writing*** this letter ***for an hour.***

妙语点睛 在例句 1) 中，有限延续动词 write 的完成进行时 have been writing 与表达较长时间的状语 for years 连用，所以可以把这里的 write 解释成重复事件，表明“我们有定期保持通信联系的习惯”，相当于说 Years ago we started writing to a pen pal. We still write to each other regularly now. 在例句 2)中，有限延续动词 write 的完成进行时 have been writing 与表达较短时间的状语 for an hour 连用，所以可以把这里的 write 解释成延续事件，表明“我在说话时刻正在做的一项活动”。

精品译文 1)我们多年来一直保持通信联系。

2)这封信我写了有一个小时了。

8 A: ***I've been running*** a mile every afternoon for the past month, but I still haven't been able to lose more than a pound or two. I wonder if it's worth it.

B: Oh, don't give up now. It always seems hard when you are just starting out.

妙语点睛 这里的有限延续动词 run 的现在完成进行时 have been running 与表达较长时间的状语 for the past month 连用，所以我们把这里的 run 解释成重复事件，尤其是时间状语 every afternoon 也表明这是一个重复活动。这表明“我养成了每天下午跑一英里的习惯，这个习惯已经有一个月了”。

精品译文 A：近一个月以来，我每天下午都要跑一英里，可是我连一两磅的体重都没减掉。我都怀疑这么跑是否真的管用。

B：哦，现在别打退堂鼓，万事开头难啊。

9 1) ***I've been jogging*** every morning ***for the last ten months.***

2) ***I've been*** jogging here ***for half an hour.***

妙语点睛 在例句 1)中，有限延续动词 jog 的完成进行时 have been jogging 与表达较长时间的状语 for the last ten months 连用，所以我们把这里的 jog 解释成重复事件，尤其是时间状语 every morning 也表明这是一个重复活动。这表明“我有慢跑锻炼的习惯，但也许在说话的时刻我并没在跑步”。在例句 2)中，有限延续动词 jog 的完成进行时 have been jogging 与表达较短时间的状语 for half an hour 连用，所以我们把这里的 jog 解释成延续事件，这并不表明“我有慢跑锻炼的习惯，只是表示在说话时刻我正做的一项运动而已”。

精品译文 1)在近 10 个月以来，我每天早晨慢跑锻炼。

2)我在这慢跑有半个钟头了。

看到这里，也许有读者会问：到底多长的时间才算是长时间呢？是几个月？几年？还是几十年？当然，这里说的“长时间”只能是一个相对的概念，尤其是针对特定的谓语动词来说的。比如“半小时”对于上面讨论过的

“慢跑(jog)”的活动是短时间，但在下面这个句子中就算是“长时间”：

10 A: I***'ve been calling*** David ***for the past half hour***, but I keep getting a busy signal.

B: Well, if you don't get him soon we'll just have to go to the movies without him.

妙语点睛　从后文的 but I keep getting a busy signal 得知，这里“我”打电话给大卫是多次重复的，而且都是在过去半个小时内多次的重复活动，所以这里“半小时”对于 call 来说就算是一个较长的时间了。

精品译文　A：近半个小时以来，我一直在给大卫打电话，但总是忙音。

B：噢，如果你不能很快地找到他，我们只好不带他去看电影了。

以下例句中的谓语动词都是有限延续动词，由于是用于表达较长时间的状语，所以都表示重复活动，请读者认真体会：

11 A: You know some TV channels ***have been rerunning*** a lot of comedies from the sixties. What do you think of those old shows?

B: Not much, but the new ones aren't so great, either.

精品译文　A：一些电视频道里一直在重播60年代的喜剧电影，你觉得那些老片子怎么样？

B：不怎么样，不过新的喜剧片也很一般。

12 That story is a legend. People ***have been telling*** it for hundreds of years. No one knows if it's true or not.

这个故事只是个传说，几百年来人们一直在讲述着，谁也不知道它是否是真的。

13 “If you sit too close to the television, you'll ruin your eyes.” Sound familiar? You might have heard this warning as a child. Mothers everywhere ***have been saying*** it for years. But is there any truth to this bit of motherly wisdom?

“如果你看电视时坐得离电视机太近，这会损害你的眼睛。”听起来熟悉吗？小的时候你可能听到过这样的警告。世界各地的母亲长久以来一直都在这样说。但是这个来自母亲智慧的忠告有多少事实根据呢？

对于一个“说话的巨人，行动的矮子”，你可以这么对他说：

14 You***'ve been saying*** that for five years. I wonder when you're going to put it into practice.

这话你都说了有五年了，我不知道你何时才能付诸实践。

如果自己也是“光说不练”的人，可以这样用英文来下决心：

15 I***'ve been talking*** about it for nearly fifty years. Now I'm going to do it.

这件事我都说了近50年了，现在我就打算去做。

如果有读者是“烟民”，那么你就可以用现在完成进行时来谈论自己“漫长的烟龄”：

16 I ***have been smoking*** for ten years.

妙语点睛　这里显然是表示“抽烟”这个习惯活动在过去的10年中不断地重复发生，而不是表示一直持续不断。同样道理，若接表达较短时间的状语，则可以解释为延续活动，比如说：I have been smoking for two minutes now. 表示“这根烟我抽了有两分钟了”，这是一个延续活动。

精品译文　我的“烟龄”已有10年了。

另外，值得注意的是，既然存在**有限延续动词**，那么就会有**无限延续动词**。在英文中，像 work, learn 和 wait 等动词并不能表现出某一具体的动作，它们近乎于一种状态的延续，把这样的动词被称为无限延续动词。对于无限延续动词来说，所接的时间状语不论表达的时间长短，都表示延续活动的意义。例如：

17 1) I***'ve been learning*** English ***for over ten years now.***

2) I***'ve been learning*** English ***for the past two hours***. No wonder I feel tired.

1) 我学英语到现在有十多年了。

2) 在过去的两个小时里我一直在学英语，所以我感到累了。

18 1) He ***has been working*** in the same job ***for 30 years.***

2) He ***has been working*** on the puzzles ***for two hours.***

1）这个工作他干了有30年了。

2）他玩这个拼图游戏有两个小时了。

19 1）A: Winter is over at last. Time to pack up my gloves and boots.

B: I'*ve been waiting* for this for months.

2）I'*ve been waiting* for you *for three hours*!

1）A: 冬天终于过去了，现在该把手套和长靴收拾起来了。

B: 我等了好几个月了！

2）我已经等了你三个小时了！

上面这些句子都是表示一个延续事件，这点在6.3.2节中讨论过。不过，即使对于这些无限延续性动词，也可能会通过其他方式来表达重复活动。比如：

20 I'*ve been working* on the night shift for several weeks.

妙语点睛 这里的work是一个典型的无限延续动词，但由于句中有on the night shift这一时间状语表示“上夜班”，又因为客观上有夜班和白班交替重复出现的情况，所以该句中的have been working表示重复活动。

精品译文 近几个星期以来我一直在上晚班。

思维总结

本节讨论了完成进行时如何表示“重复事件”。这一用法主要适用于两类动词：短暂动词和有限延续动词。不适合无限延续动词。

首先，对于短暂动词来说，它用于现在完成进行时往往表示重复事件。具体来说，就是表示到目前为止的一段时间内重复发生的某一活动（a repeated activity, a habitual action in a period of time up to the present）。需要注意的是，此时句子的谓语往往都是短暂动词，如果是延续动词则可能表示一个延续的活动。比如本节开头的那个句子，若将其谓语come改为延续动词live，说成I *have been living* in Beijing for 14 years. 则表示一个延续的living活动，意思是“我在北京生活了14年了”。简言之，短暂动词用于完成进行时，均表示一个“重复活动”。

其次，对于有限延续动词来说，它用于完成进行时要分为两种情况：若接表达较长时间的状语表示“重复活动”，若接表达较短时间的状语则表示“延续活动”。

再次，无限延续动词用于完成进行时，不论其所接时间状语表达时间的长短，都表示“延续活动”。

由此可见，have been doing的意义与动词的持续性是密切相关的，所以，这就要求读者对于某个动词的持续性特点要很敏感。

思维训练

Exercise 6.5（Key: P345）

请用括号中动词的适当的形式填空。

1. —Every Sunday they meet in the bar. They ______（go）there for ten years.
2. You ______（go）with Nancy for over three years now. Why don't you pop her the question?
3. Koreans ______（marry）US soldiers stationed here since the 1950s. The peak years ______（be）during the 1970s, when more than 4000 Koreans ______（marry）US soldiers each year.
4. I ______（hear）from my girlfriend regularly since I came to America.
5. Larry King ______（interview）important people for more than 40 years. King ______（ask）famous people questions throughout his career, having accumulated more than 40, 000 interviews. He ______（talk）with every American president since Richard Nixon.
6. I ______（run）a mile every afternoon for the past month, but I still ______（not, be）able to lose more than a pound or two. I wonder if it's worth it.
7. A: I ______（call）David for the past half hour, but I keep getting a busy signal.

   B: Well, if you don't get him soon we'll just have to go to the movies without him.

8. I ______ (smoke) for ten years.

请解释下面对话的逻辑关系。

9. A: I've been singing since I was two years old.
   B: No wonder you've lost your voice.

6.6 重复事件比较: 完成进行时与完成时

讨论完现在完成进行时表示的"重复事件"，现在自然要比较完成进行时的"重复事件"与完成时的"重复事件"。在这一节里，我们将讨论下面三个问题：

1. 重复动作的分割性：现在完成进行时表示重复活动时，不能被分割开来，即不能说出具体的次数。它的重复性是根据人们的实际经验而体会出来的。而完成时表示的重复活动，往往要说出具体的次数。因此，可以这样来看二者的差别：现在完成进行时的重复是"隐性"的，是模糊的；现在完成时的重复是"显性"的，是明确的。

2. 短暂动词的完成进行时表示重复活动。

3. 完成进行时的"重复事件"与一般现在时的"重复事件"。

因此，本节内容安排如下：

6.6.1 比较(三)：重复动作的分割性

6.6.2 比较(四)：短暂动词用于完成进行时来表示重复活动

6.6.3 完成进行时的"重复事件"与一般现在时的"重复事件"

6.6.1 比较(三)：重复动作的分割性

笔者曾经有一次和一个美国朋友喝咖啡时，聊到了英语语言的学习问题。笔者告诉她，对中国学生来说，学英语最大难点的就是复杂的时态变化。英语时态变来变去的，搞得我们晕头转向。她无辜地笑道："Tense would make me tense if I were a Chinese student. (我要是中国学生，时态一定也会让我疯掉的。)"

原因很简单，这是两种思维表达的重大差异造成的。汉语是不太重视时间表达的，所以对拥有汉语思维的中国学生来说，"三时四态"的英语精确的时间表达很难进入我们的思维。思维里既然没有时间概念，所以在用英语表达时，我们不是结结巴巴老在琢磨该用什么时态，就是撇开时态不顾，一律用一般现在时。

其实，对于 native speakers 来说，时态已融入他们的思维，他们不需要知道像"现在完成时"或"现在完成进行时" 等这样的语法术语，而是在潜意识就能够清楚地知道该用什么样的时态形式来表示什么样的时间概念。比如，笔者当时就问这位美国朋友，笔者可不可以这样说：

1 I ***have been drinking five cups of coffee*** this afternoon. 今天下午我一直喝了五杯咖啡。

她给笔者的回答是"No way(不能这样讲)"。笔者问她为什么，她则很茫然地摇摇头说："I don't know."

其实，笔者是知道为什么不能这么说的。这里涉及完成时态和完成进行时态的区别问题。完成进行时具有进行时的特点，而进行时是强调动作的持续性，因此这一活动必须是连续不断的。如果把动作分割开了看，则违背了进行时态的核心意义——持续性，所以不能用进行时态。我们在下列两种情况下就会把动作分割开：一是谈到在一段时间内一共做了多少件事情(比如说喝了五杯咖啡)；二是说明某件事发生的次数(比如下文中将要说到的去过三次洛杉矶)。因此，这两种情形下都不能使用各种进行时态，包括现在完成进行时。

所以，可以得出结论：完成进行时态不能用来谈某个动作的具体次数或几件事情。这时要用完成时态。这就解释了为什么在老外的思维里没有：

I ***have been drinking five cups of coffee*** this afternoon. *

这样的句子，而一定会这么说：I ***have drunk*** five cups of coffee this afternoon.

因为这里说出了具体的数目——五杯咖啡。

比如要说"去过三次洛杉矶"，就可以用完成时态这样说：

2 He ***has gone*** to Los Angeles three times this year. 或
He ***has been*** to Los Angeles ***three times*** this year.

但不能用完成进行时，说成：He ***has been going*** to Los Angeles three times this year. *

再比如，前面一节讲的 Larry King 的例子：

3 Larry King ***has been interviewing*** important people for more than 40 years. King ***has been asking*** famous people questions throughout his career and ***has done*** more than 40, 000 interviews. He ***has talked*** with every American president since Richard Nixon.

妙语点睛 这里 has been interviewing 和 has been asking 都是表示重复的动作，但由于并没有说明具体的次数，所以用了完成进行时态，来强调他到目前为止还一直在从事采访活动。而接下来由于说出了具体的 40, 000 次采访以及采访过每一位美国总统(every American president)，这都使得动作被分割开，强调一个结果或成就，而不是一个不间断的过程，所以改用了现在完成时 has done 和 has talked 来表达。

精品译文 拉里·金从业 40 多年来，采访过众多名人，向他们提出各种问题，累积采访达四万多人次。自从尼克松总统以来，历届美国总统都接受过他的采访。

再比如下面关于"网恋"的场景：

4 ***I've been chatting*** online for a little over three years and have met hundreds of people. One common thing of those who ***have met*** others in real life is "Don't base the rest of your life on a week or two", meaning don't spend a week or two with your online lover, then move in with them and get married.

妙语点睛 本句中的 have been chatting，因为下文说了 for a little over three years，所以 chatting 不可能是一直在不间断地延续着，而是表示重复动作。又因为没有说明聊天的具体次数，所以用完成进行时的 have been chatting 来表示这一重复活动。完成时 have met 表示重复，这里的动作已被分割，因为下文提到了 hundreds of people，所以不能说 have been meeting。

精品译文 我上网聊天已经有三年多了，也认识了很多人。那些已经和现实生活中的网友见过面的人总说："别因为一两个星期的感情就搭上你一辈子幸福"，这就是说，别仅仅因为和你的网上情人相恋一两个星期后就谈婚论嫁。

完成进行时态不能用来谈具体的几次或几件事，换句话说，它所表示的重复动作是不能被分割开来的，而只能看作是一个不间断的过程，这是进行体赋予它的特点。完成时态则常常表示间断的重复活动，可以标明具体几次或几件事，这也是完成时强调活动结果的体现。

现在完成进行时表示的重复活动都是不能说出具体次数的，而只能从上下文体会出来，或者依据我们的实际经验体会出来。比如：

5 A: ***I've been calling*** David ***for the past half hour***, but I keep getting a busy signal.

B: Well, if you don't get him soon we'll just have to go to the movies without him.

精品译文 A：近半个小时以来，我一直在给大卫打电话，但总是忙音。

B：噢，如果你不能很快找到他，我们只好不带他去看电影了。

妙语点睛 从后文的 but I keep getting a busy signal 可知，这里"我"打电话给大卫是多次的活动，而且都是在过去近半小时内发生的。这里的重复活动的意味是从下文 but 引导的分句体会出来的，但句中并没有明确说出打电话的具体次数。如果要说出具体的次数，则必须改用现在完成时态。

比如：

6 ***I've called*** David ***four times*** for the past half hour, but I keep getting a busy signal.

近半个小时以来，我给大卫打了四次电话，但每次都是忙音。

因此，可以这么来看待两种时态所表示的重复活动：**现在完成进行时的重复是"隐性"的，是模糊的，它的重复性是根据人们的实际经验体会出来的；现在完成时的重复是"显性"的，是明确的。**请比较：

7 1) ***I've been writing*** letters this morning.

2) ***I've written three*** letters this morning.

妙语点睛 在例句 1)中，复数名词 letters 表明"我上午写了不止一封信"，也即这里的现在完成进行时表示一个重复活动。但并没有具体说出是几封信。在例句 2)中，明确地说出了是三封信。

精品译文 1)今天上午到目前为止我一直在写信。
2)今天上午到目前为止我写了三封信。

再比如下面的例句：

8 1) I ***have been sitting*** in class since 8 o'clock this morning. 从早上8点钟到现在我一直在上课。
2) I ***have had three*** classes since 8 o'clock this morning. 从早上8点钟到现在我上了三门课。

6.6.2 比较(四)：短暂动词用于完成进行时来表示重复活动

6.5.1节谈到了短暂动词用于现在完成进行时可以表示一个重复活动，这时往往都会接一个表达较长的持续时间的状语。比如下面这些曾经讨论过的例句：

1 I ***have been coming*** to Beijing for 14 years.

2 I***'ve been coming*** to see him for 10 years.

3 Every Sunday they meet in the bar. They ***have been going*** there for 10 years.

4 You***'ve been going*** with Nancy for over three years now. Why don't you pop her the question?

5 Koreans ***have been marrying*** U. S. soldiers stationed here since the 1950s. The peak years were during the 1970s, when more than 4, 000 Koreans married U. S. soldiers each year.

6 Over the past few years, many towns in the United States ***have been joining*** with neighboring communities to sharc the costs of government.

7 I***'ve been hearing*** from my girlfriend regularly since I came to America.

从上面这些例句可以看到，短暂动词的完成进行时可以与持续的时间状语连用，来表示一个重复活动。但是，第五章5.6.5节讲过，短暂动词的完成时是不能与持续的时间状语连用的，因为短暂动作无法延续，这与持续的时间状语形成语义上的冲突。所以，上述句子都不可能改为现在完成时：

8 I ***have come*** to Beijing ***for 14 years.*** *

9 I've ***come*** to see him ***for 10 years.*** *

10 Every Sunday they meet in the same bar. They***'ve gone*** there ***for years.*** *

11 You***'ve gone*** with Nancy ***for over three years now.*** * Why don't you pop her the question?

12 Koreans ***have married*** U. S. soldiers stationed here ***since the 1950s.*** * The peak years were during the 1970s, when more than 4, 000 Koreans married U. S. soldiers each year.

13 ***Over the past few years***, many towns in the United States ***have joined*** with neighboring communities to share the costs of government. *

14 I***'ve heard*** from my girlfriend ***since I came to America.*** *

综上所述，短暂动词的完成进行时可以与持续的时间状语连用，来表达一个在这个时段内的重复活动；而短暂动词的完成时不能与持续的时间状语连用，不能表示重复活动。如果短暂动词的完成时要表示重复活动，如上面讨论的那样，就只能加上具体的次数。

6.6.3 完成进行时的"重复事件"与一般现在时的"重复事件"

大家知道，一般现在时也可以表示一个重复的习惯活动，比如我们说：

1 I ***run*** a mile every afternoon.

这句话表示"我每天下午都会跑一英里"，即已养成一个跑步的习惯了。现在把这个句子改为现在完成进行时：

I'***ve been running*** a mile every afternoon.

这又是什么意思呢？如何理解这个句子？还是把它简单地译成"我每天下午都会跑一英里"吗？在回答这些问题之前，可以把这个句子放在一个更完整的语境中，也就是我们上面刚刚讨论过的这个对话场景：

A: I'***ve been running*** a mile every afternoon ***for the past month***, but I still haven't been able to lose more than a pound or two. I wonder if it's worth it.

B: Oh, don't give up now. It always seems hard when you are just starting out.

大家看到，这里添加了一个持续的时间状语 for the past month，表示到目前为止的一个时间段内，重复发生"跑步"这个活动。

由此可见，当用现在完成进行时表达一个重复活动时，我们的头脑中就会有一个较明确的表示到目前为止的时间段(比如 for the past month)，而一般现在时就不能这么用。比如不能说：

2 I ***run*** a mile every afternoon ***for the past month.*** *

当用一般现在时来谈一个重复活动时，我们的头脑里没有这样的一个时间段的概念，而只表示一种泛泛的日常习惯。比如当我们说 I run a mile every afternoon. 时，只是说明 run 这个日常习惯的活动，而不知道 run 这个动作是在哪段时间内重复发生的。

所以，现在完成进行时表示"重复事件"的一个重要概念就是：**到目前为止的一个时间段内重复的活动**。有时，若上下文的语境中已暗示有一个时间段的概念，即使没有明确说出这个时间段，也要用 have been doing 来表示在这一未明示的时间段内重复的动作。例如：

3 I ***have been running*** a mile every afternoon, but I think I'll run two miles later.

这里的 but I think I'll run two miles later 就告诉我们，说话人是强调现在和将来的对比，也就是说，他头脑里是强调"到目前为止的一个时间段内每天跑一英里"，所以才有下文说"不过我想以后改为两英里"。此时就不能说：

I ***run*** a mile every afternoon, but I think I'll run two miles later. *

因此，以后遇到现在完成进行时表示的重复活动，即使没有明确的时间段出现，也要理解成这一重复活动是在从过去到目前为止的一个时间段内发生的。请比较下面两个句子：

4 1) I ***run*** a mile every afternoon.

2) I ***have been running*** a mile every afternoon.

妙语点睛 比较这两个例句，可以看到，两句中的动作没变，都是 run，但是把 run 的形式由原形 run 变为完成进行式 have been running，句子所要表达的意思也随即发生改变。在例句 2)中，加上了"到目前为止"来对应翻译英文的语言标记 have been doing 这一动词变形。另外，用现在完成进行时来说这个句子，可能会含有言外之意，比如说话人接下去要表达他要改变跑步的距离，把跑一英里改为跑两英里。

精品译文 1)我每天下午都会跑一英里。

2)到目前为止，我每天下午都跑一英里。

再比如下面类似的对比：

5 1) I ***go*** to the gym every three days.

2) I'***ve been going*** to the gym every three days, but I think I'll make it every other day from now on.

妙语点睛 在例句 1)中，用一般现在时只是单纯地谈日常习惯。在例句 2)中，用现在完成进行时表示到目前为止的一个时段内重复的活动，引出一个与将来的对比：由隔两天健身一次改为隔一天健身一次。

精品译文 1)我每三天去健身一次。

2)到目前为止，我每三天去健身一次，不过我想从今往后改为每隔一天去一次。

再比如：

6 1) Jim ***phones*** Jenny every night.

2) Jim ***has been phoning*** Jenny every night for the last week.

妙语点睛　在例句1)中，用一般现在时只是单纯地谈日常习惯——每天晚上打一次电话。在例句2)中，因为有了 for the last week 这样一个明确地表示到目前为止的一个时段，所以要用现在完成进行时，以表示在这个时段内的重复活动。

精品译文　1)吉姆每天晚上都要给珍妮打电话。

2)近一个星期来，吉姆每天晚上都要给珍妮打电话。

思维总结

本节作了两个比较。首先是比较了现在完成进行时的"重复事件"与现在完成时的"重复事件"，告诉读者二者的差别可以归纳为：现在完成进行时的重复是"隐性"的，是模糊的，是不能说出具体次数的，它的重复性只能是人们根据实际经验体会出来的；现在完成时的重复是"显性"的，是明确的，往往是要明确说出次数的。还有要注意的就是，短暂动词的完成进行时可以与持续的时间状语连用，此时表示重复事件；但是短暂动词的完成时不能与持续的时间状语连用。

其次，比较了现在完成进行时的"重复事件"与一般现在时的"重复事件"，然后告诉读者：现在完成进行时表示"重复事件"的一个重要概念就是：**到目前为止的一个时间段内重复的活动**，而当我们用一般现在时来谈一个重复活动时，我们的头脑里没有这样的一个时间段的概念，而只表示一种泛泛的日常习惯。

思维训练

Exercise 6.6（Key: P345）

请把下面中文句子翻译成英文。

1. 我每天都晨跑锻炼。
2. 近一个月来，我每天都晨跑锻炼。
3. 他们交往有三年了。
4. 10年来，我常常来看他。

6.7 完成进行时与完成时对比总结

6.7.1 比较(五)：完成进行时强调"延续过程"，完成时强调"成果"

现在完成进行时的最后一节将现在完成时与现在完成进行时的区别"算一下总账"。前面的6.4.1、6.4.2、6.6.1和6.6.2四节讨论了这两个时态在用法上的种种区别。其实那些区别都源于二者的这一根本区别：**完成进行时重在"进行(ongoing)"，即未完成(incomplete)，强调动作持续的过程(emphasis on duration)；完成时重在"完成"，即已完成(completed)，强调动作的结果或成就(emphasis on achievement)**。具体来讲，现在完成进行时所强调的是在一段时期内某项活动的持续性，强调的是动作本身；现在完成时则是强调动作产生的结果或取得的成就，而不是动作本身。

比如我们一般用现在完成进行时来谈论不断的变化和发展，这是现在进行时赋予它的这个意义，因为现在进行时可以谈不断变化的过程。例如：

1　Scientists believe that the universe ***has been expanding*** since the beginning of time.

科学家们相信，自远古时代以来，宇宙一直在不断地扩大着。

一、未完成与已完成

先来比较现在完成进行时的"未完成"与现在完成时的"已完成"。请比较下列例句：

2　1) I ***have been reading*** your grammar book. After I finish it, I'll discuss some problems with you.

2) I ***have read*** your grammar book and I have questions to ask you.

妙语点睛　在例句1)中，现在完成进行时表示 read 的动作未完成。在例句2)中，现在完成时表示 read 的动作已完成。

精品译文　1)我一直在看你的语法书，看完以后我会有一些问题要和你讨论。

2)我看过你的语法书了，现在有问题要问你。

3 1) I ***have been reading*** the book you lent me but I haven't finished it yet.

2) I ***have read*** the book you lent me, so you can have it back now.

妙语点睛 在例句1)中，现在完成进行时表示read的动作未完成，所以下文可以说but I haven't finished it yet。在例句2)中，现在完成时表示read的动作已完成，接下去就不能再说but I haven't finished it yet了。

精品译文 1)你借给我的那本书我一直在看，现在还没有看完。

2)你借我的那本书我已经看完了，所以你现在可以拿回去了。

4 1) A: ***Have*** you ***been cleaning*** the windows?

B: Yes, but I haven't finished them yet.

2) A: ***Have*** you ***cleaned*** the windows?

B: No, I haven't finished them yet.

妙语点睛 可以看到，在两组对话中，B的回答中都含有I haven't finished them yet，但是在对话1)中B的回答是肯定的Yes，而在对话2)中B的回答却是否定的No。原因分析如下：

在对话1)中，现在完成进行时have been cleaning表示"未完成"，原句的意思是"你一直在擦窗户吗"，所以，接下来可以回答说"是的，但我还没有擦完"。在对话2)中，现在完成时have cleaned表示"已完成"，原句的意思是"你把窗户擦完了吗"，所以，接下来可以回答说"没有，我还没有擦完"。

精品译文 1) A：你一直在擦窗户吗？

B：是的，但我还没有擦完。

2) A：你擦完窗户了吗？

B：没有，我还没有擦完。

再比如下面的例句，请认真体会：

5 1) Your mother is still in the kitchen. She ***has been cooking*** all morning.

2) I ***have cooked*** a lovely meal, which I'll be serving in a couple of minutes.

妙语点睛 在例句1)中，现在完成进行时表示cook的动作未完成。在例句2)中，现在完成时表示cook的动作已完成。

精品译文 1)你妈妈还在厨房，她整个一上午都一直在厨房里做饭。

2)我做完了一顿可口的饭，再过两分钟就可以上桌了。

6 1) ***I've been typing*** this report since yesterday and I'm only half way through.

2) ***I've typed*** all your letters. The job's done.

妙语点睛 在例句1)中，现在完成进行时表示type的动作未完成。在例句2)中，现在完成时表示type的动作已完成。

精品译文 1)从昨天到现在我一直在打印那份报告，现在只做完了一半。

2)你所有的信件我都打完了，此项工作已完成。

二、延续过程与结果或成果

7 1) How long ***have*** you ***been learning*** English?

2) How many words ***have*** you ***learned***?

妙语点睛 在例句1)中，询问学英语的持续时间，强调活动的持续过程，所以用现在完成进行时have been learning。在例句2)中，询问学会了多少单词，强调学习的成果，所以用现在完成时have learned。

精品译文 1)你学习英语有多久了？

2)你已经学会了多少英语单词？

8 1) How long ***have*** you ***been living*** in your present apartment?

2) How many apartments ***have*** you ***lived*** in this city?

妙语点睛 在例句1)中，询问居住的持续时间，强调活动持续的过程，所以用现在完成进行时 have been living。这里的现在完成进行时表示延续事件。在例句2)中，询问住过多少间不同的公寓，强调结果，暗指搬家的次数，所以用现在完成时 have lived。这里的现在完成时表示重复活动。

精品译文 1)你在现在这间公寓住了多久？

2)你在这座城市里都住过多少间公寓了？

9 1) Robert ***has been living*** in Pittsburgh for several years.

2) Robert ***has lived*** in many different locations.

妙语点睛 在例句1)中，说明在同一个地方居住的持续时间，强调活动持续的过程，所以用现在完成进行时 have been living。这里的现在完成进行时表示延续事件。在例句2)中，说明住过多少不同的地方，强调结果，暗指搬家的次数，所以用现在完成时 have lived。这里的现在完成时表示重复活动。

精品译文 1)罗伯特在匹茨堡生活了好几年。

2)罗伯特在很多不同的地方都生活过。

10 1) My hands are very dirty. I***'ve been painting*** the house.

2) I ***have painted*** the house green. The house was white, but now it's green.

妙语点睛 在例句1)中，表示"我一直在 painting 房屋"，painting 的活动还未结束，所以手还是脏的。这里的现在完成进行时表示延续事件。在例句2)中，则强调 paint 的结果是"房子的颜色已经变成绿色了"。这里的现在完成时表示单一事件。

精品译文 1)我的手很脏，我一直在给房子刷漆。

2)我把房子漆成了绿色。房子以前是白色的，现在变成绿色的了。

11 1) Sorry about the mess — I***'ve been painting*** the house.

2) I***'ve painted*** two rooms since lunchtime.

妙语点睛 在例句1)中，现在完成进行时 have been painting 表示 painting 的活动还没有结束，房子还没有收拾，所以屋子里很乱。这里的现在完成进行时表示延续事件。在例句2)中，现在完成时 have painted 表示 painted 的结果是"两个房间都已油漆完毕"。这里的现在完成时表示重复活动。

精品译文 1)很抱歉屋里很乱——我一直在给房子刷漆。

2)午饭时间以来我已粉刷完两个房间了。

12 1) I***'ve been gaining*** weight since last year.

2) Gosh, I really have to go on a diet. I***'ve gained*** ten pounds since last year, and everyone tells me I look fat. And if I don't lose weight now, I won't be able to get into any of my summer clothes.

妙语点睛 在例句1)中，用现在完成进行时谈"发胖"持续的过程，但不能谈具体胖了多少这样的结果。这里的现在完成进行时表示延续事件。在例句2)中，用现在完成时谈"发胖"的结果，即具体胖了多少，增重多少磅。这里的现在完成时表示单一事件。

精品译文 1) 从去年至今我一直都在发胖。

2) 天啊，我真得节食了，从去年至今我胖了10磅。现在每个人见到我都说我看起来很胖。如果我现在还不减肥，我担心夏天的衣服再也穿不进去了。

13 A: Oh, I ***have been sitting*** in the same position too long. My legs ***have fallen*** asleep.

B: Shake it a little before you get up.

妙语点睛 从A的话可以看出：由于长时间持续地 sit，即 have been sitting，造成的结果是腿 have fallen asleep。因此，完成进行时表示 sit 这个活动的延续性，而完成时强调 sit 这个动作的结果。

精品译文 A：噢，我一个姿势坐得太久了，两条腿都麻木了。

B：站起来之前，你先把腿甩甩。

14 1) I ***have been sitting*** in class since 8 o'clock this morning. 从早上8点钟到现在我一直在上课。

2) I ***have had three*** classes since 8 o'clock this morning. 从早上8点钟到现在我上了三门课。

15 1) It ***has been snowing*** all day. I wonder when it will stop.

2) We ***have had three*** major snowstorms so far this winter. I wonder how many more we will have.

精品译文 1)下了一整天的雪，不知什么时候能停。

2)今年冬天已经下了三场大雪了，不知还会不会再下雪。

16 1) The phone ***has been ringing*** for almost a minute. Why doesn't someone answer it?

2) The phone ***has rung four*** times this morning, and each time it has been for Clint.

精品译文 1)电话铃声响了有一分钟了，怎么就没有人去接呢？

2)今天上午电话铃响了四次，而且每次都是打给克林特的。

三、感情色彩的不同

由于完成进行时更强调动作的延续性，因而往往带有强烈的感情色彩，较为口语化。所以，在口语中完成进行时使用得较为普遍。而现在完成时则只是说明一个事实，一种结果，较为平铺直叙，缺乏明显的感情色彩。例如：

17 A: Why are you so late? I***'ve been waiting*** here for more than an hour!

B: Sorry to have kept you waiting. But it has been a hectic day today. I've got a million things to attend to.

妙语点睛 这里说话人A用了 have been waiting 的形式，显得较为生气。如果他说 have waited 则显得很平铺直叙，只是简单地说明"等了一个多小时"这样的事实。

精品译文 A：你怎么来得这么晚啊？我在这里一直等了有一个多小时了！

B：对不起让你久等了，因为我今天一直忙得不可开交，有一大堆事情要处理。

18 A: I just saw an ad on television that said men's suits were on sale today and tomorrow at Conrad's men's wear.

B: Great! That's what I***'ve been waiting for.***

妙语点睛 说话人B用了 having been waiting 的形式，则表明他因商场打折(on sale)而显得很兴奋。

精品译文 A：我刚刚看到电视上的一则广告说，今明两天在康拉德商场男士服装打折。

B：太棒了！我一直就等这天呢！

在2007年6月7日举行的哈佛大学的毕业典礼上，比尔·盖茨(Bill Gates)获得了学校颁发的荣誉博士学位。当时他的感言是：

19 I***'ve been waiting*** more than 30 years to say this: "Dad, I always told you I'd come back and get my degree."

妙语点睛 这里盖茨用了 having been waiting 的形式，也表明他兴奋的心情。

精品译文 我已经等了30多年才得以说这句话："老爸，我一直都在告诉你，我会回来拿到学位的。"

20 A: I***'ve been wanting*** to spend the money I got for my birthday.

B: I'm sure that money ***has been burning*** a hole in your pocket.

A: So let's go shopping.

精品译文 A：我一直想把过生日得来的那些钱花掉。

B：我相信那些钱早就不想乖乖地留在你的口袋里啦。

A：那我们一起去购物吧。

21 A: What ***have*** you ***done*** with my knife?

B: I put it back in your drawer.

A: (taking it out) But what ***have*** you ***been doing*** with it? The blade's all twisted! ***Have*** you ***been using*** it to open tins?

妙语点睛 说话人A首先用了一个现在完成时态 have done，只是单纯地询问对方是如何处理小刀的。后来在A看到小刀被弄坏了之后，他才用了现在完成进行时 have been doing 来质问对方为什么把自己的小刀弄卷刃了，显然表明了自己的气愤。最后A用了 have been using，同样表示自己生气了。

精品译文 A：你把我的刀子弄到哪里去了？

B：我把它放回你的抽屉里了。

A：(拿出小刀)可你用这刀子干什么来着？刀刃都卷了！你用它开罐头了吧？

四、重复活动：完成进行时强调持续，不讲次数；完成时强调成果，讲次数

请比较和体会下面这些例句在表示"重复事件"方面的差异：

22 1) I've ***been ironing*** my shirts this morning.

2) I've ***ironed*** five shirts this morning.

妙语点睛 这两句话都是表示重复活动。在例句1)中，现在完成进行时 have been ironing 表示重复，不能说出具体是几件衬衫，所以后面地宾语只是笼统的复数名词 shirts，以强调 iron 这个活动持续的过程。在例句2)中，现在完成时 have ironed 表示重复，说出了具体有五件衬衫，以强调 iron 这个活动的成果。

精品译文 1)我今天上午一直在熨烫我的衬衫。

2)我今天上午熨烫了五件衬衫。

23 1) Jason ***has been neglecting*** his schoolwork to spend time with Julia. Now he is failing his classes.

2) Jason ***has neglected*** his schoolwork ***three times*** this semester.

妙语点睛 这两句话都是表示重复活动。在例句1)中，现在完成进行时 have been neglecting 表示重复，不能说出具体有几次学校的作业没做，以强调 neglect 这个活动持续的过程。在例句2)中，现在完成时 have neglected 表示重复，说出了具体有三次学校的作业没做，以强调 neglect 这个活动的结果。

精品译文 1)杰森最近经常不做学校的作业，而是花时间和茱莉亚泡在一起。现在他上课都要跟不上了。

2)杰森这学期有三次没有做学校的作业了。

再体会下面的例句：

24 1) I've ***been traveling.*** 最近我一直在出差。

2) I've ***done*** a lot of travel. 最近我出了很多差。

25 1) I've ***been writing*** letters this morning. 我今天上午一直在写信。

2) I've ***written three*** letters this morning. 我今天上午写了三封信。

6.7.2 现在完成进行时与现在完成时的思维差异总结

前面各节讨论了完成进行时的两个主要的意义和用法，即表示"延续事件"和"重复事件"。这一小节将探讨这两种思维用法的渊源。这还得从"时态"这个概念说起。

一、时(tense)与态(aspect)

在《英语语法新思维初级教程——走近语法》中我们就说过，英语里的"时态"，即 tense and aspect 是两个概念，二者相互依存、密不可分，用来标志一个动作两方面的不同属性，相当于一枚硬币的不同的两面。

具体来说，谈到"时(tense)"的时候，我们关心的是这个动作发生的时间，即是在现在、过去还是将来发生的。谈到"态(aspect)"(也叫"体")的时候，我们关心的则是这个动作是固定不变的还是动态变化的(fixed or changing)；这个动作是完成了的还是在延续的 (complete or ongoing)；这个动作持续的时间是很短还是很长(lasting for only a moment or for a long time)。

二、语法体与动词体

对于上述"体(aspect)"方面的属性，英语通过两方面来表达，这也就是英语中的两类体：

一类是"语法体(grammatical aspect)"，就是读者熟悉的"进行体(continuous aspect)"、"完成体(perfect aspect)"和"完成进行体(perfect continuous aspect)"。

另一类是"动词体(lexical aspect)"，这是用来标示**动词词义本身所固有的特点**(the inherent properties of the verb's meaning)的。在这方面，英语把动词分为状态和动作(state and action)，又把动作分为短暂动作和延续动作(punctual and durative)等等。

三、完成进行时的意义

从以上两点可以推导出，某个具体时态的意义和用法，其实是"时"、"语法体"和"动词体"这三者相互作用的产物，尤其是后两者的相互作用，影响到我们对某个谓语动作含义的解释。比如，完成进行时就是由于"完成

进行体"与"动词体"的相互作用，导致了"延续事件"和"重复事件"这两种不同的意义。

我们现在就从"完成进行体"与"动词体"这两方面的结合，来解释前面各节所讨论过的完成进行时态的"延续事件"和"重复事件"这两种用法，以便让读者更加深刻地理解这两种用法，及其与完成时态或进行时态的异同。

首先，从语法体(grammatical aspect)的角度来看，完成进行体的核心意义是**有限的延续性**。关于这一点，6.2节中已经介绍过。

其次，从动词体(lexical aspect)的角度来看，完成进行时态对动词的持续性比较敏感。如果像完成时态那样，仅把动词区分为短暂动词和延续动词，已不能满足分析完成进行时态的需要，因此，前面各节对动词作了更加细致的区分，即分为**短暂动词、有限延续动词和无限延续动词**。

因此，完成进行时态的具体用法相当于是**语法体**——有限持续性——与**动词体**——短暂动词、有限延续动词和无限延续动词——相互作用之后的产物。意识到这两种"体"相互作用而导致一些典型的语义解释，这是非常重要的 (It is important to be aware of how the interaction of lexical and grammatical aspect is typically interpreted.) 具体分析如下(以现在完成进行时为例)：

1. 无限延续动词

无限延续动词(如 live)用于现在完成进行时的时候，只能表示一个延续事件。

1 I***'ve been living*** in Beijing for 20 years now.

这就是我们在 6.3.2 小节讨论过的"长期在延续的事件"。事实上，完成进行时的"有限延续性"这个核心意义与这里的长期延续事件是有语义上的冲突的。确切来说，这里的"长期延续性"并不是完成进行时所赋予的，而是无限延续动词本身所具有的特点。因此，这里即使不用现在完成进行时而用现在完成时，依然是表示一个长期在延续的事件。比如说：

2 I***'ve lived*** in Beijing for 20 years now.

这也就解释了为什么现在完成进行时的这一用法与现在完成时的关系更近，而与现在进行时的关系较远。这一语义上的冲突其实也说明：能够表示长期延续事件的现在完成进行时对谓语动词有特殊要求。换句话说，并不是所有的动词用于现在完成进行时都能表示一个长期在持续的事件。

2. 有限延续动词

这样的动词往往是一些表示单一具体活动的动词，比如 repair 这样的动词。这样的动词非常典型地反映出完成进行时的"有限延续性"的特点，因为这样的动词用于现在完成进行时，若要表示延续事件时，则只能接一个表达短暂时间的状语。比如：

3 He ***has been repairing*** his car ***since 6:00 this morning.***

而不能接一个表达较长时间的状语。如果是表达较长时间的状语，则只能解释为重复事件。比如：

4 He ***has been repairing*** cars ***for almost 20 years.***

这就是我们在 6.5.2 小节中重点讨论的内容。这说明完成进行时表示有限的延续性，除非是一些近似于状态的无限延续动词用于完成进行时，可以接表达较长时间的状语表示延续事件外，一般动词只能接表达较短时间的状语才能表示延续事件，否则会变成重复事件。

另一方面，这里的重复事件又是我们根据常识经验体会出来的。比如一个人若是修理一辆汽车，不可能是一直不间断地修了 20 年，这不符合常识，显得很荒唐。这时只能把这"修车"的活动理解为这 20 年来的一个重复发生的活动，才能讲得通。由此可见，上面讲到的语法体与动词体相互作用所产生的语义解释，在很多情况下不是明确说出来的，而是暗含的，得依靠我们自己的经验给出解释(In many cases the meaning that results from that interaction is implicated or inferred rather than stated...such an implicated meaning is based on our typical experience.)

3. 短暂动词

短暂动词与完成进行时"有限延续性"的含义发生作用后，产生了重复事件的解释。比如：

5 I ***have been coming*** to Beijing for 14 years.

这里的重复含义同样是根据我们自己的常识经验体会出来的，因为短暂动作“来(come)”不可能持续20年，所以只好把“来”这个短暂动作解释为是在20年当中重复发生的。这就是6.5.1小节重点讨论的内容。

综上所述，可见，对于完成进行时，需要对动词的体态含义非常敏感。

四、完成进行时与完成时的意义比较

大家知道，完成进行时有两个基本意义：延续事件和重复事件。而完成时有三个基本意义：延续事件、重复事件和单一事件。我们现在来一一进行比较，让读者更好地认识这两类时态的相关性。

1. 延续事件

二者最大的区别在于持续的时间状语。一方面，在带有持续的时间状语时，用两种时态几乎没有多大区别，都表示一个开始于过去的动作一直延续到现在(详见6.4.2小节)。另一方面，如果没有持续的时间状语，完成时则不表示延续至今的事件，而表示一个在过去完成了的事件(即表示“单一事件”中的过去经历)。但是，现在完成进行时在没有持续的时间状语的情况下，依然可以表示延续至今的事件。由此可见，完成进行时比完成时更强调活动本身的持续性。

另外，由于完成进行时更强调活动的持续性，因此还可以把它的延续事件进一步细分成四种不同的延续事件：长期在延续的一个一般性活动；近期在延续的活动；在说话时刻仍在延续的活动；在说话时刻之前在延续的活动，或者刚刚在延续但现在已结束的活动(详见6.3节)。

2. 重复事件

二者在表示重复事件时，最大的区别就在于事件的可分割性(详见6.6节)。现在完成进行时表示重复活动时，不能被分割开来，即不能说出具体的次数。它的重复性是根据人们的实际经验体会出来的。而完成时表示的重复活动，往往要说出具体的次数。因此，可以这样来看二者的差别：现在完成进行时的重复是“隐性”的，是模糊的；现在完成时的重复是“显性”的，是明确的。比如：

5 I ***have received 100 letters*** from my readers over the past few years.几近几年来我收到了100封读者来信。

6 I ***have been receiving letters*** from my readers over the past few years. 近几年来我不断地收到读者来信。

完成进行时表示重复事件时不能被分割，这是由它的“有限延续性”这一核心意义决定的——既然是“延续”的，那么当然就不能把某个动作断开来数具体的次数。

另外，完成进行时用于短暂动词时，是表示一个“重复事件”。而完成时用于短暂动词，则是表示“单一事件”。比如：

7 He ***has come*** to Beijing. 他已经到了北京。

8 He ***has been coming*** to Beijing for 10 years. 10年来他多次来北京。

3. 单一事件

完成时具有“单一事件”的用法，而完成进行时则没有这样的用法。不过，还是可以找到一个大概与“单一事件”对应的完成进行时的用法，这就是完成进行时表示的“刚刚在延续的事件”(详见6.3.5小节和6.4.1小节)。

二者有三个共同点：

第一，二者都表示一个事件在说话的时刻已经结束；

第二，二者都伴随有现在清晰可见的后果；

第三，二者都不接持续性的时间状语。不过，需要注意的是，现在完成进行时是可以接持续的时间状语的，但意思往往会不同；而现在完成时“单一事件”的用法是不能接持续的时间状语的。

二者最大的区别在谓语动词的延续性方面。现在完成进行时“刚刚在延续的事件”的用法所采用的动词一定都是**延续性动词**，以表示一个延续活动；现在完成时“单一事件”的用法所采用的动词都是短暂动词，或者用作短暂性的动词，不表示一个延续活动。所以，现在完成进行时是可以接持续的时间状语的，但意思往往会不同；而现在完成时“单一事件”的用法是不能接持续的时间状语的。比如：

9 He ***has just arrived.*** 他刚刚到。

10 He ***has been running.*** 他刚刚一直在跑步。

思维训练

Exercise 6.7（Key: P345）

请用括号中动词的适当的形式填空。

1. I ______（drink）five cups of coffee this afternoon.
2. He ______（go）to Los Angeles three times this year.
3. I ______（call）David four times for the past half hour, but I keep getting a busy signal.
4. I ______（call）David for the past half hour, but I keep getting a busy signal.
5. I ______（write）3 letters since lunchtime.
6. I ______（write）letters since lunchtime and am still writing now.
7. How long ______ you ______（read）that book?
8. How many pages of that book ______ you ______（read）?
9. The novel is so interesting. I ______（read）for two hours and ______（read）55 pages so far.
10. I know Jane is saving money to go on holiday. I ask her, "How long ______ you ______（save）money? How much money ______ you ______（save）?"
11. I ______（surf）online since 8 o'clock A. M. I am very tired now.
12. I ______（surf）online five times this week.
13. I ______（knock）at the door six times, but nobody answers it. I don't think anybody is in.
14. I ______（knock）at the door for two minutes, but nobody answers it.
15. I ______（read）the book you lent me but I haven't finished it yet.
16. I ______（read）the book you lent me, so you can have it back now.

请选择最佳答案。

17. I can't sleep. The people in the next apartment...
    A. have made a lot of noise.　　B. have been making a lot of noise.
18. He's been sick all week.
    A. He's stayed in bed.　　B. He's been staying in bed.
19. She is unhappy.
    A. She has just lost her job.　　B. She has been losing her job.
20. She lost her job three weeks ago. She hasn't had much free time lately because...
    A. she has looked for a new job.　　B. she has been looking for a new job.
21. My writing has been improving a lot because...
    A. I have written a composition.　　B. I have been writing compositions.
22. I meet new people everywhere: in my neighborhood, at my job, at school.
    A. I have met new people.　　B. I have been meeting new people.
23. At first she planned to move, but now she doesn't want to.
    A. She has changed her mind.　　B. She has been changing her mind.
24. Now I can pay for my car repair because I...
    A. have received a check from my insurance company.
    B. have been receiving a check from my insurance company.
25. Every week I put 20 percent of my salary in the bank. I plan to buy a house as soon as I can.
    A. I have saved my money.　　B. I have been saving my money.
26. I didn't have time to watch TV today because...
    A. I have worked on my composition.　　B. I have been working on my composition.

6.8 过去完成进行时

到目前为止，我们已经详细讨论了现在完成进行时的各种意义和用法。掌握了这些用法对于理解过去完成进行时至关重要，因为过去完成进行时与现在完成进行时的用法在本质上是相同的，区别只是将说话的“参照时间”由现在移到过去。这种“时间坐标”发生位移的情况从下面这个例子可以看出：

1 1) Your eyes ***are*** red. You'***ve been crying***, haven't you?

2) Her eyes ***were*** red. It was obvious she ***had been crying***.

妙语点睛 在例句1)中，由are可以知道，这里说话语境的时间是现在，所以后面用现在完成进行时have been crying来表达一个在“现在”说话时刻之前在延续的事件，即“现在刚刚”结束的事件，这一点在6.2.5小节讨论过。在例句2)中，由were可以知道，这里说话语境的时间是过去，此时要表达一个在“过去”说话时刻之前在延续的事件，即“过去刚刚”结束的事件就要用过去完成进行时had been crying。

所以，可以看到，这里的说话时间发生了向过去的位移，即由are变成了were。因此，对应的完成进行时态也要由现在完成进行时have been crying变为过去完成进行时had been crying。

精品译文 1)你的眼睛红红的，你刚才一直在哭吧？

2)她的眼睛当时红红的，很明显，她当时刚刚哭过。

再来看下面这个对话：

2 A: Don't you think Prof. Morison's test ***was*** too difficult?

B: Well, I must admit I ***had been expecting*** more than just a passing grade in biology.

妙语点睛 这个对话里的时态使用较为复杂：有一般现在时的think和must admit；有一般过去时的was；还有一个时间跳跃较大的过去完成进行时had been expecting。这里能够使用过去完成进行时基于以下两点：

首先，从时间的角度来看，这个过去完成进行时是谈论过去时间was之前的事件，具体来说，就是说话人B在回顾自己上次生物测验之前的心态——在考试之前以为考试会很难，所以他在考试之前只是期望成绩能及格就可以了，言外之意是因为考试并没有想象得那么难，所以成绩也很高。这个言外之意就是通过这里的过去完成进行时表达出来的。

其次，从完成进行时的意义的角度来看，这里的过去完成进行时had been expecting表达的是在was之前的一个近期延续事件，即在考试之前，他认为考试会很难，所以一直想着只要能通过就可以。

从这个例句也可以看出，过去完成进行时对一般过去时的依赖性。

精品译文 A：你不觉得莫里森教授上次的那个测验并不是太难吗？

B：是啊，我得承认，我当时还想着那次生物考试刚刚及格就可以了呢。

简单来说，过去完成进行时表示开始于过去某个时刻之前的动作持续到过去这一时刻，并继续持续下去。在意义上，过去完成进行时与现在完成进行时完全类似，可以表示延续事件(包括长期延续、近期延续、说话时刻在延续以及在说话时刻之前在延续的事件)和重复事件。在时间上，过去完成进行时类似于过去完成时，即首先要确立一个过去时间，并以此为坐标时间来谈论在此之前的事件。

6.8.1 过去时刻在延续的事件

过去完成进行时表示开始于过去某个时刻之前的动作持续到过去这一时刻，并继续持续下去。请看例句：

1 When I ***arrived*** in Inner Mongolia, it ***had been snowing*** for half a month.

妙语点睛 这里的arrived确立了过去的坐标时间，然后谈论在此之前发生的一个延续活动“下雪”，所以用过去完成进行时had been snowing。

精品译文 那次在我到内蒙古之前，雪已经下了整整半个月了。

2 She *had been studying* French for one year before she *went* to France.

妙语点睛 这里的 went 确立了过去的坐标时间，然后谈论在此之前发生的一个延续活动“学习”，所以用过去完成进行时 had been studying。

精品译文 她去法国之前已经学习了一年法语。

上述两个例句可以图示如下：

图解：

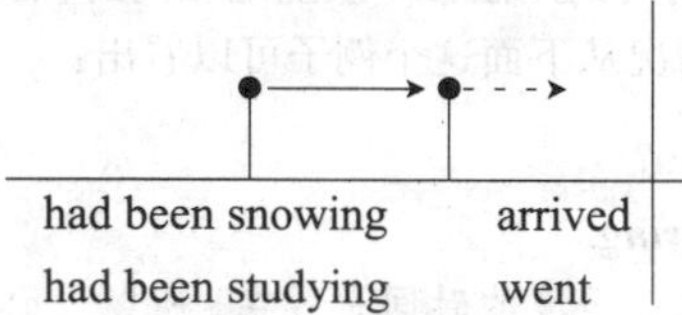

强调在过去的某一活动或时刻之前一直在持续的一项活动。

类似于现在完成进行时，过去完成进行时的延续事件同样包括长期延续、近期延续、说话时刻在延续以及在说话时刻之前在延续的事件。

一、过去的长期延续事件

1 The police *had been looking* for the murderer for two years before they *caught* him.
警察抓住这个杀人犯之前，已经找了他两年了。

2 I *had been looking* for jobs for nearly half a year before I finally *got* a position in this dot-com company.
我找工作找了将近半年，最后得到了一家网络公司的聘用。

二、过去的近期延续事件

比如上一小节讨论过的这个例子：

3 A: Don't you think Prof. Morison's test *was* too difficult?
B: Well, I must admit I *had been expecting* more than just a passing grade in biology.
A：你不觉得莫里森教授上次的那个测验并不是太难吗？
B：是啊，我得承认，我当时还想着那次生物考试刚刚及格就可以了呢。

再比如：

4 He looked so tired. I knew he *had been studying* for the final exams.
他当时看起来很累，我知道他一直在忙着准备期末考试。

三、过去说话时刻在延续的事件

5 Snowflakes *had been falling* past my window for several hours when it came time to leave for class. I pulled on two sweaters, a coat, a wool hat and boots, making for the bus stop. In this December storm it was a hard journey. As I tied around my neck the blue scarf that Grandma had knitted for me, I could almost hear her voice, "Why don't you see if you can find a lift?"

妙语点睛 这里的 came 表示过去，所以谈论在此之前的一直在延续的事件，就要用过去完成进行时，所以这里用了 had been falling，表示在说话的时刻，窗外的雪依然在下着。

精品译文 窗外的雪花纷纷扬扬地下了几个小时，上学的时间到了。我穿上两件毛衣，一件外套，头戴帽子，脚穿棉靴向公交车站走去。在12月份的这种暴风雪的天气里，这是一段艰难的路程。我用祖母为我织的蓝色围巾把脖子围紧，耳边似乎响起了她的声音：“为什么不看看是否能搭个便车呢？”

6 He told me he *had been working* on the report for hours and hadn't finished it yet. He was still working on it.
他告诉我，那个报告他已经写了好几个小时了，但还没有完成，他还在写。

7 He told me he *had been hunting* for a room since noon but with no success.
他告诉我，他从中午开始就在找住处，但一直没找到。

8 He finally ***showed*** up at nine o'clock. I ***had been waiting*** for him since six o'clock.
他最终在9点钟的时候出现了，我从6点钟开始就在等他。

9 When she ***arrived***, I ***had been waiting*** in the cold for three hours.
她到的时候，我已经在寒冷的天气里等了她三个小时了。

10 The plane, which ***had been waiting*** on the runway for hours, finally got clearance for take off.
飞机已经在跑道上等了几个小时了，终于获准起飞。

四、过去刚刚在延续的事件

11 She answered the door carrying a magazine she ***had been reading***.

妙语点睛 这里的过去完成进行时 had been reading 用得非常贴切，表示一个过去刚刚在延续的事件，即在有人敲门之前，她一直在看一本杂志。所以，整句话的意思是“她应声去开门，手里还拿着一本刚刚一直在看的杂志”。
如果这里改为过去完成时 had read，则表示杂志早已读过，那么整个句子的意思就变成“她拿着一本早已读过的杂志去开门”，这听起来显然有些奇怪，不符合正常的逻辑。

精品译文 她应声去开门，手里还拿着一本刚刚一直在看的杂志。

12 When the boys came into the house, their clothes were dirty, their hair was untidy and one of them had a black eye. I knew they ***had been fighting.*** 当时，那些男孩子走进屋里，他们的衣服很脏，头发也很乱，有个人还是个乌眼青，所以我就知道他们刚刚打架了。

13 There was nobody in the room but there was a smell of cigarettes. Somebody ***had been smoking*** in the room.
当时房间里没人但是有烟味，我知道，房间里刚刚有人抽过烟。

14 Mary's eyes ***were*** red. She ***had been crying.*** 当时玛丽的眼睛红红的，她刚刚哭过。

15 My face ***was*** hot and red because I ***had been lying*** in the sun.
当时我的脸又红又热，因为我刚刚一直在躺着晒太阳。

6.8.2 在过去时刻重复发生的事件

过去完成进行时可表示重复发生的动作。具体来说，就是表示过去某一时刻之前的一段时间内重复发生的活动。

下面这篇文章讲的是牛顿看到苹果落下，从而发现万有引力的故事。文章的观点是，科学的发展更多地依赖于科学家头脑的准备而不是科学实验。比如牛顿看到苹果落下就能发现万有引力，那是因为他多年以来一直在研究天体运动的引力问题，即他的头脑已为发现引力做好了准备。而普通人因为头脑里没有这样的准备，所以看到苹果落地可能会很快捡起来吃掉，而不会去想什么引力的问题。请看这个短文：

1 Science, in practice, depends far less on the experiments it prepares than on the preparedness of the minds of the men who watch the experiments. Sir Isaac Newton supposedly discovered gravity through the fall of an apple. Apples ***had been falling*** in many places for centuries and thousands of people ***had seen*** them fall. But Newton for years had been curious about the cause of the orbital motion of the moon and planets. What kept them in place? Why didn't they fall out of the sky? The fact that the apple fell down toward the earth and not up into the tree answered the question he ***had been asking*** himself about those larger fruits of the heavens, the moon and the planets.

妙语点睛 这里的 had been falling 和 had been asking 是表示一个长期的重复活动，而不是延续事件。另外，这里 had seen 也是表示重复活动，但由于主语 thousands of people 表明了具体次数，即动作被分割，所以不能说 had been seeing。

精品译文 实际上，科学的发展更多的是取决于观察科学实验的科学家的头脑的准备，而不是实验本身的准备。据说牛顿是因为观察到了苹果落下，然后才发现万有引力的。苹果落地这一现象在许多地方发生了几个世纪了，成千上万的人也都看到过苹果落地。但是因为牛顿多少年以来都在研究月球和行星沿着一定轨道运动的原因——是什么保持它们在适当的位置运动的？它们为什么不会落到宇宙空间的外面去？苹果向下落到地面上而不是向上掉进树里面，正好可以回答他长期以来一直在问自己的问题：像月球和行星这样的天体中的“大苹果”是如何运动的。

2 He *had been gambling* for two years before his wife found out.

妙语点睛 这里的 had been gambling 是表示一个长期的重复活动，而不是延续事件。

精品译文 在他妻子发现之前，他赌博有两年了。

3 I *had been trying* to get her on the phone. Finally she gave me a call.

我当时一直试着打电话找她，最后她给我回了个电话。

同样，这里的重复动作不能说出具体的次数。例如不能这样说：

I *had been trying five times* to get her on the phone. Finally she gave me a call. *

要表示具体次数，须改为过去完成时：

I *had tried five times* to get her on the phone before she finally gave me a call.

我曾打了五次电话去找她，最后她终于给我回了电话。

思维训练

Exercise 6.8 (Key: P345)

请用括号中动词的适当形式填空。

Firemen ______ (fight) the forest fire for nearly three weeks before they could get it under control. A short time before, great trees ______ (cover) the countryside for miles around. Now, smoke still rose up from the warm ground over the desolate hills. Winter was coming on and the hills threatened the surrounding villages with destruction, for heavy rain would not only wash away the soil but would cause serious floods as well. When the fire ______ at last ______ (put out), the forest authorities ordered several tons of a special type of grass-seed which would grow quickly. The seed was sprayed over the ground in huge quantities by airplanes. The planes ______ (plant) seed for nearly a month when it began to rain. By then, however, in many places the grass ______ (already, take root). In place of the great trees which ______ (grow) there for centuries, patches of green had begun to appear in the blackened soil.

6.9 将来完成进行时

将来完成进行时的用法与现在完成进行时基本相同，只是将“坐标时间”移到了将来。同样是强调动作的持续性，表示开始于将来某个时刻之前的动作持续到将来这一时刻，并可能继续持续下去。从时间的角度来看，将来完成进行时需要在上下文中有将来的时间坐标，这类似于过去完成进行时的过去的时间坐标。通常用“by+将来时间”或者是“by the time+ 从句(从句谓语用一般现在时)”来给出一个将来的时间坐标。请看例句：

1 My brother has promised to help me study for my exam tomorrow. I get home from school at 3:00 and he gets home from school at 5:00. I *will have been studying* for two hours *by the time* he *gets* home.

妙语点睛 这里是“by the time+ 从句”结构给出的将来的时间坐标，从句的谓语 gets 是一般现在时态，但表示将来的动作。然后在这个将来时间的基础上谈论之前的一个延续事件——一直在学习(到 5:00 时，studying 的活动仍将持续)，此时就要用将来完成进行时 will have been studying 这一较为复杂的动词形式。

图解：

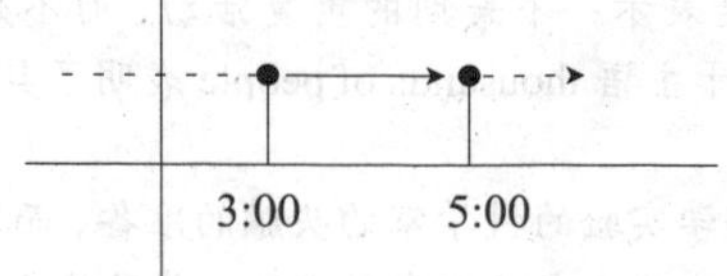

精品译文 我哥哥答应帮我学习，以准备明天的考试。我下午3点放学回家，他则是下午5点回家。所以，等他到家后，我将一直学习了两个小时了。

再看其他类似的例句：

一、长期延续的事件：

2 I'm retiring this fall. By then I'***ll have been teaching*** for 30 years.
我将于今年秋天退休，到那时，我教书就将有30年了。

3 She ***will have been taking*** care of her blind husband for 20 years by then.
到那时，她照顾她双目失明的丈夫就将有20年了。

二、说话时刻在延续的事件

4 I'm getting tired of sitting in the car. Do you realize that by the time we arrive in Beijing, we will ***have been driving*** for twenty straight hours?
我在车里都坐得累了。你有没有想到，等我们到北京的时候，我们就将一直不停地开了20个小时车了？

以上是将来完成进行时表示延续事件。将来完成进行时同样可以表示重复事件，即表示在将来某个时间之前经常重复的动作。请看例句：

5 The old man ***will have been getting*** up at 4:00 for ten years by next month.
到下个月，这老头坚持早晨4:00起床就将长达10年时间了。

6 I ***will have been attending*** Professor Smith's lectures for half a year by next week.
到下个星期，我听史密斯教授的讲座就将有半年了。

7 By tomorrow I ***will have been doing*** morning exercises for 100 days.
到明天，我坚持做早操就将有100天了。

写给读者的话

一、本章学习思路

本章内容与第五章"完成时态"密切相关。因此，读者在学习本章的过程中，要将二者结合起来比较，尤其是要重点读懂本章6.7节的内容。因为在这一节里，我们对完成进行时与完成时作了全面的比较。通过对完成进行时的学习，读者也会更加深刻地理解完成时态的用法。如果读者对于第五章的内容掌握得很好，那么学习本章就会感到比较轻松。

二、本章重点及难点

要重点掌握下面这些内容：

1. 掌握四种不同持续时间的延续事件；
2. 理解完成进行时"刚刚在延续的事件"与完成时"单一事件"的异同点；
3. 理解有限延续动词可能表示"延续事件"(接表达较短时间的状语)或"重复事件"(接表达较长时间的状语)；
4. 理解为何完成进行时表示重复活动时不能被分隔；
5. 理解完成进行时强调"延续过程"和完成时强调"成果"，并掌握由此产生的二者多方面的区别。

三、本章学习时间安排

由于本章与第五章"完成时态"密切相关，因此，读者在学习本章内容的过程中需要不断地结合完成时态的相关用法，逐一比较。这样一来，本章的学习时间可能会比较长。建议读者用8天左右的时间，先看一遍本章讲解的内容，然后再结合第五章"完成时态"，将二者进行详细的比较，这也相当于是对完成时态的复习。

综合练习（Key: P345）

请用适当的时态填空。

1. This morning I came to class at 9:00. Right now it is 10:00, and I am still in class. I ______（sit）at this desk for an hour. By 9:30, I ______（sit）here for half an hour. By 11:00, I ______（sit）here for two hours.
2. It is midnight. I ______（study）for five straight hours. No wonder I'm getting tired.
3. It was midnight. I ______（study）for five straight hours. No wonder I was getting tired.
4. Clint woke up in the middle of last night. He was frightened and didn't know where he was. He ______（dream）.
5. When I got home, I saw Clint was sitting in front of the TV. He had just turned it off. He ______（watch）TV.
6. He finally showed up at nine o'clock. I ______（wait）for him since six o'clock.
7. We were good friends. We ______（know）each other for a long time.
8. When I arrived, my girlfriend was waiting for me. She was rather annoyed with me because I was late and she ______（wait）for a very long time on such a windy day.
9. Yesterday I saw Leon sitting on the ground. He was out of breath. He ______（run）.
10. Your eyes are red. You ______（cry）?
11. Her eyes were red. It was obvious she ______（cry）.
12. My legs were stiff because I ______（sit）in the same position too long.
13. My legs are stiff because I ______（sit）in the same position too long.
14. A: Don't you think Prof. Morison's test was too difficult?
    B: Well, I must admit I ______（expect）more than just a passing grade in biology.
15. A: I kept looking for Mary at the seminar but never did see her. I can't imagine she forgot about it and she ______（talk）about it for weeks.
    B: Oh she didn't. It's just that she caught a really bad cold a couple of days ago.
16. A: ______ you ______（have）a chance to wear your new shirt yet?
    B: That reminds me. I ______（mean）to exchange it for a larger size.
17. Titanic 的发掘：

    In 1912, the "unsinkable" luxury ship Titanic ______（hit）an iceberg and ______（sink）to the bottom of the sea. Its final resting place ______（remain）a mystery for more than 70 years. You probably already know that tragic story. But do you know the whole story? Do you know who finally ______（discover）the wreck of the Titanic?

    Robert Ballard, of course. Who's Ballard? He's an explorer who ______（see）more of the ocean floor than anyone in history. He ______（explore）under the ocean waves for more than 30 years!
18. 谈辞职：
    A: So why would you want to leave?
    B: Because I feel you ______（treat）me like a person with no options.
    A: Huh?
    B: I mean, I ______（not, have）a raise in three years, or the chance to do anything new or creative. I feel stagnant. Now, if we could do something to change that...
    A: George, maybe I ______（take）you for granted. If I gave you a good raise and some new responsibilities, would you stay?
    B: I'd certainly consider it. Let's talk about it some more.
19. 谈转学：
    A: I'm thinking about transferring out of state college into another school in the spring.
    B: After only a year and a half? How come? I ______（think）you ______（like）it here.
    A: I do. But our commercial art department only ______（give）associate degrees.
    B: And you want a bachelor's, right?
    A: Right!
    B: So where do you want to go?

A: I ______ (think) about Westwater University. It has an excellent reputation. But it's probably very selective.

B: But you ______ (get) good grades in the three semesters since you ______ (be) in here at the state college, haven't you?

A: Yeah, mostly As in my major and a few Bs in sciences.

B: So what are you worried about? Just ask your art professors to write letters of recommendation for you and give you portfolio together, and you'll be set.

20. 谈旅游：

A: I ______ (study) too much and need a change. So I'm just making plans to go away during January break.

B: Really? Where are you going?

A: I ______ (plan) to visit New Mexico.

B: My sister and I ______ (have) the vacation there last year and we had a great time.

A: ______ you ______ (get) into Albuquerque?

B: Sure. Whenever we were skating.

21. 牛顿的故事：

Science, in practice, depends far less on the experiments it prepares than on the preparedness of the minds of the men who watch the experiments. Sir Isaac Newton supposedly ______ (discover) gravity through the fall of an apple. Apples ______ (fall) in many places for centuries and thousands of people ______ (see) them fall. But Newton for years ______ (be) curious about the cause of the orbital motion of the moon and planets. What kept them in place? Why didn't they fall out of the sky? The fact that the apple fell down toward the earth and not up into the tree answered the question he ______ (ask) himself about those larger fruits of the heavens, the moon and the planets.

22. 超速被罚：

A: Can I see your license and registration please?

B: What's the matter, officer? Did I do something wrong?

A: You ______ (speed).

B: I ______ (speed)?

A: You certainly were. Do you have any idea how fast you ______ (go)?

B: I'm not sure, but I think I ______ (go) about 35.

A: This street is in a 25-mile-per-hour speed zone, you know.

B: It is?

A: In this state, the speed limit in residential area is 25 unless otherwise posted. Besides, there are signs all along this street.

B: I'm sorry, officer, I guess I ______ (not, notice). I was thinking about my job interview. I'm on my way to it right now and I ______ (not, plan) to come this way.

A: What do you mean?

B: Well, I ______ (go) to come down Elm Street but the traffic was really backed up. There was some kind of construction going on. I turned on to a side street and ended up here. Give me a break. I'm nervous enough as it is.

请选择最佳答案填空。

23. I can't believe it, inspector. You mean that Smith ______ money from the till all this time!

A. stole　　B. has stolen　　C. has been stealing　　D. steals

24. You three boys look very guilty! What ______ since I ______ the room?

A. did you do/have left　　B. have you done/left

C. have you been doing/left　　D. have you been doing/ have left

25. A: You look great since you ______ those exercise classes.

B: Thanks. I've never felt better in my life.

A. took　　B. have been taking　　C. take　　D. are taking

26. A: Are you keeping current on the news from home since you ______ here?
B: I ______ weekly updates.
A. was/have got B. have been/have been getting
C. was/have been getting D. have been/have got
27. I'm having problems with David. He ______ me up in the middle of the night and ______ me his troubles.
A. has called/told B. has been calling/telling
C. has been calling/told D. called/told
28. I feel really tired. I ______ the garden for the last three hours and I ______ for a single moment.
A. weeded/didn't rest B. have weeded/haven't rested
C. have been weeding/haven't rested D. have been weeding/didn't rest
29. Don't forget that you ______ Mrs. Dawson. She ______ outside since 10:30.
A. didn't see/has waited B. haven't seen/has waited
C. haven't seen/has been waiting D. didn't see/has been waiting
30. I can't believe that you ______ three pizzas already! I ______ them in fifteen minutes ago!
A. ate/only brought B. have been eating/only brought
C. have eaten/have only brought D. have eaten/only brought
31. It's a long time since I ______ you. What ______ ?
A. saw/did you do B. have seen/have you done
C. saw/have you been doing D. have been seeing/have you been doing
32. He ______ several novels since 1985. Most of them ______ quite successful, but the last one ______ very good reviews.
A. has written/were/hasn't got B. wrote/have been/didn't get
C. has written/have been/didn't get D. wrote/were/didn't get
33. By the time you get back, great changes ______ in this area.
A. will take place B. will be taken place C. will be taking place D. will have taken place
34. By the time you ______, I ______ all my housework.
A. returned/will have finished B. return/will finish
C. return/will have finished D. returned/finished
35. When I ______ the letter, I ______ it to you.
A. wrote/will show B. wrote/would show C. have written/will show D. have written/would show
36. I ______ New York in 1986, but I ______ there since.
A. visit/hadn't been B. visited/haven't been C. visit/haven't been D. visited/hadn't been
37. I think by five o'clock the children ______ from their work.
A. will return B. had returned C. will have returned D. have returned
38. Someone ______ my book. I ______ for it for the last ten minutes, but I can't see it anywhere.
A. took/have been looking B. has taken/am looking
C. took/was looking D. has taken/have been looking
39. Just imagine, if all goes well, by Christmas we ______ in the new house for almost two months.
A. are living B. have lived C. will live D. will have been living
40. I hope you ______ all the possibilities before you make the final decision.
A. are considered B. will be considering C. will have considered D. would have considered
41. I ______ to visit them yesterday, but someone came to see me just when I was about to leave.
A. planned B. had planned C. did plan D. was planning
42. John and I ______ neighbors since we ______ children.
A. are/were B. were/have been C. have been/are D. have been/were
43. The plumber ______ here yet? Yes, but he only ______ for thirty minutes.
A. has been/has stayed B. was/has stayed C. has been/stayed D. was/stayed

44. Many years ago, he ______ in Paris with his uncle for a long period of time.
A. had been living　B. had lived　C. lived　D. has been living

45. How long ______ here? I ______ you come in.
A. do you sit/haven't seen　B. did you sit/did not see
C. have you sat/have not seen　D. have you been sitting/did not see

46. I ______ a great deal ______ I came to England.
A. have learned/before　B. have learned/since　C. learned/since　D. learn/after

47. I ______ there five minutes when all the lights ______ out.
A. was/went　B. had been/went　C. have been/go　D. have been/went

48. I ______ this crossword puzzle for the last hour, but I ______ half of it yet.
A. am doing/haven't finished　B. have been doing/haven't finished
C. did/didn't finish　D. had done/didn't finish

49. Great as Newton was, many of his ideas ______ today and are being modified by the work of scientists of our time.
A. are to challenge　B. may be challenged　C. are challenging　D. have been challenged

50. It's reported that by the end of this month the output of cement in the factory ______ by about 10%.
A. will have risen　B. has risen　C. will be rising　D. has been rising

51. That was the first time the old lady ______ her suffering to others.
A. was telling　B. had told　C. have told　D. told

52. I ______ to call on you, but was prevented from doing so.
A. mean　B. have meant　C. meant　D. had meant

53. The Olympic Games, first celebrated in Athens in 1896, ______ every four years so far this century, except during the two world wars.
A. are held　B. were held　C. had been held　D. have been held

54. It's the third time I ______ this particular aspect of grammar.
A. explain　B. explained　C. have explained　D. will explain

55. On her next anniversary she ______ married for 25 years.
A. will be　B. will have been　C. has been　D. is being

56. In two years' time he ______ his master's degree in chemistry.
A. has completed　B. will be completing　C. will have completed　D. will have been completing

57. She ought to stop work; she has a headache because she ______ too long.
A. has been reading　B. had read　C. is reading　D. read

58. It seems oil ______ from this pipe for some time, we'll have to take the machine apart to put it right.
A. had leaked　B. is leaking　C. leaked　D. has been leaking

59. ______ a rapid development in the application of laser over the last twenty year.
A. There is　B. There will be　C. There has been　D. There had been

60. By the end of this term, David ______ Chinese for four years, but he will still need more training and experience before he masters the language.
A. will be studying　B. has studied　C. will have been studying　D. has been studying

61. "I think the milkman sent us the wrong bottle." "It's likely. They ______ that many times before."
A. do　B. done　C. have done　D. are doing

62. By the year 2020, scientists probably ______ a cure for cancer.
A. have found　B. will have found　C. will be finding　D. are finding

63. I was lucky actually because that was the second time I ______ China that year.
A. have visited　B. visited　C. had visited　D. would visit

64. When the robber came in, carrying the sword, most of the passengers looked up in surprise, because they ______ anything like it before.
A. didn't see　B. have never seen　C. never saw　D. had never seen

65. If the population of the Earth goes on increasing at its present rate, by the middle of the 21st century, we ______ all the oil that drives our cars.
A. will use up B. will have been using up C. will have used up D. have used up
66. "Let's hurry. The manager is coming." "Oh, I was afraid that we ______."
A. already miss him B. had already missed him C. will miss him already D. have already missed him
67. This is the first time that I ______ really relaxed for weeks.
A. had felt B. feel C. have felt D. shall feel
68. By the time the fire engine arrived, the house ______ to the ground.
A. burned B. had burned C. has burned D. should have burned
69. Ever since the painter's paintings went on exhibit, there ______ large crowds at the museum every day.
A. is B. has been C. have been D. are being
70. Until then, Jack's family ______ from him for more than a year.
A. hadn't heard B. hasn't heard C. didn't hear D. hasn't been hearing
71. Pick me up at 6 o'clock. I ______ my bath by then.
A. may have B. can have had C. will be having D. will have had
72. By the time James ______ back from his holiday the milkman will have left twenty bottles of milk outside his doors.
A. will get B. has got C. will be getting D. will have got
73. It is amazing that the Leaning Tower of Pisa ______ for so long.
A. have stood B. stands C. has been standing D. should have stood
74. She answered the door ______ a magazine she ______.
A. carried/read B. carrying/had been reading
C. carrying/had read D. carried/was reading

请把下列各句中的中文翻译成英文。

75. 近一个月来，Jim 每天半夜都要给我打电话，向我诉苦，让我真的很烦！
76. 我们谈恋爱有三年了。
77. 最近物价一直看涨，不知是否会一直这样。
78. 最近又在熬夜？
79. 那话你都说了有五年了。
80. 我计划这次旅行有一年多了，并且和他讨论了很多次。
81. 自从上大学以来，我一直坚持早起。
82. A: Have you had a chance to wear your new shirt yet?
B: That reminds me. 我一直想换个大号的。
83. A: 我一直想检查一下眼睛。I just haven't gotten around to it yet.
B: Why don't you call for an appointment right away? Once on your calendar you will get it done.
84. A: 自从我一个人搬了那个很重的书桌以来，到现在，我肩膀疼了两三个星期了。
B: If it hasn't gotten better by now you should have it looked at.
85. A: 今年你一直住在校外的，是吧？
B: Yes, and I'm going to next year too. It's so much nicer than living in the dormitory.
86. A: You ought to see a doctor about that cough.
B: I guess I should. 我已经拖了好几天了。

Chapter 7

第七章 虚拟语气

语气(mood)是英文中谓语动词的一种变化形式，用来表示说话者的意图和态度。英文中的语气可分为三种：陈述语气(indicative mood)、祈使语气(imperative mood)和虚拟语气(subjunctive mood)。在一些场合里，当说话者谈到自己与实际情况相反的情况时，或者主观想象某事有可能发生时，或建议、要求某事发生时，就需要借助虚拟语气来表达这些心态。

虚拟语气的确比较复杂。读者在开始学习虚拟语气的时候，往往会被其较为复杂的不同形式的谓语动词变化弄得晕头转向，混淆不清。为此，请读者一定要首先了解本章的讲解思路：本章首先向读者介绍三种最基本的虚拟语气的谓语形式，即将来虚拟、现在虚拟和过去虚拟，然后介绍混合虚拟句、倒装虚拟句、跳层虚拟句，最后介绍名词从句中如何使用虚拟，以及各种要求采用虚拟语气的句型结构。具体来说，本章各节内容安排如下：

7.1 引言

7.2 将来虚拟(ZjCj)

7.3 现在虚拟(ZxCx)

7.4 过去虚拟(ZgCg)

7.5 混合虚拟(一)：主句现在＋从句过去(ZxCg)

7.6 混合虚拟(二)：主句过去＋从句现在(ZgCx)

7.7 倒装虚拟

7.8 跳层虚拟

7.9 名词从句中如何使用虚拟

7.10 各种虚拟句型

7.1 引 言

7.1.1 把U和I放在一起

相信大家都知道，英语中有 26 个字母，也知道这 26 个字母在字母表中的顺序，那就是 A, B, C, D, E...X, Y, Z。大家知道，字母排序是固定的，不可随意更改的。但是如果给你一个把字母表重新排序的机会，你会怎样排序呢？或者说，你愿意将哪两个字母放在一起并且使它们有意义呢？也许有人会说，可以把 W 和 C 放在一起，这样便构成 WC(厕所)，很有意义。但是，“如果我能把字母表重新排序，我会把 U 和 I 放在一起”：

If I could rearrange the alphabet, I would put ***U*** and ***I*** together.

U 和 I 在一起不就是“你”和“我”永远在一起嘛。当然，这只是一句玩笑话。我们是不可能改变英文字母表的顺序的。既然是不能，那上面所作的假设就是一种与事实相反的情况，或者说是一种假想的情形。这只是表示说话者的一种主观愿望、假想和建议等等，实际上并不能实现。这在英语里，用语法术语表达就叫“虚拟语气”。下面来看英文是怎样通过谓语动词的变形来传达这种虚拟假设的：

If I ***could*** rearrange the alphabet, I ***would put*** U and I together.

从上面的例句可以看到，if 引导的从句的谓语动词用了“一般过去时态(could)”，而主句的谓语动词用“would 接动词原形(put)”。实际上，英文中的虚拟语气的谓语变形比这要复杂，本章将会详细讨论。

一般来讲，英语中的虚拟语气可以分为两大体系：一是表示与事实相反的或假想的情形，通常由 if 引导，叫做“非真实条件句(unreal conditional)”，或者叫“虚拟条件句”；另一个体系是在名词从句中使用虚拟语气，表示建议、命令或要求等语气，这是一个完全不同于非真实条件句的虚拟的结构形式。虚拟语气的重点和难点都集中在虚拟条件句中，我们接下来就先对它进行简要介绍，然后在后面的各节中进行详细和深入的讨论。

7.1.2 虚拟条件句：两类三时

这里说的“两类三时”是指虚拟条件句具有两种类型，并会对三种时间进行虚拟。具体来说，虚拟条件句的两种类型是：假设条件句(hypothetical)和事实相反句(counterfactual)。

假设条件句，顾名思义，是表示一种假想的情形，表示说话者的一种主观愿望或态度等，实现的可能性不大或极小。

事实相反句，顾名思义，是表示与现在或过去的某个事实相反的情形。

对三种时间进行虚拟，即是对**将来**、**现在**和**过去**这三种时间的虚拟。

现在来分析“两类型”与“三时间”之间的关系，即假设条件句和事实相反句如何与将来、现在、过去这三个时间发生相互作用。

将来时间：将来的情形还没有发生，因而不可能成为一个事实，即谈到将来的一切情形都不是一个事实。因此，对于将来时间的虚拟不可能以事实为基础，而只能是表达说话人的一个设想或愿望。所以，对于将来的虚拟只适用于假设条件句，而不可能表达一个与事实相反的虚拟。

现在时间：对于现在的情形，既可能是事实，也可能是假设条件。因此，假设条件句和事实相反句适用于谈现在的情况。

过去时间：既然是过去了，那么谈到的一切情况都已既成事实，所以过去虚拟表达的是一个与过去事实相反的情形。

简言之，对于将来的情形只能是假设；对于现在的情形既可以是假设，也可以是谈与现在事实相反的情况；对于过去，只能是谈与事实相反的情形。下面先简单举几个例句来说明上面讨论过的观点，以便让读者更好地理解。请看例句：

1 If I ***were to have*** the time tomorrow, I ***would help*** him.

妙语点睛 这里是表示将来虚拟假设的情形。用了虚拟，就表明说话人“我”认为自己明天有时间的可能性不大，所以言外之意是“我”可能帮不了他。这里用虚拟只是说明可能性不大(unlikely)，而不是表达与事实相违背的不可能的情形(impossible)。

精品译文 如果我明天有时间，我就会帮他的。

2 If I ***had*** the time now, I ***would help*** him.

妙语点睛 这里是表示现在虚拟假设的情形。用了虚拟，就表明说话人"我"认为自己现在有时间的可能性不大，所以言外之意是"我"可能帮不了他。这里用虚拟也只是说明可能性不大(unlikely)，而不是表达与事实相违背的不可能的情形(impossible)。比如"我"现在完全可以抛开一切事情不做而去帮他，所以可能性还是存在的。

精品译文 如果我现在有时间，我就会帮他的。

3 If I ***were*** you, I ***would help*** him.

妙语点睛 这里是表示与现在事实相反的情形。因为"我"成为"你"是不可能发生的(impossible)情形，而不是可能性不大(unlikely)的情形了。

精品译文 如果我是你，我就会帮他的。

再来看下面三个表示与现在事实相反的情形：

4 If I ***were*** the President, I ***would make*** some changes.

妙语点睛 "我"现在不是"总统"，这是一个现在的事实，即这里是表示与现在事实相反的情形。

精品译文 如果我是总统，我就会做一些改革。

5 If my grandfather ***were*** alive today, he ***would experience*** a very different world.

妙语点睛 "我爷爷"现在已经去世(即 my grandfather is not alive today)，这是一个现在的事实，即这里是表示与现在事实相反的情形。

精品译文 如果我爷爷现在还活着，那他就会经历一个完全不同的世界了。

6 If my grandfather ***were*** here now, he ***would be*** angry.

妙语点睛 "我爷爷"现在不在这里，这是一个现在的事实，即这里是表示与现在事实相反的情形。

精品译文 如果我爷爷现在在这里，他会很生气的。

来看表示对过去事实虚拟的句子：

7 If I ***had had*** the time yesterday, I ***would have helped*** him.

妙语点睛 "我"昨天没有时间，这已成为一个确立的事实，不可更改。这里说"如果我昨天有时间的话"显然是与这个过去的事实相违背的情形。

精品译文 昨天我要是有时间的话，我就会帮他了。

综上所述，**假设条件句**表达的是一种在**将来或现在**可能性不大(unlikely)的情形，但不是不可能(impossible)的情形，表示说话人认为不可能，是一种比较主观的表达，而不是与客观事实相反。它尤其用来谈将来的情形，也可以谈现在。**事实相反句**表达的是一种与现在或过去的事实相违背的情形，因此是不可能发生的，而不是可能性不大。它适合谈现在或过去。由此可见，谈将来的情形，只能是假设条件句；谈现在的情形，既可能是假设条件句，也可能是事实相反句；谈过去的情形，只能是事实相反句。

7.1.3 虚拟条件句的谓语变化

我们在上一小节中讨论了两种类型的虚拟句(即假设条件句和事实相反句)与将来、现在、过去这三种时间的关系，但对于英语学习者来说，**重要的不是如何区分两种类型的虚拟句，而是要弄清楚在三种不同时间的情况下，虚拟句的主句和从句的谓语动词的复杂变形。**

现在把三种不同时间下的主、从句的谓语形式列表如下：

虚拟的时间	主句的谓语形式(Z)	IF 从句的谓语形式(C)
将来(j)	Zj：would (could, might) +do	Cj：were to do/should do
现在(x)	Zx：would (could, might) +do	Cx：did 或 were
过去(g)	Zg：would (could, might) +have done	Cg：had done 或 had been

注：1. 我们用汉语拼音字母 Z 表示主句，C 表示从句；

2. 我们用汉语拼音字母 j 表示将来时间，x 表示现在时间，g 表示过去时间；

3. 因此，Zj 表示主句为将来虚拟，Zx 表示主句为现在虚拟，Zg 表示主句为过去虚拟；Cj 表示从句为将来虚拟，Cx 表示从句为现在虚拟，Cg 表示从句为过去虚拟。

以上采用汉语拼音的首字母来标注主从句以及将来、现在、过去，是为了便于读者记忆，因为上面表格中的 6 种不同的谓语形式，必须牢牢记住，它们是正确使用虚拟语气的起点。尤其是现在和过去的四种谓语形式，更需要分别牢牢记住。这里强调要"分别"记住，是因为在实际的使用中，主从句的谓语可能会有以下四种不同的搭配组合(以 would 为例)：

1. **现在虚拟：ZxCx 型（主现从现）：*would do*+if...*did***，这里的主句和 if 引导的条件状语从句都是表示对现在的虚拟。
2. **过去虚拟：ZgCg 型（主过从过）：*would have done*+if...*had done***，这里的主句和 if 引导的条件状语从句都是表示对过去的虚拟。
3. **混合虚拟(一)：ZxCg 型(主现从过)：*would do*+if...*had done***，这里的主句是表示对现在的虚拟，而 if 引导的条件状语从句是表示对过去的虚拟，即主句与从句所虚拟的时间不一致。
4. **混合虚拟(二)：ZgCx 型(主过从现)：*would have done*+if...*did***，这里的主句是表示对过去的虚拟，而 if 引导的条件状语从句是表示对现在的虚拟，即主句与从句所虚拟的时间不一致。

关于上述这四种不同的虚拟语气的意义和用法，将分别在接下来的 7.3、7.4、7.5 和 7.6 节中详细讨论。在此之前，笔者先来和读者分享一下自己在学习虚拟语气时的心得体会。

虚拟语气是英语学习者面临的一大难题。在写作或口语交际中，要想正确地使用虚拟语气，要分"四步走"，或者说要经过下列四个步骤的考虑：

第一，是否虚拟：要敏感地把握对某一情形的阐述是否该用虚拟语气，也即要意识到这一情形是表达一个真实的情况，还是一种与事实相反的假设。这一点是中国的英语学习者最容易忽略的。因为，在汉语思维里，虚拟的表达是通过语境来实现的，而不是通过动词的变形。所以说，在汉语思维里，虚拟语气是一个天然的缺失，因此在遇到该用虚拟语气的情形时，我们的大脑不会"灵光闪现"——认为该用虚拟。克服这一点是最大的困难，这关系到意识的问题，这点想不到，下面的"三步"便无从谈起。所以，这是使用虚拟语气的前提，是一个中英文思维差异的大问题！

第二，何时虚拟：完成了上述的第一步，即想到了该用虚拟语气后，接下来就要判断虚拟的时间——是对将来、现在和过去这三种时间中的哪个时间进行虚拟。这一点对于中国的英语学习者来说也是比较难的，因为汉语里的时间表达不是很明确，主要也是依靠语境来实现的，而不像英语那样有复杂的时态变化。

第三，主句虚拟：在完成了上述的第一步和第二步之后，接下来就是判断谁是主句，谁是从句了。因为主句和从句的谓语形式是不同的，所以，第三步和第四步是要同时考虑到的。判断出是主句的，就要采用主句的三种不同时间的谓语形式，实际上有两种，即表示将来和现在的 would do，以及表示过去的 would have done。这就要求我们清楚地记住主句的这两种表达形式。

第四，从句虚拟：判断出是从句的，就要采用从句的三种不同时间的谓语形式，即表示将来的 were to do 或 should do，表示现在的过去时 did/were，表示过去的过去完成时 had done/had been。这就要求我们清楚地记住从句的这三种表达形式。

笔者把上面这四步称为"一个前提，三个变量"：第一步是前提，后面三步相当于虚拟语气的三个变量，即**时间变量、主句变量和从句变量**。

从以上的分析可知，为什么说虚拟语气对于中国的英语学习者来说是一大难题了，因为要经历四步，而且要"步步为营"，环环相扣，哪一步都不能掉链子的，否则就会用错。比如在口语交际中，要想在短短的 1 至 2 秒钟内快速地分析清楚上面的四步，这就需要熟练掌握虚拟语气！对于大多数的中国读者来说，既使说"懂"虚拟语气，也主要停留在考试时能意识到该用虚拟语气，以及知道判断主从句的不同谓语形式，但是在口语表达中就全然"无暇"顾及虚拟语气了。所以，笔者大概总结了一下中国学生对于虚拟语气的掌握过程，将其分为以下四个阶段：

1. **混沌阶段**：在这一阶段，我们知道什么叫虚拟语气，脑子里有这个概念，也大概了解主句和从句谓语的动词有各种复杂的变化，但就是记不准，头脑里对各种谓语形式模糊不清，比如不知道"过去从句"该用什么形式(had done)；"现在主句"该用什么形式(would do)；"将来从句"该用什么形式(were to do 或 should do)。各种复杂的谓语变形在头脑里是"一团浆糊"，拎不清。据笔者了解，处在这一阶段的中国学生还真不少，大多数中国的英语学习者就是对虚拟语气记不住、记不准，自然也就不会用。
2. **考试阶段**：在这一阶段，我们非常熟悉各种时间的虚拟谓语形式，在考试时也能灵活地判断选择，做对考试题。但是，如果脱离了考试这样的"提示语境"，还是想不起来该用虚拟语气。能达到这个阶段的学生，已经算是很优秀的学生了，他们的英语功底通常是非常好的，但这还不能说他们掌握了虚拟语气的思维。
3. **写作阶段**：在这一阶段，我们不仅能做对考试题，而且在语言输出(output)时，比如写作时，也能意识到何时该用何种虚拟语气。这时，虚拟语气逐渐融入了我们的思维，但还不是非常熟练，比如在即时的口语交际中，我们的头脑可能还来不及反应出该用虚拟语气。处在这一较高水平的学生并不是非常多，笔者甚至还常见到有些大学的英语老师都还用不好，在他们的论文写作中也还出现该用虚拟而"忘记"用虚拟的情况。他们不是不知道虚拟语气，只不过虚拟语气尚没有真正融入他们的思维表达中罢了。
4. **口语阶段**：在这一阶段，虚拟语气已完全成为我们思维表达的一部分了，我们完全能自如地使用各种虚拟语气，真正达到 native speaker 的思维表达水平。能达到这一阶段的英语学习者可谓凤毛麟角，没有经过多年的潜心观察、细心体会、反复操练，是达不到的。

以上的四个阶段其实就是笔者习得虚拟语气的一个过程。比如笔者在高中阶段刚接触到虚拟语气这个语法项目时，是处在"混沌阶段"，总是记不住它各种复杂的谓语变化。到了要参加高考时，终于算是记住了、记准了。这样一直到大学期间，在考试时都会灵活运用，这就是第二个阶段即"考试阶段"。由于记住了、记准了虚拟的谓语形式，于是笔者开始在写作中有意识地尝试运用虚拟语气，然后在经过了大量的笔头练习运用后，开始逐渐尝试在口语中也使用虚拟语气。但是张口还是错，常常是"言不由衷"。比如和老外说话时，本来是该用虚拟语气的场景，一张口还是没有用虚拟语气，但是能够马上在心里自责："哎，又错了，这里该用虚拟语气表达。"于是改口把刚才的话重说一遍。这就是使用虚拟语气的"写作阶段"。经过反复的这样"错了又改口"的过程，虚拟语气的思维最终逐渐成了笔者思维表达的一部分，现在说起来就非常自然，而无需多加思考和辨别了，真正可以像老外那样"潜意识"地使用虚拟语气了。这就是使用虚拟语气的"口语阶段"。要想真正达到最后这个"口语阶段"，本身是需要大量的口语实践的，而且笔者是经过了仔细的观察并用心体会了情态动词的各种微妙的表达之后，才达到这个口语熟练阶段的。现在回想起来，就笔者个人而言，前后至少是经过了五年以上的虚拟语气的训练和实践，才能达到现在的"口语阶段"，在口语的层次上能够贴切地使用虚拟语气。

总之，虚拟语气的难点在于：首先，头脑中要有"虚拟意识"；其次，要极为熟练地掌握各种复杂的主句和从句谓语时态的变化，这都需要时间、需要实践。初学虚拟语气的读者在看到上述这些复杂的组合形式后，一定会"头都大了"。的确，虚拟语气对于英语初学者来说并不容易。不过读者不要惧怕，因为后面有很多好故事在等着各位，我们一边"听"着故事一边来习得虚拟语气的思维。

7.2 将来虚拟(Z_jC_j)

下面先来讨论将来虚拟。对于将来虚拟，我们知道，它只能是谈将来的"不大可能"的情形，而不是一个与事实相反的情形。我们常常会用将来虚拟来谈一个不太可能实现的愿望。比如：

1 If I ***were to*** live my life over again, I ***would have*** you as my wife.

妙语点睛 这句将来虚拟表达的就是一个良好的愿望，但将来不会实现的。

精品译文 如果我有来生，我一定会娶你为妻。

或者用将来虚拟来谈一个说话人认为不太可能发生的情形，这表明了说话人的自信程度。比如：

2 If I ***should*** win the lottery, I ***would*** buy a house.

妙语点睛 这里说话人用 should，就是表示他对于自己赢得大奖的信心不大，但还是想碰碰运气。也相当于表达了自己将来的愿望。

精品译文 万一我赢得了彩票大奖，我就会买一栋房子。

再比如下面这句，同样表明了将来实现的可能性不大的情形：

3 Sometimes I have thought it ***would be*** an excellent rule to live each day as if we ***should*** die tomorrow. Such an attitude ***would*** emphasize sharply the values of life.

妙语点睛 有人说，每个人生来就得了一种绝症——死亡。不过，与癌症这样普通的绝症不同的是，我们无法预知自己的死期。因此，这里说“假如我们明天就会死掉”，这不是绝对不可能发生的，而只是可能性不大，所以要用将来虚拟 should die 来表达这种将来的“小概率”事件。

精品译文 我时常会想，如果我们能以明天就要告别这个世界的态度来度过每一天的话，那一定是极好的，因为这种心态会让每一个人珍视生命的意义。

事实上，对于很多将来的情况，选择用虚拟还是不用虚拟，完全取决于说话人对所陈述事件的态度，或者说虚拟语气能表明说话人的态度。比如下面这个例句：

4 What do you think ***would be*** the value of the necklace, if I ***were*** to sell it?

妙语点睛 这里“卖项链”这个事件是说话人完全可以控制的，不是像“假如我有来生”那样完全不能掌控，但说话人依然用了将来虚拟的谓语形式 were to sell，这只是向听者 / 读者表明自己这样一个态度——自己不会卖或不大可能会卖这个项链的。至于为什么不大可能卖这项链，只有说话人自己才知道，也不是听者所关心的。

精品译文 假如我把这串项链卖了，你觉得会是什么价？

既然将来虚拟在很大程度上是由说话人对事件的态度决定的，所以，将来虚拟使用起来非常灵活。比如，同样是上面这个“卖项链”的事件，如果是对于一个急需钱用而且想把自己的项链卖掉来换钱的人，若他在询问卖价，这时他就不会用将来虚拟了，而是用一般陈述的语气来这样说：

5 What do you think ***is*** the value of the necklace if I ***sell*** it to you? 如果我把这串项链卖给你，你能出什么价？

这里说话人是真想卖掉项链，所以他就用 is 和sell 这样的一般时态来询问卖价。

再来比较下列真实条件和将来虚拟条件的区别：

6 1) If it ***were to rain***, I ***would stay*** home.

2) If it ***rains***, I ***will stay*** home.

妙语点睛 这种不同语气的选择，反映了说话人对未来下雨的可能性的信心程度不同。在例句 1)中，用了虚拟语气，表明说话人认为将来不太可能会下雨。在例句 2)中，用了陈述语气，表明说话人认为将来下雨的可能性比较大。

精品译文 1)万一要下雨，那我就在家呆着。

2)如果下雨了，我就在家呆着。

再来看下面这个例句：

7 What ***would*** happen if someone ***were to*** dispose litter in a public place? “It ***would*** stir public anger and denouncement,” Sonia said. “People ***would*** look at you strangely as if you ***were*** an alien from outer space. At the same time, someone ***would*** quietly pick it up for you. Who ***wouldn't*** be embarrassed by such a scene?” 如果有人在公共场所公然乱扔垃圾，会怎样呢？索尼娅说：“这会引起公愤，招来谴责。人们会用奇怪的目光看着你，仿佛你是个外星来的怪物，而且会有人默默地替你拾起垃圾。如果置身于这样的场景之中，谁能不感到尴尬呢？”

大家看到了，这里用的都是虚拟语气，言外之意是，那里的人们不可能在公共场所乱扔垃圾，或者说这种情况极少发生。这段文字来自一篇谈论北欧国家国民素质的文章。可以想象，如果这是在谈论我们国人的情况，那笔者想就不必用虚拟语气了——因为在公共场所随地乱扔垃圾在中国是司空见惯的现象，不是不可能发生的，所以自然不必虚拟了。

思维总结

将来虚拟的谓语结构形式是：从句用 were to do 或 should do，主句用 would do。其意义是用将来虚拟谈论自己认为不太可能发生的事情。另外要注意的是，将来虚拟在很大程度上是由说话人对事件的态度决定的。所以，将来虚拟使用起来非常灵活，这一点需要读者注意了：你说话语气（虚拟还是不虚拟）的选择，反映了你的态度。

7.3 现在虚拟(Z_xC_x)

（一）

假如世界是一个村落

记得曾经读过大卫·史密斯（David J. Smith）写的一篇文章《假如世界是一个村落》(If the World Were a Village)。大卫把拥有 60 多亿人口的地球想象成一个只有 100 人的村落，他以这种独特的方式，为我们提供了一个全球的视角，让我们懂得不同民族和地域中的人们的生活是如此不同，促使我们换一个角度重新审视自己的生活。文章读来给人颇多感悟：

1 If we ***could*** shrink the earth's population to a village of precisely 100 people, with all the existing human ratios remaining the same, it ***would look*** something like the following:

There ***would be*** 57 Asians, 21 Europeans, 14 from the Western Hemisphere, both north and south, 8 Africans.

52 ***would be*** fcmalc and 48 ***would be male.***

70 ***would be*** non-white and 30 ***would be*** white.

70 ***would be*** non-Christian and 30 ***would be*** Christian.

89 ***would be*** heterosexual and 11 ***would be*** homosexual.

22 ***would speak*** Chinese, 9 ***would speak*** English and 7 ***would speak*** Spanish.

6 ***would possess*** 59% of the entire world's wealth and all 6 ***would be*** from the United States.

80 ***would live*** in substandard housing.

70 ***would be*** unable to read.

50 ***would suffer*** from malnutrition.

1 ***would be*** near death; 1 would be near birth.

1 (yes, only 1) ***would have*** a college education.

1 ***would own*** a computer.

精品译文 如果我们把全世界的人口按照现有的比例压缩为一个拥有 100 人的村子，情况就会像下面这样：

在这个村子里：

57 人是亚洲人，21 人是欧洲人，14 人来自西半球的南、北美洲，8 人是非洲人。

52 人是女性，48 人是男性。

70 人是有色人种，30 人是白人。

70 人是非基督教徒，30 人是基督徒。

89 人是异性恋者，11 人是同性恋者。

22 人说汉语，9 人说英语，7 人说西班牙语。

6 人拥有全世界 59% 的财富，而且这 6 人全是美国人。

80 人的居住环境不达标准。

70 人是文盲。

50 人营养不良。

1 人濒临死亡边缘，1 人正要出生。

1 人(是的，只有 1 人)接受大学教育。

1 人拥有电脑。

透过这张微缩的"世界村落图"，我们可以从国籍、语言、宗教信仰、种族和教育水平等众多方面更清晰地了解这个世界。通过这些比较和对照，作者希望世界人民能够彼此理解和接纳，并在书的最后告诫我们该如何去感受和珍惜现在所拥有的幸福：

2 The following is also something to ponder...

If you woke up this morning with more health than illness, you are more blessed than the million who will not survive this week.

If you have never experienced the danger of battle, the loneliness of imprisonment, the agony of torture, or the pangs of starvation...you are ahead of 500 million people in the world.

If you have food in the refrigerator, clothes on your back, a roof overhead and a place to sleep...you are richer than 75% of this world.

If you have money in the bank, in your wallet, and spare change in dish someplace...you are among the top 8% of the world's wealth.

If your parents are still alive and still married...you are very rare, even in the United States and Canada.

精品译文 再从以下角度来想想看：

如果你今天早上醒来的时候依然健康无恙，那么，比起活不过这一周的百万人来说，你真是幸福多了。

如果你未曾经历过战争的危险、入狱的孤独、严刑的折磨或者饥饿的痛苦……那么，比起世界上的 5 亿人来，你真是幸运多了。

如果你的冰箱里有食物、身上有衣服穿、头上有屋篷遮蔽、晚上有地方睡觉……那么，比起世界上 75%的人来，你真是富足多了。

如果你银行中有存款、钱包里有钱，还能下馆子就餐……你便跻身于世界上最富有的 8%的人口当中了。

如果你的父母依然健在，而且他们没有离婚还在一起生活的话……那你可真是幸运之至，因为即使是在美国和加拿大，这也是非常难得的事。

通过比较上述两部分的英文内容，可以发现，前面黑体部分英文句子的谓语形式（如 If we ***could*** shrink...it ***would look***...）与后面非黑体的英文谓语形式（如最后一句 If your parents ***are***...you ***are*** very rare...）有很大的不同：黑体部分的谓语大都采用了"would+ 动词原形"的形式，而下文没有黑体部分的谓语则采用了动词的一般现在时态。这是为什么呢？

这里其实就涉及对现在一般情况的虚拟。当大卫说：

If we ***could*** shrink the earth's population to a village of precisely 100 people, with all the existing human ratios remaining the same, it ***would look*** something like the following.

毫无疑问这是一个虚拟假设的情形，因为我们不可能把地球上的 60 多亿人口缩减到 100 人，所以作者在从句中用了过去式 could，而主句中用 would look 这样标准的一般虚拟的谓语形式。接下来的黑体部分都是虚拟主句谓语，所以都统一采用了 would 接动词原形的形式。比如：

1）There ***would be*** 57 Asians, 21 Europeans, 14 from the Western Hemisphere, both north and south, 8 Africans.

2）52 ***would be*** female and 48 ***would be*** male.

3）70 ***would be*** non-white and 30 ***would be*** white.

4）70 ***would be*** non-Christian and 30 ***would be*** Christian.

5）89 ***would be*** heterosexual and 11 ***would be*** homosexual.

6）22 ***would speak*** Chinese, 9 would speak English and 7 ***would speak*** Spanish.

7）6 ***would possess*** 59% of the entire world's wealth and all 6 ***would be*** from the United States.

8）80 ***would live*** in substandard housing.

9）70 ***would be*** unable to read.

10）50 ***would suffer*** from malnutrition.

11）1 ***would be*** near death; 1 ***would be*** near birth.

12）1（yes, only 1）***would have*** a college education.

13）1 ***would own*** a computer.

在第二部分，作者说：

If you ***woke*** up this morning with more health than illness, you ***are*** more blessed than the million who will not survive this week.

这里从句的谓语 woke 用过去式并不是表示虚拟，而是因为 this morning(今天早晨)相当于一个过去的时间，所以 woke 就是一个一般过去时态。同样，主句的谓语用了一般现在时态 are，而不是 would be 这样的虚拟形式。在接下来的几句里，作者都是在叙述真实的条件，所以都没有采用虚拟语气。比如：

14) If you ***have never experienced*** the danger of battle, the loneliness of imprisonment, the agony of torture, or the pangs of starvation...you ***are*** ahead of 500 million people in the world.

15) If you ***have*** food in the refrigerator, clothes on your back, a roof overhead and a place to sleep...you ***are*** richer than 75% of this world.

16) If you ***have*** money in the bank, in your wallet, and spare change in dish someplace...you ***are*** among the top 8% of the world's wealth.

17) If your parents ***are*** still alive and still married...you are very rare, even in the United States and Canada.

(二)

假如给我三天光明

相信大家都知道美国聋哑女作家、教育家海伦·凯勒(Helen Keller，1880-1968)的故事。她两岁时，一场大病夺取了她的听力和视力，后受业于安·沙利文·麦希(Anne Sullivan Macy)夫人。1904 年，海伦以优异的成绩毕业于剑桥大学拉德克里夫学院(Radcliffe College)。她终生致力于聋哑和盲人的公共救助事业。下面这篇短文就是选自她的《假如给我三天光明》(***Three Days to See***)，文章借助“虚拟”的假设来让人们进行换位思考，让人们真正意识到拥有健康是多么幸福：

3 I have often thought it ***would be*** a blessing if each human being ***were stricken*** blind and deaf for a few days at some time during his early adult life. Darkness ***would*** make him more appreciative of sight; silence ***would*** teach him the joys of sound.

If I ***were*** the president of a university I ***should*** establish a compulsory course in “How to Use Your Eyes”. The professor ***would*** try to show his pupils how they could add joy to their lives by really seeing what passes unnoticed before them. He ***would*** try to awake their dormant and sluggish faculties.

Suppose you set your mind to work on the problem of how you ***would*** use your own eyes if you ***had*** only three more days to see. If with the oncoming darkness of the third night you knew that the sun ***would*** never rise for you again, how ***would*** you spend those three precious intervening days? What ***would*** you most want to let your gaze rest upon?

精品译文 我常常想：如果每一个人在他生活的早期都要遭受几天的眼睛失明，耳朵失聪，那该是多么的幸福啊！黑暗会使他更加珍惜视觉；寂静无声能教会他欣赏声音的美妙。

如果我是一名大学校长的话，我会开设一门“如何用眼”的必修课。教授应该让学生们知道，因为他们能够真正看到眼前所发生的一切，这给他们的生活增添了多大的乐趣啊，他一定要唤醒学生们迟钝、麻木的感光官能。

设想你在思考这样一个问题：假如你只有三天的视力，你该如何使用你的眼睛。假如在第三天晚上，随着黑暗的降临，你知道明天太阳不会再为你升起，你将如何度过这宝贵的三天？你最想让你的目光凝视在什么上面？

读者注意上文中的这些句子表达：

...it ***would be*** a blessing if each human being ***were stricken*** blind and deaf for a few days at some time during his early adult life.

If I ***were*** the president of a university I ***should*** establish a compulsory course in “How to Use Your Eyes”.

...how you would use your own eyes if you had only three more days to see.

If with the oncoming darkness of the third night you ***knew*** that the sun ***would*** never rise for you again, how ***would*** you spend those three precious intervening days?

这些都是标准的现在虚拟句，即从句使用一般过去时态；如果是 be 动词，则不论句子的主语是单数还是复数，都是复数形式 were，而不是 was；相应地，主句用 would/should+ 动词原形。

（三）

来看下面这个幸福婚姻的秘诀：

4 It is not the lack of love that makes unhappy marriages; it is the lack of friendship. My advice to all men is "Choose in marriage a woman that ***you would choose as a friend if she were a man***". This applies to women in the same way. One tragedy in many marriages is that the romantic love on which it was based never ripened into friendship.

妙语点睛 这里作者说"如果这个女人是一个男人"，但实际上女人是无法变为男人的(当然变性手术不算在内)，所以这是一个对一般情况的虚拟。作者通过现在虚拟的句子...a woman that you ***would choose*** as a friend if she ***were*** a man，来说明夫妻之间有友情的存在对于幸福婚姻的重要性。

精品译文 婚姻不幸福并不是因为缺乏爱，而是因为婚姻中缺少了友谊。我对于男士们的建议是：选取结婚对象时，要找这样的女人——假如她们是男人的话，你愿意和他们做朋友。我的这个建议同样也适用于女人。许多婚姻的不幸往往是：作为婚姻基础的浪漫爱情没有升华成为友情。

说到美国人的极大浪费，美国环境保护专家彼得·拉文(Peter Raven)有这样一句话：

5 If everyone ***lived*** like Americans, then you ***would need*** three planet earths to sustain that level of consumption.

妙语点睛 由此可见，美国人常常指责别国破坏地球环境，浪费资源，殊不知他们自己才是破坏地球环境真正的的罪魁祸首。在这句话中，彼得就是用了虚拟语气，因为事实上我们没有三个地球来供我们浪费和糟蹋。所以，主从句的谓语分别采用了"would + 动词(need)原形"和过去式(lived)这样标准的一般虚拟形式。

精品译文 如果世界上每一个人都像美国人这般生活的话，那我们得需要三个地球方能维持这样的消费水平。

下面这句话则用虚拟语气反问，假如中国也达到美国人一般的生活水准，比如每个家庭拥有两辆小汽车、每人每年肉类的消费量达到 122 公斤，那中国该怎样应对这种需求呢？

6 How ***would*** the Chinese ***cope*** if the average family in China ***had*** two cars, and, like Americans, the average person ***ate*** 269 pounds (122 kilograms) of meat a year?

妙语点睛 由于事实上，中国目前还远没有达到这种生活水平，所以在叙述时也不要忘了使用虚拟语气，即主句用 would+cope，从句用过去式 ate。

精品译文 如果中国人也达到美国人那样的生活水平，比如平均每个家庭拥有两辆小汽车、每人每年平均消费 269 磅(122 公斤)肉类食品，中国将如何应对这种情况呢？

第五章"完成时态"的 5. 3 节谈到罗素的自传中有这个句子：

7 This has been my life. I have found it worth living, and ***would*** gladly live it again if the chance ***were*** offered me.
这就是我的一生。我已经找到了它的价值。而且如果有机会，我很愿意能再活它一次。

一个美国教授谈到语言学习时说：

8 For a North American or European, languages such as Chinese, Korean, and Japanese have what is like pictograph or ideographic type of language. Native speakers of European languages often have a very difficult time in learning one of the Asian languages, as our ears are not attuned to the sounds or characters of the language. In China, I am like a child in terms of the language, and illiterate in terms of being able to read or write Chinese. If I ***could*** read and write in Chinese, I ***would*** need to recognize at least 3, 000 or more characters.

Chinese also have a hard time learning the European languages such as English, French, Spanish, Italian, or German, because each of these languages is filled with many idioms which don't make much sense in terms of the formal language that they learn.

妙语点睛 因为这位美国教授不懂汉语，所以他用了虚拟语气说 If I ***could*** read and write in Chinese, I ***would*** need to recognize at least 3, 000 or more characters.

精品译文 对于北美人或欧洲人来说，汉语、韩语和日语等语言就像是图画语言或表意文字。以欧洲语言为母语的人往往会发现这些亚洲语言很难学，因为我们的耳朵生来就不适应这些语言的发音或写法。在中国，在语言方面我像是一个孩子，就汉语的读写能力而言，我则像是文盲。如果我希望能够具备中文的读写能力，我则需要认识至少 3,000 汉字或更多。

中国人在学习欧洲的语言方面，比如英语、法语、西班牙语、意大利语或德语等，也常常会感到困难，因为这些语言中含有大量的成语，而这些成语，如果按照他们所学的正式的外语来解释，并没有什么意思。

笔者的一位美国朋友在和笔者聊起中国学生学习英文所遭遇到的众多困惑和难题时说道：

9 From the letters I have been receiving from our Chinese readers, the problem with tense seems to be foremost. English tenses ***would make*** me tense if I ***were*** a Chinese student.

从中国读者给我的来信中看出，他们学习英文最大的难题似乎是在时态方面。如果我是一名中国学生，时态同样会让我犯憷。

的确，时态问题一直是我们学习英语的一个“老大难”问题，在复杂的时态变化的迷宫里，我们往往一筹莫展，迷失方向。于是在口语或作文中，只好把英语当成汉语一样不作谓语的变形，通篇都是“一般现在时”。虚拟语气其实就是时态问题，不过它要比一般的时态问题更难，因为它不仅需要判断谓语动作发生的时间，还要能够敏锐地“嗅出”与事实相反的虚拟“味道”来。比如上文中的“如果我是一名中国学生，时态同样会让我犯憷”这句话，从时间的角度来看，是表示一般的情况，即现在时间；从语义的角度来看，因为是一个美国人在说假如他是一名中国学生，这显然就是与事实相反的一个虚拟假设。综合这两方面，所以要用对**现在虚拟的谓语形式：主句谓语采用 would+动词原形，从句谓语采用过去式；若从句谓语是 be 动词，就多用 were，而较少用 was**。这就是对一般情形虚拟的谓语表达形式，或者叫做所谓的“语法规则”。在这里，笔者之所以不愿意说是“语法规则”，是因为很多英语学习者总是把“语法规则”当作捆住自己英语学习手脚的“死规则”，而没有把它们看成是引导和帮助我们正确使用英语的“活思维”！由此往往会造成这样的误解：以为是先有一套语法规则和教条，然后必须按照这些规则才能制造出具体的语言。而事实恰恰相反，是先有语言，然后再从大量的语言实践中总结出在使用这种语言时所遵循的一般思维规律或表达倾向，即所谓的规则。套用鲁迅先生的一句话就是：世界本无语法规则，说的人多了便成了规则。所以，语法规则不是什么不可逾越的清规戒律或天规，而是人们的思维规律或语言表达习惯。中国的英语学习者和 native speakers of English 最大的区别就是：我们懂英语语法规则却没有英语思维，而老外是在使用英语思维，尽管他们不懂语法规则。我们学的语法规则都用来对付英语考试的选择题了，而没有真正懂得规则背后的英语思维。由于没有形成真正的英语思维，所以在使用英语，如口语交际或作文时便成了“残疾人”——说不出、写不来。

这里讨论的虚拟语气尤其能考量我们的英语思维能力。在日常的口语交际中，我们会遇到大量虚拟假设的情景，此时就需要有良好的思维嗅觉能力，敏感地辨别真假情形，正确地使用语气表达。比如对于“假如我当总统，我会……”这样一个简单的句子，都要根据说话人的不同身份来选择不同的语气表达。比如，这句话若是出自一个小学生之口，他应该说成：

10 If I ***became*** President, I ***would***...

因为对于一个小学生来说，“当总统”是一个与现实相反的虚拟假设，所以这句话要借助谓语动词变化(即从句用过去式 became，主句用 would 接一个原形动词)来传达这种虚拟的情形。但若是对于一位正在竞选中的总统，比如现在(指 2004 年 9 月笔者写下这句话的时候)的美国民主党候选人约翰·克里(John Kerry)，他则要这么说：

11 If I ***become*** President, I ***will*** (make America stronger at home and more respected in the world.

如果我当了美国总统，我要(让美国变得更强大，在国际上更受尊重)。

因为他应该用表示真实条件的陈述语气来表明对自己未来总统竞选获胜的信心。如果克里用虚拟语气说：

If I ***became*** President, I ***would***...

恐怕连本来支持他的选民都要改旗易帜支持小布什了。由此可见虚拟语气的表达之精妙，它决不是一个死规则，而是一种活生生的英语思维。

思维总结

这一节讨论的是 ZxCx 型虚拟语气，即主句和从句都表示对现在一般情况的虚拟。此时，主句用 would do，而从句用一般过去时态 did；若从句的谓语是 be 动词，则一律用 were。

思维训练

Exercise 7.3（Key: P346）

请阅读下面的美文，并用括号中动词的适当形式填空。

1. **If I Were a Boy Again**

If I ______（be）a boy again, I ______（practice）perseverance oftener, and never give up a thing because it was hard or inconvenient.

If I ______（be）a boy again, I ______（school）myself into a habit of attention; I ______（let）nothing come between me and the subject in hand. I ______（remember）that a good skater never tries to skate in two directions at once.

If I ______（be）a boy again, I ______（look）on the cheerful side. Life is very much like a mirror: if you smile upon it, it smiles back upon you; but if you frown and look doubtful on it, you will get a similar look in return.

If I ______（be）a boy again, I ______（demand）of myself more courtesy towards my companions and friends, and indeed towards strangers as well. The smallest courtesies along the rough roads of life are like the little birds that sing to us all winter long, and make that season of ice and snow more endurable.

Finally, instead of trying hard to be happy, as if that were the sole purpose of life, I would, if I ______（be）a boy again, try still harder to make others happy.

请用括号中动词的适当形式填空。

2. A: The subway sure is packed this morning.

B: Yeah. It's a pain that if we all ______（drive）everyday we ______（not, be）able to breathe in this city.

3. How fast does light travel?

How fast does light travel? About 300, 000 kilometers per second. So light from the sun takes about 8 minutes to go to earth. Does this seem slow? Well, if you ______（can, drive）to the sun at 100 kilometers per hour, it ______（take）you 177 years to get there!

请回答下面问题。

4. Man: I haven't seen George all day.

Woman: Have you checked the lab? I wouldn't be surprised if he slept there.

Question: What does the woman imply about George?

A. He is probably still asleep in the lab.　　B. He spends a lot of time in the lab.

C. She needs to check his work.　　D. She has no idea where he is.

开心一刻

请阅读下面笑话故事，并找出其中使用的虚拟语气。

5. **If I were a millionaire**

The teacher asked his pupils to write an essay, telling what they would do if they had five million dollars. Every pupil except little Sammy began writing immediately. Sammy sat idle, twiddling his fingers and watching the flies on the ceiling.

Teacher collected their papers, and Sammy handed in a blank sheet.

"How is this, Sammy?" asked the teacher. "Is this your essay? Every other pupil has written two sheets or more, while you have done nothing!"

"Well," replied Sammy, "that's what I would do if I were a millionaire!"

阅读下面美文，并找出其中使用的虚拟语气。

6. If I could save time in a bottle
the first thing that I'd like to do
would be to save every day until eternity passes away
just to spend them with you
if I could make days last forever
if words could make wishes come true
I'd save every day like a treasure and then
again I would spend them with you
如果我能把时间存入一个瓶子，
我要做的第一件事就是，
把每一天都存下来直到永恒，
再和你一起慢慢度过。
如果我能把时间化作永恒，
如果我的愿望能一一成真，
我会把每天都像宝贝一样储存，
再和你一起慢慢度过。

7.4 过去虚拟(Z_gC_g)

(一)

只要有 Love，就会有 Wealth 和 Success

从前有位老妇人，有一天在自家门口发现有三个白须飘然的老头正坐在她家前院。但她并不认识他们，于是她对三个老头说道："我想我应该不认识你们，但我想你们一定是饿了，请来我家吃些东西吧(I don't think I know you, but you must be hungry. Please come in and have something to eat.)"听了老妇人的邀请，他们说道："我们三个人不会同时进去的(We do not go into a house together.)"老妇人很是纳闷，就问:"为什么呀？"

这时，有个老头就告诉她理由。他指着其中一个老头说道："他名叫'财富'(His name is Wealth.)"又指着另一个老头说："他是'成功'，我是'爱'(He is Success and I am Love.)"说完，他又补充道："现在请你回家同你丈夫商量一下，我们这三个人你们愿意邀请谁进去（Now go in and discuss with your husband which one of us you want in your home.)"

于是，老妇人回到家里告诉她老伴儿院子里发生的事，并且跟她老伴儿商量，有 Wealth, Success 和 Love 三个老头，到底该邀请谁进屋呢？她老伴儿提议说："既然这样，那我们就邀请'财富'老人进来吧，这样我们家就会充满财富(Since that is the case, let us invite Wealth. Let him come and fill our home with wealth!)"

但是老妇人对此并不同意，她说道:"老头子，我们为什么不邀请'成功'老人呢(My dear, why don't we invite Success?)"

这时，他们的儿媳妇听到了老两口的对话，说出了自己的想法："如果我们把'爱'邀请进来不是更好吗？这样我们家就会充满爱(Wouldn't it be better to invite Love? Our home will then be filled with love!)"老两口最后一商量，也都赞成儿媳妇的意见，于是老头对老妇人说："那我们出去把'爱'请进来作为我们的客人吧(Go out and invite Love to be our guest.)" 随后老妇人又来到门口准备邀请"爱"进来做客。看着三位老头，她问道："你们仨谁是'爱'呀？请进来做客吧(Which one of you is Love? Please come in and be our guest.)"

这时，老头"爱"就站起身开始朝屋里走去，但与此同时另外两个老头"财富"和"成功"也跟在"爱"的后面朝屋里走。老妇人很惊讶，就问"财富"和"成功"："我刚才只邀请了'爱'，你们俩为什么也要进来呀(Surprised, the lady asked Wealth and Success, "I only invited Love. Why are you coming in?)"

下面是这两位老人的精彩回答：

1 The old men replied together, "If you had invited Wealth or Success, the other two of us would've stayed out, but since you invited Love, wherever he goes, we go with him. Wherever there is Love, there is also Wealth and Success!"

精品译文 两位老人齐声回答道："如果你刚才只邀请了'财富'或'成功'中的任何一位，那剩下两位都将留在门外。但是，既然你已经邀请了'爱'，所以，他去哪里，我们就跟到哪里，因为只要有'爱'的地方，就会有'财富'和'成功'！"

这个故事的寓意不需在此赘述。我们再看看两位老人最后的回答：

2 If you **had invited** Wealth or Success, the other two of us **would've stayed** out.

但实际上被邀请的是Love，所以这句话说"如果你刚才邀请了'财富'或'成功'"，显然是对过去事实的一个相反的假设，也就是对过去的虚拟。**根据英文的思维表达，表示对过去的虚拟，主句的谓语要采用would have done的形式，从句的谓语则要用过去完成时态had done**。所以，上述例句正是采用了这一虚拟形式：would have stayed和had invited。

（二）

上面这个故事告诉我们："只要有爱，就会有财富和成功"。这并不是说"爱"就真的一定会给我们带来物质和金钱上的财富，而是要告诉我们，爱与被爱才真正赋予了生命的意义，就如同人们说的：Love is a reason to live. 还有一句至理名言是这样说的：Love makes the world go around. 不过下面这个故事也许会给恋爱中的你带来另外的启示：

3 "Do you love me?—Yes. Do you really, really love me?—Yes." It was a question that has been posed to many a lover. But Stephanie Powell had a special reason for asking her boyfriend, Wayne, if he loved her. Because Stephanie had just won $7 million on the lottery and wanted to make sure of Wayne's devotion before she told him the good news. "If he had known about the win I would never have known whether it was me or the money he would want to stay with," she said. "I don't know what I would have done if he hadn't answered yes. I love him and want to enjoy spending the money with him."

精品译文 "你爱我吗？——爱。你是真的爱我吗？——真的爱。"这样的问题许多恋人相互之间都问过，但是斯蒂芬妮·鲍威尔问她的男朋友韦恩是否爱她时，却是有特别的原因。因为她刚中了700万美元的彩票，想先确证她男友是否真的爱她，然后再告诉他这一好消息。她后来说："如果他先知道我赢得了这个大奖，那我就无从知晓他和我交往是因为爱我，还是因为爱我的钱。如果他当时没有回答说爱我，我真不知道该怎么办，因为我爱他，所以愿意和他分享这笔巨款。"

从这个故事我们看到，韦恩因为说了"爱"，而获得与女友一起分享700万美元巨款的机会。所以，当如果有同样的"机会"惠顾你时，记住一定要毫不犹豫地告诉他／她"爱"，因为Wherever there is Love, there is also Wealth!

故事中的斯蒂芬妮·鲍威尔说的两句话：

1）If he ***had known*** about the win, I ***would never have*** known whether it was me or the money he would want to stay with.

2）I don't know what I ***would have done*** if he ***hadn't answered*** yes.

妙语点睛 这显然是在她后来回顾这个事件时说的话，此时，这个事件已成为过去。斯蒂芬妮用了两个假设从句说"假如他知道"和"假如他没有回答'是'"，这两个从句都是表示与过去的事实相反。主句同样也是表示过去虚拟假设。因此，主句和从句的谓语分别用了would never have known和had known，以及would have done和hadn't answered这样的动词虚拟形式。

爱情是人类永恒的话题，但并不是每段美好的爱情最终都能走进幸福的婚姻。如果婚姻不幸，最终导致离婚，那对孩子的伤害应该是最大的。下面这篇短文就是英国球星贝克汉姆谈论父母离婚给他留下的阴影——他始终认为父母的离异或许是自己的错。

4 **Beckham and Divorce**

I grew up in the love of a family. Without Mum and Dad, none of my story would be here for the telling. Like any son, I ***wouldn't have grown*** up into the person I am if they ***hadn't passed*** on their values to me. Marriage and parenthood, I think, are the two most important things any of us ever take on in our lives. That explains why my parents' splitting up has been probably the most difficult episode I've ever had to face up to in my whole life. To be honest, I'm still trying to face up to it now, probably the hardest thing to deal with has been thinking — or being made to think — that the split was somehow my fault. I remember the time and the energy they both put into me as a son and as a promising footballer. Should they have given some of the attention they gave me to each other instead?

However old you are when it happens, children in a divorce always find themselves feeling guilty. I believe that what happens between husband and wife, deep down, is between husband and wife and nobody else; not even their sons and daughters can change the outcome.

The story of my parents' marriage makes me feel sad, empty inside. What was home isn't anymore. Who can tell what lies down the road for you in your own life?

精品译文 **贝克汉姆与离婚**

我是在家人的关爱中成长的。没有父母，就没有今天我在这里所说的一切。像世间任何一个子女一样，没有父母的教诲，我也就不能成为现在的"我"。我认为，婚姻和亲子关系是生命中最为重要的东西。所以，父母的离异有可能是我整个人生中必须面对的最艰难的一关。老实说，直到现在我都还在努力克服这件事带给我的影响。也许，最困难的还是自己的想法——或者说是被迫去想——认为父母的离异或许是自己的错。我仍然铭记他们俩对我付出的时间和精力，不论他们是把我看作一个儿子还是一个有前途的球员。他们是否应该把部分放在我身上的精力投到彼此身上呢？

不论父母离异时孩子有多大，孩子都会责备自己。事实上，我相信，夫妻间无论发生了什么事都是夫妻间的事，与他人无关；即使是他们的子女都不能改变这个事实。

父母的婚姻让我觉得很伤心，心里好像被掏空了。家不成家。谁又能知道在前方等待自己的又是什么呢？

从最后一句，我们能感受到，即使是现在在谈及自己的家庭时，小贝依然会黯然神伤。但对于父母在他成长过程中给予他的爱，他依然心存感激，所以他在上文中说：

Like any son, I ***wouldn't have grown*** up into the person I am if they ***hadn't passed*** on their values to me. Marriage and parenthood, I think, are the two most important things any of us ever take on in our lives.

贝克汉姆用的是过去虚拟形式 wouldn't have grown 和 hadn't passed，来表示与过去事实相反的假设，因为小贝事实是在父母的教诲下已经长大成人，而且后来成为了世界著名的球星，对此他自己也未曾料到。他曾在一次新闻发布会上说：

5 Two years ago if someone ***had turned*** round to me and said "in two years you'll be England captain", I ***would have turned*** round and said: "I don't think so!"

妙语点睛 这里同样是一个对过去事实的虚拟：两年前并没有人跟小贝说过"你将在两年后成为英格兰队的队长"，所以，小贝在这里用了虚拟语气：从句用过去完成时 had turned，主句用 would have turned。

精品译文 如果两年前，有人对我说"你将在两年后成为英格兰队的队长"，我肯定会对此一笑了之。

在这一节中我们讨论的这种过去虚拟语气，其谓语的构成形式的确有点复杂。所以，读者朋友首先需要记准它的结构形式，然后在实践中多加练习、细心体会。只有这样，虚拟语气这种汉语所没有的思维表达方式才能逐步进入我们的思维，从而为我们所运用。所以，语法的学习决不只是死记结构来应付考试，而更应该理解结构形式背后所反映的说话人真正的意念和思维。我们常常说"言为心声"，说的就是这个意思。如果只是死记规则和结构，而不去体会和领悟英语结构背后的思维规律，那我们只能永远是屈服于英语的"奴隶"，而不能成为驾驭英语的"将军"！

思维总结

这节讨论的是 ZgCg 型虚拟语气，即主句和从句都表示对过去情况的虚拟。此时，主句谓语用 would have done，而从句谓语用过去完成时态 had done。

思维训练

Exercise 7.4（Key: P347）

请用下面括号中动词的适当形式填空。

1. Tourism is an odd thing. You fly off to a strange land, eagerly abandoning all the comforts of home, and then expend time and money in a futile attempt to recapture the comforts that you ______ （not, lose）if you ______（not, leave）home in the first place.
2. If I ______（know）it would come to this, I ______（act）differently.
3. A: The coat you tried on was really nice, and reasonably priced.
   B: I ______（buy）it right away if they ______（have）it in my size.
4. If you ______（choose）where you were born and grew up, what country/culture ______（be）your choice?

请选择最佳答案填空。

5. It would have been just as satisfactory if I ______ at home. I learned nothing in class.
   A. had stayed　B. stayed　C. was staying　D. would stay
6. If you ______ Jerry Brown until recently, you'd think the photograph on the right was strange.
   A. shouldn't contact　B. didn't contact　C. weren't to contact　D. hadn't contacted

请回答下面的问题。

7. Woman: It's a shame that you didn't win your tennis match.
   Man: I might have won if I'd listened to my coach.
   Question: What does the man imply?
   A. His coach didn't help him enough.　B. He had no chance of winning.
   C. He didn't follow his coach's advice.　D. His coach didn't listen to him.
8. If I'd known he was driving downtown, I'd have asked him for a ride.
   Question: What does the speaker mean?
   A. I asked him if he needed a ride.
   B. I'm going to share the driving with him
   C. I didn't ask him for a ride since I didn't know he was driving.
   D. I asked him for a ride as soon as I found out he was going.

7.5 混合虚拟(一)：主句现在＋从句过去(Z_xC_g)

（一）

成功男人背后的女人

人们常说：每个成功男人的背后都会有一个伟大的女人，而这个伟大的女人往往就是他的妻子。这说明丈夫的成功有一半功劳应该归属于他的妻子，这就叫"军功章里有你的一半也有我的一半"。不过对于成功的女人，似乎就不那么幸运了，因为有人说：每个成功女人的背后往往都会有一个伤害她的男人。后来又有人这样调侃道：Behind every successful man, there is a woman. And behind every unsuccessful man, there are two.（每个成功男人背后都有一个女人；每个不成功男人的背后都有两个女人。）

托马斯·维勒(Thomas Wheeler)是一家大公司的CEO，有一天他和太太一同驱车出门。在路上，托马斯发现汽车油箱里没有多少汽油了，于是就把车开到路边的一个加油站去加油，然后让他太太看着车，自己到附近遛遛。过了一会，当他回来时，发现他太太和加油站的工人(gas station attendant)正聊得"火热"，显得很是亲热(As he was returning to the car, he noticed that the attendant and his wife were engaged in an animated conversation.)。但碍于面子，当着三个人，他也不好说什么。等回到车上并把车开离了加油站后，托马斯还是忍不住问道："你认识他吗？"(As they drove out of the station, Wheeler asked his wife if she knew the man.)他太太也坦诚地回答道，他们是中学同学，并且两人是彼此的初恋！听了这话，托马斯不无得意地说道：

Boy, were you lucky that I came along. If you had married him, you would be the wife of a gas station attendant instead of the wife of a chief executive officer.（你瞧，嫁给了我真是你的幸运啊，你当初要是嫁给了他，你现在就做不了总裁的太太，而只能是加油工的太太了。）

他太太也不甘示弱地回敬道：

My dear, if I had married him, he would be the chief executive officer and you would be the gas station attendant.（嘿，亲爱的，如果我当初嫁的是他，他就是总裁，而你就是加油工了。）

在上一节里我们讨论了对过去事实的虚拟，主、从句的谓语形式分别是 would have done 和 had done，但上文的最后两句话显然与此不同，请看下面黑体部分的谓语结构：

1 If you ***had married*** him, you ***would be*** the wife of a gas station attendant instead of the wife of a chief executive officer.

2 If I ***had married*** him, he ***would*** be the chief executive officer and you ***would be*** the gas station attendant.

经过分析就会发现，在这两个例句中，从句的"结婚（married）"这一活动是发生在过去，而且是**与过去事实相反**的一个假设，即是对过去的虚拟，所以谓语用的是过去完成时 had married。所不同的是，这里的主句是表示**与现在事实相反**的一个假设，即是对现在事实的虚拟，所以谓语用 would be 这样的动词形式。简言之，这里的主句是对现在的虚拟，从句是对过去的虚拟，即主句和从句的虚拟时间不同。我们**把这种主句、从句虚拟时间不一致的虚拟语气叫做"混合时间虚拟语气"**。回顾前面三节讨论过的虚拟语气，其 if 引导的从句中，谓语动词表示的动作与主句谓语动词表示的动作发生的时间是一致的，即同为将来、现在或过去，此时主从句虚拟的时间是相同的。混合时间虚拟语气的谓语变化形式比较难一些，具体来说，当主从句动作发生的时间不一致时，主句和从句各自的谓语形式要根据它们各自动作发生的时间作适当调整。这里讨论的**主句表示对现在的虚拟，谓语需要用"would+ 动词原形"，从句表示对过去的虚拟，谓语需要用过去完成时"had done"**，这种混合时间的虚拟句子是最常见的。

（二）
克林顿与希拉里

关于上面那个故事，最近笔者还看到另外一个版本，就是拿美国前总统比尔·克林顿（Bill Clinton）来调侃，把故事中夫妇两人的角色换成了克林顿和她的夫人希拉里（Hillary）。英文故事是这样讲的：

3 Bill and Hillary are vacationing in Hillary's hometown and stop at a gas station to gas up. The attendant comes out and fills up their car and when he leans over to collect the money he and Hillary recognize one another and begin making small talk.

When they finally leave, Bill asks her who she was talking to and she says it was her first boyfriend from back in high school.

Bill says that's nice and asks her, "Do you ever think about what life would be like if things had been different and you had married him instead of me?"

To which Hillary responds, "Yes I do, you would be pumping gas and he would be president."

妙语点睛 这里我们同样可以看到这种混合虚拟语气的使用，比如克林顿说：

Do you ever think about what life ***would be*** like if things ***had been*** different and you ***had married*** him instead of me?

因为主句是表示对现在的虚拟，所以主句谓语用了"would+ 动词原形"即 would be，而从句是表示对过去的虚拟假设，所以用了过去完成时 had married。希拉里的回答只有表示对现在虚拟的主句：You ***would be*** pumping gas and he ***would be*** president. 把从句省略了。

精品译文 克林顿和希拉里一起去她的家乡度假，在路上他们来到一个加油站给汽车加油。当加油工把他们的汽车加满油后，过来收钱时，发现他和希拉里彼此认识，于是两人就攀谈起来。

克林顿和希拉里离开加油站后，克林顿禁不住问希拉里，刚才和她交谈的那个人是谁。她说是她中学时代的初恋男友。

克林顿听后，问道："你想过没有，如果当初情况不同，我是说如果当初你嫁给了他，你现在的生活就完全不同了。"

对此，希拉里回答道："是不一样了，那么你就是加油工，而他就是总统了。"

（三）
帕瓦罗蒂的成功之路

虽然说每个成功男人的背后都有一个伟大的女人，但是世界著名的三大男高音之一帕瓦罗蒂(Luciano Pavarotti)把自己的成功归功于他的爸爸。我们现来看看他的成长故事：

4 When Luciano Pavarotti was a boy, his grandmother put him on her lap and said, "You're going to be great, you'll see." His mother dreamed he'd be a banker. "Instead," Pavarotti explains, "I ended up teaching elementary school and sang only infrequently. But my father constantly goaded me, said I was singing below my potential."

Finally, at age 22, Pavarotti quit teaching for selling insurance, to give him enough time to develop his vocal talent. "Studying voice was the turning point of my life," says the opera star. "It's a mistake to take the safe path in life. And yes, my teacher groomed me. But no teacher ever told me I would become famous. Just my grandmother. If I ***hadn't listened*** to my father and dropped teaching, I ***would never*** be here."

妙语点睛 在上文的最后一句里，"听从父亲的建议"显然是在过去发生的，而说"如果没有听"则是对过去的虚拟，因此帕瓦罗蒂用了过去完成时态说 If I ***hadn't listened*** to my father and dropped teaching... 而主句说"我今天就不可能站在这里了"，但事实上此刻他在这里，这显然是表示对现在事实的虚拟假设，所以他接着说 I ***would never be*** here。

精品译文 在卢西亚诺·帕瓦罗蒂小的时候，他奶奶把他放在自己的膝盖上，并对他说："你将来一定会出名的，一定会。"他妈妈梦想他将来长大后能成为一名银行家。帕瓦罗蒂说："不过，我最后还是在小学教书，只是偶尔唱唱歌。但是我父亲一直在鼓励我，说我有演唱的天赋。"

就在帕瓦罗蒂 22 岁那年，他放弃了教书，改卖保险，这样他就有时间学习演唱了。这位歌王回忆道："学习声乐是我人生中的一个转折点。人生的道路从来就不是平坦的。尽管后来有老师教我声乐，但是从来没有人告诉我，说我将来会出名，只有我奶奶。而且如果当初我没有听从我父亲的建议，放弃教书，那我今天就不可能站在这里了。"

（四）
比尔·盖茨的故事

美国人似乎总爱拿名人来调侃，下面这个故事就是拿比尔·盖茨(Bill Gates)来开玩笑的：

5 Bill Gates is hanging out with the chairman of General Motors.

"If automotive technology ***had kept*** pace with computer technology over the past few decades," boasts Gates, "you ***would now be driving*** a V-32 instead of a V-8, and it ***would have*** a top speed of 10, 000 miles per hour. Or, you ***could have*** an economy car that weighs 30 pounds and gets a thousand miles to a gallon of gas. In either case, the sticker price of a new car ***would be*** less than $50."

"Sure," says the GM chairman. "But ***would*** you really ***want*** to drive a car that crashes four times a day?"

妙语点睛 我们看到，这里通篇用的都是虚拟语气。首先，我们来看 if 引导的从句。因为汽车技术的发展在过去的几十年中并没有像计算机的发展这么快，所以，这里 if 引导的从句是表示对过去事实的虚拟，故用过去完成时态 had kept。其次，接下来的主句所设想的情形都是在这个虚拟条件下发生的，而且都是表示与现在事实相反，所以主句都用了 would 或 could 接一个动词原形，比如 would be driving, would have, could have, would be 以及 would...want。

精品译文 比尔·盖茨正在和通用公司的总裁呆在一起。

盖茨炫耀说："在过去的几十年中，如果汽车科技的发展都能像计算机技术的发展这么迅速的话，你现在开的车就是 V-32 而不是 V-8 了。这样一来，你的车速就能达到每小时一万英里这样的速度。或者，车的重量只有 30 磅(约 13. 6 公斤)，而每加仑汽油能跑一千英里。这两种情形不论出现哪一种，那么汽车的标价就会降到 50 美元以下。"

通用的总裁说："那倒是，不过，那样的话，汽车一天会碰撞四次，你还愿意开这样的车吗？"

从以上的分析我们看到，对于混合虚拟语气，可以分两步判断：首先是根据上下文的语境，要能判断出某个句子是表达了与事实相反的情形，即虚拟；其次，进而分析主从句各自的虚拟时间有何不同，从而选择各自的谓语形式来表达不同的虚拟意义。比如下面这则笑话：

6 A: I don't like my mother-in-law.

B: Listen, don't you realize that you ***couldn't have*** your wife if it ***hadn't been*** for your mother-in-law?

A: Yes, that's why I don't like her.

妙语点睛 根据主句和从句的谓语形式，我们知道这是一个混合时间虚拟语气。主句的谓语 couldn't have 表明是一个对现在的虚拟，从句的谓语 hadn't been 表明是一个对过去的虚拟。那就要思考这里为什么要用混合时间虚拟呢？该如何判断虚拟时间呢？其实，这里的主句说"你不可能有你的妻子"，但事实是现在"你有妻子"，即是一个对现在一般情况的虚拟。那么从句为什么是表示对过去时间的虚拟呢？因为从句说"如果不是因为你的岳母"，言外之意是，"如果没有你的岳母生下你的妻子"——这是发生在过去的。所以，这里的从句是表示对过去的虚拟，于是采用过去完成时 hadn't been。

精品译文 A：我不喜欢我的岳母。

B：听着，你有没有想过，如果没有你的岳母，哪来你现在的妻子啊？

A：正是因为这个所以我才不喜欢她。

再比如下面这段对话：

7 A: What an accident! If you ***had been*** careful, things ***would not be*** as they are.

B: What do you mean, it was my fault? If it were, surely I would take all responsibility for it.

妙语点睛 这里的从句是对过去的虚拟，说话人 A 是在抱怨 B 当初没有小心。主句是对现在的虚拟，谈的是眼前糟糕的处境。在 B 的回答 If it ***were***, surely I ***would take*** all responsibility for it. 中也使用了虚拟语气，主从句都是对现在的虚拟，其言外之意是：这不是他的错，所以他不会承担任何责任。

精品译文 A：多糟糕啊！如果你当初小心点，情况就不会像现在这个样子了。

B：你这是什么意思啊，这都是我的错吗？如果是，我当然会负全责。

再比如，拿笔者我个人来说，如果笔者从来没有学习过英语，那么笔者现在就不可能和读者分享语法规则了：

8 If I ***had not studied*** English, I ***would never be*** here to teach you grammar today.

如果我没有学过英语，我现在就不能在这里教你们语法了。

我们再来看其他例句，请读者认真分析其中谓语的虚拟时间：

9 If they ***had invested*** in that stock, they ***might be*** wealthy now.

如果他们当初投资了那支股票，他们现在就会很富有了。

10 If I ***had studied*** English at school, I ***could read*** the English novel now.

如果我在学校学过英语，我现在就能读英文小说了。

11 If he ***had studied*** English two years ago, he ***might have*** a chance of going abroad for further study now.

如果他两年前学过英语，他现在可能就有机会出国深造了。

的确，这种混合时间的虚拟语气对于中国学生来说是不易掌握的，因为既要判断所谈论的情形是否与事实相反，还得分别判断主句和从句虚拟的时间，所以在平时遇到时这种句子时需要细心体会，反复操练。只有这样，我们才能形成这种复杂的虚拟语气表达规律的思维，才能真正达到灵活运用的境界。

思维总结

这一节讨论的是"混合时间虚拟语气"，即主句和从句分别对不同的时间进行虚拟。在这一节里讨论的混合时间虚拟语气是 Z_xC_g 型虚拟语气，即主句对现在虚拟，用 would do 形式；从句对过去虚拟，用 had done 形式。这是最常用的一种混合虚拟语气。

在下一节里，我们将讨论另外一种混合虚拟语气，即 Z_gC_x 型：主句表过去 + 从句表现在。

思维训练

Exercise 7.5（Key: P347）

请选择最佳答案填空。

1. Had Paul received six more votes in the last election, he ______ our chairman now.
   A. must have been B. would have been C. were D. would be
2. ______ for the timely investment from the general public, our company would not be so thriving as it is.
   A. Had it not been B. Were it not C. Be it not D. Should it not be

7.6 混合虚拟(二)：主句过去 + 从句现在(Z_gC_x)

本节要讨论的混合时间虚拟语气，其主句和从句的虚拟时间正好与7.5节讨论的虚拟语气相反，即这里从句谈的是一般情况，是对一般情况的虚拟；主句谈过去，是对过去某一个具体情况的虚拟。下面先给大家讲一个故事：

约翰(John)和路易丝(Louise)是一对新婚夫妇，尽管两人很是恩爱，但丈夫John是一个沉默寡言、较为木讷而又受教育不多的人，一直以来他从未对路易丝说过I love you，他妻子路易丝因此长年郁郁寡欢。有一天他们的朋友凯斯医生(Doctor Case)来看望他们时，凯斯发现路易丝不快乐，身体也不太好。凯斯医生就问她约翰对她好不好。路易丝说，没有比约翰更好的丈夫了——只是，他不怎么爱说话，而女人都是愿意有人能与她们交谈的(Louise answered that John was the best husband any woman could ask for, only — well, he didn't say much, and a woman wants to be talked to.)

在他们婚后第三年的一天，路易丝终于病倒了。凯斯医生给她输了两次血，可她还是越来越虚弱。在医院里，路易丝面无血色地对凯斯医生说：John is so strong that he doesn't need me. If he did he would say so, wouldn't he?(*John太强了，他根本就不需要我。如果他需要我，他会说的，不是吗？*)凯斯医生对她说："约翰确实需要你，不管他说没说。"但是，路易丝却摇了摇头，闭上了眼睛。

由此，凯斯医生看出来，路易丝不想治好自己的病，因为她觉得自己的丈夫约翰并不需要她和爱她。为了治好病人，凯斯医生只好去找路易丝的丈夫约翰，于是就有了下面的一段对话（请各位读者试着用地道的英文表达出来）：

医生：约翰，你真的爱你的妻子吗？

约翰：如果我不爱她，我就不会娶她。

医生：那你告诉过她吗？

约翰：(满脸的迷惑)我不是尽力把我能给的都给她了吗？除此之外，我还能做什么？

医生：陪她说说话。

约翰：我不善言谈，她知道这个。

医生：告诉她你爱她。

对于上面这个对话，其中的一句"**如果我不爱她，我就不会娶她**"，若是不懂英文的思维规律，只按照汉语的思维表达，将其译成英文就是：

① If I don't love her, I won't marry her.

其实，这是一个彻底的Chinglish，并没有表达出原句的"言外之意"：**我当然爱她，要不我就不会娶她了。**但实际上他们已经结婚了。

这一言外之意，怎样用英文才能正确地表达出来呢？下面再提供几个译文，请读者思考：

② If I didn't love her, I wouldn't have married her.

③ If I hadn't loved her, I wouldn't have married her.

④ If I didn't love her, I wouldn't marry her.

要想正确地说出英文，先得把汉语原句的意思仔细推敲一下。“如果我不爱她”，其实这是“正话反说”，实际上约翰是爱路易丝的，而且是一直都深爱着她，因此，这在英文中就是对“现在事实”表示虚拟。我们知道，从句对现在的虚拟要用一般过去时来表示，所以，这句话用正确的英文就要说成：If I ***didn't love*** her...

“我就不会娶她”，实际上他们已经结婚了，所以，这句话是对“过去事实”表示虚拟。在英文中，主句对过去的虚拟要用 would have done 的谓语动词形式。所以，这句话用正确的英文就要说成：I ***wouldn't have married*** her。

根据以上分析，原句是一个 ZgCx（主过从现）型的混合时间虚拟语气，即主句表示对过去事实的虚拟，从句则是表示对现在事实的虚拟。因此，**“如果我不爱她，我就不会娶她”**这句话的正确英文表达应该是 2）If I ***didn't love*** her, I ***wouldn't have married*** her.

我们再来分析例句 3）：

3 If I ***hadn't loved*** her, I ***wouldn't have married*** her.

妙语点睛 按照前面介绍的英文思维规律，这是一个 Z_gC_g（主过从过）型虚拟语气，即主句和从句都表示对过去的虚拟。所以，例句 3）的含义是：在结婚时约翰是爱她的，要不然当时就不会娶她。言外之意可能是：当时能和她结婚，是因为当时爱她，但现在已经不爱了（所以离婚吧）。

我们再来分析例句 4）：

4 If I ***didn't love*** her, I ***wouldn't marry*** her.

妙语点睛 按照前面介绍的英文思维规律，这里的 would marry 表示两人还没有结婚，说的是将来的情况。所以，例句 4）的英文的真正意思是“如果我不爱她，我将来就不打算和她结婚了”。这显然是以男朋友的身份来说这话的，比如我们把这句话放在这样一个语境中：

A: Do you love your girlfriend?

B: If I didn't love her, I wouldn't marry her.

精品译文 A：你爱你的女朋友吗？

B：如果我不爱她，我将来就不打算和她结婚了。

我们现在给出上面那段对话的英文原文：

Doctor: Do you love your wife, John?

John: I ***wouldn't have married*** her if I ***didn't.***

Doctor: Have you ever told her so?

John: （John's eyes were baffled.）Haven't I given her everything I could? What more can a man do?

Doctor: Talk to her.

John: I am not a talking man. She knows that.

Doctor: Tell her that you love her.

请注意，这里说 I ***wouldn't have married*** her if I ***didn't.*** 是因为上文出现了 love，所以这里 didn't 的后面 love 被省去了。

再比如，我们在日常对话中，往往会这样责怪别人：“如果你真的理解我的话，你当时就不可能说出那种话了”。仔细分析，我们发现这也是一个 Z_gC_x（主过从现）型混合时间的虚拟语气，所以要用英文这样表达：

If you ***knew*** me better, you ***wouldn't have said*** that.

最后需要提醒读者注意的是，Z_gC_x（主过从现）型混合时间虚拟语气不如上一节讨论的 Z_xC_g（主现从过）型虚拟语气常见。

思维总结

同上一节一样，本节讨论的也是“混合时间虚拟语气”，即主句和从句分别对不同的时间进行虚拟。但与上一节不同的是，本节讨论的是 ZgCx（主过从现）型混合时间虚拟语气，即主句对过去虚拟，用 would have done 的形式；从句对现在虚拟，用 did 的形式。这正好与上一节中讨论的主句和从句所表达的虚拟时间相反。

7.7 倒装虚拟

在英文中，虚拟从句可以采用倒装结构。具体来说，当if引导的条件句省去if时，可将should, had或were置于句首，从而构成倒装虚拟句，而意义不变。请看例句：

1 Countless divorced politicians ***would have been elected*** out of office years ago ***had they even thought*** of a divorce, let alone gotten one.

妙语点睛 这里的从句用了倒装结构had they even thought...，相当于说if they had even thought...。主句的谓语是would have been elected，显然是表示对过去情况的虚拟。

精品译文 现如今很多政客都纷纷离婚，这在几年前是不可能的。那时，不要说真的离婚了，哪怕他们有离婚的想法，都一定会被赶下台。

2 For example, they do not compensate for gross social inequality, and thus do not tell how able an underprivileged youngster ***might have been had he grown*** up under more favorable circumstances.

妙语点睛 这是表示对过去的虚拟。这里的倒装结构had he grown相当于if he had grown。

精品译文 例如，它们(指测试)并不能弥补明显的社会不公；因此，它们不能说明一个物质条件差的年轻人，如果在较好的环境中成长的话，会有多大才干。

再看其他例句：

3 ***Should I*** win the lottery, I would buy a car.

= If I should win the lottery, I would buy a car. 如果我能赢得大奖，我就会买一辆车。

4 ***Were he to*** leave today, he would get there by Monday.

= If he were to leave today, he would get there by Monday. 如果他今天出发，他就能在星期一之前到达那里。

5 ***Were he to*** tell us everything, we could try to solve his problem.

= If he were to tell us everything, we could try to solve his problem. 如果他把一切都告诉我们，我们就能想办法解决他的问题。

6 ***Should you*** change your mind, no one would blame you.

= If you should change your mind, no one would blame you. 如果你改变主意的话，没有人会责怪你。

7 ***Had he*** not been promoted, he would never have remained with the company.

= If he had not been promoted, he would never have remained with the company. 如果他没有被提升，他就不会继续留在这家公司了。

8 ***Had such a disaster*** occurred, the damage would have been incalculable.

= If such a disaster had occurred, the damage would have been incalculable. 如果这场灾难发生，损失将难以估量。

也许有读者会问：为什么会出现这样的倒装结构呢？具体原因不详，但笔者个人认为，这或许和疑问句有关系。比如，在英语口语里，我们常常会使用“疑问句＋陈述句”这样的结构，如：

9 Are you ready? Okay we can leave.

意思是说“你准备好了吗？那我们现在就走”。这里的一般疑问句就相当于一个条件从句If you are ready...于是整个句子相当于说“如果你准备好了，那我们现在就走”。类似的虚拟句有：

10 Had I known? I would have come sooner.

相当于汉语说“我知道吗？那我就会早点来了！”这里的言外之意就是，如果我知道，那我就会早点来了。这就相当于一个常规的虚拟句：

If I had known, I would have come sooner.

到这一节为止，英语里常规的虚拟语气形式都已分析讨论完毕。说其是"常规"的，是因为这些虚拟句子都是由主句和 if 引导的从句组成。在接下来的几节内容中，我们将讨论另外一些特殊构造的虚拟语气形式，比如"跳层虚拟句"，它不含 if 引导的从句，而是通过其他方式来表达"非真实的虚拟条件"。

思维训练

Exercise 7.7（Key: P347）
请选择最佳答案填空。

1. Countless divorced politicians would have been elected out of office years ago had they even thought of a divorce, let alone ______ one.
   A. getting　B. to get　C. gotten　D. get
2. ______ to the doctor right away, he might be alive today.
   A. If he went　B. Had he gone　C. Were he gone　D. Should he have gone
3. ______ before we depart the day after tomorrow, we should have a wonderful dinner party.（97-1 CET-4）
   A. Had they arrived　B. Were they arriving　C. Would they arrive　D. Were they to arrive
4. The millions of calculations involved, had they been done by hand, ______ all practical value by the time they finished.
   A. could lose　B. would have lost　C. might lose　D. ought to have lost
5. There is a real possibility that these animals could be frightened, ______ a sudden loud noise.
   A. being there　B. should there be　C. there was　D. there having been

7.8 跳层虚拟

请看下面这个"脑筋急转弯"：

The Taxi Driver Mystery

Rebecca was in a taxi on her way home. Max, the taxi driver, knew she was a well-known chatterbox and didn't want to engage in conversation with her. So he pretended to be deaf and dumb. He pointed to his ears and mouth to indicate to her that he couldn't hear or speak. This ruse seemed to work. The journey was peacefully silent.

When they arrived and Rebecca had got out of the taxi, Max pointed to his meter so she would read how much she owed. Rebecca looked at the meter, read what she owed him, paid him and walked off.

But she almost immediately realized that Max couldn't have been a deaf mute.

How did she know this?

精品译文　租车司机之谜

丽贝卡是一个出了名的"话痨"，特别爱唠叨。有一天她打车回家，出租车司机麦克斯也知道她这个毛病，不想搭理她，于是就假装自己是个聋哑人。他用手指指自己的耳朵和嘴巴，示意她自己听不见，也说不了话。这一招还真管用，一路上两人就默不作声，相安无事。

等丽贝卡到了地方得下车时，麦克斯指指汽车计价器，示意她按照上面显示的数字付钱。她看罢，就按计价器所显示的付完款，准备抽身离去。这时她突然意识到，这个司机不可能是聋哑人。请问，她是怎么知道的？

这个问题的答案很简单，就是：

He ***must have heard*** her initial instructions or he ***would not have known*** where to take her.

精品译文 在她刚上车时告诉他要去哪里，他一定是听清了，否则他不会知道该把她送到哪。

我们看到，这个句子的谓语比较复杂，一个是 must have heard，另一个是 would not have known，即两个都带有情态动词。读者要注意的是，这里的 must have heard 不是虚拟语气，而是 must 表示推测的用法（详见第八章）。**在英文中，"must + have done"的结构是表示对过去的推测**。也就是说，这里谈论的是一个过去的情形。接下来有一个关键词or，表示“否则”，其后面接的就是虚拟语气。此时我们要搞清楚两点：一是虚拟的时间。由or前面的句子我们知道，这里是表示对过去的虚拟；二是句子的谓语是采用虚拟主句的谓语形式还是从句的谓语形式。因为or后面的句子相当于一个虚拟主句，所以其谓语自然要采用虚拟主句的谓语形式。搞清楚这两点，就知道为什么要说would not have known了，因为这正是一个过去虚拟的主句谓语结构形式。

由此可见，这是一类较为特殊的虚拟语气。这类虚拟句一般分为两部分，两部分在语气上截然相反，一部分虚拟，另一部分不虚拟，而用的是陈述语气，用以陈述一个事实。比如上面这个句子就是“陈述句+or+虚拟句”这样的结构。它们二者之间往往有but, or, or else或otherwise来连接。正是因为这种虚拟与不虚拟兼而有之，一部分虚拟，一部分又跳出虚拟的圈子，故笔者称之为“跳层虚拟句”。

7.8.1 陈述句+or+虚拟主句

这里的连接词除了or，还可以有or else和otherwise。需要注意的是，or前面的句子是陈述语气，而后面的句子用的是虚拟语气，而且是虚拟主句。具体的谓语搭配结构是：

1. 主语+一般现在时的谓语形式, or+主语+would do→表示对现在事实的虚拟；
2. 主语+一般过去时的谓语形式, or+主语+would have done→表示对过去事实的虚拟。

请看下面的对话：

1 Jo: You look tired. What have you been doing?

Emily: I've been burning the midnight oil. Been writing my mid-term essay.

Jo: Oh no! I feel sorry for you. I thought you'd finished it already?

Emily: Yes, I did. But my teacher wasn't happy with it. She told me to do it all again!

Jo: No way! Your teacher is mean.

Emily: Well, I ***had*** to do it. ***Otherwise***, she ***would have*** given me a low score.

Jo: I suppose if you look at it like that, then your teacher is not mean at all. After all she gave you a second chance.

Emily: Yeah, and I have to admit that my essay is better now. I really need to do well so that I can get a scholarship.

Jo: Well, good luck then.

Emily: Thanks, and I'm going to sleep like a log tonight!

妙语点睛 这里前面的had to do it表示过去的时间，otherwise后面要接一个过去虚拟的主句形式，所以谓语是would have given。

精品译文 乔： 你看上去很疲惫，最近都在忙什么？

艾米丽： 我最近一直在开夜车，写我的期中论文。

乔： 天啊！我还以为你早就写完了呢！

艾米丽： 我是写完了。可我的老师不满意，让我全部重写一遍。

乔： 不会吧！你们老师也真可恶！

艾米丽： 没办法啊，不然她就会给我很低的分了。

乔： 要是这么说的话，你们老师也还不错。毕竟她又给了你一次机会。

艾米丽： 没错，而且我必须承认，这次我的论文的确有进步了。为了得到奖学金，我必须把它做得好一点。

乔： 那么祝你好运！

艾米丽： 谢谢！我今晚得好好睡一觉！

2 Both the United States and China had reached a point in history where they shared an eagerness to start a new relationship, and where both were prepared to pay an ideological price for it. Mao Tse-tung clearly ***was*** willing to make the ideological sacrifice; ***otherwise*** he ***would not have told*** Edgar Snow in his unique interview that he would "be happy to talk with him (Nixon) either as a tourist or as a President".

妙语点睛 我们看到这里otherwise前面的句子用了过去时was，表示陈述过去的事实，而其后面用了过去虚拟的主句谓语形式would not have told。

精品译文　美国和中国都到了这样的历史时刻：双方都在渴望开始一种新的关系，并都准备为此付出意识形态上的代价。显然，毛泽东也愿意为此付出意识形态上的代价，否则他当初就不会在一次单独会见埃德加·斯诺时告诉斯诺他会"很高兴和他(尼克松)谈谈，不论是以游客的身份还是以总统的身份"。

3 We ***didn't know*** his telephone number, ***otherwise*** we would have telephoned him.

= We ***would have telephoned*** him if we ***had known*** his telephone number.

妙语点睛　这是1995年6月份的四级考试题。这里的didn't是表示陈述过去的事实，而otherwise的后面则是对过去的虚拟，且是虚拟主句的形式，因此要用would have done。

精品译文　我们不知道他的电话号码，要不然我们当时就会给他打电话了。

4 He ***must have had*** an accident, ***or*** he ***would have been*** here then.

妙语点睛　这是1990年1月份的四级考试题。这里or的前面通过用must have had这一形式，来表示对过去的推测，是属于陈述过去，而or的后面则用过去虚拟。

精品译文　他一定是出事故了，要不然早就到了。

5 Mary ***couldn't have received*** my letter; ***otherwise*** she ***would have replied*** before now.

妙语点睛　这里otherwise后面的句子表示对过去的虚拟，相应地，其前面的半个句子就是表示陈述过去，所以要用一般过去时。不过，这里情态动词的过去时态couldn't have done的形式表示对过去的推测，这类似于must表示推测。

精品译文　玛丽不可能收到我的信，要不然她现在已经给我回复了。

7.8.2 虚拟主句+but+陈述句

与or等词不同的是，这里but的前面是虚拟主句，but的后面是陈述句。该句型的使用规律是：

1. 主语 + would do, BUT+ 主语 + 一般现在时的谓语形式→表示对现在事实的虚拟；
2. 主语 + would have done, BUT+ 主语 + 一般过去时的谓语形式→表示对过去事实的虚拟。

当然，句中的would可换成should, might或could。这类跳层虚拟句的关键标志词是but，随着but一转折，句子的语气也由虚拟变为不虚拟，即but将句子一分为二，**but前面部分的句子用虚拟语气，but后面部分的句子用陈述语气。**请看例句：

1 He ***would put on weight, but*** he ***doesn't eat*** much.

= He ***would put*** on weight if he ***ate*** much.

妙语点睛　这里不用didn't，而是doesn't。因为前面的would不是表示过去时态，而是表示对现在事实的虚拟，原句相当于说If he ate much, he would put on weight. 这就解释了为什么but前面的半句话相当于虚拟主句形式了，因为but后面的陈述句相当于一个虚拟从句。

精品译文　他本来是会发胖的，但是他特别注意节食，从来不会多吃。

2 He ***could not have bought*** that limousine, ***but*** he ***inherited*** a big fortune from his father.

= He ***could not have bought*** that limousine if he ***had not inherited*** a big fortune from his father.

妙语点睛　这句话相当于说If he ***had not inherited*** a big fortune from his father, he ***could not have bought*** that limousine. 这就解释了为什么but前面的半句话相当于虚拟主句形式了，因为but后面的陈述句相当于一个虚拟从句。

精品译文　他本来是买不起那辆豪华小汽车的，不过他从他爸爸那里继承了一大笔遗产。

3 A: I thought you were going to call me last night about the train schedule.

B: Sorry. I ***would have***. But Harry and Jack stopped by and stayed past midnight.

妙语点睛　这里的I would have是一个省去了called的虚拟主句，表示对过去事实的虚拟，由but后面的陈述句的谓语stopped可得知。

精品译文　A：我还以为你昨晚要给我打电话说说火车行程的安排呢。

B：抱歉，我本来是想打电话来着，但是哈里和杰克昨晚来我这里了，他俩一直呆到后半夜才走，所以我就没有打。

4 I ***would have gone*** to visit him in the hospital, had it been at all possible, ***but I was*** fully occupied the whole of last week.

妙语点睛 这里 but 前面的句子是过去虚拟，所以采用过去虚拟主句的谓语形式 would have gone。but 后面的句子是陈述过去的事实。

精品译文 如果真的有可能，我本来是想去医院看望他的，但是我上周整个一周都很忙。

5 Some women ***could have made*** a good salary in a job instead of staying home, ***but*** they ***decided*** not to work for the sake of the family.

= Some women ***could have made*** a good salary in a job instead of staying home if they ***hadn't decided*** not to work for the sake of the family.

妙语点睛 这是 2000 年 1 月份的四级考试题。这里 but 后面的句子是陈述过去的事实，but 面的句子是对过去的虚拟，所以采用过去虚拟主句的谓语形式 could have made。

精品译文 有些妇女本来是能够挣得很高的薪水的，但是为了家庭，她们放弃了工作。

有时不用 but 来表示转折，而是用其他副词，比如下句中的 unfortunately：

6 A safety analysis ***would have identified*** the target as a potential danger. ***Unfortunately***, it ***was*** never done.

妙语点睛 这里的 unfortunately 在语义上相当于 but 表示转折，使句子从虚拟转为不虚拟。这里的 was 表示过去，因此前半部分也是表示过去，所以采用过去虚拟主句的谓语形式 would have identified。

精品译文 若是有安全分析，就可以发现这个潜在的隐患，但遗憾的是，并没有做安全分析。

思维总结

共有两类跳层虚拟句，一类是由 or 等引导的，具体的句型结构是：

1. 主语 + 一般现在时谓语形式, or + 主语 + would do→表示对现在事实的虚拟；
2. 主语 + 一般过去时谓语形式, or + 主语 + would have done→表示对过去事实的虚拟。

另一类是由 but 引导的，具体的句型结构是：

1. 主语 + would do, but + 主语 + 一般现在时谓语形式→表示对现在事实的虚拟；
2. 主语 + would have done, but + 主语 + 一般过去时谓语形式→表示对过去事实的虚拟。

注意这两类句型的前后两个分句的语气正好相反。

思维训练

Exercise 7. 8（Key: P348）

请选择最佳答案填空。

1. We didn't know his telephone number, otherwise we ______ him.（CET-4）
   A. would have telephoned B. must have telephoned
   C. would telephone D. had telephoned
2. He must have had an accident, or he ______ then.（CET-4）
   A. would have been here B. should be here
   C. had to be here D. would be there
3. Mary ______ my letter; otherwise she would have replied before now.
   A. has received B. ought to have received C. couldn't have received D. shouldn't have received
4. I would have gone to visit him in the hospital, had it been at all possible, but I ______ fully occupied the whole of last week.
   A. were B. had been C. have been D. was
5. Some women ______ a good salary in a job instead of staying home, but they decided not to work for the sake of the family.（CET-4）
   A. must make B. should have made C. would make D. could have made

6. A safety analysis ______ the target as a potential danger. Unfortunately, it was never done.
A. would identify B. will identify C. would have identified D. will have identified

7.9 名词从句如何使用虚拟

虚拟语气除了用在上述非真实条件从句以外，在特定的名词从句中也需要用虚拟语气。这里所说的“特定的名词从句”，是指这样的名词从句中均要含有特定的标志词，这些标志词可用来表示愿望、建议、命令、请求或意志等语气。而且，与非真实条件虚拟句中的主句和从句的谓语动词的形式完全不同的是，名词从句虚拟句的谓语变化的形式只有一条规律，那就是：名词从句虚拟句无论其主句的谓语动词是何种形式，从句的谓语形式均为 **should+动词原形，其中 should 可以省去**。这里特别要提醒读者注意：**不是用 would，而是用 should**。比如：

1 I *suggest* that we *should go* tomorrow.

2 I *suggested* that we *should go* the next day.

妙语点睛 上面两个例句中的 suggest 即是我们所说的标志词。这里从句中谓语的时态(should go)并没有受主句谓语时态(suggest, suggested)的影响。

精品译文 1. 我建议我们明天走。
2. 我当时建议我们第二天走。

由此可知，要掌握名词从句的虚拟句，最终归结为：记住相应的标志词即可，一旦主句中出现某一个标志词，就要注意其从句谓语须用(should)+do。

下面分别为读者列出了一些常见的标志词。

7.9.1 在下列词的宾语从句中

ask（要求，请求）, advise, beg, command, demand, decide, deserve, desire, determine, insist, move（动议，提议）, order, prefer, propose, require, recommend, request, suggest 和 urge 等。请看例句：

1 His father *urged* that he *study* medicine.

妙语点睛 注意这句话中用 study，不用 studies。

精品译文 他父亲要求他学医学。

2 The Chinese government and people have *demanded* that the U. S. Government *shoulder* all the responsibilities for the incident, *apologize* to the Chinese side and *take* effective measures to prevent the recurrence of such incidents.

精品译文 中国政府和人民要求美国政府对此事件必须承担全部责任，向中国道歉，并采取有效措施防止类似事件再次发生。

3 The instructions ask that we *not take* more than three tablets once.

妙语点睛 从句的谓语 not take 相当于 should not take，这里 should 被省去了。

精品译文 说明书要求每次服用的胶囊不超过三粒。

4 The board deemed it *urgent* that these files *should be printed* right away.

妙语点睛 这里因为有了形容词 urgent，所以从句要用虚拟语气，即用动词 should be printed 的形式。

精品译文 董事会要求把这些文件立刻打印出来。

5 Declaring that he was opposed to using this unusual animal husbandry technique to clone humans, he *ordered* that federal funds *not be used* for such an experiment — although no one had proposed to do so — and asked an independent panel of experts chaired by Prinoeton President Harold Shapiro to report back to the White House in 90 days with recommendations for a national policy on human cloning....NBAC will *ask* that Clinton's 90-day ban

on federal funds for human cloning ***be extended*** indefinitely, and possibly that it ***be made*** law.

妙语点睛 这里因为有了动词 order 和 ask，所以从句要用虚拟语气，即用动词原形。

精品译文 他宣布反对使用这项特别的生物技术来克隆人类，要求不要将联邦基金用于进行这类试验——尽管没有人提议这样做——并请求由 Prinoeton 总统哈罗德·夏皮罗领导一个独立的专家组于 90 天之后向白宫进行汇报，同时对于制定关于克隆人类的国家政策提出建议。……NBAC 将会要求克林顿的关于禁止联邦基金用于人类克隆的“90 天禁令”无限期延长，也许还会将其以法律的形式固定下来。

7.9.2 在 it is+形容词或过去分词或特定的名词+that 的主语从句中

一、形容词有：astonishing, amazing, advisable, appropriate, crucial, desirable, essential, important, imperative, keen, necessary, natural, normal, odd, proper, preferable, strange, sorry, shocked, surprising, urgent, unusual 和 vital 等。这些形容词一般表示个人对事件的反应。请看例句：

1 If we are ever going to protect the atmosphere, it is ***crucial*** that those new plants ***be*** environmentally sound.

妙语点睛 这里因为有了形容词 crucial，所以从句要用虚拟语气，即用动词原形 be。

精品译文 我们若是想保护大气层，那么就应该要求那些新开工的工厂环保。

2 It is ***natural*** that I ***should dwell*** upon his successes rather than upon his failures.

精品译文 我宁愿强调他成功的地方，而不愿突出他的失败之处，这是很自然的。

3 It is ***strange*** that he ***should not come*** here.

妙语点睛 这里的 should 只表明一种意外的语气，可译为“竟然”。

精品译文 他竟然没来，这真是太奇怪了。

4 It’s ***essential*** that people ***be*** psychologically able to resist the impact brought about by the transition from planned economy to market economy.

从心理上来讲，人们能够抗拒由计划经济转变为市场经济这一过程带来的影响，这是很明显的。

5 It is ***important*** that the hotel receptionist ***make*** sure that guests are registered correctly.

宾馆的前台接待人员应该确认客人们正确地登记注册，这是十分重要的。

6 It is quite ***natural*** that the customs of all national minorities ***be respected.***

各个少数民族的风俗习惯都应该得到尊重，这是非常自然的。

二、过去分词有：decided, desired, demanded, ordered, requested, required, recommended 和 suggested 等。请看例句：

7 It is ***requested*** that all members ***be*** present at the meeting. 要求所有的成员都出席这个会议。

8 It is politely ***requested*** by the hotel management that radios ***not be played*** after 11 o’clock at night.

宾馆的管理人员客气地要求，晚上 11 点以后不要听收音机。

三、特定的名词有：advice, decision, desire, demand, suggestion, motion, pray, resolution, wish, preference, proposal, recommendation, requirement, idea 和 order 等。请看例句：

9 It is my ***proposal*** that he ***be sent*** to study further abroad. 我建议，把他送到国外去学习。

7.9.3 在上述名词的表语从句和同位语从句中

1 Jean Wagner’s most enduring contribution to the study of Afro-American poetry is his ***insistence*** that it ***be analyzed*** in religious, as well as worldly, frame of reference.

妙语点睛 这里因为有了名词 insistence，所以从句要用虚拟语气，即用动词原形。

精品译文 让·瓦格纳对美国黑人诗歌的研究最为持久的贡献是，他坚持认为，应把此类诗歌放在宗教与世俗的框架中进行分析。

2 For my own part, it seems that the main ***requirement*** of an international language is that it ***be*** easily learned.
我个人认为，对于一门国际性的语言最主要的要求是，它必须易于学习。

3 The ***motion*** that the meeting ***be*** adjourned was adopted.
要求会议暂停的动议被批准了。

4 Reports indicate that both sides have softened their respective positions for a possible settlement. The government has backed away from ***demands*** that the software giant ***be broken up***, while Microsoft is now more willing to accept restrictions on how it manages its business.
报告显示，双方在可能签订的协议中各自作出了让步。政府已经不再支持拆分软件巨人微软公司的要求，而微软目前则更希望接受对于如何管理其企业的限制。

5 The ***suggestion*** that the mayor ***present*** the prizes was accepted by everyone. 由市长颁奖的建议被所有人接受了。

最后需要说明的是，以上所列的标志词仅是一部分比较常见的，还有很多在此并没有详细地列举出来，读者可以在今后的学习当中不断地积累，自己总结。

思维训练

Exercise 7.9（Key: P348）
请选择最佳答案填空。

1. The instructions ask that we ______ more than three tablets once.
   A. not to take　B. not take　C. won't take　D. wouldn't take
2. It is important that the hotel receptionist ______ that guests are registered correctly.（CET-4）
   A. make sure　B. made sure　C. has made sure　D. must make sure
3. It is quite natural that the customs of all national minorities ______.
   A. would be respected　B. were respected
   C. be respected　D. had been respected
4. It is politely requested by the hotel management that radios ______ after 11 o'clock at night.（CET-4）
   A. were not played　B. not be played　C. not to play　D. did not play
5. The suggestion that the mayor ______ the prizes was accepted by everyone.（CET-4）
   A. would present　B. present　C. presents　D. ought to present
6. The board deemed it urgent that these files ______ right away.
   A. had to be printed　B. should have been printed　C. must be printed　D. should be printed
7. Jean Wagner's most enduring contribution to the study of Afro-American poetry is his insistence that it ______ in religious, as well as worldly, frame of reference.
   A. is to be analyzed　B. has been analyzed
   C. be analyzed　D. should have been analyzed

辨别改错：

8. When(A) Edison died, it was proposed that the American people turned off(B) all power(C) in their homes, streets, and factories for several minutes in honor of(D) this great man.

7.10 各种虚拟句型

在英文中，虚拟语气可以分为非真实条件句（unreal conditionals）和名词从句虚拟句两大类。从7.1至7.8节，我们都是在讨论非真实条件虚拟句，在7.9节中讨论了名词从句的虚拟句。除这两大类虚拟句以外，还有其他一些句型表示的虚拟语气。由于无法归入上述任何一类中，在此将一一单列，分别讨论。

7.10.1 在wish后面的宾语从句中

这是读者非常熟悉的一个虚拟句型，它用来表示说话者难以实现的或与事实违背的愿望，具有较强的感情色彩，可分别表示对现在、过去和将来情景的虚拟。

一、对现在的虚拟

即表示对现状的愿望，从句的谓语动词用过去时。请看例句：

1 I wish I ***were*** a little younger. 我希望我能够年轻一点。

2 I wish I ***could*** travel to the moon (but I can't do that). 我希望我能够登上月球(但实际上我不能)。

3 I wish I ***knew*** his address (but I don't know his address). 我希望我知道他的地址(但实际上我不知道)。

下面这个句子很有意思：

4 Whenever something goes wrong, I just push this little Reset button and restart. I wish my whole life ***were*** like that! 每次电脑出故障的时候，我只要按一下Reset键，电脑就可以重启了。我真希望人生也能如此啊！

事实上，人生不可能如此简单。如果做错事了，想让时光倒流，重新来选择，这是不可能的。

再来看玛丽莲·梦露(Marilyn Monroe)的这句话：

5 Success makes so many people hate you. I wish it ***weren't*** that way. It would be wonderful to enjoy success without seeing envy in the eyes of those around you. 成功会让很多人讨厌你，我真希望不要这样。如果在享受成功时，看不到身旁人嫉妒的眼神，那该有多么美好啊。

二、对过去的虚拟

即对过去发生的事情表示遗憾或后悔，从句的谓语动词用过去完成时(had done)或"would/could+现在完成时"，意指从句的谓语动词所表示的动作发生在主句的谓语所表示的动作之前。请看例句：

6 I wish I ***had been*** there. 我真希望我当时在那。

7 I wish I ***had not attended*** that party. 我真希望我当时没参加那个聚会。

8 I wish I ***could have gone*** with you to the concert last night. 我真希望昨晚能和你一起去听音乐会。

9 A: I wish I ***hadn't hurt*** Mary's feelings like that. You know I never meant to.

B: The great thing about Mary is that she doesn't hold the grudge. By tomorrow she'll have forgotten all about it.

A: 我真希望我没有像那样伤玛丽的感情，你知道我从来不是故意那么做的。

B: 别担心，玛丽最大的优点就是从不记仇，到明天她准会把这事全忘记了。

三、对将来的虚拟

指对将来发生的事情表示祝愿，从句的谓语动词用"would/could+动词原形"，意指从句的谓语动词所表示的动作可能发生在主句的谓语所表示的动作之后。

10 A: It's not fun being around Debbie and Mike these days. All they do is quarrel.

B: I've noticed it, too. I wish they ***would*** keep their squabbles to themselves.

A: 这两天跟黛比和麦克呆在一起真没意思，他们整天就是吵架。

B: 我也注意到了，我真希望他们要吵就私下里吵，而不要当着大家的面吵。

11 I wish he ***could*** explain what he means. 我希望他能解释一下他是什么意思。

12 I wish you ***would*** shut up. 我希望你能闭嘴。

注意，即使将wish改为wished，上述例句谓语的时态仍然不变。

7.10.2 在if only感叹句中

if only表示"但愿"，"要是……就好了"，其用法和wish基本相同，可表示对现在、过去和将来的虚拟，只是比wish具有更强烈的感情色彩。请看例句：

1 If only the rain *would stop.*（对将来的虚拟）但愿雨能停。

2 If only I *were* taller.（对现在的虚拟）我的个子要是能高一点就好了。

3 If only he *had followed* your advice!（对过去的虚拟）他要是听从了你的建议就好了！

另外需要注意的是，可以把 only 放到句中的位置。比如说：

4 If he *had only followed* your advice!

请选择下面这句话的意思：

5 If I'*d only remembered* to lock the door.

A. I would remember if I had locked the door. B. I didn't remember to bring the door key.

C. I forgot there was a rock near the door. D. I wish I had locked the door.

正确答案 D。

精品译文 我要是记得锁门就好了。

妙语点睛 从上面这个译文，我们知道选项 D 正是表达了同样的意思。由此也看到，if only 与 wish 的用法和意义均相同，比如这里 wish 的后面也是接过去完成时来表示过去虚拟的事件。

7.10.3 在 as if/as though 引导的从句中

一、表示与现在事实相反或对现在情况有所怀疑，谓语用过去时

1 I really don't care for the way you're speaking to me. It seems as if you *were* my father.
我真的非常讨厌你和我说话的方式。你听起来就好像是我爸爸。

2 You should live each day as if it *were* the last and use every second to your advantage. That means setting goals, being involved on campus and in your community, working hard, and most importantly, never giving up! 你们应该把每一天都当作是生命中的最后一天来度过，充分利用每一秒钟。这就意味着要设定目标，融入校园和社区生活，勤奋努力，而最重要的是，永不放弃！

二、表示与过去事实相反，谓语用过去完成时

3 We have not seen each other for ten solid years, but when we encountered on the street that day, we were still so affectionate that it seemed as if not a single day *had gone* by. 我们已经有整整 10 年没见了，但是当那天我们在街上遇到时，我们仍然感到无比亲切，就好像时光并未流逝，我们还在 10 年以前那样。

注意，若从句中的情形是根据现在的迹象作出的推测，有可能发生，则用陈述语气。请看例句：

4 It is becoming dark. It looks as if it's *going to* rain. 天变黑了，似乎就要下雨。

5 It seems as if he *has been* to America. 他好像去过美国。

7.10.4 在 it is (high) time (that) 从句中

该句型表示“该是做什么事的时候了”，含有“晚了一点”的意思，从句中用过去时。请看例句：

1 Don't dawdle away your youth any more. It is time you *thought* about your future. 不要再浪费青春了，你该考虑自己的将来了。

2 It seems to be high time that this argument *were* put to an end. 现在似乎是时候结束争吵了。

3 "You are very selfish. It's high time you *realized* that you are not the most important person in the world," Edgar said to his boss angrily. 埃德加生气地对他老板说：“你太自私了。你早就应该知道，你绝对不是这个世界上最重要的人。”

请在下列对话中体会这种“晚了一点”的含义：

4 Man: The school had the football field redone over the summer.

Woman: ***It's about time.***

Question: What does the woman imply?

A. Summer is a good time for repairs. B. The field had been in poor shape.

C. It's too hot to play football in the summer. D. The work on the football field is almost finished.

正确答案 B。

妙语点睛 这里的女士既然说"早就该修了",其言外之意就是说这个足球场在修缮以前一直不是很好,这正是选项B的意思,所以B正确。

精品译文 男:学校在暑假期间把足球场重新翻修了一下。

女:早就该修了。

5 Man: Let's get this desk in order.

Woman: Yes, it's about time we ***cleared*** it off.

Question: What can be inferred about the desk?

A. It isn't placed right. B. There isn't enough time to clear it off.

C. A new desk has been ordered to replace it. D. It has needed reorganizing for quite a while.

正确答案 D。

妙语点睛 这里女士既然说"早该整理了",其言外之意就是说这个桌子一直很乱,比如桌上摆满了东西,早就需要整理了,这正是选项D的意思,所以D正确。

精品译文 男:我们把这张桌子整理一下吧。

女:是的,我们早该整理了。

7.10.5 在 would rather, would (just) as soon, would sooner, would prefer 等从句中

本节主要讨论 would rather 的各种句型。首先,would rather 后面可以接从句和接动词原形;其次,would rathe 表示将来、现在或过去时的谓语动词的不同形式。

一、would rather do sth.

would rather 的后面接动词原形,可以表示将来或现在的事件,意指"主语宁愿自己做某事"。这是 would rather 最常见的用法。请看例句:

1 I would rather ***go*** there tomorrow. 我想明天去那里。

如果要和另外一件事情来比较,这时要用 than 来引出另外的事情。比如:

2 He would rather stay at home ***than go*** to the cinema tonight. 他今晚就想在家里呆着,而不想去看电影。

注意,对该句型的否定,要在动词的前面加 not,而不是在 would 的后面加 not。例如:

3 1) He would rather ***not stay*** at home tonight. 他今晚不想在家呆着。

2) He would ***not*** rather ***stay*** at home tonight. *(错误)

二、would rather have done sth.

这是 would rather 后面接动词完成式的用法,表示过去的事件,意指"主语宁愿自己过去做了某事,但实际上没有做",因此,具有过去虚拟的意味,如同过去虚拟条件主句的谓语形式。请看例句:

4 I took Sally to the cinema last night, but I ***would rather have been*** there alone.

妙语点睛 这里的 would rather have been 表示对过去的虚拟,意思是"还不如自己一个人去",但实际上不是一个人去的。

精品译文 我昨晚带萨丽看电影去了,可是我还不如自己一个人去呢(真不该带她去)。

5 I'm eager to acquire knowledge. For my ninth birthday, my father gave me a set of the *World Book Encyclopedia.* Although I ***would rather have received*** a set of transformers, as I look back I realize that my dad made the right decision.

妙语点睛 这里的 would rather have received (a set of transformers) 表示对过去的虚拟，意思是"本来希望自己收到(一套变形金刚)"，但实际上没有收到。

精品译文 我非常渴望学习知识。记得在我九岁生日的时候，我爸爸送给了我一套《世界百科全书》。当时我还想，他倒不如送我一套变形金刚更好。但是现在回想起来，我还是觉得爸爸当时的决定是对的。

6 I ***would rather have had*** one breath of her hair, one kiss of her mouth, one touch of her hand than an eternity without it.

妙语点睛 这句话来自美国电影《天使之城》(The City of Angels)，这是由尼古拉斯·凯奇(Nicholas Cage)主演的天使说的。

精品译文 如果可以呼吸到她散发在空气中的发香、轻吻她的双唇、抚摸她的双手，那么我宁愿放弃永生。

三、would rather sb. did

这是 would rather 后面接从句的用法，意指"主语宁愿让另一个人做某事"。这里从句的谓语用一般过去式，但表示的是现在或将来的事件，如同现在虚拟条件从句的谓语形式。请看例句：

7 Don't come tomorrow. I'd rather you ***came*** next weekend.

妙语点睛 我们看到，这里的时间状语 next weekend 显然是表示一个将来的时间，但句子的谓语却用了 came 这样的一般过去式，而不用 will come，甚至也不用 would come。

精品译文 明天就别来了，我希望你下周末过来。

8 She says she'd rather he ***left*** tomorrow instead of today.

妙语点睛 同样道理，尽管有将来的时间状语 tomorrow，但句子的谓语却用了 left 这样的一般过去式，而不用 will leave，甚至也不用 would leave。

精品译文 她说她希望他明天走，而不是今天。

四、would rather sb. had done

这是 would rather 后面接从句的用法，意指"主语宁愿别人过去做了某事，但实际上没有做"。这里从句的谓语用过去完成时表示过去的事件，如同过去虚拟条件从句的谓语形式。请看例句：

9 For my ninth birthday, my father gave me a set of the *World Book Encyclopedia*. But I ***would rather he had given me*** a set of transformers. 在我九岁生日的时候，我爸爸送给了我一套《世界百科全书》，可是我倒希望他能送我一套变形金刚更好。

其他的结构，如 would (just) as soon, would sooner 和 would prefer 在接从句时，完全如同 would rather 的虚拟用法，在此不再赘述。请看例句：

10 ***I'd just as soon*** you ***didn't speak*** rudely to her. 我希望你不要那么粗鲁地对她说话。

11 ***I'd as soon*** you ***hadn't spoken*** rudely to her. 我希望你当时没有那么粗鲁地对她说话。

最后，我们再来看一个 might just as well 接完成时的虚拟表达：

12 Our holidays were ruined by the weather — we ***might just as well have stayed*** at home.

妙语点睛 这完全类似于 would rather have done 的意义和用法，都表示对过去的虚拟，意思是"还不如呆在家里"，但实际上没有这么做，而是出去度假了，但天气不好，玩得并不开心。

精品译文 因为天气的原因，我们的假期全给毁了。我们还不如就在家里呆着哪也不去呢！

思维训练

Exercise 7. 10 (Key: P348)

请选择最佳答案填空。

1. I wish I ______ with you to the concert last night.

A. could have gone B. went C. could go D. have gone

2. Sometimes I wish I ______ in a different time and a different place. (CET-4)

A. be living B. were living C. would live D. would have lived

3. Look at the terrible situation I am in! If only I ______ your advice.（CET-4）
A. follow B. had followed C. would follow D. have followed
4. It seems to be high time that this argument ______ put to an end.
A. must be B. is C. were D. should be
5. "You are very selfish. It's high time you ______ that you are not the most important person in the world," Edgar said to his boss angrily.（CET-4）
A. realized B. have realized C. realize D. should realize
6. You don't have to be in such a hurry. I would rather you ______ on business first.（CET-4）
A. would go B. will go C. went D. have gone
7. Wouldn't you rather your child ______ to bed early?（CET-4）
A. go B. went C. would go D. goes

写给读者的话

一、本章学习思路

虚拟语气是英语谓语动词的重要变化形式之一，也是比较难以理解和掌握的一大类语法项目，原因是汉语的思维表达中天然缺失虚拟语气。

另一方面，虚拟语气其实也是情态动词的一种用法，所以读者应该把本章内容和下一章有关情态动词的内容结合起来学习，这样就可以更加全面而深入地理解情态动词的用法。

本章内容相当于是情态动词的虚拟用法。该用法的内容包括三部分：

第一，非真实条件虚拟句（unreal conditionals），这包括从7.1至7.8节的所有内容，这是虚拟语气的重点内容，占据虚拟语气内容的90%。

第二，名词从句虚拟句，就是在7.9节中讨论的内容。

第三，除了上述这两大类虚拟句外，还有其他一些用于虚拟的句型结构，就是在7.10节中讨论的内容。

二、本章重点及难点

在上述三大类虚拟的内容中，重点要掌握非真实条件句。读者首先要熟练掌握三种基本的虚拟结构：7.2节中讨论的将来虚拟（Z_jC_j）、7.3节中讨论的现在虚拟（Z_xC_x）以及7.4节中讨论的过去虚拟（Z_gC_g）。然后在此基础上，熟练辨别和把握7.5节中讨论的混合虚拟(一)：主句现在＋从句过去(Z_xC_g)、7.7节中讨论的倒装虚拟和7.8节中讨论的跳层虚拟句。

三、本章学习时间安排

本章的内容多而且也是比较难的，因此读者需要下功夫、花时间学好。建议读者可以花3周的时间来研读本章所讲解的所有内容，边读边思考、消化和总结，并做相应的练习。读者需要反复阅读和理解本章的内容，至少四遍以上，要真正做到融会贯通，全面理解和掌握。但是，若要真正达到我们前面提到的使用虚拟语气的"口语阶段"，则需要多多实践，方能做到运用自如，从而真正地把虚拟语气融入成为自己的思维表达中，成为自己思维的一部分。

综合练习（Key: P349）

1. George would certainly have attended the proceedings ______.
A. had he not had a flat tire B. had the tire no flattened itself
C. if the flat tire hadn't happened D. if he didn't get a flat tire
2. Nelson ______ the fight, with a little more training and a better manager.
A. would win B. had won C. could have won D. won
3. If I ______ my own clothes, I ______ a lot of money.
A. had made/would save B. could make/would save C. can make/would save D. could make/will save

4. Thank goodness, it's all over. I ______ it if I ______ it was going to take me so long.
A. would never have done/had known　B. would never do/knew
C. would never have done/knew　D. would never do/had known
5. He was fully occupied yesterday, otherwise he ______ to the sales conference.
A. would come　B. would have come　C. came　D. had come
6. Without computers, the world ______ what it is today.
A. would be　B. would not be　C. won't be　D. hadn't been
7. ______ I realized the consequences, I would never have contemplated getting involved.
A. If　B. Had　C. When　D. Unless
8. He had to drive fast yesterday; otherwise he ______ his plane.
A. had missed　B. would be missing　C. would have missed　D. would miss
9. ______ the sense of someone watching them, Ralph would have shouted at his wife.
A. Despite　B. Except　C. But for　D. Except for
10. Any man in his position ______ like that.
A. has done　B. would have done　C. does　D. would be done
11. We didn't know his address; otherwise we ______ an invitation to him.
A. would have sent　B. must have sent　C. had sent　D. would send
12. Sometimes I have thought it would be an excellent rule to live each day as if we ______ tomorrow.
A. should die　B. are to die　C. were dying　D. must die
13. The boy would have died, ______ on him without delay.
A. if the doctor didn't operate　B. if the doctor wouldn't operate
C. would the doctor not operate　D. had the doctor not operated
14. If Greek civilization ______ all of Europe, English wouldn't contain so many Greek words.
A. hadn't influenced　B. doesn't influence　C. hasn't influenced　D. didn't influence
15. If television ______ a thousand years ago, would nations be significantly more homogeneous than they are now?
A. were invented　B. was invented　C. has been invented　D. had been invented
16. At the conference, it has been decided that she ______ an opportunity to go abroad as a sales representative.
A. is going to have　B. have　C. will have　D. has
17. It is extremely urgent that they ______ from the mountain before dark.
A. must rescue　B. be rescued　C. will be rescued　D. shall be rescued
18. The women's magazines, deploring the statistics, urged that courses on marriage, and marriage counselors, ______ in the high schools.
A. installed　B. be installed　C. have been installed　D. installing
19. I intend to move that our committee ______ Tom as chairman, and I hope that you will second my motion.
A. will appoint　B. appoint　C. appoints　D. has appointed
20. The dean approved of the requirement that every student ______ on social investigation after summer vacation.
A. reports　B. report　C. reported　D. reporting
21. I second Mr. Wang's motion that a special committee ______ to examine the problem.
A. be established　B. established　C. was to establish　D. was established
22. "I wish you ______ the play last night."
"It's a shame that I ______."
A. had attended / didn't　B. attended / didn't　C. had attended / hadn't　D. could attend / haven't
23. The picture exhibition bored me to death. I wish I ______ to it.
A. have not gone　B. had not gone　C. didn't go　D. should not have gone
24. It was a lovely day yesterday. I ______ I had been at the seaside then.
A. think　B. wish　C. hope　D. expect
25. It's about time I ______ something about home-decorating.
A. learn　B. learned　C. have learned　D. should learn

26. If only we ______ a phone! I'm tired of queuing outside the public phone box.
A. had B. had had C. would have D. have had

27. The manager would rather his daughter ______ in the same office.
A. had not worked B. not no work C. does not work D. did not work

28. He would rather ______ than worked last night.
A. have slept B. has slept C. sleep D. slept

29. Frankly, I'd rather you ______ anything about it for the time being as it has not yet been decided.
A. did B. didn't do C. didn't D. don't

30. She would rather that you ______ last night.
A. not arrive B. do not arrive C. had not arrived D. did not arrive

31. In the United States a law requires that a warning label ______ on cigarette packages.
A. ought to be printed B. needs to be printed C. must be printed D. should be printed

32. It is high time that the third world countries ______ a more active part in economic affairs of the world.
A. play B. were playing C. played D. had played

33. If the United States had built more homes for people in 1995, the housing problems now in some parts of this country ______ so serious.
A. wouldn't be B. will not have been C. wouldn't have been D. would have not been

34. At the last conference, the motion that the chairman of the International Olympic Games ______ was defeated.
A. would be dismissed B. be dismissed C. were dismissed D. was dismissed

35. If the climate had been more favorable, the crops ______ still better.
A. would have grown B. would be growing C. would be grown D. will grow

36. These facts suggested that women ______ in opportunity for physical exercise by cultural taboos.
A. should been limited B. had been limited C. be limited D. have been limited

37. I would very much like to have gone to see the movie, but I ______ a ticket.
A. shall not have B. haven't had C. don't have D. didn't have

38. The result has turned still worse than it ______
A. would otherwise have been B. would be otherwise
C. has otherwise been D. had otherwise been

39. The stubborn young man did not follow the advice that he ______ on his behavior since he refused to believe he had done anything wrong.
A. reflect B. had reflected C. would reflect D. must reflect

40. ______ for your help, we'd never have been able to get over the difficulties.
A. Had it not been B. Had it not C. If it were not D. If we had not been

41. The storm delayed us. ______ the storm we would have been in time.
A. For B. Were it not for C. Had it not been for D. But

42. The party ______ at my house, but the central heating broke down, and we had to have it at John's place.
A. would be B. would have been C. was to be D. were

43. We are all for your proposal that the discussion ______.
A. be put off B. was put off C. should put off D. is to put off

44. He turned down her proposal that she ______ at the conference.
A. should offer B. offer C. offered D. offering

45. What do you think of Tom's proposal that ______ put on the play at tonight's English evening?
A. we will not B. we not C. we hadn't D. we wouldn't

46. The school board listened quickly as John read the demands that his followers ______ for.
A. be demonstrating B. demonstrate C. had been demonstrating D. have demonstrated

47. It was suggested at the meeting that effective measures ______ to solve the problem.
A. be taken B. were taken C. must be taken D. take

48. It is desirable that the doctor ______ there at the moment.
A. be B. would be C. will be D. must be
49. I propose that a woman ______ deputy to the district congress.
A. would be nominated B. was nominated C. is nominated D. be nominated
50. Her mother insists that she ______ skating with her brother.
A. went B. go C. goes D. will go
51. I move that he ______ discharged for his serious mistake.
A. be to be B. was to be C. is to be D. would be
52. These national parks are very important for preserving many animals, who would ______ run the risk of becoming extinct.
A. instead B. nevertheless C. therefore D. otherwise
53. We went to work on foot yesterday, though we ______ by bus.
A. could have gone B. must have gone C. ought to have gone D. had better to
54. One of the requirements for a fire is that the material ______ to its burning temperature.
A. is heated B. will be heated C. be heated D. would be heated
55. It is advisable that a general announcement ______ to the teaching staff.
A. will be made B. should make C. be made D. have been made
56. Abraham Lincoln insisted that ______ not just on mere opinion but on moral purpose.
A. to base democracy B. for democracy to be based
C. democracy be based D. whenever democracy is based
57. Mr. Smith didn't phone me last night, but he ______.
A. might have to B. would do C. had to D. should have
58. It is essential that these application forms ______ back as early as possible.
A. must be sent B. will be sent C. are sent D. be sent
59. I'd rather you ______ make any comment on the issue for the time being.
A. don't B. wouldn't C. didn't D. shouldn't
60. Had he worked harder, he ______ the exams.
A. must have got through B. would have got through C. would get through D. could get through
61. I don't think it advisable that Tim ______ to the job since he has no experience.
A. is assigned B. will be assigned C. be assigned D. has been assigned
62. If only the committee ______ the regulations and put them into effect as soon as possible.
A. approve B. will approve C. can approve D. would approve
63. It is vital that enough money ______ to fund the project.
A. be collected B. is collected C. must be collected D. can be collected
64. You ______ her in her office last Friday; she's been out of town for two weeks.
A. needn't have seen B. must have seen C. might have seen D. can't have seen
65. Jean doesn't want to work right away because she thinks that if she ______ a job she probably wouldn't be able to see her friends very often.
A. has to get B. were to get C. had D. could have got
66. The local peasants gave the soldiers clothes and food, without which they ______ of hunger and cold.
A. would dead B. will die C. would be dead D. would have died
67. It is recommended that the project ______ until all the preparations have been made.
A. is not started B. will not be started C. not be started D. is not to be started
68. I wish I ______ longer this morning, but I had to get up and come to class.
A. could have slept B. slept C. might sleep D. have slept
69. We desire that the tour leader ______ us immediately of any change in plans.
A. inform B. informs C. informed D. had informed

70. He suggested ______ to tomorrow's exhibition together.
A. us to go B. we went C. we shall go D. we go

71. John's score on the test is the highest in the class; he ______ hard last weekend.
A. should have studied B. must have studied C. would have studied D. should study

72. The room is in a terrible mess; it ______ cleaned.
A. can't have been B. shouldn't have been C. mustn't have been D. wouldn't have been

73. Sally can't have been in Paris, or ______
A. I met B. I'd met C. I'll meet him D. I'd have met

74. Research findings show we spend about two hours dreaming every night, no matter what we ______ during the day.
A. should have done B. would have done C. may have done D. must have done

75. To be frank, I'd rather you ______ in the case.
A. not to be involved B. not involved C. will no be involved D. were not involved

76. It seems to be high time that this argument ______ put to an end.
A. must be B. is C. were D. should be

77. The dentist said that my tooth went worse and I ______ it pulled out.
A. should have had B. might have had C. needn't have had D. mustn't have had

78. The business is risky. But ______, we would be rich.
A. should we succeed B. would we succeed C. might we succeed D. could we succeed

79. If we hadn't been interrupted the day before yesterday, we ______ the job.
A. would do B. would not have done C. had done D. would have done

80. It is decided that no smoking ______ in public places from now on.
A. be allowed B. is allowed C. will be allowed D. should have been allowed

81. The Reform club proposed that wages ______.
A. would be raised B. were raised C. would have been raised D. be raised

82. Through worldly loss he came to an insight into spiritual truth to which he might ______ have been a stranger.
A. no more B. no less C. neither D. otherwise

83. ______ yesterday, I would have asked him not to do that.
A. Had he come B. Provided he came C. If he came D. Has he come

84. It is highly necessary that the rocket ______ until all the preparations have been made.
A. is not to be launched B. not be launched C. were not launched D. is not to be launched

85. I had intended to go to the airport yesterday, in which case I ______ the guests.
A. might meet B. would meet C. might have met D. had met

86. It is generally thought to be necessary to a college student that he ______ at least on foreign language.
A. know B. knows C. knew D. would know

辨别改错:

87. I'd rather you would go (A) by train, because I can't bear (B) the idea of your being (C) in an airplane in such (D) bad weather.

88. Your math instructor would have been (A) happy to give you a makeup examination had you gone (B) and explained (C) that your parents had been (D) ill at the time.

89. I don't think it (A) advisable that he will be assigned (B) to the job since he has no (C) experience whatsoever (D).

90. The law I am referring to requires (A) that everyone (B) who owns (C) a car has (D) accident insurance.

Chapter 8

第八章 情态动词

本章将详细讨论英文的情态动词(modal auxiliary verbs，简称 modals)。第七章讨论了虚拟语气的意义和用法，这其实就是情态动词用法的一部分。确切来说，就是 would, could, might 和 should 这四个情态动词用于表示虚拟的意义和用法。这四个情态动词还有其他不是表示虚拟语气的用法，本章将详细讨论。

情态动词的难点在于其微妙变化的各种情态意义，以及各个不同的情态动词之间的相互关系，这些都是本章中详细讨论的问题。本章内容安排如下：

8.1 引言：多情多义的情态动词

8.1.1 情态动词的"全家福"

首先，我们还是简单地了解一下英文情态动词的全貌。下面给出一个它的"全家福"：

情态动词		情态动词短语
现在式	过去式	
can	could	be able to
may	might	be allowed to
must	——	have (got) to
shall	should	be supposed to/ought to
will	would	be going to

从以上表格看到：

1. 最基本的情态动词有五个：can, may, must, shall 和 will(见第一栏)；

2. 除了 must 以外，其他四个情态动词都有对应的一般过去式，分别是：could, might, should 和 would(见第二栏)；

3. 这五个情态动词都有对应的情态动词短语，分别是：be able to, be allowed to, have (got) to, be supposed to/ought to 和 be going to(见第三栏)。

需要注意的是，四个过去形式的情态动词 could, might, would 和 should 只是在形式上是 can, may, will 和 shall 的过去式，而在意义上并不是完全对应于 can, may, will 和 shall。具体来说，一方面，现在式和过去式这两类情态动词的意义并不完全对等。例如，can 和 could 的意义并不完全等同，它们既有共同的用法，如表示"能力"，也有各自不同的用法。另一方面，这四个过去形式的情态动词并不一定表示过去的时间(实际上通常都不是)。关于它们具体的意义和用法，将在以后各节中详细讨论。

思维训练

Exercise 8.1.1 (Key: P350)

请找出下列短文中的情态动词及情态动词短语，并把短文翻译成中文。

Would you stop complaining about things? We're supposed to do our best and we should be able to finish this work before the boss has to start screaming at us again. If you could just concentrate on getting finished, we might be allowed to leave early this afternoon. You know he's not going to let us leave early if we can't get the work done.

8.1.2 情态动词的意义

见识了情态动词的"长相"后，下面再简单地了解一下它们都有什么样的"脾气"和"秉性"——即它们有何意义。

简言之，情态动词(modals)用在实义动词(main verb)的前面，以增添某种意思。下面请比较下列句子用与不用情态动词在意义上的差别：

1 1) John isn't in class. He ***is*** sick.

2) John isn't in class. He ***must be*** sick.

妙语点睛 在例句1)中，没有使用情态动词，只用了一般现在时态的is，表达的是一个客观事实。在例句2)中，用了情态动词must，则是表示说话人的主观猜测。我们看到，因为有了must，使得例句2)比例句1)更带有主观色彩，意思也不同了。

精品译文 1)约翰今天没上课，他病了。

2)约翰今天没上课，他一定是病了。

我们再看下列例句：

2 I ***must*** go to school today.

妙语点睛 比较上面的例句2)和本句，我们发现两句中相同的情态动词must的意思是不一样的：例句2)中的must表示推测，而本句中的must没有推测的意思，而是表示"必须"。

精品译文 今天我一定得上学去。

有时，就是对于同一个句子来说，可能会因为语境不同，其中的情态动词会有不同的理解。比如：

3 He ***must*** drink a lot of milk.

妙语点睛 这句话该如何理解呢？没有上下文的语境，我们很难判断。比如，这句话如果是出自一个医生之口，我们显然就会把它理解成是医生对病人提的一个忠告或建议，这时我们就把这句话理解为"他得多喝牛奶"。言外之意，就是说明喝牛奶对健康是有好处的。因此，此时的must是"必须"之意。我们再想象这句话可能出现的另一个场景，比如，有一天我们在商店里看到一个人买了很多牛奶，这时我们就可以推断说He must drink a lot of milk. 显然这时要说的意思是"他准是爱喝很多牛奶"。因此，此时的must表示的是推测。

精品译文 译文一：他得多喝牛奶。

译文二：他准是爱喝很多牛奶。

从以上分析可知，情态动词的意思不止一个。事实上，每个情态动词都有很多的意思，而意思不同就有不同的用法。尽管如此，经过多年来对英语语言资料的收集、观察、分析和总结，笔者发现情态动词的含义大致可以分为以下两大类：

一类是表示"逻辑可能性"，笔者称之为**推测用法**，即表示人们对于某件事情发生的可能性大小所作的判断。比如上述例句1)中的must即是推测用法。几乎每个情态动词都有推测用法，这是情态动词的共性。

另一类是各个情态动词有各自基本的意思，比如，can意为"能够"，must意为"必须"(如在上述例句2中的意思)，should意为"应该"等等。情态动词的这层意思是读者较为熟悉的，因为这些情态动词的意思往往就是我们词典中的第一个意思。这是情态动词的"个性"意义和用法，我们称之为情态动词的**基本用法**。这一用法尤其适用于社会交往中。当涉及与别人相关的某事时，我们往往就用情态动词，来表示出不同程度的文明礼貌。比如，请别人"允许"自己做某事或准许别人做某事；"规劝"别人做某事或接受别人的劝告；对别人提出"请求"和"建议"，或答应别人的请求和提议等等。情态动词的这一用法相当灵活，因为与交际双方的社会关系密切相关。

我们下面进一步通过举例来比较说明这两类情态意义的根本差别。比如上面讨论的例句1，即关于"约翰生病"的例子：

4 1) John isn't in class. He ***is*** sick.

2) John isn't in class. He ***must be*** sick.

3) John isn't in class. He ***may be*** sick.

妙语点睛 这里，例句1)没有使用情态动词，只用了一般现在时态的is，这表明说话人只是在陈述一个客观事实，即"约翰生病了"。这句话没有表明说话人的态度(the speaker's attitude)。而例句2)和3)这两句使用了情态动词，则表明了说话人的态度。例句2)用的是must，意为"一定是"，"准是"，这表明了说话人对于"约翰生病了"这件事是很有把握和信心的一个推断(deduction)。例句3)用的是may，意为"可能是"，"或许是"，这表明了说话人对于"约翰生病了"这件事是比较没有把握和信心的一个推断。说话人推断"约翰生病了"，只是为他今天没有来上课，这提供了一种可能的解释或原因，也许还有其他很多原因导致他今天没有来上课。所以，我们看到，这里说话人可以对"约翰生病了"这件事从三个不同的角度(perspective)来表达：

1)简单地陈述事实(is)；

2）很有把握的推断(must be)；
3）比较没有把握的推断(may be)。

现在自然有这么一个问题：是什么决定了说话人可以采用不同的角度来表达“约翰生病了”？答案自然是：根据说话人自己掌握的信息情况。比如对于例句1)，可能是说话人刚刚从医院看望约翰之后回来，这时别人问他约翰今天为什么没有来上课，他自然就会说He is sick. 对于例句2)，说话人并不是100%地肯定约翰生病了，但是可能是根据约翰一贯的表现，他从来都不缺课，这次是唯一一次没来上课，所以说话人就很自信地推断，除非是约翰生病了，否则他不会不来上课的。对于例句3)，可能是说话人知道约翰常常不来上课，缺课对于约翰来说是常有的事，所以这次没有来上课，可能有多种原因，他生病了可能只是其中一个原因（John isn't in class today. He could be at home, or at the library, or he may be sick — nobody knows.）因此，说话人根据这样一些信息情况，他比较没有把握地推断约翰可能是生病了。

精品译文 1）约翰今天没上课，他病了。
2）约翰今天没上课，他一定是病了。
3）约翰今天没上课，他可能是病了。

总之，对于情态动词的推测用法，说话人是基于一定的信息情况来对某个事件发生的可能性进行推断。说话人不同的肯定程度(different degrees of certainty)是以说话人所掌握的不同信息情况为基础的。所以，情态动词的推测用法是以信息为基础的(The speaker's deduction is based on what is known, or ***knowledge-based.***)。

另一方面，对于情态动词的基本用法，我们接着上面的例句3，即关于“喝牛奶”的例子来讨论。比如：

5 1）You ***must drink*** some milk.
2）You ***may drink*** some milk.

妙语点睛 我们可以想象这样一个场景：一对父母要求自己的孩子多喝牛奶，这时他们就会说“你必须多喝牛奶”，即例句1)的意思。这里的must表达一个孩子应尽的“义务(obligation)”。而如果是孩子向他们要东西喝，这时他们就可以回答说“你可以喝点牛奶”，即例句2)的意思。这里的may表达一个“许可(permission)”。这里，说话人能用must(必须)或may(允许)这样的词，是基于他自己的社会角色——父母，作为父母他可以控制孩子的行为(the general social authority of parents in determining their child's behavior)。对于情态动词的这些基本用法，或者说社交功能的用法，交际双方都会根据彼此之间确定的社会关系（some established social relationship)，比如父母—孩子、老板—雇员、陌生人之间等等，来选择使用情态动词。所以，情态动词的基本用法是基于特定的社会关系的，或者说是由社会关系决定的（The root meaning of modals is based on what is socially determined or ***socially-based.***)，而不是基于说话人对某一事实情况的认知(not based on the speaker's knowledge of facts)。

精品译文 1）你必须多喝牛奶。
2）你可以喝点牛奶。

不论是推测用法(即***knowledge-based***，以信息为基础的)，还是基本用法（即***socially-based***，以社会关系为基础的)，英文的情态动词都表达了说话人的态度或角度——对所描述的情景或事件的态度。所以，情态即说话人的心态，反映了说话人微妙的心态变化。native speakers就是通过运用各种功能强大的情态动词，极其微妙的方式来“言传心声”的。对于我们这些学英语的“老外”来说，如果不是深谙情态动词的丰富意义和用法，那么在用英语交流时，就不明白该如何表达自己的态度或心态，这就是一个大问题。所以，情态动词甚至比我们前面讨论过的众多时态还要变化多端，纷繁复杂。因此，情态动词也是更让中国学生“摸不着头脑”的一种英语谓语的变化形式。

最后需要说明的是，第七章中讨论的虚拟语气其实就是情态动词could, might, would和should的用法的一部分，这一虚拟用法其实是属于推测用法中的一个重要分支。因此，如果把虚拟用法从推测用法中独立出来，那么情态动词就有三大类用法：**推测用法、基本用法和虚拟用法**。

在具体地分类阐述情态动词各个不同的意义和用法之前，脑子里有一个关于情态动词的逻辑框架是非常重要的。既然其虚拟用法已经讨论过了，所以本章不再系统地讨论情态动词的虚拟用法了，而只是在必要时简单提及，以便于与其他用法作一比较。

8.1.3 情态动词的结构搭配与意义关系

在8.1.1小节中了解到，情态动词有对应的情态动词短语；在8.1.2小节中初步了解到，情态动词有推测用法和基本用法这两种区分。本节将讨论情态动词后面所接的动词的形式与情态意义之间的关系，这与8.1.1小节和8.1.2小节的内容都密切相关。

在笔者长期的观察和研究中，笔者发现情态动词的结构搭配与意义之间的关系有下列三点：

一、情态动词+一般式

这结构就是在情态动词后面接一个动词原形。上面讨论的所有例句都属于这一结构搭配，比如：

6 He ***must*** drink a lot of milk.

译文一：他得多喝牛奶。

译文二：他准是爱喝很多牛奶。

在"情态动词＋一般式"这个结构搭配中，情态动词可以是推测意义，也可以有基本含义。比如这里的must可以表示推测含义"准是"，也可以表示基本含义"必须"。

二、情态动词+完成式/进行式/完成进行式

在这一结构搭配中，完成式如may ***have done***；进行式如should ***be doing***；完成进行式如must ***have been doing***。请看例句：

7 I think I ***may have annoyed*** Mary. 我想我可能是惹玛丽生气了。

8 He ***should*** still ***be working*** right now. 他现在应该还在工作。

9 ***Could*** he ***be waiting*** for us at the station? 他会不会正在车站等我们呢？

10 You look very tired. You ***must have been working*** all day. 你看起来很累，你准是忙了一整天了。

从以上的例句我们发现，在情态动词接完成式、进行式或完成进行式的时候，情态动词都是具有推测意义，而没有各自的基本意义。比如上面例句中的may, should, could和must都是用于推测意义。具体来说，这里的may不是"许可"的意思，而是表示推测的"可能"；should不是表示义务的"应该"的意思，而是表示推测的"应该"；could不是表示"能力"，也不是表示过去，而是表示对现在的推测；must不是表示"必须"，而是表示推测的"准是"。

也许有读者怀疑：这个发现可以推而广之吗？回答是肯定的。也就是说当情态动词的后面接了完成式、进行式或完成进行式时，它往往只是表示推测的含义。换句话说，用于基本意义的情态动词，其后面一般只接动词的一般式，而不接完成式、进行式或完成进行式。对此，读者今后不妨自己观察、检验和总结。

另外需要说明的是，四个过去形式的情态动词would, could, might和should接完成式(have done)可以表示对过去的虚拟，此时情态动词不是推测的意义，而是虚拟含义。不过，将来虚拟是表达某件事发生的可能性极小——这也是一种推测，这就表明推测意义与虚拟意义还是有某种联系的。从这一点我们得到启示：如果把虚拟意义看作是推测意义的一种特例——推测某种可能性不存在，此时也就与情态动词的推测用法有联系了，这样就依然证明了笔者上面发现的规律：在情态动词接完成式、进行式或完成进行式的时候，情态动词都具有推测意义，而没有各自的基本意义。对此，读者要灵活把握。

就出现的频率来说，最常用的是情态动词与一般式的搭配，其次是与完成式的搭配；与进行式的搭配较少，而与完成进行式的搭配最少用到。

我们将在8.4节中讨论"情态动词＋完成式"，在8.5节中讨论"情态动词＋(完成)进行式"。

三、情态动词＋情态动词短语

在8.1.1小节中讲到，情态动词对应于这样一些短语：be able to, be allowed to, have(got) to, be supposed to/ought to和be going to。这些短语可以用在情态动词后面。比如，在8.1.1小节的练习中看到的这些句子：

11 We're supposed to do our best and we ***should be able to*** finish this work before the boss has to start screaming at us again. 我们得竭尽全力，在老板再次冲我们大喊大叫之前完成这项工作。

12 If you could just concentrate on getting finished, we ***might be allowed to*** leave early this afternoon. 如果你们集中精力做完这项工作，可能就会允许我们今天下午早点走。

13 He ***may be able to*** help. 他或许能够帮忙。

14 You ***might have to*** work late. The others ***may be allowed to*** leave early. 你可能得加班，其他人或许可以早走。

从上面这些句子我们看到，情态动词接短语，此时的情态动词往往也是只有推测的意义，而没有基本意义。

思维总结

本节向读者展示了情态动词的概况。

第一，情态动词有 can, may, must, will 和 shall，除 must 以外它们各自对应的过去形式是 could, might, would 和 should，以及对应的情态短语，如 be able to 等。

第二，总结出了两大类情态意义：基本意义(root meaning)和推测意义(deduction meaning)。

第三，总结出了意义与结构搭配之间的关系。如基本意义一般仅限于用在“情态动词＋一般式”的结构中。这一结构也是情态动词最常见的结构搭配。推测意义可存在于“情态动词＋一般式”、“情态动词＋完成式 / 进行式 / 完成进行式”以及“情态动词＋短语情态动词”这三类结构中。

第四，在“情态动词＋情态动词短语”(如 may be able to)这样搭配中，情态动词也是只有推测意义。

思维训练

Exercise 8. 1 (Key: P350)

请判断下列句中情态动词是“推测意思”，还是“基本意思”。

1. I've got a lot to do so I ***might*** be late.
2. All students ***must*** wear school uniforms.
3. Oh hello, you ***must*** be the new teacher!
4. Smoking ***may*** cause serious illness.
5. Yes, you ***may*** smoke, buy only over there.
6. Your friend ***can*** come in and play with you.
7. Because of the rain, the roads ***will*** be dangerous.
8. You ***will*** do what you are told, or else!

请解释下列各句可能有的含义。

9. His mother says he may go.
10. His mother says he may have gone.

请判断下列句子中情态动词在使用形式上是否正确，错误的请予以改正。

11. He can to speak English well.
12. He can spoke English well.
13. He can speaking English well.
14. He can speaks English well.
15. He cans speak English well.
16. He doesn't can speak English well.
17. Does he can speak English well?
18. They must don't do that again.
19. They must did the work yesterday.
20. They musted do the work yesterday.

8.2 推测用法(一):现在推测(情态动词+一般式)

尽管情态动词的意思众多,但他们有一个共性的用法——表示推测,也就是表示说话人对某件事发生的可能性的大小作出判断。在英文中,对现在或当前的情况进行推测,要用"情态动词+一般式"这一结构。同时要注意,对现在的肯定推测与否定推测所使用的情态动词也不尽相同,所以下面分别讨论对现在推测的肯定形式与否定形式。

8.2.1 对现在的肯定推测

一、must 表示"推测"及其他含义

请看下面这些对现在的肯定推测的例子:

1 A: Why isn't John in class?

B: He ***must be*** sick.

A:约翰今天怎么没来上课呢?

B:他一定是病了。

2 A: I've had no sleep for 48 hours.

B: You ***must be*** exhausted.

A:我48个小时没有合眼了。

B:你一定筋疲力尽了。

3 You've been traveling all day. You ***must*** be tired. 你跑了一天了,一定累了。

4 Carol ***must*** get very bored in her job. She does the same thing every day. 凯萝尔一定烦透了她的工作,她每天都做着同样的事。

5 The computer is on, so someone ***must*** be using it. 电脑开着,肯定是有人在用。

6 Look at that house! Those people ***must*** have a lot of money. 你看他们那房子!那些人一定很有钱。

7 It ***must*** be hot in there with no air-conditioning. 那里没有空调,一定很热。

8 What is your favorite color? Do you like yellow, orange, red? If you do, you ***must be*** an optimist, a leader, an active person who enjoys life, people and excitement. 你最喜欢什么色彩?你喜欢黄色、橙色和红色吗?倘若如此,你准是一个乐观的人,一个领导者,一个享受人生、乐于交往、容易激动、积极向上的人。

9 Winter ***must*** be cold for those with no warm memories. 对于那些没有温暖回忆的人们来说,冬天一定会很冷。

must 除了表示"推测"之外,还有另一个常见的用法是表示"责任"或"义务",译成"必须"。这其实是 must 的基本用法,由于它与"推测"的用法形成了一个很好的对比,所以在此对这一含义和用法作一个介绍。

must 在表示"必须"时,可以是非常"强烈的义务(strong obligation)",比如法律规定:

10 You ***must*** wear a seat belt while driving. 开车时必须系安全带。

或者是一些规章制度或某些规定等。比如:

11 Door ***must*** be closed when machine is in operation. 机器运转时门必须关闭。

12 Students ***must*** pay course fees before attending classes. 学生必须先交费,然后才能上课。

以上这些句中 must 的语气是非常强烈的。must 也可以是表示说话人主观认为某事是重要的、必须完成的"义务"。比如:

13 You ***must*** concentrate on one thing at a time. 做事时你必须一心一意。

这里 must 表示“义务”的意味就要比上面例句中法律规定的“义务”要弱很多。还有“义务”的含义更弱的情况，即把 must 用于描述说话人自身的情况。比如：

14 I ***must*** remember to feed the cat later. 我得记住一定要喂猫。

15 I ***must*** try harder next time. 我下次必须更努力。

以上其实区分了三种“强烈”程度不同的“义务”的含义。在现代英语口语中，还有一种语气更弱的“义务”，用来谈未来的“安排(arrangement)”。比如：

16 You ***must*** come to see us one of these days. 你这几天得来看看我们啊。

17 We ***must*** get together for lunch sometime. 我们得找个时间聚一聚，吃个午饭。

总之，关于 must 表示“必须”时，大致可以区分为以上四种不同的强烈程度，对此读者不妨体会一下。

最后，简单地比较一下 must 的“推测”用法和“必须”的用法之间的关系：

第一、表示“推测”时，must 不能表示将来，而只能表示对现在的推测和对过去的推测(见 8.4 节)。若是表示对现在的推测，其谓语形式是“must + 一般式”，即 must do；或“must + 进行式”，即 must be doing。若是表示对过去的推测，其谓语形式是“must + 完成式”，即 must have done。

第二、表示“必须”时，must 不能谈过去的事件，而只能谈现在和将来的事情。其谓语形式都是“must + 一般式”，即 must do。不能用“must + 进行式或完成式”，即 must ***be doing*** 或 must ***have done*** 中的 must 一定不会译成“必须”，而只能是表示推测。must 表示“必须”的意义时是没有过去时态的，要表示“过去必须”，则要借用 had to来表达。

第三、在表示“必须”时，must 后面的谓语动词一般是表示动作(action)的，具体来说，就是现在的动作或将来的动作(present and future actions)，不会是表示状态。在表示“推测”时，must 后面的谓语动词可以是动作，也可以是状态。比如：

18 He must ***be*** dead.

妙语点睛 因为这句话的谓语动词 be 是表示状态，所以这句话不会译成“他必须死掉”，而只能译成“他一定是死了”，即表示推测。

精品译文 他一定是死了。

与 must 相关的一个情态短语是 have (got) to。它同 must 一样，既可以表示“推测”，也可以表示“必须”。比如下面两句中的 have to 都表示“推测”：

19 Look at that house! Those people ***have to*** have a lot of money.

妙语点睛 这里的 have to 表示推测。

精品译文 你看他们那房子！那些人一定很有钱。

20 He is really big; he ***has to*** be over seven feet tall.

妙语点睛 这里的 have to 表示推测。

精品译文 他是个大块头，一定得有超过 7 英尺高。

用 had to 表示对过去的推测，如：

21 He was really big; he ***had to*** be over seven feet tall.

用 have to 表示“必须”时，与 must 主要存在两点区别：

第一、在时态的表达上，must 只能谈现在或将来，不能谈过去。must 没有时态的变化，而 have to 有各种时态的变化，比如过去时 had to，将来时 will have to，现在完成时 have had to，过去完成时 had had to 等。请看例句：

22 When I was in school, we ***had to*** wear school uniform.

妙语点睛 这里的 had to 表示“过去必须”。

精品译文 我上学那时，我们都得穿校服。

23 A: Do we really have to go to this meeting?

B: Yes, and we ***will have to*** present our report.

妙语点睛 这里的 will have to 表示“将来必须”。

精品译文 A：我们真的一定得去参加这个会议吗？

B：是的，因为我们得展示我们的报告。

第二、如果是来自外界的不可控的行为(uncontrollable external behavior)，此时要用 have to。比如，“要打喷嚏”是我们无法控制的，所以要说：

24 Excuse me, but I ***have to sneeze***. 对不起，我要打喷嚏。

此时，一般不用 must。

除了以上两点，还需要注意的是，must(“必须”)的否定形式 mustn't 不是表示“不必”，而是“千万别做某事”的意思，表示“不必”要说 don't have to。因此，可以说 must(“必须”)的否定是 don't have to(“不必”)。另外，must 的推测用法“一定是”的否定不是 mustn't，而是 can't(“不可能是”)(见 8. 2. 2 小节)。

在口语中，have got to 作为 have to 的口语形式更为常用，同样可以有两个意思：推测和必须。比如：

25 They***'ve got to*** try harder next time.

妙语点睛 这里的 have got to 表示“必须”。

精品译文 他们下次得更努力些。

26 You***'ve got to*** be joking!

妙语点睛 这里的 have got to 表示“推测”。

精品译文 你准是在开玩笑！

不过需要注意的是，have to 有各种时态的变化，而 have got to 没有时态的变化（只能表示现在或将来，这一点同 must 表示“必须”意义时相同)，比如不说 had got to* 等。

二、其他表示推测的情态动词

当然，我们还可以用其他的情态动词来表示对现在的推测，这些情态动词有 may, might 和 could 等。比如：

27 A: I wonder where Tom is.

B: He ***may/might/could*** be in the library.

精品译文 A：我不知道汤姆在哪里。

B：他或许在图书馆。

我们再来看下面这个笑话：

28 Michael: Teacher, is there life after death?

Teacher: Why do you ask?

Michael: I ***may need*** the extra time to finish all this homework you gave us.

精品译文 迈克尔：老师，人死后有来生吗？

老师：为什么问这个问题？

迈克尔：因为我可能需要额外的时间才能完成你给我们布置的所有这些作业。

请再看其他例句：

29 While this ***might*** explain some cases, it is not universally applicable.

精品译文 这种观点或许可以解释某些情况，但它并非放之四海而皆准。

30 Nonverbal information comes from facial expression, eye contact, body posture and hand movements. If a person is smiling or laughing, he ***may*** be telling a joke. If a person is yawning, then he ***may*** be tired of the conversation.

精品译文 非语言信息是指来自面部表情、眼神接触、身体姿势和手势等方面的信息。比如，若有人在微笑或大笑，这说明他可能是在开玩笑；而如果有人在打哈欠，则可能说明他对这个交谈感到乏味。

读者需要注意的是，不同的情态动词所表达的可能性的程度是不一样的。下面大致给出这样一个肯定程度的差别比较：

A: Why isn't John in class?

B: He *is* sick.（100%肯定，对客观事实的陈述）

He ***must*** be sick.（90%肯定，很有把握的陈述）

He ***may*** be sick.（50%肯定，不太有把握的陈述）

He ***could/might*** be sick.（25%肯定，很没有把握的陈述，只是提供一种可能）

当然，以上数字不是绝对的，只是为了让大家比较直观地了解不同的情态动词所表达的确定程度的差别而已。比如，用 must 肯定要比用 could 或 might 表示说话人的把握大得多。用 could 或 might，说话人只是为约翰没来上学提供一种解释而已，他的言外之意会是：

He ***might be*** sick. I don't really know. He ***could be*** at home watching TV. He ***might be*** at the library. He ***could be*** out of town. 他有可能病了，但我真的不肯定，他也有可能是在家看电视，也有可能是在图书馆，还有可能不在城里。

所以，这里到底要用什么词，比如是 must 还是 might 或是 may，完全取决于说话人当时的确信程度，或根据自己掌握的信息情况，因为正如在 8.1.2 小节中讲过的，情态动词的推测用法是以信息为基础的（The speaker's deduction is based on what is known, or knowledge-based.）。再比如：

31 A: Do you think the plane will be on time?

B: I don't know. It ***may/might/could*** be delayed by fog.

妙语点睛 这里说话人 B 已经说明自己不知道了，所以他不会用 must 这样肯定的语气来推测。

精品译文 A：你认为飞机会准时吗？

B：我不知道，可能会因为大雾而晚点吧。

笔者记得以前在大学的英语角（English Corner）上，为了让"哑巴"学生张口说句英文，外教可是想尽了各种办法。其中一个绝招就是做各种游戏，这样我们可以一边做游戏一边用英语讨论、交流，从而也就练习了口语。有一个游戏是这样的：让小组里一位同学在脑子里想一个常见或常用的物品，然后其他组员去猜。但猜的时候，要用一般疑问句对这个东西的性质特征进行发问，比如 Is it white?而不能问 Is it white or black?这样的选择问句，也不能问 What color is it?这样的特殊疑问句，因为对方只能回答 Yes / No。我们就这样一边发挥想象，一边围绕它的特征一点点地追问，这样逐渐把思考的范围缩得越来越小，最终才能猜到答案。比如，一个同学提示道：

32 A: I am thinking of something made of metal that you can find in my pocket. 我在想的东西是金属做的，你们可以在我的口袋里找到。

然后围绕这个线索，其他同学就跟着猜。但也有同学因为不知道规则，一上来就七嘴八舌地这样猜起来：

B: It ***could*** be a pen. 可能是笔。

C: It ***could*** be some keys. 可能是钥匙。

D: It ***might*** be a paper clip. 可能是曲别针。

E: It ***may*** be a small pocket-knife. 可能是小刀。

F: It ***could*** be a coin. 可能是硬币。

……

因为就这样漫无目的地瞎猜，所以在这样的场合中用 must 这个极为确信的词就不合适了。当然这样直接猜是违反游戏规则的，不过，我们也就因此学会了情态动词的推测用法。

再如在《老友记》（Friends）里，有一场戏是钱德勒（Chandler）正在搞网恋，他在网上认识了一个女孩，两人的感情似乎正在急剧升温。这时菲比（Phoebe）却给他泼冷水，提醒钱德勒不要当真，因为对方可能是一个 90 岁的老人，或者是一个双头怪物，甚至是一个男人也说不定。我们来看这个对话：

33 Phoebe: Are you the cutest?

Chandler: I'm afraid I might just be.

Phoebe: You know, what I think is so great that you are totally into this person and yet for all you know she ***could*** be like 90 years old, or have two heads, or it ***could*** be a guy.

Chandler: Okay, it's not a guy, all right, I know her.

Phoebe: It ***could*** be like a big giant guy.

妙语点睛 当然，菲比在这里只是故意打击钱德勒而已，因此这里她的推测纯属胡诌，不足为信，因而她也就选用了肯定程度最低的一个词 could，而没有用 may 甚至是 must。

精品译文 菲比： 你是最可爱的吗？

钱德勒：我觉得我恐怕就是呢。

菲比： 你知道，我在想的是，你完完全全迷上了这个人，不过她有可能是个 90 岁的老人，或者有两个脑袋，或者是个男人呢。

钱德勒：哦，那人不是男的，嗯，我了解她。

菲比： 对方可能是一个彪形大汉呢。

8.2.2 对现在的否定推测

我们也可以对当前的情况作一个否定的推测。比如：

A: The restaurant is always empty.

B: It ***isn't*** good.（100%肯定，对客观事实的陈述）

It ***can't/couldn't*** be good.（90%肯定，很有把握的陈述）

It ***may not*** be good.（50%肯定，不太有把握的陈述）

It ***might not*** be good.（25%肯定，很没有把握的陈述，只是提供一种可能）

纵观以上阐述，我们发现以下四点是值得注意的：

1. 在否定推测中没有 must，因为 must 表示推测一般只用在肯定句中，而否定的 mustn't 常用于表示“命令别人不要做什么”，译为“千万别”。

2. 与 must 相反，can 表示推测时不能用在肯定句中，只用在否定句和疑问句中。关于这一点，在 8.6 节中将有详细的分析和解释。因此，must 不能在否定句表示推测这一空白正好由 can't 来填补，也就是说表示推测的 must，否定时要改为 can't，而不是 mustn't。比如：

You ***must*** be joking. You ***can't*** be serious. 你准是在开玩笑，你不可能当真吧。

3. 在肯定推测时，could 的肯定程度很低；但在否定推测时，couldn't 则表示十分确信，译为“不可能”。

4. could 和 might 虽然是过去式，但在这里并不是表示对过去的推测，而是表示对现在的推测，或者是对将来的推测(见 8.3 节)。

8.2.3 对现在推测的其他情态动词

表示对现在的推测，常用的情态动词是 must, may, might 和 could，在否定句中还有 can't（来替换 must）。不过 will 和 should 也可以用来表示对现在的推测，其肯定程度等同于 must。比如：

1 Ring his home number. He***'ll*** be at home now.

妙语点睛 这里用 will，表示“我肯定他在家”，相当于 He must be at home now.

精品译文 给他家打电话吧，他现在会在家。

2 A: Someone is knocking at the door.

B: That***'ll*** be the postman.

精品译文 A：有人在敲门。

B：准是邮递员。

3 It's no use asking Tom; he ***won't*** know.

妙语点睛 相当于说“我肯定他不知道。”

精品译文 这事问汤姆没用，他不会知道的。

4 A: This ***should*** be State Street up here.

B: It's not. I think you should have turned left at the last intersection.

精品译文 A：这应该就是国家大街了。

B：不是。你应该在上一个十字路口左转。

will 表示对现在的推测很少用，主要是表示对将来的"预测"。should 表示推测还有其他限制，详见下一节内容。

思维总结

本节主要讨论了情态动词对现在的推测的用法。读者需要掌握推测现在的结构，即"情态动词＋一般式"，以及肯定与否定推测时不同的情态动词所表示的确信程度不同。

思维训练

Exercise 8. 2（Key: P350）

口语练习：请与你的英语伙伴，针对下列情景做出推测。

例如：

A: I am thinking of something made of metal that you can find in my pocket. What ***could*** it be?

B: It ***could*** be a pen. It ***could*** be some keys. It ***might*** be a paper clip. It ***may*** be a small pocket-knife. It ***could*** be a coin.

A: I was thinking of the keys in my pocket.

1. Something has four legs and is found on a farm.
2. Something is sweet and you can eat it.
3. Something you can play on a large field.
4. Something that has wheels

请用 **must not** 或 **don't have to** 填空。

5. I've already finished all my homework, so I ______ study tonight.
6. You ______ forget to take your keys with you.
7. You ______ introduce me to Dr. Smith. We've already met.
8. A person ______ become rich and famous in order to live a successful life.
9. A person ______ get married in order to lead a happy and fulfilling life.
10. You ______ play with sharp knives.
11. We ______ go to the concert if you don't want to, but it might be good.
12. I ______ go to the doctor. I'm feeling much better.
13. In order to be a good salesman, you ______ be rude to a customer.
14. This is an once-in-a-lifetime opportunity. We ______ let it pass. We must act.

请判断下列句子中的 **must** 是"推测"还是"必须"。

15. My watch has stopped. It must be broken.
16. With that accent, you must be from Scotland.
17. You must come up and see me sometime.
18. No ifs or buts, you must wear a helmet.
19. Wayne left. He must have been feeling ill.
20. I mustn't forget to send him a gift.
21. Someone must have borrowed my dictionary.
22. What goes up must come down.

请阅读下面文章，体会其中的情态动词推测含义。

小知识

23. Did You Know?

When baby sharks are born, they quickly swim away from their mothers. This is because their mothers ***might*** see them as prey and eat them.

开心一刻

下面这个笑话讲到了古老的中华饮食文化。

24. Moshe was eating in a Chinese restaurant and was chatting to his Chinese waiter.

Moshe commented upon what a wise people the Chinese were.

"Yes," replied the waiter, "we're wise because our culture is 4,000 years old. But Jewish people are also very wise, are they not?"

Moshe replied, "Yes, we are. Our culture is 5, 000 years old."

The waiter was surprised to hear this. "That ***can't*** be true," he replied, "where did your people eat for a thousand years?"

8.3 推测用法(二)：将来预测(情态动词+一般式)

(一)

对将来的推测，更确切地说应该是"预测(prediction)"，谓语形式也是用"情态动词 + 一般式"，这与上一节讨论的对现在推测的谓语形式一样。实际上，除了 must，情态动词如 will, should, may, might 和 could 都可以表示对将来的推测。比如：

1 A: What did the weatherman say?

B: It ***will*** rain tomorrow.

It ***should*** rain tomorrow.

It ***may*** rain tomorrow.

It ***might / could*** rain tomorrow.

上述例句的确信程度同样是由高到低。比如，should 在表示推断时，没有用 will 表示推断时的自信心强：

2 1) Tom ***will know*** the address. 我肯定汤姆知道。

2) Tom ***should know*** the address. 我想汤姆会知道。

比如，《时代》(Time)周刊对 21 世纪所作的预测中提到：

3 It is a near certainty that science ***will*** discover the aging gene and find out how to turn it off. The ethical problems of who shall live and who shall die and who can have children in a crowded world ***will*** be monumentally difficult to solve.

妙语点睛　这里我们看到，因为该周刊对人类将会发现致衰老基因及将会面临的问题很确信，所以都用了 will。

精品译文　几乎可以肯定的是，未来的科学会发现人类的致衰老基因，并知道如何消除这一基因。到那时，由此引出的各种问题，比如让什么人长生不老，让什么人寿终正寝，以及在这样拥挤的地球上谁可以生孩子，这些都将是难以解决的伦理问题。

我们再看看下列句子：

4 A: I hear Mary isn't getting much support in her running against Steve in the election.

B: It is not over yet. I think she ***will*** make a come back.

妙语点睛　说话人 B 在这里用了 will，表明自己相信玛丽一定会反败为胜(Speaker B expects Mary to win.)

精品译文 A：我听说玛丽在与史蒂夫选举对决中，并没有获得很多的支持。
B：现在选举还没结束呢，我想她最终会反败为胜的。

5 A: Think it'***ll*** rain tomorrow? I am sure it ***won't***.
B: But according to the weather report, it ***will*** rain tomorrow.
妙语点睛 说话人A很自信地说I am sure...，所以他在后面用了will (won't)。
精品译文 A：你认为明天会下雨吗？我肯定不会下雨的。
B：可是天气预报说明天要下雨的。

6 This movie ***will*** be popular in China because it explores some of the differences between Western and Eastern culture and the changing from the traditional to the modern world.
精品译文 预计这部电影将在中国大受欢迎，因为它探讨了东西方文化的差异以及从传统社会过渡到现代社会这一过程中所发生的变化。

7 If much more snow accumulates, the roads ***will*** have to be closed.
如果再有更多的雪堆积起来，那么肯定要封路的。
would表示肯定程度较大的预测。请看例句：

8 **New Year's Superstitions**
In many European countries, people believe that the first visitor on New Year's Day ***would*** bring them either good luck or bad luck. A dark-haired man ***would*** bring good luck. A woman or a man with light hair ***would*** bring bad luck. So some towns ***would*** choose a man with dark hair to go quickly from house to house. After he makes his rounds, the houses ***would*** be open to other visitors.
妙语点睛 这里的前三个would都是表示推测。注意，在So some towns ***would*** choose a man with dark hair to go quickly from house to house. After he makes his rounds, the houses ***would*** be open to other visitors. 一句中，这里的两个would不是表示推测，而是表示"意愿"，即属于情态动词的基本用法。
精品译文 新年的迷信
在许多欧洲国家，人们相信，在新年这天你遇到的第一个人将会给你带来不是好运就是厄运。若是遇到一头黑发的男子，这就意味着好运。若是遇到浅色头发的女子或男子，则意味着是厄运。因此，有的城镇就会专门挑选出一名深色头发的男子迅速地挨家挨户走动。等他转一圈下来之后，屋门才会打开，迎接其他客人。

should表示肯定程度较大的预测，相当于说"很可能将会这样了(most probably the case)"。请看例句：

9 The results are expected tomorrow. We ***should*** know the results tomorrow.
结果明天就出来了。我们明天就该知道结果了。

10 He ***should*** have plenty of time to get to the station. 他应该有足够多的时间去车站。

11 They ***shouldn't*** have any difficulty in finding the house. 找这个房子他们不应该有太大的困难。

12 The job ***should*** be finished by next Monday. 这项工作到下周一之前应该能够完成。

13 He is the best runner, so he ***should*** win the race. 他是最佳的跑步运动员，所以应该能赢得这个比赛。

14 The journey ***should*** take two or three days. 行程应该需要两到三天。

15 Your laundry ***should*** be ready for pick-up tomorrow. 你送洗的衣服明天就应该可以来取。

注意，should在表示推测时，也翻译成"应该"，但这并不是表示义务或责任的"应该"，而是表示说话人的主观判断或推测。

may表示约50%肯定的预测。请看例句：

16 Tomorrow's computers ***may*** have something for your nose to enjoy.
未来的计算机可能就会使你的鼻子能够闻到气味。

17 This bridge ***may*** collapse in an earthquake. 这座桥在地震中可能就会坍塌。

18 We ***may*** go camping this summer. 今年夏天我们可能去野营。

could/might 表示很不肯定(如只有 25%)的预测。请看例句:

19 There ***might/could*** be a strike next week. 下周可能会有罢工。

20 I ***might*** be given a new job soon. 不久我也许就会找到新的工作。

21 Look at those dark clouds. It ***could*** start raining any minute. 看这满天乌云密布的,说不定随时会下雨。

2003 年 3 月 20 日,美国开始空袭伊拉克。当天中午,布什总统随即发表电视讲话,在讲话中他说:

22 A campaign on the harsh terrain of a nation as large as California ***could*** be longer and more difficult than some predict.

妙语点睛 这里小布什用的是肯定程度最低的情态动词 could,来表示对未来战争局势的预测。可以理解,他不可能在战争一开始就很肯定地告诫美国士兵,这场战争 will be longer and more difficult than some predict(一定会持久而艰难)。尽管后来事实证明战争并没有像美国预想的那样很快结束,直到现在美国依然没有完全从伊拉克战争中抽出身来,有人预计未来五年内美国都很难完全从伊拉克撤军。

精品译文 在一个面积同加利福尼亚州一样大的、并且充满险恶地形的国家里进行战争,意味着战争的时间可能比人们预想的要长,困难要大。

再比如,《时代》周刊对 21 世纪所作的预测中,提到在未来,父亲和母亲的角色恐怕会像恐龙一样消失:

23 Between invitro fertilization and cloning, dads ***could*** become dinosaurs. Moms, too, with the possibility looming of an artificial womb.

妙语点睛 当然,这只是一种对将来不是十分肯定的预测,所以《时代》周刊用词很谨慎,用了 could,而不是 will 或 should。真是难以想象,如果没有了 mom and dad,人类的社会伦理将会是什么样子。

注意这个句子的结构:Moms, too, with the possibility looming of an artificial womb. 相信很多读者不理解。该句完整的说法应该是:Moms could also become dinosaurs, with the possibility of an artificial womb ***looming***. 所以这里的介词短语 of an artificial womb 应该接在 possibility 后面,表述"人造子宫的可能性"。looming 是一个分词,表示"可能存在"。整个短语 with the possibility of an artificial womb ***looming*** 其实是一个分词短语,作原因状语,来说明原因——为什么说母亲的角色也可能会消失。

精品译文 由于体外受精和克隆技术的发展,父亲的角色可能将会像恐龙一样从地球上消失。另外,由于人造子宫将会发明,母亲的角色也将可能成为历史。

同样要注意,在否定句中,can't/couldn't 要比 may not/might not 的否定语气强烈。试比较:

24 1) We ***may not/might not*** go camping this summer. 今年夏天我们可能不去野营。

2) We ***can't/couldn't*** go camping this summer. 今年夏天我们不可能去野营。

(二)

值得注意的是,should 表示说话人的一种合理的假设(the speaker's reasonable assumption),因此它是用来对说话人所希望发生的事进行推断的。若将来的事件不是他所期望发生的,则不用 should 表示这种推测。比如上面例句 22 讲到的小布什对未来战争局势的预测,他就不会说美伊这场战争 ***should*** be longer and more difficult than some predict,如果他用 should 这样说,就意味着小布什希望战争"越持久越艰难越好"。请比较下面的例句:

25 1) Let's not go to the movie. It ***could*** be bad.

2) Let's go to the movie. The film ***should*** be really good.

妙语点睛 在例句 1)中,"电影可能不好"并不是说话人所期望的,所以不说 It ***should*** be bad. * 在例句 2)中,"电影好看"自然是人人希望的,所以说话人用 should。

精品译文 1）我们别去看电影了，它或许不好看。
2）我们去看那电影吧，它应该很好看。

再如说：

26 There ***should be*** another disaster shortly. *

这样说话显得很别扭，因为它暗示说话人对灾难持赞许的态度。所以正确的说法应该是：

There ***could be*** another disaster shortly. 很快就会发生另一场灾难。

27 A: I have flushed cheeks and a slight fever.

B: You ***should*** be coming down with something. *

精品译文 A：我脸颊发红，有些低烧。
B：你应该是生病了。

妙语点睛 B的回答有问题，因为他用了should，暗示A的生病症状是他所希望的，这显然不妥，所以B最好用could, might, may或must来表达。从上面的译文中我们也看到，尽管在汉语中可以说"应该"来表达不好的事情，但英文中不可以这样。

28 A: These summer days are getting to be more than I can take. It was even too hot to go to the pool yesterday.

B: Hold on, according to the weather report we ***should*** have some relief by the end of the week.

妙语点睛 "天气转凉"是人们所希望发生的，所以用了should。

精品译文 A：这夏天热得让我越来越受不了了。昨天热得都无法去游泳池了。
B：别急，天气预报说，到这个周末，可能就会凉快点。

思维总结

首先，表示对将来的推测的情态动词较多，除了must外都可以，比如could和might等这样的过去形式的情态动词都可以表示对将来的推测。

其次，不同的情态动词所表示的确信程度不同。

最后，要理解should用来对说话人所希望发生的事进行推断。

思维训练

Exercise 8.3（Key: P351）

请判断下列句中should是表示"义务"的"应该"，还是"推测"的"应该"。

1. Should I invite our neighbors to the wedding?
2. Dogs should be kept on a leash in public.
3. If they mailed it last week, it should be here by now.
4. Those who have studied should find the test quite easy.
5. Why should we always do what they say?
6. She should have said "thank you" for the gift.
7. How long should it take to complete the task?
8. They say you should serve red wine with steak.

开心一刻

9. Is He a Good Student?

I have one teacher who is so forgetful he gave the same test three weeks in a row. If he does that two more times, I ***may*** pass it.

8.4 推测用法(三)：过去推测(情态动词+完成式)

(一)

肯尼迪遇刺之谜

1963年11月22日，美国历史上最年轻的总统约翰·肯尼迪(John F. Kennedy)携同夫人杰奎琳参加完一次竞选活动后，来到得克萨斯州的达拉斯市。数声枪响之后，肯尼迪随之倒在了杰奎琳的膝上，从此告别了人世。

在事发后不到48小时，中央情报局就在达拉斯市抓获了一名"嫌疑犯"——李·哈维·奥斯瓦尔德(Lee Harvey Oswald)。但可疑的是，美国政府并没有对他提起诉讼，并且不久以后，这名刺杀肯尼迪的重要嫌疑犯在众目睽睽之下被人枪杀。

1964年，美国政府就此案公布的官方调查报告《华伦报告》认定，奥斯瓦尔德是肯尼迪遇刺时唯一的凶手，他从得克萨斯州图书大楼向肯尼迪开了三枪。但15年后，美国众议院调查委员会重新对此案进行调查后得出结论称，当时刺客共向肯尼迪开了四枪，其中三枪来自图书大楼，另外一枪则来自另一个地点，这一结论进一步增加了人们对奥斯瓦尔德是单独作案的怀疑。

如今距离美国前总统约翰·肯尼迪遇刺已经有40多年，然而这场惊天谋杀案的真相至今仍迷雾重重。有调查显示，在过去的40多年里，关于肯尼迪遇刺的内幕至少有36种不同的版本，但至今没有一种版本真正令人信服，没有一种说法被证明属实。下面这篇短文就是人们围绕这个历史之谜所作的种种猜测：

On November 22, 1963, President John F. Kennedy, the thirty-fifth President of the United States, was assassinated in Dallas, Texas, while he was riding in an open car. Many people think it was foolish of him to be in an open car. He ***should have had*** a covered bulletproof car, as most world leaders do today. His death ***could have been prevented***.

Immediately after the assassination, a suspect, Lee Harvey Oswald, was arrested. Two days later, as Oswald was being transferred to a jail, he himself was killed by a gunman in the crowd. An investigation took place to find out the truth behind the assassination. After examining a lot of evidence and questioning many people, the investigating committee determined that Lee Oswald ***must have been*** the person who shot Kennedy. However, many theories have been made about why he did it. Some people think Oswald ***could have been*** a crazy person who thought he could get attention by killing a famous man. Another theory states that he ***might have been*** the agent of another government, possibly Russia or Cuba. According to another theory, organized crime (the Mafia) ***may have been*** behind the assassination.

Some witnesses report gunshots coming from two different directions. If this is true, Oswald ***could not have acted*** alone; there ***must have been*** more than one gunman.

Even though the assassination occurred many years ago, people are still fascinated with this event. Books and movies have appeared through the years offering new theories about this mysterious tragedy. Because Oswald was killed before he went to trial, many questions have remained unanswered.

精品译文 1963年11月22日，美国第35任总统约翰·肯尼迪在得克萨斯州的达拉斯市被暗杀，当时他正坐在一辆敞篷车里。很多人认为，他乘坐敞篷车是非常愚蠢的，他应该像如今的各国政要那样，乘坐封闭的防弹汽车才对，这样他也就不会丧命了。

暗杀发生后不久，嫌疑犯李·哈维·奥斯瓦尔德被抓获。两天以后，就在奥斯瓦尔德被送往监狱的路上，他被混藏在人群中的枪手枪杀。随后展开调查，以期查明刺杀背后的真相。在调查了大量的证据并询问了诸多证人之后，调查委员会认为李·奥斯瓦尔德一定就是刺杀肯尼迪总统的真凶。然而，关于他刺杀肯尼迪的原因众说纷纭。有人认为，奥斯瓦尔德可能是个疯子，他是想通过刺杀名人来使自己出名；还有一种理论认为，他可能是别国政府（比如当时的苏联或古巴)的间谍。另外还有理论认为，这次刺杀行动的背后可能另有主谋，比如黑手党。

几名目击者报告称，枪击来自两个方向。如果这种说法正确的话，那么奥斯瓦尔德不可能是单独行动的，当时一定还有另外的枪手。

尽管这次暗杀事件已是多年以前的事了，但人们对它仍旧兴趣盎然。多年来，关于这个神秘的悲剧事件的书籍和电影层出不穷，不断地提出各种新的理论。由于奥斯瓦尔德在前往监狱的路上被枪杀，因此许多问题成了永远的谜。

上文中黑体部分的句子除了前两个句子(***should have had, could have been prevented***)外，其他的都是表示对过去的推测。比如：

1 The investigating committee determined that Lee Oswald ***must have been*** the person who shot Kennedy.
调查委员会认为，李·奥斯瓦尔德一定就是刺杀肯尼迪总统的真凶。

2 Some people think Oswald ***could have been*** a crazy person who thought he could get attention by killing a famous man. 有人认为奥斯瓦尔德可能就是个疯子，他是想通过刺杀名人来使自己出名。

3 Another theory states that he ***might have been*** the agent of another government, possibly Russia or Cuba.
还有一种理论认为，他(奥斯瓦尔德)可能是别国政府(比如当时的苏联或古巴)的间谍。

4 According to another theory, organized crime (the Mafia) ***may have been*** behind the assassination.
另外还有理论认为，这次刺杀行动的背后可能另有主谋，比如黑手党。

5 If this is true, Oswald ***could not have acted*** alone; there ***must have been*** more than one gunman.
如果这种说法正确的话，那么奥斯瓦尔德不可能是单独行动的，当时一定还有另外的枪手。

由以上例句我们看到，表示对过去的推测，英文的谓语形式要用“情态动词＋完成式”，常用的情态动词有must, may, might 和 could，所以要说成：***must have been***, ***could have been***, ***might have been*** 和 ***may have been*** 等形式；若是在否定句中，则需要将 must 换成 can 或 could，说成 ***can't*** have done 或 ***couldn't*** have done，比如上文中的 ***could not have acted***。显然，表示对过去的推测的谓语形式不同于在上一节中所讨论过的表示对现在的推测的谓语形式“情态动词＋一般时态”，这一点请读者朋友一定要注意。所以，在上述表示过去的场景中，所作的推测就不能这样表达：

*The investigating committee determined that Lee Oswald ***must be*** the person who shot Kennedy.

*Some people think Oswald ***could be*** a crazy person who thought he could get attention by killing a famous man.

*Another theory states that he ***might be*** the agent of another government, possibly Russia or Cuba.

*According to another theory, organized crime (the Mafia) ***may be*** behind the assassination.

*If this is true, Oswald ***could not acted*** alone; there ***must be*** more than one gunman.

其中情态动词所表达的推测的肯定程度与对现在的推测中所说的一样，即 must 表示非常肯定的推测，may 其次，might 或 could 最不肯定。比如：

6 A: Why wasn't John in class yesterday? 约翰昨天怎么没来上课？
B: He was sick. 他病了。
He ***must have been*** sick. 他一定是病了。
He ***may have been*** sick. 他可能病了。
He ***could/might have been*** sick. 他或许是病了。

(二)

虚拟还是推测？

另外值得注意的是，上文中前两个黑体部分的句子：

7 He ***should have had*** a covered bulletproof car, as most world leaders do today.
他(约翰·肯尼迪总统)应该像如今的各国政要那样，乘坐封闭的防弹汽车才对。

8 His death ***could have been prevented***. 他(约翰·肯尼迪总统)也就不会丧命了。

根据对上下文的分析，这两句话并不是表示对过去的推测，而是表示一个与过去事实相反的假设，即表示对过去的虚拟。事实上，英语中四个过去形式的情态动词 would, could, might 和 should 既可以表示推测，也可以表示虚拟。具体来说，would/could/might/should ***do*** 可以表示对现在或将来的推测，也可以表示对现在或将来的虚拟；would/could/might/should ***have done*** 可以表示对过去的推测，也可以表示对过去的虚拟。请比较例句：

9 1）I don't know who killed John, but I guess his wife Mary ***could have killed*** him.

2）You ***could have killed*** me I hope you know.

妙语点睛 在例句 1)中，根据上下文语境知道，could have killed 是表示对过去的推测，"玛丽杀死丈夫约翰"存在一定的可能性。在例句 2)中，根据上下文语境知道，could have killed 是表示对过去的虚拟，事实上"我"没有死，即不存在"我过去死"的可能性。

精品译文 1）我不知道是谁杀死了约翰，但我猜测他的妻子玛丽可能杀了他。

2）你差点要了我的命，我希望你知道这一点。

所以，对于某些谓语带有 would, could, might 和 should 的句子，在没有具体语境的情况下，可能会在"推测"与"虚拟"之间产生歧义。比如：

10 He ***could have sent*** a message.

这个句子既可以理解为对过去的虚拟，因而可译成：他本来可以事先捎个口信过来的（但实际上没有这么做，表示抱怨）。

也可以理解成对过去的推测，因而可译成：他可能已经捎口信过去了。

再如：

11 He ***might have been drowned***.

精品译文 译文 1：他当时差点就淹死了(虚拟)。

译文 2：他可能已经淹死了(推测)。

当然，如果我们说：

12 You ***might have been drowned***!

妙语点睛 此时，因为主语是 you，所以，这句译成虚拟的意思较为妥当。

精品译文 你当时差点就被淹死了！

再如：

13 You ***shouldn't have drunk*** that wine. You ***might have been drugged***.

妙语点睛 这里有两处采用了"情态动词＋完成式"的结构：shouldn't have drunk 和 might have been drugged。该如何理解这两句话的意思呢？其实同样存在"虚拟"与"推测"之间的歧义：如果是虚拟，则可以理解成"你不应该喝那酒，要是里面放有迷药把你迷倒了怎么办"，而实际上酒里没有迷药。这反映了说话人一种事后的担心和后怕，言外之意是告诫听话人以后不要乱喝酒。如果是推测，则可以理解成"你不应该喝那酒，你可能已经被其中的迷药迷倒了"。若这么理解，表明此时"你"已经出现了被迷药迷倒了的症状，于是说话人推测可能是因为"你"喝的那酒造成的。

精品译文 译文 1：你不应该喝那酒，要是里面放有迷药把你迷倒了怎么办(虚拟)。

译文 2：你不应该喝那酒，你可能已经被其中的迷药迷倒了(推测)。

对于读者非常熟悉的 should have done 句型，一般会被理解成"本来应该做，但实际没有做"。比如上面这个例句中的 shouldn't have drunk 就是表示虚拟，意思是"你本来不应该喝那酒的，但实际上你已经喝过了"，这其实是它的虚拟含义。不过，我们也可以用它来表示对过去的推测，表示说话人所希望发生的事。请比较：

14 1）You ***should have received*** four letters by now.

2）I ***should have received*** four letters from them, but I got none.

妙语点睛 在例句 1)中，说话人是在推断说"到现在你们应该收到过四封信"，他用 should 来表示非常自信的推测，言外之意是，如果不出意外，四封信应该已经在你们手里了。当然，也许会出现万一的情况，导致你们没有收到来信。这就是 should 的推测用法：信很可能收到，也可能没有收到。在例句 2)中，说话人是在用虚拟语气抱怨说"我应该收到他们的四封信，但实际上我一封也没有收到”。这里的should表示虚拟，就不像例句1)中的推测那样存在“信很可能收到，也可能没有收到”这两种可能性，而只有一个现实：“我”一封信都没有收到。

精品译文 1）到现在你们应该收到过四封信。

2）我应该收到他们的四封信，但实际上我一封也没有收到。

请看例句：

15 The letter ***should have arrived*** by now. 我相信现在该到了。

16 He ***should have finished*** by now. 他现在该完成了。

建议读者结合在第七章“虚拟语气”中讨论的内容来比较would, could, might, should do/have done可能有的推测或虚拟的歧义。可以这样来分辨是推测还是虚拟：知道确切结果的是表示虚拟，而不知道确切结果，即存在两种可能性的是表示推测。结合这一点，请读者自己回头再看看上面例句的意思。

但是，现在形式的情态动词must, can, may和will不能表示虚拟，所以must/can/may/will have done只能是表示对过去的推测，而不能表示对过去的虚拟。

请看下面这篇小短文，这是笔者的一个澳大利亚朋友在讲述自己在中国湖北孝感任教的经历时说的一番话。这位朋友虽然是澳大利亚人，但他的大部分时间都是在其他国家度过的，足迹遍布了世界各地。但不知出于什么原因，他觉得到了中国之后，自己有一种回家的感觉，所以他在下文中说“我上辈子一定是一个中国人”：

17 My year in China turned out to be one of the most memorable periods in my varied life. I sometimes thought I ***must have been*** born a Chinese in a past life because I felt more at home in China than any of the other countries where I lived.

My one regret was that my wife hadn't been able to come with me because I know she ***would have liked*** the whole experience as much as me.

I suspect there ***may have been*** an element of luck in being reassigned to Xiaogan rather than Chengdu but, for whatever reason fate took a hand, it proved to be a really marvelous experience.

妙语点睛 我们看到，上文中三处黑体的句子分别用了***must have been***, ***would have liked***和***may have been***这种“情态动词＋完成时态”的形式，其中***must have been***和***may have been***表示的就是对过去的推测，而***would have liked***则是表示对过去的虚拟，因为他的夫人当时没有和他一同来中国，所以说她...liked the whole experience as much as me只能是一种假设。

精品译文 我在中国一年的任教经历，是我这辈子丰富人生经历中最值得回味的部分。有时我就想，我上辈子一定是一个中国人，因为在我所生活过的国家中，中国让我感觉更像回家。

我唯一的遗憾是，我的夫人当时并没有和我一同去中国，要不然，我想她一定也会和我一样热爱中国的。

我本来是要去成都任教的，但后来被分配到湖北孝感，这好像冥冥之中有命运在安排，但不管怎样，这段经历最让人难忘。

我们再看看下列场景中对过去推测的表达：

18 A: I ***must have lost*** some weight. Look, how baggy my pants are. 我准是瘦了不少，你看我穿这裤子现在显得多肥。

B: They don't look that loose to me. 可是我看它并不显得肥。

19 A: Why are the windows open? 窗户怎么是开着的？

B: A burglar ***must have broken in***. 一定有贼闯进来了。

20 A: The money has disappeared! Who ***could have taken*** it? 钱没了！会是谁拿的呢？

B: John ***could have*** (taken it); he was here alone yesterday. 可能是约翰，他昨天一个人在这里。

21 Oh no, a traffic jam. There ***must have been*** an accident. 哦，又是堵车，一定是发生交通事故了。

22 The guests ***will/would have arrived*** by that time. 到那时，客人将已经到了。

23 They ***might not have received*** our letter yet. 他们或许还没有收到我们的信。

24 I suppose I ***may have been*** rather critical. 我想我当时可能是太苛刻了。

另外需要提醒大家注意的是，"情态动词 +have done"的结构不一定相当于一个现在完成时。例如：

25 You ***must have seen*** him.（你一定见过他了。）

可以相当于：

I assume now you ***have seen*** him before.

I assume now you ***saw*** him last night.

I assume now you ***had seen*** him before you came here.

我们看到，在 must have seen 这个结构中的 have seen，在时间上可以相当于一个现在完成的动作 have seen，也可以相当于一个过去的动作 saw，甚至可以相当于一个过去完成的动作 had seen。

思维总结

本节重点讨论了情态动词推测过去的结构和用法。首先，读者需要掌握，表示对过去的推测，需要用"情态动词 + 完成式"这一结构。这里的情态动词既可以是现在形式的 may, can 和 will，也可以是过去形式的 might 和 could 以及 would 和 should。

但是，对于过去形式的情态动词 could, might, would 和 should，在没有具体语境的情况下，可能会在"推测"与"虚拟"之间产生歧义。建议读者结合在第七章"虚拟语气"中讨论的内容来比较 would, could, might, should do/have done 可能有的推测或虚拟的歧义。我们可以这样来分辨是推测还是虚拟：知道确切结果的是表示虚拟，而不知道确切结果，即存在两种可能性的是表示推测。

思维训练

Exercise 8. 4（Key: P351）

请用动词适当形式填空，以表示推测语气，注意肯定程度的不同。

1. It rained every day during their holiday, so they ______（not/have）a very nice time.
2. The restaurant ______（be）very good. It's always full of people.
3. The phone rang but I didn't hear it. I ______（be）asleep.
4. There ______（be）a bad accident here. Look at all the broken glass.
5. Jane walked past me without speaking. She ______（not/see）me.
6. Joe isn't at work today. He ______（be）ill.
7. Joe wasn't at work last week. He ______（be）ill.
8. When I woke up this morning, the light was on. I ______（forget）to turn it off.
9. The lights were red but the car didn't stop. The driver ______（not/see）the red light.
10. She knew everything about our plans. She ______（listen）to our conversation.
11. I can't find my umbrella. I ______（leave）it in the restaurant last night.
12. I left my bike outside the house last night and this morning it wasn't there any more. Somebody ______（take）it.
13. A: He says he saw you at the theater yesterday.
    B: He ______（not see）me. I wasn't there.
14. A: He has been working the whole morning.
    B: He ______（be）very tired
15. A: Did you hear me come in last night?
    B: No, I ______（be）asleep.

请判断下列句子是否有虚拟意味，并用 may 或 can't 来改写句子。

16. I could have left my office keys at home because I can't find them anywhere.
17. I could have married anybody I wanted to.

18. Jim started smoking last year. He might have picked up this bad habit from his friends.
19. It's a pity you didn't ask because I could have helped you.
20. The letter might have arrived by now.
21. You could have helped me!
22. You could have received four letters by now.
23. Your mother could have called when you were out.
24. You might have left your umbrella in the restaurant.
25. You screamed in your sleep last night. You might have had a terrible dream.
26. You might have drowned!
27. I suppose I might have been rather critical.
28. They might not have received our letter yet.
29. Some women could have made a good salary in a job instead of staying home, but they decided not to work for the sake of the family.
30. I could have become a millionaire, but I decided not to.
31. I can't find my sunglasses. I might have left them at the restaurant yesterday.
32. I don't know who rang, but it could have been Jim.
33. I could have bought that car, but I decided to look at a few others.
34. Peter wasn't here, so he couldn't have broken your vase.
35. The test was no problem at all. It couldn't have been easier, in fact!
36. The package is gone. Someone could have picked it up by mistake.
37. A: Donna, you said you'd take this package to accounting yesterday
    B: Oh, no. It could have slipped my mind.
38. A: Why are the windows open?
    B: A burglar might have broken in.
39. A: It took me five days to drive down to Florida.
    B: Five days? I could've walked there in less time.
40. A: I haven't seen you like this in weeks.
    B: The committee finally reached a decision, and I couldn't have hoped for a better outcome.
41. A: I could have seen this play five times. Don't you think it's great?
    B: Not that great.
42. A: I might have lost some weight. Look how baggy my pants are.
    B: They don't look that loose to me.
43. A: I'm sorry I missed your soccer game. But I had the flu.
    B: Don't worry about it. We couldn't have played worse.

8.5 推测用法(四):情态动词+(完成)进行式

在 8. 1. 3 小节讲过,情态动词接完成式、进行式及完成进行式,此时的情态动词均是表示推测的含义。所以,情态动词与进行式或完成进行式连用时,表达的意思与相应的进行时态或完成进行时态的意思差不多,只是增加了情态的意义——推测含义。比如:

1 I can't reach my friend. His line is always busy. He ***might be using*** the Internet now.

这里是说,“我”打电话找我的朋友找不到,电话总数占线,于是“我”就推测他现在可能正在上网,所以占用了电话线。如果“我”是很确信他在上网,那就可以说成:

He ***must be using*** the Internet now.

或者不是很确信地说:

He ***may be using*** the Internet now.

当然，如果知道他确实就在上网，则可以不用情态动词，而直接用现在进行时态说成：

He ***is using*** the Internet now.

从以上的例句我们看到，“情态动词 + 进行式”同一般进行时态一样，表达的是一个现在正在进行的活动，只是因为有了情态动词而增添了情态的意义——推测含义。

在《老友记》(Friends)中有这样一个场景：罗斯(Ross)的前妻凯萝尔(Carol)要临产了，罗斯、雷切尔(Rachel)、钱德勒(Chandler)、乔伊(Joey)和莫尼卡(Monica)等众人在医院的休息室里等候凯萝尔和她的同性恋女友苏珊(Susan)的到来。罗斯见她们迟迟未到，焦急地说道：

2 She's not here yet. She's not here. She's having my baby and she's not here. God, I don't believe this. She ***could be giving*** birth in the cab.

妙语点睛 这里罗斯说 could be giving 即是情态动词接进行式，表示在说话的时刻可能发生的事件。我们也看到，这里罗斯用了最不肯定的词 could，一方面表明他不希望他的前妻在出租车上生孩子这件事真的发生，另一方面也说明了他的焦急程度——急得如此胡思乱想！如果他希望这件事发生，他就会用 should 了。

精品译文 她还没有到，她还没有到，她就要生下我的孩子了，可她现在却还没有到。天啊，真不敢相信。她现在或许正在出租车上生产了。

我们再来看其他例句：

3 A: Congratulations! I understand you got a job. When do you start work?

B: You ***must be thinking*** of someone else. I'm still waiting to hear.

A: 恭喜你！我知道你找到新工作了，什么时候开始上班啊？

B: 你想的一定是别人，我还在等着听信呢。

4 I am afraid he hasn't found a job yet. He ***must still be checking*** the papers.

我恐怕他现在还没有找到工作，他一定还在翻着报纸找呢。

5 The plane ***should be landing*** now. 飞机现在肯定在降落。

6 They ***can't be having*** dinner right now. 他们现在不可能还在吃晚饭。

“情态动词 + 进行式”也可以用在虚拟语气中。比如下面这个面试的场景：

7 A man is applying for a job. Here is the talk between the director and him.

Director: What's your name, please?

Man: Greg Bulmash.

Director: What's your favorite position?

Man: Whatever's available. Well, if I were a picky person, I ***wouldn't be applying*** here in the first place.

Director: What salary do you expect?

Man: $ 185, 000 a year plus stock options and a long vacation.

精品译文 一个人应聘一份工作。下面是公司主任与他的谈话。

主任：请问您的名字？

应聘者：格雷格·布尔马什。

主任：您最喜欢的职位是什么？

应聘者：什么职位都可以。我要是个很挑剔的人，我现在就不会在这里申请工作了。

主任：你期望的薪水是多少？

应聘者：年薪 18.5 万美元，外加股票期权和带薪长假。

我们再来看看情态动词与 have been doing 连用的情形。请看例句：

8 A: Oh, I ***must have been sitting*** in the same position too long. My legs have fallen asleep.

B: Shake it a little before you get up.

妙语点睛 这里 must 的后面接完成进行时表示推测，而且这里的完成进行式就相当于一个现在完成进行时态 have been sitting，表示一直持续的一个动作或状态。

精品译文 A：噢，我一定是同样一个姿势坐得太久了，我的两条腿都麻了。
B：站起来之前，你先把腿甩甩。

请看其他例句：

9 You ***must have been dreaming***. 你刚才一定是一直在做梦。

10 You ***can't/couldn't have been swimming*** all day. 你不可能一整天都一直在游泳。

"情态动词+完成进行式"也可以用在虚拟语气中。比如：

11 You ***shouldn't have been following*** him so closely; you should have kept your distance.
你本不该一直跟着他那么近，你应该和他保持一定的距离。

8.6 基本用法(一)：现在或将来的能力

本节开始讨论情态动词的基本意义和用法。首先，来讨论读者非常熟悉的一个基本意义——能力。

说到表示"能力"的情态动词，相信很多读者立即会想到 can。能这么联想自然没错，不过，如果把 can 与"能力"完全等同起来，那就不对了。原因有二：首先，can 的含义远不止"能力"这一个意思；其次，即使是表示"能力"，这个"能力"又该如何理解呢？

看到这里，很多读者也许开始纳闷了："能力"就是"能力"嘛，这还需要有什么过多的解释吗？

其实不然，英语表达的"能力"和汉语是有差别的，而且差别很大，以至于需要通过本节以及接下来的 8.7 和 8.8 共三节的内容来详细讲解。只有这样，读者才能真正明白英语的"能力"的含义。

在开始讨论 can 的意义和用法之前，首先要说明的是，从核心意义(core meaning)的角度来看，can 强调的是"潜在可能性"，而不是真正去实施(the potential to perform an action, not the actual performance)。真正理解这一核心意义非常重要！在后面的内容中，笔者都将反复强调这一核心概念。

传统语法书上说，can 主要有三个意义，即"能力(ability)"、"可能(possibility)"和"许可(permission)"，其实都是源自"潜能(potential)"这一核心意思。比如下面句中的 can 表示"能力"：

1 A: My son ***can*** play the piano.
B: My daughter is only four and she ***can*** ride a bicycle.
C: Hey, that's nothing. My dog ***can*** count to ten.

妙语点睛 这里的三个 can 都是强调具备这样的"潜能"，或说"潜在的可能性"，而不是强调真正去实施。比如说话人 C 不会去牵来他家的狗，真的让它数数。

精品译文 A：我儿子能够弹钢琴。
B：我女儿才四岁，就能够骑自行车了呢。
C：嘿，这都没什么。我家的狗能够数到 10 呢！

再比如下面句中的 can 表示"可能"：

2 Don't take the tube in London. That ***can*** be very dangerous.

妙语点睛 这里的 can 表示"可能"。伦敦地铁在 2005 年 7 月 7 号爆炸过，以后还可能遭到恐怖袭击，因而再次发生爆炸，即有潜在的可能。

精品译文 在伦敦别坐地铁了，那可能很危险。

再比如下面句中的 can 表示"许可"：

3 You ***can*** use my car tomorrow.

妙语点睛 这里的 can 表示"许可"——"我"允许你用"我"的车，但实际上你并不一定就用，只是一种潜在的可能。

精品译文 你明天可以用我的车。

所以，上述三个例句都只是表明主语有完成某一行为的“潜在可能”，而并不一定真正去实施，或者表示某事可能存在(如伦敦地铁可能再次发生爆炸)。

本节主要讨论现在或将来的“能力”，在8.8节讨论过去的“能力”，在8.7节讨论“可能”，在8.9节讨论“许可”。

就“能力”的含义而言，can的核心意思是表示“潜在的”能力(The core concept of CAN is about “potential”.)用来说明因为具备某些特点或条件，某人能够完成某件事或某事是可能存在的，而并不强调何时或怎样实施这种潜在的行为。所以，can既可以表示“能力(ability)”，也可以表示“可能(possibility)”。比如：

4 I don't know how she knows, but Mom ***can*** always detect when I'm lying.
我不知道妈妈是怎么知道的，每次我撒谎的时候，她总是能够察觉出来。

5 Phil doesn't know why his back hurts. He hopes his doctor ***can*** determine the problem.
菲尔不知道他的背为什么疼，他希望医生能够查出问题的原因。

6 The theater ***can*** seat 10, 000 people. 这家剧院可坐10, 000人。

7 This car ***can*** go faster with this fuel. 用这种燃油，这辆车子能跑得更快。

显然，上述例句都只是表明主语有完成这一行为的“潜能”，而并没有真正去实施，或者表示某事可能存在。我们还可以把“能力”区分为“先天的能力”或者说“天赋的能力”，及“后天获得的能力”。比如：

8 A fish ***can't*** walk, but it ***can*** swim. (天赋的能力)鱼不能走，但是会游泳。

9 Dogs ***can*** bark, but they ***cannot*** talk. (天赋的能力)狗会叫，但不会说话。

10 Bob ***can*** play the piano. He has taken lessons for many years. But I ***can't***.
(后天获得的能力)鲍勃会弹钢琴，他学琴已经有很多年了。但是我不会弹。

11 I ***can*** sing in English. (后天获得的能力)我会唱英文歌。

12 I ***can*** drive a car. (后天获得的能力)我会开车。

表示“潜在的可能性”或者说“可能”，意思就是因为具备某些特点或条件，某人能够完成某件事或某事是可能存在的。比如：

13 John is strong. He ***can*** lift that heavy box.
妙语点睛 因为约翰足够健壮，所以他“能够”举起重箱子。
精品译文 约翰很强壮，他能举起沉重的箱子。

14 The theater ***can*** seat 10, 000 people.
妙语点睛 因为这个剧院的面积够大，所以它“能够”容纳10, 000人。
精品译文 这家剧院可坐10, 000人。

15 I ***can*** walk to school. It's not far.
妙语点睛 因为距离不远，所以我“能够”走到学校去。
精品译文 我能走到学校去，因为它不远。

16 You ***can*** see fish at an aquarium.
妙语点睛 因为水族馆就是用来养水生动物的，否则就不叫水族馆了，所以你“能够”在那里看到鱼。
精品译文 你能再水族馆里看到鱼。

17 You ***can*** buy stamps at the post office, but you ***can't*** buy shoes there.
妙语点睛 因为邮局就是经营邮件、邮票之类业务的，所以你“能够”在那买到邮票。如果能买到鞋，那就叫鞋店了。
精品译文 你可以在邮局买到邮票，但是买不到鞋。

以上这些解释就是表示因为具备某些特点或条件，使得某人能够做某事，或某事可能发生。这就是“能力”

的真正含义，即表示“潜能”！尤其是当句子的主语是有生命动作的执行者(an animate agent)时，即人类或者是动物，此时的“潜能”往往就会解释成“能力”。

思维总结

在这一节，读者要真正能够理解 can 的核心意义(core meaning)，即 can 强调的是“潜在的可能性”，而不是真正去实施(the potential to perform an action, not the actual performance)。理解了这个核心意义，将会为学习下两节内容打下基础。

8.7 基本用法(二)：现实“可能”与理论“可能”

笔者相信，很多读者一定认为 can 是一个很简单的情态动词，只是表示“能够”的意义，其实并不这么简单。上一节强调了 can 的核心意义是表示“潜能(potential)”，另外 can 可以表示“能力”，也可以表示“可能”。其实，“能力”可以看作是“可能”的一种特殊情况，即在这种情况下，动作的可能性与主语所指的对象的技巧或能力有关。

can 表示“能力”时还是比较好理解的，但表示“可能”则比较难了。本节将要讨论的问题可以说是“超难”的，绝对是挑战智商和理解力的。

愿意接受挑战的读者请比较下面这些中文句子里的“可能”在含义上的差别：

1 这孩子可能会很淘气。

2 这孩子脸色煞白，他可能是病了。

3 这里的交通有时可能会很拥堵。

4 约翰现在还没到，他可能是在路上堵车了。

请问各位聪明的读者：你能看出上面这四句话里，“可能”在含义上的差别吗？要知道，它们之间存在的还不是细微的差别，而是巨大的差别！

看完上述例句中的“可能”，也许有读者还是一头雾水，看不出这些“可能”有什么不同。我们还是从 can 的核心意义——潜在的可能性——来分析。can 既然是强调“潜在的可能”，所以它是强调在理论上某事发生的可能性是存在的，而与说话时的实际情况无关。比如说“这孩子可能会很淘气”，就是从一般的理论意义上来说的，而与这孩子当时的行为表现毫无关系。比如即使这孩子当时正在甜美地熟睡着，我们仍然可以指着他说“这孩子有时可能会很淘气”。同样，当我们说“这里的交通有时可能会很拥堵”时，我们并不需要考虑说话当时的交通状况，即使是在夜里没有车辆通行的情况下，我们依然可以说“这里的交通有时可能会很拥堵”。因此，can 具有“偶然的可能性”或“理论上的可能性”的含义，而不是“实际上的可能性”。一般可以把这时的 can 翻译成“有时会”，“可能会”。

由此可见，can 所表示的“可能”与前文讲过的 could, may 和 might 所表示的“推测”是完全不同的。尽管在汉语中都可译成“可能”，但两者的内涵是有巨大差别的。前面讨论的 could, may 和 might 所表示的“推测”，是强调“实际上的可能”。说话人是要紧密结合当时的实际情形，来判断某事发生的“确定程度(degrees of certainty)”的大小，从而选择 might, could 以及 may，甚至是 must 来表达不同的确信程度。此时，我们往往是表示根据现有事件的某种结果来推断其发生的原因。比如我们说“这孩子脸色煞白”，对这一说话时的现状，我们推断其原因可能是“他可能是病了”。同样，对于“约翰现在还没有到”这一现有的结果，我们可以推测出各种原因，其中一个原因是“他可能是在路上堵车了”。

从以上的讨论发现，区分“理论上的可能”与“实际上的可能”的一个关键点，是看所说的可能情况与说话时的现状是否有联系。与说话时的现状有联系的，则是“实际上的可能”。这时往往是谈论一个具体的事件，所以也可称之为“具体的可能”，尤其是用来针对一个现状或后果来推断其产生的原因。与说话当时的现状无关的，则是“理论上的可能”。

由于 can 具有“潜能”这一特性，决定它只能用来表示“理论上的可能”，而不能表示“实际上的可能”，即不能具体地谈一个事件。所以，在前面的 8.2、8.3 和 8.4 等几节关于“推测”的讨论中，都没有提到用 can，而说的是 could, might 和 may。所以，上述中文句子应分别译成：

1 The boy ***can*** be very naughty.（理论上、潜在的可能）

2 The boy looks pale. He ***could*** be sick.（实际上、现实的可能）

3 There are times when the traffic here ***can*** be very heavy.（理论上、潜在的可能）

4 John isn't here now. He ***could*** be caught in the traffic jam.（实际上、现实的可能）

其实，can 表示这种"理论上的可能"是非常常见的。原因很简单：在理论上，大多数事情都有可能发生，这就是人们常说的"世事无绝对"。对此，请读者日后不妨在英语阅读中多加细心观察、体会，这里也多举几例来说明。

在现代通讯手段发达的时代，大多数城市人都在使用电子邮件(e-mail)。但同时，信息又是如此泛滥，比如每天邮箱里都充斥着大量的垃圾邮件(junk mail or spam)。因此，有人说 e-mail 现在成了 e-jail(电子监狱)：

5 **E-mail or E-jail?**

E-mail ***can*** be e-jail. You might spend hours writing and responding to e-mails when you should be hitting the books for an upcoming exam. Or, you might be signed up for so many daily services, such as horoscopes, news services, or personals, that your mailbox is so filled up with "junk mail", that finding the important e-mails through your mailbox may take hours.

妙语点睛 这里的 can 就是表示一种理论上的可能。因为它与说话当时的情况无关，只是在谈一种泛泛存在的可能性。

精品译文 **电子邮件还是电子监狱？**

电子邮件可能会成为"电子监狱"。马上就要考试了，你本应为此刻苦攻读，可是你可能得花上几个小时回电子邮件。或者，你可能注册了太多的日常服务项目，诸如占星预测、新闻服务、征友等等，你的电子邮箱中因而塞满了大量的"垃圾信件"，要从电子信箱中找到重要信件就可能需要几个小时的时间。

很喜欢下面这篇短文所讲的道理：

6 Remember, it's not what happens to us that makes the difference in the quality of our lives. I believe that everything that happens ***can*** be a lesson. Next time things don't seem to be going the way you want, ask yourself what the positive aspect is. What's the benefit in the adversity? You'll have greater enjoyment and learn more in the process.

妙语点睛 这里的 can 就是表示一种理论上的可能。因为它与说话当时的情况无关，只是在谈一种泛泛存在的可能性。

精品译文 记住，并不是发生在我们身上的事情影响了我们的生活质量。我相信任何事情的发生都可能成为我们的经验财富。以后，如果事情的发展不随你愿，那你就得问问自己：这件事情积极的一面是什么？这一逆境将给我带来何种益处？在这个过程中，你就可以收获更多的快乐，学到更多的东西。

请看下面关于食物营养的短文：

7 The body uses protein to build muscles, and it uses fat to absorb the vitamins in food. Protein and fat are found in foods like milk, cheese, meat, fish, and eggs. Too much fat, however, ***can*** be harmful.

妙语点睛 这里的 can 就是表示一种理论上的可能。表示太多的脂肪有时候或许也会对我们的健康造成危害，尽管脂肪是我们的身体必不可少的。

精品译文 我们的身体需要蛋白质来促进肌肉的生长，同时利用脂肪来促进对食物中的维生素的吸收。在牛奶、奶酪、肉类、鱼类以及蛋类等食物中含有蛋白质和脂肪。不过，太多的脂肪有时可能会造成危害。

我们再来看下面各个句子，这些句子中的 can 都是表示"理论上的可能"，即只要在一定的条件下，就有偶尔发生的可能。对此，请读者结合给出的译文认真体会。请看例句：

8 Grammar *can* be fun!

妙语点睛 这里的 can 就是表示一种"理论上的可能"。比如说现在市面上有太多枯燥乏味的英语语法书，而且往往有很多讲的内容是语焉不详、含糊不清的。于是笔者就想说"语法可能也会很有趣的"，并且笔者一直在努力这么做。只不过，这种理论上的可能，在实践中是要下一番苦功夫的。

精品译文 语法也可能会很有趣的！

9 Even experienced teachers *can* make mistakes. 即使是再有经验的老师也有可能犯错误。

10 Measles *can* be quite dangerous. 麻疹有可能很危险。

11 Prolonged exposure to the sun *can* burn your skin. 长时间在太阳底下曝晒有可能会晒伤你的皮肤。

12 Don't stay outside too long on hot days. Too much exposure to the sun *can* be dangerous. 在大热天在外面呆的时间不要过长，因为长时间晒太阳会很危险。

13 Winter here *can* be really cold. 这里的冬天会非常的冷。

14 It *can* sometimes get very cold here in winter. 这里的冬天有时候会非常的冷。

15 It *can* be quite cold in Kunming in January. 昆明一月份时有时可能会很冷。

16 Such an accident *can* happen. 这样的事故完全有可能发生。

17 You *can* be very critical sometimes. 你这人有时候还真的很挑剔啊。

18 A woman *can* do anything when jealous. 女人在妒忌的时候，什么事情都可能做得出来。

19 He *can* be very rude. 他这人的态度有时会非常粗鲁。

20 A visit to the dentist *can* be frightening. 去看牙医对某些人来说可能会很恐怖。

21 Things *can* get crazy around here sometimes. 这里有时情况会变得很疯狂。

注意，can 这种"理论上的可能"往往只适用于肯定句中，不宜用于否定句。为什么？笔者思考过背后的原因，认为应该是：正如上文说过的，这种"理论上的可能"就意味着"世事无绝对"这样一个普遍的真理。如果用 can't 来否定，就相当于说"什么事情都不可能发生"，这显然有悖于一般真理。比如不宜说：

Even experienced teachers *can't* make mistakes. *

这就表示"即使再有经验的老师都不会犯错误"，这显然不符合常理，这在中文里也讲不通。

再比如我们不宜说：

Too much fat, however, *can't* be harmful. *

这就表示"再多的脂肪都不可能有害"，这显然也违反了营养学的道理。

再比如我们不宜说：

Measles *can't* be quite dangerous. *

这就表示"麻疹不可能很危险"，这显然不符合医学常识。

再比如我们不宜说：

Prolonged exposure to the sun *can't* burn your skin. *

这就表示"长时间在太阳底下曝晒不可能晒伤你的皮肤"，这显然不符合皮肤保健常识。

以上这些句子在语法上没错，但不符合现实情况或科学道理。由此可见，can 表示"理论上的可能"这个意义时都不宜用在否定句中。

如果真的要用 can't 来否定一个"可能性"，这个"可能性"一般就是"实际上的可能"或者说"具体的可能"，即是针对具体特定的一件事情来否定的，而不是否定一般的真理。这其实就是在 8.2、8.3 和 8.4 等几节中谈到的 can't 表示否定推测的"不可能"，表示说话人的信心非常大，对应的是肯定推测的 must。或者说 can't 是用来帮助 must 构成否定句的。比如：

22 A: This *must* be the way to the post office.

B: This *can't* be the way to the post office.

妙语点睛 这里的 can't 显然就是表示"具体的可能"。

精品译文 A：这一定是去邮局的路。

B：这不可能是去邮局的路。

23 A: The restaurant is always empty.

B: It ***isn't*** good.（100%肯定，客观事实的陈述）

It ***can't*** be good.（90%肯定，很有把握的陈述）

精品译文 A：这家餐馆总是很冷清。

B：它不怎么样。

它一定是不怎么样。

所以，can 表示"理论上的可能"时一般只适用于肯定句中。如果是在否定句中，则意味着 can't 是用于表示"具体的可能"。比如上面这个句子，说话人就不能用 can 来这么说：

A: The restaurant is always empty.

B: It ***can*** be bad. *

因为这里是一个"具体的可能"。此时，可以用 must, may, could 或 might 来表示"推测"，即"具体的可能"。比如说：

A: The restaurant is always empty.

B: It ***must*** be bad.

It ***may*** be bad.

It ***could*** be bad.

It ***might*** be bad.

我们再来看下面表示"具体的可能"的例子：

24 A: Do you know where John is now? 你知道约翰现在哪里吗？

B: I don't know. He ***could*** be in the library.（实际上真的可能）我不知道，他可能在图书馆吧。

这时同样不能用 can 说：I don't know. He ***can*** be in the library. *

以上谈到 can 表示"理论上的可能"通常只用于肯定句，不适用于否定句，也解释了这背后的原因。当然，肯定句可以变成一个疑问句。比如说：

25 ***Can*** measles be quite dangerous? 麻疹有可能很危险吗？

26 ***Can*** prolonged exposure to the sun burn my skin? 长时间在太阳底下曝晒有可能会晒伤我的皮肤吗？

所以，can 的这种"理论上的可能"也可用于疑问句中。不过同时要注意的是，在疑问句中，can 还可以表示"实际上的可能"。比如：

27 A: Do you think he ***can*** be right?

B: He ***can hardly*** be right.

妙语点睛 这里的两个 can 都是表示"具体的可能"，因为与说话时的现状都有联系。比如说他做数学题得出一个答案，你提出质疑说："你觉得他可能对吗？"这显然是"具体的可能"，而 can 用于疑问句中表示这一"具体的可能"。

精品译文 A：你觉得他可能对吗？

B：不太可能对。

28 Someone is knocking at the door. Who ***can*** it be?

妙语点睛 这里的 can 是表示"具体的可能"，因为与说话时的现状——外面有人正在敲门——有联系。

精品译文 有人在敲门，可能会是谁呢？

综上所述，can 表示"理论上的可能"主要是用在肯定句中，很少用在否定句中，因为在否定句中往往会造成语义不通或悖论。在否定句中，can't 往往只是表示"推测"，也就是这里说的"具体的可能"，这在 8.2、8.3 和 8.4 节中讨论过，取代 must 的肯定推测，帮助 must 构成否定句。在疑问句中，can 既可以表示"理论上的可能”，也可以表示“具体的可能”。

在前面的8.2、8.3和8.4三节中讨论的could, may和might用于表示“推测”，就相当于这里讨论的“实际上的可能”。但could, may和might也可以表示“理论上的可能”。

请看下面这篇有关互联网的文章：

29 **Internet *May* Cause Depression**

Internet use ***may*** cause a decline in psychological well-being, according to research at Carnegie Mellon University.

The fact that Internet use reduces time available for family and friends ***may*** account for the drop in well-being, researchers hypothesized. Faceless, bodiless "virtual" communication ***may*** be less psychologically satisfying than actual conversation, and the relationships formed through it ***may*** be shallower. Another possibility is that exposure to the wider world via the Net makes users less satisfied with their lives.

"But it's important to remember this is not about the technology per se; it's about how it is used," says psychologist Christine Riley of Intel, one of the study's sponsors. "It really points to the need for considering social factors in terms of how you design applications and services for technology."

妙语点睛　这里的5个may都是表示一种理论上的可能。因为它们与说话当时的情况都无关，只是在谈一种泛泛存在的可能性。比如第一句话中的may完全可以改成can说成：Internet use can cause a decline in psychological well-being。

精品译文　**上网可导致抑郁**

根据卡内基·麦伦大学的研究，使用因特网可能会导致心理健康程度下降。

研究者推测说，实际的情况是，上网减少了网民和家人及朋友共度的时光，这也许可以解释他们心理健康状况下降的原因。和面对面的交谈相比，这种见不着面、看不见人的“虚”的交流可能会使人从心理上缺乏满足感，人们通过这种交流结下的友谊也不会太深。还有一种可能是，网民通过互联网所了解到的广阔世界使他们对自己的生活不那么满意了。

“然而，重要的是不要忘记这与技术本身是无关的，问题在于如何使用互联网。”这项研究的发起人之一、心理学家、英特尔公司的克里斯廷·赖利说，“这的确表明，在考虑从技术上如何设计应用和服务时有必要把社会因素考虑进去。”

下面这篇有关学校教育的短文也很有意思，其中提到“我们的大学教育都是在培养‘废物’”这个观点，不禁让人们反思：

30 A student acquires knowledge mainly from the textbook and in class. When he graduates from school he ***can*** do nothing. Everything is different from what teachers told him. He ***may be*** disappointed. He ***may be*** frustrated. He ***may be*** afraid to face the real world. Our universities have turned out people of no use.

妙语点睛　显然，这里的may并不是针对现在实际的结果来推测其发生的原因的，而是表示一般理论上的“可能”。

精品译文　学生主要是从书本和课堂上获得知识。可是当他们从学校毕业走上社会后，他们就感觉自己什么也不会，社会上的一切都与老师课堂上讲的不同。这时，他们可能就会感到失望，或者是有很大的挫败感，甚至是害怕面对现实社会。由此看来，我们的大学都是在培养“废物”，而不是人才。

再如：

31 Don't go there; it ***could / may / might*** be dangerous!

妙语点睛　这句话如果是针对眼前的某一具体情况来说“别去那里，可能会很危险”，则表示具体的可能；但是，若没有具体所指，只是泛泛在谈，则是表示理论上的可能。

精品译文　别去那里，可能会很危险！

最后，我们再来看下面这句话：

32 You ***may*** be one person to the world, but you ***may*** also be the world to one person.

妙语点睛 这句话里的 may 显然不是表示与现状有任何联系的"实际上的可能"，而是表示"理论上的可能"。这句话我们可以按照字面上的意思把它译成：

精品译文 在这个世界上，你可能只是一个普通的人，但对于某些人来说，你也可能是一个世界。

笔者曾经在新东方的课堂上讲过这个例句，有同学说不懂这话说的是什么意思。但这个看似普通的句子，据说是出现在一位英国士兵的墓碑上，他在二战中阵亡，这是他深爱的女友为他献上的一句话。有了这样的故事背景，我们不妨可以把这句话译成：

哪怕只是沧海一粟，爱人眼里你是全部。

现在，这句话似乎成了一句很经典的 words for lovers，笔者见过有人在情人节的贺卡上这样写道：

To the world you may just be one person, but to me, you mean the world!

所以，读者朋友不妨也模仿引用。

思维总结

综上所述，可以得出下列结论：

1. 与说话当时现状有联系的，则是"实际上的可能"；与说话当时现状无关的，则是"理论上的可能"。

2. can 因为是表示"潜能"，所以主要用来谈论"理论上的可能"。在肯定句中，不能谈"实际上的可能"。在否定句中，can't 主要是谈"实际上的可能"，相当于 must 的否定形式。在疑问句中，can 既可以表示"理论上的可能"，也可以表示"具体的可能"。

3. could, might 和 may 可以用来谈论"具体的可能"和"理论上的可能"。

思维训练

Exercise 8.7（Key: P352）

请判断下列句中 can 用的是否正确，错误的请改正。请注意区别"理论上可能"与"实际上的可能"。

1. Even expert drivers can make mistakes.
2. Measles can be quite dangerous.
3. Winter here can be really cold.
4. It can be quite cold in Cairo in January.
5. You can be very critical sometimes.
6. He can still be waiting for a bus.
7. Clint isn't in class today. He can be ill.
8. Such an accident can happen.
9. If you look carefully, you can spot some deer through those trees.
10. A: Do you think the plane will be on time?
    B: I don't know. It can be delayed by fog.
11. A woman can do anything when jealous.
12. The weather here can be extremely cold.
13. The light switch doesn't work well. There can be something wrong with it.
14. Prolonged exposure to the sun can burn your skin.
15. Don't stay outside too long on hot days. Too much exposure to the sun can be dangerous.
16. Tom can sometimes be very rude.
17. I wonder where Tom is. He can be in the library.

8.8 基本用法(三)：过去的能力

2005 年 9 月 12 日，香港迪斯尼乐园(Disneyland)开幕，这是继美国加州本土、法国巴黎和日本东京之后，世界上的第四个迪斯尼乐园。相信迪斯尼乐园是很多人梦想去的地方，比如我们可以这样畅想：

1 I hope I ***can*** go to Hong Kong Disneyland one day. 我希望将来有一天我能够去香港迪斯尼乐园。

如果是“今天我能够去迪斯尼乐园”，用英语可以这么说：

2 Today I ***can*** go to Disneyland.

或者说：Today I ***am able to*** go to Disneyland.

在 8.6 节中讲过说过，can 强调的是“潜在的可能性”，而不是真正去实施(the potential to perform an action, not the actual performance)，所以这句话其实是说“尽管理论上可以去，但实际上我可能去，也可能不去”。

我们现在把时间改为“昨天”，来表达一个确定的事实，即“我昨天终于能够去了迪斯尼乐园”，这时要怎么说呢？

也许有读者会认为，只要把 can 改成过去式 could 就可以了。比如这样说：

3 Yesterday I ***could*** go to Hong Kong Disneyland. *

其实是不可以这么讲的，或者说在英文中不存在上面这样的句子。如果一个 native speaker 听到了这个句子，他或许还会进一步问你“昨天到底是去了还是没有去”。如果是去了，则他会让你这么说：

Yesterday I ***was able to*** go to Hong Kong Disneyland.

如果是要表达“我昨天本来是可以去，但结果没有去成”这样的虚拟意思，则要说成：

Yesterday I ***could have gone*** to Hong Kong Disneyland.

所以，在英语中不存在 Yesterday I ***could*** go to Hong Kong Disneyland. 这样的句子。

看到这里，一定有读者要问：换成过去时态后，用 could 为什么就不再正确呢？为什么只能用 was able to?

这个问题涉及 could 和 was able to 在表达“过去的能力(past ability)”时的区别。

看到 can/could，读者的第一反应可能就是“能够”的意思。但这是不够的，因为这样并没有真正掌握 can/could 的核心意思。比如汉语里完全可以说“昨天能够怎样怎样”，但在英文里却不能说 Yesterday I could...这样的句子。因为在 8.6 节中强调过，can/could 的核心意思是表示一种“潜能”(The core concept of CAN is about “potential”.)强调的是“潜在的可能性”，而不一定真正去实施(the potential to perform an action, not the actual performance)。具体来说就是表示因为具备某些特点或条件，某人能够完成某件事或某事是可能存在的，而并不是强调何时或怎样实施这种潜在的行为。比如下面短文中的 can 就是表示这种“潜在的可能”：

4 When Disney began designing its newest kingdom in Hong Kong, planners decided Mickey’s magic wasn’t enough for success. The park needed an extra boost from “*feng shui*”. In Hong Kong, “*feng shui*” has played a large part in the park’s design. A master moved its main gate so it was facing the right direction, put a bend in its walkway so that “*qi*” or energy does not flow into the South China Sea and does not have the unlucky number “four” in its elevators. It’s a tricky business, but few dare to ignore it in Hong Kong. Many believe bad feng *shui* ***can*** cause financial ruin, and Disney wasn’t about to risk it, Tom Morris, a chief designer at Hong Kong Disneyland, said.

妙语点睛 该短文讲到了美国迪斯尼集团为了融入中国的本土文化(fit into the local culture)，在建造香港迪斯尼乐园时就充分考虑了中国的“风水”文化。比如在修建香港迪斯尼乐园的新入口时，迪斯尼集团的管理层决定把前门方位调整 12 度。之所以这样做，是因为他们咨询了一名中国的风水大师。另外，从火车站到大门的走道上，迪斯尼还专门设计了一个拐弯，以确保“气”不会溜过入口而跑到南海里。在香港，迪斯尼乐园每建好一座建筑，就会举行焚香仪式；同时还专门挑选了被认为是黄道吉日的 9 月 12 日作为首次开放的时间。在我们的风水文化里，认为“风水不好，就有可能会造成财务亏损(bad *feng shui* ***can*** cause financial ruin)”，因此迪斯尼集团也不敢冒这个险而甘愿向风水“折腰”(ancient Chinese *feng shui* magic guides Disney design)。这里的 can 显然是表示一种“潜在的可能性”。

精品译文 当迪斯尼开始设计其在香港的新乐园时，策划者认为，仅靠米老鼠的神奇号召力是不够的，乐园需要“风水”的额外帮助。在香港，“风水”在整个乐园的设计中起着重要的作用。一个风水大师把正门的方向改动了一下，这样它就朝向合适的方向；又在走到上设计了一个拐弯，这样“气”或者说能量就不会泄入南海里。另外，乐园的电梯上没有“4”这个不吉利的数字。这是一种迷信，但是在香港，没人胆敢忽视它。很多人认为，风水不好，就有可能会造成经营亏损，迪斯尼也不愿冒这个险。香港迪斯尼乐园的总设计师汤姆·莫里斯如是说。

请再看下面的短文：

5 Disney executives have said China ***can*** support two Disneylands, but they have said no other park would open on the mainland before 2010. The world's best-known entertainment company is counting on these increasingly affluent mainland Chinese tourists in its third international venture, and its second in Asia after Japan. It is also hoping it ***can*** export its magic to China, where there is no deep knowledge of its culture.

妙语点睛 该短文说到，迪斯尼的管理层认为，中国这个巨大的市场足以支持两个迪斯尼乐园。因此，说不定某一天在中国内地也会建起一个迪斯尼乐园，但是迪斯尼方认为这只可能是在2010年以后了。其实，迪斯尼公司在香港建园，就是为了通过香港迪斯尼乐园来向中国人普及迪斯尼的相关知识，以便为将来进军中国内地做好铺垫，因为，在亚洲的大部分地区，人们对迪斯尼的很多商品和相关角色并不是很了解。同样，我们看到句中的两个 can 均表示一种"潜在的可能"，强调的是一种 potential，相当于说 China has the ***potential to support*** two Disneylands and Disney has the ***potential possibility of exporting*** its magic to China. 而这些都不是 actual performance。

精品译文 迪斯尼的管理层认为，中国能够支持两座迪斯尼乐园，但他们还说，2010年之前不会在中国大陆建造新的迪斯尼乐园了。迪斯尼这个世界最为知名的娱乐公司期待着，中国大陆逐渐富裕起来的旅游者们能够到其全球第三家、继日本东京迪斯尼乐园之后的亚洲第二家迪斯尼乐园来探险。他们还希望，他们能够向中国推广迪斯尼的相关知识，因为中国对于迪斯尼的文化并不十分了解。

现在回头看本章开头的两个例句：

1) I hope I ***can*** go to Hong Kong Disneyland one day.

2) Today I ***can*** go to Disneyland.

"将来能够"或者是"今天能够"去迪斯尼乐园，强调的都是一种"潜在的可能性"，而不一定真正去实施。也就是说，尽管理论上"我"可以去迪斯尼乐园，但实际上"我"可能去，也可能不去。但如果我们谈一个具体的过去的事件，如"昨天能够去迪斯尼乐园"，则是表达一个确定的事实，没有"潜在的可能"的意思了，这就违背了 can 的"潜能"这一核心意思。故不能说出：Yesterday I ***could*** go to Hong Kong Disneyland. * 这样的句子。

所以，从"将来能够"或"今天能够"变为"昨天能够"，改变的不仅是时态问题，更重要的是其中 can 所蕴含的"潜在的可能性"这一核心思维改变了。当用 can 谈将来的事件或现在的事件时，这种"潜在的可能性"自然是一直存在的，以至于让我们忽略了 can 的这一重要思维。但是，若谈论过去的事件时，这种"潜在的可能性"有可能(但不是必然)会丧失。这个问题涉及在表达"过去的能力(past ability)"时，could 和 was able to 的区别。

简单来说，二者的区别是：could 表示"过去的一般能力"，was able to 表示"过去的具体能力"。具体地说，所谓"过去的一般能力"就是指在过去有能力想做某件事就随时可以去做，但并不说明真正实施了这个行为，即强调的是一种"潜能"，而不是某一次具体的过去行为。(When used to denote past ability, COULD does not refer to a single instance of ability on a particular occasion, but rather, it signifies ***an ability in a very general sense***.)例如：

6 I ***could*** run after a bus and catch it twenty years ago, but I can't do that now.

妙语点睛 这里只是说明"我"过去有"追上汽车"这个能力，而并没有强调"我"真的实施了"追车"这个行为，即表示的是一种"潜能"或"一般能力"，所以用 could 来表示"潜在的可能"。这里不能用 can，因为 can 不能表示过去。

精品译文 20年前我可以追上汽车，但现在不行了。

所谓过去的"具体的能力"，即表示主语在过去的某个特定场合所实施的具体行动，此时没有"潜在的可能性"，所以不能用 could，而要用 was/were able to，表示"成功地做成了某事"。因此 was/were able to do 可用 succeeded in doing 或 managed to do 替换。(The successful demonstration of ability on a particular past occasion is expressed by means of be able to, manage to do, succeed in, etc.)例如：

7 I ran after the bus yesterday and ***was able to*** catch it.

妙语点睛 这里用 was able to 表示的正是过去的一次具体的行为，说明具体实施了"追车"这一行为，而且成功地追上了，即表示"具体的能力"，而不是过去的"潜能"。

精品译文 昨天我追赶了一辆汽车，而且成功地追上它了。

下面是迪斯尼乐园的创始人沃特·迪斯尼(Walt Disney)先生在谈到迪斯尼乐园的设想时的原话:

8 I think what I want Disneyland to be most of all is a happy place, a place where adults and children ***can*** experience together some of the wonders of life, of adventure, and feel better because of it. 我想，我希望迪斯尼乐园首先是要成为一个充满快乐的地方，无论是成年人还是孩子，都能在这里体验到生命和探险的神奇，并因此而感到愉快。

我们现在可以用过去时这样来转述他的话:

Walt Disney revealed that his Disneyland Park would be an environment where parents and children ***could*** have fun together and ***could*** experience some of the wonders of life and adventure. 沃特·迪斯尼说，他的迪斯尼乐园将会是一个父母与孩子能在这里找到快乐的地方，能在这里体验到生命和探险的神奇。

两个句子都不是表示一次"实际的行动"，而是传达一种"潜在的可能"，所以用 can/could。如果是谈过去一次具体的活动，则要用 be able to。比如回忆自己的一次游览迪斯尼乐园的经历:

9 I ***was able to*** experience the wonders of life and adventure in Hong Kong Disneyland last week. 上周我终于去了香港迪斯尼乐园疯玩了一把。

我们再来看下面这篇短文:

10 **Volcanoes**

Haroun Tazieff, the Polish scientist, has spent his lifetime studying active volcanoes and deep caves in all parts of the world. In 1948, he went to Lake Kivu in the Congo to observe a new volcano which he later named Kituro. Tazieff ***was able to*** set up his camp very close to the volcano while it was erupting violently. Though he ***managed to*** take a number of brilliant photographs, he ***could not*** stay near the volcano for very long. He noticed that a river of liquid rock was coming towards him. It threatened to surround him completely, but Tazieff ***managed to*** escape just in time. He waited until the volcano became quiet and he ***was able to*** return two days later. This time, he ***managed to*** climb into the mouth of Kituro so that he ***could*** take photographs and measure temperatures. Tazieff has often risked his life in this way. He has been able to tell us more about active volcanoes than any man alive.

妙语点睛 我们看到，这里 was able to 与 managed to 进行了多次互换使用。其中还有 could 表示过去的一般能力。

精品译文 火山

波兰科学家哈鲁恩·塔齐夫终生致力于研究世界各地的活火山和深洞。1948 年，他前往刚果境内的齐乌湖，去观察那里的一座新火山，他后来将这座火山命名为齐图鲁。塔齐夫能够将帐篷搭建在一座正在猛烈喷发的火山近旁。尽管他设法拍摄了大量精美的照片，但还是无法在火山旁边呆得太久。他注意到一条岩浆流正在朝他涌来，会将他完全包围，但是塔齐夫还是及时逃脱了。他一直等到火山不再喷发。两天后，他又能够回到火山那里去了。这一次，他设法爬到了齐图鲁火山的火山口处，这样他就能拍照并测量那里的温度了。塔齐夫经常这样冒险，较之其他人，他能告诉我们更多的关于活火山的事情。

综上所述，could 同 can 一样，表示的是一种"潜能"或者说"过去的一般能力"，而不是"实际行动"；was/were able to 则更多地是用来表示过去的"实际行动"或者说"具体的能力"。但注意，也可以用 was/were able to 表示"潜能"，但不如 could 常用。请再看更多的例句:

一、表示过去的"潜能"

11 He ***could / was able to pull*** down a bull and acknowledged as a man with superman strength.

妙语点睛 这里只是说他"曾经能够"，并没有具体说是哪次活动，所以是"潜能"，不是"实际行动"。

精品译文 他曾能够拉倒一头牛，被公认为是具有神力的人。

12 I ***could / was able to*** recite several poems when I was 3 years of age. 我在三岁的时候就能背诵好几首诗歌。

13 Fred ***could / was able to*** speak Russian when he was 6 years old. 弗雷德六岁的时候就能说俄语。

14 In those days few workers ***could*** support their families. 那时很少有工人能够养家糊口。

二、表示过去的"实际行动"(均不能用 could)

15 They ***were able to*** get tickets to the Rolling Stones concert last week. 上周他们搞到了滚石乐队的演唱会的票。

16 How ***were*** you ***able to*** convince him to come to the exhibition last week? 你上周是怎么说服他去看展览的？

17 With the aid of the wood, he ***was able to*** swim across the river. 借助这块木头，他就能游过河去了。

18 I applied everywhere and finally I ***was able to*** get a good job. 我四处应聘，终于找到了一份不错的工作。

19 He hurried to the station, and he ***was able to*** catch the train. 他赶到车站，赶上了火车。

20 The fire spread through the building quickly but everybody ***was able to*** escape.
大火在大楼中迅速蔓延，但是所有人都逃脱了。

21 The two boys tried many ways to catch that sly fox and ***were able to*** do so at last.
两个孩子试用了多种方法抓那只狡猾的狐狸，最后终于成功了。

22 Although the pilot was badly hurt he ***was able to*** explain what had happened.
飞行员的伤势虽然很严重，但是他还能够解释所发生的一切。

23 Tom has started an exercise program. He ***was able to*** run two miles yesterday without stopping or slowing down.
汤姆开始了他的训练计划。昨天他一口气跑了两英里，且速度未减。

24 He didn't agree with me at first but I ***was able to*** persuade him.
起初他并不同意我的意见，但最后我成功地说服了他。

对于某些句子，既可以用 could，又可以用 were able to，此时的含义自然是不同的。比如：

25 1) I ***could*** repair the old car.
2) I ***was able to*** repair the old car.

妙语点睛 在例句 1)中，用 could 表达的是过去的一般能力，即表示"我过去是能够修理旧汽车的"，这里是泛指任何一辆旧汽车。在例句 2)中，用 was able to 表达的是过去的具体能力，即表示"我终于把那辆旧汽车修理好了"，这里是具体指某一辆特定的旧汽车。

精品译文 1) 我过去是能够修理旧汽车的。
2) 我终于把那辆旧汽车修理好了。

我们再来看下面这篇短文：

26 **Over the South Pole**

In 1929, three years after his flight over the North Pole, the American explorer, R. E. Byrd, successfully flew over the South Pole for the first time. Though, at first, Byrd and his men ***were able to*** take a great many photographs of the mountains that lay below, they soon ran into serious trouble. At one point, it seemed certain that their plane would crash. It ***could*** only get over the mountains if it rose to 10, 000 feet. Byrd at once ordered his men to throw out two heavy food sacks. The plane ***was*** then ***able to*** rise and it cleared the mountains by 400 feet. Byrd now knew that he ***would be able to*** reach the South Pole which was 300 miles away, for there were no more mountains in sight. The aircraft ***was able to*** fly over the endless white plains without difficulty.

精品译文 **飞越南极**

美国探险家 R. E. 伯德在飞越北极三年之后，于 1929 年第一次成功地飞越了南极。虽然开始时伯德和他的助手们拍下了飞机下面连绵群山的大量照片，但他们很快就陷入了困境。在一个地方，飞机似乎肯定要坠毁了。只有在飞至 10,000 英尺的高度时，它才能飞过这些山头。伯德马上命令他的助手们把两个沉重的食物袋扔掉，于是飞机可以上升了，它在离山头 400 英尺的高度飞越了过去。这时，伯德知道他能够顺利飞抵 300 英里以外的南极了，因为前面没有山了，飞机可以毫无困难地飞过这片茫茫无际的白色原野！

有趣的是，上述 could 和 was/were able to 的区别仅限于肯定句中，在否定句中 could 和 was/were able to 可以互换使用，没有区别。比如可以说：

27 I ran after the bus yesterday, but ***wasn't able to/couldn't*** catch it. 我昨天追赶公共汽车，但是没赶上。

28 I applied everywhere and I ***wasn't able to/couldn't*** get any good job. 我四处应聘，但是没能找到好工作。

29 The fire spread through the building quickly and people ***wasn't able to/couldn't*** escape. 大火在大楼中迅速蔓延，人们没能逃脱。

30 Though he ***managed to*** take a number of brilliant photographs, he ***could not*** stay near the volcano for very long. 尽管他设法拍摄了大量精美的照片，但还是无法在火山旁边呆得太久。

尽管这里是表示过去的具体场合，但依然用了 could，因为有否定的 not，即 couldn't 表示过去具体的能力。

思维总结

首先，在 can/could 表示"能力"时，二者均表示"潜能"或者说"一般能力"。其中，can 表示将来或现在的一般能力，could 表示过去的一般能力。

其次，could 表示"过去的一般能力"，不表示"过去具体的能力"；was/were able to 既可以表示"过去的一般能力"，也可以表示"过去具体的能力"。

再次，结合 8. 7 节中讨论的"可能"的含义，我们发现，虽然 could 不能谈"过去具体的能力"，但可以表示"具体的可能"（如 He could be sick. 表示现在或将来的具体可能，或 He could have been sick. 表示过去的具体可能）。所以，could 可以用来谈论"具体的可能"，"理论上的可能"，以及"过去的一般能力"，但不能谈"过去具体的能力"。另外值得注意的是，could 表示"推测"时，本身不能表示"过去"，而是用 could have done 来表示过去的可能。但 could 表示"能力"时，本身就表示"过去"，即"过去的一般能力"。

最后，在否定句中，couldn't 和 wasn't/weren't able to 没有区别，即 couldn't 可以谈过去具体的能力，表示在过去的某一个特定场合"未能"完成某事。

思维训练

Exercise 8. 8（Key: P352）

请在合适的地方填上 could 或 couldn't 或 was/were able to。

1. I applied everywhere and finally I ______ get a good job.
2. Although the pilot was badly hurt he ______ explain what had happened.
3. Tom has started an exercise program. He ______ run two miles yesterday without stopping or slowing down.
4. I ______ run two miles without stopping or slowing down when I was in my 20s.
5. He didn't agree with me at first but I ______ persuade him.
6. Fred ______ speak Russian when he was six years old.
7. They ______ get tickets to the Rolling Stones concert last week.
8. After waiting for an hour, I finally ______ see the doctor.
9. I ______ see anything in all that smoke. But then a fireman emerged from the darkness and saved my life.
10. I tried to persuade Grace to come with us, but I ______ convince her.
11. A: Did you see the exhibit at the art center?
    B: I sure did. And I ______ make heads or tails of it.
12. A: I lived with my sister this summer and didn't have to pay rent. So I ______ save most of my salary.
    B: Not me. The more I earned, the more I spent.
13. They didn't want to come with us at first but we ______ persuade them.
14. Jack was an excellent tennis player. He ______ beat anybody.
15. Jack and John had a game of tennis yesterday. John played very well but in the end Jack ______ beat him.
16. I looked everywhere for the book but I ______ find it.

17. I looked everywhere for the book and finally I ______ find it.
18. Sue wasn't at home when I phoned but I ______ contact her at her office.
19. My mother loved music. She ______ play the piano very well.
20. A girl fell into the river but fortunately we ______ rescue her.
21. I had forgotten to bring my camera so I ______ take any photographs.
22. Although I forgot to bring my camera that day, I ______ take some nice photographs with John's camera.
23. When I worked as a secretary, I ______ type 60 words a minute without making a mistake. My typing skills aren't nearly as good now.
24. Yesterday I typed these reports for my boss. I don't type very well, but I ______ finish the reports without making too many mistakes.
25. When I ran into Mr. Smith yesterday, I ______ recognize him even though I hadn't seen him for years.
26. At the sale yesterday, I ______ get this shirt for half price. Quite a bargain, don't you think?
27. My grandfather was a merchant all his life. He knew how to make a sale by using psychology. He ______ convince anyone to buy anything, whether they needed it or not.
28. Volcanoes

    Haroun Tazieff, the Polish scientist, has spent his lifetime studying active volcanoes and deep caves in all parts of the world. In 1948, he went to Lake Kivu in the Congo to observe a new volcano which he later named Kituro. Tazieff ______ set up his camp very close to the volcano while it was erupting violently. Though he ______ take a number of brilliant photographs, he ______ stay near the volcano for very long. He noticed that a river of liquid rock was coming towards him. It threatened to surround him completely, but Tazieff ______ escape just in time. He waited until the volcano became quiet and he ______ return two days later. This time, he ______ climb into the mouth of Kituro so that he ______ take photographs and measure temperatures. Tazieff has often risked his life in this way. He has been able to tell us more about active volcanoes than any man alive.

请翻译下列句子，并比较两句含义的差别。

29. I was able to go to the library last night.
30. I could have gone to the library last night.

8.9 基本用法(四)：许可

用情态动词表示"许可"，以下三点是非常重要的：

1. 可以用的情态动词有 may, might, can 和 could，但多用 can 或 be allowed to do 表示许可；
2. 表示"许可"一般用陈述句(若用疑问句则表示"请求〈request〉"，见 8.12 节)；
3. 肯定的陈述表示允许某人做某事；否定的陈述则表示不允许某人做某事。

8.9.1 肯定句——给予许可

1 We ***can*** borrow these books from the library.

相当于说：We ***are allowed to*** borrow these books from the library.

精品译文 我们可以从图书馆借出这些书。

2 You need to get a license before you ***can*** drive a car in this country.

相当于说：You need to get a license before you ***are allowed to*** drive a car in this country.

精品译文 在这个国家，你需要先取得驾照然后才可以开车。

3 I ***can*** leave the office as soon as I have finished.

相当于说：I ***am allowed to*** leave the office as soon as I have finished.

精品译文　我工作一结束就可以离开办公室。

4 You ***can*** use my car tomorrow.

相当于说：You ***are allowed to*** use my car tomorrow.

精品译文　明天你可以用我的车。

当然也可以用 may 来表示"许可"。比如：

5 A: ***May*** I turn on the TV?

B: Yes, of course you ***may***.

妙语点睛　这里 may 用在疑问句中表示"请求许可"，用在肯定的陈述句中表示"给予许可"。

精品译文　A：我可以打开电视吗？

B：当然可以。

6 You ***may*** only register for two classes. 你只能报两门课。

不过，在口语中，我们更多的还是用 can 来表达"许可"。而 may 表示"许可"会用在非常正式的文体中，所以在口语中比较少见。

※ can 表示"许可"和"能力"的辨别

can 表示"许可"，可以和表示将来的时间状语连用。尽管前面讲过，can 可以表示将来的能力，不过此时一般不与表示将来的时间状语连用。若有表示将来的时间状语，要说 will be able to do。请比较：

7 You ***can*** use my car ***tomorrow***.

妙语点睛　该句中的 can 是表示"许可"，所以可以与 tomorrow 连用。

精品译文　明天你可以用我的车。

再比如下面这个句子：

8 You ***can*** pass your driving test next time you take it.*

妙语点睛　因为该句中的 can 是表示"能力"，所以不宜与表达将来的从句 next time you take it 连用，最好改为：You ***will be able to*** pass your driving test next time you take it.

精品译文　下次你参加路考应该就能通过了。

我们来看下面家长与孩子之间颇为有意思的对话：

9 Child: ***Can*** I leave the table now?

Parent: I'm sure you ***can***, but you ***may*** not.

妙语点睛　这里孩子用 can，他的意思是用 can 的"许可"含义，这里用在疑问句中，是表示"请求"家长"许可"他离开饭桌。而家长用的 can 是表示"能力"的含义，may 是表示"许可"。家长在这里似乎是故意通过曲解孩子的"许可"，而将其曲解为"能力"的 can，来和孩子开了个玩笑，意思是说"你长腿了，当然'能够'离开饭桌，但我不允许你离开"。

精品译文　孩子：我现在可以离开饭桌了吗？

家长：你是能够离开，但我不允许你离开。

8.9.2 否定句——拒绝许可，甚至禁止

1 A: May I borrow your car?

B: No, I'm afraid you ***may not***.

妙语点睛　may 用在疑问句中表示"请求许可"，用在否定的陈述句中表示"拒绝许可"。

精品译文　A：我可以借用你的车吗？

B：恐怕不行。

2 You ***may not*** smoke in here.

=You ***are not allowed to*** smoke in here. 这不让抽烟。

3 You *can't* take the test paper out of the classroom.
=You *are not allowed to* take the test paper out of the classroom. 试卷不允许带出教室。

4 You *can't* take your camera into the museum. 照相机不让带进博物馆。

我们还可用 must not 表示强烈的拒绝许可——禁止，但 must not 比 cannot 或 may not 的语气强烈。比如：

5 Students *must not* take the test papers out of the classroom. 任何学生都不得把试卷带出教室。

8.9.3 could 一般不用来表示现在的许可，而表示过去的许可

表示过去的一般许可，could 与 was/were allowed to do 可以互换。比如：

1 I *could / was allowed to* read what I liked when I was a child. 我小的时候爱看什么书，就看什么书。

不过，若表示过去允许进行某项特定的活动时，要用 was/were allowed to do，这一区别与表示"能力"时的 could 和 was/were able to 的区别类似。比如：

2 Yesterday evening, Peter *was allowed to* watch TV for an hour.

但不说：Yesterday evening, Peter *could* watch TV for an hour. *
同理，might 在表示"许可"时，也只能是表示过去的一般许可，而不能表达具体场合的某一个活动。不能说：Yesterday evening, Peter *might* watch TV for an hour. * 昨晚，允许彼得看一个小时电视。

请比较：

3 1) They *might* have a break after lunch.
2) They *were allowed to* have a break after lunch.

妙语点睛 在例句 1)中，用 might 是表示过去一般的许可，所以该句的意思是：他们在过去的一段时期内，是被允许在吃完午饭后休息一会儿的。在例句 2)中，用 were allowed to 可以表示过去一般的许可。但若表示过去具体的许可，则该句的意思是：在过去的某一天他们被允许在吃完午饭后休息了一次。

精品译文 1) 那时，他们吃完午饭后是可以休息一会儿的。
2) 那次，他们吃完午饭后被允许休息了一会儿。

8.10 基本用法(五)：建议与忠告

在英语中，表示建议与忠告的情态动词比较多，比如可以用 could, shall 和 should 等。本节内容安排如下：

8.10.1 could 表示建议
8.10.2 Shall I? Shall we?
8.10.3 may (just) as well, might (just) as well
8.10.4 should 和 ought to 表示忠告
8.10.5 should 表示"忠告"与 could 表示"建议"比较
8.10.6 had better 表示忠告

8.10.1 could 表示建议

前面讨论了 could 可以表示"推测"(可用于将来、现在及过去时间)、过去的"能力"、过去的"许可"。这里我们来看 could 用于表示"建议"，此时，could 并不表示过去。比如：

1 A: I've been invited to a dinner party at Janet's. Do you think I should bring something?
B: You *could* pick up a cake. Chocolate is her favorite.

妙语点睛 说话人 A 是在征求 B 的建议，于是 B 通过 could 来提出自己的建议，建议 A"买一份蛋糕"。

精品译文 A：我受到邀请去珍妮特家参加晚宴，你认为我该带点什么东西去吗？
B：你可以买一份蛋糕嘛，巧克力口味的她最喜欢。

其他例句比如：

2 A: What shall we do this evening? 我们今晚做些什么？
B: We *could go* to the cinema. 我们可以去看电影。

3 It is a nice day. We *could go* for a walk. 今天天气不错，我们可以出去散散步。

4 We *could go* to that new restaurant opposite the cinema. 我们可以去电影院对面那家新开的餐馆吃饭。

5 We *could go* to the theater instead.
=How about going to the theater instead? 我们可以改去剧院。

8. 10. 2 Shall I...? Shall we...?

shall 用于第一人称的一般疑问句中，表示征求对方的“建议”。请看例句：

1 ***Shall I*** open the window?
=***Would you like me to*** open the window? 要不要我把窗子打开？

2 ***Shall we*** leave at two? Is that OK? 我们两点钟走如何？怎么样？

关于 shall I/we 的其他用法，详见 8. 15. 1 小节。

8. 10. 3 may (just) as well, might (just) as well

这组情态动词表示“建议换另一种方式做某事”，可译成“倒不如”，“不妨”。请看例句：

1 A: I'll go on Monday by train. 我将在周一坐火车去。
B: You ***might just as well*** wait till Wednesday and go by plane. 你不妨等到周三坐飞机去。

2 We ***may as well*** stay here tonight. 我们今晚不如在这过夜。

另外，may/might as well 还有一种多少有些勉强或讥讽的意味，表示“在没有其他更好的选择的情况下，只好为之”之意(May/might as well describes the only thing left to do, something that the speaker is not enthusiastic about.)比如：

3 It's no use waiting here. We ***might as well*** start walking. 在这里干等没用，我们还不如开始步行回去。

4 Nobody else is going to turn up now for the lesson, so you ***may as well*** go home. 没有其他人会到场来上课了，所以你还是回家吧。

5 You ***might as well*** tell the truth (as continue to tell lies).
妙语点睛 这里言外之意是“别再继续撒谎了”，相当于说 There is no point in your continuing to tell lies.
精品译文 (与其继续撒谎)你不妨还是实话实说了吧。

8. 10. 4 should 和 ought to 表示忠告

should 最主要的意义和用法就是表示“建议”，“忠告”或者说“规劝”，表示“某事是应该做的或恰当的(appropriate behavior)”。比如：

1 You ***should*** brush your teeth twice a day. 你应该每天刷牙两次。

2 We ***should*** call them before we go there. 去那之前我们应该给他们打个电话。

3 You ***should*** do as you are told. 你应该按照告诉你的那样去做。

4 We ***should*** study harder because the finals are near. 快要期末考试了，我们得更用功了。

此时的 should 往往也会含有"责任"和"义务"的含义。比如：

5 Drivers ***should*** obey the speed limit. 司机应该遵守车速限制(的规定)。

这种"责任"的意味比 must 要轻。请比较：

6 Drivers ***must*** obey the speed limit. 司机必须遵守车速限制(的规定)。

这种表示"责任"的 should 也常见于疑问句中，表示否定一个"责任"。比如：

7 Why ***should*** I do what everyone else does? 我为什么非得跟其他人一样啊？

8 Why ***should*** I go there when I'm quite happy here? 我在这里很快乐，为什么非要去那里啊？

总之，should 的基本含义是表示进行恰当的行为(expressing appropriate behavior)、正确地做事(correct ways of doing things)，所以可以用来表示规劝、建议或忠告等等。

另外，上述例句也都可以用 ought to，只不过它更多地是出现在口语中，而不是书面语中。

8.10.5 should 表示"忠告"与 could 表示"建议"比较

should 表示强烈的、明确的忠告；could 表示建议某事的可能性。

1 A: Hi, Tom. How is your chemistry paper going?

B: It's coming along. But I've been staring at this computer screen for hours and my eyes hurt.

A: Yeah. Doing that can make your eyes really dry and tired. You ***should*** take a break.

B: I can't. I have to get this paper written. It's due tomorrow.

精品译文 A：嗨，汤姆，你的化学论文进展如何？

B：正在写，不过我盯着电脑屏幕看几个小时了，现在眼睛很痛。

A：是啊，一直看电脑会让你的眼睛又干又累，你应该歇会儿。

B：可是不行啊，我得把这篇论文写完，明天我得交。

2 A: John doesn't feel good. He has a bad stomachache.

B1: He ***should*** see a doctor.

B2: Well, he ***could*** see a doctor, or he ***could*** simply stay in bed for a day and hope he feels better tomorrow.

精品译文 A：约翰不舒服，他胃疼得厉害。

B1：他应该看医生去。

B2：嗯，他可以看医生去，也可以卧床休息一天，但愿他明天能感觉好一点。

从上面这个对话看到，用 should 表示只有一种选择，而 could 表示可以有很多种选择。再如：

3 A: I need to get to the airport.

B1: You ***should*** take the airport bus. It's cheaper than a taxi.

B2: Well, you ***could*** take the airport bus. Or you ***could*** take a taxi. Maybe Clint ***could*** take you. He has a car.

精品译文 A：我得去机场。

B1：你应该坐机场大巴，比坐出租车便宜。

B2：嗯，你可以坐机场大巴，也可以坐出租车。克林特也许能送你去，他有车。

所以，总体来说，could 比 should 的语气要弱得多，只是为听话者提供一种参考意见，听话人可以有多种选择。而 should 则是表示听话人最好应该采用的一种选择。

8.10.6 had better 表示"忠告"

常用于口语中，后面接动词原形，否定用 had better not do。

1 We ***had better*** study harder, or we'll probably fail in the exam. 我们最好用功学习，不然考试就有可能不及格。

需要注意的是，had better 在表示"忠告"时，有时会暗含"如果不这么做，就会有不良后果"的意思，而

should 则更为中性。比如：

2 You *had better* return the book to the library.

妙语点睛 这相当于警告对方，如果不及时还书，图书馆就会有惩罚措施，比如罚款。

精品译文 你最好把书还给图书馆。

3 You *had better* do your homework.

妙语点睛 言外之意是，如果不做作业就会受到批评，或是考试受影响等。

精品译文 你最好去写作业。

但是若用 should，则更多地是表示个人的责任或义务，比如借书归还是每个人应该尽到的责任。比如说：

4 You *should* return the book to the library. 你应该把书还给图书馆。

5 You *should* do your homework. 你应该写作业。

8.11 基本用法(六)：意愿、意图与执意

在《英语语法新思维初级教程——走近语法》第八章中，笔者讨论过 will 主要的两个意义和用法：预测和意愿。比如在下面打电话的场景中：

1 A: The phone's ringing.

B1: That*'ll* be for me.

B2: I*'ll* get it.

妙语点睛 这里 B 的第一种回答方式，是表示很肯定的预测，即“肯定是我的电话”。而 B 的第二种回答方式，则是表示自己愿意去接这个电话，是表示意愿，即“我来接”。

精品译文 A：电话铃在响。

B1：肯定是我的电话。

B2：我来接。

再如：

2 We*'ll* carry those for you if he *won't*.

妙语点睛 表示意愿。

精品译文 如果他不愿意，我们会帮你拿那些东西的。

3 Think it *will* rain? I'm sure it *won't*.

妙语点睛 表示预测。

精品译文 你觉着要下雨？我肯定不会下雨的。

关于 will 的这两种用法，请读者参看《英语语法新思维初级教程——走近语法》，在此不再赘述。在本节中，笔者主要来分析 will 另外的意义和用法：意图和执意。

8.11.1 意图(intention)

表示“意图”往往涉及将来准备好的事件(“Intention” clearly involves a future event that is planned.)，请看例句：

1 I *will* borrow some money and buy a car.

妙语点睛 这里 will 表示说话人的意图和打算，而不是在预测或表达意愿。这句话相当于说 I intend to borrow some money and buy a car.

精品译文 我要借钱买辆车。

也许读者不大好理解什么是“意图”。为了帮助大家理解，现在，我们把“意图”的含义向两个极端——承诺

与威胁——延展开来。在表达意图时，如果是希望的行为(desirable action)，则可解释为一种“承诺(promise)”；若是不希望的行为(undesirable action)，则解释成为一种“威胁(threat)”。请比较：

2 I *will* make dinner for tomorrow night.

妙语点睛 这里的 will 表达的是一种承诺。

精品译文 明晚我来做晚饭。

3 I'*ll* call the police if you don't leave.

妙语点睛 这里的 will 表达的是一种威胁。

精品译文 如果你不离开，我就要叫警察了。

说话人也可能意图不明确，比如下面对话中的 B 半开玩笑的回应：

4 A: I'*ll* talk to you about this later.

B: Is that a threat or a promise?

妙语点睛 这里说话人 A 用 will 可能引起听话人的迷惑。比如 will 若表示威胁，则 A 的意思可以理解为“这个我以后再找你算账”；如果 will 表示承诺，则 A 的意思可以理解为“这个我以后再和你商量”。这里我们把该句的意思译成模棱两可的，比如“这个我以后再跟你说”。

精品译文 A：这个我以后再跟你说。

B：你这是在威胁还是答应了？

8.11.2 执意(insistence)

will 表示“执意”，来源于它的“意图”的含义，因为当某人坚持自己的“意图”而不愿意改变时，就变成了“执意”(“Will/won't” can be used to emphatically tell someone of the speaker's intention, or to forbid an action.)。此时，肯定的 will 表示“某人坚持要做某事”，比如说 I will 相当于 I insist(“I will” can mean “I insist”.)；否定的 won't 表示“某人坚持不愿意做某事或禁止做某事”，比如说 I won't 相当于 I refuse(“I won't” can mean “I refuse”.)。请看例句：

1 If they *will* pay in cash, we have to accept it although it'*ll* cause trouble to both sides.

妙语点睛 这里 if 引导的从句中的 will 就是表示执意。一般来讲，在 if 引导的条件状语从句中是不能用将来时态 will 的，但这里 will 用于 if 引导的条件状语从句中了。究其原因，就是因为这里的 will 不是表示将来时态，而是侧重于表示“执意”这样的情态含义。另外，although 引导的从句中的 will 是表示说话人的预测。

精品译文 如果他们非要坚持用现金支付，那我们也没办法，只好接受了，尽管这会给双方都造成麻烦。

类似上面这个句子，我们可以造一个 will not 的否定句，来表示说话人拒绝做某事。比如：

2 If they *will not* accept a check, we shall have to pay cash, though it would be much trouble for both sides.

妙语点睛 这里 if 引导的条件状语从句中，will not 就是表示“执意不做某事”，相当于 refuse。

精品译文 如果他们就是不愿意接受支票，那我们也没办法，只好付现金了，尽管这会给双方都造成麻烦。

2007 年，日本以“文化传统”为由开始大肆捕杀鲸鱼(slaughtering whales)，这遭到了很多动物保护组织的强烈抗议。有人提出，如果日本不停止捕鲸活动，将发起抵制日货运动：

3 If Japan *won't* stop, a boycott of Japanese goods would not be unreasonable.

妙语点睛 这里 if 引导的条件状语从句中，will not 就是表示“执意不做某事”，相当于 refuse。另外，这里主句的谓语用 would，具有虚拟假设的意味。

精品译文 如果日本不停止(捕鲸)，抵制日货大概也不算过分。

请再看其他例句：

4 If you *will* go out without your overcoat, what can you expect?

如果你一定要不穿外套就出门，你还能指望有什么好结果啊？（比如说你当然就会冻感冒）

5 If you ***will*** keep your watch half an hour slow it is hardly surprising that you are late for your appointments. 如果你一定要让你的表慢半个小时，你约会时总迟到就不足为怪了。

我们再看下面的对话：

6 A: I'***ll*** take the money anyway.

B: You ***won't***!

A: I ***will***!

妙语点睛 这里第一句 I'll take the money anyway. 中的 will 表示"意图"甚至"执意"；第二句中的 won't 则表示"执意"的否定；第三句 will 则是表示"执意"的肯定，语气非常强烈。

精品译文 A：不管怎样，这钱我要拿走。

B：你办不到！

A：我非得要拿走！

再比如下面的对话：

7 A: I ***won't*** do it 我不做。

B: Yes, you ***will***. 没门，你一定得做。

注意，当 will 用于表达"执意"这样强烈的感情色彩时，一方面不要缩写成 'll，而要用 will；另一方面，will 要重读。比如上面例句中表示"执意"的 will 都没有缩写。其中 I'll take the money anyway 中的缩写 'll 则更多地含有"意图"的意思。

will 这种表示"执意"的用法对应于过去，则用 would，即 would 也有类似表示"执意"的用法。请看例句：

8 We all tried to stop him smoking in bed but he ***would*** do it. 我们大家都尽力阻止他在床上抽烟，但是他就是非得要这么做。

同理，这里的 would 不能缩略写成 'd，而且要重读。

思维训练

Exercise 8. 11（Key: P352）

请判断下列的 will 是"意图"、"意愿"还是"预测"。

1. I'll do what I can to help, I promise.
2. There will be blue birds over the white cliffs of Dover.
3. Give it to Mikey, he'll eat anything.
4. Don't call too early; I'll still be sleeping.
5. My pen won't write. Will you lend me yours?
6. I'll stop them making all that noise!
7. Her parents won't let her stay out late.
8. By now you will probably have heard enough about modal verbs.

8.12 基本用法(七)：请求

（一）

在日常生活交往中，我们往往会请求别人为我们做某事，此时，我们当然要表现出我们的礼貌或委婉，而不能直截了当地，甚至是粗鲁地提出"强求"。为了表示礼貌，就需要借助情态动词。首先来比较下面的两个对话，体会一下情态动词表示礼貌请求的作用：

1 A: Hey, you! Open this door!

B: It's locked. Want we get the key?

A: Yeah. Get it. Fast!

精品译文 A：嘿，说你呢，把门打开！
B：门锁了。想要钥匙？
A：去给我拿，快点！

我们看到，这种直接而唐突的表达，显然缺乏礼貌，显得说话人很粗俗。但是如果借助情态动词及其相关句型，就可以使我们的请求显得客气和委婉。比如这样稍微改写一下：

2 A: Excuse me, ***would*** you please open this door?
B: I'm afraid it's locked. ***Shall*** I get a key?
A: Please, if you ***wouldn't*** mind, as quickly as you can.

精品译文 A：对不起，你能把门打开吗？
B：恐怕门被锁上了，要我替你把钥匙拿来吗？
A：太好了，那就麻烦你快点去拿，好吗？

通过对比上面这两个对话，我们看到，用了情态动词的对话非常礼貌与客气，显然是每个人都乐意接受的。再如，请陌生人不要抽烟，需要很礼貌地说：

3 A: Excuse me, sir. I realize you have the right to smoke here. But ***could*** you put out your cigarette, please? Your smoke is coming right at us.
B: Well, sorry, I am in the smoking section, and I was here before you. If you ***wouldn't*** mind, you ***could*** go to the non-smoking section.
A: OK. Just asking.

精品译文 A：对不起，先生，我知道你有权在这抽烟，但是，我还是想请你把烟熄了，好吗？你的烟味直冲着往我这来。
B：哦，不好意思，我这是在吸烟区，而且我先来的。你要是不介意的话，你能去那边的无烟区吗？
A：好吧，我只是说说而已。

上面的对话无论是提出请求的A，还是委婉拒绝的B，都使用了情态动词来表示自己的礼貌，显得相当有修养，易于让人接受。请再来比较一下如果没有情态动词，那会是一种什么样的口气：

4 A: Damn it! Put out your cigarette! Your smoke is coming right at us!
B: Fuck off! I am in the smoking section, and I was here before you.

精品译文 A：你他妈的，把烟给我掐灭！你的烟直冲我这来！
B：滚开！这是吸烟区，而且我比你先来的。

像上面这样对话，没有使用一个情态动词，A这样直截了当地提出"强求"，当然让人难以接受，所以B同样以牙还牙，断然拒绝，说不定两人最后还要剑拔弩张，打斗起来。

通过上述这些对话的比较，我们看到，情态动词在表示礼貌的请求时所起到的作用有多么重要。在下面的内容里，笔者将系统地总结英语里用情态动词表示请求的常用句型。

(二)

用第一人称(I/we)和第二人称(you)来提出请求。当用第一人称时，可以用四个情态动词：can/could 和 may/might，表示"请求对方允许我们做某事"。比如：

Can/Could I...?
May/Might I...?

请注意它们在用法上的一些区别：

第一、May I...?和Could I...?表示较正式、很礼貌地提出请求。比如在询问陌生人的姓名时：

5 ***May*** I have your name, please? 请问您怎么称呼？

再如，在售票窗口买票时，可以这样礼貌地提出请求：

6 ***Could*** I have two tickets, please? 请给我两张票好吗？

再如警察要看你的驾照，他可以这样说，表示礼貌：

7 ***Could*** I see your driving license? 可以给我看看您的驾照吗？

第二、Can I...?是非正式的请求允许，一般用于说话人与对方相当熟悉的情况下。比如和朋友之间的对话：

8 ***Can*** I use your pen? 我能用一下你的钢笔吗？

9 A: Hi, Jenny. ***Can*** I join you? 嗨，珍妮，我能坐在你这吗？

B: Sure, Michael. Please sit down.发当然可以，迈克尔。请坐吧。

第三、Might I...?显得过于正式和客气，所以一般很少用。

当用第二人称时，请注意要用的情态动词是：can/could 和 will/would，这是"请求对方为我们做某事"。比如：

Can/Could you...?

Will/Would you...?

同样要注意这几个词表达不同的礼貌程度，Would you...?和 Could you...?都是用来表示很客气地请求对方，客气程度相同。比如上面对话中出现的两句：

10 ***Would*** you please open this door? 你能把门打开吗？

11 ***Could*** you put out your cigarette, please? 请你把烟熄了，好吗？

Will you...?不如 Would you...?客气，比如较熟悉的朋友之间的对话：

12 A: I am on duty this afternoon. ***Will*** you please cover for me? I have a doctor's appointment.

B: I am sorry I can't. My term paper is due tomorrow.

精品译文 A：今天下午我值班，你能替我一下吗？我得去看医生。

B：对不起，我替不了你。我明天得交学期论文。

Can you...?常用于非正式场合、熟人之间。比如，在吃饭的餐桌上，你对你母亲说：

13 ***Can*** you pass me the salt, Mom? 妈妈，把盐递给我好吗？

综上所述，在"请求"时，不同人称所使用的情态动词不尽相同。can/could 可以同时用于两个人称，如 Can/Could I...?或者 Can/Could you...?但 may/might 只能用于第一人称，不能说 May/Might you...?而 will/would 只能用于第二人称，不能说 Will/Would I...?

I will 表示"意愿"	Will you...? 表示"请求"
you may 表示"许可"	May I...? 表示"请求"
you can/could 表示"许可"	Could/Can I...? 表示"请求"
I can/could 表示主动提出帮助	Could/Can you...? 表示"请求"

其实，表示"请求"的用法与情态动词的其他意义是密切相关的，具体相关性如下：

以上表格中的对应关系就解释了在表示"请求"时，为什么特定的情态动词要与特定的人称搭配使用。比如表示"请求"的 will 只能用于第二人称 you，是因为 will you 句型来源于表示"意愿"的 I will。在变成一般疑问句时，我们自然要把 I 变成 you，于是便有了 will you。在表示"意愿"时，英文中没有 you will，因为"意愿"一定是句子的主语自己发出的(from the ***Subject***)。既然没有用 you will 表示"意愿"的，那么自然就不会有 will I 表示"请求"的了。但 you will 可以表示"预测"，因为"预测"总是由说话人作出的(from the ***speaker***)，而与句子的主语无关。

在英文中表示"请求"往往都是用一般疑问句式，因为"请求"的含义有三个来源：

1. 询问听话人是否愿意，这就是 Will/Would you...?表示“请求”(questioning someone's “willingness” to make a request)；

2. 询问听话人是否许可“我”做某事，这就是 May I...?或 Could/Can I...?表示“请求”(questioning someone's “permission” to make a request)；

3. 询问听话人是否能够帮助，这就是 Could/Can you...?表示“请求”(questioning someone's “offer to help” to make a request)。

(三)

表示请求时，在语气上越是不肯定或犹豫，就越显得礼貌。所以，由“直截了当”到“极为犹豫不决”，可以用不同的情态动词句型来表达不同程度的礼貌。以下都是表示很礼貌的请求句型：

Could you do...?

Could you please do...?

Could you ***possibly*** do...?(注意副词)

Would you do...?

Would you please do...?

Would you ***kindly*** do...?(注意副词)

Would you mind doing...?

Would you be good/kind enough to do...?

Would you be so kind as to do...?

Do you think I could...?

Do you think you could/would do/would mind doing...?

我们来看看，在下面的短文中，作者描述了自己为什么不愿意轻易请别人帮助，比如搭便车：

14 A thousand reasons why I didn't want to ask someone for a lift came into my mind: I don't know my neighbors; I don't like to impose; I feel funny asking for favors. Pride would not let me knock on a door and say, “It's a 10-minute ride by car but a long wait for the bus, and it's a 30-minute bus ride, so ***could you possibly*** give me a lift to school?”

精品译文 一千个不请别人让自己搭便车的理由跳进我的脑海：我不认识我的邻居，我不喜欢打扰别人，我觉得请人帮忙很可笑。自尊心不允许我敲开别人家的门说：“搭便车只需要10分钟，但等公共汽车就要很久了，而且行程要30分钟，所以我能搭你的车去学校吗？”

后来有一次，在迫不得已的情况下，作者只好请求别人帮助：

15 She was wearing a brown coat and had a set of keys in her hand. Obviously she had a car, and just as obviously, she was going out. In that split second, desperation overcame pride, I blurted, “***Could you possibly*** give me a lift?” I hurriedly explained, “I never ask anybody for a lift, but...”

精品译文 我看到她穿了件褐色的大衣，手里拿了一串钥匙。显然，她有车，而且正准备出门。就在那一刹那，绝望战胜了我的自傲，我脱口而出：“您能让我搭个便车吗？”我又赶忙解释：“我从没向别人这样要求过，可是……”

在两段短文中，作者都是用了 Could you possibly...?这样很礼貌的句型来请求陌生人让自己搭便车。当然还可以用其他的句型，比如，在大街上向一个陌生人借手机用，你可以这样礼貌地说：

16 Excuse me, but ***would you kindly*** lend me your mobile phone? 对不起，你能把手机借我用一下吗？

再比如下面这个对话：

17 A: ***Do you think you could*** give me a ride to the library tonight?

B: I'd like to, but I'm heading the other direction. I'm meeting Jean tonight.

精品译文 A：今晚你能顺便开车捎我去图书馆吗？

B：本来是可以，不过我正好去反方向，我今晚要去接吉恩。

从以上例句看到，表示请求的句型通常是一般疑问句。但也可以用 wonder 的各种陈述句型来表示比上述例句更加礼貌的请求：

I wonder if I could do...

I wondered if I could do...

I was wondering if I could do...

I wonder if you could/would do/would mind doing...

I wondered if you could/would do/would mind doing...

I was wondering if you could/would do/would mind doing...

比如上面那个借手机的例子。如果你告诉对方你要借他的手机，从中国往美国打一个国际长途，这时你就应该用上述这些更为礼貌的(尤其是最后一个“超级”礼貌的)句型来表达你的这一“过分请求”，以显得你“极为犹豫不决”和不好意思：

18 Excuse me, sir, ***I was wondering***...um...if you...er...***if you could possibly*** lend me your mobile phone, coz I really need to make a long distance call to America right now.

精品译文 对不起，先生，我想……嗯……您能不能……呃……您能不能把手机借我用一下，因为我现在急着要往美国打个长途。

我们再看看在以下例句中，学生在向老师提出请求时，是如何通过犹豫不决的语气和句型来显示出自己的礼貌态度的：

19 A: Hello, I know Doctor Wilson's out of town at a conference, but I ***was wondering***...um...since she won't be back till next week, if you...***if you could*** check in your computer records and find out how I did on her midterm exam?

B: I'm sorry, Miss. But I'm not authorized to give out that kind of information.

精品译文 A：您好，我知道威尔逊博士出差开会去了，但因为她下周才能回来，所以，我想……嗯……您能否……您能否在您的电脑记录里帮我查看一下，她的那门课我这次期中考试考得怎么样？

B：对不起，小姐，我无权向你透露这样的信息。

20 A: Oh, Professor Jackson, I ***was wondering***...but uh...well, ***if uh...I could*** have a chance yet to uh...look at my thesis proposal.

B: Well, I know you gave it to me over a week ago, but to be honest, I have been swamped with other things.

精品译文 A：哦，杰克逊教授，我想请问您……呃……嗯，如果……我何时才有机会……看到我上次交给您的我的论文选题。

B：嗯，我知道你一个星期前就把它给我了，可是说句实话，最近我一直忙着别的事了。

在上面这两个对话中，两个学生对老师的态度是非常之礼貌，因为都是用了极为委婉的请求句型 I was wondering if...could...

下面这个对话是一部美国喜剧电影《旅行冒险记》(*Planes, Trains and Automobiles*)里的一个场景：感恩节来临，尼尔(Neil)要打车赶去机场坐飞机回家与家人团聚，但当时正是下班高峰时间，而且还下着大雪。可想而知，在这样的天气和这个特殊的时候，出租车是多么难打到。等了半天，好不容易有了一辆空车，于是出现上百人奋力拼抢一辆车的壮观场面。不幸的是，尼尔 Neil 没有抢到这辆空车，但由于飞机快要起飞了，所以，他希望那位抢到车的陌生人能把出租车让给他坐。可以想象，在这种情景下，把一辆空车让给别人是一个多么大的恩惠，于是尼尔便“极尽礼貌之能事”地采用了 I was wondering if I could...这样的委婉句型提出了他的请求：

21 Neil: Sir? Sir? Excuse me, I know this is your cab, but I'm desperately late for a plane and I ***was wondering if I could*** appeal to your good nature and ask you to let me have it.

Stranger: I don't have a good nature. Excuse me.

Neil: ***Could I*** offer you $10 for it? Twenty, I'll give you $20 for it.

Stranger: I'll take fifty...anyone who would pay $50 for a cab would certainly pay seventy-five.

Neil: Not necessarily. All right, seventy-five. You're a thief.

Stranger: Close. I'm an attorney.

精品译文 尼尔：先生，先生，对不起，我知道这是您的车，但是我想求您发发慈悲，行行好让给我坐，好吗？因为我急着去赶飞机。

陌生人：（这个陌生人都没抬眼看尼尔，就很冷漠地说道）对不起，我没有慈悲之心。

尼尔：那我给你10块钱，你让给我坐行吗？（这时陌生人才稍微斜眼瞥了一下尼尔，尼尔见他还是不同意，于是又马上说道）20块，我给你20块行吗？

陌生人：我要50块……（说完，他见尼尔毫不犹豫就准备掏钱，于是他又提高了价码）既然50块你同意，那75块一定也没问题，我现在要75块就让你坐这车。

尼尔：（这明摆着是在敲诈啊，尼尔当然不愿意）不一定吧。（但是没办法，最后只好任人宰一刀）好吧，好吧，就给你75，你这个强盗。

陌生人：（奸诈地笑道）差不多，因为我是律师。

我们再来看电影《初恋50次》（*50 First Dates*）中的一个场景：男主角亨利·罗斯（Henry Roth）生活在美丽的夏威夷，每天有大量去那里度假的美女相伴。不过，在他爱上露茜（Lucy）之后，就告别了他花花公子般的生活。遗憾的是，露茜有短时记忆丧失的病症，所以她永远都无法记住亨利与她交往过，这样使得亨利每天都得重新追求露茜。在下面这个对话中，就是亨利又一次主动与露茜搭讪（Henry Roth lives in Hawaii and enjoys the company of women who vacation there. But, he leaves the playboy life behind after he falls for Lucy, who suffers from short-term memory loss. Since she can never remember meeting him, Henry has to woo Lucy every single day and hope that she falls for him. In the following dialogue, he tries to strike up a conversation with Lucy.）

22 Henry: I see you're sitting here by yourself, and ***I was wondering if I could*** join you for breakfast.

Lucy: Oh, that would be nice, but I have a boyfriend. I'm sorry.

Henry: You're making up a boyfriend just to get rid of me?

Lucy: No. I'm not.

Henry: Oh yeah, what's his name then?

Lucy: Ringo.

Henry: Oh yeah? What's his last name, Starr?

Lucy: No. McCartney.

精品译文 亨利：我看你一个人坐在这里，那我可以和你一起坐在这吃早饭吗？

露茜：哦，可以呀，不过我有男友了，很抱歉。

亨利：你瞎编说自己有男朋友就是为了摆脱我吧？

露茜：不是啊。

亨利：哦，是吗？那他叫什么名字？

露茜：林戈。

亨利：哦，是吗？他姓什么？姓斯塔？

露茜：不是，他姓麦卡特尼。

妙语点睛 我们看到，这里亨利用了 ***I was wondering if I could*** 这样的委婉句型提出了他的请求。在美国的很多电影中，男主角在约女主角出去的时候，大多是采用这个句型，读者在以后看美剧的时候不妨多多注意。

另外需要说明的是，要想真正理解这个对话的含义，需要有一点些文化背景知识。

亨利说 Oh yeah. 的字面意思是“哦，是吗？”但在这里，他明显带有嘲讽的语气，潜台词是：行，你就瞎编故事吧，有本事你继续编。这里露茜说她的男朋友叫林戈，这可不是一般的人物，林戈·斯塔（Ringo Starr）是六七十年代风靡全球的“甲壳虫（The Beatles）”乐队的鼓手，也是该乐队目前仍旧在世的两名成员之一。林戈是个少见的名字，所以很明显露茜是在编造。于是亨利也语带讽刺地说道：“姓斯塔？”但露茜却说她的男朋友姓麦卡特尼，这就更绝了，因为甲壳虫乐队仍旧在世的另一名成员即是保罗·麦卡特尼（Paul McCartney）。所以，这里利用把两个名人 ***Ringo*** Starr 和 Paul ***McCartney*** 的名字错位成 ***Ringo McCartney*** 来制造讽刺幽默的效果。而如果没有上述背景知识，恐怕就笑不起来了。

最后，我们来看看下面这个对话。在这个对话中，乔治（George）对他弟弟吉姆（Jim）得寸进尺地提出了一系列的“请求”。乔治先以“你能帮我一个忙吗？（***Would you*** do me a big favor?）”这样一个礼貌的请求开始，然后很狡猾地找出各种理由，让他弟弟替自己完成了整个洗衣服的程序：

先让吉姆把他的衣服放进洗衣机；

然后再让吉姆往洗衣机里放入洗衣粉，并开始洗衣；

还告诉吉姆，衣服洗完后，把它们从洗衣机拿出来；

再让吉姆把衣服放进烘干机；

然后又是让吉姆等衣服烘干后，从烘干机里拿出来，并帮他叠好。

至此，他弟弟吉姆都一一答应了他的请求。但最后当乔治提出让吉姆给自己做晚饭时，吉姆终于忍无可忍了，断然拒绝了乔治的无理要求。我们现在就来看看乔治是如何使用上述各种情态动词的礼貌句型让自己的弟弟吉姆屡屡中招的：

23 George: Jim, ***would you*** do me a big favor?

Jim: What?

George: ***Could you*** just take my clothes down and drop them in the washing machine?

Jim: Sure. No problem.

George: Oh, and ***if you don't mind, do you think you could*** just put some detergent in the machine and get it going?

Jim: Okay. I think I can do that.

George: Oh, and if I'm out when the wash cycle finished, ***would you please*** take my clothes out of the washing machine?

Jim: Okay.

George: And if it's not too much of a bother, ***I wonder if you would mind*** putting them in the dryer?

Jim: No. I guess I can do that.

George: Also, if I'm still not back by the time my clothes are dry, ***I was wondering if you could*** take them out of the dryer and fold them. You know, my shirts will wrinkle if they aren't folded right away.

Jim: Okay, okay.

George: One more thing — if I'm still out at about 6:00, ***would you mind*** taking the steaks out of the freezer?

Jim: George, my dear brother, I'll agree to do your laundry, this once, but I'm not making your dinner. Sorry.

妙语点睛 我们看到，乔治在不断地提出各种请求的过程中，他所用的句型是越来越礼貌的，由开始的Would you...?进而说 Do you think you could...?直到后来的 I wonder if you would mind...?后来又变 wonder 为 was wondering 说 I was wondering if you could...? 这样就更显得犹豫不决，显得非常礼貌。

精品译文 乔治：吉姆，你能帮哥哥一个忙吗？

吉姆：什么事？

乔治：你能帮我把我的衣服拿下来，然后放进洗衣机吗？

吉姆：当然可以，没问题。

乔治：好，如果你不介意，你能往洗衣机里再放些洗衣粉然后打开洗衣机开始洗吗？

吉姆：好的，我想可以。

乔治：哦，如果洗衣程序结束之后我还没有回来的话，你能帮我把衣服从洗衣机里拿出来吗？

吉姆：好的。

乔治：还有，如果不太麻烦的话，我不知道你是否愿意帮我把衣服放到烘干机里烘干。

吉姆：不介意，我想我可以做到。

乔治：还有啊，如果我衣服烘干了之后我还没有回来，不知道你能否帮我把衣服从烘干机里拿出来，然后帮我把衣服叠好，因为你知道，我的衬衫如果干了之后没有立即叠好，就会起皱的。

吉姆：好的，好的。

乔治：还有一件事，如果我6点钟的时候还在外面没回来，你介意把牛排从冰柜里拿出来吗？

吉姆：乔治，我亲爱的哥哥，这次我答应帮你洗衣服，但我不想给你做晚饭。对不起了。

对于上述所讨论的用情态动词表达请求的句型，希望读者能熟练掌握，并能在实际生活会话中，根据语境和说话的对象灵活地运用。

思维总结

这部分总结了英文中情态动词用于表示礼貌请求的句型，具体有四大类：

1. 第一人称：Can/Could I...? May/Might I...?
2. 第二人称：Can/Could you...? Will/Would you...?
3. 文中其他各种疑问句形式的请求句型；
4. 文中带有 wonder 的陈述句所表示的礼貌的请求句型。

思维训练

Exercise 8.12（Key: P353）

请根据所给情景做出礼貌请求。

1. You want to ask your teacher a question.
2. You're at your friend's apartment. You want to use the phone.
3. You want your boyfriend to meet you in front of the library at three this afternoon.
4. You knock on your professor's half-open door. He's sitting at his desk. You want to go in.
5. You are at a gas station. You want thc attendant to check the oil.
6. You want to see your deskmate's dictionary for a minute.
7. You want a stranger in an airport to keep eye on your luggage while you get a drink of water.

8.13 基本用法(八)：过去习惯

（一）

第七章着重讨论了情态动词 would 的虚拟假设用法，那么是不是句中一出现 would，就都可以把它理解为虚拟的意思呢？在回答这个问题之前，我们先来看看特蕾萨修女（Sister Teresa）在回忆自己父母时说的这番话：

1 My own mother used to be very busy the whole day, but as soon as evening came, she ***would*** move very fast to get ready to meet my father. At that time we didn't understand; we ***would*** laugh; we ***would*** tease her; but now I remember what a tremendous, delicate love she had for him. It didn't matter what happened that day; she was ready with a smile to meet him.

精品译文 以前，我母亲每天总是忙忙碌碌的，但是只要到了傍晚时分，她就会很快地把家里的一切都料理好，以准备迎接我父亲回家。那时我们对此都不理解，因而常常取笑她。但现在我终于明白了，这是母亲对父亲多么深厚、细腻的爱啊！不论每天发生什么事，她总是微笑着去迎接父亲回家。

（作者注：特蕾萨修女是生于阿尔巴尼亚的印度修女，她献身于扶助印度贫困无助和濒临死亡的人们，并于 1950 年建立了一个罗马天主教修女组织——慈善传教会 <the Missionaries of Charity>。她于 1979 年获诺贝尔和平奖。）

从以上短文来看，这里的 would 并不能解释为虚拟假设的情形，因为句中特蕾萨修女说的都是她自己小时候的真实经历。所以，并不是任何时候只要句中出现了 would 就是虚拟用法，would 在句中的含义要依据上下文的语境而定。其实，这里的 would 是表示过去反复发生或习惯性的动作（habitual or repeated action in the past）。

当回顾自己的孩提时代时，我们也许会这样说：

2 When I was a child, my mother ***would*** read me a story at night before bed.
小时候，晚上睡觉前妈妈常常会给我讲故事。

或许小时候我们都有过这样的经历：

3 When I was a child, I ***would*** take a flashlight to bed with me so that I could read comic books without my parents' knowing about it. 小时候，我常常会拿着手电筒在床上看连环画，这样爸妈就不会发觉了。

我们再来看看下面这篇描写父女亲情的短文：

4 Joan Benny remembers Sunday mornings as being her “special time” with her father, Jack Benny:
Daddy ***would*** wake me up for breakfast about 7:30. Then we ***would*** head outside to go for a drive. Daddy ***would*** get into the car and turn the ignition key. Inevitably, nothing ***would*** happen. He ***would*** push and pull every button on the dashboard, twist all the knobs, and pump the accelerator, but the motor still ***wouldn't*** start. At length he ***would*** sigh and say to me, “Honey, the car just won't start until you give me a kiss.” So I did, and it did, and off we went. For a long time I believed there was some kind of scientific connection between kissing and car starting.

妙语点睛 在这里，作者不厌其烦地使用了七个 would，表示关于父亲的情形发生过不止一次，而是每个周日早晨都会重复同样的情况，以至于有了后来她还一直以为“在亲吻和汽车发动之间有某种必然的科学联系”。通过这些细致的描写，浓浓的父女之情跃然纸上，让我们读起来不禁为之感动。如果没有 would 来传达这种重复的情形，而只是用一般过去时，那原文顿觉索然无味。

精品译文 琼·本尼依然记得每个周日的早晨，自己和父亲杰克·本尼度过的幸福时光：
“小时候，爸爸总是在 7:30 左右把我叫醒吃早饭，然后我们就开车出去兜风。爸爸先是钻进车里，准备发动汽车。可每次总是发动不起来，于是他就把汽车的仪表板上的每个按钮东拉一下、西拽一下，弄弄把手，踩踩油门，可是汽车依旧无法发动。最后，爸爸就会叹一口气，然后对我说‘宝贝，车子就是发动不了，除非你吻我一下。’于是，我就吻他一下，汽车果然就发动起来了，然后我们就开车出去了。如此一来，以至于很长一段时间内，我一直以为在亲吻和汽车发动之间有着某种必然的科学联系呢！”

（作者注：杰克·本尼〈1894-1974〉，美国喜剧演员，以迟钝的喜剧口才和在广播〈1932-1955〉及电视〈1950-1965〉中的表演而著称，其滑稽剧的特色以虚构的吝啬为主要题材。他的演艺生涯共 39 年，同时还是业余小提琴手。）

我们再看看，在下面这篇文章中，作者是如何通过 would 来传达出只有三岁的“我”是怎样与母亲进行情感交流的：

5 As a child, I loved talking, listening, and interacting with others. I was sensitive to other people's feelings and intuitively knew how to say the right things to make them feel better. Because I was mature for my age, grown-ups treated me more like a peer than a child and often told me about their problems. I recently learned that my mother used me as a sounding board when I was only three years old. When something was bothering her she ***would*** take me for long walks and talk to me about her problems. We ***would*** stop for a soda and I ***would*** look at her as though I totally understood, pat her on the back and say, “Everything will be all right, mother baby.” She said she actually believed me and ***would*** feel better. Obviously, these personality traits were evident early in my life but I had no idea they would be the very natural strengths and talents that would lead me to the work I love.

妙语点睛 这里有四处 would 都是表示过去习惯的活动：would take, would stop, would look 和 would feel。另外，在宾语从句 they would be...和定语从句 that would lead...中的两个 would 不是表示过去习惯的动作，而是表示过去将来时态，具有将来“预测”的意味。

精品译文 小时候，我喜欢跟人交流，听人说话。我对别人的感觉很敏感，凭直觉就能知道说什么话能让他们高兴。由于我的心理年龄比较成熟，大人们都把我看成是他们的同辈，而不是一个小孩，他们常向我倾诉他们的苦恼。现在我渐渐回想起，妈妈在我三岁大的时候就已把我当成她的倾诉对象了。当她感到苦恼时，她便常带我去散步，向我倾诉。我们会在途中停下来喝杯汽水，我会以一种完全理解的目光看着她，拍拍她的背说：“一切都会好起来的，妈妈宝贝。”她说她完全相信我的话，会感觉好多了。很显然，在我小的时候，我就已具备了这种品格特质，但没想到的是，这种与生俱来的优点和天赋会引领我找到自己喜欢的工作。

请再来看下面这篇文章：

6 Winters I spent indoors in solace. My flat mates—the only friends I had—worked day and night. They were accustomed to leaving the soul behind, the need for money was so official. I ***would*** spend nights in the strange house, with creaks of a wall I did not know, and sit by the phone that our landlord had locked and think of

conversations of the past, of my mother's voice ringing, of my best friend whom I ***would*** lose contact with, and I ***would*** write letters—letters I ***would*** never send, letters that clutched the truth—that only I knew. I ***would*** cry — tears staining the ink, a smudged idea of love. I was temping then, doing mindless data entry, tapping words into a computer and moving on wondering what worth there was and how to find it. My flat mates ***would*** come home just before midnight—Mark and Craig, my two best friends. I ***would*** smile inwardly and outwardly make them tea, a sandwich, sit with them and live their lives, hear their stories—flourish in company. Sleep ***would*** be eschewed, I yearned for comfort, and company eased the etching of loneliness.

妙语点睛 上文中的 would 都是过去常常发生的活动，用来表示作者曾经的痛苦经历。

精品译文 冬天，我独自躲在屋里。我的室友，我仅有的朋友们，每天从早忙到晚，他们习惯了没有思想，赚钱才是天经地义的事。我一夜又一夜地一个人呆在这个陌生的屋子里，只有墙壁发出些莫名其妙的声音。我坐在被房东锁上了的电话机旁，回忆着过去的一些对话，回忆着妈妈响亮的声音，还有已失去联络的好友。我写信，写从来不曾寄出去的信，里面全是只有我才知道的真心话。我哭，泪水把字迹化掉，模糊的字迹记载了我的爱念。那时我正在打一份临时工，每天机械地把资料输入电脑，边打字边质疑着做这些工作的价值，以及如何才能找到它的价值。我的室友马克和克雷格——我最好的两个朋友，要到午夜时分才回来。我会带着满心的欢喜和满脸的笑容，帮他们泡茶，做三明治，和他们坐在一起，感受他们的生活，听他们的故事，和他们一起手舞足蹈。睡眠也被省略了，我渴望安慰，和别人呆在一起才能缓解孤独的侵蚀。

（二）

另外，用 would 表示过去习惯或重复的动作时，还可以是某人一贯的行为(typical of a person)。这时，往往用来表示批评人们的行为或表示对他人的行为怀有某种恼怒的情绪(an annoying habit)，此时 would 要重读。比如：

7 A: Jack ***would*** get lost, wouldn't he? 杰克老是迷路，是吧？
B: It's typical. 可不是嘛！

8 We all tried to stop him smoking in bed but he ***would*** do it.
我们都试图不让他在床上抽烟，可他每次偏偏这么做。

9 He was a nice boy, but he ***would*** talk about himself all the time. 他人还不错，但就是老喜欢谈论他自己。

10 A: Bill objected. 当时比尔反对。
B: He ***would***! 他老是反对！

值得注意的是，也可用 used to 来表示过去习惯的动作。但二者之间的区别是：used to 可以表示过去重复的动作，也可以指过去存在的状态，有"现在不再"的含义。would 常用来表示过去重复的动作，不表示过去的状态。我们再看看上面关于特蕾萨修女的例子中的第一个句子：

11 My own mother ***used to*** be very busy the whole day.

妙语点睛 这里作者用的是 used to，而不是 would，因为 be very busy 是过去存在的一种状态，不是动作。

精品译文 以前，我母亲每天总是忙忙碌碌的。

再如：

12 Illiteracy is still a problem in my country, but it ***used to be*** much worse.

妙语点睛 一般就不说 it ***would be*** much worse，因为 be much worse 同样表示的是一种状态。

精品译文 文盲在我们国家仍然是一个问题，但在过去更为严重。

思维总结

本节讨论了 would 表示过去反复发生或习惯性的动作(habitual or repeated action in the past)。此时，与 used to 表示的过去在用法上的区别是：used to 不仅可以表示过去的动作，还可以表示过去的状态；而 would 只表示过去的动作。

思维训练

Exercise 8. 13（Key: P353）

请在合适的地方填上 would 或 used to。

1. I ______ be very shy. Whenever a stranger came to our house, I ______ hide in a closet.
2. When I was a child, I ______ take a flashlight（手电筒）to bed with me so that I could read comic books without my parents' knowing about it.
3. I remember my aunt very well. Every time she came to our house, she ______ give me a big kiss and pinch my cheek.
4. I ______ be afraid of flying. My heart ______ start pounding every time I stepped on a plane. But now I'm used to flying and enjoy it.

请分析下列三段短文中 would 的含义与用法。

5. 为了帮助全世界饥饿的儿童，1975 年成立了"救助饥饿儿童基金会"。下面这篇短文——Help the Suffering Children in War-torn Iraq（救助战乱中受苦的伊拉克儿童）——是该基金会一位成员描述自己在救助伊拉克孩子时的情景：

   It was strange to drive in a city without law and order. Litter and rubbish were everywhere. Cars ***would*** drive on the sidewalks or on the wrong side of the roads. Banks, business and homes ***would*** be burnt and robbed. Cars ***would*** be hijacked. Every now and again, we ***would*** hear the sound of gunfire or large explosions. People told us that it was too dangerous to deliver relief aid items. We ***would*** be attacked and our items ***would*** be robbed.

6. 下面这篇短文是对美国著名黑人歌星 Quincy Jones 的采访：

   Q: How did you get started in music?

   QUINCY JONES: It was during World War II...I started as a singer in a little gospel street-corner group. I started at 12 years old, or so. Seattle was very hot because everybody went to Japan from there during the war.

   I met Ray Charles when I was 14, he was 16, so we came up together. And we'***d*** work three different clubs a night. We'***d*** do the tennis clubs with the society music and all that stuff, and classical music, then we'***d*** do some rhythm and blues clubs, with strip dancers, and comics and everything. Then at three o'clock in the morning we'***d*** go down to Jackson Street, where we'***d*** play bebop for nothing. It just never stopped. It was around the clock. We'***d*** rehearse all day and then start the cycle all over again. It was a fantastic spawning ground.

7. 美国的一个节日——阵亡战士纪念日：

   As the summer begins, Americans celebrate Memorial Day as national holiday, the last Monday of May, to honor all of the country's war dead. As a child, my parents ***would*** drive to southern Indiana where my mother ***would*** put many bouquets of red, white and pink peonies on the graves of her and my father's dead families. There ***would*** be a little parade in the cemetery with the town's high school band, and we ***would*** have a picnic there.

8.14 基本用法（九）：should 的特殊用法

8. 10 节讨论了 should 的很多用法，比如通常把 should 译为"应该"，表示忠告或规劝，这是 should 的常规用法。但 should 还有另外一些比较特殊的用法，不表示劝告，这时不能译成"应该"，而是表示"竟然"和"万一"。

8. 14. 1 should 表示"竟然"

用在下列形容词后面的从句中的 should，带有一种很"惊奇"的感情色彩，含有"竟然"的意思。比如：It is/was absurd, amazing, annoying, funny, ludicrous, odd, ridiculous, strange, surprising, unthinkable that...等。

1. It is ridiculous that we ***should be*** short of water in a country where it is always raining. 在经常下雨的国家里，我们竟然会缺水，这简直是荒谬！
2. It is unthinkable that he ***should*** be so careless. 真不可思议，他竟然如此粗心大意！

3 It's strange that you ***should*** be staying in the same hotel! 真奇怪，你竟然呆在同一个酒店！

4 It's odd that you and I ***should*** have the same name. 很奇怪，我们的名字竟然相同。

此时，从句中也可以用现在时态或过去时态：

5 It is ridiculous that we ***are*** short of water in a country where it is always raining.

也常用在下列结构的从句里，放在 can't think why, I don't know why, I see no reason why 等的后面。比如：

6 I don't know why he ***should*** think that I did it. 我真不知道他凭什么竟然会认为这件事是我干的。

7 I see no reason why you ***should*** interfere in their quarrel. 我真不明白你有什么理由竟然会介入他们的争吵。

8 I can't think why he ***should*** have been so angry. 我现在搞不明白他当时为什么竟然那么生气。

9 You can't imagine that a well-behaved gentleman ***should*** be so rude to a lady.
你真无法想象，一个举止优雅的绅士竟然会对一个女子如此态度粗鲁。

10 Why ***should*** anyone object to her enjoying herself? 为什么竟然有人反对她过得开心呢？

11 Why ***should*** anyone bother to risk losing his treasure to help a stranger?
为什么竟然会有人冒着失去自己财产的危险而去帮助一个陌生人呢？

8.14.2 should 表示"万一"

should 常常用在lest, for fear that 和 in case 引导的从句中，表示"万一"。比如：

1 I've brought my umbrella in case it ***should rain***. 我把伞带着了，以防万一下雨。

不过，此时，从句中的谓语也可用正常时态，如一般现在时或一般过去时。比如：

2 I've brought my umbrella in case it ***rains***.

8.15 基本用法(十)：shall 的特殊用法

有一个关于"警察与小偷"的故事：

一个警察，一天抓住了一个小偷。正当他准备给小偷戴上手铐时，一阵狂风把他的帽子吹掉了。这时小偷立即拍马屁说道：

Shall I go and fetch it?（要不要我去帮你把帽子捡回来啊?）

这雕虫小技哪能糊弄得了警察，警察说道："你把我当傻瓜啊？你在这里等着，我自己去捡！"

我们看到小偷这里用了情态动词 shall，这是 shall 的一个用法。本节将对 shall 的用法详细讲解。

8.15.1 用于第一人称的疑问句中：Shall I/we...?

当 shall 用于第一人称时，此时的 shall 可以表示主动提供帮助、提供建议或请求给予指示。具体如下：

一、主动提供帮助

此时的 Shall I...?相当于 Would you like me to do sth?比如上面故事中的小偷说：

1 ***Shall I*** go and fetch it?

相当于说：***Would you like me to*** go and fetch it? 要不要我去帮你把帽子捡回来啊?
再比如：

2 ***Shall I*** open the window?

相当于说：***Would you like me to*** open the window? 你要不要我把窗户打开?

3 ***Shall we/I*** deliver the goods to your home address? 你要我(们)把货物送到你家去吗？

二、主动提供建议

4 ***Shall we*** meet at the theater? 我们是否在剧院见面呢？

可以说成：

Let's meet at the theater, ***shall we***? 我们在剧院见面吧，好吗？

Shall we leave at two? 我们两点钟走如何？

What ***shall we*** do this evening? ***Shall we*** go to the theater? 我们今晚做些什么？去剧院好吗？

三、表示请求给予指示

5 How ***shall I*** cook it? 这东西该怎么做着吃？

6 Where ***shall we*** put this? 我们该把这东西放在哪里？

8.15.2 用于第三人称的疑问句中

在表示提供建议或请求给予指示的意思时，shall 可以用于第三人称。比如：

1 A man wants to see you, sir. ***Shall he*** wait outside?

相当于说：***Would you like him to*** wait outside? 你要不要让他在外面等呢？

2 ***Shall he*** come with us?

相当于说：***Would you like him to*** come with us? (你)要不要让他和我们一起去呢？

8.15.3 用于第二、三人称的陈述句中

一、表示"命令"

在法律条文、规章制度中，常用 shall 表示"命令"，这主要用于第三人称。此时，shall 在意思上接近 must。比如：

1 It has been announced that candidates ***shall*** remain in their seats until all the papers have been collected.
已经宣布，在所有试卷全部收齐之后，考生方能离开自己的座位。

2 The license of a person who is arrested for driving while intoxicated ***shall*** be suspended.
因醉酒驾车而被捕的司机，其驾照应该被吊销。

3 The author ***shall*** prepare a manuscript which ***shall*** meet the following requirements. 作者准备的手稿须满足下列要求。

4 Each competitor ***shall*** wear a number. 每位参赛人员必须佩戴号码。

5 Members ***shall*** enter the names of their guests in the book provided. 会员必须把所邀客人的名字登记在提供的本子上(比如某俱乐部的规则)。

6 The Chairman ***shall*** be elected once every four years. 主席须每四年改选一次。

7 No player ***shall*** knowingly pick up or move the ball of another player. 不得故意捡起或移动其他球员的球。

这样使用的 shall 很正式，若是在不是很正式的场合，可以用 must 或 are to do 来代替 shall。

二、表示说话人的许诺

shall 用于第二、三人称的陈述句中，表示说话人的许诺。请看例句：

8 You ***shall*** have the money back next week.

相当于说：***I promise you will*** have the money back next week. (我答应)你下周一定能拿回这钱。

9 If he passes the examination he ***shall*** have a bicycle.

相当于说：***I promise he will*** have a bicycle.（我答应）只要他能通过考试，就可以得到一辆自行车作为奖励。

10 The boss has promised that every employee ***shall*** have a rise in income. 老板已经答应给每一位员工涨工资。

三、表示说话人强烈的意愿，甚至威胁

shall 用于第二、三人称的陈述句中，表示说话人强烈的意愿，甚至威胁。请看例句：

11 They ***shall*** do as they are told. 他们一定要按照吩咐他们的去做。

12 He ***shall*** be punished if he disobeys. 若他不服从，定将受到处罚。

13 You ***shall*** do exactly as I say. 你一定得按我说的去做。

14 You ***shall*** pay for this. 你一定得为此付出代价！

附录：

开心一刻

A detective（侦探）arrested a thief and was about to handcuff（给……戴上手铐）him when a huge gust（一阵狂风）of wind blew off the detective's hat.

"Shall I go and fetch it?" the criminal asked.

"Do you take me for a fool?" asked the detective. "You wait here while I go and get it!"

8.16 基本用法(十一)：may 的特殊用法

may 的含义主要有："可能"，"许可"和"请求"，这在前文中都已讨论过。may 还有一种特殊的用法，即用在 may...but 这样的结构中，表示让步（May can be used to express ***although*** clauses.）。请看例句：

1 We ***may*** have our differences from time to time, ***but*** basically we trust one another's judgment.

这里的 may 多少已失去了"可能"的含义，而是表示被认为是真实的陈述，所以上句应改写为：

We admit that we have our differences, but basically we trust one another's judgment.

或者：Although we have our differences, basically we trust one another's judgment.

而不是改写成：***It is possible*** that we have our differences, but basically we trust one another's judgement.

精品译文 尽管我们常常有分歧，但是我们基本上还是信任彼此的判断。

人们之所以习惯用 may have 这一情态动词结构，而不是用一般现在时 have，主要是出于礼貌或委婉表达的考虑。再比如：

2 You ***may*** have good reasons, ***but*** that doesn't make it legal.

=Although you have good reasons, that doesn't make it legal. 尽管你有很好的理由，但这并不意味着就合法。

3 She ***may*** be the boss, ***but*** that is no excuse for shouting like that.

=Although she is the boss, that is no excuse for shouting like that.

尽管她是老板，但这决不是她那么大声嚷嚷的理由。

4 You ***may*** be older than me, ***but*** that doesn't mean you're cleverer.

=Although you are older than me, that doesn't mean you're cleverer.

尽管你比我年长，但这并不意味着你就更聪明。

5 You ***may*** be in charge, ***but*** it doesn't give you the right to be rude.

=Although you are in charge, it doesn't give you the right to be rude.

尽管是你负责，但这并不说明你就有权对人态度粗鲁。

曾经看到一位身材矮小的学生干部的茶杯壁上写着这样一句话：

6 I *may* be small, ***but*** I am influential. 尽管我身材矮小，但我是很有影响力的。

基于may可以表示让步，因此它常常用于各种结构的让步状语从句中。比如：

7 But ***however*** amazed our descendants ***may be*** at how far from Utopia we were, they will look just like us.

妙语点睛 这个句子本来的结构是：Our descendants ***may be amazed*** at how far from Utopia we were, they will look just like us. 现在因为有了连词however，所以amazed和however一同提到了句首。这里however引导一个让步状语从句，从句的谓语含有may。

精品译文 但是不管我们的后代对我们离乌托邦之遥远感到多么吃惊，他们的长相将和我们一样。

8 When a new movement in art attains a certain fashion, it is advisable to find out what its advocates are aiming at, for, however farfetched and unreasonable their principles ***may seem*** today, it is possible that in years to come they may be regarded as normal.

妙语点睛 这个句子有一定的难度。关键是要知道这里的for是表示原因的连词，引导原因状语从句，而在这个for引导的原因状语从句里面又套有一个however引导的让步状语从句。这个让步从句原本的结构是：their principles ***may seem farfetched and unreasonable*** today，现在因为有了连词however，所以farfetched and unreasonable和however一同提到了句首。

精品译文 当一种新的艺术运动达到某种程度的流行时，我们最好搞清楚这个运动倡导者们的目标是什么，因为不管他们的原则现在看来是如何牵强和不合理，很可能在将来它们会被视为正常的规范。

这里的may(或might)是用来加强让步语气的，相当于汉语中说"可能会多么的"。此外，有时甚至是把may或might省去，只剩下一个动词原形。请看下列例句：

9 Try as he will, no man breaks wholly loose from his first love, no matter who ***she be***...We've only one virginity to lose and where we lost it there our hearts will be!

妙语点睛 这里no matter who ***she be***就相当于no matter who ***she might be***这种加强语气的形式，这里的no matter who引导的是一个让步状语从句。此外，该句中的try as he will也是一个让步状语从句的结构。

精品译文 不管怎么样，没有一个男人能够完完全全地忘却自己的初恋，不管她是谁。因为，我们的童贞只有一次，我们永远不会忘记自己奉献出的第一次。

思维训练

Exercise 8. 16（Key: P353）

请判断下面句子中的may或might含义是"许可"、"推测"还是"让步"？

1. I may be wrong, but that's what I think.
2. These pills may cause dizziness.
3. I'd like to take this chair, if I may.
4. We may be old-fashioned, but we believe in good manners.
5. Might I trouble you for a glass of water?
6. They might decide it isn't worth the effort.
7. Customers may smoke in designated areas only.
8. These exercises, as difficult as they may seem to be, are really good for you.

8.17 情态动词的否定

本节将探讨情态动词的否定问题。这看似一个简单的问题——因为把否定词not直接置于情态动词的后面即构成否定结构，但是并不简单——因为在意义理解上是有差别的。根据含义的不同，可以把情态动词的否定区分为"内部否定"和"外部否定"两种。

8.17.1 情态动词否定意义的深层结构——内部否定和外部否定

关于情态动词的否定句，在前面各节中已接触到很多。比如：

1 A: The restaurant is always empty. 这家餐馆总是很空。
B1: It *can't* be good. 那这家餐馆不可能好。
B2: It *may not* be good. 那这家餐馆可能不好。

这里用 can't 和 may not 所表达的肯定程度不同，can't 是表示 90%肯定，是很有把握的陈述；而 may not 是表示 50%肯定，是不太有把握的陈述，所以导致翻译时有“不可能”和“可能不”的区别。

从译文的差别，应该能够觉察出否定词 not 在情态动词前后位置的差异：对于“cannot + 谓语动词”的结构，真正的否定意义的结构是“否定 + 情态动词 + 谓语动词”，即“NOT+CAN+VERB（不可能）”；而对于“may not + 谓语动词”的结构，真正的否定意义结构是“情态动词 + 否定 + 谓语动词”，即“MAY+NOT+VERB（可能不）”。

现在，可以推而广之，用 MODAL 来代表“情态动词”，于是可以得出两种不同的否定结构：

1. NOT+MODAL+VERB
2. MODAL+NOT+VERB
这就是情态动词否定意义的深层结构。

为了接下来讨论方便，我们现在为这两种不同的否定结构定义两个术语：以否定词 NOT 的位置为标准，把否定词 NOT 在外部的 NOT+MODAL+VERB 称为外部否定（external negation）；相应地，把否定词 NOT 在中间的 MODAL+NOT+VERB 称为内部否定（internal negation）。在外部否定的结构中，被否定的是情态动词，比如把 cannot 译成“不 + 可能 + 好（be good）”，而不是谓语动词。在内部否定的结构中，被否定的是谓语动词，比如 may not 译成“可能 + 不 + 好（be good）”，而不是情态动词。

所以，尽管在表层结构上，否定词 not 都是跟在情态动词的后面，但在深层结构上是不同的。因此，对于某些句子来说，就可能会在外部否定与内部否定这两种结构上产生歧义。比如：

2 Paul *won't* come.

如果把该句理解成外部否定，即：Paul NOT will come.
这里被否定的是情态动词 will 即 NOT+will，这就表示“保罗不愿意来”。
如果把该句理解成内部否定，即：Paul will NOT come.
这里被否定的是谓语动词 come 即 NOT+come，这就表示“保罗将来不了”。

精品译文 外部否定：保罗不愿意来。
内部否定：保罗将来不了。

所以 Paul won't come. 这句话就产生了歧义，比如把该句放在下面两个不同的语境中：

3 1）Paul won't come because he doesn't want to. 保罗不愿意来，因为他就是不想来。
2）Paul won't come because he's too busy. 保罗将来不了，因为他太忙。

在陈述句中，不论是外部否定还是内部否定，not 总是要紧跟在情态动词后面。但是，若在疑问句中，就能看出外部否定和内部否定在句子结构上的差别。请比较：

4 1）*Could* you *not* come?
2）*Couldn't* you come?

妙语点睛 从句子的结构上来看，例句 1）采用的是内部否定，在变成疑问句时，只能把情态动词 could 提前，而把否定词 not 留在被否定的谓语动词 come 之前，这就露出了该句的“庐山真面目”。但例句 2）采用的是外部否定，在变成疑问句时，要把否定词与被否定的情态动词一起拿到句首。
所以，例句 1）否定的是谓语动词，意思是“能 + 不来”；例句 2）否定的是情态动词，意思是“不能 + 来”。

精品译文 1）你能不来吗？（不希望你也来）
2）你不能来吗？（非常希望你也能来）

如果不看上面提供的译文，也许读者会认为例句 1）和 2）这两句的意思没有差别，其实差别很大：例句 1）是表示说话人不希望“你”跟着过来；而例句 2）则是表示说话人非常希望“你”能过来。所以，例句 1）和 2）的意思完全相反。

再如：

5 1）***Could*** we ***not*** go together?

2）***Couldn't*** we go together?

妙语点睛 显然，这两句话的意思完全相反。比如，如果你的女友用例句1）对你说“我们能不走在一起吗？”你自然就会犯嘀咕了：为什么不能走在一起？想分手吗？这意味着你可能要被她甩了。但如果她用例句2）对你说“我们难道就不能走在一起吗？”这表明你不愿意和她走在一起，这就意味着要被甩的可能就是她了。

精品译文 1）我们能不走在一起吗？

2）我们难道就不能走在一起吗？

这两种不同的否定结构，尤其常用在表示“请求”或“要求”的句型中，比如上面的疑问句都是表示“请求”的意思。从以上例句的意思能发现这样的规律：

如果否定词not没有与情态动词的缩写形式一起被提置句首，而是直接置于谓语动词之前，这时被否定的就是谓语动词，即“某事不应该做”；而当否定词与情态动词的缩写形式放在一起时，被否定的就是情态动词，是用来加强“请求”的情态含义，强调“某事应该做”。

再比如：

6 1）***Will*** you please ***not*** get into the room?

2）***Won't*** you please get into the room?

妙语点睛 在例句1）中，相当于说Please don't get in. 在例句2）中，相当于说Please do get in.

精品译文 1）你能不进这个房间里来吗？（不希望你进这个房间）

2）你难道就不能进这个房间里来吗？（非常希望你进这个房间）

7 1）***Could*** I please ***not*** go to the party?

2）***Couldn't*** I please go to the party?

妙语点睛 在例句1）中，相当于说I don't want to; please don't force me. 在例句2）中，相当于说I want to go; please let me go.

精品译文 1）我能不来参加聚会吗？（我不想参加聚会）

2）难道我不能来参加聚会吗？（我非常想参加聚会）

8 1）***Could*** you ***not*** tell him? 你能不告诉他吗？（不希望你告诉他）

2）***Couldn't*** you tell him? 你难道就不能告诉他吗？（非常希望你告诉他）

以上举的例子都是一般疑问句，现在再举几个特殊疑问句的例子。在《老友记》(Friends)里有这样一个场景：莫尼卡(Monica)有一次一不小心和一个比自己小很多的处男埃森(Ethan)上了床，事后她才知道原来埃森才十多岁，这让她有点于心不忍，于是她质问道：How could you not tell me?（你怎么能不告诉我你的实际年龄呢？）请看下面的对话：

9 Monica: What we did was wrong. Oh god, I just had sex with somebody that wasn't alive during the Bicentennial.

Young Ethan: I just had sex.

Monica: Ethan, focus. How ***could*** you ***not tell*** me?

Young Ethan: Well, you never told me how old you were.

Monica: Well, that's different. My lie didn't make one of us a felon in 48 states. What were you thinking?

Young Ethan: I wasn't thinking. I was too busy fallin'...

Monica: Don't say it. (closes Ethan's mouth with her hand)

Young Ethan:...in love with you.

妙语点睛 我们看到，这里莫尼卡说How ***could*** you ***not tell*** me?采用的就是一个内部否定，表示“你怎么能不告诉我呢？”我们现在来看，如果用外部否定说成：How couldn't you tell me?

那是什么意思呢？这句话是表示“你怎么就不能告诉我呢？”

比较这两句话的意思，我们可以看出，“你怎么能不告诉我呢？”应该是在事后知道某一实情才说的话。比如上面的对话里，莫尼卡知道埃森年龄非常小之后才这么质问他的。而“你怎么就不能告诉我呢？”则往往表示在事前不知道某一情况，并希望对方告诉自己这一情况才说的。言外之意，相当于说 I want to know。所以，两句话的意思完全不同。

精品译文 莫尼卡：我们做得不对。哦，天啊，我竟然和一个毛头小伙子发生了关系。
年轻的埃森：我不过是做做爱而已。
莫尼卡：埃森，听着。你怎么能不告诉我你的实际年龄呢？
年轻的埃森：嗯，你从没告诉我你多大。
莫尼卡：哦，那不一样。我的谎言在48个州都不算犯罪，你是怎么想的？
年轻的埃森：我什么也没想。我忙着与你……
莫尼卡：别说了！（用手捂住埃森的嘴）
年轻的埃森：……相爱。

这句 How could you not tell me?也出现在下面这个场景对话中：傻大姐菲比(Phoebe)乐于助人。有一次，为了帮助一个男同性恋朋友获得美国绿卡而竟然和他结了婚。这事莫尼卡后来知道了，她来质问菲比为什么不告诉她：

10 Joey: This is unbelievable Phoebs, how can you be married?
Phoebe: Well, I mean, I'm not married married, ya know, he's just a friend and he's gay and he's just from Canada and he just needed a green card.
Monica: I can't believe you married Duncan. I mean how ***could you not tell*** me? We lived together, we told each other everything.
Phoebe: I'm sorry, Monica, but I knew if I told you, you'd get really, like, judgmental and you would not approve.
Monica: Of course I wouldn't approve, I mean, you were totally in love with this guy who, hello, was gay. I mean, what the hell were you thinking?
Ross: You see, and you thought she'd be judgmental.
Phoebe: OK, I wasn't in love with him and I was just helping out a friend.

精品译文 乔　伊：这个菲比真叫人难以置信，你怎么就结婚了呢？
菲　比：其实，我并没有真正意义上的结婚。你知道，他只是我的一个朋友，是个同性恋，他刚从加拿大过来，需要拿到绿卡。
莫尼卡：我真不敢相信你嫁给了邓肯。我是说，你怎么能不告诉我呢？我们住在一起，我们俩什么话都说的啊。
菲　比：很抱歉，莫妮卡，因为我知道，如果我和你讲了，你就一定会对这事评头论足的，而且一定不会同意。
莫尼卡：我当然不会同意的，我是说，你爱的是一个同性恋啊，这怎么可能？我是说，你到底是怎么想的？
罗　斯：你看，你想的是对的，莫妮卡就是爱这么评论。
菲　比：不是，我并不是爱他，我只是在帮助一个朋友。

下面两个女人争一个男人的故事：

11 She could totally find it in her heart to forgive poor, lonely Serena — after all, who ***could not*** fall in love with Nate? Besides, and most of all, Serena had no chance of coming between them ever again.
其实，在内心深处，她完全可以原谅这个可怜而又孤独的塞莉娜——毕竟，谁能不爱上内特呢？此外最重要的是，塞莉娜不会再有机会插足于她与他俩之间了。

注意，could not 往往要分开写，并且要重读。

8.17.2 内部否定和外部否定的使用规律

搞清楚了有关情态动词的外部否定和内部否定，有读者也许还会进一步追问：那怎么判断什么时候适宜按外部否定来理解和翻译，什么时候按内部否定来理解和翻译呢？

笔者自己也琢磨过，发现这两种否定结构与情态动词的两种基本意义有关：推测用法和基本用法。一般具有这样的规律：

1. 推测用法的情态动词，一般是内部否定，即否定的是谓语动作；

2. 基本用法的情态动词，一般是外部否定，即否定的是情态意义。

比如上面讨论过的例句：

12 1）Paul won't come because he doesn't want to.

2）Paul won't come because he's too busy.

妙语点睛 在例句1)中，won't表示"不愿意"，这里的will表示"愿意(willingness)"，属于will的基本含义和用法，所以这里采用了外部否定，即否定的是情态意义"愿意"。在例句2)中，won't表示"将不来"，这里的will表示"预测(prediction)"，属于will的推测用法，所以这里采用了内部否定，即否定的是谓语动作"来"。

精品译文 1）保罗不愿意来，因为他就是不想来。

2）保罗将来不了，因为他太忙。

请再看其他例句：

13 1）You can leave now, but he ***may not*** leave.

2）Tom will come, but John ***may not*** come.

妙语点睛 在例句1)中，may表示"许可(permission)"，是基本用法，所以may not是外部否定，译成"不可以"。在例句2)中，may表示"可能(possibility)"，是推测用法，所以may not是内部否定，译成"可能不"。

精品译文 1）你现在可以走了，但他不可以走。

2）汤姆将会来，但约翰可能不来了。

再比如下列内部否定的例句：

14 It ***won't*** rain.

妙语点睛 这里will表示推测，所以won't是内部否定。

精品译文 天将不会下雨。

15 It ***shouldn't*** last long.

妙语点睛 这里should表示推测，所以shouldn't是内部否定。

精品译文 应该不会太久的。

再比如下列外部否定的例句：

16 He ***won't*** help us.

妙语点睛 这里will表示"意愿"，属于基本用法，所以won't是外部否定。

精品译文 他不愿意帮我们。

17 You ***can't*** smoke here.

妙语点睛 这里can表示"许可"，属于基本用法，所以can't是外部否定。

精品译文 你不能在这里抽烟。

我们再看下面这个句子：

18 You ***can't*** be serious.

妙语点睛 这里can表示推测，属于推测用法。但这里can't是外部否定"不可能"，而不是内部否定"可能不"。但按照上面的规律——表示推测用法，应该是内部否定。由此可见，can不适用于上述规则。

精品译文 你不可能是当真的吧。

同样，对于must，上述规则也不适用。因为must用于推测用法时，本身没有否定，即不能说mustn't。当must用于基本含义表示"必须"时，其否定形式mustn't的意思是"千万别做某事"，这里否定的是谓语动作，即一个内部否定，而不是上面规则说的外部否定，即含义为"不必"。must的外部否定"不必"应说成don't have to。对此，读者了解即可。

最后，需要提醒读者注意的是还有这样特殊的否定句：

19 Rachel:（to Ross）I can't believe you don't want to know. I mean, I ***couldn't not know***, I mean, if, if the doctor knows, and Carol knows, and Susan knows...

妙语点睛 这里的 couldn't not 是一个双重否定，很像汉语里说的"不能不"。这种否定比较罕见。

精品译文 雷切尔：(对罗斯说)我真不敢相信，你都不想知道。我的意思是说，就是说，既然医生知道了，凯萝尔也知道了，苏珊也知道了，我就不能不知道。

思维总结

读者需要了解何谓外部否定和内部否定，并掌握这两种否定结构的使用规律：

1. 推测用法的情态动词，一般是内部否定，即否定的是谓语动作；
2. 基本用法的情态动词，一般是外部否定，即否定的是情态意义。

思维训练

Exercise 8.17（Key: P353）

请正确翻译下面句子，并说明每个句子是采用了外部否定还是内部否定。

1. Could you not tell him?
2. Paul won't come because he doesn't want to.
3. Tom will come, but John may not come.
4. Couldn't you tell him?
5. Couldn't we go together?
6. Paul won't come because he's too busy.
7. Could we not go together?
8. You can leave now, but he may not leave.

8.18 总结：英文情态与中文情态的简单对比

从前面各节讨论的内容看到，每个情态动词都有很多的意思，而不同的意思有不同的用法。所以，情态动词的用法和词义变化多端，纷繁复杂，情态动词因此也是让中国学生"摸不着头脑"的一种英语谓语的变化形式。这也可以理解，因为情态动词即是说话人微妙心态变化的反映，native speakers 就是通过运用各种功能强大的情态动词以极其微妙的方式来"言传心声"的。本节将简单地比较中文情态与英文情态的用法和意义。

8.18.1 英文情态意义与中文情态意义的对应性

英语中的情态动词的某些意义能在中文中找到比较好的对应表达，比如 can 对应于"能够"，should 对应于"应该"。对于这样一些中文思维里也有的情态意义，中国学生一般使用地比较好。比如：

1 I ***can*** speak good English. 我能够讲很好的英文。

2 You ***should*** study English. 你应该学习英文。

但是对于下面这些句子中的情态意义就不甚了解或不知道了：

3 Women ***can*** do anything when jealous.

妙语点睛 这里的 can 表示"潜在的可能"或者说"理论上的可能"。显然，这里的 can 不是中文的情态动词"能够"所能表达的意思。

精品译文 女人要是妒忌了，什么事都可能做得出来。

4 It's strange that you ***should*** say this.

妙语点睛 这里的 should 表示惊讶之意——"竟然"。显然，这里的 should 在中文里没有对应的情态动词。

精品译文 你竟然这么说，真是奇怪。

5 We ***should*** be grateful if you ***could*** do it.

妙语点睛 这里的 should 和 could 用于委婉地提出请求，很正式的用语。这里的 should 没有含义，只是一个礼貌的表达形式。

精品译文 如果您能这么做，我们将非常感激。

6 He ***might*** come.

妙语点睛 这里的 might 表示把握不大的推测。

精品译文 他或许会来吧。

7 1) I ***would*** be happy to help you.

2) I ***am*** happy to help you.

妙语点睛 这里说 I ***would be*** happy to help you. 要比 I ***am*** happy to help you. 委婉得多。

在例句 1）中，would 表达一种委婉假设的含义，意思是说"如果你真的需要我帮忙，我会很乐意帮助你的"。这么用 would 来说这句话，只是告诉对方你主观上愿意帮助他。至于对方是否需要你来帮助，那是他的选择。在例句 2)中，说 am 就显得比较直截了当，不给对方选择的余地，好像在强迫别人找你帮忙一样，有点把自己的主观意愿强加于对方的感觉(impose yourself on people who don't want your help)。比如，也许对方真的是需要有人帮忙，但他出于自尊心的原因不一定非得找你帮忙。所以，用例句 2)也许会让人感觉你把自己当作救世主一样，但例句 1)就绝不会让人有这种误解。

精品译文 1）如果需要的话，我会非常乐意帮你的。

2）我想要帮你(有困难一定要找我啊)。

笔者曾经告诉自己的一个外国朋友笔者正在写英语语法书，他在电子邮件里回复说：I ***would be*** happy to have a read. 他这么说的言外之意是：如果笔者愿意把自己的书稿通过电子邮件发给他看看的话，他会非常乐意拜读一下的。他这里用 would be happy 这么说就显得非常礼貌，没有强迫笔者非得把书稿发过去给他看的意思。如果他说 I ***am*** happy to have a read. 则显得他很想让笔者把书稿发给他看，有点强人所难的意味。

上面笔者解释了这么多，相信读者以后读到类似的含有 would 的句子，应该有更深刻、更准确的理解了。显然，这里的 would 在中文中也没有很好的对应词，不是一个简单的"将愿意"就能表达 would 如此微妙的内涵的。

8 Let me see if I ***could*** help work this out.

妙语点睛 这里的 could 表示非常礼貌和谦虚。即使你认为对方的某个问题是小菜一碟，你能轻而易举地解决，你也不妨用 could 来显示你的谦虚谨慎。比如，你是公司新来的一名员工，大家对于某个电脑技术难题都无法解决，而你很清楚该怎么处理。面对那么多的公司老前辈和领导，你只是一个初出茅庐的新手，如果你很骄傲地说 I ***can*** work this out. It's a piece of cake.（这个我能解决，对我来说简直是小菜一碟。)这样说就显得你过于自负，当然会让你的领导及其他老员工脸面上很难堪。但如果你用 could 说 Let me see if I ***could*** work this out. 则显得你为人谦虚，这样给周围同事的感觉自然大不一样。另外，万一这个问题你也解决不了，你用 could 这样委婉地表达也是给自己留了余地，因为 could 表明了你不肯定是否能完成。由此可见，can 与 could 在语气上的巨大差异。这里的 could 在中文里也没有很好的对应词，不是一个简单的"能够"就能表达 could 的含义的。

精品译文 我来看看是否能够帮忙解决。

请看下面这个例句：

9 I ***wouldn't*** pay them a penny.

妙语点睛 这句话是英国伦敦市长肯·利文斯通(Ken Liverstone)说的，他如此直言不讳地批评 2012 年伦敦奥运会会徽的设计者。这里的 would 用于虚拟假设，所以在译文中增添了"要是我"这样的条件表达。这里的 would 没有对应的汉语情态动词。

精品译文 要是我，一分钱也不会给他们。

对于上面这些情态动词的微妙含义，没有很好的英语思维基础的中国学生是很难理解和把握的，他们往往不能理解这些情态动词所潜含的各种微妙的含义。

总的来说，英语的情态动词所表达的含义要比中文多很多。因此，很多英语的情态意义在中文找不到对应的情态表达，而只能通过其他字词来传达其含义，比如表示惊讶的情态意义的 should，在汉语中就取“竟然”来翻译。这就是为什么中国学生往往在口头或书面表达中“忘记”使用或不会使用英语的情态动词来微妙地言传心声的原因。

8.18.2 英文情态动词的委婉表达在汉语中的缺失

英文表达往往要求采用比较礼貌的表达形式，尤其是在“指示(instructions)”、“邀请(invitations)”、“请求(requests)”和“建议(suggestions)”等语境中，此时正是情态动词发挥魅力的时候。但中国学生往往在这些该用情态动词的场合中不使用情态动词，这样使英语的表达显得较为生硬、突然(abrupt)，甚至不礼貌。比如汉语里常这样说话：

1 请看一下这篇文章。

2 我们希望你明天能过来和我们一起吃午饭。

3 请你过来坐在这。

4 我建议你去和他说一下。

对于上面的这些中文句子，读者在口语中是不是常常这么说？而且这些表达在汉语里听起来已经够礼貌和客气了。但是如果直接生硬地译成英语，则显得并不十分礼貌。大家来看下面的简单直接的对译：

5 Please read this article.

6 We hope that you will come and have lunch with us tomorrow.

7 You come and sit here, please.

8 I suggest that you have a word with him.

这样简单的“死译”，其重要原因就在于不会灵活地应用英文的情态动词。这些句子其实可以表达得更礼貌。比如同样的意思，若用英文表达，下列表达会显得更自然而礼貌：

9 You ***may*** like to read this article.

10 We ***were wondering whether you could*** come and have lunch with us tomorrow.

11 ***Would you*** come and sit here, please?

12 You ***might*** want to have a word with him.

当然，上面这些句子还有其他更多礼貌的表达形式，这时都得采用情态动词。比如，对于最后一句的“提建议”，还可以这样说：

13 I ***would suggest*** that you have a word with him.

14 ***May I suggest*** that you have a word with him?

如果是在正式的交际场合，比如商务谈判中，往往要借助情态动词来更委婉地，或者说比较“外交辞令”地表达意思，而不会不采用任何情态动词就这么直接而生硬地交流。请比较：

15 1) That's impossible.

2) ***Unfortunately*** that ***wouldn't be*** possible.

妙语点睛 这两句是在拒绝对方。

在例句 1)中，谓语动词用的是 is，显得说话的语气非常直白和生硬，容不得对方商量。这自然就会让对方难以接受。在例句 2) 中，首先是借助 would 来“软化”生硬的口气。其次，把

impossible 换成 not possible，给人感觉有商量的余地。再次，因为是在拒绝对方，所以用副词 unfortunately 来表达遗憾，给对方以安慰。

由此可见，为了使话语显得礼貌，采用了上述三个方面的处理。

精品译文 1）这是不可能的。

2）很遗憾，这恐怕不太可能。

16 1）It is a good idea to agree on a price before we go any further.

2）***Wouldn't it*** be a better idea to agree on a price before we go any further?

妙语点睛 这两句是在提建议。

在例句 1)中，谓语动词用的是 is，it is a good idea 表示"……这样做好"，用这种方式来向对方提出建议，显得有些自负而傲慢，有把自己的观点强加于对方的味道。在例句 2)中，首先，借助 would 来"软化"生硬的口气。其次，把肯定句变为否定句，给对方很大的选择余地。再次，用否定的 wouldn't 来提问，更具商量的口吻。第四，把 good 变成 better 也显得更礼貌。

由此可见，为了使话语显得礼貌，我们采用了上述四个方面的技术处理。

精品译文 1）我们还是先商定好价格然后再继续往下谈吧，这样比较好。

2）在继续往下讨论之前，如果我们能先商定一下价格，是不是更好些？

17 1）We ***can't*** go higher than 7 per cent.

2）We ***would find it*** (***quite***) ***difficult*** to go any higher than 7 per cent.

妙语点睛 这两句是在讨价还价。

在例句 1)中，直接说"不能(can't)"，没有给对方回旋的余地。在例句 2)中，首先，借助 would 来"软化"生硬的口气。其次，difficult 相当于委婉地说 impossible，从而比较礼貌地拒绝对方的要求。

精品译文 1）我们无法再高于 7%了。

2）如果这样的话，我们发现很难再高于 7%了。

18 1）We ***need*** a commitment from you now.

2）We ***would like*** some kind of commitment from you now.

妙语点睛 这两句是在向对方提要求。

在例句 1)中，用 need 显得比较直截了当地提出自己的要求。在例句 2)中，用 would 来委婉地说出自己的需要。其次，增添了 some kind 来缓和语气。

精品译文 1）我们现在就需要你的承诺。

2）现在我们想知道你能不能给我们一些承诺。

19 1）You***'ll*** have to pay more if you want that.

2）You ***may*** have to pay slightly more if you (really) want that.

妙语点睛 在例句 1)中，用 will 显得语气比较强硬。在例句 2)中，用委婉的 may，表示"或许"来缓和语气。其次，增添了 slightly 来轻描淡写，以及 really 来加强语气，这两个词都起到了"软化"语气的作用。

精品译文 1）如果你想那样的话，那你就必须得多付钱。

2）如果你真的是想那样的话，那么你或许得需要稍微多付点钱。

20 1）It ***will*** be difficult to get my boss to agree to this.

2）It ***might*** not be very easy to get my boss to agree to this.

妙语点睛 在例句 1)中，用 will 显得语气比较强硬。在例句 2)中，用委婉的 might，表示"或许"来缓和语气。其次，把 difficult 改成 not very easy，给对方的感觉更好。

精品译文 1）这样就一定很难得到我们老板的同意了。

2）这样或许不太容易得到我们老板的同意。

21 1）We ***should*** spend more time looking for a compromise here.

2）***Shouldn't*** we spend a little more time looking for a compromise here?

妙语点睛 这两句是在提建议。

在例句 1)中，用 should 显得语气比较强硬。在例句 2)中，用 shouldn't 委婉地否定反问，显得是在和对方商量，给人以礼貌的感觉。

精品译文 1) 在这一点上，我们双方应该多花时间来寻找一个折中的办法。

2) 在这一点上，我们双方是不是应该多花点时间来寻找一个折中的办法呢？

从以上各对例句的比较中，我们看到，在进行委婉的表达时，各类情态动词在其中起了根本的作用，其次才是结合疑问句式以及增添某些词语来共同表达委婉的语气。对于情态动词礼貌的表达作用，读者需要多加观察和用心体会。

尽管在本章中对于情态动词的意义和用法已作了较为详尽和系统的分析与比较，但不可能包括所有的用法。正如在"引言"里指出的，情态动词即是说话人微妙心态变化的反映，老外就是通过运用各种功能强大的情态动词以极其微妙的方式来"言传心声"的。所以，希望读者在英语学习过程中，继续观察、分析和体会情态动词这种微妙的使用规律，以逐渐习得英语思维。

写给读者的话

一、本章学习思路

正如在前面讲过的，对于情态动词的学习，可以从两个方面入手。一方面，以情态动词的推测用法和基本用法为主线，来探讨各个情态动词之间的相关性。另一方面，可以单独以各个情态动词为主线，对每个情态动词可能具有的语义功能给予总结和归纳。

由于在本章采用的主要是第一种阐述方式，因此，读者可以此作为主要的学习途径。

另外，在涉及情态动词的虚拟用法时，读者应该结合第七章的相关内容来学习。

二、本章重点及难点

总体来说，情态动词的意义和用法都是比较难的，非常微妙。在诸多内容中，建议读者重点掌握下面这些用法：

1. 对现在推测的用法；
2. 对过去推测的用法；
3. 在表示过去的能力时，could 与 was/were able to 的区别；
4. 表示"请求"的各个句型。

最后，对其他用法要有所了解。

三、本章学习时间安排

读者可以用两周左右的时间研读完所讲解的内容，并做完每节后面的练习，然后从头复习一遍或两遍，最后用两天左右的时间来做后面的综合练习，并结合所给的答案搞清楚每题的考点及情态动词的意义。

综合练习 (Key: P353)

请根据句义，选出正确的情态动词。

1. We are enjoying our holiday, though the weather (could, must) be better.
2. We (could, might) go to that new restaurant opposite the cinema.
3. How about going to the theater instead. We (could, should) go to the theater instead.
4. I don't know how she knows, but Mom (can, may) always detect when I'm lying.
5. Nobody else is going to turn up now for the lesson, so you (have to, may as well) go home.
6. No member of the association (shall, will) remove official documents from these premises without written permission.
7. The peace conference (may, has to) find a solution to the problem.

8. Rule 6. No member (shall, should) enter the bar area wearing sports kit.
9. The heating comes on automatically. You (must not, don't have to) turn it on.
10. It's a lovely hotel. And the staff (couldn't, might not) be more helpful.
11. You (could, may) be right, but I still don't agree with you!
12. I am sure Nick wasn't there. That (can't have been, shouldn't have been) Nick that you saw.
13. You (had to give, might have given) me a hand!
14. I caught a later train because I (had to see, must have seen) a client.
15. I suppose Bill (should have lost, might have lost) his way.
16. I don't know who rang, but it (could, must) have been Jim.
17. The situation was bad but it (could be, may have been, could have been) worse.
18. It's a pity you didn't ask because I (could help, could have helped) you.
19. It's your own fault, you (can't have, shouldn't have gone) to bed so late.
20. I was so angry that I (might, may) have killed her.
21. You screamed in your sleep last night. You (might have, might have had) a terrible dream.
22. Harry studies a lot. He (should know, should have known) all the answers.

请选出与所给句子在意思上最接近的解释。

23. It's possible that we'll know the answers tomorrow.
    A. We may know all the answers tomorrow. B. We should know all the answers tomorrow.
24. It's possible that the decision will be announced next week.
    A. The decision might be announced next week. B. The decision will be announced next week.
25. I know. Why don't we go out to eat instead.
    A. I know. We must go out to eat instead. B. I know. We could go out to eat instead.
26. Perhaps these are the keys.
    A. These might be the keys. B. These must be the keys.
27. I think it's wrong for you to work so hard.
    A. You don't have to work so hard. B. You shouldn't work so hard.
28. You needn't come if you don't want to.
    A. You won't come if you don't want to. B. You don't have to come if you don't want to.
29. It would be quite wrong for us to lock the dog in the house for a week.
    A. We'd better not lock the dog in the house for a week.
    B. We can't lock the dog in the house for a week.
30. I don't think you should ring him now. It's rather late.
    A. You might not ring him now. It's rather late. B. You'd better not ring him now. It's rather late.

请根据句义填空。

31. Peter wasn't here, so he ______ (break) your vase.
32. I'm sure Jack didn't mean to ignore you. He ______ (notice) you.
33. That was a lucky escape! We ______ (kill)!
34. The meat is a bit burnt. You ______ (cook) it for so long. I did tell you!
35. There were plenty of tickets left for the concert. We ______ (buy) them in advance.
36. Sally got home at four o'clock this morning. The party ______ (be) really good.
37. Thank you very much for buying me flowers. You ______ (buy) me flowers.
38. I don't believe that you have lost your keys again! You ______ (lose) your keys again.
39. Mary was a talented violinist at the age of ten. She ______ (play) the violin very well when she was ten.
40. Perhaps they didn't notice the tire was flat. They ______ (notice) the tire was flat.
41. Our worrying so much was a waste of time. We ______ (worry) so much.
42. It's possible that the last person to leave didn't lock the door. The last person to leave ______ (lock) the door.
43. They hurried there, only to find the meeting was cancelled. In fact, they ______ (go) there.

44. She paid him and walked off. Then she realized that he ______ (not, be) a deaf mute. How did she know? He must have heard her initial instructions or he ______ (not, know) where to take her.
45. A: It seems to rain. I guess I ______ (bring) my umbrella.
B: It would be nice to have one but how ______ you ______ (know) that this morning?
46. "If you sit too close to the television, you'll ruin your eyes." Sound familiar? You ______ (hear) this warning as a child. People sit too close to the television because they already can't see very well. This may give them tired eyes or a headache, but it won't make their eyesight any worse.

请选择最佳答案填空。

47. As it turned out to be a small house party, we ______ so formally.
A. needn't dress up B. did not need have dressed up
C. did not need dress up D. needn't have dressed up
48. You can't imagine that a well-behaved gentleman ______ be so rude to a lady.
A. might B. need C. should D. would
49. It has been announced that candidates ______ remain in their seats until all the papers have been collected.
A. can B. will C. may D. shall
50. It is unthinkable that he ______ be so careless.
A. will B. would C. shall D. should
51. The boss has promised that every player in NBA ______ have a rise in income.
A. would B. might C. shall D. should
52. A man wants to see you, sir. ______ he wait outside?
A. Will B. Shall C. Would D. Ought
53. He was a good swimmer so he ______ swim to the river bank when the boat sank.
A. could B. might C. succeeded to D. was able to
54. Oh, I'm not feeling well in the stomach. I ______ so much fried chicken just now.
A. shouldn't eat B. mustn't have eaten C. shouldn't have eaten D. mustn't eat
55. Several cases have been reported recently of people who ______ read and detect colors with their fingers.
A. should B. can C. will D. could
56. No one expect his secretary ______ go straight into his office without permission.
A. can B. is able to C. will D. is not allowed to
57. She was absent for the first time yesterday. She ______ sick.
A. must be B. has been C. is D. must have been
58. He did very badly on the exam. He ______ harder.
A. must study B. must have studied C. should study D. should have studied
59. I ______ to him because he phoned me shortly afterwards.
A. ought to have written B. must have written C. couldn't have written D. needn't have written
60. He ______ ten lectures on American history, but he only gave two because of his illness.
A. had given B. would give C. must have given D. should have given
61. We did hold a meeting yesterday, but you ______. So we did not inform you.
A. did not need attending B. needn't attending C. did not need to attend D. needn't attend
62. We came early and had to wait two hours before the ceremony began. We ______.
A. should not hurry B. must not have hurried C. need not hurry D. need not have hurried
63. "Have you paid your telephone bill?"
"No, but I ______ yesterday."
A. ought to pay it B. ought to have paid it C. must pay it D. must have paid it
64. He ______ pull down a bull and acknowledged as a man with superman strength.
A. used to be able to B. would be able to C. should be able to D. might be able to
65. Some women ______ a good salary in a job instead of staying home, but they decided not to work for the sake of

the family.

A. must make B. should have made C. would make D. could have made

66. I didn't send out my application form last week, but I ______.

A. had B. would do C. should have D. might have to

67. Mary ______ my letter; otherwise she would have replied before now.

A. has received B. ought to have received C. couldn't have received D. shouldn't have received

68. You ______ him so closely; you should have kept your distance.

A. shouldn't follow B. mustn't follow

C. couldn't have been following D. shouldn't have been following

附录 答案解析

第一章 简单句与复合句

Exercise 1. 1（P2）

1. 这里是对介词短语 with one hand 所作的成分有不同的解释。在说话者 A 的话语中，with one hand 是作状语，修饰谓语 lift，表示“用一只手就能够把一头猪举起来”。但在 B 的话语中，with one hand 是作定语，修饰 pig，表示“只有一条腿的猪”。
2. 这里是对介词短语 with a wooden leg 所作的成分有不同的解释。在顾客的话语中，with a wooden leg 是作定语，修饰 man，表示 “装有一支木头假腿的男子”。但理发师把 with a wooden leg 误解成是作状语，修饰 shaved，表示“用一支木头腿来给一个男子刮脸”。于是，他立即否定说道“不是，我总是用剃刀来给他刮脸”。

Exercise 1. 2（P9）

1. 她独身一辈子，直到去世都未嫁人。
2. 他 18 岁到北京，当时身无分文，但现在已是一家跨国公司的总裁了。
3. 这本书过期一周了，我一定要被罚款了。
4. 史密斯先生死的时候已经是一个大学的校长了。
   相当于说“Mr. Smith was a university president when he died.”
5. 他当时在装傻。
6. 他当时的行动非常愚蠢。
7. C。表示行为愚蠢，所以要用副词 foolishly 来修饰 acted。
8. A。act 是系动词，后接形容词 sick 作表语。
9. A。形容词 safe 是补充说明主语，作主语补足语。
10. B。stay 是系动词，所以其后接形容词，作表语。

Exercise 1. 5（P15）

1. a thief 是间接宾语；enough rope 是直接宾语。可以用 to 改写成：Give enough rope to a thief。
   精品译文：多行不义必自毙。
2. me 是间接宾语；a good novel 是直接宾语。可以用 to 改写成：Can you recommend a good novel to me?
   精品译文：你能给我推荐一部好的小说吗？
3. them 是间接宾语；a hut 是直接宾语。可以用 for 改写成：He built a hut for them.
   精品译文：他为他们建造了一个小木屋。
4. himself 是间接宾语；a bottle of champagne 是直接宾语。可以用 for 改写成：He ordered a bottle of champagne for himself.
   精品译文：他为自己点了一瓶香槟。
5. me 是间接宾语；an interesting novel 是直接宾语。可以用 for 改写成：Will you choose an interesting novel for me?
   精品译文：你愿意为我挑选一本有趣的小说吗？
6. me 是间接宾语；a few minutes of your valuable time 是直接宾语。可以用 for 改写成：Can you spare a few minutes of your valuable time for me?

精品译文：我能占用你几分钟宝贵的时间吗？

7. me 是间接宾语；anything 是直接宾语。可以用 to 改写成：Jack doesn't owe anything to me.
   精品译文：杰克不欠我任何东西。
8. you 是间接宾语；a favor 是直接宾语。可以用 of 改写成：May I ask a favor of you?
   精品译文：我能请你帮个忙吗？
9. you 是间接宾语；a lot of time 是直接宾语。可以用 for 改写成：That will save a lot of time for you。
   精品译文：那样会为你节省很多时间。
10. the author 是间接宾语；a Nobel Prize 是直接宾语。可以用 for 改写成：The novel won a Nobel Prize for the author。
    精品译文：这部小说为其作者赢得了诺贝尔奖。
11. me 是间接宾语；three dollars 是直接宾语。该句不能改写。
    精品译文：这花了我三美元。

Exercise 1.6 (P17)

1. grow fonder 是宾语补足语；不带 to 的不定式作宾补。
   精品译文：久别情深。
2. thirty-three times their original size 是宾语补足语；名词短语作宾补。
   精品译文：17 世纪的望远镜能够把物体放大 33 倍。
3. speechless 是宾语补足语，形容词作宾补。
   精品译文：这名男生一番刻薄的话让老师无言以对。
4. over 是宾语补足语，副词作宾补。
   精品译文：主席宣布会议结束。
5. medium 是宾语补足语，形容词作宾补。
   精品译文：我喜欢牛排半分熟。
6. free 是宾语补足语，形容词作宾补。
   精品译文：迪克把笼中的动物放跑了。
7. black 是宾语补足语，形容词作宾补。
   精品译文：锅说水壶黑 / 半斤八两 / 五十步笑百步。

综合练习 (P19)

1. B。本题考查复合宾语结构：consider A B，表示"把 A 看作是 B"。
   精品译文：Willa Cather 认为她那部描写 19 世纪内布拉斯加州生活的小说《我的安东尼奥》是她最好的一部作品。
2. B。本题考查复合宾语结构：make A B，表示"使 A 成为 B"。
   精品译文：Carrie Mae Weems 在拍摄照片时，常常把自己的家人作为照片拍摄的对象。这些照片深刻反映了非洲裔美国人的经历，并表达了对他们的深厚情感。
3. B。本题考查复合宾语结构：name A B，表示"任命 A 成为 B"。
   精品译文：尤利塞斯·格兰特上台成为美国总统的第一个任命就是，任命塞内卡族首领 Donehogawa 作为处理印度事务的特使。
4. C。本题考查复合宾语结构：consider A B，表示"把 A 看作是 B"。
   精品译文：小说家 Edith Wharton 认为作家 Henry James 对自己的作品有很大的影响。
5. C。本题考查复合宾语结构：make A B，表示"使 A 成为 B"。
   精品译文：蓝宝石可以使紫外线和红外线的辐射穿透，这使得其在光学仪器中得到广泛的应用。
6. C。本题考查复合宾语结构：appoint A B，表示"授予 A 成为 B"。
   精品译文：在 1993 年，美国国会图书馆授予作家 Rita Dove 美国"桂冠诗人"称号。

7. D。本题考查双宾语结构：win somebody something。这里 D 选项中 a work 是作为同位语，补充说明 The Old Man and the Sea。然后在 work 后边接一个定语从句。

   精品译文： 在 1952 年，欧内斯特·海明威发表了小说《老人与海》，这部作品为他赢得了 1954 年度的诺贝尔文学奖。

8. C。本题考查双宾语结构：win somebody something。A 和 B 选项有 was 作谓语，错误；D 选项误用了介词 for，应该说成：win something for somebody，而不是 for something。

   精品译文： Barbara McClintock 在遗传学领域的研究成果，为她赢得了 1983 年的诺贝尔奖。

第二章 名词从句

Exercise 2. 1 (P27)

1. Whether she comes is unimportant to me.
2. Whether we shall have the match remains uncertain.
3. I wonder whether we should wait for him.
4. No one knows exactly whether there is life on other planets.
5. I am interested in the question whether people will live on the moon someday.
6. My question is whether we have enough time to go to the movie.
7. Do you know whether sound travels faster than light?
8. I don't know how old he is.
9. What he was talking about was interesting.
10. Do you know what's on TV tonight?
11. Please tell me where you live.
12. I wonder why dinosaurs became extinct.
13. What she said wasn't true.
14. What he told you is true.
15. Why they refused to cooperate with us is still a mystery.
16. Do you know when they are coming?
17. I can't remember how much it costs.
18. Let's ask him which book he wants.
19. I don't know who is coming to the party.
20. I don't know who are those people.
21. Do you know whose pen this is?
22. Why they left the country is a secret.
23. Where she went is none of your business.
24. What happened on the morning of September will be forever etched in our memories?
25. I don't remember how many letters there are in the English alphabet.
26. I need to find out how old a person has to be to get a driver's license.
27. The little boy wants to know whether animals have the same emotions as human beings
28. The little boy wants to know why the water of the sea is salty.

Exercise 2. 2 (P30)

1. It is a fact that the word is round.
2. It is true that smoking can cause cancer.
3. It is true that English is becoming an international language.

4. It was strange that Clint failed his English exam.
5. It is a serious matter that he has been late for work over and over again.

综合练习（P34）

1. B。这是 how 引导的宾语从句，其中 how 在从句中充当方式状语，修饰 began。
2. D。这是“It is + 形容词 + that”固定的主语从句句型。
3. C。这是“It is + 名词 + that”固定的主语从句句型。D 不正确，因为有冠词 a，但没有名词。
4. C。这是“It is + 过去分词 + that”固定的主语从句句型。
5. B。这是 what 引导的主语从句，what 需要充当成分。这里 what 充当从句的主语。
6. A。这是 what 引导的表语从句，其中 what 充当从句谓语 solve 的宾语。连词 that 不充当成分，故 B 错误。
7. B。这是主语从句的固定句型“It + be 动词 + 过去分词 + that 从句”。
8. D。这是 what 引导的宾语从句，what 作表语。
9. B。这是 what 引导的宾语从句，其中 what 作 do 的宾语。A 错误，是因为 that 和 what 是两个连词，但后边只有一个从句。
10. B。这是 what 引导的宾语从句，其中 what 作 says 的宾语。
11. A。这是 that 引导的宾语从句，that 不充当任何成分。
12. B。这是 when 引导的宾语从句，其中 when 修饰 return。A 错，是因为两个连词，但只有一个从句。C 错，是因为 if or not 一般不连用，可以说 whether or not。
13. C。这是 what 引导的表语从句，其中 what 在从句中充当主语。
14. B。这里是 what 引导的主语从句：What can be dangerous。其中，what 在从句中充当主语。
15. B。这是关于 what 引导的宾语从句，其中 what 充当 know 的宾语。
16. B。这里含有两个名词从句。一个是 what 引导的主语从句，其中 what 充当从句谓语 tell 的宾语；另一个是 that 引导的表语从句，that 不充当任何成分。
17. B。这是 what 引导的主语从句，其中 what 充当从句谓语 adopt 的宾语。
18. A。这是 what 引导的表语从句。这里 what 用法较特殊，其后接有名词 measure，what measure 充当从句谓语 adopt 的宾语。
19. B。这是 where 引导的表语从句，表示地点。
20. C。在 reason 后边的表语从句一般不用 because，而用 that。故 C 正确，而 D 不正确。这与汉语思维有差异，请读者注意比较。
21. D。这是从句的嵌套结构。首先是 how 引导一个表语从句，然后在 how 从句中，嵌套一个 what 引导的主语从句。其中 what 充当从句谓语 learn 的宾语。
22. A。这是 that 引导的同位语从句，补充说明先行词 signs。
23. C。这是“It is + 过去分词 + that”固定的主语从句句型。
24. B。这是“It is + 过去分词 + that”固定的主语从句句型。
25. B。这是 that 引导的同位语从句，补充说明先行词 news。
26. what。这里 what 引导的是表语从句，且 what 在从句中充当主语。
27. whether。这里 whether 引导的是主语从句，被放在了句末。
28. why。这里 why 引导的是主语从句，被放在了句末。
29. that。这里 that 引导的是表语从句。因为前面有 reason，后边不能用 because。
30. that。这里 that 引导的是同位语从句，补充说明 conclusion。
31. what。这里 what 引导的是同位语从句，补充说明 idea，且 what 在从句中充当主语。
32. that。这里 that 引导的是同位语从句，补充说明 idea。
33. that, what, what。这里 that 引导的是一个定语从句，且在从句中作主语。这里两个 what 引导的都是表语从句，并且 what 在从句中充当主语。
34. what, what, what。这里三个都是 what 引导的表语从句，并且 what 在从句中充当主语。
35. B，改为 that。这里 that 引导的是同位语从句，补充说明 proof。

    精品译文：要说植物所需要的食物与动物的不同，有证据表明这一点吗？

36. A，改为 what。这里 what 引导的是主语从句，且 what 在从句中充当 doing 的宾语。

精品译文：如果一个人他所热衷从事的工作却被社会认为是毫无价值或毫无意义的，那么他就不可能真正快乐。

37. C，改为 that。这里 that 引导的是同位语从句，补充说明 fact。

精品译文：越来越多的人已经意识到这样的事实：心脏病与人们的生活方式有关系。

第三章 定语从句

Exercise 3. 1（P39）

Passage 1

这里定语从句包括：

1. I like guys who aren't too serious and who have a good sense of humor.

这里有两个定语从句：who aren't too serious 和 who have a good sense of humor，都是修饰同一个先行词 guys，关系词是 who。

2. I'd prefer someone who I have something in common with—who I can talk to easily.

这里有两个定语从句：who I have something in common with 和 who I can talk to easily，都是修饰同一个先行词 someone，关系词是 who。

Passage 2

这里定语从句包括：

1. I'm talking about friends who care deeply about each other, who support each other, who make life worth living.

这里有三个定语从句：who care deeply about each other，who support each other 和 who make life worth living，都是修饰同一个先行词 friends，关系词是 who。

2. I'm talking about friends who you can share almost everything with.

这里定语从句 who you can share almost everything with 修饰先行词 friends，关系词是 who。

精品译文：友谊是很难处理的，有时还会带来麻烦。事实上，我想说的是，友谊与爱情甚至婚姻一样难以处理。当然了，我这里所说的友谊不是那种"来得快去得也快"泛泛之交，而是那种彼此之间能真正互相关心的朋友，能够互相支持的朋友，能够让你的人生更有意义的朋友，是那种你和他们几乎可以分享一切的朋友。

Passage 3

这里定语从句包括：

1. And yet when anyone of us has seen that which to him is beautiful

这里定语从句 which to him is beautiful 修饰先行词 that，关系词是 which。

2. he has known an emotion which is in every case the same in kind.

这里定语从句 which is in every case the same in kind 修饰先行词 emotion，关系词是 which。

3. these are the drops of rain that keep the human spirit from death by draught.

这里定语从句 that keep the human spirit from death by draught 修饰先行词 the drops of rain，关系词是 that。

4. They are a stealing and silent refreshment that we perhaps do not think about but which goes on all the time.

这里有两个定语从句：that we perhaps do not think about 和 which goes on all the time，都是修饰同一个先行词 stealing and silent refreshment，关系词分别是 that 和 which。

精品译文：审美标准，因人而异。但一旦美在眼前出现，我们对美的感受却并无二致。扬帆的航船，绽放的鲜花，夜晚的小镇，优美的诗行，婆娑的树影，孩童的烂漫，满天的繁星，春天的果树——这些使我们潜生美感的万千景象，仿佛雨露般滋润着我们干涸的心田。它们悄然而来，在我们不经意中荡涤尘寰，绵延不断。美是大地的笑容，人人得以享受，只要我们用眼去捕捉，用心去感受。

Exercise 3. 2（P42）

1. 可以与f搭配，从而构成这样句子：It would be fun to go out with a person who is a really good conversationalist.
   精品译文：与善于交谈的人出去约会，应该是非常有趣的事情。
2. 可以与a搭配，从而构成这样句子：For me, the ideal spouse is someone who doesn't mind doing housework.
   精品译文：对我来说，理想的伴侣应该是不介意做家务的人。
   可以与c搭配，从而构成这样句子：For me, the ideal spouse is someone that I can trust completely.
   精品译文：对我来说，理想的伴侣应该是我能够完全信任的人。
   可以与f搭配，从而构成这样句子：For me, the ideal spouse is someone who is a really good conversationalist.
   精品译文：对我来说，理想的伴侣应该是真正善于交流的人。
3. 可以与c搭配，从而构成这样句子：I'd really like to find a friend that I can trust completely.
   精品译文：我真想找到一个我能够完全信任的朋友。
4. 可以与e搭配，从而构成这样句子：I hope I never have a boss I can't talk to about my problems.
   精品译文：我希望我不要有一个无法和他谈论我的问题的老板。
5. 可以与b搭配，从而构成这样句子：I don't want to be friends with anyone I have nothing in common with.
   精品译文：我不想同那些与我没有任何共同点的人做朋友。
   可以与e搭配，从而构成这样句子：I don't want to be friends with anyone I can't talk to about my problems.
   精品译文：我不想同那些无法和他谈论我的问题的人做朋友。
6. 可以与d搭配，从而构成这样句子：The perfect English teacher is someone that doesn't criticize me all the time.
   精品译文：一个真正好的英语老师是不会总是批评我的。
7. 错误。应改为He is the man who is teaching us English。
8. 错误。应改为I'd really like to find a friend that I can trust completely。
9. 错误。应改为I'd really like to find a friend I can share almost everything with。
10. 关系词作从句的主语：I like people who always keep their promise.
    关系词作从句的动词宾语：I like people who I can trust.
    关系词作从句的介词宾语：I like people who I can have fun with.
11. 关系词作从句的主语：I don't like teachers who do not have sense of responsibility.
    关系词作从句的动词宾语：I don't like teachers who I can't understand well in class.
    关系词作从句的介词宾语：I don't like teachers who I can't talk to about my problems.
12. 关系词作从句的主语：A good friend is a person who is always there to support you.
    关系词作从句的动词宾语：A good friend is a person who you can have by your side supporting you while you are in trouble.
    关系词作从句的介词宾语：A good friend is a person who you can share almost everything with.
13. 关系词作从句的主语：I have a good friend who is always ready to help me when I am in trouble.
    关系词作从句的动词宾语：I have a good friend who I can trust completely.
    关系词作从句的介词宾语：I have a good friend who I can always rely on.

Exercise 3. 3（P47）

1. The girl who won the race is happy.
2. The student who sits next to me is from America.
3. The boy who fell from a tree was not badly hurt.
4. The taxi driver who took me to the airport was friendly.
5. I can't remember the name of the person to whom I gave the money.
6. The employees who had reached the age of sixty-five had to retire.
7. The teacher spoke to the boys whose work was below standard.
8. The people whose houses I rented were friendly.

9. He is the professor whose grammar course I am taking.
10. That is the man whose son died in that air crash.
11. The man whose car was stolen called the police.
12. The man whose picture is in the newspaper is famous.
13. I have a neighbor whose dog barks all day long.
14. The girl whose camera I borrowed is a good friend of mine.
15. The church where we were married was built in 1400.
16. She told me her address, which I wrote down on a piece of paper.
17. We are studying sentences which contain adjective clauses.
18. The exhibition which my friend took me to see was not very interesting.
19. John isn't home yet, which worried me.
20. Jack was fired from his job, which surprised all of his co-workers.
21. My roommate always plays music at the dorm, which really gets on my nerves.
22. 错误。应改为：I enjoy the music that we are listening to.
23. 错误。应改为：The people who live next to me are friendly.
24. 错误。应改为：He is the man who taught me English.
25. 错误。应改为：I gave the book to him that he needed.
26. 错误。应改为：The airline has a booklet which will tell you most of the important things about a trip to Europe.
27. 错误。应改为：The man who told me the news refused to give me his name.
28. 错误。应改为：The book which I bought at the bookstore was very useful.
29. 错误。应改为：The woman that I met yesterday was nice.
30. 错误。应改为：I met a woman whose husband is a famous lawyer.
31. 错误。应改为：Let ABC be a triangle whose sides are of unequal length.
32. 错误。应改为：Do you know the people who live in that house?
33. 错误。应改为：The people who I met at the party last night were interesting.
34. 错误。应改为：He dropped in on an old friend that day when he visited his club.
35. 错误。应改为：The day, which began brightly, ended with a violent storm.
36. The girl who answered the phone was polite. 这里 who 作主语，因而不可以省去。
37. I didn't know any of the people（who）Bill invited to his party. 这里 who 作宾语，因而可以省去。
38. The woman（who）I saw in the park was feeding the pigeons. 这里 who 作宾语，因而可以省去。
39. I like the barber who usually cuts my hair. 这里 who 作主语，因而不可以省去。
40. The person（who）I admire most is my father. 这里 who 作宾语，因而可以省去。
41. The people（who）I met at the party last night were very nice. 这里 who 作宾语，因而可以省去。
42. The people（who）live next to me have three cars. 这里 who 作主语，因而不可以省去。
43. The soup（which）I had for lunch was too salty. 这里 which 作宾语，因而可以省去。
44. The pill（which）I took made me sleepy. 这里 which 作宾语，因而可以省去。
45. My daughter asked me a question（which）I couldn't answer. 这里 which 作宾语，因而可以省去。
46. The man（who）my sister goes out with is tall, dark and handsome. 这里 who 作宾语，因而可以省去。
47. I couldn't understand the woman（who）I talked to on the phone. 这里 who 作宾语，因而可以省去。

Exercise 3. 4（P51）

1. Monday is the day when we will come.
2. He arrived in Shanghai on the day when I left.
3. July is the month when the weather is usually the hottest.
4. April Fool's Day is that special day of the year when you should play a joke on someone!
5. March 10, 1876 was the day when the first complete sentence was sent over a telephone.
6. The city where we spent our vacation was beautiful.

7. That is the restaurant where I will meet you.
8. The town where I grew up is small.
9. This is the house where they put their tools.

10. when	11. which	12. which	13. which	14. when	15. where
16. which	17. which	18. where	19. which	20. where	21. which

Exercise 3. 5 (P55)

1. 应该添加逗号，改为非限制性定语从句：Seoul, which hosted the 1988 Summer Olympics, is well known for its shopping.
2. 不需要添加逗号，保留限制性定语从句。
3. 应该添加逗号，改为非限制性定语从句：There are many temples and shrines in Kyoto, which used to be the capital of Japan.
4. 应该添加逗号，改为非限制性定语从句：Kyoto, which was the country's capital from 794 until 1868, has around 2, 000 temples and shrines.
5. 应该添加逗号，改为非限制性定语从句：Brasilia, which is the capital of Brazil, is less than 50 years old.
6. 不需要添加逗号，保留限制性定语从句。
7. 应该添加逗号，改为非限制性定语从句：Bangkok, which is the capital of Thailand, has many beautiful temples.
8. 应该添加逗号，改为非限制性定语从句：Mexico City, which has a population of around 20, 000, 000, is the largest urban area in the Americas.
9. 应该添加逗号，改为非限制性定语从句：Salvador, which lies in the northeast, was the country's busiest port from 1500 to 1815.
10. 不需要添加逗号，保留限制性定语从句。
11. 不需要添加逗号，保留限制性定语从句。
12. 不需要添加逗号，保留限制性定语从句。
13. 应该添加逗号，改为非限制性定语从句：The teacher, who comes from Canada, teaches us English.
14. 不需要添加逗号，保留限制性定语从句。
15. 限制性或非限制性均可

    I saw him stand under the apple tree which was behind the house. 用限制性定语从句表明屋子周围有多棵树。

    I saw him stand under the apple tree, which was behind the house. 用非限制性定语从句表明屋子周围只有一棵树。
16. 限制性或非限制性均可

    The teacher thanked the students who had given her some flowers. 用限制性定语从句表明老师对部分学生表示感谢。

    The teacher thanked the students, who had given her some flowers. 用非限制性定语从句表示补充，说明感谢的原因。
17. 限制性或非限制性均可

    He has a daughter who works in a hospital. 用限制性定语从句表明他有多个女儿。

    He has a daughter, who works in a hospital. 用非限制性定语从句表明他只有一个女儿。
18. 应该添加逗号，改为非限制性定语从句：An elephant, which is the earth's largest land mammal, has few natural enemies other than human beings.
19. 不需要添加逗号，保留限制性定语从句。
20. 不需要添加逗号，保留限制性定语从句。
21. 应该添加逗号，改为非限制性定语从句：Rice, which is grown in many countries, is a staple food throughout much of the world.
22. 限制性或非限制性均可

    Jane was delighted when she opened the present which was from her ex-boyfriend. 用限制性定语从句表明 Jane 收到了多份礼物。

Jane was delighted when she opened the present, which was from her ex-boyfriend. 用非限制性定语从句表明 Jane 只收到了一份礼物。

23. 不需要添加逗号，保留限制性定语从句。
24. 应该添加逗号，改为非限制性定语从句：Linda Watson, who earned a cumulative grade point average of 3. 7, was graduated with highest honors.
25. 不需要添加逗号，保留限制性定语从句。

Exercise 3. 6（P56）

1. 这是定语从句。关系词 that 充当 offered 宾语，因而可以把 that 省去，或改为 which。
2. 这是同位语从句。连词 that 后边是一个完整的陈述句，因而 that 在从句中不充当任何成分，不能把 that 省去，也不能改为 which。
3. Studies show that...宾语从句；the things that contribute...定语从句。

   精品译文：研究表明，真正让我们感到幸福的是金钱无法买到的，比如：美满的家庭生活、纯真的友谊和工作上的称心如意。
4. 同位语从句。

   精品译文：尽管大多数人认为核战争是愚蠢的行为，但这并不意味着核战不会爆发。
5. 同位语从句。

   精品译文：生命早在 38 亿年前就已经存在的证据在这些古老的岩石中被发现了。
6. 同位语从句。

   精品译文：在伦敦以南 45 英里处发现有一只美洲狮出没的通知送到伦敦动物园时，人们对此并没有重视。
7. 在主语部分 The idea that some groups of people may be more intelligent than others，其中的 that 从句是同位语从句，补充说明 idea。

   在表语部分 one of those hypotheses that dare not speak its name，其中的 that 从句是定语从句，后置修饰 hypotheses。

   精品译文：认为某些特定人群要比其他人群更聪明，这个观点一般是不敢公开宣扬的。
8. The rumor that...同位语从句；warned that...宾语从句；any man that...定语从句；all the men that...定语从句；one little man that...定语从句；see that we have...宾语从句。

   精品译文：古时候，有位国王，他想证明，在他统治的国度里并非向人们谣传的那样：妇人统治丈夫。他把王国里所有的男人都召到跟前，并警告说，如果谁不说实话将遭到严厉的惩罚。然后，他让所有听从夫人命令的男人站到王宫的左侧。结果所有的男人都去了左边，只有一个矮小的男人站在右边。"太好了，"国王说，"我们的国度里还有一个真正的男人。告诉那些胆小鬼们，你为什么站在右边。""陛下，"他尖着嗓子说，"微臣出门之前，夫人有令，人多的地方不能去。"

综合练习（P57）

1. Yesterday I bought a book whose author was blind.
2. My office, which is small, is on the second floor of this building.
3. The book that you lent me yesterday is very interesting.
4. The teacher teaches me English, who comes from Canada.
5. The girl I work with has a boyfriend.
6. Please tell me the reason why you were late this morning.
7. They arrived on the day when it was raining.
8. He is the man who you can depend on.
9. What is the name of the hotel where you live?
10. The man who answered the phone told me that you were away.
11. C。先行词是 the professor and her achievement，包含有人和物，此时只能用 that 引导定语从句。
12. A。先行词是 anything，此时只能用 that 引导定语从句。

13. B。先行词 voice 有最高级 the loudest 修饰，此时只能用 that 引导定语从句。
14. B。先行词 book 有最高级 the best 修饰，此时只能用 that 引导定语从句。
15. A。表示所属关系，用关系词 whose。也可以说 of which the name 或 the name of which。
16. C。先行词是整个主句 the meeting was postponed，此时只能用 which 引导定语从句。如果没有，则可以采用并列句，故 C 正确。
17. A。这里 for whom 来自于 work for 搭配。
18. A。先行词是 much，用 that 引导定语从句。
19. D。这里是根据句子意思来选择介词，from the cover of which 表示“从书的封面(可以判断)”。
20. A。先行词是表示时间，用 when 引导定语从句。
21. A。这里 for which 相当于 why，表示原因。
22. C。A 的先行词是 address，但关系词是 who，故错误；B 的先行词是 address，与谓语 order“订购”语义不搭配，故错误；D 的先行词是 lady，但关系词是 which，故错误。
23. C。这里先行词是 time，表示时间，故 when 正确。
24. C。先行词被 no 修饰，常用 that 引导定语从句。
25. D。这里 that 引导的是同位语从句，补充说明 certainty。
26. C。名词 Venus 是表示地点，因此要用关系副词 where 来引导定语从句，在从句中作地点状语。
27. D。名词 reason 是表示原因，因此要用关系副词 why 来引导定语从句，在从句中作原因状语，修饰 died。
28. A。名词 shop 是表示地点，因此要用关系副词 where 来引导定语从句，在从句中作地点状语，修饰谓语buy。
29. B。这里虽然先行词是 reason，但它充当 gave 的宾语，所以该用 that 引导定语从句。
30. D。关系词充当从句中 about 的宾语，故要用关系代词 which 引导定语从句。
31. D。这里定语从句是修饰指人的 those。
32. D。这里 that 引导同位语从句，补充说明 evidence。
33. C。这里定语从句是修饰 food crop。
34. D。这里定语从句是修饰前面整个句子 they helped us time and again。
35. D。这里 the one 相当于说 the one which，关系词被省去。
36. D。这里 that 引导同位语从句，补充说明 reports。
37. C。考查 whose 的用法。这里 whose 指代 feathers，whose colors 作主语，而 blend 是动词，作谓语。
38. C。这是省去了关系词的定语从句，相当于说...that a person may have...，修饰 freedoms and rights。
39. D。这里是省去关系词的定语从句，相当于说 that the average person could afford。

40. who　41. who　42. where　43. who
44. who　45. where　46. where

精品译文：阿拉伯传说中有两个朋友在沙漠中旅行，在旅途中的某点他们吵架了。一个还给了另外一个一记耳光。被打的觉得受辱，一言不语，在沙子上写下：“今天我的好朋友打了我一巴掌。”他们继续往前走. 直到到了沃野，他们就决定停下，洗个澡。

被打巴掌的那位差点淹死，幸好被朋友救起来了。被救起后，他拿了一把小剑在石头上刻了：“今天我的好朋友救了我一命。”

一旁好奇的朋友问说：“为什么我打了你以后，你要写在沙子上。而现在要刻在石头上呢？”

另外一个笑笑的回答说：“当被一个朋友伤害时，要写在易忘记的地方，风会负责抹去它；相反如果被帮助，我们要把它刻在心里的深处，那里任何风都不能抹灭它。”朋友的相处，伤害往往是无心的，帮助却是真心的。忘记那些无心的伤害，铭记那些对你的帮助，你会发现这世上你有很多真心的朋友。

47. what　48. what　49. that　50. 不填　51. that　52. which/tha
53. why　54. 不填　55. which/that　56. which/that　57. which/that　58. that
59. that　60. that　61. what　62. how　63. which/that　64. why
65. which/that　66. that

第四章 状语从句

Exercise 4. 1（P67）

1. B。考查时间状语从句的各类句型结构。比如还有 no sooner...than...，hardly...when...等。
2. D。考查表示“一……就……”的时间连词。
3. C。考查表示“一……就……”的时间连词。
4. A。考查 when 的用法特点。When 在这里表示“突然，意外”含义。
5. A。这是 1991 年考研语法题。本题不难，只要考生熟悉 when 表示过去时间的一个固定搭配用法，即 hardly had something done when something did...这样一个倒装句型，它表示“一……就……”。请注意主从句的时态搭配：主句用过去完成时态，且常倒装，而从句用一般过去时态。其他类似结构有：scarcely……when、no sooner……than 等。

   精品译文：他刚要开始发言，这时观众就打断了他。
6. D。这是 1998 年考研语法题。本题不难，只要考生熟悉 when 的一个固定搭配用法，即 when it comes to...这一结构，表示“当提到……”。

   精品译文：做家庭作业当然是一个提高考试成绩的好办法，这尤其是对课堂测试来说。
7. C。这是 2000 年考研语法题。这一题比上两道稍微难点，考点是要求考生掌握 when 的时态搭配关系。在众多 when 的主从句时态搭配中，有这样一种搭配关系：一般过去时与过去进行时搭配，短暂动词用一般过去时，如这里的 noticed，而延续动词用过去进行时，如这里 was driving。这一时态配套使用所表示的意义是——在一个延续背景动作过程中（如 was driving）突然发生了一个短暂动作。

   精品译文：在一个雨天，我正驾着车往北穿越佛蒙特州，这时我突然看见一个年轻男子，手里举着牌子，上面写着“波士顿”。
8. B。这是一道四级考题。这里从句的动词 patted 是一个短暂动作，所以不能用 while，而要用 when。

   精品译文：当时我正在路上走，突然有人从后面拍了我的肩膀。
9. C。本题考查时间状语从句中要用一般现在时态来表示将来的动作。
10. A。考查表示“一……就……”的时间连词。
11. B。本题考查句子之间的逻辑语义关系。这里表示时间，所以用 while。

Exercise 4. 2（P68）

1. C。本题考查句子之间逻辑语义关系，这里是表示地点，故用 where。
2. C。本题考查地点状语从句的构成，在四个选项中，只有 C 才是地点状语从句，故 C 正确。
3. B。本题考查句子之间逻辑语义关系，这里是表示地点，故用 where。

Exercise 4. 3（P70）

1. B。本题考查原因状语从句的连词的用法特点。
2. C。本题考查表示原因的介词。
3. C。本题考查表示原因的连词与介词的用法区别。
4. A。本题考查表示原因的连词，这里 for 表示补充说明原因。
5. A。本题考查原因连词的用法区别，这里 since 表示众所周知的原因。
6. D。本题考查原因连词的用法区别，这里是强调句型，只能用 because。

Exercise 4.4（P71）

1. I'm going to leave the party early so that I can get a good night's sleep.
2. Harry brought his umbrella so that he could not get wet.
3. I turned on the TV in order that I could listen to the news.
4. The little boy pretended to be sick so that he could stay home from school.
5. Clint took some change from his pocket so that he could buy a newspaper.
6. I put the milk in the refrigerator so that it wouldn't spoil.
7. I unplugged the phone so that I wouldn't be interrupted while I was sleeping.

Exercise 4.5（P73）

1. This tea is so good that I will have another cup.
   This is such good tea that I will have another cup.
2. The car was so expensive that we couldn't afford to buy it.
   It was so expensive a car that we couldn't afford to buy it.
   It was such an expensive car that we couldn't afford to buy it.
3. It was such a cold day that I had to wear my coat.
   It was so cold a day that I had to wear my coat.
4. We are having such beautiful weather that I don't feel like going to class.
5. She talked so fast that I couldn't understand her.
6. The black leopard is so dark that its spots are difficult to see.
7. I've met so many people in the last few days that I can't remember all of their names.
8. There was such little traffic that it took us only ten minutes to get there.
9. There were so few people at the meeting that it was cancelled.
10. I have so much trouble that I need your help.
11. The classroom has such comfortable chairs that the students find it easy to fall asleep.
12. D。这是 2001 年考研真题。这是结果状语从句的倒装结构。这句正常语序为：The children become so involved with their computers that leaders...，另外，这里 C 选项虽然也是一个倒装结构，但时态不对，因为从句谓语是 have to 一般现在时态，不可能与过去完成时态搭配。
    精品译文：这些孩子们是如此迷恋于电脑，以至于计算机夏令营里的带队老师们常常要强迫他们停止玩电脑，以便参加体育活动和做游戏。
13. B。考查 so 与 such 用法区别。修饰不可数名词要用 such。
14. B。考查 so 与 such 用法区别。修饰复数名词要用 such。
15. A。考查 so 与 such 用法区别。修饰形容词要用 so。
16. B。考查 so 与 such 用法区别。修饰单数可数名词时，such 结构是"such a + 形容词 + 单数名词"，而 so的结构是"so + 形容词 + a + 单数名词"。

Exercise 4.6（P75）

1. A。这是 1993 年考研真题。分析两个句子之间逻辑关系，我们知道这是表示条件，故 A 正确。
   精品译文：你可以早点去北京开会，只要你不介意坐夜班火车。
2. D。这是一道 2000 年 12 月四级考题，前后句是条件关系。
   精品译文：只要我们放手让他按照自己的方式去做，他一定能够准时完成这个工作的。
3. B。本题考查条件从句的连词用法。这里 supposing 表示"假如……"。
4. A。本题考查条件从句的连词用法。这里前后两个分句是表示"只要……"，A 符合句义。

Exercise 4.7（P79）

1. D。本题考查的就是 as 引导的让步从句。这里没有选择 B，而选择了 D，显然是因为在这样的倒装句中不能用 although 代替 as。

   精品译文：尽管他很喜欢她，但是他有时也会对她很生气。
2. B。本题考查 although 与 but 不能连用的用法。
3. D。本题考查表示让步关系的连词与介词的用法区别。注意句中 play 是谓语动词，所以这里该用连词 although，而不能用介词 in spite of。
4. A。本题考查表示让步关系的连词与介词的用法区别。这里因为是名词短语，所以只能用介词，而不能用连词。
5. B。本题考查表示让步关系的介词的用法。这里 for all 表示"尽管"。
6. A。本题考查 as 引导的倒装句表示让步关系。该句正常语序是"Though search techniques were sophisticated, the policeman still has good command"。
7. B。本题考查表示让步关系的倒装句型。在这句型中，连词常用 as，也可以用 though，但不可以用 although。
8. C。本题考查 as 引导的倒装句表示让步关系的用法。这里 much 是副词，被前置。
9. A。本题考查表示让步关系的连词的用法。
10. A。本题考查表示让步关系的连词与介词的用法区别。这里因为是 what 从句，相当于一个名词短语，所以只能用介词，而不能用连词，故 A 正确。
11. C。本题考查表示让步关系的连词与介词的用法区别。这里因为是分词短语，相当于一个从句，所以只能用连词，而不能用介词，故 C 正确。
12. B，应改为：his，即把 but 去掉。本题考查的是 although 和 but 不能连用这一知识点。这与汉语思维习惯不同。

    精品译文：尽管史密斯先生在巴黎是学习绘画艺术的，但他的文学作品要比他的绘画更为引人关注。
13. A，应改为：Though 或 Although。本题考查的是让步状语从句连词的用法。这里 despite 是介词，不能引导从句，故要改成连词。

    精品译文：尽管动物脂肪和植物油都是重要的能量来源，但是医学研究表明饱和脂肪可能会导致动脉硬化。

Exercise 4.8（P85）

1. A。本题考查原级比较 as...as 句型。
2. C。本题考查比较级 the more...the more 句型。
3. A。本题考查比较级 more...than 句型。
4. C。本题考查倍数比较句型："倍数 + as...as"结构。
5. D。本题考查"as + 形容词 + a(n) + 可数名词单数 + as"结构。
6. D。本题考查倍数比较句型："倍数 + as...as"结构。
7. A。本题考查比较对象的一致性。这里比较对象是 South 和 North，因此 A 正确，does the North 是一个倒装结构，相当于说 the North receives。
8. D。这是 1996 年考研真题。本题考查的是倍数比较关系的表达。适用的句型是"倍数 + 名词"的结构句型。此题有一定的难度，就是看比较对象的判断。比较对象是"今年报名参加马拉松比赛的人数"与"去年报名参加马拉松比赛的人数"。这里的名词是 the number of registered participants，但为了避免重复，可以用 that 来指代。所以 D 正确。

   精品译文：今年报名参加马拉松比赛的人数是去年的一半。
9. A。than does 是一个倒装结构，句子的主语是 heavily polluted outside air。

   精品译文：室内或写字楼里的空气，往往比室外严重污染的空气污染物含量还要高。
10. A。本题考查 as...as 句型的倒装结构。这里主语是 its soils and the water of its lakes, rivers and oceans 这个复数名词短语，所以谓语动词要用 are。

    精品译文：地球周围的大气层，就如同地球上的泥土及地球上湖泊、河流、海洋中的水一样，都是地球的组成部分。

11. A。这是1996年考研真题。as good as 是一个完整结构，不能省去 as，原句相当于说 I find records are often as good as an actual performance, if they are not better than it，由此可见，if not better than 是一个省略句。

精品译文：你喜欢听唱片吗？我发现唱片的音响效果与现场演出效果一样好，甚至可能更好。

12. D，改为 than。本题考查比较级的形式，因为前面有 more，所以后边要接 than 来呼应。

综合练习（P87）

1. A。这里 that 替换了 as，引导一个倒装句，表示让步。
2. C。本题考查表示让步关系的连词与介词的用法区别。这里因为是形容词短语，相当于一个从句，所以只能用连词，而不能用介词，故 C 正确。
3. A。本题考查表示让步关系的连词与介词的用法区别。这里因为是形容词短语，相当于一个从句，所以只能用连词，而不能用介词，故 A 正确。
4. B。本题考查 not until 的倒装结构。
5. B。本题考查分句间的逻辑语义关系，这里是表示地点，故 where 正确。
6. B。本题考查分句间的逻辑语义关系，这里是表示地点，故 where 正确。
7. A。given that 表示"既然"。
8. B。本题考查目的状语从句，根据句义，lest"以免"才正确。
9. D。本题考查目的状语从句，这里 that 相当于 so that 的省略形式。
10. A。本题考查 so 和 such 用法区别以及结果状语从句。这里 so many 是固定搭配，不说 such many*。
11. D。本题考查句间逻辑语义关系，这里表示目的，只有 D 表示目的，故正确。
12. B。本题考查目的状语从句，根据句义，lest"以免"才正确。
13. B。本题考查目的状语从句，根据句义，lest"以免"才正确。选项 D 中多了 not。
14. C。考查 in that 表示原因。
15. C。考查表示让步关系的连词与介词的用法区分。这里 his learning 是一个名词短语，应该用介词 for all。
16. B。考查 as 引导的倒装句表示让步关系。
17. A。考查 it was not until...that...句型，表示时间。
18. C。考查 as 引导的倒装句表示让步关系的用法。
19. D。考查 as 引导的倒装句表示让步关系的用法。
20. B。考查句间逻辑语义关系，这里是表示地点，故 where 正确。
21. D。考查句间逻辑语义关系，以及 as 引导的倒装句表示让步关系。
22. D。考查句间逻辑语义关系，这里是表示条件，故 D 正确。
23. A。本题考查 no sooner...than...引导时间状语从句的用法。
24. B。考查 it was not until...that...句型，表示时间。
25. A。本题考查 the more...the more 句型。这里前半部是省略 is 的结构：The lower the level of lighting is in a room，所以其中的 the level of lighting 是充当句子主语。
26. C。本题考查句间逻辑语义关系，这里是表示让步，所以 C 正确。
27. C。考查分句间的逻辑语义关系。这里是表示让步，故 C 正确。
28. C，改为 many，即把 therefore 去掉。因为 since 与 therefore 不能同时出现在一个句子中。
29. C，改为 so。有 so...that 表示结果的句型，但没有 too...that...* 句型。
30. A，改为 so。有 so...that 表示结果的句型，但没有 very...that...* 句型。
31. C，改为 as。考查 not so...as 原级比较句型。
32. D，改为 that of。指代单数名词 diameter 应该用 that。

第五章 完成时态

Exercise 5.3（P97）

1. 从 So here we are at the end of the 20th century 我们知道，这个对话是发生在 20 世纪末。换句话说，这是站在世纪之末来“回顾”整个 20 世纪，即具有回顾性特点，因而用了现在完成时态 has been。

   精品译文： A：我们现在到了 20 世纪末了，现在回想看看，快要过去的这 20 世纪发生了多么巨大的变化啊！

   B：是啊，比如像汽车、飞机、电影、收音机、电视机、电话、录像机以及因特网等等这些我们现在习以为常的东西，可在 20 世纪之初谁会想象得到呢！

   A：不知道未来 21 世纪会是什么样子。

   B：从近几年的科技发展来看，我相信未来我们将会进入一个充满奇迹和变化的黄金时代。

   A：是的，到下个世纪，人们生活一定很棒！
2. has been
3. has been
4. will be 因为是在年初时说的这番话，是在预测，所以要用 will。这里说话的时间点对于时态的正确使用非常重要。由此可见，英语时态是一个与说话的时间点和语境密切相关的活生生的思维表达，而不是僵化的死规则。

Exercise 5.5（P113）

1. has been, has called。这里 has been 表示延续状态；has called 表示重复活动，并且具体说出重复六次。
2. have told。have told 表示重复活动，并且具体说出重复五次。

   精品译文： 这个电脑程序如何使用我已跟你讲了五遍，可是你却一再犯同样的错误。
3. have killed。这里 have killed 表示重复活动，因为火灾造成的死亡人数不是一次完成的，而是多次火灾导致众多死亡的累积。

   精品译文： 根据统计显示，今年第一季度全国发生火灾 36，832 起，死亡 971 人，伤 1，228 人，造成直接经济损失 3.1 亿元。
4. has nearly killed。have killed 表示重复活动，并且具体说出重复四次。
5. has released, has produced, has been nominated, has won。这里的四个现在完成时都是表示重复活动。
6. have already bought。从这个对话语境中 next month，我们知道 exhibit 还没有结束，是要持续到将来某个时间。不过，“买票 buy”动作已经发生了，它的影响会一直持续到现在及未来直到 exhibit 结束，所以用了现在完成时态。如果这个展览结束了，就要用一般过去时态，比如说“I bought a ticket to see it”。

   精品译文： A：十八世纪绘画展今天开幕了，这里有一篇关于它的报道文章你看了吗？

   B：看过了，而且我还已经买了票准备下个月去看呢。
7. has been delayed。这里的“飞机延误”是已经发生了并且要持续到“将来”的四点钟，同样是与将来有联系，所以要用现在完成时态。

   精品译文： A：刚刚通知说，这个航班要一直延误到四点钟。

   B：真倒霉，那这两个小时我们怎么过呢？
8. have...had, have had。

   精品译文： A：这个月到目前为止你面试过几次了？

   B：这个月到目前为止我有过两次面试。
9. did...have, had。

   精品译文： A：上个月你面试过几次了？

   B：上个月我有四次面试。
10. starred。

Exercise 5. 6. 1（P119）

1. 这个笑话英文讲述得很含蓄，只是借助上帝之母前后不同的电话回答：This is Virgin Mary/This is the Immaculate Mary（我是圣母玛利亚）与 This is Mary（我是玛利亚），道出了风流倜傥的肯尼迪总统 insatiable appetites for women 的这一癖好，而没有露骨地提到一个“sex”。这里完成时态 has President Kennedy arrived yet? 其中 arrived 是一个短暂动作，其发生在过去，但这个过去短动作对现在有很大的影响：使圣洁的上帝之母由 Virgin Mary 变成了 Mary。所以，他的同僚们最后还没等 Mary 回答，就直接 put down the phone，然后断定“The President is in Heaven”。
2. 这个故事最后一句：Someone has stolen our tent!这里完成时态表示一个短暂的过去事件（has stolen our tent），但这个过去事件对现在的影响很多，比如正是因为没了帐篷，所以华森才能“看到了无数颗星星”，以及下文中他一番长篇大论的“推断”。

   精品译文：　　　　　　野营

   一天，英国大侦探夏洛克·福尔摩斯和华森医生去野营。晚上一顿酒足饭饱之后，他们开始休息睡觉。过了几个小时，福尔摩斯用肘轻轻地碰了他忠实的朋友。

   “华森，看看天空，然后告诉我你看到了什么。”

   “我看到了无数颗星星，福尔摩斯。”华森答道。

   “那么由此你可以推断出什么？”

   华森想了想。

   “嗯，从天文学角度来说，这告诉我那里有成百万个星系以及可能潜在的几十亿颗恒星；就占星术角度来说，我看到土星正位于狮子座；而从时间上推算，现在该是三点一刻了；从气象上来讲，我想明天会是一个好天气；就神学角度来说，我看到上帝是万能的，而我们只是宇宙中极微不足道的一分子。你有什么推断呢，福尔摩斯先生？”

   福尔摩斯沉默了一会儿，然后说道，“华森，你这个笨蛋！有人偷走了我们的帐篷！”
3. 这句话表示“他的腿跌断了”，对于这里现在完成时态 has broken 所产生的“现在影响”，我们可以想象为：Now he is still in hospital, so he can’t go for an outing with his classmates（他现在还在住院，所以不能和同学们一起出去郊游）。如果说：He broke his leg（他腿摔断过），则单纯是叙述过去的一种经历，与现在无关，现在腿已好了。
4. happen 动作发生在过去，短暂动作，对现在的影响是 Jane 在哭。
5. 因为买到了便宜货，所以很高兴。买东西是在过去，但他现在高兴。

Exercise 5. 6. 2（P121）

这句话表明，对于现在完成时态所表示的过去短暂动作，有时候，具体到某一个句子，动作发生时间离现在的“远近”要看上下文。这里可以指“远的过去”，比如可以译成“你考过驾照吗？”；也可以指“近的过去”，即刚刚参加完考核之后有人这么问你，此时该句意思相当于“你驾照考试通过了吗？”。比如下列两句都可能回答这个提问：

Yes, I passed it when I was 17.

Yes, I passed it yesterday.

Exercise 5. 6. 3（P125）

1. has broken, did...happen, fell
2. has spilt, wasn’t, didn’t do, was

Exercise 5. 6. 4（P130）

1. A: Have you ever worked in a restaurant?

   B: Yes. I*’ve worked* in many ones.

   B: Yes. I *worked* in a French one last year.

2. A: Have you ever been to the Great Wall?

   B: Yes. I***'ve been*** there many times.

   B: Yes. I ***went*** there last spring.

3. A: Have you read this book?

   B: Yes. It ***was*** interesting.

4. A: Have you ever taken a French course?

   B: Yes. I ***took*** a French course in high school.

5. A: Have you graduated from college?

   B: Yes, I ***studied*** French for two years.

6. Have you ever lent money to a friend?
7. Have you ever been on television?
8. Have you ever met a famous person?
9. Have you ever broken an arm or leg?
10. Have you ever gone to court?
11. Have you ever found money on the street?
12. Have you ever been cheated?
13. Have you ever told a lie?
14. Have you ever taken a flight?
15. Have you ever been to Disneyland?
16. Have you ever studied abroad?
17. Have you ever order products over the Internet?
18. A: ***Have*** you ***ever worked*** as a security guard before?

    A: How many years of experience ***have*** you ***had*** as a security guard?

    A: ***Have*** you ***had*** experience monitoring alarm systems?

    B: Yes. I ***have monitored*** several types of alarm systems in my previous job.

19. A: What jobs have you had?

    B: Well, I once had a job on a cruise ship.

    A: What did you have to do?

    B: I organized activities for the passengers.

    A: What did you like about it?

    B: Well, working on a cruise ship was terrific. I really enjoyed...

    A: Were there any bad points?

    B: Oh, sure. Every job has its bad points. I didn't like...

20. Isabel: I went to Sunrise Beach last week. Have you ever been to Sunrise Beach, Andy?

    Andy: Yes, I have. It's beautiful. Did you go there on the weekend?

    Isabel: Yeah, I did. I went on Sunday. I got up at 4:00 a. m.

    Andy: Wow! I've never woken up that early!

    Isabel: Oh, it wasn't so bad. I got to the beach early to see the sun rise. Have you ever seen sunrise, Andy?

    Andy: No, I haven't. I prefer sunsets to sunrises.

    Isabel: Really? Then I went swimming around 6:00, but there were some strange dark shadows in the water. Have you ever heard of sharks at Sunrise Beach?

    Andy: Yes, I have. I heard a news report about sharks last summer.

    Isabel: Gee! Maybe I had a lucky escape on Sunday morning! Why don't you come with me next time?

    Andy: Are you kidding?

Exercise 5. 6. 5（P134）

1. have never seen 2. 've never seen 3. hasn't eaten 4. 've never seen
5. 've never seen 6. 've never seen 7. hasn't been cleaned

Exercise 5. 7（P143）

1. 2. 3. He has come here 是"动作表达"，用于现在完成时态在意思上相当于"状态表达"的一般现在时，如：He is here。所以，这句话意思是"他来了"（人在这里）。

He has been here 是"状态表达"，用于现在完成时态表示"曾经经历"，这句话意思是"他来过这里"（人现在不在这里）。

He has been here for three hours 是"状态表达"，接有持续时间状语表示"延续"，意思是"他来这里有三个小时了"（人现在还在这里）。

4. Have...made 5. Do...have 6. Have...made 7. Do...have

8. 通常认为此句错误。因为肯尼迪被刺杀已经是很久以前的事情了，不是刚刚发生，所以宜用一般过去时态（Kennedy was assassinated on 22 Nov. 1963）。这句话只有在一个极为特殊的语境中才正确，即表示"曾经经历"的语境：回顾历史上有多少位美国总统曾经是被暗杀的（People are discussing American presidents and recalling how many of them have been assassinated so far.），比如把这个句子放在下面这样的语境中：

Many American presidents have been assassinated. Let's see, Lincoln has, Kennedy has, Garfield has and Mckinley has. You know, I've recently read an online article that says their ill fates have to do with the curse by a cacique of some tribe. But I can't believe it. （许多美国总统都是遭暗杀身亡的。比如有林肯、肯尼迪、加菲尔德和麦金利。你知道吗，我最近看到网上一篇文章说，他们这些人的悲惨命运与某个部落的一位首长的诅咒有关。但对此我并不相信）。所以，我们看到，这里用了 Kennedy has（been assassinated）。

9. 错误。因为"死亡"不具有重复性，人不能死而复活，这违背了现在完成时可重复性的特点。

10. 错误。因为"衰老"不具有重复性，人不能返老还童，这违背了现在完成时可重复性的特点。

11. 这句既可以理解成最近一次动作——"我被开除了"，也可以理解成曾经的经历——"我曾经被开除过"。歧义产生是因为这个句子的谓语 be fired 既可以作为动作，也可以作为状态。

12. 这句既可以理解成最近一次动作——"我已经把车洗干净了"，也可以理解成曾经的经历——"我曾经洗过汽车"。歧义产生是因为这个句子的谓语 clean 既可以作为动作，也可以作为状态。

Exercise 5. 8（P146）

1. 've come 2. has knocked 3. 've had
4. 've ever read 5. 've ever seen 6. 've ever seen

7. This is the best wine I have ever drunk.
8. It is the worst book I have ever read.
9. This is the hardest job I have ever had.

Exercise 5. 9（P151）

1. A：你不当老师有多久了？
   B：你当老师有多久了？
2. A：我病好以来，他常常给我写信。
   B：自从我生病以来，他常常给我写信。
3. 三年来我都没有休过假。

Exercise 5. 10. 1（P157）

1. had just sat, heard, opened, saw

2. had just poured, rang, came, was, had drunk, thrown
3. called, had been held up
4. has...been, operated, had lost
5. arrived, had thanked
6. had lost
7. hadn't had
8. has fallen, hadn't stopped

Exercise 5. 10（P163）

精品译文： **爱的约会**

在纽约地铁中心总站，咨询处上方的时钟指向了5点54分。年轻高大的陆军中尉抬起黝黑的脸庞，眯着眼睛看上面的时间。一颗心激动得怦怦直跳，6分钟后，他就要见到那个女人了——在过去的13个月里一直占据着他心灵某个特殊位置的女人。虽然他们素未谋面，但她的信却一直是他的精神支柱。

布兰福德中尉记得那天，战斗最艰苦的时刻，他的飞机被敌机重重包围。他曾在一封信里对她坦言，他经常会感到畏惧。就在战斗打响的前几天，他收到了她的回信："你当然会畏惧……勇士们都会那样，下次在你不自信时我希望你能听到我为你朗诵的声音：'啊，是的，尽管我要走过死亡之谷但我将勇往直前，因为你与我同在。'……"他记得，正是那封信使他重新振作。

此时，他就要听到她真实的声音了，还有4分钟就6点了。

一个女孩走近他，布兰福德中尉一惊。她戴着一朵花但不是他们约好的那种红色玫瑰。这女孩只有18岁左右，而霍丽丝·梅内尔告诉过他，她已30岁。"有什么关系呢，"他还回信说："我32岁"，其实他只有29岁。

他又想到了在训练营时看过的一本书——《人性的枷锁》，书里有一个女人写的批注。他难以相信，一个女人竟能如此透彻地读懂男人的心。书签上有她的名字：霍丽丝·梅内尔。于是他找来一本纽约市电话簿，查到了地址，给她写信，并收到了回信。因为执行任务，第二天就坐船离开了，但他们仍然保持通信。

13个月里，她始终诚挚地给他回信，通常是他的信还未到，她的信就来了。因此，他深信，他们彼此深爱着。

然而，她拒绝送他照片，并解释说："如果你真心对我，我的外表并不重要。如果我长得很漂亮，我会认为，你是爱我的外貌，那样会令我很反感。如果我长相平凡(你必须承认这个更有可能)，就会担心，你和我通信，是因为内心孤独，无人倾诉。别向我要照片，你来纽约时就可以看到我了，可以在那时做出某些决定。"

还有1分钟就6点了……布兰福德猛抽了一口烟，心跳更加快了。

一位年轻的女士向他走来，她身材苗条，金黄的卷发拢在小巧的耳后，双唇红润，下巴精致，眼睛深蓝动人。她穿着淡绿的西装，浑身散发着春天的气息。

……

答案：略

综合练习（P166）

1. have taught, had taught, will have taught
2. will have spent
3. had already gone
4. went
5. went
6. had gone
7. broke
8. were driving, had broken
9. had written, had never relied
10. had just come
11. had never flown
12. get, will already have arrived
13. had been
14. has written
15. have taken
16. have ever done
17. will have read
18. has phoned
19. have lost
20. lost, have found

21. have been seen
22. will have risen
23. will have gone
24. thought, was, has shrunk
25. is snowing, have ever seen, doesn't snow
26. got, don't know, did, have been
27. Have...arrived, ordered.
28. Have...seen, was
29. meant, doesn't hold, will have forgotten
30. 'll drive, has already left
31. has qualified, has helped, has competed, had almost lost, assured
32. 错误，应改为：I have been in the university for two years，或者用一般过去时态说成：I entered the university two years ago.
33. 错误，应改为：He has been here for three hours.
34. 错误，应改为：The old lady has been dead for ten years.
35. 错误，应改为：He has been away from his native place for three years.
36. 错误，应改为：I have been married for one year.
37. 错误，应改为：He has been in the army for five years.
38. 错误，应改为：I have been in Beijing for seven years.
39. Have you taken a flight before?
40. Have you skied from the top of the mountain before?
41. I've already had lunch.
42. Have you found a job yet?
43. I haven't finished yet.
44. I am afraid he has gone out.
45. 这是完成时态表示延续事件。
46. 这是单一事件的否定，相当于一个延续事件。
47. 这是完成时态表示单一事件，这是远的过去单一事件，表示一个过去的经历。
48. 这是完成时态表示单一事件，这是近的过去单一事件。
49. I've been in America for three months now. I've made many good friends, but all of them are boys. I wish I could get to know some girls.
50. Have you been on a diet? You're nothing but skin and bones.
51. China has always opposed terrorism in any form.
52. For the past few nights he has slept on the floor.
53. I don't think I've ever seen you in that sweater before. My grandmother made it for me years ago.
54. I thought you were going to read this book by today. I have.
55. I'd considered going to Tokyo or Singapore, but I've never regretted my decision.
56. Our basketball team's won every game so far.
57. I don't know how to solve this math problem. Every method that I've tried just leads to a dead end.
58. But it has won so many awards.
59. But we've invited him three times and he hasn't come once.
60. I've tried several times, but the line's been busy.

第六章 完成进行时态

Exercise 6. 3 (P184)

1. Have...been running 2. have...been doing 3. has been playing 4. have...been doing

Exercise 6. 4 (P188)

1. have been cleaning 2. have been writing 3. have been painting 4. have painted

Exercise 6. 5 (P194)

1. have been going 2. have been going 3. have been marrying, were, married
4. have been hearing 5. has been interviewing, has been asking, has talked
6. have been running, haven't been 7. have been calling 8. have been smoking
9. 这里说话人 A 和 B 对其中的完成进行时态 have been singing 的含义有各自不同的理解。A 说 have been singing 意思是表示一个“重复活动”，即自己是从两岁开始唱歌，一直唱到现在，但并不是时刻不停地唱，而是一个习惯性、重复性的活动。但 B 故意将 have been singing 理解为一个“延续活动”，从而制造幽默，因此他说“难怪你的嗓子哑掉了(因为你从两岁开始一直唱到现在)”。

Exercise 6. 6 (P199)

1. I jog every morning. 2. I've been jogging every morning for the last month.
3. They have been dating for three years now. 4. I have been coming to see him for ten years.

Exercise 6. 7 (P206)

1. have drunk 2. has gone 3. have called 4. have been calling
5. have written 6. have been writing 7. have...been reading 8. have...read
9. have been reading, have read 10. have...been saving, have...saved
11. have been surfing 12. have surfed 13. have knocked 14. have been knocking
15. have been reading 16. have read
17. B 18. B 19. A 20. B 21. B
22. B 23. A 24. A 25. B 26. B

Exercise 6. 8 (P210)

had been fighting, had covered, had...been put out, had been planting,
had already taken root, had been growing

综合练习 (P212)

1. have been sitting, had been sitting, will have been sitting
2. have been studying 3. had been studying 4. had been dreaming 5. had been watching
6. had been waiting 7. had known 8. had been waiting 9. had been running
10. have been crying 11. had been crying 12. had been sitting 13. have been sitting
14. had been expecting 15. has been talking 16. Have...had, have been meaning
17. hit, sank, remained, discovered, has seen, has been exploring
18. have been treating, haven't had, have been taking

19. thought, liked, gives, have been thinking, have gotten, have been
20. have been studying, am planning, had, Did...get
21. discovered, had been falling, had seen, had been, had been asking
22. were speeding, was speeding, were going, was going, didn't notice, hadn't planned, was going

23. C	24. C	25. B	26. B	27. B	28. C	29. C
30. D	31. C	32. C	33. D	34. C	35. C	36. B
37. C	38. D	39. D	40. C	41. B	42. D	43. C
44. C	45. D	46. B	47. B	48. B	49. D	50. A
51. B	52. D	53. D	54. C	55. B	56. C	57. A
58. D	59. C	60. C	61. C	62. B	63. C	64. D
65. C	66. B	67. C	68. B	69. C	70. A	71. D
72. B	73. C	74. B				

75. Jim has been calling me up in the middle of the night over the past month and telling me his troubles. I really feel upset.
76. We've been going together for three years.
77. The price has been going up recently. I wonder whether it will remain so.
78. You've been staying up late again?
79. You've been saying that for five years.
80. I've been planning this trip for more than a year and have discussed it with him many times.
81. I've been getting up early since I entered the college.
82. I've been meaning to exchange it for a larger size.
83. I have been meaning to get my eyes checked.
84. My shoulder's been hurting for a couple of weeks now ever since I moved that heavy desk by myself.
85. You've been living off campus this year, haven't you?
86. I've been putting it off for days.

第七章 虚拟语气

Exercise 7. 3 (P228)

1. were, would practice; were, would school, would let, would remember; were, would look; were, would demand; were.

   精品译文：

   假如我再回到童年，我会更多地培养自己的毅力，决不会因为事情艰难或麻烦而轻言放弃。

   假如我再回到童年，我会培养自己专心致志的习惯；一旦手头有事，决不会让任何东西使我分心。我会牢记：一位优秀的溜冰手从不试图同时滑向两个不同的方向。

   假如我再回到童年，我会凡事都看其光明的一面。生活就像一面镜子：你朝它微笑，它也会朝你微笑；你朝它皱眉，它也会朝你皱眉；如果你用怀疑的目光看待它，它也会用怀疑的目光看待你。

   假如我回到童年，我会要求自己对待同伴和朋友更有礼貌，而且对待陌生人也同样如此。在坎坷的人生道路上，最细小的礼貌也犹如漫长的冬季里为我们歌唱的鸟儿，使得冰雪寒冬易于忍受。

   最后，假如我再回到童年，我不会只是为自己寻找幸福——这似乎是人生的唯一目标，而是更加积极为他人谋求幸福。

2. drove, wouldn't be
3. could drive, would take

   精品译文：光的速度有多快？大约每秒30万公里。因此，从太阳发出的光约8分钟可以到达地球。感觉这个速度很慢是吗？我们换一个角度来看：如果你以100公里的速度开车去太阳的话，你要花177年才能到达那里！

4. B。说话人用虚拟语气说 I wouldn't be surprised if he slept there"如果他睡在那里，我都不觉得奇怪"，这是表明 George 花在实验室的时间很多，而不是说明 George 可能还在实验室睡觉，所以 A 不对。
5. 这里虚拟语气有：telling what they ***would do*** if they ***had*** five million dollars 和 that's what I ***would do*** if I ***were*** a millionaire。
6. 这里虚拟语气如黑体部分所示：

If I ***could save*** time in a bottle
the first thing that I'd like to do
would be to save every day until eternity passes away
just to spend them with you
if I ***could make*** days last forever
if words ***could make*** wishes come true
I'***d save*** every day like a treasure and then
again I ***would spend*** them with you

Exercise 7.4 (P232)

1. wouldn't have lost, hadn't left。这里是表示对过去事实的虚拟。这段话道出了我们生活的矛盾性，很有意思。比如还有这样一些矛盾之处：We get bored with childhood, we rush to grow up, and then we long to be children again. We lose our health to make money—and then lose our money to restore our health. By thinking anxiously about the future, we forget the present, such that we live in neither the present nor the future.
精品译文：旅游这事很奇怪，你飞往一个陌生的地方，急切地放弃了家里的舒适，然后想尽办法费时费钱地又想得到家里的舒适。可是这些舒适，你原本不会失去的，要是你当初不离家出游。
2. had known, would have acted
精品译文：早知今日，何必当初。
3. would have bought, had had
4. could have chosen, would have been
5. A。这里是表示对过去事实的虚拟，从句要用过去完成时态，故 A 正确。
精品译文：我呆在家里而不去上课还更好些，因为我在课堂上什么也学不到。
6. D。这里是对过去事实的虚拟，从句应该用过去完成时态，故 D 正确。
精品译文：要是你最近一直没有和 Jerry 联系过的话，你一定会认为右边这张照片很奇怪。
7. C　　8. C

Exercise 7.5 (P236)

1. D。本题考查混合虚拟语气。这里从句谓语是一个倒装结构：Had Paul received，表示对过去虚拟。主句里有 now 时间状语，表示对现在虚拟，即这是一个混合时间虚拟句，故选 D。
精品译文：假如 Paul 在上次选举中多得六票的话，他就是我们现在的主席了。
2. A。这里主句谓语是 would not be，是表示对现在虚拟。对于从句，从逻辑关系来看，应该是表示过去的虚拟，因为投资人的投资应该发生在过去。这里还考查了虚拟倒装句，故 A 正确。
精品译文：若不是因为当时有大众及时投资，我们公司就不会像现在这样景气了。

Exercise 7.7 (P239)

1. C。这里从句用了倒装结构 had they even thought...，主句谓语是 would have been elected，显然是表示对过去情况的虚拟。这里 let alone 后面接的应该是与从句谓语 had thought 并列的，同样表示对过去的虚拟，但为了避免重复，可以省去 had，从而只保留 gotten，故 C 正确。
精品译文：现如今很多政客都纷纷离婚，这要是在几年前是不可能的。那时，就不说真的离婚了，只要他们有离婚的想法，都一定会被选下台。

2. B。
3. D。
4. B。这里虚拟倒装句是 had they been done，表示过去虚拟，对应的主句也是表示对过去虚拟，所以选择 B。
   精品译文：这其中所涉及到的百万次运算，若是都用手工来做的话，那在我们还未计算完成之前，就早已失去了实用价值。
5. B。这里是对将来的虚拟，从句应该用 should 或 were to，故 B 正确。这里 should there be 是一个倒装结构。
   精品译文：万一突然有一声巨响，这些动物完全有可能会受惊吓的。

Exercise 7. 8 (P242)

1. A。这里 didn't 是表示陈述过去事实，而 otherwise 后边则是过去虚拟，且是虚拟主句的形式，因此要用 would have done 而不是 had done，故 A 正确。
   精品译文：我们不知道他的电话号码，要不然我们当时就给他打电话了。
2. A。这里 or 前边通过用 must have had 这一形式，来表示对过去推测，属于陈述过去，而 or 后边则用过去虚拟，故 A 正确。
   精品译文：他一定是出事故了，要不然早就到了。
3. C。这里 otherwise 后边句子表示对过去虚拟，相应地其前半句子就是表示陈述过去，所以要用一般过去时态。不过，这里情态动词的过去时态 couldn't have done 的形式，表示对过去的推测。这类似于上述讨论的 must 推测。
   精品译文：玛丽不可能收到我的信，要不然她现在已经给我回复了。
4. D。这里 but 前边句子是过去虚拟，but 后边句子是陈述过去事实。故用一般过去时态 was，D 正确。
   精品译文：如果真的有可能，我本来是想去医院看望他的，但是我上周整个一周都很忙。
5. D。这里 but 后边句子是陈述过去事实，but 前边句子是过去虚拟。故 D 正确。
   精品译文：有些妇女本来是能够挣得很好的薪水的，但是为了家庭，他们放弃了工作。
6. C。这里的 unfortunately 在语义上相当于转折，使句子从虚拟转为不虚拟。我们从 was 就可以判断这里是表示过去的，因此前半部分也是表示过去，但表示的是过去虚拟，故 C 正确。
   精品译文：若是有安全分析，就可以发现这个潜在隐患，但遗憾的是，没有做安全分析。

Exercise 7. 9 (P245)

1. B。本题含有虚拟标志词 ask。
2. A。本题含有虚拟标志词 important。
3. C。本题含有虚拟标志词 natural。
4. B。本题含有虚拟标志词 requested。
5. B。本题含有虚拟标志词 suggestion。
6. D。这里因为有了形容词 urgent，所以从句要用虚拟语气，即用动词 should be printed 的形式。
   精品译文：董事会要求这些文件需要紧急打印出来。
7. C。这里因为有了名词 insistence，所以从句要用虚拟语气，即用动词原形。
8. B，改为：turn off 或 should turn off。这里因为有了动词 proposed，所以从句要用虚拟语气，即用动词原形 turn off。
   精品译文：当爱迪生过世时，人们都提议，美国人民把自家的、街道上、工厂里的电停掉几分钟，以此来悼念这位伟人。

Exercise 7. 10 (P249)

1. A　　2. B　　3. B　　4. C　　5. A
6. C　　7. B

综合练习（P250）

1. A　2. C　3. B　4. A　5. B
6. B　7. B　8. C　9. B　10. B
11. A　12. A　13. D　14. A　15. D
16. B　17. B　18. B　19. B　20. B
21. A　22. A　23. B　24. B　25. B
26. A　27. D

28. A 本题考查 would rather have done 的虚拟句型，本题相当于 He would rather have slept than have worked last night，后边的 have 被省去了。

29. B　30. C　31. D　32. C　33. A
34. B　35. B

36. B 这里的 suggested 是"表明，显示"而不是"建议"的意思，因而不用虚拟语气。

37. D

38. A 这里有 otherwise，表明要用虚拟，且是虚拟的主句形式。另根据句义判断，这里是表示过去虚拟，故要用 would have done 形式，所以 A 正确。

39. A　40. A　41. C　42. B　43. A

44. C 这里 that she...at the conference 是一个定语从句，不是同位语从句，因而不需要用虚拟语气，而是用正常的时态。这里是表示过去，所以 C 正确。

45. B

46. C 这里 that his followers ______ for 是一个定语从句，不是同位语从句，因而不需要用虚拟语气，而是用正常的时态。这里是表示过去完成进行，所以 C 正确。

47. A　48. A　49. D　50. B　51. A
52. D　53. A　54. C　55. C　56. C
57. D　58. D　59. C　60. B　61. C
62. D　63. A

64. D 这里其实是情态动词表示过去推测，不是虚拟语气。读者需要对此进行区分，关于情态动词对过去的推测用法，详见 8.4 节。

65. C　66. D　67. C　68. A　69. A　70. D

71. B 这里其实是情态动词表示过去推测，不是虚拟语气。读者需要对此进行区分，关于情态动词对过去的推测用法，详见 8.4 节。

72. A 这里其实是情态动词表示过去推测，不是虚拟语气。读者需要对此进行区分，关于情态动词对过去的推测用法，详见 8.4 节。

73. D

74. C 这里其实是情态动词表示过去推测，不是虚拟语气。读者需要对此进行区分，关于情态动词对过去的推测用法，详见 8.4 节。

75. D　76. C　77. A　78. A　79. D　80. A
81. D　82. D　83. A　84. B　85. C　86. A

87. A，改为 went　　88. D，改为 were
89. B，改为(should) be assigned　　90. D，改为 have

第八章 情态动词

Exercise 8. 1. 1（P256）

情态动词有：would, should, could, might, can't

情态动词短语有：are supposed to, be able to, has to, be allowed to, is going to

精品译文：你能不能不要再抱怨了？我们应该竭尽全力，这样才能够干完工作，免得老板又得对我们嚷了。如果你集中精力干完活儿，我们今天下午或许能够早点离开。要知道，如果我们活儿完不了，他是不会放我们走的。

Exercise 8. 1（P260）

1. 该句 might 表示推测含义。
2. 该句 must 表示“必须”，属于基本含义。
3. 该句 must 表示推测含义。
4. 该句 may 表示推测含义。
5. 该句 may 表示“许可”，属于基本含义。
6. 该句 can 表示“许可”，属于基本含义。
7. 该句 will 表示根据当前情况所作出的具有十分把握的推测，属于推测含义。
8. 该句 will 表示强烈的个人意图，有“威胁”的意思，属于基本含义。
9. 该句有歧义。第一，可以理解成“他妈妈说他可以去”，此时的 may 表示许可，属于基本含义。第二，可以理解成“他妈妈说他可能会去。”，此时的 may 表示现在或将来推测，属于推测含义。
10. 该句意思是“他妈妈说他可能去了”，这是表示过去推测，即 may 属于推测含义。
11. 错误。应该把 to 去掉。
12. 错误。情态动词后边只能接动词原形，所以要把 spoke 改为 speak。
13. 错误。情态动词后边只能接动词原形，所以要把 speaking 改为 speak。
14. 错误。情态动词后边只能接动词原形，所以要把 speaks 改为 speak。
15. 错误。情态动词本身没有单复数的变化，所以要把 cans 改为 can。
16. 错误。情态动词的否定是直接在后边加 not，所以要把 doesn't can 改为 cannot。
17. 错误。带有情态动词的句子，在变成疑问句时，是直接把情态动词提置句首，所以把这里 Does he can...改为 Can he...。
18. 错误。情态动词的否定是直接在后边加 not，所以要把 must don't 改为 must not。
19. 错误。情态动词后边只能接动词原形，所以 must did 是错误的。另外，must 没有过去时态，但这里要表示过去时间的动作，可以用 had to，所以要把 must did 改为 had to do。这时句子意思是“他们昨天必须得工作”。或者，把 must did 改为 must have done，此时 must 表示推测含义，这时句子意思是“他们昨天一定是做了这项工作”。
20. 错误。情态动词 must 本身没有过去时态，因此不能说 musted。可以按照上述改为 They had to do the work yesterday 或者 They must have done the work yesterday。

Exercise 8. 2（P266）

1- 4 略

5. don't have to
6. mustn't
7. don't have to
8. don't have to
9. don't have to 其实这里也可以填 mustn't，但两者意思是不同的。用 don't have to 表示“一个人要想生活幸福美满，不一定非得要结婚”；用 mustn't 表示“一个人要想生活幸福美满，那就千万不要结婚”。因此，具体填入哪个，这取决于每个人的婚姻价值观了。
10. mustn't
11. don't have to
12. don't have to
13. mustn't
14. mustn't

15. 推测　16. 推测　17. 必须　18. 必须　19. 推测
20. 必须　21. 推测　22. 推测　23. might 表示推测
24. can't 表示推测，一个否定的推测，表示非常有把握，意思是"不可能"

Exercise 8. 3（P270）

1. 表示"义务"(obligation)的"应该"
2. 表示"义务"(obligation)的"应该"
3. 表示"推测"(probability)的"应该"
4. 表示"推测"(probability)的"应该"
5. 表示"义务"(obligation)的"应该"
6. 表示"义务"(obligation)的"应该"
7. 表示"推测"(probability)的"应该"
8. 表示"义务"(obligation)的"应该"
9. may 表示将来的推测

Exercise 8. 4（P275）

1. can't have had
2. must be
3. must have been
4. must have been
5. can't have seen 或 may not have seen
6. must be 或 may be
7. must have been 或 may have been
8. must have forgotten
9. can't have seen 或 may not have seen
10. must have listened
11. may have left 或 must have left
12. must have taken
13. can't have seen 或 couldn't have seen
14. must be
15. must have been
16. 这里 could 没有虚拟意味，只是表示推测，所以可以把 could 替换为 may。
17. 这里 could 具有虚拟意味，所以不能把 could 替换为 may。
18. 这里 might 没有虚拟意味，只是表示推测，所以可以把 might 替换为 may。
19. 这里 could 具有虚拟意味，所以不能把 could 替换为 may。
20. 这里 might 可以表示推测，意思是"这封信现在可能已经到了"，此时可以把 might 替换为 may。也可以表示虚拟，意思是"这封信本来现在已经早到了"(但实际上并没有到)，此时则不可以替换为 may。
21. 这里 could 具有虚拟意味，所以不能把 could 替换为 may。这里显然是表示抱怨。
22. 这里 could 解释为推测比较自然，意思是"到现在你或许已经收到四封信了"，所以可以把 could 替换为may。
23. 这里 could 解释为推测比较自然，意思是 "你刚才出去的时候，可能是你妈妈打电话来了"，所以可以把 could 替换为 may。
24. 这里 might 可以表示推测，意思是"你或许是把伞忘在了饭馆"，此时可以把 might 替换为 may。也可以表示虚拟，意思是"你本来可以把伞放在饭馆的"(而不必带在身上这么麻烦)，此时则不可以替换为 may。
25. 这里 might 没有虚拟意味，只是表示推测，所以可以把 might 替换为 may。
26. 这里 might 具有虚拟意味，所以不能把 might 替换为 may。
27. 这里 might 解释为推测比较自然，意思是"我现在想当时我可能是有点挑剔了"，所以可以把 might 替换为 may。
28. 这里 might 解释为推测比较自然，意思是"他们当时或许还没有收到我们的信件"，所以可以把 might not 替换为 can't(当然在语气上 can't 强烈)。
29. 这里 could 具有虚拟意味，所以不能把 could 替换为 may。
30. 这里 could 具有虚拟意味，所以不能把 could 替换为 may。
31. 这里 might 没有虚拟意味，只是表示推测，所以可以把 might 替换为 may。
32. 这里 could 没有虚拟意味，只是表示推测，所以可以把 could 替换为 may。
33. 这里 could 具有虚拟意味，所以不能把 could 替换为 may。
34. 这里 could 没有虚拟意味，只是表示推测，所以可以把 couldn't 替换为 can't。
35. 这里 could 具有虚拟意味，所以不能把 couldn't 替换为 can't。
36. 这里 could 没有虚拟意味，只是表示推测，所以可以把 could 替换为 may。
37. 这里 could 没有虚拟意味，只是表示推测，所以可以把 could 替换为 may。
38. 这里 might 没有虚拟意味，只是表示推测，所以可以把 might 替换为 may。

39. 这里 could 具有虚拟意味，所以不能把 could 替换为 may。
40. 这里 could 具有虚拟意味，所以不能把 couldn't 替换为 can't。
41. 这里 could 没有虚拟意味，只是表示推测，所以可以把 could 替换为 may。
42. 这里 might 没有虚拟意味，只是表示推测，所以可以把 might 替换为 may。
43. 这里 could 具有虚拟意味，所以不能把 couldn't 替换为 can't。

Exercise 8. 7 (P285)

1. 表示理论上的可能，所以用 can 正确。
2. 表示理论上的可能，所以用 can 正确。
3. 表示理论上的可能，所以用 can 正确。
4. 表示理论上的可能，所以用 can 正确。
5. 表示理论上的可能，所以用 can 正确。
6. 表示实际上的可能，所以用 can 错误，可以改成 may 或 could 等。
7. 表示实际上的可能，所以用 can 错误，可以改成 may 或 could 等。
8. 表示理论上的可能，所以用 can 正确。
9. 表示理论上的可能，所以用 can 正确。
10. 表示实际上的可能，所以用 can 错误，可以改成 may 或 could 等。
11. 表示理论上的可能，所以用 can 正确。
12. 表示理论上的可能，所以用 can 正确。
13. 表示实际上的可能，所以用 can 错误，可以改成 may 或 could 等。
14. 表示理论上的可能，所以用 can 正确。
15. 表示理论上的可能，所以用 can 正确。
16. 表示理论上的可能，所以用 can 正确。
17. 表示实际上的可能，所以用 can 错误，可以改成 may 或 could 等。

Exercise 8. 8 (P290)

1. was able to
2. was able to
3. was able to
4. could 或 was able to
5. was able to
6. could 或 was able to
7. were able to
8. was able to
9. couldn't
10. couldn't
11. couldn't
12. was able to
13. were able to
14. could 或 was able to
15. was able to
16. couldn't
17. was able to
18. was able to
19. could 或 was able to
20. were able to
21. couldn't
22. was able to
23. could 或 was able to
24. was able to
25. was able to
26. was able to
27. could 或 was able to
28. was able to, was able to, could not, was able to, was able to, was able to, could
29. **精品译文**：我昨晚终于能够去图书馆了。
    这句话有言外之意，比如说之前因为没有学生卡，所以不能进入图书馆，而现在学校发卡了，可以刷卡进去了。
30. **精品译文**：我昨晚本来是要去图书馆的。
    言外之意是，因为有别的事情，而事实上没有去。

Exercise 8. 11 (P298)

1. 意图(intention)
2. 预测(prediction)
3. 意愿或预测或两者兼而有之(willingness or prediction or even both)
4. 预测(prediction)
5. 意愿(willingness)
6. 意图(intention)
7. 意愿(willingness)
8. 预测(prediction)

Exercise 8.12（P305）

1. Could I ask you a question?
2. Can I use your phone?
3. Could you meet me in front of the library at three this afternoon?
4. I was wondering if I could come in.
5. Will you check the oil?
6. Can I use your dictionary for a minute?
7. Would you please keep eye on my luggage while I get a drink of water?

Exercise 8.13（P308）

1. used to, would　2. would　3. would　4. used to, would
5. 这里的 would 都是表示过去常常发生的活动。
6. 这里 'd 都是 would 的缩写，Quincy 用 would 来回顾自己初涉乐坛时的种种经历，即这里 would 是表示过去常常发生的活动。
7. 这里作者用 would 来回顾自己小时候庆祝 Memorial Day 的经历。

Exercise 8.16（P312）

1. 让步（concession）　2. 推测（weak possibility）　3. 许可（permission）　4. 让步（concession）
5. 许可（permission）　6. 推测（weak possibility）　7. 许可（permission）　8. 让步（concession）

Exercise 8.17（P317）

1. 内部否定，否定谓语 tell。
   精品译文：你能不告诉他吗？
2. 外部否定，否定情态动词 will。
   精品译文：保罗不愿意来，因为他就是不想来。
3. 内部否定，否定谓语 come。
   精品译文：汤姆将会来，但约翰可能不来了。
4. 外部否定，否定情态动词 could。
   精品译文：难道你就不能告诉他吗？
5. 外部否定，否定情态动词 could。
   精品译文：我们不能一起走吗？
6. 内部否定，否定谓语 come。
   精品译文：保罗将来不了，因为他太忙。
7. 内部否定，否定谓语 go。
   精品译文：我们能不走在一起吗？
8. 外部否定，否定情态动词 may。
   精品译文：你现在可以走了，但他不可以走。

综合练习（P321）

1. could　2. could　3. could　4. can
5. may as well　6. shall　7. may　8. shall
9. don't have to　10. couldn't　11. may　12. can't have been
13. might have given　14. had to see　15. might have lost　16. could
17. could have been　18. could have helped　19. shouldn't have gone　20. might
21. might have had　22. should know

23. A　24. A　25. B　26. A
27. B　28. B　29. B　30. B
31. can't have broken　32. can't have noticed
33. might have been killed　34. shouldn't have cooked
35. needn't have bought　36. must have been
37. shouldn't have bought　38. can't have lost
39. could play　40. may not have noticed
41. needn't have worried　42. may not have locked
43. needn't have gone　44. can't have been, wouldn't have known
45. should have brought, could...have known　46. might have heard
47. D　48. C　49. D　50. D　51. C　52. B
53. D　54. C　55. B　56. A　57. D　58. D
59. D　60. D　61. C　62. D　63. B　64. A
65. D　66. C　67. C　68. D

结　语

自从我在2002年出版了《英语语法新思维》初级、中级和高级三本书以来，至今有6年多时间过去了。那套书出版以后，让我有两个"没想到"：没想到那套书能如此深受读者的喜爱，以至于6年后的今天还在畅销；也没想到这期间有那么多读者给我来信，他们一封封鼓励的信或充满众多英文疑惑的信，让我有一种责任感和使命感——要为广大英语爱好者写出更好的语法书，于是便有了现在改版后的《英语语法新思维》。

虽说是改版，其实我是完全重新创作了。因为6年过去了，其间我也经历了很多，如在新东方教书、去英国剑桥大学深造等等。但我一直没有中断对英语的研究，对英语的认识也有了很大的提高，同时也积累了很多好的语言素材，这些都融进了我这套书的创作当中。这套书可以说是我学习和研究英语十多年的心得的总结。因此，书中有些内容，也许不是读者看完一遍就能深刻理解的，需要读者边看边认真思考并加以练习。有时，甚至需要读者多读几遍，方能加深对书中内容的理解和运用。记得曾经看过这样的一个观点，大意是说，真正的好书不是作者一个人完成的，而是需要读者和作者一起共同完成。为什么这么说？因为好书是要能够激发读者去思考，去感受，所以，真正的好作品，不是作者写完就完成了，而是读者读完也没完成，只完成一半。好多年过去，又读了两遍，和作者的心相通了，会心一笑，这时作品才完成了。所以，读者和作者的思想交流和碰撞是一次完成不了的。虽然不敢奢望我的书能够达到这样的境界，但我希望我的这套书能够对读者有所启发，能激发广大的英语学子重新审视自己的英语学习经历和学习方法，并能更明智和高效地学习英语，能做到这一点，便感到足矣。人们常说诗人的功夫在诗外，同样，功夫在书外。把这套书读完了，真正的学英语也许才刚刚开始。

写书，对我来说是件快乐且辛苦的事。因为，我是个做事认真的人，尤其是在写书方面，更加要求自己做到一丝不苟、决不敷衍。因为，在我看来，书，是架在读者和作者之间的一座沟通的桥梁，所以我希望尽我所能，写出好书，这样读者与我可以进行高质量的沟通。若是读者把银子和宝贵时间浪费在我粗制滥造的书上，我会深感内疚的。我可以很欣慰地说，这套书我一直是在用心写的，相信读者在阅读时也会看到我的用心。

另一方面，出书，也是一件令人遗憾的事，因为每本书出来，总会有它不足的地方，这包括书中的各种错误、疏漏、表达不当、条理欠佳等等。因为，我在写书时，脑中会同时有很多的想法，都想一股脑儿说出来，这时就很难字斟句酌。因此，说出来的句子，有时自己懂了，但读者也许难以理解。另外，自己的文章，看过三四遍之后，也很难发现有什么错误或不妥的地方。正因为这个原因，我在给杂志写稿子时，文章写完后，我都要搁起来几天后再看，或者是请我的太太帮我细读、修改。但对于书的创作，很难有这样好的待遇。所以，请读者朋友在读这套书的时候，如果发现有任何不妥的地方，烦请提出或指点，以便再印时订正。在此先感谢您了！

研究英语，总结规律，比较英汉表达差异，以及与广大英语爱好者分享我的研究成果，是一件非常快乐的事情。我从内心希望，通过我的微薄努力，能够对广大英语学习者有所帮助，我愿意充当你们英语学习道路上的一块铺路砖，希望你们踩在我这块砖上，在英语之路上能够走得顺利些。

最后，如果读者对于本套书中各章节的内容存有疑问，我们可以通过邮件交流。请发邮件发至：zhangmansheng@hotmail.com。我还会把大家的问题发布到我的个人英语学习网站上：www.zhangmansheng.com，与广大读者分享。如果问题很多，需要更直接的交流，我们可以进行电话沟通。到时我愿意为大家作详细讲解，以便最大限度地帮助大家学好英语。因为，我真心希望，你们看完我的这套三本书之后，对英语语法不再有困惑与不解，并逐渐建立和培养良好的英语思维习惯！

张满胜

新东方大愚基础英语系列精品图书推荐

英语词汇速记大全系列：

《英语词汇速记大全 1——词根+词缀记忆法》

《英语词汇速记大全 2——词形拓展记忆法》

《英语词汇速记大全 3——同形近形比较法》

《英语词汇速记大全 4——同义同类归纳法》

（各含光盘 1 张） **俞敏洪 编著**

囊括绝大部分常考单词，适用于各类英语考试，所选词汇具有较强的实用性和发散性。对词汇的研究独到而深刻，是新东方创始人俞敏洪多年词汇研究的精华。

新东方词汇进阶系列：

《Vocabulary Basic》

《Vocabulary 6000》

《Vocabulary 12000》

《Vocabulary 23000》

（各含光盘 1 张） **包凡一 王玉梅 编著**

精选四级、六级、研究生入学考试、TOEFL、GRE、GMAT 核心精品词汇，突破以往词汇书籍单调的形式，在包含音标、例句、同义词的基础上，采用“助记法”、“联想记忆”帮助记忆，举一反三。

新概念英语之全新全绎系列：

（1–4 册）（各含光盘 1 张）

周成刚 翁云凯 主编

- ◎ 按图索骥，追溯字根词源
- ◎ 说文解字，洞悉语句内涵
- ◎ 语法简述，化解疑难考点
- ◎ 文化拓展，补充同类知识
- ◎ 测试练习，对应同级考试

新概念英语之小题大做系列：

（1–4 册）（各含光盘 1 张）

周成刚 翁云凯 主编

本套丛书是《新概念英语》的配套练习丛书，以练习为主，涵盖听、说、读、写，特配 MP3 光盘，与《新概念英语之全新全绎》系列丛书配套使用，效果更佳。

《新概念英语（2）精讲笔记》

张少云 编著

- ◎ 遵照语言学习的普遍规律，单词入手，语法铺陈，实例巩固，步步为营
- ◎ 根据知识点的重要性及考查频率来安排编写体例，大而全面，精到明晰

定价：35 元 开本：32 开 280 页

《新概念英语句典》（2、3 册）

戴愫 编著

本书是针对《新概念英语》的学习辅导书，旨在帮助读者通过学习经典句型写出好文章。书中精选了《新概念英语》中每课的经典句子，并举出读者表达同样意思时常用的平庸句子，两相对比，找出《新概念英语》的文章中所选句子的亮点。

职场技能速成读本系列：

（中英对照）（1–10 册）

Douglas Gordon 等 著

人生就像一场战争，职场是每一个现代人的主战场。本丛书是一套职场指导全辑（共 10 册），以专题讨论的形式全面、系统地介绍了实用的职场策略和个人技能提升方法，并配有经典案例，视角新颖，重点突出。

朗文新思维英语教程系列：

（1–4 册）（各配光盘） **Ken Beatty 著**

教程组成：

- ◎ 学生用书 （1–4）
- ◎ 教师用书（1–4）（附学生用书后，含教学建议、练习答案及参考译文）
- ◎ 录音 CD （1–4）
- ◎ 测试光盘 CD-ROM Test Bank
- ◎ 网址：www.read-and-think.com

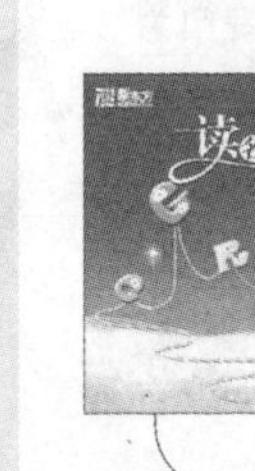

英语诵读菁华系列：

《读名言·学语法》/《箴言妙语诵读》

《英文哲理故事精读》/《英语诵读菁华》

这里收集了大量闪烁着智慧光芒的双语美文，它就像一道精致的阅读快餐，清新芬芳，让你的心灵在阅读中品味到人生的点点滴滴……

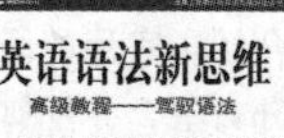

新东方英语美文背诵系列：

《生而为赢》

《摘取梦想的启明星》

《希望长着翅膀》

（各含光盘 1 张）

俞敏洪 编审 王强 录音

新东方英语美文背诵系列是“新东方英语美文背诵大赛”唯一指定用书。本套图书精选了多篇脍炙人口的英语美文，或阐释人生哲理，或抒发缱绻情怀，发人深省，感人肺腑。全书配中文参考译文和生词注释，适合英语爱好者学习、诵读。本书语音部分由新东方资深英语教学专家、美语思维学习法创始人王强老师朗读。

英语语法新思维教程系列：

《英语语法新思维高级教程——驾驭语法》

《英语语法新思维中级教程——通悟语法》

《英语语法新思维初级教程——走近语法》

张满胜 编著

◎ 传统语法书教给你“死规则”，《英语语法新思维》告诉你“活思维”。

◎ 传统语法书“大而全”地罗列死规则，《英语语法新思维》“少而精”地点透活思维。

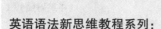

朗文英语语法系列：

（含初级、中级、高级 3 册）

Betty Schrampfer Azar 等 著

《朗文英语语法》系列是专门为英语学习者量身定做的一套语法教材，分为初级、中级、高级三个级别，并配有对应的强化训练册。该系列教材自 20 世纪 80 年代出版以来，深受英语学习者喜爱，在国际上享有盛誉。

朗文英语语法强化训练系列：

（含初级、中级、高级 3 册）

Betty Schrampfer Azar 等 著

《朗文英语语法强化训练》是《朗文英语语法》的配套练习册，它针对《朗文英语语法》各章节中的重要语法点设计了丰富、多样的练习。

《英语语法高手的 24 堂必修课》

石黑昭博 编著

本书是在日本畅销不衰的英语语法读本，契合亚洲读者的学习特点。

定价：38 元 开本：32 开 页码：608 页

《600 词走遍英联邦——最新英语口语学习词典》（含光盘 1 张）

段立新 编著

◎ 全面收录英联邦国家高频率的日常英语口语

◎ 详尽、真实地展现英语口语原生态

定价：32 元 开本：32 开 页码：520 页

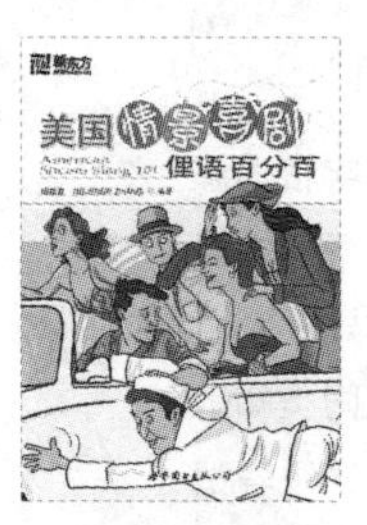

《美国情景喜剧俚语百分百》

邱政政 Jessie Zhang 编著

◎ 书中具体介绍了情景喜剧的特点和美国最受欢迎的七大情景喜剧，包括其内容、角色及经典对白

定价：15 元 开本：32 开 页码：168 页

《新理念美语语音强化教程》

Marnie Reed 等 编著 李莘 译

◎ 清晰透彻的美语发音概念

◎ 丰富多彩的情景听说练习

定价：45 元 开本：16 开 页码：324 页

《跟我唱英文》(含光盘1张)

翟梦　著

◎ 唱会即背会，唱准即发准，乐感即语感

◎ 当你大声唱会一首首歌曲，你就掌握了一个个口语话题的核心句型。

定价：29.8元　开本：24开　页码：120页

《话里画外学美国俚语》(含光盘1张)

朱方庆　编著

◎ 本书遵循以下四个标准：①时效性。②通用性。③实用性。④个性化。

◎ 本书的一大特色是“画说”：给尽可能多的俚语配上幽默滑稽、形象生动的插图，期望读者能够开动“右脑思维”，不看注解和范例就可把俚语的意思猜个八九不离十，从而强化刺激、提高兴趣、帮助记忆。

定价：28元　开本：32开　页码：208页

《美语脱口秀》

陈晶　编著

◎ 美语健身房：品读原汁原味的情景喜剧

◎ 晶晶西游记：展现大洋彼岸的校园生活

◎ 和晶晶一起过节/上学/打工：浓缩美国社会的人生百态

◎ 文化哈哈镜：迸发文化撞击的灿烂火花

定价：19.8元　开本：16开　页码：232页

《美国口语超强纠错》

邱政政　JESSIE ZHANG　编著

◎ “M7”理论与实践的水乳交融！

◎ 追求听说“无极限”！

◎ 实现交流“零误区”！

定价：15元　开本：32开　页码：208页

《美音纠音、透析与突破》

(含光盘一张)

邱政政　郑咏滟　编著

◎ “M7”理论与实践的结合

◎ 全面透析美语发音规律

◎ 丰富的语料实例练就您的完美发音

定价：18元　开本：32开　页码：188页

《从零快乐学英语》(含光盘1张)

李露　琚晋蓉　杨爽　编著

本书从成人学英语的实际出发，语言浅显，内容简单、实用。内容有“字母启蒙”、“点滴积累”、“认识音标”、“发音规则”、“情景对话”、“语法”、“绕口令”、轻松一下”、“话里话外”和“课堂活动”。

定价：29元　开本：32开　页码：292页

《英美报刊英语精读》(1–2册)

◎ 中文导读——帮你抓住主题

◎ 背景知识——帮你开拓视野

◎ 阅读要求——帮你知己知彼

◎ 阅读练习——帮你掌握技巧

《奥林匹克文化之旅》(含光盘一张)

刘忻　编著

《奥林匹克文化之旅》是一本用英语普及奥林匹克知识的教材。同时它也可以供有兴趣的读者了解奥林匹克运动是什么。内容选编上基本上包括了与奥运会有关的内容。英语运用上偏向于通俗实用。

定价：28元　开本：16开　页码：256页

《挑战翻译》

谷约　编著

◎ 从翻译实践出发，分析读者翻译中常犯的典型错误

◎ 深入浅出地传授种种翻译技巧，讲解生动有趣，让翻译理论不再枯燥

◎ 扩充讲述了中国近现代著名翻译家的故事以及相关背景知识

◎ 提供来自优秀译者的翻译实践经验介绍，贴近读者水平，更有助于读者借鉴学习

定价：20元　开本：32开　页码：216页

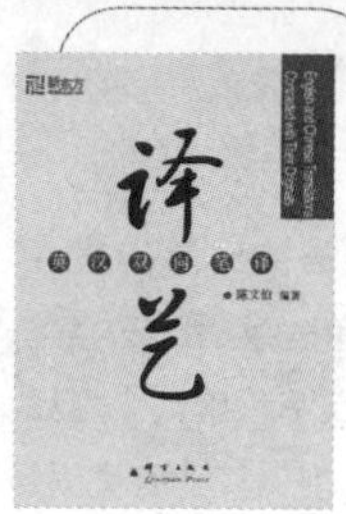

《译艺：英汉双向笔译》
陈文伯　编著

结合翻译文本讲翻译理论，通俗易懂；既讲英译汉，又讲汉译英，双管齐下；外交学院教授陈文伯老师长期致力于英汉翻译的教学与研究之结晶；译法要点讲解精辟而细致，全面提升翻译水平；所选文本或趣味横生，或极富哲理，学习翻译方法的同时获得美的阅读体验。

定价：32 元　开本：32开　页码：392 页

《英语论文成功写作》
孙钰（美）Sheryl Holt　编著

本书着重介绍专业英语论文的写作。其宗旨是帮助中国科研人员、研究生和留学生提高专业英语论文写作质量，促进与国际同行间的交流，增加论文发表的几率。

定价：25 元　开本：32开　页码：242 页

《16 天英语入门》
张隽　卓佳　编著

◎ 针对成人英语零起点学习编写
◎ 纠正英语发音，掌握语音知识
◎ 口腔、口形图利于读者模仿发音要领
◎ 语法讲解深入浅出，易于初学者掌握

定价：16 元　开本：32开　页码：156页

《美国名校毕业演说集萃》
许轶　编著

本书收录了美国著名大学的毕业演说。这些站在美国顶级名校毕业典礼讲台上的演说者们，来自政界、商界、学术界、娱乐界……他们在这里“齐聚一堂”，侃侃而谈，以他们的视角、经历和感悟来传道、授业、解惑。

定价：20 元　开本：32 开　页码：224 页

《我的哈佛日记》　张杨　著

一个出生在 80 年代的年轻人，带着梦想独立地自我规划，走进了中国和世界上的顶级学府。这本书既沉淀了他生活中最真实的感受，也记录了他通过激烈的考验和出国申请的竞争，靠自己的努力蜕变成一个年轻的“国际中国人”的独特历程。

定价：25 元　开本：32 开　页码：304 页

《我的美利坚本科岁月》马俏　著

本书记述了作者从高考前的抉择到美国一流名校的留学生涯，从充实、和谐的美国社区见闻到充满冒险及人文关怀的异国游记，从单纯、快乐的校园生活到险象环生的求职之路，全方位展现了一位优秀的 80 后留学生的奋斗路程。同时，通过作者对生活的细腻观察，从一个女留学生的视角展示了现代美国及美洲国家的生活风貌。

定价：25 元　开本：32 开　页码：304 页

《带你去耶鲁》
曹蕴　马征　著

总统的摇篮——美国常青藤名校耶鲁大学。这里，是美国第一所具有授予博士学位资格的大学；这里，拥有全美大学中最早的博物馆、最古老的艺术馆和全世界规模第二大的大学图书馆；这里，走出了普林斯顿、康奈尔等著名大学的创始人，被誉为“美国学院之母”；这就是缔造了 300 多年传奇历史，以“光明与真知”为校训的学术圣殿——耶鲁大学。让我们一起走进耶鲁，揭开她神秘的面纱……

定价：22 元　开本：32 开　页码：252 页

《永不言败》　俞敏洪　著

这本书里的俞敏洪，不仅是一位站在中国民办教育行业前沿的领军人物，也不仅是新东方团队的领导者和新东方神话的缔造者，他更是一位睿智的长者、一位辛勤的教师、一位慈祥的父亲、一位千百万学子心中可敬可爱的朋友。他会为你指出《生命的北斗星》，引导你突破《局限》，避开《习惯的陷阱》，最终走出人生的沙漠……

定价：18 元　开本：16 开　页码：200 页

读者反馈表

尊敬的读者：

您好！非常感谢您对**新东方大愚图书**的信赖与支持，希望您抽出宝贵的时间填写这份反馈表，以便帮助我们改进工作，今后能为您提供更优秀的图书。谢谢！

为了答谢您对我们的支持，我们将对反馈的信息进行随机抽奖活动，当月将有20位幸运读者可获赠《**新东方英语**》期刊一份。我们将定期在新东方大愚图书网站 www.dogwood.com.cn 公布获奖者名单并及时寄出奖品，敬请关注。

来信请寄：北京市海淀区海淀中街6号新东方大厦750室　北京新东方大愚文化传播有限公司

图书部收

邮编：100080　　E-mail：club@dogwood.com.cn

姓名：________ 年龄：________ 职业：________ 教育背景：________ 邮编：________

通讯地址：________________ 联系电话：________

E-mail：________________ 您所购买的书籍的名称是：________________

1. 您是通过何种渠道得知本书的（可多选）：
   □书店 □新东方网站 □大愚网站 □朋友推荐 □老师推荐 □其他________
2. 您是从何处购买到此书的？ □书店 □邮购 □图书销售网站 □其他________
3. 影响您购买此书的原因（可多选）：
   □封面设计 □书评广告 □正文内容 □图书价格 □新东方品牌 □新东方名师 □其他________
4. 您对本书的封面设计满意程度： □很满意 □比较满意 □一般 □不满意 □改进建议________
5. 本书配哪种音像资料更适合您？ □磁带 □光盘 □MP3 □其他________
6. 您认为本书的内文在哪些方面还需改进？ □结构编排 □难易程度 □内容丰富性 □内文版式
7. 本书最令您满意的地方：□内文 □封面 □价格 □纸张
8. 您对本书的推荐率：□没有 □1人 □1－3人 □3－5人 □5人以上
9. 您更希望我们为您提供哪些方面的英语类图书？
   □四六级类 □考研类 □雅思考试类 □GRE、GMAT类 □NEW SAT类 □实用商务类
   □休闲欣赏类 □初高中英语类 □其他________
   您目前最希望我们为您出版的图书名称是：________
10. 您在学习英语过程中最需要哪些方面的帮助？（可多选）
    □词汇 □听力 □口语 □阅读 □写作 □翻译 □其他
11. 您最喜欢的英语图书品牌：________________
    理由如下（可多选）：□版式漂亮 □内容实用 □难度适宜 □价格适中 □对考试有帮助 □其他________
12. 看到“新东方”三个字，您首先想到什么？________________
13. 您的其他意见和建议（可附在本页背面）：________________
14. 填表时间：________年______月____日